5th Workshop on Open-Source Arabic Corpora and Processing Tools with a Shared Tasks on Qur'an QA and Fine-Grained Hate Speech Detection (OSACT 2022)

Held at LREC 2022

Marseille, France
20 June 2022

Editors:

Hend Al-Khalifa
Tamer Elsayed
Hamdy Mubarak
Abdulmohsen Al-Thubaity
Walid Magdy
Kareem Darwish

ISBN: 978-1-7138-6131-7

Printed from e-media with permission by:

Curran Associates, Inc.
57 Morehouse Lane
Red Hook, NY 12571

Some format issues inherent in the e-media version may also appear in this print version.

Printed with permission by Curran Associates, Inc. (2023)

For permission requests, please contact the Association for Computational Linguistics at the address below.

Association for Computational Linguistics
209 N. Eighth Street
Stroudsburg, Pennsylvania 18360

Phone: 1-570-476-8006
Fax: 1-570-476-0860

acl@aclweb.org

Additional copies of this publication are available from:

Curran Associates, Inc.
57 Morehouse Lane
Red Hook, NY 12571 USA
Phone: 845-758-0400
Fax: 845-758-2633
Email: curran@proceedings.com
Web: www.proceedings.com

LREC 2022 Workshop
Language Resources and Evaluation Conference
20-25 June 2022

The 5th Workshop on Open-Source Arabic Corpora and Processing Tools with Shared Tasks on Qur'an QA and Fine-Grained Hate Speech Detection

PROCEEDINGS

Editors:
Hend Al-Khalifa, Tamer Elsayed, Hamdy Mubarak,
Abdulmohsen Al-Thubaity, Walid Magdy, and Kareem Darwish

Proceedings of the LREC 2022 5th Workshop Open-Source Arabic Corpora and Processing Tools with Shared Tasks on Qur'an QA and Fine-Grained Hate Speech Detection (OSACT 2022)

Edited by:
Hend Al-Khalifa, Tamer Elsayed, Hamdy Mubarak, Abdulmohsen Al-Thubaity, Walid Magdy, and Kareem Darwish

For more information:
European Language Resources Association (ELRA)
9 rue des Cordelières
75013, Paris
France
http://www.elra.info
Email: lrec@elda.org

Preface

Given the success of the first, second, third, and fourth workshops on Open-Source Arabic Corpora and Corpora Processing Tools (OSACT) in LREC 2014, LREC 2016, LREC 2018, and LREC 2020, the fifth workshop comes to encourage researchers and practitioners of Arabic language technologies, including computational linguistics (CL), natural language processing (NLP), and information retrieval (IR) to share and discuss their research efforts, corpora, and tools. The workshop gives special attention to Multilingualism and Language Technology for All, which is one of LREC 2022 hot topics. In addition to the general topics of CL, NLP and IR, the workshop gives a special emphasis on two shared tasks, namely, Qur'an QA and Fine-Grained Hate Speech Detection.

OSACT5 had an acceptance rate of 53%, where we received 15 regular papers from which 8 papers were accepted, in addition to 21 shared task papers. We believe that the accepted papers are of high quality and present a mixture of interesting topics. This year, we introduced two shared tasks: (1) the shared task on Qur'an QA 2022: Answering Questions on the Holy Qur'an, and (2) the Second Shared Task on Offensive Language and Hate Speech Detection. The Qur'an QA shared task aims to trigger state-of-the-art question answering and reading comprehension research on the Holy Qur'an. Thirty teams have registered for the task; thirteen of them submitted runs (total of 30 runs), and twelve of them eventually submitted papers for the task. The task is defined as a machine reading comprehension task on the Holy Qur'an. The participating systems are expected to provide answers to questions (posed in Modern Standard Arabic) on given passages (sets of consecutive verses) from the Holy Qur'an, where an answer is a span of text extracted from the given passage.

The other shared task aims to push the research on detecting offensive language and hate speech on Arabic Twitter in addition to determining the fine-grained hate speech type. We define offensive language as any kind of socially unaccepted language (vulgar, insults, threats, etc.). When a tweet has offensive language that targets people based on common characteristics such as race, ethnicity, ideology, gender, etc., this is considered as hate speech. We annotated data for six types of Hate Speech: Race, Religion, Ideology, Disability, Social Class, and Gender. The shared task is divided into 3 subtasks. In Subtask A ("offensive" versus "clean" tweets), 40 teams registered, and 17 teams submitted results (a total of 120 runs). In Subtask B ("hate speech" versus "no hate speech" tweets), 26 teams registered, and 12 teams submitted results (a total of 66 runs). In Subtask C ("fine-grained hate speech type"), 23 teams registered, and 10 teams submitted results (a total of 54 runs). 10 teams submitted papers describing their participation in one subtask or more, and 8 papers were accepted.

Finally, we would like to thank everyone who in one way or another helped in making this workshop a success. Our special thanks go to the members of the program committee, who did an excellent job in reviewing the submitted papers, and to the LREC organizers. Last but not least, we would like to thank our authors and the workshop participants.

This volume documents the Proceedings of the 5th Workshop on Open-Source Arabic Corpora and Processing Tools, held on 20 June 2022 as part of the LREC 2022 conference (International Conference on Language Resources and Evaluation).

Hend Al-Khalifa, Tamer Elsayed, Hamdy Mubarak,
Abdulmohsen Al-Thubaity, Walid Magdy, and Kareem Darwish
OSACT5 Organizing Committee

Organizing Committee

Hend Al-Khalifa, King Saud University, Saudi Arabia
Tamer Elsayed, Qatar University, Qatar
Hamdy Mubarak, Qatar Computing Research Institute, Qatar
Abdulmohsen Al-Thubaity, KACST, Saudi Arabia
Walid Magdy, University of Edinburgh, UK
Kareem Darwish, aiXplain Inc., US

Program Committee

Abdelmajid Ben-Hamadou, Sfax University, Tunisia
AbdelRahim Elmadany, The University of British Columbia, Canada
Abdullah Alrajeh, King Abdulzziz City for Science and Technology, KSA
Abdulrahman Almuhareb, King Abdulzziz City for Science and Technology, KSA
Adel Alshehri, King Abdulzziz City for Science and Technology, KSA
Alexis Nasr, University of Marseille, France
Aloulou Chafik, Univeristé de Sfax, Tunisia
Areeb Alowisheq, Saudi Data and Artificial Intelligence Authority, KSA
Azzeddine Mazroui, University Mohamed I, Morocco
Bassam Haddad, University of Petra, Jordan
El Moatez Billah Nagoudi, The University of British Columbia, Canada
Fatima Haouari, Qatar University, Qatar
Fethi Bougares, Le Mans University, France
Fouzi Harrag, Ferhat Abbas University, Algeria
Hamada Nayel, Benha University, Egypt
Ibrahim Abu Farha, University of Edinburgh, Scotland
Imed Zitouni, Google, USA
Karim Bouzoubaa, Mohammad V University, Morocco
Khaled Shaalan, The British University in Dubai, UAE
Maram Hasanain, Qatar University, Qatar
Mourad Abbas, CRSTDLA, Algeria
Mucahid Kutlu, TOBB University, Turkey
Muhammad Abdul-Mageed, The university of British Columbia, Canada
Mustafa Jarrar, Bir Zeit University, Palestine
Nada Ghneim, Higher Institute for Applied Sciences and Technology, Syria
Nizar Habash, New York University Abu Dhabi, UAE
Nora Al-Twairesh, King Saud University, KSA
Omar Trigui, University of Sousse, Tunisia
Reem Suwaileh, Qatar University, Qatar
Sahar Ghannay, LIMSI, France
Sakhar Alkhereyf, King Abdulzziz City for Science and Technology, KSA
Salam Khalifa, New York University Abu Dhabi, UAE
Salima Harrat, École Normale Supérieure (Bouzaréah), Algeria
Salima mdhaffar, Le Mans University, France
Samhaa R. El-Beltagy, Newgiza University, Egypt
Saud Alashri, King Abdulzziz City for Science and Technology, KSA
Shammur Absar Chowdhury, Qatar Computing Research Institute, Qatar
Wajdi Zaghouani, Hamad Bin Khalifa University, Qatar
Waleed Alsanie, King Abdulzziz City for Science and Technology, KSA
Watheq Mansour, Qatar University, Qatar
Wissam Antoun, American University of Beirut, Lebanon
Younes Samih, Heinrich Heine Universität Düsseldorf, Germany

Table of Contents

Workshop Program

Monday 20 June 2022

Session 1: Main Workshop

9:00–9:10 *Workshop Opening*
Hend Al-Khalifa, Tamer Elsayed, Hamdy Mubarak, Abdulmohsen Al-Thubaity, Walid Magdy, and Kareem Darwish

9:10–9:50 *Keynote Talk: A proposal to accelerate innovation for Arabic Speech and Language Processing*
Hassan Sawaf, aiXplain.com

9:50–10:10 *TURJUMAN: A Public Toolkit for Neural Arabic Machine Translation*
El Moatez Billah Nagoudi, AbdelRahim Elmadany and Muhammad Abdul-Mageed

10:10–10:30 *Detecting Users Prone to Spread Fake News on Arabic Twitter*
Zien Sheikh Ali, Abdulaziz Al-Ali and Tamer Elsayed

Session 2: Main Workshop (Cont.)

11:00–11:20 *AraSAS: The Open Source Arabic Semantic Tagger*
Mahmoud El-Haj, Elvis de Souza, Nouran Khallaf, Paul Rayson and Nizar Habash

11:20–11:40 *AraNPCC: The Arabic Newspaper COVID-19 Corpus*
Abdulmohsen Al-Thubaity, Sakhar Alkhereyf and Alia O. Bahanshal

11:40–12:00 *Pre-trained Models or Feature Engineering: The Case of Dialectal Arabic*
Kathrein Abu Kwaik, Stergios Chatzikyriakidis and Simon Dobnik

12:00–12:20 *A Context-free Arabic Emoji Sentiment Lexicon (CF-Arab-ESL)*
Shatha Ali A. Hakami, Robert Hendley and Phillip Smith

12:20–12:40 *Sa'7r: A Saudi Dialect Irony Dataset*
Halah AlMazrua, Najla AlHazzani, Amaal AlDawod, Lama AlAwlaqi, Noura Al-Reshoudi, Hend Al-Khalifa and Luluh AlDhubayi

12:40–13:00 *Classifying Arabic Crisis Tweets using Data Selection and Pre-trained Language Models*
Alaa Alharbi and Mark Lee

Monday 20 June 2022 (continued)

Session 3: Qur'an QA Shared Task

14:00–14:20 *Qur'an QA 2022: Overview of The First Shared Task on Question Answering over the Holy Qur'an*
Rana Malhas, Watheq Mansour and Tamer Elsayed

14:20–14:30 *DTW at Qur'an QA 2022: Utilising Transfer Learning with Transformers for Question Answering in a Low-resource Domain*
Damith Premasiri, Tharindu Ranasinghe, Wajdi Zaghouani and Ruslan Mitkov

14:30–14:40 *eRock at Qur'an QA 2022: Contemporary Deep Neural Networks for Qur'an based Reading Comprehension Question Answers*
Esha Aftab and Muhammad Kamran Malik

14:40–14:50 *GOF at Qur'an QA 2022: Towards an Efficient Question Answering For The Holy Qu'ran In The Arabic Language Using Deep Learning-Based Approach*
Ali Mostafa and Omar Mohamed

14:50–15:00 *LARSA22 at Qur'an QA 2022: Text-to-Text Transformer for Finding Answers to Questions from Qur'an*
Youssef MELLAH, Ibtissam Touahri, Zakaria Kaddari, Zakaria Haja, Jamal Berrich and Toumi Bouchentouf

15:00–15:10 *LK2022 at Qur'an QA 2022: Simple Transformers Model for Finding Answers to Questions from Qur'an*
Abdullah Alsaleh, Saud Althabiti, Ibtisam Alshammari, Sarah Alnefaie, Sanaa Alowaidi, Alaa Alsaqer, Eric Atwell, Abdulrahman Altahhan and Mohammad Alsalka

15:10–15:20 *niksss at Qur'an QA 2022: A Heavily Optimized BERT Based Model for Answering Questions from the Holy Qu'ran*
Nikhil Singh

15:20–15:30 *QQATeam at Qur'an QA 2022: Fine-Tunning Arabic QA Models for Qur'an QA Task*
Basem Ahmed, Motaz Saad and Eshrag A. Refaee,

15:30–15:40 *SMASH at Qur'an QA 2022: Creating Better Faithful Data Splits for Low-resourced Question Answering Scenarios*
Amr Keleg and Walid Magdy

15:40–15:50 *Stars at Qur'an QA 2022: Building Automatic Extractive Question Answering Systems for the Holy Qur'an with Transformer Models and Releasing a New Dataset*
Ahmed Sleem, Eman Mohammed lotfy Elrefai, Marwa Mohammed Matar and Haq Nawaz

15:50–16:00 *TCE at Qur'an QA 2022: Arabic Language Question Answering Over Holy Qur'an Using a Post-Processed Ensemble of BERT-based Models*
Mohamemd Elkomy and Amany M. Sarhan

Monday 20 June 2022 (continued)

Session 4: Fine-Grained Hate Speech Detection Shared Task

Proceedings of the OSACT 2022 Workshop @LREC2022, pages 1–11
Marseille, 20 June 2022

TURJUMAN:
A Public Toolkit for Neural Arabic Machine Translation

El Moatez Billah Nagoudi[⋆] **AbdelRahim Elmadany**[⋆] **Muhammad Abdul-Mageed**[⋆]
Deep Learning & Natural Language Processing Group
The University of British Columbia
{moatez.nagoudi,a.elmadany,muhammad.mageed}@ubc.ca

Abstract

We present TURJUMAN, a neural toolkit for translating from 20 languages into Modern Standard Arabic (MSA). TURJUMAN exploits the recently-introduced text-to-text Transformer AraT5 model, endowing it with a powerful ability to decode into Arabic. The toolkit offers the possibility of employing a number of diverse decoding methods, making it suited for acquiring paraphrases for the MSA translations as an added value. To train TURJUMAN, we sample from publicly available parallel data employing a simple semantic similarity method to ensure data quality. This allows us to prepare and release AraOPUS-20, a new machine translation benchmark. We publicly release our translation toolkit (TURJUMAN) as well as our benchmark dataset (AraOPUS-20).[1]

Keywords: Machine Translation, Neural Machine Translation, Arabic, Arabic NLP, Open Source, TURJUMAN, Toolkit.

1. Introduction

Natural language processing (NLP) technologies such as question answering, machine translation (MT), summarization, and text classification are witnessing a surge. This progress is the result of advances in deep learning methods, availability of large datasets, and increasingly powerful computing infrastructure. As these technologies continue to mature, their applications in everyday life become all the more pervasive. For example, neural machine translation (NMT), the focus of the current work, has applications in education, health, tourism, search, security, recreation, etc. Similar to other areas, progress in NMT is contingent on high-quality, standardized datasets and fast prototyping. Such datasets and tools are necessary for meaningful comparisons of research outcomes, benchmarking, and training of next generation scholars. Off-the-shelf tools are also especially valuable both as stand-alone and enabling technologies in all research and development. Although various tools have been developed for Arabic NLP tasks such as those involving morphosyntactic analysis (Pasha et al., 2014; Darwish and Mubarak, 2016; Obeid et al., 2020b) and detection of social meaning (Abdul-Mageed et al., 2019; Farha and Magdy, 2019), there has not been as much progress for MT. More specifically, there is shortage of publicly available tools for Arabic MT. The goal of this work is to introduce **TURJUMAN**, a new publicly available Arabic NMT toolkit that seeks to contribute to bridging this gap.

Recent advances in NMT leverages progress in Transformer-based encoder-decoder language models, and TURJUMAN takes advantage of such a progress. In particular, encoder-decoder models such as MASS (Song et al., 2019), BART (Lewis et al., 2020), and T5(Raffel et al., 2019), and their multilingual counter-parts have all

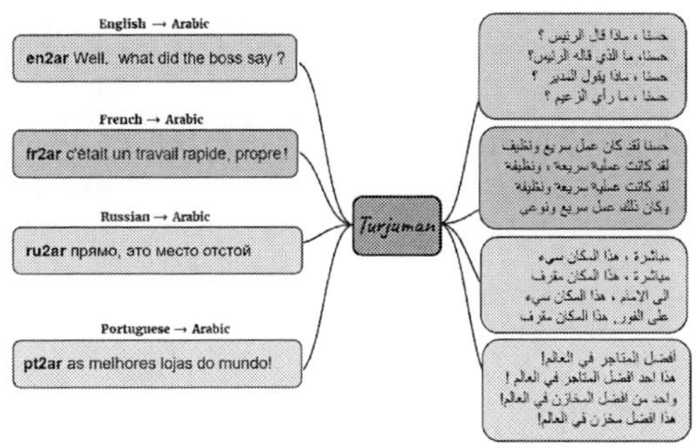

Figure 1: Our TURJUMAN neural machine translation toolkit illustrated with four prompt MT tasks: English, French, Russian, and Portuguese → Arabic. For each source sentence, we employ four decoding methods to produce output: *greedy search, beam search, top-k sampling*, and *top-p sampling*.

been shown to remarkably benefit NMT. For this reason, TURJUMAN is built off AraT5 (Nagoudi et al., 2022). AraT5 is a recently released text-to-text Transformer model. For comparisons, we benchmark AraT5 against a number of baselines on a new parallel dataset that we also introduce as part of this work. Importantly, we do not intend TURJUMAN as a tool for delivering state-of-the-art (SOTA) translations. For this reason, we do not use all parallel datasets at our disposal. Rather, we introduce TURJUMAN as an extensible framework. For example, it can be further developed to produce SOTA performance by fine-tuning its backend model on larger datasets.

In the context of creating our tool, we also prepare and release **AraOPUS-20**. AraOPUS-20 is a reasonably-sized parallel dataset of 20 language pairs (with X → Arabic) for NMT. We extract AraOPUS-20 from OPUS (Tiedemann, 2012). Since OPUS is known to involve noisy translations, we propose a simple quality assurance method based on semantic similarity to remove this noise from the dataset. We

[1] `https://github.com/UBC-NLP/turjuman`
⋆All authors contributed equally.

release AraOPUS-20 in standard splits, thereby making it well-suited for Arabic MT model comparisons.

TURJUMAN also integrates recent progress in diverse decoding, such as *greedy search* (Cormen et al., 2009), *beam search* (Koehn, 2009), *top-k sampling* (Fan et al., 2018), and *nucleus sampling* (Holtzman et al., 2019). This makes it possible to use TURJUMAN for generating various translations of the same foreign sequence. As such, TURJUMAN can also be used for producing paraphrases at the Arabic side (see Figure 1).

To summarize, we make the following contributions:

1. We prepare and release ***AraOPUS-20***, an MT benchmark that we extract from the freely available parallel corpora OPUS (Tiedemann, 2012). AraOPUS-20 consists of bitext between Arabic and 20 languages. The languages paired with Arabic include high-resource languages such as English, French, and Spanish and low-resource ones such as Cebuano,[1] Tamashek,[2] and Yoruba[3].

2. We introduce ***TURJUMAN***, a python-based NMT toolkit for translating sentences from 20 languages into Arabic. TURJUMAN fine-tunes AraT5 (Nagoudi et al., 2022), a powerful Arabic text-to-text Transformer language model. Our toolkit can be used off-the-shelf as a strong baseline, or as an enabling technology. It is also extensible. For example, it can be further developed through additional fine-tuning on larger amounts of data.

3. We endow TURJUMAN with a diverse set of decoding capabilities, making it valuable for generating paraphrases (Fadaee et al., 2017) of foreign content into Arabic.

The rest of the paper is organized as follows: We provide an overview of works related to Arabic machine translation in Section 2. We introduce AraOPUS-20 MT benchmark in Section 3. We describe TURJUMAN in Section 4., and Section 6. is where we conclude.

2. Related Work

Our work is related to research on MT datasets and tools, and language models on which these tools may be fine-tuned. Hence, we start our coverage of related work by presenting most of the popular Arabic MT datasets for both MSA and Arabic dialects. We then provide an overview of Arabic MT systems and tools. Finally, we review both Arabic and multilingual encoder-decoder pre-trained language models since these are most relevant to the translation task.

[1]Language spoken in the southern Philippines

[2]Tamashek or Tamasheq is a variety of Tuareg, a Berber macro-language widely spoken by nomadic tribes across North Africa countries.

[3]Yoruba is a language spoken in West Africa, primarily in Southwestern Nigeria.

2.1. MSA MT Resources

Open Parallel Corpus (OPUS). Tiedemann (2012) propose the large, multi-lingual, parallel sentences datasets OPUS. OPUS contains more than 2.7 billion parallel sentences in 90 languages including Arabic.[4] We extract AraOPUS-20 from OPUS. A number of additional MSA datasets involving Arabic have also been proposed. Although we do not make use of any of these, we review them here both for completeness and since they can be exploited for extending TURJUMAN.

United Nations Parallel Corpus. Ziemski et al. (2016) introduce a manually translated united nations (UN) documents corpus covering the six official UN languages: *Arabic, Chinese, English, French, Russian,* and *Spanish.* The corpus consists of development and test sets only, each of which comprise 4K sentences that are one-to-one alignments across all official languages.

IWSLT Corpus. Several Arabic to English parallel datasets were released during IWSLT[5] evaluation campaigns. These include IWSLT 2012 (Federico et al., 2012), IWSLT 2013 (Cettolo et al., 2013), IWSLT 2016 (Cettolo et al., 2016), and IWSLT 2017 (Cettolo et al., 2017).

Arab-Acquis. Habash et al. (2017) propose Arab-Acquis. It consists of 12k English and French sentences extracted from the JRC-Acquis corpus (Steinberger et al., 2006). The foreign sentences are translated into Arabic by two professional translators. JRC-Acquis is a publicly available parallel collection of legislative text of the European Union and is written in the 22 official European languages.

MSA MADAR Corpus. Proposed by Bouamor et al. (2018), this dataset. It consists of 10k MSA-English evaluation sentences manually translated using the Crowdsourcing platform *crowdFlower.com*.[6]

2.2. Dialectal MT Resources

There are also a number of available dialectal datasets that can be used to extend TURJUMAN. We also briefly review these here.

APT Corpus. Zbib et al. (2012) present an Arabic-English dataset[7] covering MSA and two other Arabic dialects. It comprises 8.11M MSA-English sentences, 138k Levantine-English sentences, and 38k Egyptian-English sentences. The dataset was collected from Arabic weblogs and translation was carried out through Amazon Mechanical Turk.[8]

Qatari-English Speech Corpus. This parallel corpus comprises 14.7k Qatari-English sentences collected by Elmahdy et al. (2014) from talk-show programs and Qatari TV series and translated into English.

Multi-dialectal Parallel Corpus (MDPC). Bouamor et al. (2014) construct MDPC by selecting 2k Egyptian-English sentences from the APT corpus (Zbib et al., 2012). Then, native speakers from Palestine, Syria, Jordan, and Tunisia

[4]https://opus.nlpl.eu/

[5]https://wit3.fbk.eu.

[6]http://www.crowdflower.com/.

[7]https://catalog.ldc.upenn.edu/LDC2012T09.

[8]https://www.mturk.com.

MSA sentences	English sentences	Sim
ألمانيا	The annex to the present report.	-0.12
إساءة استغلال مركز الهيمنة	Abuse of dominance	0.02
البند ٣ (أ) من جدول الأعمال	Draft resolution submitted by Argentina	0.11
ألف - آراء بشأن تنظيم الدورة	plenary meetings have been made.	0.27
نفس الوطن .	the same home, yes! we are brothers!	0.43
خامساً اعتماد التقرير	Adoption of the report	0.52
ألبانيا والكاميرون.	Albania, Cameroon.	0.70
مشاورات غير رسمية	Informal consultation	0.72
نوارة نجم تقع في حب أحمد مكي:	Nawara Negm is falling in love with Mekki	0.74
نتيجة التصويت كما يلي:	The voting was as follows:	0.77
المجموعة العربية	Arab Group	0.91
وتشمل هذه التكاليف ، تكاليف الصيانة	These costs include, maintenance	0.94

Table 1: A sample of MSA-English parallel sentences extracted from the Open Parallel Corpus (OPUS). We report semantic similarity on each pair of sentences using the multilingual sentence transformer model SBERT. **Green:** Selected sentences. **Red:** Ignored sentences.

were asked to translate the sentences into their respective native dialects.

Parallel Arabic Dialect Corpus (PADIC). Meftouh et al. (2015) offers PADIC, a multi-dialect corpus including MSA, Algerian, Tunisian, Palestinian, and Syrian. PADIC consists of 6.4K parallel sentences between MSA and all the listed dialects.

Dial2MSA. Mubarak (2018) release this parallel dialectal Arabic corpus for converting dialectal Arabic to MSA. The dataset has 6K tweets from four Arabic dialects: Egyptian, Levantine , Gulf ,and Maghrebi. Each of the dialects is translated into MSA by native speakers of each dialect.

DIA MADAR Corpus. Bouamor et al. (2018) introduce this commissioned corpus. Arabic native speakers from 25 Arabic cities were tasked to translate 2k English sentences each into their own native dialect. The sentences are selected from the Basic Traveling Expression Corpus (Takezawa et al., 2007). We now review systems for Arabic MT.

2.3. Arabic MT Systems

MSA MT. Arabic MT went through different stages, including rule-based systems (Bakr et al., 2008; Mohamed et al., 2012; Salloum and Habash, 2013) and statistical MT (Habash and Hu, 2009; Salloum and Habash, 2011; Ghoneim and Diab, 2013). There has been work on Arabic MT employing neural methods. For example, Almahairi et al. (2016) propose an Arabic $\leftrightarrow$ English NMT using a vanilla attention-based NMT model of Bahdanau et al. (2014). Also, Junczys-Dowmunt et al. (2016) report an experimental study where phrase-based NMT across 30 translation directions including Arabic is investigated. Other sentence-based Arabic $\leftrightarrow$ English NMT systems training on various datasets are presented in Akeel and Mishra (2014), Durrani et al. (2017), and Alrajeh (2018). A number of Arabic-related NMTs were also proposed to translate from languages other than English into Arabic. This includes from Chinese (Aqlan et al., 2019), Turkish (El-Kahlout et al., 2019), Japanese (Noll et al., 2019), and four foreign languages[9] into MSA (Nagoudi et al., 2022).

Dialectal MT. Some work has focused on translating between MSA and Arabic dialects. For instance, Zbib et al. (2012) show the impact of combined MSA and dialectal data on dialect/MSA $\rightarrow$ English MT performance. Sajjad et al. (2013) use MSA as a pivot language for translating Arabic dialects into English. Salloum et al. (2014) investigate the effect of sentence-level dialect identification and several linguistic features for dialect/MSA $\rightarrow$ English translation. Guellil et al. (2017) propose an NMT system for Arabic dialects using a vanilla recurrent neural network encoder-decoder model for translating Algerian Arabic written in a mixture of Arabizi and Arabic characters into MSA. Baniata et al. (2018) present an NMT system to translate Levantine (Jordanian, Syrian, and Palestinian) and Maghrebi (Algerian, Moroccan, and Tunisia) into MSA. Sajjad et al. (2020) introduce AraBench, an evaluation benchmark for dialectal Arabic to English MT and several NMT systems using several training settings: fine-tuning, data augmentation, and back-translation. Farhan et al. (2020) propose an unsupervised dialectal NMT where the source dialect is not represented in training data (i.e., zero-shot MT (Lample et al., 2018)). More recently, Nagoudi et al. (2021) introduce a transformer-based MT system for translating from code-

[9]English, French, German, and Russian.

mixed Modern Standard Arabic and Egyptian Arabic into English. Nagoudi et al. (2022) Finally, propose three Arabic text-to-text transformer (AraT5) models dedicated to MSA and a diverse set of Arabic dialects. The models are used in several dialects → English MT tasks. To the best of our knowledge, neither MSA nor dialectal machine translation systems described in this section have been made publicly available for research.

2.4. Open Source Arabic Tools

There have been many efforts to develop tools to support Arabic NLP. Some tools target morphosyntax such as in morphological analysis, disambiguation, POS tagging, and diacritization (Pasha et al., 2014; Darwish and Mubarak, 2016; Obeid et al., 2020a), while others focus on social meaning tasks such as sentiment analysis, emotion, age, gender, and sarcasm detection (Farha and Magdy, 2019; Abdul-Mageed et al., 2019). For MT, we do not know of any publicly available Arabic MT tools (let alone ones that afford many-to-Arabic translations nor diverse decoding). We now review Transformer-based Arabic and multilingual encoder-decoder models since these can be fine-tuned for MT.

2.5. Pre-Trained Language Models

mBART50 (Liu et al., 2020) is a multilingual encoder-decoder model primarily intended for MT. It is pre-trained by denoising full texts in 50 languages, including Arabic. Then, mBART is fine-tuned on parallel MT data under three settings: many-to-English, English-to-many, and many-to-many. The parallel MT data used contains a total of 230M parallel sentences and covers high-, mid-, and low-resource languages.

mT5 (Xue et al., 2020) is the multilingual version of **T**ext-**to**-**T**ext **T**ransfer **T**ransformer model (T5) (Raffel et al., 2019). The basic idea behind this model is to treat every text-based language task as a "text-to-text" problem, (i.e. taking text format as input and producing new text format as output), where a multi-task learning set-up is applied to several NLP tasks: question answering, document summarization, and MT. The mT5 model is pre-trained on the "mC4: Multilingual Colossal Clean Crawled Corpus", which is $\sim$ 26.76TB for 101 languages (including Arabic).

AraT5 (Nagoudi et al., 2022) is an Arabic text-to-text Transformer model dedicated to MSA and Arabic dialects. Again, AraT5 is an encoder-decoder Transformer similar in configuration and size to T5 (Raffel et al., 2019). AraT5 was trained on more than 248GB of Arabic text (70GB MSA and 178GB tweets). In addition to Arabic, AraT5's vocabulary covers 11 others languages. Namely, the model covers vocabulary from Bulgarian, Czech, English, French, German, Greek, Italian, Portuguese, Russian, Spanish, and Turkish.

3. AraOPUS-20 Parallel Dataset

In this section, we describe AraOPUS-20 (the dataset we use to develop TURJUMAN) and the cleaning process we employ to ensure high quality of the data.

xx→ar	Orig. OPUS	Filtering	Train	Dev	Test
bg	2M	sim	1M	2K	2K
bs	2M	rand	1M	2K	2K
cs	2M	sim	1M	2K	2K
da	2M	sim	0.93M	2K	2K
de	2M	sim	0.99M	2K	2K
el	2M	sim	1M	2K	2K
en	2M	sim	1M	2K	2K
es	2M	sim	1M	2K	2K
fr	2M	sim	1M	2K	2K
hi	2M	sim	0.81M	2K	2K
it	2M	sim	1M	2K	2K
ko	2M	sim	0.83M	2K	2K
pl	2M	rand	1M	2K	2K
pt	2M	sim	1M	2K	2K
ru	2M	sim	1M	2K	2K
tr	2M	sim	1M	2K	2K
ceb	83.1K	all	82.1K	200	200
gd	19.9K	all	19.5K	200	200
tmh	2.6K	all	2.8K	100	100
yo	1.4K	all	1.2K	100	100

Table 2: OPUS filtering process and data distribution in AraOPUS-20. Filtering methods: **(1)** ***sim:*** keep only 1M sentences with semantic similarity between [0.7,0.99] ***(2) random:*** if the language is not supported by SBERT model, we pick a random 1M pair of sentences. ***(3) all***: for the low resource languages, we keep all the parallel data. **ar**: Arabic **bg**: Bulgarian. **bs**: Bosnian. **cs**: Czech. **da**: Danish. **de**: German. **el**: Greek. **en**: English. **es**: Spanish. **fr**: French. **hi**: Hindi. **it**: Italian. **ko**: Korean. **pl**: Polish. **pt**: Portuguese. **ru**: Russian. **tu**: Turkish. **ceb**: Cebuano. **gd**: Scots Gaelic. **tmh**: Tamashek. **yo**: Yoruba.

3.1. Training Data.

As mentioned earlier, in order to develop our TURJUMAN tool, we use AraOPUS-20. AraOPUS-20 is extracted from OPUS (Tiedemann, 2012) as follows:

1. We randomly pick 2M Arabic parallel sentences from the 16 highest-resource languages from among our 20 languages. Namely, we extract parallel data involving Arabic (mainly MSA) and Bulgarian, Czech, English, French, German, Greek, Italian, Portuguese, Russian, Spanish, Hindi, Polish, Korean, and Turkish.
2. We also use available data form the four low resource languages: Cebuano (Philippine), Scots Gaelic (Scotland), Tamashek (Mali), and Yoruba (Nigeria).[10]

3.2. Quality of Parallel Data.

In order to investigate the quality of OPUS Arabic parallel sentences, we measure semantic similarity between the parallel sentences by running a multilingual sentence Transformer model (Reimers and Gurevych, 2020) on each pair of sentences,[11] keeping only pairs with a semantic

[10]We list the country where a language is mostly spoken, otherwise a given language can be spoken in more than one country.

[11]We exclude the low-resource data from our semantic similarity steps as these languages are not supported in Reimers and Gurevych (2020) model.

similarity score between 0.70 and 0.99. This allows us to filter out sentence pairs whose source and target are identical (i.e., similarity score = 1) and those that are not good translations of one another (i.e., those with a cross-lingual semantic similarity score < 0.70). Manually inspecting the data, we find that a threshold of $> 0.70\%$ safely guarantees acquiring semantically similar (i.e., good translations) and distinct pairs of sentences (i.e., sentences from two different languages). Table 1 shows a sample of MSA-English parallel sentences extracted from OPUS, along with their measured semantic similarity. We pick the top 1M sentences[12] (i.e., sentences with high semantic similarity score and satisfy our semantic similarity condition) from each language. We then split the resulting dataset into Train, Dev, and Test (see next section) and refer to the resulting benchmark that covers 20 languages as *AraOPUS-20* as we explained.

3.3. Development and Test Data.

For each of development and test split, we randomly pick 2k sentences form AraOPUS-20 (after filtering). We do this for all of the high resource languages. Regarding the low-resources languages, if the training split has more than 15K sentences, we randomly pick 200 sentences each for Dev and Test. Otherwise, we consider only 100 sentences for each of these splits per language. More details about the AraOPUS-20 parallel data distribution are given in Table 2.

4. TURJUMAN Tool

TURJUMAN is a publicly available toolkit for translating sentences from 20 languages into MSA. The package consists of a Python library and related command-line scripts. In this section, we discuss: **(1)** the training and evaluation processes of TURJUMAN's backbone MT model and **(2)** how we design the TURJUMAN tool itself and its different settings.

4.1. Approach

Training. For all the 20 languages, we fine-tune AraT5 (Nagoudi et al., 2022) with training data of AraOPUS-20 (see in Section 3.). That is, we train a single *multilingual* model that translates from a given foreign language into MSA (many-to-MSA). Currently, a user needs to specify the identity of the input language.[13] We train our models on 96 AMD MI50 GPUs (16GB each) for 25 epochs with a batch size of 32, maximum sequence length of 256 tokens, and a learning rate of $5e^{-5}$.

Evaluation. In order to evaluate our TURJUMAN model, we use two datasets (AraOPUS-20 and United Nations Parallel Corpus, both described in Section 3.3.).[14] As a rule, for all datasets we identify the best model on our Dev data[15] and blind-test it on our Test split for each language separately. For the two datasets, we report results on both Dev and Test splits as shown in Tables 5 and 6 respectively.

Baselines. For comparison, we use three baselines:

- **Baseline I**. A vanilla sequence-to-sequence (S2S) Transformer (Vaswani et al., 2017) as implemented in Fairseq (Ott et al., 2019). We train this model from scratch using AraOPUS-20 training data
- **Baseline II**. We fine-tune the multilingual encoder-decoder model mT5 (Xue et al., 2020) on the same training data as our second baseline.
- **Baseline III**. We use the mBART-50 many-to-many multilingual MT model for our third baseline. We do not fine-tune this model on AraOPUS-20 Train data as it is a checkpoint of mBART-large-50 (Liu et al., 2020) already fine-tuned on a multilingual MT dataset covering high-, mid-, and low-resource languages. In total, this model is fine-tuned with 230M parallel sentences from these 50 languages.

4.2. Implementation

We distribute TURJUMAN as a modular toolkit built around standard libraries including PyTorch (Paszke et al., 2019) and HuggingFace (Lhoest et al., 2021).

Command-Line Tools. We provide several command-line tools for translation and evaluation:

- *turjuman_interactive:* This interactive command line facility can be used for quick sentence-by-sentence translation exploiting our fine-tuned NMT model (TURJUMAN's backbone translation model).
- *turjuman_translate:* This is the same as the interactive command. However, a path to a file containing source sentences is required.
- *turjuman_score:* This evaluates an output translation (output translations) against reference translation(s) in terms of a BLEU score.

4.3. Decoding Support

We also endow TURJUMAN with support for MT-based *paraphrase* generation by adding four decoding methods at the decoder side. We implement a number of prominent decoding methods used in the literature. Namely, we implement *greedy search*, *beam search* (Koehn, 2009), *top-k sampling* (Fan et al., 2018), and *nucleus sampling* (Holtzman et al., 2019). Table 3 shows example translations with TURJUMAN exploiting each of the four decoding methods. We now briefly describe each of these methods.

[12]For low resource languages we use all available sentences.

[13]We plan to incorporate a language ID module into TURJUMAN in the future.

[14]We exclude the Chinese language as it is not included in our training data.

[15]We merge all the development data for all the 20 languages.

# Decoding	Source/Translated Sentences
en2ar:	*She sort of grew up in front of everyone in Arkansas. Then as the spokesman for President Trump*
GS	لقد نشأت في وسط كل شخص في أركنساس ، ثم أصبحت متحدثة باسم الرئيس ترامب.
BS	لقد نشأت أمام الجميع في أركنساس ، ثم أصبحت متحدثة باسم الرئيس ترامب.
Top-k	لقد نشأت في وسط كل شخص في أركنساس ، ثم أصبحت متحدثة باسم الرئيس ترامب.
Top-p	ترعرعت ، بجانب كل شخص في أركنساس ، ثم أصبحت الناطق باسم الرئيس ترمب ،
fr2ar:	*Match Algérie et Cameroun : la grande victoire des fake news.*
GS	مباراة الجزائر والكاميرون : النصر الكبير للأخبار الكاذبة.
BS	مباراة الجزائر والكاميرون : الانتصار الكبير للأخبار المزيفة.
Top-k	مباراة الجزائر والكاميرون : النصر الكبير للأخبار الكاذبة.
Top-p	مباراة الجزائر والكاميرون : البطولة الرئيسة للأخبار المزيفة.
pt2ar:	*Já o governo federal não explicou os motivos da manutenção dos contratos*
GS	لم تعد الحكومة الاتحادية تفسر أسباب استمرار العقود.
BS	لم تعد الحكومة الاتحادية تفسر أسباب الإبقاء على العقود.
Top-k	لم تعد الحكومة الاتحادية تفسر أسباب استمرار العقود.
Top-p	لم تعد الحكومة الاتحادية تشرح أسبابه المتعلقة بالمحافظة على العقود بعد الآن.
ru2ar :	*Резкий скачок цен на зерновые из-за войны: что будет с ценами на продовольствие?*
GS	ارتفاع أسعار الحبوب بسبب الحرب : ماذا عن أسعار الغذاء ؟
BS	ارتفاع حاد في أسعار الحبوب بسبب الحرب : ماذا عن أسعار الغذاء ؟
Top-k	ارتفاع أسعار الحبوب بسبب الحرب : ماذا عن أسعار الغذاء ؟
Top-p	تناقص حاد في أسعار الأمونيا بسبب الحرب : ماذا لو تناقصت أسعار الغذاء ؟
tr2ar :	*Türkiye ile Ermenistan arasında, son dönemde yeniden başlayan doğrudan uçuşlardan birindeyiz.*
GS	نحن في رحلة طيران مباشرة بين تركيا وأرمينيا ، التي بدأت في الآونة الأخيرة.
BS	بين تركيا وأرمينيا ، نحن في واحدة من الرحلات الجوية المباشرة التي بدأت من جديد خلال الفترة الأخيرة.
Top-k	نحن في رحلة طيران مباشرة بين تركيا وأرمينيا ، التي بدأت في الآونة الأخيرة
Top-p	حيث أنه يتم نقل معظم الركاب الطيارين ضمن عصر النقل الجوي الداخلي.

Table 3: A sample of sentences from five foreign languages along with their MSA translations using four decoding methods. **GS**: Greedy Search. **BS**: Beam Search. **Top-k**: top-k sampling. **Top-p**: top-p sampling. **en2ar:** English to Arabic. **fr2ar** French to Arabic. **pt2ar:** Portuguese to Arabic. **ru2ar:** Russian to Arabic. **tr2ar:** Turkish to Arabic.

Greedy Search. Is a simple heuristic strategy aiming to selects the word with the highest conditional probability as its next word at each timestep as shown in Formula (1):

$$w_t = argmax_w P(w|w_{1:t-1}) \quad (1)$$

Beam Search. Beam search is an improved version of greedy search that uses a hyper-parameter num_beams. It is based on exploring the solution space and reduces the risk of missing hidden high probability word sequences by keeping the most likely num_beams of hypotheses sequences.

Top-k Sampling. A probabilistic decoding method proposed by Fan et al. (2018) that aims to avoid repetitions during decoding. This method also increase diversity of the output by using a simple, yet powerful sampling stochastic scheme called ***top-k*** sampling. First, the top k words with the highest probability are selected. Then, we sample from this shortlist of words. This allows the other high-scoring tokens a chance of being picked. Formula (2) describe top-k sampling, where $V^{(k)}$ is the top-k vocabulary.

$$w_t = \sum_{w \in V^{(k)}} P(w|w_{1:t-1}) \quad (2)$$

Top-p Sampling. Also called *nucleus-sampling*, this method is proposed by Holtzman et al. (2019). It shares the same principle as the *top-k* method, and the only difference between the two is that Top-p sampling chooses from the smallest possible set of words the sum of whose probability is greater than a certain probability p (i.e., threshold). This method is described in Formula (3), where $V^{(p)}$ is the top-p vocabulary.

$$w_t = \sum_{w \in V^{(p)}} P(w|w_{1:t-1}) \geq p \quad (3)$$

Arguments	Description	Command-line	Required
- - *help or -h*	show the help message and exit	interactive, translate	no
- - *text or -t*	translate the input text into Arabic	translate	yes
- - *input_file*	path of input file	translate	yes
- - *batch_size or -bs*	the number of sentences translated in one iteration	translate	no
- - *seq_length or -s*	generate sequences of maximum length *seq_length*	interactive, translate	no
- - *search_method or -m*	decoding method [*'greedy'*, *'beam'*, *'sampling'*]	interactive, translate	no
- - *n_beam*	beam serach with a size of *n_beam*	interactive, translate	no
- - *top_k or -k*	sampling using *top-k*	interactive, translate	no
- - *top_p or -p*	sampling using *top-p*	interactive, translate	no
- - *no_repeat_ngram_size*	ngram size cannot be repeated in the generation	interactive, translate	no
- -*max_outputs or -o*	number of hypotheses to output	interactive, translate	no
- - *cache_dir or -c*	path of the cache directory	interactive, translate	no
- -*logging_file ot -l*	the logging file path	interactive, translate	no
- - *hyp_file or -p*	path of hypothesis file	score	yes
- - *ref_file or -g*	path of references file	score	yes

Table 4: *Required* and *optional* arguments for each of TURJUMAN command-line tools.

Model	Split	bg	bs	cs	da	de	el	en	es	fr	hi	it	ko	pl	pt	ru	tr	ceb	gd	tmh	yo
S2SMT	Dev	5.45	4.14	4.73	5.04	4.28	6.17	7.08	6.42	7.64	4.45	5.27	3.85	6.59	7.24	5.41	4.27	1.67	0.13	0.23	2.59
	Test	5.25	4.44	4.38	5.94	4.61	6.77	7.42	6.22	6.98	4.59	5.24	3.58	6.93	7.15	5.65	4.25	1.98	0.17	0.0.25	2.48
mBART	Dev	-	-	0.98	-	0.71	-	8.02	1.23	1.45	0.39	0.22	0.47	1.18	1.82	1.93	2.03	-	-	0.02	-
	Test	-	-	1.03	-	0.88	-	8.38	1.36	1.66	0.40	0.32	0.39	1.38	1.86	1.78	2.15	-	-	0.06	-
mT5	Dev	8.13	6.63	9.71	10.94	16.64	14.28	25.41	21.12	19.04	4.29	15.17	6.08	3.29	10.96	26.63	10.84	10.23	2.37	0.58	3.45
	Test	12.85	6.60	7.79	10.94	14.90	**15.33**	25.24	21.12	20.74	**4.80**	12.90	**8.27**	**6.41**	21.13	27.94	11.77	7.53	**3.20**	**0.43**	**5.24**
TURJ	Dev	8.68	7.94	9.83	11.30	16.84	13.82	25.80	21.57	21.43	2.86	16.99	2.18	3.43	12.00	29.67	11.75	9.89	2.32	0.64	5.11
	Test	**13.64**	**7.87**	**8.32**	**11.30**	**16.05**	15.06	**25.46**	**21.57**	**22.43**	3.29	**14.92**	3.44	6.38	**23.64**	**31.68**	**13.05**	**8.43**	2.41	0.29	4.39

Table 5: Results of TURJUMAN in BLEU on Dev and Test splits of AraOPUS-20 dataset. **Bolded**: best result on Test. Underlined: best result on Dev. **bg**: Bulgarian. **bs**: Bosnian. **cs**: Czech. **da**: Danish. **de**: German. **el**: Greek. **en**: English. **es**: Spanish. **fr**: French. **hi**: Hindi. **it**: Italian. **ko**: Korean. **pl**: Polish. **pt**: Portuguese. **ru**: Russian. **tu**: Turkish. **ceb**: Cebuano. **gd**: Scots Gaelic. **tmh**: Tamashek. **yo**: Yoruba. **Dash** (−): language is not supported by mBART50 many-to-many.

Model	Split	en	es	fr	ru
S2SMT	Dev	19.79	17.03	13.47	15.84
	Test	18.66	17.56	14.38	14.61
mBART	Dev	9.95	1.78	2.03	1.27
	Test	9.65	1.86	2.12	1.96
mT5	Dev	27.68	23.54	20.22	20.09
	Test	29.93	25.49	21.66	20.94
TURJ	Dev	30.54	26.21	22.82	22.87
	Test	**32.07**	**28.16**	**24.11**	**23.95**

Table 6: Results of TURJUMAN in BLEU on Dev and Test splits of UN dataset. **en**: English. **es**: Spanish. **fr**: French. **ru**: Russian.

4.4. TURJUMAN Arguments.

Each of the command-line tools (i.e., *turjuman-interactive, turjuman-translate,* and *turjuman-score*) support/require several arguments. Table 4 presents the required and optional arguments for each of these TURJUMAN tools.

4.5. Discussion

Results reported in Table 5 show that TURJUMAN achieves best BLEU score in 13 out of the 20 tests splits, outperforming all our baselines: S2SMT, mBART, and mT5 with +8.07, +11.28, and +0.53 BLEU points on average. We also note that mT5 outperforms AraT5 mostly in the languages that were not included in AraT5 vocabulary. Namely, we observe this in Hindi, Polish, Korean, Scots Gaelic, Tamashek, and Yoruba (see Section 2.5.). In addition, as Table 6 shows, TURJUMAN outperforms *all* baselines in UN-Test data in the four investigated MT tasks: English, French, Spanish, and Russian → Arabic.

5. TURJUMAN: Getting Started

5.1. Installation

TURJUMAN is implemented in Python and can be installed using the pip package manager.[16] It is compatible with *Python 3.6* and later versions, *Torch 1.8.1*, and *HuggingFace Transformers 4.5.1 library*.[17]

```
> pip install turjuman
```

5.2. Turjuman Command Line Examples

As explained, TURJUMAN provides several command-line tools for translation and evaluation. Each command supports multiple arguments. In the following, we provide a number of examples illustrating how to use TURJUMAN command-line tools with different arguments.

- **turjuman_interactive.** In the following two examples we use *turjuman_interactive* to generate translations interactively for an English and Portuguese sentences, respectively. Here, we use beam search with a beam size of 5, a maximum sequence length of 300, and a number of targets to output at 3.

```
> turjuman_interactive
```

Output

```
> Turjuman Interactive CLI
> Loading model from UBC-NLP/turjuman
> Type your source text or (q) to STOP:

> She thought a dark moment in her past was forgotten.
> target1: اعتقدت أن لحظة مظلمة في ماضيها قد نسيت.
> target2: لقد اعتقدت أن لحظة مظلمة في ماضيها قد نسيت.
> target3: كانت تعتقد أن لحظة مظلمة في ماضيها قد نسيت.

> Type your source text or (q) to STOP:
> Esta é uma lista de estados soberanos
> target1: هذه قائمة الدول ذات السيادة
> target2: هذه قائمة بالدول ذات السيادة
> target3: قائمة الدول ذات السيادة هذه
```

- **turjuman_translate.** In the following we show how to use turjuman_translate with two modes of input:

(1) Text. A raw text is passed to the turjuman model directly troughs command line using the argument *-text* or *-t*. Translation will display directly on the terminal.

```
> turjuman_translate --text "Je peux payer
   le traitement de votre fille"
```

Output

```
> Turjuman Translate CLI
> Translate from input sentence
> Loading model from UBC-NLP/turjuman
> target: يمكنني أن أدفع ثمن علاج ابنتك.
```

(2) File. The argument *-input_file* or *-f* can be used to import a set of sentences from a text file. Translation will be saved on a JSON file format.

```
> turjuman_translate --file
   ./sample.txt
```

Output

```
> Turjuman Translate CLI
> Translate from samples.txt
> Loading model from UBC-NLP/turjuman
> Translation is saved in samples.json
```

- **turjuman_score.** This evaluates an output translation (output translations) against reference translation(s) in terms of a BLEU score.

```
> turjuman_score -p
   "translated_targets.txt" -g
   "gold_targets.txt"
```

Output

```
> Turjuman Score CLI
> hyp_file=translated_targets.txt
> ref_file=gold_targets.txt
> bleu score: 43.573826221233
```

6. Conclusion

We presented TURJUMAN, an open-source Python-based package and command-line tool for Arabic neural machine translation. In the context of developing TURJUMAN, we also extracted and prepared a high quality 20 language pairs benchmark for MSA MT (*AraOPUS-20*). We exploit AraOPUS-20 to fine-tune an Arabic text-to-text Transformer model, AraT5. Our resulting multilingual model outperforms competitive baselines, demonstrating the utility of our tool. In addition to its translation ability, TURJUMAN integrates a number of decoding methods. This allows for use of the tool for paraphrasing foreign sentences into diverse Arabic sequences. TURJUMAN is extensible, and we plan to train it with larger datasets and further enhance its functionality in the future. We also plan to explore adding new language pairs to TURJUMAN.

Ethical Considerations

TURJUMAN is developed using publicly available data. Hence, we do not have serious concerns about personal information being retrievable from our trained model. Similar to many NLP tools, TURJUMAN can be misused. However, the tool can be deployed for a wide host of useful application such as in education or travel. We do encourage deploying TURJUMAN in socially-relevant scenarios.

[16] *pip install turjuman*

[17] Installation instructions and documentation can be found at: https://github.com/UBC-NLP/turjuman.

Acknowledgements

We gratefully acknowledge support from the Natural Sciences and Engineering Research Council of Canada (NSERC; RGPIN-2018-04267), the Social Sciences and Humanities Research Council of Canada (SSHRC; 435-2018-0576; 895-2020-1004; 895-2021-1008), Canadian Foundation for Innovation (CFI; 37771), Compute Canada (CC),[18] UBC ARC-Sockeye,[19] and Advanced Micro Devices, Inc. (AMD). Any opinions, conclusions or recommendations expressed in this material are those of the author(s) and do not necessarily reflect the views of NSERC, SSHRC, CFI, CC, AMD, or UBC ARC-Sockeye.

7. Bibliographical References

Abdul-Mageed, M., Zhang, C., Hashemi, A., and Nagoudi, E. M. B. (2019). AraNet: A Deep Learning Toolkit for Arabic Social Media. *arXiv preprint arXiv:1912.13072*.

Akeel, M. and Mishra, R. (2014). Ann and rule based method for english to arabic machine translation. *Int. Arab J. Inf. Technol.*, 11(4):396–405.

Almahairi, A., Cho, K., Habash, N., and Courville, A. (2016). First Result on Arabic Neural Machine Translation. *arXiv preprint arXiv:1606.02680*.

Alrajeh, A. (2018). A Recipe for Arabic-English Neural Machine Translation. *arXiv preprint arXiv:1808.06116*.

Aqlan, F., Fan, X., Alqwbani, A., and Al-Mansoub, A. (2019). Arabic–chinese neural machine translation: Romanized arabic as subword unit for arabic-sourced translation. *IEEE Access*, 7:133122–133135.

Bahdanau, D., Cho, K., and Bengio, Y. (2014). Neural machine translation by jointly learning to align and translate. *arXiv preprint arXiv:1409.0473*.

Bakr, H. A., Shaalan, K., and Ziedan, I. (2008). A hybrid approach for converting written egyptian colloquial dialect into diacritized arabic. In *The 6th international conference on informatics and systems, infos2008. cairo university*.

Baniata, L. H., Park, S., and Park, S.-B. (2018). A neural machine translation model for arabic dialects that utilizes multitask learning (mtl). *Computational intelligence and neuroscience*, 2018.

Bouamor, H., Habash, N., and Oflazer, K. (2014). A multidialectal parallel corpus of arabic. In *LREC*, pages 1240–1245.

Bouamor, H., Habash, N., Salameh, M., Zaghouani, W., Rambow, O., Abdulrahim, D., Obeid, O., Khalifa, S., Eryani, F., Erdmann, A., et al. (2018). The madar arabic dialect corpus and lexicon. In *Proceedings of the Eleventh International Conference on Language Resources and Evaluation (LREC-2018)*.

Cettolo, M., Niehues, J., Stüker, S., Bentivogli, L., and Federico, M. (2013). Report on the 10th iwslt evaluation campaign. In *Proceedings of the International Workshop on Spoken Language Translation, Heidelberg, Germany*.

Cettolo, M., Jan, N., Sebastian, S., Bentivogli, L., Cattoni, R., and Federico, M. (2016). The iwslt 2016 evaluation campaign. In *International Workshop on Spoken Language Translation*.

Cettolo, M., Federico, M., Bentivogli, L., Jan, N., Sebastian, S., Katsuitho, S., Koichiro, Y., and Christian, F. (2017). Overview of the iwslt 2017 evaluation campaign. In *International Workshop on Spoken Language Translation*, pages 2–14.

Cormen, T. H., Leiserson, C. E., Rivest, R. L., and Stein, C. (2009). Introduction to algorithms.

Darwish, K. and Mubarak, H. (2016). Farasa: A new fast and accurate Arabic word segmenter. In *Proceedings of the Tenth International Conference on Language Resources and Evaluation (LREC'16)*, pages 1070–1074, Portorož, Slovenia, May. European Language Resources Association (ELRA).

Durrani, N., Dalvi, F., Sajjad, H., and Vogel, S. (2017). Qcri machine translation systems for iwslt 16. *arXiv preprint arXiv:1701.03924*.

El-Kahlout, I. D., Bektaş, E., Erdem, N. Ş., and Kaya, H. (2019). Translating between morphologically rich languages: An arabic-to-turkish machine translation system. In *Proceedings of the Fourth Arabic Natural Language Processing Workshop*, pages 158–166.

Elmahdy, M., Hasegawa-Johnson, M., and Mustafawi, E. (2014). Development of a tv broadcasts speech recognition system for qatari arabic. In *LREC*, pages 3057–3061.

Fadaee, M., Bisazza, A., and Monz, C. (2017). Data augmentation for low-resource neural machine translation. *arXiv preprint arXiv:1705.00440*.

Fan, A., Lewis, M., and Dauphin, Y. (2018). Hierarchical neural story generation. *arXiv preprint arXiv:1805.04833*.

Farha, I. A. and Magdy, W. (2019). Mazajak: An online arabic sentiment analyser. In *Proceedings of the Fourth Arabic Natural Language Processing Workshop*, pages 192–198.

Farhan, W., Talafha, B., Abuammar, A., Jaikat, R., Al-Ayyoub, M., Tarakji, A. B., and Toma, A. (2020). Unsupervised dialectal neural machine translation. *Information Processing & Management*, 57(3):102181.

Federico, M., Cettolo, M., Bentivogli, L., Michael, P., and Sebastian, S. (2012). Overview of the iwslt 2012 evaluation campaign. In *IWSLT-International Workshop on Spoken Language Translation*, pages 12–33.

Ghoneim, M. and Diab, M. (2013). Multiword expressions in the context of statistical machine translation. In *Proceedings of the Sixth International Joint Conference on Natural Language Processing*, pages 1181–1187.

Guellil, I., Azouaou, F., and Abbas, M. (2017). Neural vs statistical translation of algerian arabic dialect written with arabizi and arabic letter. In *The 31st Pacific Asia Conference on Language, Information and Computation PACLIC*, volume 31, page 2017.

Habash, N. and Hu, J. (2009). Improving arabic-chinese statistical machine translation using english as pivot lan-

[18] https://www.computecanada.ca

[19] https://arc.ubc.ca/ubc-arc-sockeye

guage. In *Proceedings of the Fourth Workshop on Statistical Machine Translation*, pages 173–181.

Habash, N., Zalmout, N., Taji, D., Hoang, H., and Alzate, M. (2017). A parallel corpus for evaluating machine translation between Arabic and European languages. In *Proceedings of the 15th Conference of the European Chapter of the Association for Computational Linguistics: Volume 2, Short Papers*, pages 235–241, Valencia, Spain, April. Association for Computational Linguistics.

Holtzman, A., Buys, J., Du, L., Forbes, M., and Choi, Y. (2019). The curious case of neural text degeneration. *arXiv preprint arXiv:1904.09751*.

Junczys-Dowmunt, M., Dwojak, T., and Hoang, H. (2016). Is neural machine translation ready for deployment. *A case study on*, 30.

Koehn, P. (2009). *Statistical machine translation*. Cambridge University Press.

Lample, G., Ott, M., Conneau, A., Denoyer, L., and Ranzato, M. (2018). Phrase-based & neural unsupervised machine translation. *arXiv preprint arXiv:1804.07755*.

Lewis, M., Liu, Y., Goyal, N., Ghazvininejad, M., Mohamed, A., Levy, O., Stoyanov, V., and Zettlemoyer, L. (2020). Bart: Denoising sequence-to-sequence pretraining for natural language generation, translation, and comprehension. In *Proceedings of the 58th Annual Meeting of the Association for Computational Linguistics*, pages 7871–7880.

Lhoest, Q., del Moral, A. V., Jernite, Y., Thakur, A., von Platen, P., Patil, S., Chaumond, J., Drame, M., Plu, J., Tunstall, L., et al. (2021). Datasets: A community library for natural language processing. In *Proceedings of the 2021 Conference on Empirical Methods in Natural Language Processing: System Demonstrations*, pages 175–184.

Liu, Y., Gu, J., Goyal, N., Li, X., Edunov, S., Ghazvininejad, M., Lewis, M., and Zettlemoyer, L. (2020). Multilingual denoising pre-training for neural machine translation. *Transactions of the Association for Computational Linguistics*, 8:726–742.

Meftouh, K., Harrat, S., Jamoussi, S., Abbas, M., and Smaili, K. (2015). Machine translation experiments on PADIC: A parallel Arabic DIalect corpus. In *Proceedings of the 29th Pacific Asia Conference on Language, Information and Computation*, pages 26–34, Shanghai, China, October.

Mohamed, E., Mohit, B., and Oflazer, K. (2012). Transforming standard arabic to colloquial arabic. In *Proceedings of the 50th Annual Meeting of the Association for Computational Linguistics (Volume 2: Short Papers)*, pages 176–180.

Mubarak, H. (2018). Dial2msa: A tweets corpus for converting dialectal arabic to modern standard arabic. In *OSACT 3: The 3rd Workshop on Open-Source Arabic Corpora and Processing Tools*, page 49.

Nagoudi, E. M. B., Elmadany, A., and Abdul-Mageed, M. (2021). Investigating code-mixed Modern Standard Arabic-Egyptian to English machine translation. In *Proceedings of the Fifth Workshop on Computational Approaches to Linguistic Code-Switching*, pages 56–64, Online, June. Association for Computational Linguistics.

Nagoudi, E. M. B., Elmadany, A., and Abdul-Mageed, M. (2022). Arat5: Text-to-text transformers for arabic language generation. Online, May. Association for Computational Linguistics.

Noll, E., Oudah, M., and Habash, N. (2019). Simple automatic post-editing for arabic-japanese machine translation. *arXiv preprint arXiv:1907.06210*.

Obeid, O., Zalmout, N., Khalifa, S., Taji, D., Oudah, M., Alhafni, B., Eryani, F., Erdmann, A., and Habash, N. (2020a). Camel tools: An open source python toolkit for arabic natural language processing. 05.

Obeid, O., Zalmout, N., Khalifa, S., Taji, D., Oudah, M., Alhafni, B., Inoue, G., Eryani, F., Erdmann, A., and Habash, N. (2020b). CAMeL tools: An open source python toolkit for Arabic natural language processing. In *Proceedings of the 12th Language Resources and Evaluation Conference*, pages 7022–7032, Marseille, France, May. European Language Resources Association.

Ott, M., Edunov, S., Baevski, A., Fan, A., Gross, S., Ng, N., Grangier, D., and Auli, M. (2019). fairseq: A fast, extensible toolkit for sequence modeling. *arXiv preprint arXiv:1904.01038*.

Pasha, A., Al-Badrashiny, M., Diab, M., El Kholy, A., Eskander, R., Habash, N., Pooleery, M., Rambow, O., and Roth, R. (2014). MADAMIRA: A fast, comprehensive tool for morphological analysis and disambiguation of Arabic. In *Proceedings of the Ninth International Conference on Language Resources and Evaluation (LREC'14)*, pages 1094–1101, Reykjavik, Iceland, May. European Language Resources Association (ELRA).

Paszke, A., Gross, S., Massa, F., Lerer, A., Bradbury, J., Chanan, G., Killeen, T., Lin, Z., Gimelshein, N., Antiga, L., et al. (2019). Pytorch: An imperative style, high-performance deep learning library. *Advances in neural information processing systems*, 32:8026–8037.

Raffel, C., Shazeer, N., Roberts, A., Lee, K., Narang, S., Matena, M., Zhou, Y., Li, W., and Liu, P. J. (2019). Exploring the limits of transfer learning with a unified text-to-text transformer. *arXiv preprint arXiv:1910.10683*.

Reimers, N. and Gurevych, I. (2020). Making monolingual sentence embeddings multilingual using knowledge distillation. In *Proceedings of the 2020 Conference on Empirical Methods in Natural Language Processing (EMNLP)*, pages 4512–4525.

Sajjad, H., Darwish, K., and Belinkov, Y. (2013). Translating dialectal arabic to english. In *Proceedings of the 51st Annual Meeting of the Association for Computational Linguistics (Volume 2: Short Papers)*, pages 1–6.

Sajjad, H., Abdelali, A., Durrani, N., and Dalvi, F. (2020). Arabench: Benchmarking dialectal arabic-english machine translation. In *Proceedings of the 28th International Conference on Computational Linguistics*, pages 5094–5107.

Salloum, W. and Habash, N. (2011). Dialectal to standard arabic paraphrasing to improve arabic-english statistical machine translation. In *Proceedings of the first workshop on algorithms and resources for modelling of di-*

alects and language varieties, pages 10–21.

Salloum, W. and Habash, N. (2013). Dialectal arabic to english machine translation: Pivoting through modern standard arabic. In *Proceedings of the 2013 Conference of the North American Chapter of the Association for Computational Linguistics: Human Language Technologies*, pages 348–358.

Salloum, W., Elfardy, H., Alamir-Salloum, L., Habash, N., and Diab, M. (2014). Sentence level dialect identification for machine translation system selection. In *Proceedings of the 52nd Annual Meeting of the Association for Computational Linguistics (Volume 2: Short Papers)*, pages 772–778.

Song, K., Tan, X., Qin, T., Lu, J., and Liu, T.-Y. (2019). Mass: Masked sequence to sequence pre-training for language generation. *arXiv preprint arXiv:1905.02450.*

Steinberger, R., Pouliquen, B., Widiger, A., Ignat, C., Erjavec, T., Tufiş, D., and Varga, D. (2006). The jrc-acquis: A multilingual aligned parallel corpus with 20+ languages. In *Proceedings of the Fifth International Conference on Language Resources and Evaluation (LREC'06).*

Takezawa, T., Kikui, G., Mizushima, M., and Sumita, E. (2007). Multilingual spoken language corpus development for communication research. In *International Journal of Computational Linguistics & Chinese Language Processing, Volume 12, Number 3, September 2007: Special Issue on Invited Papers from ISCSLP 2006*, pages 303–324.

Tiedemann, J. (2012). Parallel data, tools and interfaces in opus. 2012:2214–2218.

Vaswani, A., Shazeer, N., Parmar, N., Uszkoreit, J., Jones, L., Gomez, A. N., Kaiser, Ł., and Polosukhin, I. (2017). Attention is all you need. In *Advances in neural information processing systems*, pages 5998–6008.

Xue, L., Constant, N., Roberts, A., Kale, M., Al-Rfou, R., Siddhant, A., Barua, A., and Raffel, C. (2020). mt5: A massively multilingual pre-trained text-to-text transformer. *arXiv preprint arXiv:2010.11934.*

Zbib, R., Malchiodi, E., Devlin, J., Stallard, D., Matsoukas, S., Schwartz, R., Makhoul, J., Zaidan, O., and Callison-Burch, C. (2012). Machine translation of arabic dialects. In *Proceedings of the 2012 conference of the north american chapter of the association for computational linguistics: Human language technologies*, pages 49–59.

Ziemski, M., Junczys-Dowmunt, M., and Pouliquen, B. (2016). The united nations parallel corpus v1. 0. In *Lrec.*

Proceedings of the OSACT 2022 Workshop @LREC2022, pages 12–22
Marseille, 20 June 2022

Detecting Users Prone to Spread Fake News on Arabic Twitter

Zien Sheikh Ali[1], **Abdulaziz Al-Ali**[1,2], **Tamer Elsayed**[1]
[1]Computer Science and Engineering Department, Qatar University
[2]KINDI Center for Computing Research, Qatar University
{zs1407404, a.alali, telsayed}@qu.edu.qa

Abstract

The spread of misinformation has become a major concern to our society, and social media is one of its main culprits. Evidently, health misinformation related to vaccinations has slowed down global efforts to fight the COVID-19 pandemic. Studies have shown that fake news spreads substantially faster than real news on social media networks. One way to limit this fast dissemination is by assessing information sources in a semi-automatic way. To this end, we aim to identify users who are prone to spread fake news in Arabic Twitter. Such users play an important role in spreading misinformation and identifying them has the potential to control the spread. We construct an Arabic dataset on Twitter users, which consists of 1,546 users, of which 541 are prone to spread fake news (based on our definition). We use features extracted from users' recent tweets, e.g., linguistic, statistical, and profile features, to predict whether they are prone to spread fake news or not. To tackle the classification task, multiple learning models are employed and evaluated. Empirical results reveal promising detection performance, where an F1 score of 0.73 was achieved by the logistic regression model. Moreover, when tested on a benchmark English dataset, our approach has outperformed the current state-of-the-art for this task.

Keywords: Misinformation, Social Media, Source Credibility, Fake News

1. Introduction

Twitter has evolved into a popular social media platform for news sharing. It allows tweets to reach a larger audience quickly through retweets and likes. The platform is commonly used by news outlets, governments, and public figures to communicate the latest news in a brief manner and engage with their followers (Vosoughi et al., 2018). While Twitter can be an effective tool to express thoughts and engage with authorities and organizations, it is also misused to generate fabricated information and occasionally manipulate the public opinion.

Misinformation can spread faster, deeper and wider in social networks compared to traditional media sources (Vosoughi et al., 2018). This wide spread of misinformation causes a serious impact on society and individuals. In the past few years, Arabic social media has been utilized to spread state propaganda, attack political parties, and mislead the society (Jones, 2019). Moreover, with the recent COVID-19 outbreak, health related misinformation has proliferated on Arabic social media (Jones, 2020). Spreading anti-vaccine misinformation has contributed in large public hesitancy, which is now hindering the national global efforts to fight the pandemic. Misinformation nowadays is not only used as a political weapon, but it also poses a serious risk to society and public health.

Previous studies have targeted misinformation on Arabic social media from a content-based perspective, by verifying the content of a single post or a tweet (El Ballouli et al., 2017; Nakov et al., 2021; Harrag and Djahli, 2022; Haouari et al., 2021a). However, only a few studies explored this task from a source-based perspective. The spread of misinformation can be effectively mitigated by identifying the credibility of the source of the information (Shu et al., 2020). In social media, users are contributing to the spread of fake news by retweeting and engaging with the information. It was found by Shao et al. (2018) that fake news tends to attract both malicious and normal users. The goal of malicious users is to achieve personal benefits, while normal users often spread misinformation unintentionally. Contrary to previous studies that target malicious users that intentionally spread misinformation (e.g., bots (Yang et al., 2020) and trolls (Mihaylov et al., 2015)), our work is concerned with users that are prone to spread fake news. We define them as *users that contribute in the diffusion and amplification of misinformation on Twitter, either intentionally or unintentionally*. Recognizing that type of users on Twitter is an important task that can be employed to combat the spread of fake news. For example, a tool to identify fake news spreaders can be an explicit addition to fake news detection systems.

In this paper, we aim to identify users prone to spread fake news on Arabic Twitter. Our objective is to classify a user as either prone to spread fake news, or not. Due to the lack of Arabic datasets for this task, we proposed a data collection pipeline to collect claims, tweets, and users for this task. We explored a range of different features extracted from the user timeline, such as textual, profile, statistical, and emotional features. Finally, we evaluated the performance of multiple learning models on our Arabic dataset, as well as publicly available English benchmark dataset.

The contributions of this paper are three-fold:

- We propose a method for constructing a user dataset using a set of previously-verified claims.

- We propose the first model to detect users prone to spread Arabic fake news.
- We made the source code and features used in our experiments publicly available for reproducibility and further research.[1]

The rest of the paper is organized as follows. Section 2 summarizes related work. Section 3 describes our user data collection process. Section 4 outlines our methodology. Section 5 shows our experimental evaluation and results, and Section 7 concludes.

2. Related work

In this section, we review the literature for related work on the task of detecting misinformation spreaders on social media. We discuss efforts on profiling users that spread misinformation (Section 2.1). Second, we review the different approaches that collect datasets of Twitter users to identify their role in spreading fake news (Section 2.2).

2.1. Classifying Misinformation Spreaders on Social Media

The task of classifying misinformation spreaders remains under-explored. Recent attention has focused on identifying social media users that spread fake news. Rangel et al. organized an Author Profiling Shared task at CLEF 2020 (Rangel et al., 2020). The task is defined as follows, given a Twitter user's recent tweets, determine whether they are keen to spread fake news or not. The authors provide a corpus of Twitter users and their recent 100 tweets. The languages covered are English and Spanish only. The task received 66 participants, and the highest Accuracy scores achieved were 75% on the English dataset and 82% on the Spanish dataset. It is worth mentioning that the highest performance was achieved using a stacked ensemble classifier of five machine learning algorithms; four of the base models use character n-grams as features, while the fifth model uses features based on statistics of the tweets such as the average length of the tweets (Buda and Bolonyai, 2020). All of the highest six participants in the task used a combination of n-grams and traditional machine learning approaches.

Rath et al. (2020) proposed a fake news spreader detection model using an inductive representation framework. Given a tweet and a directed social network, users that are more likely to spread misinformation are identified. They built a social graph of twitter users and defined modular communities using Community Health Assessment (CHA) model. Their approach identifies fake news spreaders based on a given tweet, while our approach identifies users independently.

Shu et al. (2019) investigated the role of user profiles for fake news detection. Their experiments show that user features such as registration time, account verification, political bias and personality type could make a significant impact in detecting fake news.

2.2. Annotated User Datasets

Current Twitter fake news datasets are catered for verification of tweets (tweet-level verification) (Haouari et al., 2021a). Limited datasets identify the role of users in the spread of fake news. We summarize the different approaches to collect Twitter users next.

Rangel et al. (2020) constructed a corpus of 500 English users and 500 Spanish for PAN 2020 shared task to detect users keen to spread fake news on Twitter. The corpus was constructed as follows: first, false claims debunked by fact-checking websites (e.g. PolitiFact and Snopes) are collected. Then, Twitter is searched to find tweets relevant to these claims, where the tweets are labeled as supporting a claim or not. After annotating the tweets, the users are labeled as keen to spread fake news or not based on whether they shared at least one tweet supporting a fake claim. Finally, users with the most annotated tweets were selected.

Labelling users based on annotated tweets was similarly adopted by Shao et al. (2018), where users who are super-spreaders are identified as users that continuously spread misinformation. Another contribution by Shu et al. (2019) used verified tweets from FakeNewsNet dataset (Shu et al., 2018) to label users as likely to spread fake-news or likely to spread real-news.

The studies presented thus far provide solutions for profiling users who try to spread misinformation. There is however insufficient research on addressing users spreading misinformation on Arabic Twitter. To fill this gap, our study focuses on identifying users that are prone to spread Arabic fake news. While previous work has focused on misinformation datasets for the task of tweet-level verification, very few studies worked on constructing datasets for user-level verification.

3. Data Collection

In this section, we describe the user data collection and annotation methodology. Our goal is to collect a set of users that are prone to spread fake news, and users that are not prone to spread fake news. To build the dataset, we modified the method used in the shared task at PAN 2020 for profiling fake news spreaders on Twitter, as described in Section 2.2. We constructed the dataset in three main stages. First, we collected sets of previously-verified Arabic claims from multiple resources. We then used those claims to find tweets that are spreading them. Finally, we identify users associated with those tweets and label them based on tweet frequencies. These stages are detailed in the next three subsections.

3.1. Claim Collection

In this stage, we aim to collect real claims from the Arab world and then search for tweets that are spread-

[1] https://gitlab.com/bigirqu/ArPFN

Figure 1: Example of a tweet obtained from AraFacts. The claim translates to "Dr. Mohammed Mashali has passed away." However, the tweet is only questioning whether the claim is true or not.

ing them. To do so, we leveraged two existing Arabic rumor datasets, namely, ArCOV19-Rumors (Haouari et al., 2021b), and AraFacts (Sheikh Ali et al., 2021).

ArCOV19-Rumors covers claims related to COVID-19 from multiple topical categories such as social, political, sports and, entertainment. The dataset contains 138 verified claims from fact-checking websites, and 9,414 tweets relevant to those claims.

AraFacts is the first large collection of Arabic naturally-occurring claims from 5 different Arabic fact-checking websites. The claims are annotated and verified by professional fact-checkers. It contains 6,222 claims that were posted between 2016 and 2021. Claims are crawled from each fact-checking website along with their factual label, description, and 10 additional meta-data. We selected claims from AraFacts that have the labels *True* and *False* only. Overall, we have collected 5,371 claims from both datasets with 299 of them being True and 5,072 being False.

3.2. Tweet Collection

After collecting the claims, the next step is to find tweets that are relevant to them. We utilized the manually-annotated tweets from ArCOV19-Rumors dataset, where only tweets labeled as *True* or *False* were kept, and the rest were discarded, resulting in 3,025 tweets.

In the AraFacts dataset, we used the claim URLs data field, which contains URLs to Web pages that spread each claim. We identified URLs pointing to tweets and obtained their tweet IDs. The tweets were then crawled using the Twitter API yielding 2,981 tweets that are related to 1,213 claims.

After collecting the tweets from AraFacts, we manually inspected a subset of 100 tweets to verify that the tweets are indeed relevant to their corresponding claims. Surprisingly, some of the tweets were not associated with their claims, or not expressing them. Figure 1 shows one such example. Arguably, a user that is questioning the correctness of a claim is neutral towards it and not spreading it. Out of the 100 tweets that we inspected, 9 were found to be irrelevant to their claims. This has prompted us to manually annotate all tweet-claim pairs to verify their relevancy to the claim. The annotation task was performed by one annotator who was asked to read the tweet and the claim, then label the tweet as: *Expressing the claim*, *Negating the claim* or *Other*. The detailed annotation guidelines can be found in Appendix 8.

The results of the annotation task are presented in Table 1. Evidently, 95% of the tweet-claim pairs were labeled correctly by the fact-checkers and 4.5% tweets were labeled as *Other*; meaning they are not relevant or not spreading the claim. We unexpectedly identified 7 tweets negating the claim which could have been added erroneously by the fact-checkers.

Annotation	Number of tweets
Expressing the claim	2,474
Other	125
Negating the claim	7

Table 1: Results for tweet-claim annotation task.

Once annotation was complete, we eliminated the tweets that are labeled as *Other* and changed the label of tweets that are labeled as *Negating* (i.e., a tweet that negates a True claim is labeled False and vice versa). Finally, we collected retweets of all the verified tweets from AraFacts using Twitter API.[2] Unlike AraFacts, the retweets for ArCOV19-Rumors are publicly available.[3] The total number of collected retweets is **35,698**.

3.3. User Collection

Since our annotated tweet collection is limited to only ArCOV19-Rumors tweets and a small subset of AraFacts claims (only 1,213 claims have annotated tweets), this step aims to capture more associated claims to each user by searching the users' timelines for occurrences of other claims from our collection.

We started by using the collected tweets to identify unique users with at least 1 tweet in ArCOV19-Rumors or AraFacts. Consequently, 4,176 unique users were found. For each user, we used Twitter API to collect their timelines. The maximum number of tweets that can be crawled per user is 3,200 tweets.

We then searched the users' timelines for claims using all 5,371 claims from our collection. For each user timeline, we used the ElasticSearch engine[4] to retrieve tweets that have high similarity with the claims' text or description. The retrieved tweets, with BM25 similarity score above 15, were manually annotated using the same annotation guidelines mentioned in Section 3.2, and then appended to the tweet collection.

Table 2 summarizes our tweet collection statistics. We also visualize our collection of verified tweets (tweets

[2]https://developer.twitter.com/en/docs/twitter-api/tweets/retweets/introduction

[3]https://gitlab.com/bigirqu/ArCOV-19/-/blob/master/ArCOV19-Rumors/tweet_verification

[4]https://www.elastic.co/elasticsearch/

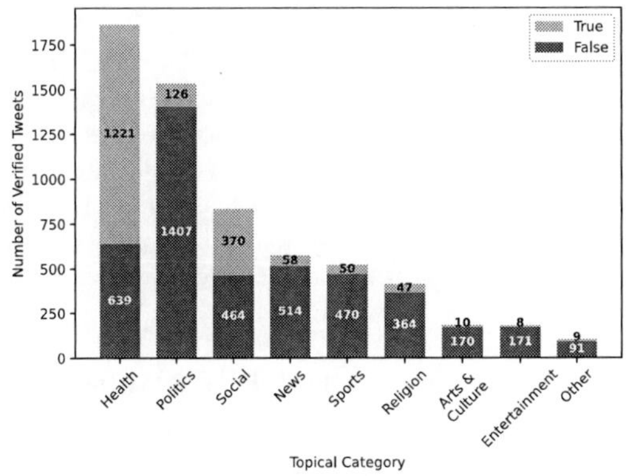

Figure 2: Distribution of the verified tweets and their topical categories and veracity labels.

related to verified claims) in Figure 2 by demonstrating all 9 topical categories and their label distributions. Notably, the majority of tweets are related to Health or Politics and most Fake claims are political.

Tweet Source	True Tweets	False tweets
ArCOV19-Rumors	1,625	1,948
AraFacts	191	2,431
Manually annotated tweets	133	114
All	1,949	4,493

Table 2: Summary of the verified tweets collection.

Next, we investigate the user collection after adding the newly annotated tweets. We count the number of users in terms of their number of verified tweets or retweets. Table 3 summarizes our user collection.

Table 3: Number of users in terms of the number of verified tweets and retweets (RTs) they shared.

Users that shared ...	X			
	1	2	3	4
at least X true tweets or RTs and 0 false tweets or RTs	**1,005**	204	71	35
at least X false tweets or RTs	3,171	**541**	166	73

To construct our final *labeled* user dataset, we identify users as **prone to spread fake news** if they *shared at least two false tweets or retweets*. On the other hand, users are considered **not prone to spread fake news** if they *shared at least one true tweet or retweet and have no record of spreading false tweets or retweets*. The assumption is that users associated with frequent false tweets or retweets are more likely to be prone to spread fake news than others. Although we choose a threshold of *two* false tweets or retweets for users prone to spread fake news, this threshold can be adjusted by the practitioner to suit the task at hand. The threshold for users not prone to spread fake news was set to at least one true tweet. Admittedly, this criterion may introduce noise to this class, as we do not have enough evidence that those users did not spread any fake news that are not included in our verified set of claims.

4. Methodology

In this section, we describe our features and models used to automatically identify users that are prone to spread fake news on Twitter.

4.1. Feature Extraction

For each user, we obtain recent tweets and user's metadata using Twitter API. Features that capture information about the user's activity, popularity, and linguistic style are extracted. These features can be classified into the following five main categories:

4.1.1. Textual Features

To obtain textual features, the user's recent tweets are first concatenated as one "document". We then performed light pre-processing on the text. In particular, we removed all non-alphanumeric characters, replaced URLs or media links with #URL# and #MEDIA#, and used tashaphyne library[5] to clean the text by removing any figuration and normalizing elongated words.

From each user's document, we derived tf-idf word n-grams, and eliminated words that appear in less than 50 documents (across all users). Additionally, we tested multiple n-gram ranges (unigrams, bigrams, and unigrams and bigrams) as a hyper-parameter for each trained model. Using n-grams as textual features was proven to be effective in PAN author profiling task (Rangel et al., 2020).

4.1.2. Contextualized Embeddings

We used contextualized embeddings to represent each user's recent 100 tweets. The use of contextualized embeddings as features is motivated by the work of An et al. (2021) to predict hateful users on Twitter. They obtain a user-level representation by computing Sentence-BERT (S-BERT) (Reimers and Gurevych, 2019) embeddings for each user's tweet then averaging all tweet embeddings into one 768-dimensional vector. In our experiments, we used transformer models to generate embeddings, namely, the different variations of Bidirectional Encoder Representations from Transformers (BERT) to compute embeddings. Three different BERT-based models that support Arabic were tested: AraBERT (Antoun et al., 2020), MARBERT (Abdul-Mageed et al., 2021), and S-BERT.

[5] `https://github.com/linuxscout/tashaphyne/`

4.1.3. Statistical Features

This category of features is derived from users' recent 3,200 tweets. We used features that describe the user impact, motivated by the work proposed by Lampos et al. (2014), in addition to timeline features that describe the user's activities. The proposed statistical features are listed below. The last three features are newly proposed in this work.

- Proportion of tweets with hashtags.
- Average number of hashtags per tweet.
- Proportion of tweets with mentions.
- Number of unique mentions in user's timeline.
- Proportion of tweets that are replies to other users.
- Proportion of tweets that contain URLs.
- Proportion of tweets that contain media, e.g., images or videos.
- Proportion of tweets that are retweets.
- Proportion of tweets that are quote retweets.
- Average engagement of the user, computed as the average number of retweets and likes per tweet.
- Average number of days between each two consecutive tweets.

4.1.4. Profile Features

For each user, we used some meta-data from the user's JSON object as features and derived 10 additional features related to the user. The features used have been implemented in previous studies that profile users (Shu et al., 2019; Yang et al., 2020; Castillo et al., 2011). Table 9 summarizes the extracted profile features, their type, and description.

4.1.5. Emotional Features

Several researchers have utilized emotional signals for credibility assessment (Ghanem et al., 2020; Zhang et al., 2021). Moreover, multiple participants in PAN author profiling task (to detect users keen to spread fake news) used emotional signals to address the task (Rangel et al., 2020; Fersini et al., 2020; Moreno-Sandoval et al., 2020). We similarly extracted emotional signals from the text of each user's recent 100 tweets. For the Arabic experiments, we used the emotion functionality in ASAD tool (Hassan et al., 2021). The extracted 11 features are: anger, anticipation, disgust, fear, joy, love, optimism, pessimism, sadness, surprise, and trust. For the English experiments, we used NRC emotion Lexicon.[6] Specifically, we used the python library NRCLex[7] to retrieve raw emotions count given a text. The extracted features include eight basic emotions (anger, fear, anticipation, trust, surprise, sadness, joy, and disgust) and two sentiments (positive and negative).

[6]https://saifmohammad.com/WebPages/NRC-Emotion-Lexicon.htm

[7]https://pypi.org/project/NRCLex/

4.2. Models

We trained multiple machine learning models over a combination of the features described in Section 4.1. The models we experiment with are known to achieve high performance in different text classification tasks (Shwartz-Ziv and Armon, 2022; Islam et al., 2019), namely, XGBoost (HGB), Random Forests (RF), Logistic Regression (LR), and Feed-forward Neural Networks (NN).

5. Experimental Evaluation

In this section, we conduct experiments to answer the following research questions:

RQ1 How effective are traditional machine learning methods in automatically detecting users that are prone to spread fake news on Arabic Twitter?

RQ1.1 How effective are the existing baselines for the task?

RQ1.2 Which feature category combination exhibits the best performance?

RQ1.3 How does the classifier perform when contextualized embeddings are used instead of word n-grams?

RQ2 What is the effect of increasing the number of user tweets, considered for feature extraction, on the performance of the classifier?

RQ3 How effective is our methodology on an English dataset?

5.1. Experimental Setup

5.1.1. Datasets

The datasets used in our experiments are listed below and summarized in table 4.

- Arabic Dataset (**ArPFN**): This is our Arabic user dataset described in Section 3.3.
- English Dataset (**EN_PAN**): We use the English dataset constructed for PAN author profiling task to predict users keen to spread fake news.[8] The provided dataset consists of hashed user ids, the text of their recent 100 tweets, and the user label.

Dataset	PFN	NPFN	Total Users
ArPFN	541	1,005	1,546
EN_PAN	250	250	500

Table 4: Datasets used in our experiments. PFN/NPFN denotes the number of users that are prone/not prone to spread fake news.

[8]https://zenodo.org/record/4039435#.YlV0g-hBw2x

5.1.2. Training and Evaluation Measures

We evaluated our models using Positive-F_1 (F_1^+) score, where users prone to spread fake news constitute the positive class. We additionally report Macro-F_1 score. Experiments on **ArPFN** were performed using nested 10-fold cross validation to tune the hyper-parameters of model. For that, we optimized for F_1^+ score. Since the dataset is imbalanced and the positive class is the minority, we over-sampled the positive class in training folds only. The reported results on **ArPFN** are the average over the 10-folds used in cross validation.

For the experiments on **EN_PAN**, we used the same data splits provided PAN for easy comparisons. Additionally, we evaluated our models using 10-fold cross validation to be able to perform significance tests.

For statistical significance tests, we performed two-tailed paired t-test on F_1^+ score, using the scores over the 10 folds, with a 5% significance level.

5.1.3. Baselines

We compare the performance of our models against the following baselines:

1. **Majority:** A classifier that always predicts the label of the majority class.
2. **PAN_2020**: The winning participation at PAN author profiling task (Buda and Bolonyai, 2020). They proposed an ensemble of five machine learning models. They replaced the typical majority voting with a logistic regression classifier that takes the outputs of the ensemble models as the input vector. The first four models (Logistic Regression, Support Vector Machine, Random Forest and XGBoost) use word n-grams as features, while the fifth model (XGBoost) uses statistical features. All features are derived from the user's recent 100 tweets only. We used the authors' implementation.[9]
3. **PAN_2020+**: An improved version of **PAN_2020** that we proposed. First, we eliminated the XGBoost model from the ensemble, as it was shown by Buda and Bolonyai (2020) that it has the least impact on the performance as per the Logistic Regression coefficients. Additionally, for the remaining models that use only tf-idf as features, we expand the feature vector by including emotional signals. We trained four models individually with the same feature vector of word n-grams and emotions, then we stack the four models into a Logistic Regression ensemble as done in **PAN_2020**.

5.2. Classification of Users Prone to Spread Arabic Fake News (RQ1)

To address **RQ1**, we trained our baselines and individual models to predict if a user is prone to spread fake news or not. We tried four models: Random Forest (RF), XGBoost (XGB), Logistic Regression (LR), and Feed-forward Neural Networks (NN). We used the Arabic dataset **ArPFN** for this experiment, where the textual features are extracted from each user's recent 100 tweets.

Table 5 summarizes the performance of the baseline models. We note that **PAN_2020** and **PAN_2020+** clearly outperform majority baseline. Moreover, **PAN_2020+** performs slightly better than **PAN_2020**; however, the difference is not statistically significant. To answer **RQ1.1**, the baseline models identify users prone to spread fake news with a F_1^+ score of 0.63.

Model	F_1^+	Macro-F_1
Majority	0.00	0.40
PAN_2020	0.61±0.05	0.71
PAN_2020+	**0.63**±0.06	**0.73**

Table 5: Baseline performance on **ArPFN**.

Next, we perform an ablation study to evaluate the impact of different feature category combinations and find the best combination for this task. We tried the following combinations:

- Textual features only.
- Non-textual-based features (profile and statistical).
- Textual, profile, and statistical features.
- All feature categories.

Table 6 summarizes the results of these experiments. We performed significance tests to compare the performance of each combination with respect to **PAN_2020+**. We use the $*$ symbol to denote a statistically significant improvement over that baseline.

The results clearly show that training the models using textual features only produces similar (in case of XGB and NN) to or better results (in case of RF and LR) than the baseline model. Moreover, RF still yields even better performance with non-textual-based features than the baseline and also the other models. However, the improvements were not statistically significant.

Interestingly, we observe that when textual features are combined with profile and statistical features, XGB, LR, and NN models outperformed the baseline with statistically-significant improvements. Moreover, adding the emotional features (i.e., using all the feature categories) yield an even further improvement in both F_1^+ and Macro-F_1 for the XGB model.

In conclusion, to answer **RQ1.2**, combining textual and non-textual features yields better results in general. More specifically, the best achieved performance (F_1^+= 0.70) is obtained when the XGB classifier is trained on all feature categories.

[9]https://github.com/pan-webis-de/bolonyai20

Features	Model	F_1^+	Macro-F_1
-	**PAN_2020+**	0.63±0.06	0.73
Textual	RF	0.64±0.05	0.75
	XGB	0.63±0.05	0.74
	LR	0.65±0.05	0.75
	NN	0.63±0.05	0.74
Profile +Statistical	RF	0.65±0.05	0.76
	XGB	0.63±0.05	0.73
	LR	0.60±0.03	0.59
	NN	0.63±0.04	0.66
Textual +Profile +Statistical	RF	0.66±0.06	0.76
	XGB	0.68*±0.04	0.78
	LR	0.68*±0.04	0.77
	NN	0.67*±0.05	0.78
Textual +Profile +Statistical +Emotions	RF	0.67±0.05	0.77
	XGB	**0.70***±0.05	**0.79**
	LR	0.68*±0.04	0.76
	NN	0.64±0.06	0.75

Table 6: Performance on **ArPFN** with different feature category combinations. The asterisk (*) indicates statistically-significant improvement over the baseline model.

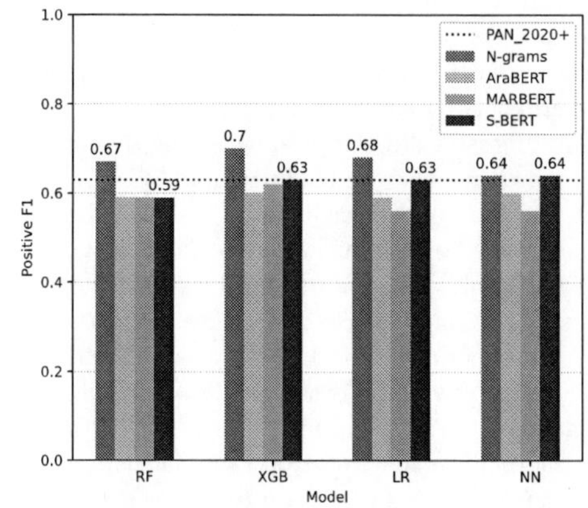

Figure 3: Performance of different models trained using mean-pooling BERT embeddings with profile, statistical, and emotional features on **ArPFN**.

Lastly, we investigate the performance of the classifiers when contextualized embeddings are used as features instead of word n-grams. We used the 768-dimensional embeddings vector that represents the average of the embeddings of each user's tweet. We concatenate the embeddings vector to the profile, statistical, and emotional features. Figure 3 compares the F_1^+ score of using *different* embeddings (i.e., generated from different pre-trained language models) in training our four models. The figure also illustrates the performance of the models trained with all feature categories when the textual features are word n-grams (same scores as in Table 6) for the sake of comparison.

The figure shows that S-BERT embeddings yield the best performance among all other types of embeddings. However, the models trained on the embeddings are all outperformed by the models trained on the word n-grams. Answering **RQ1.3**, the replacement is then deemed ineffective, at least in the way we generated the embeddings vector as the average of the embeddings vectors of the individual user's tweets.

5.3. Effect of Considering Longer User's Timeline (RQ2)

We explore the effect of using more tweets from the user's timeline on classifying the users. Identifying the ideal number of tweets is important in time-sensitive applications, as it determines the number of requests using Twitter API, which allows the retrieval of 100 tweets per request with a rate limit of 900 requests within a 15-minute window.[10]

We conduct experiments by gradually increasing the number of tweets per user and evaluating the performance of each model. We test the model performance on 100, 500, 2,000 and 3,200 user tweets. The experiments are conducted only on **ArPFN**, as **EN_PAN** is only limited to 100 tweets and the usernames are hashed so we were unable to expand it.

For these experiments, we chose the best models from Table 6, namely XGB and LR, trained on all features (with word n-grams). Figure 4 shows the performance after increasing the number of tweets for both models. The figure clearly shows that increasing the number of considered tweets of the timeline results in a monotonically-improving performance for both models. The most notable improvement (which is also statistically-significant) was achieved by the LR model whose performance jumped from F_1^+ score of 0.68 with 100 tweets to 0.73 with 3,200 tweets, yielding the highest performance in all of our experiments. Answering **RQ2**, considering more tweets in extracting the textual features yield better performance; however this requires more API requests, hence more time.

5.4. Performance on English (RQ3)

We aim to validate the effectiveness of our methodology by testing it on datasets of other languages. To this end, we used **EN_PAN** dataset to conduct our experiments on English. **EN_PAN** is limited to the text of the recent 100 tweets from each user, and the usernames were hashed to maintain their privacy. So, we were unable to extract all the features we described in Section 4.1. In this experiment, we compare the performance

[10] `https://developer.twitter.com/en/docs/twitter-api/rate-limits`

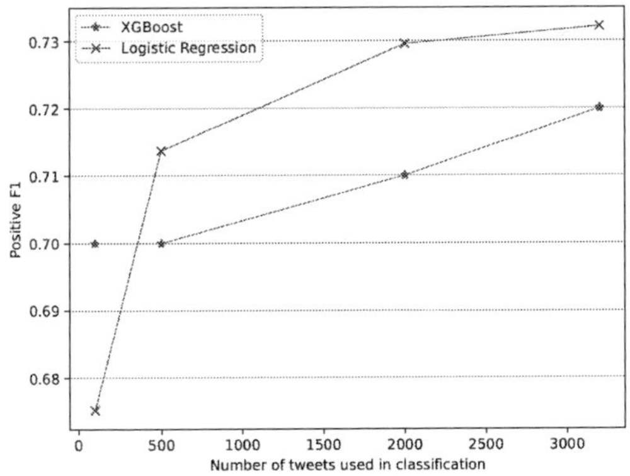

Figure 4: Performance on **ArPFN** after increasing the number of user's tweets for classification.

of the main baseline **PAN_2020** and the improved baseline **PAN_2020+**.
Table 7 reports the results of our experiment on the same PAN data splits. It is shown that our methodology of combining textual features with emotional signals has improved the F_1^+ scores by 5 points. To validate our results, we also perform 10-fold cross validation. The results of that setup are summarized in Table 8, showing that our improved baseline **PAN_2020+** outperforms **PAN_2020**, which constitute the current state-of-the-art. However, the improvement was not statistically-significant.

Model	F_1^+	Macro F_1
PAN_2020	0.74	0.73
PAN_2020+	0.79	0.77

Table 7: Performance on **EN_PAN** using PAN train-test splits.

Model	F_1^+	Macro F_1
PAN_2020	0.73±0.05	0.73
PAN_2020+	0.75±0.03	0.75

Table 8: Performance on **EN_PAN** using 10-fold cross validation.

6. ArPFN Dataset Release

To enable further research, we have made the extracted features of all 1,546 users in **ArPFN** publicly available. Additionally, we shared the folds used in our experiments to enable the reproducibility of our experimental results. To maintain the confidentiality of the users, and in accordance to Twitter content redistribution policy,[11] we do not share the text of the tweets.

[11] `https://developer.twitter.com/en/developer-terms/agreement-and-policy`

7. Conclusion

In this paper, we explored the task of identifying users who are prone to spread fake news in Arabic Twitter. While most related work on fake news detection systems focus on tweet verification, we instead explore the source of the tweet. We constructed the *first* Arabic users dataset **ArPFN** for this task by leveraging two Arabic misinformation datasets, ArCOV19-Rumors and AraFacts. We also proposed the *first* Arabic-specific classifier to identify users prone to spread fake news on Arabic Twitter. Our experiments showed that combining all feature categories yields the best classification performance. Moreover, we established that increasing the number of considered user tweets increases detection accuracy. The best model has achieved an average F_1^+ score of 0.73 using 10-fold cross validation on our Arabic dataset. We also showed that our method is effective even on English datasets, as it has outperformed the current state-of-the art and achieved an F_1^+ score of 0.79.
This study offers important insights on the subject of user credibility on Twitter, a topic that undoubtedly has ethical consequences. As a result, the use of any such prediction system to assess an individual's credibility must be done with caution. We would like to emphasize that the user labeling heuristic in this paper was established by taking the opinion of multiple individuals rather than one. Ultimately, the choice of heuristics to label users is subjective and may differ based on the use case of the target application.

Acknowledgements

This work was made possible by NPRP grant No.: NPRP11S-1204-170060 from the Qatar National Research Fund (a member of Qatar Foundation). The statements made herein are solely the responsibility of the authors.

8. Bibliographical References

Abdul-Mageed, M., Elmadany, A., et al. (2021). Arbert & marbert: Deep bidirectional transformers for arabic. In *Proceedings of the 59th Annual Meeting of the Association for Computational Linguistics and the 11th International Joint Conference on Natural Language Processing (Volume 1: Long Papers)*, pages 7088–7105.

An, J., Kwak, H., Lee, C. S., Jun, B., and Ahn, Y.-Y. (2021). Predicting anti-asian hateful users on twitter during covid-19. In *Findings of the Association for Computational Linguistics: EMNLP 2021*, pages 4655–4666.

Antoun, W., Baly, F., and Hajj, H. (2020). Arabert: Transformer-based model for arabic language understanding. In *Proceedings of the 4th Workshop on Open-Source Arabic Corpora and Processing Tools, with a Shared Task on Offensive Language Detection*, pages 9–15.

Buda, J. and Bolonyai, F. (2020). An ensemble model using n-grams and statistical features to identify fake news spreaders on twitter. In *CLEF*.

Castillo, C., Mendoza, M., and Poblete, B. (2011). Information credibility on twitter. In *Proceedings of the 20th international conference on World wide web*, pages 675–684.

El Ballouli, R., El-Hajj, W., Ghandour, A., Elbassuoni, S., Hajj, H. M., and Shaban, K. B. (2017). Cat: Credibility analysis of arabic content on twitter. In *WANLP@ EACL*, pages 62–71.

Fersini, E., Armanini, J., and D'Intorni, M. (2020). Profiling fake news spreaders: Stylometry, personality, emotions and embeddings. In *CLEF (Working Notes)*.

Ghanem, B., Rosso, P., and Rangel, F. (2020). An emotional analysis of false information in social media and news articles. *ACM Transactions on Internet Technology (TOIT)*, 20(2):1–18.

Haouari, F., Hasanain, M., Suwaileh, R., and Elsayed, T. (2021a). ArCOV-19: The First Arabic COVID-19 Twitter Dataset with Propagation Networks. In *Proceedings of the Sixth Arabic Natural Language Processing Workshop*, pages 82–91.

Haouari, F., Hasanain, M., Suwaileh, R., and Elsayed, T. (2021b). ArCOV19-Rumors: Arabic COVID-19 Twitter Dataset for Misinformation Detection. In *Proceedings of the Sixth Arabic Natural Language Processing Workshop*, pages 72–81.

Harrag, F. and Djahli, M. K. (2022). Arabic fake news detection: A fact checking based deep learning approach. *Transactions on Asian and Low-Resource Language Information Processing*, 21(4):1–34.

Hassan, S., Mubarak, H., Abdelali, A., and Darwish, K. (2021). Asad: Arabic social media analytics and understanding. In *Proceedings of the 16th Conference of the European Chapter of the Association for Computational Linguistics: System Demonstrations*, pages 113–118.

Islam, M. Z., Liu, J., Li, J., Liu, L., and Kang, W. (2019). A semantics aware random forest for text classification. In *Proceedings of the 28th ACM International Conference on Information and Knowledge Management*, pages 1061–1070.

Jones, M. O. (2019). The gulf information war—propaganda, fake news, and fake trends: The weaponization of twitter bots in the gulf crisis. *International journal of communication*, 13:27.

Jones, M. O. (2020). Disinformation superspreaders: the weaponisation of covid-19 fake news in the persian gulf and beyond. *Global Discourse: An interdisciplinary journal of current affairs*, 10(4):431–437.

Lampos, V., Aletras, N., Preoţiuc-Pietro, D., and Cohn, T. (2014). Predicting and characterising user impact on twitter. In *Proceedings of the 14th Conference of the European Chapter of the Association for Computational Linguistics*, pages 405–413.

Mihaylov, T., Georgiev, G., and Nakov, P. (2015). Finding opinion manipulation trolls in news community forums. In *Proceedings of the nineteenth conference on computational natural language learning*, pages 310–314.

Moreno-Sandoval, L. G., Del Puertas, E. A. P., Quimbaya, A. P., and Alvarado-Valencia, J. A. (2020). Assembly of polarity, emotion and user statistics for detection of fake profiles. In *CLEF (Working Notes)*.

Nakov, P., Da San Martino, G., Elsayed, T., Barrón-Cedeño, A., Míguez, R., Shaar, S., Alam, F., Haouari, F., Hasanain, M., Mansour, W., et al. (2021). Overview of the clef–2021 checkthat! lab on detecting check-worthy claims, previously fact-checked claims, and fake news. In *International Conference of the Cross-Language Evaluation Forum for European Languages*, pages 264–291. Springer.

Rangel, F., Giachanou, A., Ghanem, B., and Rosso, P. (2020). Overview of the 8th author profiling task at pan 2020: Profiling fake news spreaders on twitter. In *CLEF*.

Rath, B., Salecha, A., and Srivastava, J. (2020). Detecting fake news spreaders in social networks using inductive representation learning. In *2020 IEEE/ACM International Conference on Advances in Social Networks Analysis and Mining (ASONAM)*, pages 182–189. IEEE.

Reimers, N. and Gurevych, I. (2019). Sentence-bert: Sentence embeddings using siamese bert-networks. In *Proceedings of the 2019 Conference on Empirical Methods in Natural Language Processing and the 9th International Joint Conference on Natural Language Processing (EMNLP-IJCNLP)*, pages 3982–3992.

Shao, C., Ciampaglia, G. L., Varol, O., Yang, K.-C., Flammini, A., and Menczer, F. (2018). The spread of low-credibility content by social bots. *Nature communications*, 9(1):1–9.

Sheikh Ali, Z., Mansour, W., Elsayed, T., and Al-Ali, A. (2021). AraFacts: The First Large Arabic Dataset of Naturally-Occurring Professionally-Verified Claims. In *Proceedings of the Sixth Arabic Natural Language Processing Workshop*. Association for Computational Linguistics.

Shu, K., Mahudeswaran, D., Wang, S., Lee, D., and Liu, H. (2018). FakeNewsNet: A data repository with news content, social context and spatialtemporal information for studying fake news on social media. *arXiv preprint arXiv:1809.01286*.

Shu, K., Zhou, X., Wang, S., Zafarani, R., and Liu, H. (2019). The role of user profiles for fake news detection. In *Proceedings of the 2019 IEEE/ACM international conference on advances in social networks analysis and mining*, pages 436–439.

Shu, K., Bhattacharjee, A., Alatawi, F., Nazer, T. H., Ding, K., Karami, M., and Liu, H. (2020). Combating disinformation in a social media age. *Wiley*

Interdisciplinary Reviews: Data Mining and Knowledge Discovery, 10(6):e1385.

Shwartz-Ziv, R. and Armon, A. (2022). Tabular data: Deep learning is not all you need. *Information Fusion*, 81:84–90.

Vosoughi, S., Roy, D., and Aral, S. (2018). The spread of true and false news online. *Science*, 359(6380):1146–1151.

Yang, K.-C., Varol, O., Hui, P.-M., and Menczer, F. (2020). Scalable and generalizable social bot detection through data selection. In *Proceedings of the AAAI Conference on Artificial Intelligence*, volume 34, pages 1096–1103.

Zhang, X., Cao, J., Li, X., Sheng, Q., Zhong, L., and Shu, K. (2021). Mining dual emotion for fake news detection. In *Proceedings of the Web Conference 2021*, pages 3465–3476.

Appendix

The annotation guidelines used to annotate the AraFacts tweets are described below:
Given a claim X, label the tweet T as:

- **Expressing the same claim**: if the author of the tweet is sharing, restating, or rephrasing the same claim X. In other words, the author is believing the claim and participating in sharing it. (i.e., T = X).
- **Negating the same claim**: if the author of the tweet is disagreeing or denying the claim. In other words, the author is debunking the claim and stating that it is incorrect. (i.e., C = not X).
- **Other**: if it is not one of the above, for example:
  - Author of the tweet is sharing the claim and questioning whether it is true or fake
  - Author of the tweet is sharing multiple claims including the main claim
  - The tweet is referring to a deleted image or video and the text of the tweet is insufficient to annotate the claim

Annotation steps:

1. Read claim text.
2. Read the tweet text.
3. Determine if tweet is expressing the claim, negating the claim or neither.

Notes:

- If the claim is related to an image or video, we recommended to check the URL of the claim and the URL of the tweet to compare if both links refer to the same image or video.
- We recommend considering the claim publication date and tweet posting date into considerations. If the tweet is posted after the claim has been verified, make sure that the tweet is still relevant to the same claim and that the claim is still holding the same label when it was verified.

Table 9: Profile features extracted from users' profiles. Features marked with ⋆ are the 10 features derived using fields from the User's JSON meta-data, while the remaining features are fields from the user's JSON object without modifications.

Feature	Type	Description
default_profile	Boolean	If the user has changed the default theme or background of their profile or not.
verified	Boolean	If the user has a verified account or not.
followers_count	Integer	Number of followers the account has.
following_count	Integer	Number of users that the account is following.
favourites_count	Integer	Number of tweets that were liked by the user.
listed_count	Integer	Number of lists the user has been added to.
statuses_count	Integer	Number of tweets posted by the user.
tweet_frequency⋆	Float	Frequency of the users tweets, calculated as *tweets_count* divided by the account age in months.
follower_ growth_rate⋆	Float	Rate of followers growth, calculated as *followers_count* divided by the account age in months.
following_ growth_rate⋆	Float	Rate of followings growth, calculated as *following_count* divided by the account age in months.
listed_ growth_rate⋆	Float	Rate of lists growth, calculated as *lists_count* divided by the account age in months.
followers_following_ratio⋆	Float	Number of followers compared to the number of following
screen_name_length⋆	Integer	Number of characters in the users screen name.
digits_in_screen_name⋆	Integer	Number of digits in the users screen name
name_length⋆	Integer	Number of characters in the name of the user.
digits_in_name⋆	Integer	Number of numerical digits in the name of the user.
description_length ⋆	Integer	Number of characters in the user's description (biography).

Proceedings of the OSACT 2022 Workshop @LREC2022, pages 23–31
Marseille, 20 June 2022

AraSAS: The Open Source Arabic Semantic Tagger

Mahmoud El-Haj, Paul Rayson, Elvis de Souza[*], Nouran Khallaf[†] and Nizar Habash[‡]

Lancaster University, UK
[*]Pontifical Catholic University of Rio de Janeiro, Brazil
[†]University of Leeds, UK
[‡]New York University Abu Dhabi, UAE
{m.el-haj, p.rayson}@lancaster.ac.uk,[*]elvis.desouza99@gmail.com,
[†]mlnak@leeds.ac.uk, [‡]nizar.habash@nyu.edu

Abstract

This paper presents (AraSAS) the first open-source Arabic semantic analysis tagging system. AraSAS is a software framework that provides full semantic tagging of text written in Arabic. AraSAS is based on the UCREL Semantic Analysis System (USAS) which was first developed to semantically tag English text. Similarly to USAS, AraSAS uses a hierarchical semantic tag set that contains 21 major discourse fields and 232 fine-grained semantic field tags. The paper describes the creation, validation and evaluation of AraSAS. In addition, we demonstrate a first case study to illustrate the affordances of applying USAS and AraSAS semantic taggers on the Zayed University Arabic-English Bilingual Undergraduate Corpus (ZAEBUC) (Palfreyman and Habash, 2022), where we show and compare the coverage of the two semantic taggers through running them on Arabic and English essays on different topics. The analysis expands to compare the taggers when run on texts in Arabic and English written by the same writer and texts written by male and by female students. Variables for comparison include frequency of use of particular semantic sub-domains, as well as the diversity of semantic elements within a text.

Arabic, English, Semantics, Corpus Linguistics, Taggers

1. Introduction

Semantic tagging is the process of associating an element of text data to a well-formed ontology or a lexicon (Rayson and Wilson, 1996; Rayson et al., 2004). While in other types of semantic annotation, the tagging can be applied to a whole text or to text fragments (e.g. sentences, words), in this paper we consider only the case of assigning labels (or tags) to words and multi-word expressions. The tags are assigned based on a pre-defined semantic lexicon indicating coarse-grained word senses. A lexicon refers to the component of a Natural Language Processing (NLP) system that contains semantic or grammatical information about individual words or word strings (Guthrie et al., 1996). This annotation can be considered as a tool for semantic enrichment of the text which facilitates the development of various types of NLP applications especially allowing a better performance for semantic search (Kogalovskii, 2018; Rayson et al., 2004). Moreover, semantic annotation is an important task in NLP, with the original semantic tagger being developed for English (Piao et al., 2015b; Piao et al., 2016b).

Unlike English and despite the increasing interest in research related to Arabic NLP, there is still a lack of well developed NLP tools and techniques that are required to advance the computational study or application of semantics. This is partly due to features of Arabic morphology and orthography which are very different to English and other Indo-European languages, as well as the lack of available corpus resources over time. Arabic is morphologically rich and complex (Habash, 2010; El-Haj and Rayson, 2016). In addition to its rich inflectional and derivational systems, Arabic has a large number of attachable clitics such as prepositions, and pronouns. Arabic orthography uses optional diacritical marks to indicate short vowels, and consonantal gemination. But these diacritics are almost never used beyond religious texts and children's books. The combination of rich morphology and underspecified orthography leads to a high degree of ambiguity: the Standard Arabic Morphological Analyzer (SAMA) (Graff et al., 2009), e.g., returns 12 analyses per word on average. This ambiguity comes on top, and independently, of the kind of polysemy that is common in many languages (e.g. "set", "run" and "get" have multiple related meanings in English). For example the undiacritized Arabic word ولعين *wlςyn*[1], returns four lemmas and 83 analyses using the CALIMAStar Arabic analyzer (Taji et al., 2018) inside of CamelTools (Obeid et al., 2020). The lemmas correspond to the *vocables*: لَعِين *laςiyn* 'cursed' (adjective), عَين *ςayn* 'Ain' (proper noun), وَلِع *waliς* 'passionnate' (adjective), and عَين *ςayn* 'eye' (noun). The effect of morphological inflection and cliticization together with underspecified vowels can be demonstrated by contrasting two of these readings: وَلِعِينَ *waliςiyna* 'passionnate [masc.pl]' and وَلِعَينٍ *wa+li+ςaynĩ* 'and+for+an-eye'. When consider-

[1]Arabic Transliteration in the HSB Scheme (Habash and Rambow, 2005).

ing polysemy, the lemma عَيْن *ʕayn* by itself has around 50 meanings out of context (ibn Mukarram ibn Manzūr, 1290): besides 'eye', 'eighteenth letter of the Arabic alphabets', 'spy', 'envy', 'sun', 'rain' and 'water spring'. In this paper, we introduce the first open source Arabic Semantic tagger (AraSAS). Throughout the paper, we describe the process of creating, validating and evaluating AraSAS. In addition we analyse the semantic fields or domains of words used in ZAEBUC[2] corpus (Palfreyman and Habash, 2022; Habash and Palfreyman, 2022) which contains text written by bilingual students writings from different cities in the United Arab Emirates (UAE) who had just joined Zayed University. The text was created by undergraduate Arabic-English bilingual students as part of their degree, where the written assignment was to assess their language skills. The assignments written by the students formed the ZAEBUC corpus. The analysis provides semantic annotation to ZAEBUC as a new gold-standard language resource to increase the understanding of texts, especially through machine learning and NLP. In addition, the analysis helps in widening and supporting both comparative research and studies of the Arabic language from the perspective of English. Fuller details of the application of this tagger to ZAEBUC are presented in (Khallaf et al., 2022).

AraSAS is the Arabic equivalent to the well established English UCREL Semantic Analysis System (USAS) (Rayson et al., 2004). The USAS lexicon (Rayson et al., 2004) contains 21 major semantic fields (see Figure 1) with 232 sub-classes as the reference semantic ontology. USAS was used in the first prototype of AraSAS tagger (Mohamed et al., 2013), which was never been publicly released. The authors used the Buckwalter Arabic Morphological Analyser (Buckwalter, 2004) to compile a list of Arabic lemmas. Buckwalter also provides English glosses (equivalent translations) of those lemmas. The English translations were used to match against the entries in the USAS English lexicon, where they then compiled a lexicon entry for each Arabic lemma containing the union of all tags from the entries of all its possible equivalents. Although the authors managed to match 71% of the lemmas to the USAS lexicon, the process itself was error prone due to the out-of-context matching process (Zawahreh, 2013). The process resulted in a lexicon containing 37,312 lemmas. A post-editing process was performed on just 4% of the total lemmas. The lemmas were sorted by lemma frequencies in the Leeds Corpus of Contemporary Arabic (CCA) (Al-Sulaiti and Atwell, 2006), with the post-editing being focused on the most frequent lemmas in order to maximise coverage of typical texts. Our new release of AraSAS provides a much extended and edited semantic lexicon and an open source semantic tagger tool that is developed for the Arabic language. AraSAS has been inte-

[2]http://www.zaebuc.org

A general and abstract terms	B the body and the individual	C arts and crafts	E emotion
F food and farming	G government and public	H architecture, housing and the home	I money and commerce in industry
K entertainment, sports and games	L life and living things	M movement, location, travel and transport	N numbers and measurement
O substances, materials, objects and equipment	P education	Q language and communication	S social actions, states and processes
T Time	W world and environment	X psychological actions, states and processes	Y science and technology
Z names and grammar			

Figure 1: USAS Tagger Major Discourse Fields

grated with CAMeL Tools[3] to provide a Python platform for researchers working on Arabic NLP (Obeid et al., 2020).

Both AraSAS and USAS will help in analysing the semantic domains of words used in ZAEBUC by the bilingual university-level students in Arabic and English. The taggers will help in annotating each word in those texts by giving each word a semantic domain/sub-domain (e.g. "B2: Health and disease" or "A6.1 Comparing: Similar/different")[4].

2. Related Work

Semantic tagging is an umbrella term for a wide variety of other terms and tasks related to linguistic annotation of corpora. These can include mark up tasks such as Named Entity Recognition (locations, names, dates, times and organisations), semantic role labelling (goals, agents and results), word sense disambiguation (fine-grained dictionary senses), summarisation (reducing the length of a text while retaining its core meaning), or sentiment analysis (annotation for positive and negative opinions about a product or service).

A core task implemented by the UCREL Semantic Annotation System (USAS) (Rayson et al., 2004), is to assign coarse-grained semantic fields to all words and phrases in a text. Originally applied for content analysis of market research interview transcripts, the USAS tagger is a knowledge based system incorporating manually curated semantic information in large single word and multi-word expression (MWE) lexicons, approximately 80,000 words and MWEs in total. The job of the tagger is then to select the contextually appropriate semantic tag to best represent the broad semantic field of a word or MWE. The semantic tags are taken from a

[3]CAMeLTools: An Open Source Python Toolkit for Arabic Natural Language Processing which offers a robust Arabic morphological analysis, dialect identification, named entity recognition and sentiment analysis.

[4]The categories are based on a hierarchical semantic tag set. The first letter shows the major discourse field as shown in Figure 1 (e.g. B refers to 'the body and the individual', while the 6 in B6 refers to the sub-category 'health and disease'.

Word	Gloss	POS	Lemma	Semantic Tags
تشهد *tšhd*	witnesses	verb	شَهِد_1 *šahid*	S9 A10+@ X3.4 G2.1 Q2.1 S7.1-@ X3.2
دولة *dwlħ*	state	noun	دَوْلَة_1 *dwlħ*	G1.1c W3 F4/M7 M7
الإمارات *AlǍmArAt*	Emirates	noun	إِمَارَة_1 *ǍimArah̄*	Q1.1 A6.2+ X4.1 Q1.2 O4.1 S9 B2
العربية *Alςrbyħ*	Arab	adj	عَرَبِيّ_1 *ςrabiy~*	Z2/Q3
المتحدة *AlmtHdħ*	United	adj	مُتَّحِد_1 *mut~aHid*	S5+ A1.1.1
تطورا *tTwrA*	development	noun	تَطَوُّر_1 *taTaw~ur*	A5.1+/A2.1 T2++ A2.1+ H1 A3+/A11.1
كبيرا *kbyrA*	great	adj	كَبِير_1 *kabiyr*	N3.2+ N5+ A11.1+ A5.1+ X5.2+ A13
.	.	punc	.	PUNC

Table 1: Example of tagging an Arabic sentence (POS: part-of-speech tag).

taxonomy of 232 labels grouping together word senses that are connected to the same topic, e.g. the 'education' tag P1 is assigned to words and MWEs such as 'academic', 'coaching', 'coursework', 'deputy head', 'exams', 'PhD', 'playschool', and 'revision notes'. The English tagger performs this task at around 91% accuracy (Rayson et al., 2004).

Using a similar knowledge-based model with manually created lexicons, semantic taggers for other languages were created e.g. Finnish (Löfberg, 2017) and Russian (Mudraya et al., 2006). More recently, bootstrapping approaches have been evaluated to more quickly generate prototype semantic lexicons in new languages (Piao et al., 2015a), alongside crowd-sourcing methods to see whether non-expert native speakers could assist in the creation and checking of such resources (El-Haj et al., 2017). This has resulted in a proliferation of semantic taggers in multiple languages (Piao et al., 2016a), as well as applying further contextual disambiguation methods to apply more fine-grained taxonomies in a historical context (Piao et al., 2017), and multi-task machine learning methods to derive annotation knowledge from manually tagged corpora and pre-trained embeddings (Ezeani et al., 2019). For a more detailed discussion of the development of USAS, see (Löfberg and Rayson, 2019).

Other than the previous work on AraSAS, most research on Arabic semantic annotation is limited to semantic role labelling (Al-hadi et al., 2016). Similarly, semantically annotated corpora and other tools for Arabic are still in the early stages of creation, with very few available resources (Saleh and Al-Khalifa, 2009).

3. AraSAS Semantic Tagger

The new Arabic Semantic Annotation System (AraSAS) was developed in *Python* 3 and makes use of several other Python packages in its pipeline. The AraSAS pipeline to transform raw Arabic text into semantically tagged output is illustrated in Figure 2.

As shown in Figure 2, the first part of the pipeline is sentence segmentation, which is performed using the Natural Language Toolkit (NLTK) (Loper and Bird,

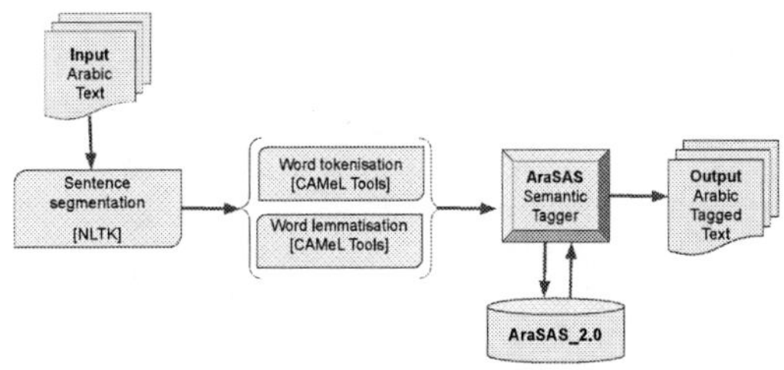

Figure 2: AraSAS pipeline

2002). For the segmentation to work properly for Arabic texts, we also needed to replace right-to-left with left-to-right punctuation marks (e.g. the Arabic question mark '؟' to the English/Latin question mark '?').

Once sentences are identified, AraSAS calls CAMeL Tools (Obeid et al., 2020) to tokenise the sentences into tokens. Those tokens are then disambiguated using a morphological analyser, which ranks the most probable analysis for a word based on its lemmatisation and part of speech annotation.

As an example we used AraSAS to tag the following Arabic sentence from ZAEBUC: تشهد دولة الامارات العربية المتحدة تطورا كبيرا 'The United Arab Emirates is witnessing a great development.' The result of the semantically tagged sentence is shown in Table 1, where each token is displayed in a new line and each semantic tag is separated by a white space. Besides the use of a lexicon, a few regular expressions are also applied to finding punctuation and numbers, both receiving their own distinct semantic tags.

We have made AraSAS freely available open source for academic use[5]. AraSAS is also available as a web-tool, where users can type in or paste their text to be tagged[6].

3.1. AraSAS Lexicon Creation

We used the first draft of the AraSAS lexicon (henceforth, `AraSAS_1.0`) (Mohamed et al., 2013) to cre-

[5] `https://github.com/UCREL/AraSAS`

[6] `http://ucrel-api.lancaster.ac.uk/`

	Lemma	Translation	POS	Semantic Tag
AraSAS_1.0	عَلِيّ *ςaliy∼*	supreme, high, Ali	–	A1.1.1 A5.1+++ Z1m
AraSAS_2.0	عَلِيّ *ςaliy∼*	supreme, high	adjective	A1.1.1 A5.1+++
	عَلِيّ *ςaliy∼*	Ali	proper noun	Z1m

Table 2: Lemma representation in both original and CAMeL list annotated with Semantic tags

ate a verified lexicon that we can use with the newly created AraSAS semantic tagger (henceforth, `AraSAS_2.0`).

One of the main shortcomings of the `AraSAS_1.0` lexicon is that it used a reduced basic representation of Arabic lemmas. In contrast, the CAMeL database, which is based on BAMA/SAMA, provides number markings for different meanings of a lemma. For example, the lemma عَلِيّ *ςaliy∼* has two variants: *ςaliy∼_1* 'supreme;high (adj)', and *ςaliy∼_2* 'Ali (proper noun)'. These two variants are collapsed into one lemma in `AraSAS_1.0`. Most of these number ids overlap with POS distinctions as in the above example. In the CAMeL database, there are 42,226 (lemmas with ids and POS), corresponding to 37,613 basic lemmas (no ids), and 40,795 basic lemmas with POS. We keep the lemma disambiguation markers and POS while building the `AraSAS_2.0` lexicon as much as possible in an attempt to increase the precision of the semantic tagging process. Originally, when creating the English USAS lexicon, words with their POS tags were used for lexicon entries, and gradually this was updated to include lemmas with POS once a lemmatiser was included in the English processing pipeline.

We began by creating a list of the most frequent lemmas in the Penn Arabic Treebank (PATB) (Maamouri et al., 2004) and cross matched it to the lemmas in `AraSAS_1.0`. The PATB lemma-list was created by selecting 32,000 words from the full PATB words list, which was done to match the number of Arabic words in ZAEBUC (212 documents with each containing an average of 160 Arabic words). We then lemmatised the words and normalised digits using CAMeL tools, which resulted in a PATB lemma-list of 4,500 lemmas. Matching `AraSAS_1.0` to PATB lemma-list we ended up with 200 new lemmas, which were found in PATB lemma-list but not in `AraSAS_1.0`. We then combined the `AraSAS_1.0` lemmas with the new 200 lemmas to create an updated list of lemmas as in Figure 3.

We asked a linguist, who is also the fourth author of this paper, to manually check the validity of given semantic tags for a random sample of 150 lemmas from `AraSAS_1.0`. The linguist found that a large number of the lemmas were assigned unrelated semantic tags. This was mainly due to the fact that a single word may have multiple meanings. This was not accounted for in `AraSAS_1.0` where the authors compiled a lexicon entry for each Arabic lemma containing the union of all tags from the entries of all its possible equivalents

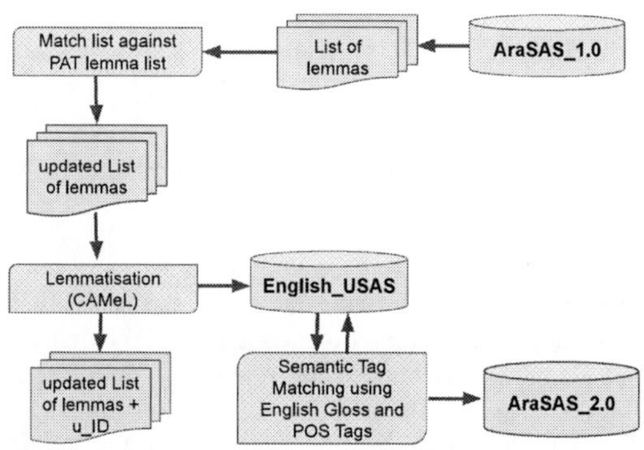

Figure 3: The process of creating `AraSAS_2.0` lexicon

in English. Although this would result in a higher coverage, it reduced precision and accuracy (Mohamed et al., 2013). To overcome this problem we decided to use CAMeL tools lemmatiser and part of speech (POS) tagger to help capture the different meanings of all lemmas in the updated list of lemmas as illustrated in Figure 3. For a single lemma with different possible meanings, the CAMeL lemmatiser follows each of those meanings with a unique number (u_ID) to help differentiate between them (e.g. work_1, work_2) (Obeid et al., 2020). The process resulted in the *Updated List of Lemmas + u_ID* as shown in Figure 3.

To sustain the different meanings, we included u_ID in a new column in the lexicon to help identify such differences as shown in Table 2. As with the Buckwalter Morphological Analyser, CAMeL also provides the English glosses (equivalent translations) of those lemmas, which we used to match against the USAS English lexicon in order to produce a more accurate AraSAS lexicon (`AraSAS_2.0`).

The linguist validated the same 150 lemmas as in `AraSAS_1.0` by comparing to `AraSAS_2.0`, but this time considering the different meanings for a single lemma using u_ID. The linguist found that the lemmas from `AraSAS_2.0` provided a clear division between the senses, since each entry with a different meaning was treated as a different lemma.

The second step after that was to match `AraSAS_2.0` entries against USAS English lexicon using POS tags and English gloss for each lemma. The process resulted in an addition of 4,260 entries on top of the original 37,312 entries found in `AraSAS_1.0` (the new 200 lemmas from the Penn Arabic Treebank are included in the 4,260 lemmas). The reason for this increase in AraSAS_2.0 was due to the use of u_ID, which resulted in a total of 41,572 entries.

3.2. Validating AraSAS_2.0

AraSAS_1.0 was based on lemmas appearing in the Leeds Corpus of Contemporary Arabic (CCA) (Al-Sulaiti and Atwell, 2006). This lexicon required some modifications in order to maximise its coverage, as well as normalise the lemmas to be compatible with CAMeL Tools (Obeid et al., 2020). Firstly, we compared the semantic tags attached to the first one thousand lemmas in the AraSAS_1.0 list with AraSAS_2.0. Areas where significant differences have been found include both lemmatisation and semantic tags. For instance, as represented in Table 2 the two variants of the lemma عَلِيّ *ςaliy∼* with their different POS tags were collapsed in AraSAS_1.0, but are distinguished in AraSAS_2.0. This lemma division has a high impact on the semantic annotation process. On the other hand, in AraSAS_1.0 there was some disagreement upon some annotated semantic tags such as in lemma مع *mς* 'with/together' which was wrongly annotated with T1.1.2 (Referring to Time: General: Present; simultaneous), we believe there are no cases for time correlated with this Arabic lemma. However, this meaning is correlated with the English word 'together', which refers to 'at the same time'. For this reason, a manual modification of the semantic tags for the first most frequent 1000 Arabic lemmas involved removing or adding a semantic sense and rearranging the previously annotated senses according to the new added lemmas.

Secondly, the process of building AraSAS_2.0 was challenging in terms of matching and aligning the lemmas to AraSAS_1.0. In this case we matched both lists using the English translation provided in AraSAS_1.0 and the English gloss provided by the CAMeL analysis along with the POS tags to produce the new merged list. Moreover, in AraSAS_1.0 common orthographic inconsistencies, e.g., among various Alif-Hamza forms: آإأا *AÂǍĀ*, resulted in mismatches between the two lists.

Matching using the English translations and glosses resulted in adding 286 new untagged lemmas that were not analysed by CAMeL POS tagger. Starting with manual analysis and semantically tagging these lemmas, we found they are usually due to transliteration and misspellings. Examples include (a) English words written with Arabic letters such as هاوس *hāwis* 'house' and تيليفيجن *tīlīfijan* 'television'; (b) English proper nouns written in Arabic letters such as رولاند *Rūlāand* 'Roland'; and (c) misspelled words such as اوكسترا *Ūksitrā* rather than اوركسترا *Ūrksitrā* 'orchestra'.

This validation process was followed by manually analysing the 10,023 lemmas assigned the Z99 semantic tag, which is used when there is no match (unmatched category) to any of the tags found in AraSAS_2.0 tagging list. We manually annotated the 1,300 most frequent PATB lemmas in order to prioritise our efforts in assigning a tag other than Z99 as widely as possible. Around 600 lemmas of the manually checked 1,300 Z99 lemmas were found to be Personal-Names (Z1), Geographic-Names (Z2) or Other-Proper-Names (Z3).

3.3. AraSAS Evaluation

We evaluated AraSAS lexical coverage by tagging two different sets of texts in Arabic: one from Arabic blogs (composed of 1,114,535 tokens, according to CAMeL Tools tokeniser) and another from Arabic newspapers (1,108,058 tokens).

Running the lexical coverage experiment, we found that AraSAS lexical coverage ranges from 96% of tokens in blogs texts to 96.8% in news texts. The results shows that AraSAS_2.0 to have a high lexical coverage.

Additionally, using the ZAEBUC dataset (described in Section 4.), we evaluated the proportion of untagged words from the English sub-corpus (annotated by the English original USAS) and the Arabic sub-corpus (annotated by the recently developed AraSAS_2.0). The English tagger showed a lexical coverage of 99.3%, while applying AraSAS resulted in coverage of 98.3%. For future work we will work on manually tagging a larger set of AraSAS entries and calculating recall, precision and F-measure scores to assess the tagging quality.

Originally, English USAS as well as USAS in other several languages, have been assessed and evaluated to measure tagging quality. The work her is a release of the AraSAS semantic tagger tool, which we believe is going to be useful for researchers working on Arabic NLP and Arabic semantics. In previous, work we report the process used to evaluate the quality of lexicon bootstrapping for different languages, including Arabic, as shown in (El-Haj et al., 2017) and (Piao et al., 2016b).

4. ZAEBUC Corpus

Zayed Arabic-English Bilingual Undergraduate Corpus (ZAEBUC) is composed of bilingual students writings from different cities in the United Arab Emirates (UAE) who just joined Zayed University. The students were asked to do two assignments to assess their language skills, one in Arabic and another in English. Their essays, that are part of the assignment, were collected to compose the bilingual writers corpus of ZAEBUC.

Students could choose from three different topics and they did not have to choose the same topic for the writings in Arabic and English, although most of them did. The resulting ZAEBUC corpus is not balanced– there are more female than male authors, more English than Arabic essays, and most of the students chose the 'social media' topic over 'development' and 'tolerance'.

Despite the differences, we were still able to establish fruitful comparisons by looking at their writings in terms of semantic domains.
The students essays were manually validated by academics who detected spelling mistakes replaced them by the corrected words for the sake of the experiments described in this paper, as otherwise the semantic tagging would be less accurate.

5. Experimental Work

As mentioned earlier, Arabic texts from ZAEBUC were semantically annotated using AraSAS, while the English ones were tagged by the original English USAS. Both systems share the same tagset and tagging methodology. The ZAEBUC dataset is unbalanced, it is composed of 603 essays,[7] of which 215 were written in Arabic and 388 in English. The coverage percentage for each language is shown in Table 3. Tokens not tagged by AraSAS were later manually annotated and added into the lexicon to improve its coverage.

	Arabic	English
Texts	215	388
Tokens	34,442	97,994
Tagged	33,887	97,354
Untagged	555	640
Coverage	98.4%	99.3%

Table 3: ZAEBUC Composition

To compare the AraSAS and USAS we a modified version of the Type Token Ratio (TTR) formula (Richards, 1987), where instead we consider the total number of unique semantic tags rather than words (types). We call the updated formula the Semantic Token Ratio (STR) as shown in the following formula:

$$STR = \frac{N_{tag}}{T} \tag{1}$$

where STR is the Semantic Token Ratio, N_{tag} is the number of tokens that received a given semantic tag, and T is the total number of tokens in the sub-corpus, allowing the comparison of unbalanced sub-corpora like the ones featured in ZAEBUC.

5.1. Comparing Texts from Bilingual Authors

As stated earlier, the authors from ZAEBUC are Arabic-English bilingual speakers, but not all of them wrote in both Arabic and English as shown in the corpus description in Table 3. The number of texts in the English sub-corpus exceeds the number of Arabic texts by around 80%. As shown in the table, the number of tokens is far more unbalanced than the texts, there are 184% more tokens in English than in Arabic. This resulted in an average of 252 tokens for each text in English, while Arabic texts have an average of 160 tokens per article due to the high use of clitics and affixes/suffixes in Arabic (García-Barrero et al., 2013)
Figure 4 shows the eight most frequent semantic tags in texts written in Arabic and English after running AraSAS and USAS. Semantic tags related to punctuation and grammar are not featured as otherwise they would represent most of the relative occurrences while not being relevant to the discussion.
The Y axis in Figure 4 shows the percentage of the sample that the semantic tag occupies. For example, the most frequent semantic tag in texts written in Arabic is `M6` (Location and direction), which represents 13.7% of all tokens in the Arabic sub-corpus, while the most frequent semantic tag in English is `A3` (Being)[8].

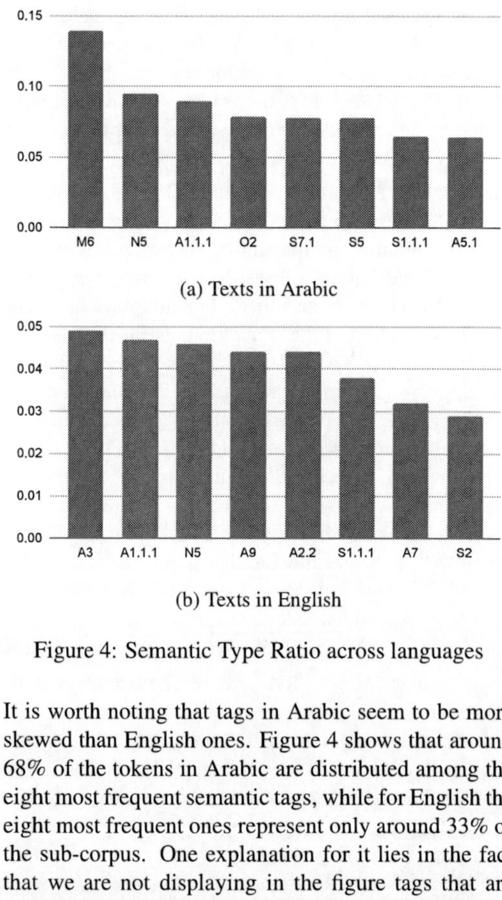

(a) Texts in Arabic

(b) Texts in English

Figure 4: Semantic Type Ratio across languages

It is worth noting that tags in Arabic seem to be more skewed than English ones. Figure 4 shows that around 68% of the tokens in Arabic are distributed among the eight most frequent semantic tags, while for English the eight most frequent ones represent only around 33% of the sub-corpus. One explanation for it lies in the fact that we are not displaying in the figure tags that are grammatical – `Z5` (Grammatical bin) represents 33% in English and only 25% in Arabic, while `Z8` (Pronouns etc.) represents 11% in English and only 7% in Arabic. The semantic tag `M6` (Location and direction), while the most used in Arabic, is not be found in the eight most frequent tags in the English sub-corpus. At the

[7]These numbers are based on an early release of the ZAEBUC Corpus v0.1.

[8]Full list of tags used by USAS and AraSAS: https://ucrel.lancs.ac.uk/usas/USASSemanticTagset.pdf

Tag	Label	MFT	STR
Z5	Grammatical bin	.	0.25
M6	Location and direction	في *fy* 'in/inside	0.13
N5	Quantities	فرد *frd* 'one/individual	0.09
A1.1.1	General actions, making	موقع *mwqς* 'location'	0.08
02	Objects generally	رد *rd* 'to reply'	0.07
S7.1	Power, organizing	كبير *kbyr* 'large'	0.07
S5	Groups and affiliation	مجتمع *mjtmς* 'community'	0.07
Z8	Pronouns etc.	أنّ *Ân* 'that'	0.07
S1.1.1	General	اجتماعي AjtmAςy 'social'	0.06
A5.1	Evaluation: Good/bad	سلبّي *slby* 'negative'	0.06

Table 4: Semantic tags in Arabic texts (10 out of 222 tags) *MFT: Most Frequent Token, STR: Semantic Type Ratio*

same time, the fact that A3 (Being) is the most frequent tag for texts in English is likely due to the grammatical role of the verb "to be", making it not as much as frequent in Arabic. Interestingly, the semantic tags N5 (Quantities), A1.1.1 (General actions, making, etc.) and S1.1.1 (General) are frequent in both languages, although always mostly more used in Arabic.
The English sub-corpus showed particular preference for A9 (Getting & giving; possession), A2.2 (Affect: Cause/Connected), A7 (Definite (+ modals)) and S2 (People), while Arabic show more usage other semantic tags such as, O2 (Objects generally), S7.1 (Power, organising), S5 (Groups and affiliation) and A5.1 (Evaluation: Good/bad). Tables 4 and 5 show the 10 most frequent semantic tags in the Arabic and English sub-corpora and including the Z tagset subcategories Z5 Z8 that are used to refer to grammatical items and pronouns.

Tag	Label	MFT	STR
Z5	Grammatical bin	the	0.33
Z8	Pronouns etc.	it	0.11
A3	Being	be	0.04
A1.1.1	General actions, making	way	0.04
N5	Quantities	many	0.04
A9	Getting&giving; possession	have	0.04
A2.2	Affect: Cause/Connected	have	0.04
S1.1.1	General	social	0.03
A7	Definite (+ modals)	can	0.03
S2	People	people	0.03

Table 5: Semantic tags in English texts (10 out of 210 tags) *MFT: Most Frequent Token, STR: Semantic Type Ratio*

5.2. Comparing Texts Written by Male and Female Authors

We are also able to compare ZAEBUC texts by their authors' gender so we can assess any possible gender bias in the students' writings. The number of texts for each gender is extremely unbalanced, as seen in Table 6 show the distribution of authors by gender, where 90% of the students identified themselves as females.

	Texts	Tokens
Female (Arabic)	199	32,115
Female (English)	344	87,804
Male (Arabic)	16	2,327
Male (English)	44	10,190

Table 6: Distribution authors by gender

Figure 5 shows the six most frequent semantic tags in texts from male and female authors in both languages. Once again, semantic tags related to punctuation and strictly grammatical ones are not shown.

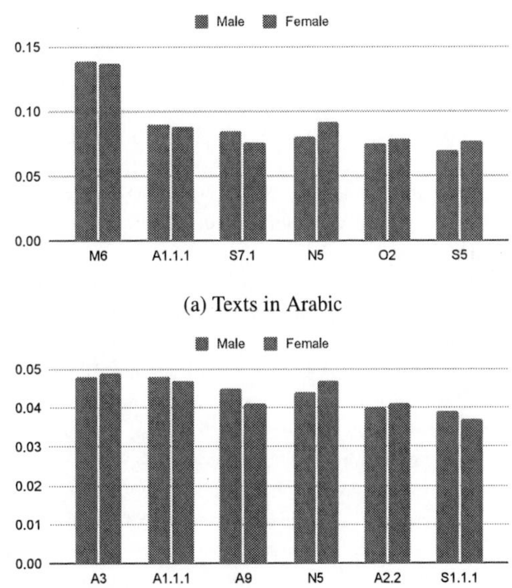

(a) Texts in Arabic

(b) Texts in English

Figure 5: Semantic Type Ratio across authors' gender

The Y axis in the figure shows the percentage of the sample that the semantic tag occupies. The most frequent semantic tag in texts from authors from both genders in Arabic is `M6` (Location and direction), representing 13.65% for the female writers and 13.92% for male writers. As for the English texts, both genders used `A3` (Being) the most, as expected and explained when we compared languages in Section 5.1.. Texts by female writers show more frequent use of the semantic domain of `N5` (Quantities) than texts by male writers, while `A1.1.1` (General actions, making etc.) was used in a comparable proportion in both but more frequently in texts by male writers. Additionally, `O2` (Objects generally) and `S5` (Groups and affiliation) were more frequently used by female writers, although the semantic domain of `S7.1` (Power, organizing) was used more frequently by male writers than female writers.
When it comes to English texts, other relevant semantic tags are `N5` (Quantities) and `A2.2` (Affects: Cause/Connected), it was found that female writers used those tags more than the male writers, while `A1.1.1` (General actions, making etc.) was more applied by males, along with `A9` (Getting & giving; possession) and `S1.1.1` (General).

6. Conclusion and Future work

In this paper, we have presented the first open source Arabic Semantic Tagger (AraSAS). Building on prior work, we have significantly improved and extended the semantic lexicon which forms the linguistic knowledge base on which the AraSAS tagger relies. We have also created a new software tool in Python, which uses NLTK for sentence segmentation, and CAMeL Tools for tokenisation, and morphological analysis in terms of lemmatisation and POS tagging. The semantic taxonomy applied to words and multi-word expressions is the same as that used in the English and other language semantic taggers meaning that cross-lingual comparisons become possible at the level of coarse-grained semantic fields. We have made AraSAS freely available open source for academic use[9]. AraSAS is also available as a web-tool, where users can type in or paste their text to be tagged[10].
In terms of evaluation, we first considered the coverage of the semantic lexicon in terms of how many tokens in a corpus are present and matched in the lexicon. Very good coverage figures were obtained, 96% of tokens in blogs and 96.8% in news texts, which are comparable to the English USAS tagger. In addition, we performed a number of experiments on a corpus of Arabic-English writing (603 essays) by bilingual students in the UAE. Using AraSAS facilitates comparison of concepts and topics across the two languages in general, and to compare texts written by male and female authors. This serves to illustrate just the beginnings of the analysis possibilities that having comparable semantic tagging systems in two or more languages.
In terms of future work, we will focus on extending the single word lexicon along with a lexicon of multiword expression patterns, and develop and apply further methods for bootstrapping the coverage, e.g., using word vectors, and for disambiguation, e.g., by applying deep learning methods.

[9] `https://github.com/UCREL/AraSAS`
[10] `http://ucrel-api.lancaster.ac.uk/`

7. Bibliographical References

Al-hadi, M., Ba-Alwi, F., Al-Baltah, I., Sana'a, Y., and Al-Gaphari, G. (2016). Survey of semantic annotation of arabic text. In *1st Scientific Conference on Information Technology and Networks(SCITN'2016)*.

Al-Sulaiti, L. and Atwell, E. S. (2006). The design of a corpus of contemporary arabic. *International Journal of Corpus Linguistics*, 11(2):135–171.

Buckwalter, T. (2004). Buckwalter Arabic Morphological Analyzer Version 2.0. LDC catalog number LDC2004L02, ISBN 1-58563-324-0.

El-Haj, M. and Rayson, P. (2016). Osman—a novel arabic readability metric. In *Proceedings of the Tenth International Conference on Language Resources and Evaluation (LREC'16)*, pages 250–255.

El-Haj, M., Rayson, P., Piao, S., and Wattam, S. (2017). Creating and validating multilingual semantic representations for six languages: Expert versus non-expert crowds. In *Proceedings of the 1st Workshop on Sense, Concept and Entity Representations and their Applications*, pages 61–71, Valencia, Spain, April. Association for Computational Linguistics.

Ezeani, I., Piao, S., Neale, S., Rayson, P., and Knight, D. (2019). Leveraging pre-trained embeddings for Welsh taggers. In *Proceedings of the 4th Workshop on Representation Learning for NLP (RepL4NLP-2019)*, pages 270–280, Florence, Italy, August. Association for Computational Linguistics.

García-Barrero, D., Feria, M., and Turell, M. T. (2013). Using function words and punctuation marks in arabic forensic authorship attribution. In *Proceedings of the 3rd European Conference of the International Association of Forensic Linguists*, pages 42–56.

Graff, D., Maamouri, M., Bouziri, B., Krouna, S., Kulick, S., and Buckwalter, T. (2009). Standard Arabic Morphological Analyzer (SAMA) Version 3.1. Linguistic Data Consortium LDC2009E73.

Guthrie, L., Pustejovsky, J., Wilks, Y., and Slator, B. M. (1996). The role of lexicons in natural language processing. *Communications of the ACM*, 39(1):63–72.

Habash, N. and Palfreyman, D. (2022). ZAEBUC: An annotated Arabic-English bilingual writer corpus. In *Proceedings of the Language Resources and Evaluation Conference (LREC)*, Marseille, France.

Habash, N. and Rambow, O. (2005). Arabic tokenization, part-of-speech tagging and morphological disambiguation in one fell swoop. In *Proceedings of the Conference of the Association for Computational Linguistics (ACL)*, pages 573–580, Ann Arbor, Michigan.

Habash, N. Y. (2010). Introduction to arabic natural language processing. *Synthesis Lectures on Human Language Technologies*, 3(1):1–187.

ibn Mukarram ibn Manzūr, M. (1290). Lisan al-arab.

Khallaf, N., de Souza, E., El-Haj, M., and Rayson, P. (2022). Semantic domains across topics, genders and languages.

Kogalovskii, M. (2018). Semantic annotating of text documents: Basic concepts and taxonomic approach. *Automatic Documentation and Mathematical Linguistics*, 52(3):134–141.

Löfberg, L. and Rayson, P., (2019). *Developing multilingual automatic semantic annotation systems*, pages 94–109. Cambridge University Press, June.

Löfberg, L. (2017). *Creating large semantic lexical resources for the Finnish language*. Ph.D. thesis, Lancaster University.

Loper, E. and Bird, S. (2002). Nltk: the natural language toolkit. *arXiv preprint cs/0205028*.

Maamouri, M., Bies, A., Buckwalter, T., and Mekki, W. (2004). The penn arabic treebank: Building a large-scale annotated arabic corpus. In *NEMLAR conference on Arabic language resources and tools*, volume 27, pages 466–467. Cairo.

Mohamed, G., Hardie, A., and Potts, A. (2013). Arasas: a semantic tagger for arabic. In *Second Workshop on Arabic Corpus Linguistics*.

Mudraya, O., Babych, B., Piao, S., Rayson, P., and Wilson, A. (2006). Developing a russian semantic tagger for automatic semantic annotation, October. Also published in Russian (pp. 282-289); Corpus Linguistics 2006 ; Conference date: 10-10-2006 Through 14-10-2006.

Obeid, O., Zalmout, N., Khalifa, S., Taji, D., Oudah, M., Alhafni, B., Inoue, G., Eryani, F., Erdmann, A., and Habash, N. (2020). Camel tools: An open source python toolkit for arabic natural language processing. In *Proceedings of the 12th language resources and evaluation conference*, pages 7022–7032.

Palfreyman, D. and Habash, N. (2022). Zayed arabic-english bilingual undergraduate corpus (zaebuc).

Piao, S., Bianchi, F., Dayrell, C., D'Egidio, A., and Rayson, P. (2015a). Development of the multilingual semantic annotation system. In *Proceedings of the 2015 Conference of the North American Chapter of the Association for Computational Linguistics: Human Language Technologies*, pages 1268–1274, Denver, Colorado, May–June. Association for Computational Linguistics.

Piao, S. S., Bianchi, F., Dayrell, C., D'egidio, A., and Rayson, P. (2015b). Development of the multilingual semantic annotation system. In *Proceedings of the 2015 Conference of the North American Chapter of the Association for Computational Linguistics: Human Language Technologies*, pages 1268–1274.

Piao, S., Rayson, P., Archer, D., Bianchi, F., Dayrell, C., El-Haj, M., Jiménez, R.-M., Knight, D., Křen, M., Löfberg, L., Nawab, R. M. A., Shafi, J., Teh, P. L., and Mudraya, O. (2016a). Lexical coverage evaluation of large-scale multilingual semantic lexicons for twelve languages. In *Proceedings of the Tenth International Conference on Language Resources and Evaluation (LREC'16)*, pages 2614–2619, Portorož, Slovenia, May. European Language Resources Association (ELRA).

Piao, S. S., Rayson, P., Archer, D., Bianchi, F., Dayrell, C., El-Haj, M., Jiménez, R.-M., Knight, D., Křen, M., Löfberg, L., et al. (2016b). Lexical coverage evaluation of large-scale multilingual semantic lexicons for twelve languages. In *Proceedings of the Tenth International Conference on Language Resources and Evaluation (LREC'16)*, pages 2614–2619.

Piao, S., Dallachy, F., Baron, A., Demmen, J., Wattam, S., Durkin, P., McCracken, J., Rayson, P., and Alexander, M. (2017). A time-sensitive historical thesaurus-based semantic tagger for deep semantic annotation. *Computer Speech and Language*, 46:113–135, November.

Rayson, P. and Wilson, A. (1996). The acamrit semantic tagging system: progress report. In *Language engineering for document analysis and recognition, LEDAR, AISB96 workshop proceedings*, pages 13–20.

Rayson, P., Archer, D., Piao, S., and McEnery, A. M. (2004). The ucrel semantic analysis system.

Richards, B. (1987). Type/token ratios: What do they really tell us? *Journal of child language*, 14(2):201–209.

Saleh, L. M. B. and Al-Khalifa, H. S. (2009). Aratation: an arabic semantic annotation tool. In *Proceedings of the 11th International Conference on Information Integration and Web-based Applications & Services*, pages 447–451.

Taji, D., Khalifa, S., Obeid, O., Eryani, F., and Habash, N. (2018). An Arabic morphological analyzer and generator with copious features. In *Proceedings of the Fifteenth Workshop on Computational Research in Phonetics, Phonology, and Morphology*, pages 140–150, Brussels, Belgium, October. Association for Computational Linguistics.

Zawahreh, F. A. S. (2013). A linguistic contrastive analysis case study: Out of context translation of arabic adjectives into english in efl classroom. *International Journal of Academic Research in Business and Social Sciences*, 3(2):427.

Proceedings of the OSACT 2022 Workshop @LREC2022, pages 32–40
Marseille, 20 June 2022

AraNPCC: The Arabic Newspaper COVID-19 Corpus

Abdulmohsen Al-Thubaity, Sakhar Alkhereyf, Alia Bahanshal
The National Center for Data Analytics and Artificial Intelligence
King Abdulaziz City for Science and Technology (KACST)
Riyadh, Saudi Arabia
{aalthubaity, salkhereyf, abahanshal}@kacst.edu.sa

Abstract

This paper introduces a corpus for Arabic newspapers during COVID-19: AraNPCC. The AraNPCC corpus covers 2019 until 2021 via automatically-collected data from 12 Arab countries. It comprises more than 2 billion words and 7.2 million texts alongside their metadata. AraNPCC can be used for several natural language processing tasks, such as updating available Arabic language models or corpus linguistics tasks, including language change over time. We utilized the corpus in two case studies. In the first case study, we investigate the correlation between the number of officially reported infected cases and the collective word frequency of "COVID" and "Corona." The data shows a positive correlation that varies among Arab countries. For the second case study, we extract and compare the top 50 keywords in 2020 and 2021 to study the impact of the COVID-19 pandemic on two Arab countries, namely Algeria and Saudi Arabia. For 2020, the data shows that the two countries' newspapers strongly interacted with the pandemic, emphasizing its spread and dangerousness, and in 2021 the data suggests that the two countries coped with the pandemic.

Keywords: Arabic corpora, language resources, text analytics, language models

1. Introduction

Recent advances in Natural Language Processing (NLP) are attributed to deep learning. However, such advances cannot be achieved without the availability of large amounts of textual data known as corpora. The various transformers-based language models are good examples for such a case: BERT (Devlin et al., 2018), GPT-2 (Radford et al., 2019), AraBERT (Antoun et al., 2020), and CAMeLBERT (Inoue et al., 2021).

The availability of large corpora, when classified based on time, country, and topic, can be beneficial for applications such as text clustering (Behpour et al., 2021) and text analytics such as detecting trends (Curiac et al., 2022), as well as corpus linguistics studies that include detecting neologisms (Amiruddin et al., 2022) and semantic change (Kutuzov et al., 2022), studying of language variations among countries (Deuber et al., 2021), and investigating language changes over time (Baker and Heritage, 2021).

The benefits of using large corpora increase when covering texts from a recent time period because they will give us not only a clear picture of the language but can demonstrate the validity of previously implemented models.

With the emergence of the coronavirus disease of 2019 (COVID-19) and its global negative effect, several research questions may arise from an NLP perspective. For example, will pre-trained language models on available datasets at that time have the same performance as the language models that may be pre-trained using data covering the COVID-19 period? How has the language changed to reflect the pandemic and its impact on societies? Can we build an effective model to detect global effect events based on textual data?

There are several newspaper-based corpora for English and other languages covering COVID-19; see for example (Davies, 2021; de Melo and Figueiredo, 2020); however, to the best of our knowledge, there is no Arabic newspaper corpus covering this period.

In this paper, we present the Arabic Newspapers COVID-19 Corpus (AraNPCC) comprising more than 2 billion words and 7.2 million texts, covering the time from 1st of January 2019 until 31st of December 2021 collected from 88 Arabic newspapers published in 12 Arabic countries. The text and its metadata, namely web link, title, date of publication, and topic, are available in a CSV format file for each newspaper.

The importance of AraNPCC lies in four main aspects: (a) its large size, (b) the fact that it was collected from reliable and quality sources, i.e., official and well known Arabic newspapers, (c) the availability of metadata for each text, and (d) its coverage of a significant period as it covers one year before the COVID-19 pandemic (i.e., 2019) and two years after the emergence of the pandemic (i.e., 2020 and 2021). These four aspects qualify AraNPCC for different NLP, computational linguistics, and corpus linguistics studies/applications, such as building new Arabic language models or extending the available models; text clustering and classification across topics and countries; Arabic language changes after the pandemic; and the response of different Arab countries to COVID-19 among different fields of life as reflected in text topics.

The remainder of this paper is organized as follows. Sections 2 and 3 discuss the procedure followed to generate AraNPCC and its basic statistics. section 4 illustrates two case studies as examples of the practical use of AraNPCC. section 5 presents some of the recent and related corpora and section 6 summarizes the conclusions and future work.

2. Method

To construct AraNPCC, we followed these steps:

1. For each Arab country, we identified newspapers based on three criteria: (a) The newspaper is a widely circulated and reliable source for news, such as *Okaz* newspaper from Saudi Arabia or *Alahram* newspaper from Egypt; (b) The newspaper has an archive covering 2019 up to the date of starting collecting data [1]; (c) Each article can be accessed based on an incremental identifier for easy iteration and retrieval of articles. Note, however, that we were able to cover only 12 Arab countries, namely Algeria, Bahrain, Egypt, Iraq, Jordan, Kuwait, Morocco, Oman, Saudi Arabia, Sudan, Tunisia, and Yemen. For the United Arab Emirates, Lebanon, Palestine, and Qatar, we could not find a way to retrieve articles from any newspaper because we could not iterate over their websites (see c above). In addition, we could not identify resources meeting these criteria for Libya, Mauritania, and Syria either due to political instability or information technology infrastructure issues.

2. For each newspaper, we used the "*beautifulsoup4*" python package version (4.10.0) [2] to retrieve newspaper articles; for each article, we parsed the web page to identify article text, title, topic, and date of publication. Note that when no topic is extracted, the topic value is set to *No_Class*.

3. For each newspaper, we store a copy of each article in a text file using UTF-8 encoding. The file name for each file is a combination of newspaper name, topic, date, and serial number. We also store each text alongside its metadata in one row of a CSV file. Text metadata includes title, URL, date, topic, newspaper name, and text file name saved in external storage. The purpose of saving articles as text files on external storage is to maintain reliable data if the CSV files are deleted for any reason.

4. For each newspaper, we remove duplicate texts and normalize the date format [dd-mm-yyyy]. To ease file handling and processing, we save the data for each year in a separate CSV file.

3. Data

AraNPCC is an opportunistic corpus where there are no limits on its size growth nor any restriction on its design criteria except the language (Arabic) and text genre (newspapers). However, AraNPCC can be considered a snapshot corpus, i.e., a corpus that covers a short period of time (3 years).

Following the construction steps outlined in section 2 above, we built a corpus of more than 2 billion words comprising more than 7.2 million text files. Table 1 contains the basic statistics for AraNPCC.

Country	Newspapers	Texts	Tokens
Algeria	11	439,204	133,040,389
Bahrain	4	571,162	201,409,392
Egypt	6	2,926,693	747,884,209
Iraq	4	48,178	12,879,456
Jordan	5	538,461	161,970,053
Kuwait	8	368,574	107,963,207
Morocco	4	268,827	101,124,149
Oman	7	203,542	76,634,312
Saudi Arabia	8	826,323	214,865,053
Sudan	11	178,461	58,500,490
Tunisia	10	509,427	92,404,722
Yemen	10	398,673	125,990,973
Total	88	7,277,525	2,034,666,405

Table 1: Number of newspapers, number of texts, and the total number of words for each Arab country in AraNPCC.

Topic	Texts	Tokens
Society	1,497,237	379,143,518
International	1,239,692	332,492,650
Economy	975,847	301,421,854
Politics	881,825	254,434,561
Sports	927,381	211,049,481
Culture	579,951	180,933,718
No_Class	520,857	160,654,866
Health	448,608	114,527,652
Religion	85,136	44,191,143
Opinion	70,526	42,878,753
Other	36,295	7,195,575
Reports	8,012	4,004,529
Sci_Tech	6,158	1,738,105
Total	7,277,525	2,034,666,405

Table 2: Texts and tokens distribution over main topics.

The data shows that there are 43 classes for text topics in the AraNPCC; however, it is possible to combine different classes under a single class. For example, "Art," "Arts," and "Culture" can be combined under the class "Culture"; "Technology," "Sci_Tech," and "Science_Tech" can be combined under the "Sci_Tech" class. Combining different classes in this manner yields the 13 classes shown in Table 2.

To increase the freedom of usability, we kept all texts and metadata as is with no changes or preprocessing except for date normalization (see section 2 above).

Since copyright is a serious matter, we strive to maintain the copyright and the usability of the corpus for research purposes. This Corpus was created in Saudi Arabia, and according to Saudi Arabian Executive Reg-

[1] We started collecting data in July 2020. However, in 2021, some newspaper sites declined to crawl.

[2] `https://pypi.org/project/beautifulsoup4/`

ulations of Copyright Protection Law [3], news reports are protected by law; however, "Daily News Facts are excluded of this protection." In addition, we considered the following:

- All collected texts were available for reading and downloading free of charge [4]. In addition, no subscriptions or passwords were needed to access these texts.
- Web sites links for all texts are available with all necessary metadata to maintain the credits to newspapers.
- The use of AraNPCC is strictly for research purposes and is purely non-commercial.
- We do not claim ownership of any of the content within AraNPCC

4. Case Studies

There are many tasks that can be applied using AraNPCC including: building large language models, topic modeling, and corpus spatio-temporal analysis. For illustrating the usage of AraNPCC for spatio-temporal analysis, we present in this section two case studies. In the first case study, we will test if there is a positive correlation between COVID-19 reported cases and COVID-related words in the corpus, namely the terms COVID "كوفيد" and Corona "كورونا". In the second case study, we evaluate the use of keyword extraction to evaluate how the pandemic affects the Arab countries. Such analysis presented in the two case studies can be applied to other Corpus Linguistics and text analysis tasks.

In both case studies, we use the NLTK *word_tokenize()* function (Bird et al., 2009) for extracting tokens without any further preprocessing.

4.1. First Case Study: Response to the Pandemic

We investigate the correlation between the number of confirmed COVID-19 cases as reported by official agencies and the frequency of COVID-related terms in the newspaper articles. We then group the examples in the corpus into countries and months.

For COVID-related terms, we use two words: "كوفيد" (COVID) and "كورونا" (Corona). Next, we compute per million ratios (PM) to the total number of tokens for each month and country. For example, if the term has a frequency of 20 in a given month in which there are 100 thousand tokens, the PM for this term is 200.

For COVID confirmed cases, we use the Johns Hopkins dataset (Dong et al., 2020), which has been collected from official health agencies. We compute new cases for each month and country and use the daily updated CSV file "*time_series_covid19_confirmed_global.csv*" from the GitHub data repository "*CSSEGISandData/COVID-19*"[5].

Country	Pearson	Kendall	Spearman
Saudi Arabia	0.577	0.688	0.857
Oman	0.449	0.615	0.776
Algeria	0.448	0.597	0.771
Tunisia	0.413	0.546	0.734
Bahrain	0.391	0.629	0.802
Kuwait	0.372	0.551	0.744
Egypt	0.368	0.499	0.694
Sudan	0.355	0.577	0.734
Jordan	0.316	0.387	0.589
Yemen	0.281	0.499	0.675
Morocco	0.216	0.495	0.695
Iraq	0.011	0.405	0.594

Table 3: Correlation between PM and the frequency of COVID-19 terms using three methods for computing correlation scores.

To compute the correlation between the usage of COVID-19 terms and the number of confirmed cases, we compute the per million (PM) ratios of COVID-19 terms in a given month and the total number of confirmed cases in that month. Then, we apply three correlation coefficients commonly used in the literature: Pearson's rho, Kendall's tau, and Spearman's rho (Arabzadeh et al., 2021; Imran and Sharan, 2010; Sonowal, 2020; Baron et al., 2009). We report the correlation using the three correlation measures as that each of them has its own strengths, limitations, and distributional assumptions that might not be satisfied in corpora (Gries, 2010) including AraNPCC.

We have a total of 36 months covering the period of January 2019 and December 2021 and 36 pairs of time series for PM scores and the number of confirmed cases for each country. Table 3 shows the results of the correlation between the number of COVID-19 words and the number of reported cases using the three statistical correlation metrics. We observe that there is a strong correlation between the number of cases and the frequency of COVID-19 related words for most countries. Note that Saudi Arabia has the highest correlation ratio for all metrics. For the Pearson correlation score, most countries have a moderate to a weak correlation between the reported number of cases and the occurrence of COVID-19 terms, except Iraq. We observe higher scores for other correlation metrics (i.e., Kendall and Spearman) than for Pearson.

To test how the usage of COVID-related terms correlates in different countries, we analyze the correlation coefficient between the PM ratios in two countries: Al-

[3] https://externalportal-backend-production.saip.gov.sa/sites/default/files/2022-02/IMPLEMENTING-REGULATIONS-Of-Copyright-Law-.pdf

[4] https://archive.org/details/AraNPCC

[5] https://github.com/CSSEGISandData/COVID-19

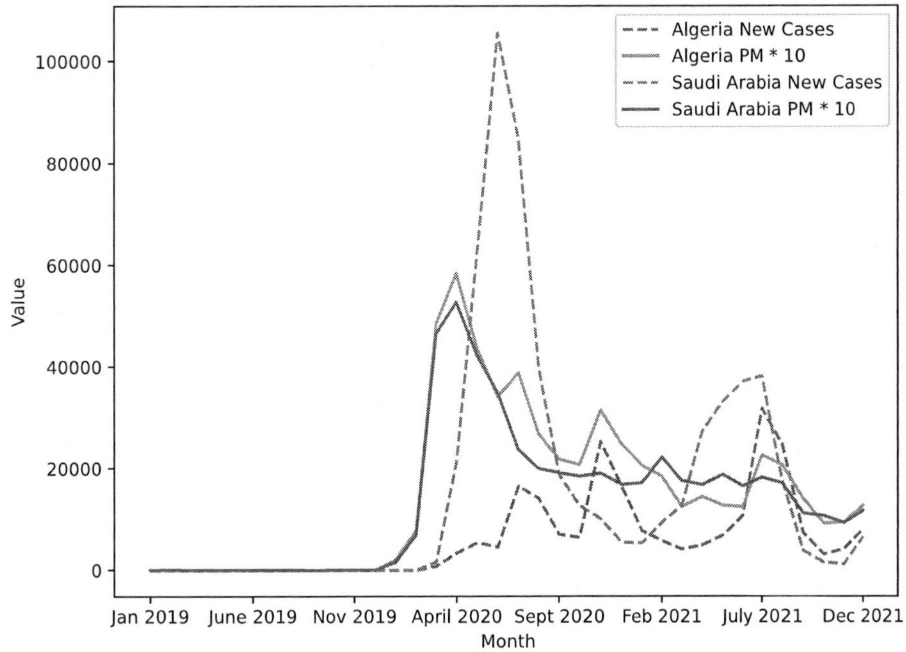

Figure 1: Ratio of COVID-related terms and the number of confirmed COVID cases for two countries, Algeria and Saudi Arabia, from the beginning of January 2019 until the end of December 2021. Dotted lines represent the number of cases while solid lines represent the per ten million (PM * 10) ratio for two words related to Covid: COVID "كوفيد" and Corona "كورونا".

geria and Saudi Arabia. We represent the PM ratios as a pair of two time series of length 36 (one for each country) covering a period of 36 months. Also, we study the correlation of the number of cases between the two countries in a manner similar to the one just discussed but using the number of confirmed cases instead of the PM value.

We choose Saudi Arabia as it has the highest correlation between the number of cases and COVID-related terms, while the next country based on the highest correlation is Oman, which is in the same region (Gulf region). To analyze diverse content, we choose the next country outside the region: Algeria.

Method	Pearson	Kendall	Spearman
PM	0.97 **	0.82 **	0.94 **
# Cases	0.38 *	0.65 **	0.82 **

Table 4: Correlation between the two countries: Algeria and Saudi Arabia in the usage of COVID-19 terms and the number of confirmed cases. * $p < 0.05$ ** $p < 0.001$.

Table 4 shows the correlation between the PM scores in the two countries as well as the correlation of the confirmed number of cases between the two countries using the three correlation metrics. The results show that there is a strong correlation in using COVID-19 terms over time in the newspapers from the two countries. In particular, the Pearson's correlation coefficient between the PM scores in the two countries over months is 0.97 with a p-value < 0.001. For the number of confirmed cases, the Pearson's correlation score is 0.38 with a p-value < 0.05.

Figure 1 is a graph for the number of reported cases and the frequency of COVID-related terms over months for the two countries: Algeria and Saudi Arabia. From January 2019 to December 2021. For a visualization purpose, we use the frequency of terms per 10 million (PM * 10) instead of PM to scale the graphs and make them visually easier to interpret.

According to the Johns Hopkins dataset, from the beginning of 2019 until January 2020, the number of confirmed cases was zero, which was before COVID-19 became a global pandemic. February 2020 was the first month with a confirmed case in the Arab world. The first mentions of COVID-19 terms date back to the beginning of January 2019 (the first month in the corpus). The reason behind this apparent discrepancy is that some newspapers discussed the Middle East Respiratory Syndrome (MERS), which is usually referred to as "كورونا" (Corona) in Arabic, before COVID-19. However, the PM values before COVID-19 were insignificant. In particular, the highest PM in 2019 was 84 in Saudi Arabia, which has the highest number of MERS cases [6].

We observe that in early 2020, when the pandemic started in these countries, the PM values significantly increased and peaked in April 2020. Also, the number of confirmed cases increased and peaked in June 2020 for Saudi Arabia. After that, the PM value started to decline, but it fluctuated with time, and the PM for COVID-19 terms increased as attention to COVID-19 returns with new variants (e.g., the Delta variant in late 2020).

Overall, the analysis results show that there is a positive correlation between the mention of COVID-19 related terms and the confirmed number of cases. The strength of the correlation differs among Arab countries.

4.2. Keywords and phrases

As we mentioned in the Introduction section, large corpora can be used for text analytics. One of the methods that can be used for text analytics is keywords analysis. Keywords are the words whose frequency is significantly different in a corpus of interest (primary corpus) than their frequency in another corpus (reference corpus).

In this study, we use keywords to identify the distinctive topics in 2020 and 2021 in Arabic newspapers to see how the Arabic countries cope with the COVID-19 pandemic. Studying the effect of COVID-19 on all Arab countries is out of the scope of this paper; therefore, we focus only on two countries, namely Algeria and Saudi Arabia. We choose these countries because they have the highest correlation between the confirmed number of cases and the frequency of COVID-related terms.

Since witnessing the COVID-19 pandemic, we can specifically judge the extracted keywords and their representativeness for the studied case and briefly show how large corpora, when classified with metadata, can be used for text analytics specifically for main topics detection.

To extract keywords, we need two corpora: (a) a primary corpus, which is the corpus we want to extract keywords from, and (b) a reference corpus that we compare with the primary corpus to find keywords.

In Corpus Linguistics, there are various measures to extract keywords for a given primary corpus by comparing it with another reference corpus. In this study, we use the Log-Likelihood measure to extract keywords. The values of the Log-Likelihood measure can be calculated using contingency tables of observed frequencies and the expected frequencies in primary and reference corpora.

Corpus	w	$\neg w$	Total
Primary	O_{11}	$O_{12} = N_1 - O_{11}$	N_1
Reference	O_{21}	$O_{22} = N_2 - O_{21}$	N_2
	$C_1 = O_{11} + O_{21}$	$C_2 = N - C_1$	$N = N_1 + N_2$

Table 5: Observed values contingency table.

Corpus	w	$\neg w$	Total
Primary	$E_{11} = (N_1 * C_1)/N$	$E_{12} = N_1 - E_{11}$	N_1
Reference	$E_{21} = (N_2 * C_1)/N$	$E_{22} = N_2 - E_{21}$	N_2
	$C_1 = E_{11} + E_{21}$	$C_2 = N - C_1$	$N = N_1 + N_2$

Table 6: Expected values contingency table .

Given that we know the size of the primary corpus (N_1), the size of the reference corpus (N_2), the actual frequency of the word in the primary corpus (O_{11}), and the actual frequency of the word in the reference corpus (O_{21}), the cells of contingency tables can be easily computed as shown in Tables 5 and 6

The Log-Likelihood (LL) for any word in the primary corpus is given by the following equation:

$$LL = 2 \sum_{ij} O_{ij} \log \frac{O_{ij}}{E_{ij}}$$

To extract keywords for 2020 and 2021 (primary corpora), we compare them to 2019 and 2020 (reference corpora), respectively. To decide the keyness of a word in the primary corpus, we used the following criteria:

- We use a 99.9999 significant level for Log-Likelihood, i.e., the value of LL is greater than or equal to 24.
- The frequency of the word in the primary corpus is greater than or equal to 20.
- The ratio of the word's relative frequency in the primary corpus to its relative frequency in the reference corpus is greater than or equal to 10.

After applying the above criteria for all words, we remove numbers, symbols, and non-Arabic words from the list.

Country	Primary corpus *	# of keywords
Saudi Arabia	2020	7,449
Saudi Arabia	2021	1,023
Algeria	2020	906
Algeria	2021	205

Table 7: Number of keywords for 2020 and 2021 for Saudi Arabian and Algerian newspapers. * Reference corpora for 2020 is 2019; and for 2021 is 2020.

Table 7 illustrates the primary corpus and number of keywords for Saudi Arabian and Algerian newspapers. The data suggests that the numbers of keywords for

[6] https://www.who.int/health-topics/middle-east-respiratory-syndrome-coronavirus-mers

Saudi Arabian newspapers for both 2020 and 2021 are far greater than the number of keywords for Algerian newspapers. This large difference in the number of keywords can be attributed to the diversity of subject matters that are covered by Saudi Arabian newspapers. Furthermore, for both countries, data suggest that the number of keywords for 2020 is also far greater than the number of keywords for 2021. The difference can be attributed to the effect of the COVID-19 pandemic and its significant influence on all aspects of life in the two countries.

Since the top-ranked keywords identify the main topics of the primary corpus and, therefore, the interests of the newspapers in 2020 and 2021, such as in our case, we restricted our analysis to the 50 top-ranked keywords. Table 8 and Table 9 illustrate 2020 Keywords for Algerian and Saudi Arabian newspapers, respectively.

الوباء , الحجر , كوفيد , فيروس , كورونا
جائحة , تفشي , وباء , بفيروس , الفيروس
الكمامات , بالفيروس , الجائحة , جراد , المستجد
فورار , المنزلي , لفيروس , الظل , التباعد
بكورونا , للحجر , الكمامة , الوبائية , البروتوكول
للفيروس , المؤكدة , كمامة , الاحترازية , تعقيم
الأقنعة , الواقية , بكوفيد , ووهان , التعقيم
السميد , الواقي , كوفيد٩١ , والتباعد , بالحجر
دودة , الكورونا , للوباء , بالوباء , التاجي
عطار , كمامات , الوبائي , بوباء , واجعوط

Table 8: 2020 Keywords for Algerian newspapers.

الاحترازية , كوفيد , المستجد , فيروس , كورونا
انتشار , بفيروس , الفيروس , الجائحة , حالة
تفشي , إصابة , فايروس , الصحة , الوباء
حالات , التجول , العشرين , الإجراءات , الوقائية
بالفيروس , وباء , الإصابات , وفاة , الوفيات
لفيروس , للحد , التباعد , الحالات , الفايروس
تسجيل , أزمة , والتدابير , الأزمة , العدوى
والمقيمين , منع , الحجر , اللقاح , لقاح
الصحي , الإصابة , أعراض , بفايروس , الكمامات
بالإجراءات , جديدة , للوقاية , العزل , بايدن

Table 9: 2020 Keywords for Saudi newspapers.

For 2020, the data shows that all 50 keywords are directly related to the COVID-19 pandemic, its effects, and its health countermeasures except 7 and 3 keywords (in red) for Algerian and Saudi Arabian newspapers, respectively. To check the meaning of these keywords, we study their contexts.

For Algerian newspapers, the 7 keywords that are not directly related to the COVID-19 pandemic are indirectly related to the pandemic. Five of these keywords, namely "جراد" (Jarad), "فورار" (Fourara), "دودة" (Doudah), "واجعوط" (Wajatot), "عطار" (Attar), are the family names for new ministers in the Algerian government—and their position in the government were important to countermeasures the effects of COVID-19. The keyword "سميد" (semolina) came in the context of the Algerian government's efforts to provide basic foodstuffs as well as news that says it is scarce or unavailable. The keyword "الظل" (shadow) came in the context of the Algerian government's efforts to take care of marginalized areas or "shadow areas" that suffer from economic difficulties.

For Saudi Arabian newspapers, the two keywords are not related to the COVID-19 pandemic, namely "العشرين" (the twenty) and "بايدن" (Biden). This first keyword, "العشرين" related to Saudi Arabia's Presidency and hosting of G20 Summit for 2020. The second keyword, "بايدن" refers to the President of the United States of America. This keyword shows the effect and importance of the American President to the relationship between Saudi Arabia and the USA. The third keyword "المقيمين" (residents) (i.e., non-Saudis living in Saudi Arabia either legally or not) is indirectly related to the pandemic. It refers to all actions and measures for freely extending their residency in Saudi Arabia and including them in medication and vaccinations as Saudi nationals. Note that non-Saudis contribute more than 30% of the population in Saudi Arabia.

After returning the pandemic keywords to their stem, the data suggests that these keywords are referencing to:

- disease name: كورونا، كوفيد، المستجد، التاجي (Corona, Covid, novel/new, coronary)
- disease cause: فيروس، ووهان (virus, Wuhan)
- countermeasures: احترازية، وقاية، إجراءات، تدابير، للحد، تجول، حجر، عزل، تباعد، منزلية، منع، كمامة، الأقنعة، لقاح، تعقيم، (precautionary, prevention, procedures, measures, to limit, roam, quarantine, isolate, distancing, household, prevent, muzzle, mask, vaccine, sterilization)

2021 Keywords for Algerian and Saudi Arabian newspapers are shown in Table 10 and Table 11, respectively. The data suggest that Algeria and Saudi Arabia coped with the COVID-19 pandemic. Unlike 2020 keywords, all keywords for 2021 are not related to the COVID-19 pandemic except 7 and 13 keywords for Algerian and Saudi Arabian newspapers, respectively.

لمحليات , ميستورا , بوغالي , الدبيبة , **أوميكرون**
أمكيدش , لوموتي , **بالمتحور** , **المتحورات** , دبيبة
اللاي , والمسافة , نابسا , لوحايدية , **متحورات**
ستافان , تونغيث , مرابي , الإرهابيتين , **للمتحور**
, تونغيت , مانولوفيتش , **السلالتين** , أديوي
الجنحاوي , **بمتحور** , بالتشريعيات , بيليم , التحضير
غورديل , بانكولي , أولطاش , للتوقيعات
مشرارة , كونتال , الأسيهار , والاستفتائية
, عبوبو , دراغي , إيفانكو , اينمبا , الميثادون
وبتصويت , أوفرت , أوبوكو , كوكالا , نقيش
بونابي , سجاتي , بوجعدار

Table 10: 2021 Keywords for Algerian newspapers.

The pandemic related keywords can be classified into two topics:

افتتاحيتها , **المتحورة** , بلينكن , **دلتا** , **أوميكرون**
الدبيبة , **متحور** , **جرعتي** , قرداحي , **محصن**
حامدي , ممتثل , **إعطاؤها** , ميقاتي , **المتحورات**
الكابيتول , الـ١٩ , ميكالي , **الجرعتين** , **المعطاة**
وتجريف , صيفنا , **متحورات** , **التنشيطية** , تاليسكا
شربل , **متحورة** , جوك , ماريغا , مانو
إخلائها , واستخفافها , الصفري , كونترا , هورفات
لبعثاتهم , إكستريم , القولف , بالإبعاد , بوهانج
إثيوبيو , تحديها , المنفي , العبدية , لمحاولتهم
, أجمك , وتدنيا , لابورتا , تراكتور , ليندركينغ

Table 11: 2021 Keywords for Saudi newspapers.

- the new variant of the virus "أوميكرون" (Omicron), "دلتا" (Delta) and different forms of the stem "متحور" (variant) and "السلالتين" (the two strains).
- vaccination as represented by "المعطاة" and "إعطاؤها" (administered), "الجرعتين" and "جرعتي" (two doses), and "محصن" (vaccinated person).

The keywords not related to the pandemic varies between the two countries, but in both countries, they are mainly related to political matters. For Algerian newspapers, the three most important topics were local government affairs "بوغالي" (Boughali: the assembly president of Algeria), the neighborhood Libya "الدبيبة" (Al-Dbeibeh: the prime minister of Libya's interim Government of National Unity), and the Western Sahara "ميستورا" (Mistura: UN personal envoy to Western Sahara).
For Saudi Arabian newspapers, the main three topics were American relationships and affairs: "بلينكن" (Blinken: The United States secretary of state), Saudi Lebanese relationships: "قرداحي" (Kordahi: Minister of Information of Lebanon), "ميقاتي" (Mikati: Prime Minister of Lebanon), and Libyan affairs: "الدبيبة" (Al-Dbeibeh: the prime minister of Libya's interim Government of National Unity).

5. Related Work

Corpora are crucial resources for building NLP, computational linguistics systems, and language studies. In this section, we review related work on corpus construction, focusing on the Arabic corpora, corpora covering a significant period of time, and COVID-19 corpora.
One of the largest Arabic corpora is arTenTen (Belinkov et al., 2013), a web-crawled corpus of Arabic gathered in 2012 and a member of the TenTen Corpus Family (Jakubíček et al., 2013). The arTenTen corpus consists of 5.8 billion words loaded into Sketch Engine (Kilgarriff et al., 2004), a corpus query tool. The corpus covers various genres and uses texts from Arabic Wikipedia and other Arabic web-pages while implementing different language identification methods. Similar to arTenTen, ArabicWeb16 (Suwaileh et al., 2016) is another web-crawled corpus collected in 2016 from more than 150 Arabic million web pages covering MSA and various Arabic dialects. However, unlike AraNPCC, both corpora (i.e. arTenTen and ArabicWeb16) texts are not categorized by topic or time.
Similar to arTenTen, the King Abdulaziz City for Science and Technology Arabic Corpus (KACSTAC) (Al-Thubaity, 2015) provides a user interface with various tools for corpus linguistics. KACST comprises more than 1.2 billion words dated from the era before Islam until 2011 (more than 1400 years). Each text in KACSTAC is categorized according to its source, topic, country, and time span publication date.
The main difference between AraNPCC and ArTenTen, and KACST is that our corpus entirely downloadable without using a corpus query tool as Sketch Engine. This allows interested researchers to freely work with the corpus without being restricted by a tool. Furthermore, AraNPCC covers a new time span not covered by any of these corpora.
Another widely used Arabic corpus is the Arabic GigaWord corpus 5th edition (Parker, Robert, et al., 2011). It consists of more than a billion words from 3.3 million articles obtained from various Arabic news resources. It was collected by the LDC over a period of more than a decade and is considered the largest licensed Arabic corpus. Both AraNPCC and Arabic GigaWord corpus share the same text genre: Arabic newspapers. However, AraNPCC is larger in size, covering more Arabic news resources and more Arab regions. AraNPCC is freely available and covers the period of 2019 to 2021 to study the language changes due to the Covid-10 pandemic. Moreover, our corpus maintains the meta-data such as the article category, publication time, and country of origin.
Besides arTenTen, KACST, and Arabic GigaWord, there have been several other attempts in building free Arabic corpora. For example, (El-Khair, 2016) released the "1.5 billion words Arabic Corpus," a contemporary Arabic corpus of 1.5 billion words collected from newspaper articles in ten major news sources from eight Arabic countries, over a period of fourteen years. Similar to Abu El-khair corpus, the OSIAN corpus (Zeroual et al., 2019) is an Arabic newspaper-based corpus comprising around 1 billion words and consists of about 3.5 million articles. Like our corpus, both corpora are newspaper based; however, our corpus is larger in size and supported by the metadata of each text.
The Arabic part of the OSCAR corpus (Suárez et al., 2020), which is extracted from the CommonCrawl [7], is another freely available Arabic corpus comprising more than 6.1 billion words and more than 8.7 million documents collected from Arabic websites. The new version of OSCAR covers the COVID-19 pandemic until September 2021. However, the text genres and other useful metadata for language study of OSCAR corpus

[7] https://commoncrawl.org

are not available for all texts.

Since the COVID-19 pandemic started in late 2019, researchers in corpus linguistics and NLP began studying the pandemic-related content. In particular, (Davies, 2021) released the Coronavirus Corpus, an English collection from 20 English-speaking countries with more than 1.4 billion words. The corpus allows searching for the frequency of words over time and several other search tools. Furthermore, the user can freely download the entire corpus. Similar to our corpus, the Coronavirus Corpus is based on newspaper articles; however, it only includes the articles that contain specific terms such as "COVID", "COVID-19", and "coronavirus" only. Our corpus does not implement such a filter: we consider all articles published during the pandemic to study its effect on all aspects of life by analyzing the texts that contain COVID-19 related terms and to know the size of this effect by comparing to other articles that do not contain COVID-19 related terms. We believe this wide coverage will give AraNPCC more flexibility and usability from a corpus linguistics perspective.

Recently, language models that use temporal information have gained the attention of the research community. (Rosin and Radinsky, 2022), for example, proposed a temporal attention mechanism that can be applied to transformer language models and make use of the time tags of documents. (Müller et al., 2020) release the COVID-Twitter-BERT (CT-BERT) transformer-based model, pre-trained on a corpus of more than 160 million tweets related to COVID-19. (Hebbar and Xie, 2021) propose CovidBERT, a transformer model based on BERT for relation extraction from biomedical papers. AraNPCC can be used to build Arabic COVID-19 language models or to update available Arabic language models.

Unlike our work, most of the previous work focuses on the textual content while ignoring the metadata content. On the other hand, we provide such information, including title, date of publication, country, URL, and topic. These kinds of metadata information are extremely useful for various applications, including studying language change.

6. Conclusion

In this paper, we have presented AraNPCC, a large Arabic newspaper COVID-19 corpus, automatically collected from 88 Arabic newspapers from 12 Arab countries. AraNPCC comprises more than 2 billion words and 7.2 million news articles. We have analyzed the correlation between the frequency of Coivd-related terms and the number of confirmed cases for each month and country. The results of this analysis show that correlation scores differ among Arab countries. We have also extracted keywords for 2020 and 2021 for Algerian and Saudi Arabian newspapers; the data suggests that the list of the top-ranked keywords for both countries for 2020 is dominated by COVID-related terms. However, for 2021, when people coped with the pandemic, we observed different keywords among newspapers from these two countries that were primarily about national and international issues. To the best of our knowledge, the AraNPCC is the only modern standard Arabic corpus covering the period of COVID-19 from the beginning of 2019 to the end of 2021. The corpus will be freely available [8] for researchers and can be used for various tasks, including the training of specialized language models and spatio-temporal analysis of corpora.

Possible directions for future work include: adding more articles covering the post-pandemic period, pre-training temporal language models, and analysis of the language change for the COVID-19 pandemic period.

7. Bibliographical References

Al-Thubaity, A. O. (2015). A 700m+ Arabic corpus: KACST Arabic corpus design and construction. *Language Resources and Evaluation*, 49(3):721–751.

Amiruddin, N., Yassi, A. H., and Sukmawaty, S. (2022). Covid-19 blends: A new phenomenon in English Neologisms. *Journal of Language and Linguistic Studies*, 17(3).

Antoun, W., Baly, F., and Hajj, H. (2020). Arabert: Transformer-based model for arabic language understanding. *arXiv preprint arXiv:2003.00104*.

Arabzadeh, N., Khodabakhsh, M., and Bagheri, E. (2021). Bert-qpp: Contextualized pre-trained transformers for query performance prediction. In *Proceedings of the 30th ACM International Conference on Information & Knowledge Management*, pages 2857–2861.

Baker, P. and Heritage, F. (2021). How to use corpus linguistics in sociolinguistics: A case study of modal verb use, age and change over time.

Baron, A., Rayson, P., and Archer, D. (2009). Word frequency and key word statistics in corpus linguistics. *Anglistik*, 20(1):41–67.

Behpour, S., Mohammadi, M., Albert, M. V., Alam, Z. S., Wang, L., and Xiao, T. (2021). Automatic trend detection: Time-biased document clustering. *Knowledge-Based Systems*, 220:106907.

Belinkov, Y., Habash, N., Kilgarriff, A., Ordan, N., Roth, R., Suchomel, V., et al. (2013). arTenTen: a new, vast corpus for Arabic. *Proceedings of WACL*, 20.

Bird, S., Klein, E., and Loper, E. (2009). *Natural language processing with Python: analyzing text with the natural language toolkit.* " O'Reilly Media, Inc.".

Curiac, C.-D., Banias, O., and Micea, M. (2022). Evaluating research trends from journal paper metadata, considering the research publication latency. *Mathematics*, 10(2):233.

[8] `https://archive.org/details/AraNPCC`

Davies, M. (2021). The Coronavirus corpus: Design, construction, and use. *International Journal of Corpus Linguistics*.

de Melo, T. and Figueiredo, C. M. (2020). A first public dataset from Brazilian twitter and news on COVID-19 in portuguese. *Data in brief*, 32:106179.

Deuber, D., Hackert, S., Hänsel, E. C., Laube, A., Hejrani, M., and Laliberté, C. (2021). The norm orientation of English in the Caribbeana comparative study of newspaper writing from ten countries. *American Speech*, pages 1–40.

Devlin, J., Chang, M.-W., Lee, K., and Toutanova, K. (2018). Bert: Pre-training of deep bidirectional transformers for language understanding. *arXiv preprint arXiv:1810.04805*.

Dong, E., Du, H., and Gardner, L. (2020). An interactive web-based dashboard to track COVID-19 in real time. *The Lancet infectious diseases*, 20(5):533–534.

El-Khair, I. A. (2016). 1.5 billion words Arabic corpus. *arXiv preprint arXiv:1611.04033*.

Gries, S. T. (2010). Useful statistics for corpus linguistics. *A mosaic of corpus linguistics: Selected approaches*, 66:269–291.

Hebbar, S. and Xie, Y. (2021). Covidbert-biomedical relation extraction for Covid-19. In *The International FLAIRS Conference Proceedings*, volume 34.

Imran, H. and Sharan, A. (2010). Co-occurrence based predictors for estimating query difficulty. In *2010 IEEE International Conference on Data Mining Workshops*, pages 867–874. IEEE.

Inoue, G., Alhafni, B., Baimukan, N., Bouamor, H., and Habash, N. (2021). The interplay of variant, size, and task type in arabic pre-trained language models. *arXiv preprint arXiv:2103.06678*.

Jakubíček, M., Kilgarriff, A., Kovář, V., Rychlỳ, P., and Suchomel, V. (2013). The TenTen corpus family. In *7th International Corpus Linguistics Conference CL*, pages 125–127.

Kilgarriff, A., Rychly, P., Smrz, P., and Tugwell, D. (2004). Itri-04-08 The Sketch Engine. *Information Technology*, 105(116).

Kutuzov, A., Touileb, S., Mæhlum, P., Enstad, T. R., and Wittemann, A. (2022). NorDiaChange: Diachronic semantic change dataset for Norwegian. *arXiv preprint arXiv:2201.05123*.

Müller, M., Salathé, M., and Kummervold, P. E. (2020). Covid-twitter-bert: A natural language processing model to analyse covid-19 content on twitter. *arXiv preprint arXiv:2005.07503*.

Radford, A., Wu, J., Child, R., Luan, D., Amodei, D., Sutskever, I., et al. (2019). Language models are unsupervised multitask learners. *OpenAI blog*, 1(8):9.

Rosin, G. D. and Radinsky, K. (2022). Temporal attention for language models. *arXiv preprint arXiv:2202.02093*.

Sonowal, G. (2020). Detecting phishing sms based on multiple correlation algorithms. *SN Computer Science*, 1(6):1–9.

Suárez, P. J. O., Romary, L., and Sagot, B. (2020). A monolingual approach to contextualized word embeddings for mid-resource languages. *arXiv preprint arXiv:2006.06202*.

Suwaileh, R., Kutlu, M., Fathima, N., Elsayed, T., and Lease, M. (2016). ArabicWeb16: A new crawl for today's Arabic web. In *Proceedings of the 39th International ACM SIGIR conference on Research and Development in Information Retrieval*, pages 673–676.

Zeroual, I., Goldhahn, D., Eckart, T., and Lakhouaja, A. (2019). OSIAN: Open source international Arabic news corpus-preparation and integration into the clarin-infrastructure. In *Proceedings of the Fourth Arabic Natural Language Processing Workshop*, pages 175–182.

8. Language Resource References

Parker, Robert, et al. (2011). *Arabic Gigaword Fifth Edition*. Linguistic Data Consortium, ISLRN 494-144-988-211-3.

Proceedings of the OSACT 2022 Workshop @LREC2022, pages 41–50
Marseille, 20 June 2022

Pre-trained Models or Feature Engineering: The Case of Dialectal Arabic

Chatrine Qwaider (Kathrein Abu kwaik)[*] , Stergios Chatzikyriakidis[◇*], Simon Dobnik[*]
[*]Centre for Linguistic Theory and Studies in Probability, FLoV, University of Gothenburg
{kathrein.abu.kwaik, simon.dobnik}@gu.se
[◇]Department of Philology, University of Crete
{Stergios.Chatzikyriakidis}@uoc.gr

Abstract

The usage of social media platforms has resulted in the proliferation of work on Arabic Natural Language Processing (ANLP), including the development of resources. There is also an increased interest in processing Arabic dialects and a number of models and algorithms have been utilised for the purpose of Dialectal Arabic Natural Language Processing (DANLP). In this paper, we conduct a comparison study between some of the most well-known and most commonly used methods in NLP in order to test their performance on different corpora and two NLP tasks: Dialect Identification and Sentiment Analysis. In particular, we compare three general classes of models: a) traditional Machine Learning models with features, b) classic Deep Learning architectures (LSTMs) with pre-trained word embeddings and lastly c) different Bidirectional Encoder Representations from Transformers (BERT) models such as (Multilingual-BERT, Ara-BERT, and Twitter-Arabic-BERT). The results of the comparison show that using feature-based classification can still compete with BERT models in these dialectal Arabic contexts. The use of transformer models have the ability to outperform traditional Machine Learning approaches, depending on the type of text they have been trained on, in contrast to classic Deep Learning models like LSTMs which do not perform well on the tasks.

Keywords: Dialect Identification, Sentiment Analysis, Machine learning, Deep Learning, Feature engineering, Language modelling

1. Introduction

The last decade has not only seen the emergence and development of social media platforms, but also, and relating to the latter, an increased interest in the automatic processing of Arabic dialects. A number of researchers have investigated several tasks related to Dialectal Arabic (DA) Natural Language Processing (NLP) that range from purely theoretical issues of syntax and morphology (Chiang et al., 2006; Habash et al., 2005) to more applied tasks like language generation and machine translation (Zbib et al., 2012; Meftouh et al., 2015; Diab and Habash, 2014).

Regardless of the increase in the interest of processing Arabic dialects, this research is still in its developing stage and the lack of significant and valuable resources is well-known. Currently, a lot of the NLP research handles the problem of Dialectal Arabic by introducing and building different kind of resources, e.g. lexicons, corpora, tree-banks and others that are usually focused on the specific task they attempt to address (Guellil et al., 2019). Dialectal Arabic resources are still suffering from the lack of available data that would enable a full investigation of the newly introduced Deep Learning (DL) networks on it.

Furthermore, the research that supports DA differs in terms of the tasks and the datasets used, a fact that leads to different results that are hard to compare. Some researchers and developers still support the use of traditional ML techniques in Arabic NLP given the limited size of available corpora (Abdul-Mageed et al., 2014), while others try to overcome and fine-tune complex DL networks (Heikal et al., 2018). In the case of corpora that are of limited size, feature-based ML approaches still give better results than DNNs for DA NLP tasks(Qwaider et al., 2019). In this paper, we investigate the performance of different approaches on DA on two NLP tasks: Dialect Identification (DI) and Sentiment Analysis (SA). We explore various datasets that have different sizes, balanced and imbalanced, hand-crafted and user-generated. In addition, we employ several features such as n-gram language models, pre-trained word embeddings, and pre-trained language models (Devlin et al., 2018). For classification tasks, we try traditional ML algorithms like Support Vector Machine (SVM), fully connected dense layers and Long Short Term Memory (LSTM) networks. For Sentiment Analysis, we achieve the state-of-the-art on the corpora used. In addition, our approach is one of the few that applies BERT for the Dialect Identification task.

The paper is organised as follows: Section 2 discusses recent related work in DI and SA, while Section 3 introduces the datasets used throughout our experiments. Section 4 presents the experiments, settings and, results. The section is in Section 5, while the conclusions can be found in Section 6.

2. Related work

In this paper we focus on two NLP tasks: Dialect Identification and Sentiment Analysis. Three main approaches are presented: (i) traditional ML with feature engineering, (ii) LSTM DL architectures and (iii) pre-trained language models.

The vast majority of research as regards Dialect Identification, uses traditional ML with feature engineering

(Tachicart et al., 2017; Obeid et al., 2019; Zaidan and Callison-Burch, 2014). Recently, after the introduction of the MADAR corpus (Bouamor et al., 2018), which covers 25 Arabic dialects, a good amount of research followed. Salameh et. al; (2019) present a fine-grained Dialect Identification model, where a character-gram language model with Multinomial Naive Bayes (MNB) classifier is used to identify the label of 25 dialects is used. The top five ranked systems at the MADAR shared task, focus on traditional character feature classification (Abu Kwaik and Saad, 2019; Meftouh et al., 2019; Ragab et al., 2019; Mishra and Mujadia, 2019). All these papers conclude that neural methods did not do as well as traditional ML approaches which is likely the result of limited training data. However, despite this inability of DL architectures to outperform traditional ML models, a number of researchers have turned towards straightforward DL architectures. For example, (Ali, 2018) proposes a deep learning CNN network based on character feature extraction to distinguish among MSA and dialects. De Francony et al. (2019), compare two approaches for Arabic fine-grained Dialect Identification, one using an RNN (BLSTM, BGRU) with hierarchical classification and and another using a voting classifier approach based on NB and Random Forest. In the same vein, (Fares et al., 2019) try different combinations of deep learning networks with different kinds of features on the MADAR corpus. These last two works both conclude, in line with the results from the MADAR task systems, that traditional ML algorithms outperform deep learning networks arguing that this might be because of the small size of the used corpus.

Recently, pre-trained language models such as BERT have been used for Dialect Identification. In (Zhang and Abdul-Mageed, 2019; Talafha et al., 2020; Beltagy et al., 2020), different Dialect Identification models based on BERT are introduced for the MADAR (Bouamor et al., 2019) and the NADI shared tasks[1].

Sentiment Analysis is a supervised classification task where a proposed model should be able to classify a sentence into two or more sentiment classes. The dominant approach for Arabic Sentiment Analysis in the last couple of years, as in the case of Dialect Identification, has been the feature-based and language modelling approach using ML classification algorithms like SVM, Multinomial Naive Bayes Classifier and others (Mountassir et al., 2012; Aly and Atiya, 2013; Omar et al., 2013; Elawady et al., 2014; Al-Saqqa et al., 2018). Some works use linguistics features such as the stems, lemmas, or part-of-speech, in addition to the Arabic variety (MSA, dialect), while others use more specific features depending on the kind of the dataset, e.g. userID (person, organisation) and the gender of the user found in datasets that use Twitter data (Abdul-Mageed et al., 2014; Shoukry and Rafea, 2012). However, most research uses language models by extracting words and character n-grams and investigating different ML classifiers (Duwairi et al., 2014).

Recently, as for Dialect Identification, researchers and developers started using deep learning networks for Sentiment Analysis with word embeddings and pre-trained language models. A CNN feature extractor and transformation network was proposed in (Soumeur et al., 2018) to determine the sentiment of Algerian users' comments on various Facebook brand pages of companies in Algeria, while (Baly et al., 2017) present an LSTM network with pre-trained word embeddings to build a 5-scale Sentiment Analysis model for 4 Arabic dialects. A combination of word and document embeddings in addition to a set of semantic features were used in (Abdullah et al., 2018) for Arabic tweets. The features are applied into a CNN-LSTM network followed by a fully connected layer. Heikal et al., (2018) propose an ensemble DL model that combines an LSTM with a CNN to predict the sentiment class of Arabic tweets exploiting the Arabic Sentiment Tweets Dataset (ASTD). Deep LSTM-CNN networks were used in (Mohammed and Kora, 2019) and a new 40K-tweets dataset collected from Twitter focusing on Egyptian dialects. Similarly, (Kwaik et al., 2019) propose a DL model that uses AraVec word embeddings with two Bi-LSTMs followed by 15 parallel CNN layers.

With the advent of pre-trained language models, a considerable amount of research concentrated on building and training their dialectal models by applying Arabic BERT as a first layer of the model instead of using a word-embeddings layer. In (Antoun et al., 2020) a Transformer-based Model for Arabic Language Understanding called AraBERT is proposed and applied on different Dialectal Arabic NLP tasks such as Sentiment Analysis and Question Answering. Some projects have built their own dialectal BERTs to be used in their specific models such as DziriBERT for Algerian dialects (Abdaoui et al., 2021) and ARabiziBERT where Arabizi is a written form of spoken Arabic that relies on Latin characters and digits (Baert et al., 2020).

Despite a large number of work on DA Dialect Identification and Sentiment Analysis, it is still an open question whether using old-fashion ML algorithms with feature engineering is better than using more sophisticated deep learning networks and pre-trained language models. This is because the results reported in the literature are based on models that are trained on datasets that differ in terms of size, the dialects covered, classification methods, or even the quality of the dataset. In this paper, we make a comparison using the same corpora on which we apply several models.

3. Datasets

We will use a number of well-known corpora. For the task of Dialect Identification we use the following:

- PADIC (Meftouh et al., 2015): a Parallel Arabic Dialect Corpus (PADIC) that was collected from Algerian telephone conversations, transcribed and

[1]https://sites.google.com/view/nadi-shared-task

then translated to other dialects. It is composed of 6.400 sentences for each dialect. The corpus contains five dialects where two of them present Algerian dialects (Algeria, Annaba), one from Tunisia and two dialects from Levantine (Palestine, Syria), in addition to MSA.

- SHAMI (Kwaik et al., 2018): a Levantine dialect corpus, includes 66.251 documents which were collected from different domains such as sports, social life, cooking, and others and it covers the four Levantine dialects. The corpus is unbalanced in term of number of documents per dialect with 10.830, 37.760, 10.643, 7.018 for Lebanese, Syrian, Palestinian and Jordanian respectively.
- MADAR-6 (Bouamor et al., 2018): a parallel corpus in the travel domain that covers, in addition to MSA, five different Arabic dialects from five Arabic cities: Beirut (BEI), Cairo (CAI), Doha (DOH), Rabat (RAB), Tunisia (TUN), therefore it is called MADAR-6. The corpus is composed of 10.000 documents for each dialect.

We focus on binary classification where the document is classified as either positive or negative. The three corpora we use are:

- ATSAD (Kwaik et al., 2020): an Arabic Tweets Sentiment Analysis Dataset (multi-dialects). The corpus has been collected from Twitter during April 2019 and employs emojis as seeds for extraction of candidate instances. It is a balanced binary corpus which was partly annotated by human experts and then self training techniques were applied to annotate the rest of tweets. The corpus contains 18.173 and 18.695 negative tweets and positive tweets respectively.
- 40-K tweets (Mohammed and Kora, 2019): an Egyptian binary balanced corpus where all tweets were pre-processed and cleaned manually by two experts. The total size is 40,000 tweets, where 20.002 tweets are negative and 19.998 are positive.
- ASTD (Nabil et al., 2015): an Arabic Sentiment Tweets Dataset focusing on the Egyptian dialect. The corpus is composed of 10k tweets classified for objective and subjective sentiment. It is unbalanced dataset since there are 1.681 negative documents and 818 positive ones.

4. Experiments

In this section we describe our experiments and the models used for both Dialect Identification and Sentiment Analysis on dialectal Arabic. For both tasks, we make use of three corpora as shown in the previous section. We split the datasets into 90% for training set and 10% for testing. The 90% training part is further split into 80% for training and 20% for validation. Tables 1 and 2 show the total size of the corpora alongside the number of sentences for every set: training, validation, and testing.
We investigate the performance and the differences between the models. We performed a number of experiments where we focus on some common popular architectures. First of all, we apply BERT as a pre-trained language model followed by a classification layer. Then we compare it with a model with pre-trained word embeddings (AraVec) (Soliman et al., 2017) and an LSTM network. We also investigate the performance of feature extraction language model on both traditional ML algorithms like SVM and on a fully connected classification layer. Figure1 shows a diagram summarising all the experiments.
In order to evaluate the performance of the models, we use accuracy together with the following two measures:

- Mathews correlation coefficient (MCC): A measure used in ML to measure the quality of classification model (Matthews, 1975). It is a balanced measure which could also be used for imbalanced classification problem (Boughorbel et al., 2017). The MCC has a value between -1 (total disagreement between prediction and observation) to +1 (perfect prediction), and 0 value indicate random prediction. MCC is calculated from the confusion matrix according to Equation 1

$$MCC = \frac{TP \times TN - FP \times FN}{\sqrt{(TP+FP)(TP+FN)(TN+FP)(TN+FN)}} \quad (1)$$

- F-score: also a well-known measure for classification success in ML. The F-score is the harmonic mean between the precision and the recall (Derczynski, 2016). Through all the experiments we chose the F-score to optimize on the validation set, as some of datasets are not balanced, so accuracy could not be a good choice for optimization.

4.1. BERT for Dialectal Arabic

The main component of BERT or Bidirectional Encoder Representations from Transformer (Devlin et al., 2018) is a Transformer which is an encoder-decoder attention mechanism that has been build to learn the contextual relations between sequence of words in any text and generate a language model. It takes a sequence of words (sub-words) as an input layer. These tokens are embedded into vectors and then go through the transformer encoder. The output of BERT is a sequence of vectors, where each vector presents an input token. To apply fine-tuning on BERT for any classification task or language generation task, a fully connected classification layer with a soft-max activation function is built on top of the output vectors.
As we work on Dialectal Arabic, a natural thing to do is to use the Arabic versions of BERT. On top of the BERT model we add a classification layer for our two tasks which are trained separately. We use the following BERT models:

Dataset	# Dialects	Total size	Train_set	Val_set	Test_set
PADIC	6	33,502	25,560	6,391	3551
Shami	4	66,251	47,699	11,925	6,626
MADAR-6	6	60,000	43,200	10,800	6,000

Table 1: Corpora statistics for the Dialect Identification task

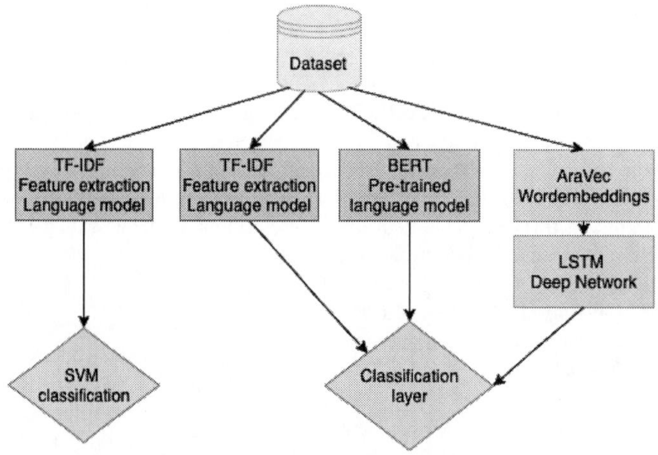

Figure 1: Fours different models used in the classification tasks in the experiments

Dataset	Total	Train	Val	Test
ATSAD	22,542	16,229	4,058	2,255
40-K	40,000	28,800	7,200	4,000
ASTD	2499	1,799	450	250

Table 2: Corpora statistics for the Sentiment Analysis task

1. Multilingual-BERT[2]: This is the multi-lingual version of BERT, which contains the top 100 languages with the largest Wikipedia content, including Modern Standard Arabic.

2. Arabic-BERT (Safaya et al., 2020): consists of 4 models of different sizes (Large, Base, Medium and Mini). We use the base model for the experiments. Arabic-BERT has been built with 8,2B words from the OSCAR data (Suárez et al., 2020) and the recent data dump from Wikipedia.

3. AraBERT-Twitter-base (Antoun et al., 2020): AraBERT is an Arabic pre-trained language model based on Google's BERT architecture. It also uses the same BERT-base configuration. There are two versions of AraBERT v1 and v2 where they differ in term of segmentation techniques. AraBERT-Twitter-base is the dialectal version of AraBERTv2. It contains 60M Multi-Dialect Tweets in addition to 200M from the AraBERTv2-base.

[2]https://github.com/google-research/bert/blob/master/multilingual.md

The same parameters are used through all the experiments in order to get a reasonable comparison. We use the Adam optimiser where the learning rate is 5e-5 and epsilon is equal to 1e-8 through all the BERT models. We set the batch size to be 32 for multi-lingual BERT and 16 for both Arabic BERT and Twitter-AraBERT models. The preferred number of epochs for fine tuning Multi-BERT is between 2 to 4 (Devlin et al., 2018). In our case 4 epochs was the best choice for Sentiment Analysis, while for Dialect Identification the best number of epochs was 10. For Arabic BERT and Twitter-AraBERT, the number of epochs is between 8 to 10 and we employ early stopping and save the best performed epoch. We also explore max sequence lengths for both tasks and decide on 77 for Sentiment Analysis and 130 for Dialect Identification using Multi-lingual BERT, and 280 and 256 for ArabicBERT and Twitter-AraBERT respectively.

We build the first model by employing Multi-Lingual BERT as a basic layer, and then have a softmax fully connected layer for classification purposes. Table 3 and Table 4 present the output results for the Accuracy, MCC and F-score for the two tasks. For Dialect Identification the accuracy ranges between 0.72 to 0.89 with 10 epochs and has very short training time compared to an end-to-end neural network. In case of Sentiment Analysis we get an accuracy between 0.8 to 0.83 where the model outperforms the state of the art result using deep learning on the ASTD corpus (Heikal et al., 2018; Kwaik et al., 2019).

Dataset	Accuracy	MCC	F-score
PADIC	0.72	0.67	0.72
Shami	0.88	0.81	0.83
MADAR-6	0.89	0.87	0.89

Table 3: Results of applying Multilingual-BERT on Dialect Identification task

Data_set	Accuracy	MCC	F-score
ATSAD	0.80	0.6	0.80
40-k Tweets	0.83	0.66	0.83
ASTD	0.81	0.51	0.75

Table 4: Results of applying Multilingual-BERT on Sentiment Analysis task

The Multi-Lingual model was not only built for the purpose of Arabic-NLP. For comparison we implement the second model using Arabic-Bert. We used the basic version of Arabic-BERT and then the same soft-max classification layer. The three test measurements (Accuracy, MCC, F-scores) for Dialect identification and Sentiment Analysis are presented in Tables 5 and 6 respectively. The accuracy for DI models range from 0.71 to 0.80 which is less than the previous Multilingual BERT model. This is may be because the later model was trained on different languages so it is easier to fine-tune it to identify or classify languages or dialects. On the other hand, on Sentiment Analysis the models performed better than those using Multilingual-BERT where the accuracy is in the range of 0.83 to 0.90.

Both Multilingual BERT and Arabic-BERT have been trained on MSA data that was collected mainly from news websites and Wikipedia documents. We conduct a third experiment with BERT which was trained on dialectal data, the Twitter-AraBERT. Table 7 shows the test accuracy on the Dialect Identification task. The model is the best among those described previously.

Data_set	Accuracy	MCC	F-score
PADIC	0.71	0.66	0.72
Shami	0.87	0.78	0.81
MADAR-6	0.80	0.76	0.80

Table 5: Results of applying Arabic-BERT on Dialect Identification task

Data_set	Accuracy	MCC	F-score
ATSAD	0.93	0.87	0.93
40-k Tweets	0.83	0.66	0.83
ASTD	0.84	0.63	0.81

Table 6: Results of applying Arabic-BERT on Sentiment Analysis task

The accuracy is now in the range of 0.77 and 0.91. Table 8 shows the accuracy of Sentiment Analysis models which ranges from 0.88 to 0.97. The model outperforms the state-of-the-art on the 40K tweets dataset (Mohammed and Kora, 2019). Here, the authors achieve an average accuracy of 0.81 using LSTM models. In addition, it outperforms the state-of-the-art on the ASTD corpus (Heikal et al., 2018). Among the three BERT models, Twitter-AraBERT is the best performing model when the data used for training is mostly dialectal.

Data_set	Accuracy	MCC	F-score
PADIC	0.77	0.73	0.77
Shami	0.91	0.86	0.87
MADAR-6	0.91	0.90	0.91

Table 7: Results of applying Twitter-AraBERT on Dialect Identification task

Data_set	Accuracy	MCC	F-score
ATSAD	0.97	0.94	0.97
40-k Tweets	0.91	0.82	0.91
ASTD	0.88	0.74	0.87

Table 8: Results of applying Twitter-AraBERT on Sentiment Analysis task

4.2. LSTM Baseline

We build a simple LSTM baseline and apply it to the corpora for the two tasks. We employ the AraVec (Twitter-CBOW 300) which are pre-trained Arabic word embeddings as a first layer (Soliman et al., 2017), followed by an LSTM layer with 70 nodes and a dropout of 0.25%. This is followed by a fully connected dense layer with 30 nodes. The last layer is also a fully connected dense layer where the output depends on the number of classes in each task. For Dialect Identification, there are 6, 6 and 4 output classes for PADIC, MADAR-6 and SHAMI respectively. For the Sentiment Analysis task, we use the binary classification task. Table 9 shows the LSTM baseline settings.

Parameter	Value
Max_length	130 (DI), 77 (SA)
Optimiser	Adam (DI), RMSprop(SA)
Word_embeddings	AraVec (Twitter-CBOW 300)
LSTM_nodes	70
Drop_out	0.25
Dense_nodes	30
Activation_function	Sigmoid
Loss	Categorial_crossentrapy (DI), Binary_crosentrapy (SA)
Batch_size	32
Epochs	up to 100, Early_stopping

Table 9: LSTM baseline network settings

We use the loss with a minimum value to monitor the model and to save the best performance weights. Tables 10 and 11 show the results of applying the baseline into the corpora in concern. It is clear that a baseline LSTM with Arabic pre-trained word embeddings is not able to perform well with dialectal Arabic NLP tasks. The accuracy does not exceed 0.6 in any corpus. Moreover, the MCC shows zero values through all the corpora which means that the classifier is not able to correctly classify the documents and it is no better than random prediction. For Shami corpus the accuracy is high (comparing to other datasets) while the F-score is equally low 0.18, which suggests that Shami is more imbalanced and the model is not doing well on recall on minority classes.

Data_set	Accuracy	MCC	F-score
PADIC	0.17	0	0.14
Shami	0.57	0.004	0.18
MADAR-6	0.17	0	0.29

Table 10: Results of applying LSTM baseline on Dialect Identification task

Data_set	Accuracy	MCC	F-score
ATSAD	0.52	0	0.34
40-k Tweets	0.49	0	0.33
ASTD	0.69	0	0.41

Table 11: Result of applying LSTM baseline on Sentiment Analysis task

4.3. Feature-Based Classification for Dialectal Arabic

In addition to BERT and LSTM experiments we also investigate the performance of traditional Machine Learning algorithms on Dialectal Arabic. An SVM machine learning model (linear SVC) was built and proposed in (Qwaider et al., 2019) for dialectal Arabic Sentiment Analysis. We employ the same approach for both tasks. The models apply various n-gram features as follows:

- Word-gram features with uni-gram, bi-grams and tri-grams, the transformation weight is 0.8.
- Character-gram features with word boundary consideration from bi-grams to 5-grams and the transformation weight of 0.5
- Character-gram features without word boundary consideration from bi-grams to 5-grams and the transformation weight of 0.4.

For the SVM ((linear SVC) classifier, we set a linear kernel and use the default squared_hinge loss function, we set tolerance to be 1e-5, other parameters are kept as default. The results after training and testing the model are presented in Table 12 and 13.

Data_set	Accuracy	MCC	F-score
PADIC	0.72	0.66	0.72
Shami	0.90	0.84	0.86
MADAR-6	0.89	0.87	0.89

Table 12: Results of applying the feature-based model (SVM) on the Dialect Identification task

Data_set	Accuracy	MCC	F-score
ATSAD	0.96	0.92	0.96
40-k Tweets	0.84	0.67	0.84
ASTD	0.80	0.45	0.71

Table 13: Results of applying the feature-based model (SVM) on the Sentiment Analysis task

We further investigate the effect of feature based approaches by placing a fully connected classification layer on the top of the language model rather than using a traditional machine learning algorithm such as SVM or NB. The model seems like BERT, but instead of the pre-trained language model layers we use the feature extraction language model discussed before, followed by a classification layer. Table 14 and 15 show the results of this experiment. Table 16 and 17 report the results for all the aforementioned experiments.

Data_set	Accuracy	MCC	F-score
PADIC	0.73	0.68	0.74
Shami	0.57	0	0.50
MADAR-6	0.89	0.87	0.89

Table 14: Results of the feature-based model with fully connected classification layers on the Dialect Identification task

Data_set	Accuracy	MCC	F-score
ATSAD	0.96	0.91	0.95
40-k Tweets	0.82	0.63	0.82
ASTD	0.77	0.49	0.73

Table 15: Results of the feature-based model with fully connected classification layers on the Sentiment Analysis task

5. Discussion

The LSTM model is the worst performing model among all the models with a huge evaluation gap between that and the other models. The low performance of the LSTM network might be due to the usage of the AraVec pre-trained word embeddings. The percentage of OOV words is high (from 30% to 70%). We try to overcome this problem by replacing the embedding vector for the missing word with the embedding vector for the least lexical-distance word. To compute the lexical distance, we apply the Levenshtein distance algorithm and set the distance to at most two characters.

	PADIC			SHAMI			MADAR-6		
	Acc	MCC	F	Acc	MCC	F	Acc	MCC	F
Multilingual-BERT	72	67	72	88	81	83	89	87	89
Arabic-BERT	71	66	72	87	78	81	80	76	80
Twitter-BERT	**77**	**73**	**77**	**91**	**86**	**86**	**91**	**90**	**91**
LSTM	17	0	14	57	0.4	18	17	0	29
TFIDF + SVM	72	66	72	90	84	86	89	87	89
TFIDF+ Dense	73	68	74	57	0	50	89	87	89

Table 16: Performance measurements for all the experiments on Dialect Identification.

	ATSAD			40K tweets			ASTD		
	Acc	MCC	F	Acc	MCC	F	Acc	MCC	F
Multilingual-BERT	80	60	80	83	66	83	81	51	75
Arabic-BERT	93	87	93	83	66	83	84	63	81
Twitter-BERT	**97**	**94**	**97**	**91**	**82**	**91**	**88**	**74**	**87**
LSTM	52	0	34	49	0	33	69	0	41
TFIDF + SVM	96	92	96	84	67	84	80	45	71
TFIDF+ Dense	96	91	95	82	63	82	77	49	73

Table 17: Performance measurements for all the experiments on Sentiment Analysis

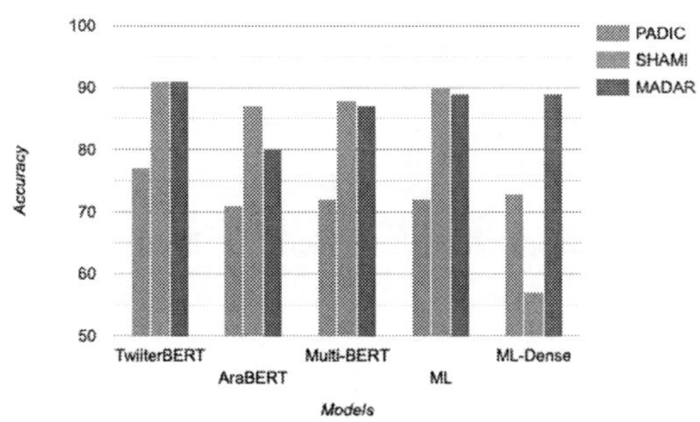

Figure 2: Accuracy of different Dialect Identification models

This makes the LSTM network not perform well even when the word embeddings layer is set to be trainable. The network is also biased towards the majority class. This is very clear in the case of SHAMI, which is the most unbalanced dataset of all.

As we see from the experiments, feature-based classification methods can compete with the pre-trained language models followed by a fully connected layer and sometimes even outperform them. Figure 2 plots the accuracy for the Dialect Identification models as well as the used corpora. The LSTM is not shown, as it is the worst of all and the MCC was 0. Although the results are close in some cases, the Twitter-AraBERT outperforms all the models on all corpora. The Twitter-AraBERT model and the ML models are close to each other in terms of accuracy especially for SHAMI, a non-parallel and unbalanced corpus. It is clear that the size of the corpus has an effect on the performance of the DI task. For example, ML with feature based and svm algorithm is doing better on SHAMI and MADAR than PADIC. However, for a corpus of reasonable size, even with unbalanced data like SHAMI, ML algorithms (SVM) have the ability to compete with pre-trained language models. On well structured and human annotated corpora like PADIC and MADAR both feature-based approaches do nearly the same regardless of whether they are using an SVM or a classification layer. Both corpora have handcrafted examples that increase the power of n-gram language models.

Figure 3 plots the accuracy for the Sentiment Analysis task. Also here Twitter-AraBERT is the best over all the corpora. Sentiment Analysis is a task that does not depend on the structural properties of language as much but rather on the context where emotions are expressed. On the ATSAD corpus where emojis were used as weak labels for annotation Twitter-AraBERT performs very well. Twitter-AraBERT is also able to deal efficiently with the problem of imbalanced datasets like ATSD which is of small size. When it comes to the composition of dialects in the datasets, the 40k-tweets dataset as well as ASTD include Egyptian data. In this case, Twitter-BERT performs better than ML methods. In contrast, in a multi-dialect corpus like ATSAD, feature-based approaches are also a good choice, achieving results very close to those obtained with Twitter-BERT.

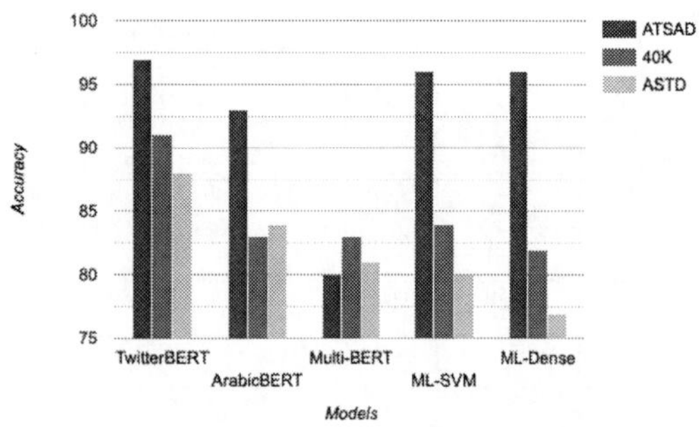

Figure 3: Accuracy of different Sentiment Analysis models

In general, applying pre-trained language models on dialectal Arabic NLP tasks leads to reasonable results.
Many factors play a role on the decision of which model to choose for an NLP task: The size of the dataset, the sources and the quality of the data, the data balance, whether the corpus contains MSA or multi-dialectal Arabic data, as well as the number of classes. For under-resourced languages we show that traditional ML approaches perform well and that they are still a highly competitive choice over more complicated and time and resource intensive deep neural models.

6. Conclusion

In this study, we discuss the issue of choosing the best methods for Dialectal Arabic NLP tasks, taking into consideration the differences among the resources. We implemented various approaches from traditional ML to the most recent approaches using BERT, and using different corpora. We wanted to measure the performance of pre-trained models compared to feature-based ML methods. Firstly, we proposed the use of a pre-trained language model like BERT into Dialectal Arabic. Two DA-NLP tasks were used in this study (Dialect Identification and Sentiment Analysis) on six different corpora (3 for each task). Fine-tuning BERT for DA can produce acceptable results on all corpora. Using BERT that supports Arabic saves effort and time to build deep learning models for dialectal Arabic from scratch.
The second part of the study investigates other classification approaches and compares them to the BERT models. We build an LSTM baseline with the support of the pre-trained AraVec word embeddings which does not perform well. The usage of AraVec with a large OOV dialectal words does not facilitate the model in being retrained and fine-tuned for DA. We also built feature-based models either using the SVM or using a fully connected neural network layer. The usage of a tailor-made feature extractor can compete end-to-end feature training in BERT. In summary, after investigating feature-based and feature-pre-trained machine learning approaches, we can say that training DL models such as LSTMs directly from data is not a good solution for the specific tasks and datasets for DA. BERT-pre-trained models appear to be a good solution for dialectal Arabic tasks but feature-pre-training is nearly matched by traditional feature-based models. However, not all BERT-pre-trained models perform equally well. There is a preference for the model that was trained on social media which contains dialectal linguistic variation. However, the use of pre-trained models does not necessarily mean getting better results all the time. In some experiments the use of the SVM algorithm with feature-based classification does surprisingly well and produces very competitive results. In the future, we intend to consider performing error analysis to have a deep look into the proposed approaches, especially on the LSTM approach, since the performance was surprisingly too low. In addition, make more effort to implement an effective LSTM model that can compete with the aforementioned models. Moreover, we want to compare more between BERT models and Feature-based engineering models, for example, in terms of running or inference time., so researchers can decide on the chosen model based on their preferences criteria.

7. Acknowledgements

The research reported in this paper was supported by a grant from the Swedish Research Council (VR project 2014-39) for the establishment of the Centre for Linguistic Theory and Studies in Probability (CLASP) at the University of Gothenburg.

8. Bibliographical References

Abdaoui, A., Berrimi, M., Oussalah, M., and Moussaoui, A. (2021). Dziribert: a pre-trained language model for the algerian dialect. *arXiv preprint arXiv:2109.12346.*

Abdul-Mageed, M., Diab, M., and Kübler, S. (2014). SAMAR: Subjectivity and sentiment analysis for Arabic social media. *Computer Speech & Language*, 28(1):20–37.

Abdullah, M., Hadzikadicy, M., and Shaikhz, S. (2018). SEDAT: Sentiment and Emotion Detection in Arabic Text Using CNN-LSTM Deep Learning. In *2018 17th IEEE International Conference on Machine Learning and Applications (ICMLA)*, pages 835–840. IEEE.

Abu Kwaik, K. and Saad, M. K. (2019). ArbDialectID at MADAR Shared Task 1: Language Modelling and Ensemble Learning for Fine Grained Arabic Dialect Identification. *ArbDialectID at MADAR Shared Task 1: Language Modelling and Ensemble Learning for Fine Grained Arabic Dialect Identification*, (Proceedings of the Fourth Arabic Natural Language Processing Workshop).

Al-Saqqa, S., Obeid, N., and Awajan, A. (2018). Sentiment Analysis for Arabic Text using Ensemble Learning. In *2018 IEEE/ACS 15th International Conference on Computer Systems and Applications (AICCSA)*, pages 1–7. IEEE.

Ali, M. (2018). Character level convolutional neural network for Arabic dialect identification. In *Proceedings of the Fifth Workshop on NLP for Similar Languages, Varieties and Dialects (VarDial 2018)*, pages 122–127.

Aly, M. and Atiya, A. (2013). Labr: A large scale arabic book reviews dataset. In *Proceedings of the 51st Annual Meeting of the Association for Computational Linguistics (Volume 2: Short Papers)*, volume 2, pages 494–498.

Antoun, W., Baly, F., and Hajj, H. (2020). Arabert: Transformer-based model for arabic language understanding. *arXiv preprint arXiv:2003.00104*.

Baert, G., Gahbiche, S., Gadek, G., and Pauchet, A. (2020). Arabizi language models for sentiment analysis. In *Proceedings of the 28th International Conference on Computational Linguistics*, pages 592–603, Barcelona, Spain (Online), December. International Committee on Computational Linguistics.

Baly, R., El-Khoury, G., Moukalled, R., Aoun, R., Hajj, H., Shaban, K. B., and El-Hajj, W. (2017). Comparative evaluation of sentiment analysis methods across arabic dialects. *Procedia Computer Science*, 117:266–273.

Beltagy, A., Wael, A., and ElSherief, O. (2020). Arabic dialect identification using bert-based domain adaptation. *arXiv preprint arXiv:2011.06977*.

Bouamor, H., Habash, N., Salameh, M., Zaghouani, W., Rambow, O., Abdulrahim, D., Obeid, O., Khalifa, S., Eryani, F., Erdmann, A., et al. (2018). The MADAR Arabic dialect corpus and lexicon. In *Proceedings of the Eleventh International Conference on Language Resources and Evaluation (LREC 2018)*.

Bouamor, H., Hassan, S., and Habash, N. (2019). The MADAR shared task on Arabic fine-grained dialect identification. In *Proceedings of the Fourth Arabic Natural Language Processing Workshop*, pages 199–207.

Boughorbel, S., Jarray, F., and El-Anbari, M. (2017). Optimal classifier for imbalanced data using Matthews Correlation Coefficient metric. *PloS one*, 12(6):e0177678.

Chiang, D., Diab, M., Habash, N., Rambow, O., and Shareef, S. (2006). Parsing Arabic dialects. In *11th Conference of the European Chapter of the Association for Computational Linguistics*.

de Francony, G., Guichard, V., Joshi, P., Afli, H., and Bouchekif, A. (2019). Hierarchical Deep Learning for Arabic Dialect Identification. In *Proceedings of the Fourth Arabic Natural Language Processing Workshop*, pages 249–253.

Derczynski, L. (2016). Complementarity, F-score, and NLP Evaluation. In *Proceedings of the Tenth International Conference on Language Resources and Evaluation (LREC'16)*, pages 261–266.

Devlin, J., Chang, M.-W., Lee, K., and Toutanova, K. (2018). Bert: Pre-training of deep bidirectional transformers for language understanding. *arXiv preprint arXiv:1810.04805*.

Diab, M. and Habash, N. (2014). Natural language processing of Arabic and its dialects. In *Proceedings of the conference on empirical methods in natural language processing (EMNLP). Doha, Qatar*, page 10. Citeseer.

Duwairi, R. M., Marji, R., Sha'ban, N., and Rushaidat, S. (2014). Sentiment analysis in Arabic tweets. In *2014 5th International Conference on Information and Communication Systems (ICICS)*, pages 1–6. IEEE.

Elawady, R. M., Barakat, S., and Elrashidy, N. M. (2014). Different feature selection for sentiment classification. *International Journal of Information Science and Intelligent System*, 3(1):137–150.

Fares, Y., El-Zanaty, Z., Abdel-Salam, K., Ezzeldin, M., Mohamed, A., El-Awaad, K., and Torki, M. (2019). Arabic Dialect Identification with Deep Learning and Hybrid Frequency Based Features. In *Proceedings of the Fourth Arabic Natural Language Processing Workshop*, pages 224–228.

Guellil, I., Saâdane, H., Azouaou, F., Gueni, B., and Nouvel, D. (2019). Arabic natural language processing: An overview. *Journal of King Saud University-Computer and Information Sciences*.

Habash, N., Rambow, O., and Kiraz, G. A. (2005). Morphological analysis and generation for Arabic dialects. In *Proceedings of the ACL Workshop on Computational Approaches to Semitic Languages*, pages 17–24.

Heikal, M., Torki, M., and El-Makky, N. (2018). Sentiment analysis of Arabic Tweets using deep learning. *Procedia Computer Science*, 142:114–122.

Kwaik, K. A., Saad, M., Chatzikyriakidis, S., and Dobnik, S. (2018). Shami: A corpus of levantine arabic dialects. In *Proceedings of the Eleventh International Conference on Language Resources and Evaluation (LREC 2018)*.

Kwaik, K. A., Saad, M., Chatzikyriakidis, S., and Dobnik, S. (2019). LSTM-CNN Deep Learning Model for Sentiment Analysis of Dialectal Arabic. In *International Conference on Arabic Language Processing*, pages 108–121. Springer.

Kwaik, K. A., Chatzikyriakidis, S., Dobnik, S., Saad, M., and Johansson, R. (2020). An arabic tweets sentiment analysis dataset (atsad) using distant supervision and self training. In *Proceedings of the 4th Workshop on Open-Source Arabic Corpora and Processing Tools, with a Shared Task on Offensive Language Detection*, pages 1–8.

Matthews, B. W. (1975). Comparison of the predicted and observed secondary structure of T4 phage lysozyme. *Biochimica et Biophysica Acta (BBA)-Protein Structure*, 405(2):442–451.

Meftouh, K., Harrat, S., Jamoussi, S., Abbas, M., and Smaili, K. (2015). Machine translation experiments on PADIC: A parallel Arabic dialect corpus. In *The 29th Pacific Asia conference on language, information and computation*.

Meftouh, K., Abidi, K., Harrat, S., and Smaili, K. (2019). The SMarT Classifier for Arabic Fine-Grained Dialect Identification.

Mishra, P. and Mujadia, V. (2019). Arabic Dialect Identification for Travel and Twitter Text. In *Proceedings of the Fourth Arabic Natural Language Processing Workshop*, pages 234–238.

Mohammed, A. and Kora, R. (2019). Deep learning approaches for Arabic sentiment analysis. *Social Network Analysis and Mining*, 9(1):52.

Mountassir, A., Benbrahim, H., and Berrada, I. (2012). An empirical study to address the problem of unbalanced data sets in sentiment classification. In *2012 IEEE international conference on systems, man, and cybernetics (SMC)*, pages 3298–3303. IEEE.

Nabil, M., Aly, M., and Atiya, A. (2015). Astd: Arabic sentiment tweets dataset. In *Proceedings of the 2015 conference on empirical methods in natural language processing*, pages 2515–2519.

Obeid, O., Salameh, M., Bouamor, H., and Habash, N. (2019). ADIDA: Automatic dialect identification for Arabic. In *Proceedings of the 2019 Conference of the North American Chapter of the Association for Computational Linguistics (Demonstrations)*, pages 6–11, Minneapolis, Minnesota, June. Association for Computational Linguistics.

Omar, N., Albared, M., Al-Shabi, A. Q., and Al-Moslmi, T. (2013). Ensemble of classification algorithms for subjectivity and sentiment analysis of Arabic customers' reviews. *International Journal of Advancements in Computing Technology*, 5(14):77.

Qwaider, C., Chatzikyriakidis, S., and Dobnik, S. (2019). Can Modern Standard Arabic Approaches be used for Arabic Dialects? Sentiment Analysis as a Case Study. In *Proceedings of the 3rd Workshop on Arabic Corpus Linguistics*, pages 40–50.

Ragab, A., Seelawi, H., Samir, M., Mattar, A., Al-Bataineh, H., Zaghloul, M., Mustafa, A., Talafha, B., Freihat, A. A., and Al-Natsheh, H. (2019). Mawdoo3 AI at MADAR Shared Task: Arabic Fine-Grained Dialect Identification with Ensemble Learning. In *Proceedings of the Fourth Arabic Natural Language Processing Workshop*, pages 244–248.

Safaya, A., Abdullatif, M., and Yuret, D. (2020). Kuisail at semeval-2020 task 12: Bert-cnn for offensive speech identification in social media. In *Proceedings of the Fourteenth Workshop on Semantic Evaluation*, pages 2054–2059.

Shoukry, A. and Rafea, A. (2012). Sentence-level Arabic sentiment analysis. In *2012 International Conference on Collaboration Technologies and Systems (CTS)*, pages 546–550. IEEE.

Soliman, A. B., Eissa, K., and El-Beltagy, S. R. (2017). Aravec: A set of arabic word embedding models for use in arabic nlp. *Procedia Computer Science*, 117:256–265.

Soumeur, A., Mokdadi, M., Guessoum, A., and Daoud, A. (2018). Sentiment Analysis of Users on Social Networks: Overcoming the challenge of the Loose Usages of the Algerian Dialect. *Procedia computer science*, 142:26–37.

Suárez, P. J. O., Romary, L., and Sagot, B. (2020). A monolingual approach to contextualized word embeddings for mid-resource languages. *arXiv preprint arXiv:2006.06202*.

Tachicart, R., Bouzoubaa, K., Aouragh, S. L., and Jaafa, H. (2017). Automatic identification of Moroccan colloquial Arabic. In *International Conference on Arabic Language Processing*, pages 201–214. Springer.

Talafha, B., Ali, M., Za'ter, M. E., Seelawi, H., Tuffaha, I., Samir, M., Farhan, W., and Al-Natsheh, H. T. (2020). Multi-Dialect Arabic BERT for Country-Level Dialect Identification. *arXiv preprint arXiv:2007.05612*.

Zaidan, O. F. and Callison-Burch, C. (2014). Arabic dialect identification. *Computational Linguistics*, 40(1):171–202.

Zbib, R., Malchiodi, E., Devlin, J., Stallard, D., Matsoukas, S., Schwartz, R., Makhoul, J., Zaidan, O., and Callison-Burch, C. (2012). Machine translation of Arabic dialects. In *Proceedings of the 2012 conference of the north american chapter of the association for computational linguistics: Human language technologies*, pages 49–59.

Zhang, C. and Abdul-Mageed, M. (2019). No Army, No Navy: Bert Semi-supervised Learning of Arabic Dialects. In *Proceedings of the Fourth Arabic Natural Language Processing Workshop*, pages 279–284.

Proceedings of the OSACT 2022 Workshop @LREC2022, pages 51–59
Marseille, 20 June 2022

A Context-free Arabic Emoji Sentiment Lexicon (CF-Arab-ESL)

Shatha Ali A. Hakami [1 2], Robert Hendley[1], Phillip Smith[1]
[1]University of Birmingham, UK [2]Jazan University, Saudi Arabia
{sah624, r.j.hendley, p.smith.7}@cs.bham.ac.uk, sahakami@jazanu.edu.sa

Abstract

Emoji can be valuable features in textual sentiment analysis. One of the key elements of the use of emoji in sentiment analysis is the emoji sentiment lexicon. However, constructing such a lexicon is a challenging task. This is because interpreting the sentiment conveyed by these pictographic symbols is highly subjective, and differs depending upon how each person perceives them. Cultural background is considered to be one of the main factors that affects emoji sentiment interpretation. Thus, we focus in this work on targeting people from Arab cultures. This is done by constructing a context-free Arabic emoji sentiment lexicon annotated by native Arabic speakers from seven different regions (Gulf, Egypt, Levant, Sudan, North Africa, Iraq, and Yemen) to see how these Arabic users label the sentiment of these symbols without a textual context. We recruited 53 annotators (males and females) to annotate 1,069 unique emoji. Then we evaluated the reliability of the annotation for each participant by applying sensitivity (Recall) and consistency (Krippendorff's Alpha) tests. For the analysis, we investigated the resulting emoji sentiment annotations to explore the impact of the Arabic cultural context. We analyzed this cultural reflection from different perspectives, including national affiliation, use of colour indications, animal indications, weather indications and religious impact.

Keywords: Emoji, Lexicon, Arabic, NLP, Sentiment Analysis, Social Media

1. Introduction

Emoji are pictographic characters that people use in text-based communication to address the issue of the lack of nonverbal cues (e.g. facial expressions, body language, and voice tones) in text communication. The unseen coding skeleton for emoji is the Unicode standard, which is the foundation for text in all modern writing systems. Currently, there are more than three thousand emoji in the Unicode standard list. Each emoji has a point code in a Unicode transformation format (e.g., U+1F602), and a name (e.g., 'face with tears of joy'), but they lack a standard graphical appearance. To generate the graphical appearance (e.g., ), each platform has to render the UTF point codes to produce emoji. As a consequence, the shape, the colour, and the availability of emoji differs across platforms.

The accessibility of emoji in almost all social media platforms leads the users to adopt them to, for instance, initiate/close conversations, indicate celebration, express approval of a message, signal task fulfilment or to respond to thanks/complimenting expressions (Al Rashdi, 2018). Linguistically, researchers have found that emoji can be used to disambiguate the intended sense (Riordan, 2017), manipulate the original meaning (Donato and Paggio, 2017; Njenga, 2018), infer some contextual information (Dresner and Herring, 2010; Skovholt et al., 2014), add sentiment to a message as a writer (Shiha and Ayvaz, 2017) and to ease the understanding of the expressed sentiment as a reader (Dresner and Herring, 2010; Skovholt et al., 2014). This has led natural language processing (NLP) researchers to realise the importance of emoji as sentiment features in text and to include them in their analysis.

Sentiment analysis has become an important tool in classifying and interpreting text. It has important applications in social media analysis, consultation systems, text classification and many other areas. Sentiment analysis can be defined as a process that analyses text and builds an interpretation of the sentiment that it is intended to convey. Usually, this is a two dimensional measure from negative to positive and often it is mapped to just three values: negative, neutral or positive. Studies on emoji within textual context mainly focus on three areas: the usage of emoji, their meaning and the sentiment they convey.

According to Hakami et al. (2020), emoji can be a true sentiment indicator, which is the conventional assumption of most existing sentiment analysis approaches with emoji. This is the approach used by most of the existing work and of implementations of software to perform sentiment analysis of text with embedded emoji. However, some of the most frequently used emoji also occur with many other, unconventional, roles. They may act as either multi-sentiment indicators or as ambiguous sentiment indicators. This is because, depending on the context, emoji sometimes have a very negative effect, and sometimes a very positive one. Furthermore, in some cases, the sentiment of an emoji can be neglected within a text. They may be dominated by the sentiment of the text or be dominated by the sentiment of the other emoji in that text. In this case, such emoji are considered as No-sentiment indicators.

Semantically, although some emoji may have a clear standard, defined meaning, there is, in practice, no constant, universal agreement on their interpretation. Their interpretation varies over time and across users. Many factors can affect the semantic interpretation of emoji: age, level of education, language etc. Indeed, the functional meaning of some emoji is culture-sensitive, and the sender-receiver cultural background is one of the essential contextualization aspects that can affect emoji-text sentiment analysis. For instance, the 'Thumbs Up' emoji (i.e., ) has a positive meaning in Asia and North America, while it can be interpreted as an insult in Iraq or Greece (i.e., means 'up yours') (Danesi, 2017).

Eastern and Western cultures are different in their use of mouth versus eye cues when interpreting emotions (Gao and VanderLaan, 2020). These researchers found that such differences extend to written para-linguistic signals such as emoji and, consequently, this has implications for digital communication. Also, although cultures might share similar emoji sentiment indications (i.e., with emoji that represent common human behaviours or basic emotions), there are other emoji where their sentiments might be affected by a cultural-specific aspect, such as those for food, symbols, and human activities (Hakami et al., 2021).

In this work, we present a context-free emoji sentiment lexicon for Arabic with 1,069 emoji. The lexicon is made freely available for research use[1]. We describe a preliminary study which analyses the impact of the Arabic culture on such an emoji sentiment annotation. The rest of this paper is organized as follows. Section 2 reviews related work upon which we build; Section 3 presents the study's design; Section 4 presents the analysis of the results and the discussion. Finally, in Section 5 we draw conclusions from this work along with highlighting its limitations as well as some recommendations for future work.

2. Related Work

Emoji can be treated as non-verbal emotional indicators within texts. This means that emoji are a valuable feature in sentiment analysis approaches. There has been some work that has utilized emoji in their sentiment analysis methodologies. This has been done in different languages, but little that has investigated their use in Arabic. Here we present an analysis of the research in sentiment analysis for Arabic that includes emoji (and/or emoticons) in their studies.

Refaee and Rieser (2014) investigated a distant supervision approach for both subjective and sentiment analysis of Arabic tweets. Two data-sets were manually and automatically annotated. Emoticons (i.e., a sequence of ASCII characters that represent nonverbal behaviors, such as facial expressions) were utilized to collect and annotate a data-set of Arabic tweets. Several features were used including bag-of-words (BOW) and both morphological and semantic features. Emoticons were considered as semantic features but were excluded when evaluating the automatically annotated data-set. The authors reported that the emoticon-based distant supervision approach to subjectivity and sentiment analysis in Arabic can perform significantly better than a fully supervised approach and can be useful for annotating larger amounts of data.

Hussien et al. (2016) utilised emoji to analyze emotions in Arabic texts. They claimed that training a classifier to detect emotions in automatically annotated tweets (based on emoji) is better than training it on manually annotated tweets. In their methodology, they collected 22,752 tweets with emoji, extracted the most frequently occurring emoji (58 emoji) and assigned a sentiment weight to each, based on the AFINN sentiments lexicon (Nielsen, 2011). Afterward, each emoji was categorized into one of the four emotion categories: joy, sadness, anger and disgust. For the automatic labelling approach, they labelled each tweet with an emotional label based on the sum of the weights of the emoji it contains. For manual labelling, they selected 2,025 tweets which were human annotated into the four adopted emotional labels. Then, they applied two machine learning classification models (support vector machine and multinomial naive Bayes) on both automatically and manually labelled training data-sets. Finally, they evaluated each model's results on a test data-set. Their results showed that the performance of the machine learning classifiers on the automatic labelled data (using emoji) outperformed the one with the manually labelled data.

Al-Azani and El–Alfy (2018b) aimed at analysing the impact of combining emoji-based features (including some emoticons) with text-based features on sentiment classification of Arabic texts. They used bag-of-words (BOW), latent semantic analysis (LSA) and word embedding as feature extraction models. The data-set they used was 1,101 tweets containing 120 emoji and emoticons. For sentiment classification, they applied a sequential minimal optimization-based support vector machine (SMO-SVM) classifier (with and without feature selection) to examine the effect of fusing emoji with texts as features. They concluded that merging emoji with word-embedding and a selection of the most relevant subset of features as input to a simple sentiment classifier, like a SVM, can produce good classification results.

In other work, Al–Azani and El–Alfy (2018) explored a new approach for sentiment polarity detection in Arabic text using non-verbal emoji-based features while addressing the class imbalance problem. The proposed method was based on a Bootstrap Aggregating (Bag-ging) algorithm and a Synthetic Minority Oversampling Technique (SMOTE) to build and combine multiple models from the training data-set. Three different classifiers were evaluated as single and ensemble classifiers: naive Bayes, k-NN, and decision trees. The performance was evaluated and compared on three data-sets with a varying imbalance ratio ranging from two to more than seven. This study concluded that the proposed approach performs better than other approaches in most of the considered cases.

Al-Azani and El-Alfy (2018c) extended their previous work mentioned above by expanding the dataset with more instances from Twitter and YouTube comments to become 2,091 texts with 429 unique emoji. All instances were manually annotated as positive or negative, and each has at least one emoji. For feature extraction, they used two techniques: ReliefF and Correlation-Attribute Evaluator (CAE). For classification, they generated 429 emoji-based feature vectors and used them to construct and evaluate various machine learning classifiers, including: naive Bayes (NB), multi-nomial naive Bayes (MNB), stochastic gradient descent (SGD), sequential minimal optimization-based support vectors machines (SMO-SVM), decision trees (C4.5 and REP trees), repeated incremental pruning to produce error reduction (RIPPER), and random forests (RF). By testing the performance of these eight machine learning classifiers, the experimental results demonstrated that emoji-based features alone can be a very effective means for detecting sentiment polarity with high performance.

Moreover, relying on their extended data-set, Al-Azani and El-Alfy (2018a) empirically evaluated two state-of-the-art

[1] https://github.com/ShathaHakami/Context-Free-Arabic-Emoji-Sentiment-Lexicon

models of deep recurrent neural networks to detect sentiment polarity of Arabic micro-blogs using emoji as features. In this work, they applied both unidirectional and bidirectional Long Short-Term Memory (LSTM) and its simplified variant Gated Recurrent Unit (GRU). Then, they compared the performance to baseline traditional learning methods and deep neural networks. The experimental results revealed that LSTM and GRU based models significantly outperformed other classifiers with a slight difference between them with best results attained when using bidirectional GRU.

Abdellaoui and Zrigui (2018) used ten subjective emoji from the Euro-ESL (Kralj Novak et al., 2015) along with the Arabic word sentiment lexicon Ar-SeLn (Badaro et al., 2014) to construct and annotate a large-scale dataset for Arabic sentiment analysis. Their process used a dataset of Arabic tweets with a vocabulary of 602,721 distinct entities. They named their dataset TEAD and released a subset of it for public use.

From another research perspective, hate speech and offensive language in Arabic texts has been analyzed using emoji (Husain, 2020). The study's approach was based on applying intensive pre-processing techniques to their data-set before processing it further and feeding it into the classification model. One of these techniques was converting emoji and emoticons into their Arabic labels (i.e., their official Unicode names) and using them as sentiment features to train their Linear SVM-based classifier for hate speech and offensive language detection. Their results reported better performance than another model that did not consider emoji conversion.

Similarly, Mubarak et al. (2022) employed the paralinguistic information embedded in the emojis to collect a large number of offensive texts containing hate speech and vulgar or violent content. Then, they used their data-set as a benchmark for detecting offensive and hate speech using different transformer architectures. For evaluation, they used a different data-set that had been collected separately. They found that the data collected using emoji captures universal characteristics of offensive language. Further, as a benefit of using emoji, their findings showed the common words used in offensive communications, common targets for hate speech and specific patterns in violent tweets. This study also highlighted the common classification errors due to the need to understand the context, consider cultural-background and the presence of sarcasm among others.

It is worth mentioning that almost all of the work listed here agreed on the need for an Arabic-specific emoji sentiment lexicon and they recommended constructing such a lexicon upon which to build their further work. Thus, our work is trying to fulfil this target.

3. STUDY DESIGN

The objective of this work, is to construct a context-free Arabic emoji sentiment lexicon, annotated manually by Arabic native speakers. This was done through the following steps.

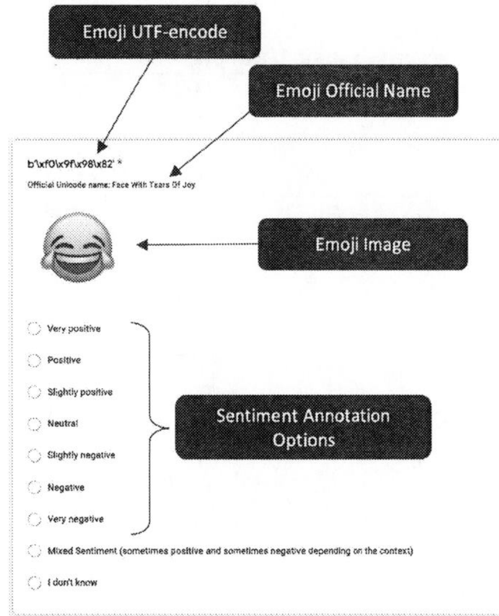

Figure 1: The interface for context-free emoji sentiment annotation.

3.1. Emoji Selection

A collection of 1,034 emoji extracted from the context-sensitive Arabic emoji sentiment lexicon Arab-ESL [2] (Hakami et al., 2021) was used. These emoji have been extracted from 14 different Arabic datasets that contain tweets from the Twitter platform. The tweets have a variety in dialect, aspect, topic, and emoji used within the text. In addition, we added 35 extra emoji that we believe are important to be included in this lexicon. In total, we ended up with 1069 emoji.

3.2. Annotation Interface Setup

To perform an easier and more efficient emoji sentiment annotation, it was important to set up a user-friendly annotation interface. This was done using *Google Forms*, an online web-based survey administration service provided by *Google*. We created two sets (each with five forms): one with the emoji's official names and the other without. Each set containing all of the 1069 emoji. We think that by adding official names (i.e., emoji descriptions), the uncertainty towards an emoji's meaning will be decreased. However, only a subset of the participants were provided with the forms that contained the emoji descriptions; to test whether this procedure is beneficial for emoji sentiment annotation.

To provide a consistent representation of the emoji's graphical appearance, the Apple platform emoji rendering was used throughout. We uploaded the emoji to the forms as images rather than using the locally rendered Unicode characters. This is to unify the visual appearance and the displayed size of the emoji on the various web browsers

[2] `https://github.com/ShathaHakami/Arabic-Emoji-Sentiment-Lexicon-Version-1.0`

Negative Emoji	Annotator ID					κ-Alpha	Recall
	1002	negative	negative	negative	negative	1.00	1.00
	1003	negative	negative	negative	negative	1.00	1.00
	1004	negative	negative	negative	negative	1.00	1.00
	1005	negative	negative	negative	negative	1.00	1.00
	1007	negative	negative	negative	negative	1.00	1.00
Neutral Emoji	**Annotator ID**					**κ-Alpha**	**Recall**
	1002	neutral	neutral	neutral	neutral	1.00	1.00
	1003	neutral	neutral	neutral	neutral	1.00	1.00
	1004	neutral	neutral	neutral	neutral	1.00	1.00
	1005	**positive**	neutral	neutral	neutral	0.80	0.75
	1007	neutral	neutral	neutral	**disregard**	0.87	0.75
Positive Emoji	**Annotator ID**					**κ-Alpha**	**Recall**
	1002	positive	positive	positive	positive	1.00	1.00
	1003	positive	positive	positive	positive	1.00	1.00
	1004	positive	positive	positive	positive	1.00	1.00
	1005	positive	positive	positive	positive	1.00	1.00
	1007	positive	positive	positive	positive	1.00	1.00

Table 1: A sample showing reliability and validation test results for human annotators. The annotations in blue are outliers.

and operating systems used by the annotators. Consequently, we converted each emoji's official name into its UTF-encoding and used it as an emoji identifier within the forms. This is to ease identifying and extracting each emoji with all of its corresponding annotations by all annotators after the entire annotation task is completed.

For the annotation options, we chose to use a seven-point fine-grained sentiment label scale, ranging from "Very Positive" to "Very Negative", including "Neutral". Two extra options were added, which are "Mixed Sentiment" and "I don't know". Figure 1 illustrates the details of the annotation interface.

3.3. Participants Recruitment and Annotation Process

We recruited participants from all over the Arabic regions. Some of the participants were directly asked to volunteer while others were hired via Khamsat[3], the largest Arabic marketplace for digital services. Initially, we recruited 83 native Arabic speakers, males and females, from the Gulf, Egypt, Levant, Sudan, Magharib, Iraq, and Yemen. Each participant was provided with the URLs of five Google Forms. In addition to the emoji annotation section, the first form collected demographic information and obtained informed consent. After analysing the forms, as will be described later, we found that one participant disagreed on the informed consent; 27 participants did not completed all the five forms; one was dyslexic; and one failed in the self-agreement annotation tests and was considered as an unreliable annotator. Thus, the total number of approved participants was 53 (28 females, and 25 males).

As a post-sentiment-annotation procedure, in the last form (i.e., the fifth form), we asked the participants the following. First, to provide us with the five emoji that they used most. Second, to answer a question regarding the impact of including the emoji's official names along with their symbols in the emoji sentiment annotation process. The answer options to this question were: "Partially important"; "Very important"; "Not important"; and "Causing a confusion".

3.3.1. Demographics and Consent

Each participant was asked to provide the following information: gender, age, native country of residence, current country of residence, religion, educational qualifications, employment status, some health issues (i.e., dyslexia and colour blindness) and social media usage. We also asked about the currently used device, operating system, and browser, as part of the technical setup for the annotation task. After providing their demographic information, each participant was asked to agree or disagree to the use of the provided information for the purpose of scientific research.

3.3.2. Emoji Annotation

Each of the five forms contained around 200 emoji, which are drawn from 1,069 emoji in total. Each participant was asked, independently, to complete the five forms within seven days. They were asked to select one option, from a list, which represents their interpretation of the sentiment of each emoji. The list contains the following options: *Very Positive, Positive, Slightly Positive, Neutral, Slightly Negative, Negative, Very Negative, Mixed Sentiment*, and *I don't know*, presented as radio buttons (see Figure 1). The annotation process was estimated at roughly 21 seconds per emoji, which is about 50 minutes per form. The whole data collection task was completed by all participants within a period of six weeks.

3.4. Validity and Reliability Annotation Tests

To test an individual annotator's self-agreement, we used the Recall for sensitivity measure (Su, 1994), and the Krippendorff's Alpha (κ-Alpha) for consistency measurement (Krippendorff, 2004). We applied these measurements, for

[3]https://khamsat.com/

Emoji	Emoji Class	N	P_negative	P_neutral	P_positive	Sentiment Score	Sentiment Label
💔	Heart	53	0.767857	0.178571	0.053571	-0.714286	negative
😭	Facial Expression	53	0.553571	0.339286	0.107143	-0.446429	negative
😂	Facial Expression	53	0.017857	0.125000	0.857143	0.839286	positive
❤️	Heart	53	0.017857	0.053571	0.928571	0.910714	positive
👇	Body Language	53	0.120000	0.800000	0.080000	-0.040000	neutral
👈	Body Language	53	0.056604	0.849057	0.094340	0.037736	neutral

Table 2: A sample of the context-free Arabic emoji sentiment lexicon. **N** denotes the number of times an emoji has been annotated. P_negative, P_neutral, and P_Positive denote the relative frequency probability $\mathbf{p_c}$ in negative, neutral, and positive sentiment classes, respectively.

each annotator, on the three sentiment label norms: negativity, neutrality, and positivity. We chose the following groups of emoji: (😔, 😢, 😞, 😟), (🕛, 🕒, 🕕, 🕘), and (❤️, 🖤, 💖, 💝), for negativity, neutrality, and positivity self-agreement tests, respectively. If either the Recall value or the κ-Alpha value for an annotator, in any of the three sentiment norms, is less than 0.75, then we considered the annotator as unreliable, and her/his annotation results as invalid. Thus, such an annotator will be excluded from the analysis. Table 1 displays a sample of the results of the two tests.

3.5. Sentiment Scores and Labels Calculation

To associate each emoji with each sentiment class, we, first, unified the group of sentiment labels under one sentiment norm as one sentiment label. For example, we unified the labels "Very Positive", "Positive" and "Slightly Positive" under the *positive* label. The same applied to the labels under the negative sentiment norm, which were unified as *negative*. For the neutral sentiment norm, we unified the labels "Neutral" and "Mixed Sentiment" to be *neutral*. lastly, any emoji label found to be "I don't know" was disregarded from the sentiment label count.

The sentiment score calculation was applied by following the approach of Kralj Novak et al. (2015). We started by identifying the frequency with which each emoji is associated with human sentiment annotation labels (negative, neutral and positive). Equation (1) captures the sentiment distribution for the set of sentiment annotations for an emoji across annotators, as follows:

$$N(c), \sum N(c) = N, \, c \in \{-1, \, 0, \, +1\} \tag{1}$$

N denotes the number of times an emoji has been annotated with one of these labels: *negative*, *neutral*, or *positive*. **N(c)** are the occurrences of an emoji with the sentiment label **c**, where **c** is either *negative*, *neutral* or *positive*. From the above we formed a discrete probability distribution:

$$(p_-, \, p_0, \, p_+), \sum_c p_c = 1 \tag{2}$$

The components of the distribution, i.e., p_-, p_0, and p_+ denote the negativity, neutrality, and positivity of the emoji, respectively. $\mathbf{p_c}$ are the probabilities that are estimated from relative frequencies as follows:

$$p_c = \frac{N(c)}{N} \tag{3}$$

Since we are dealing with small samples (i.e., the maximum **N** is 53, which is the maximum number of annotation agreed on a sentiment class), we used the Laplace estimate (also known as the rule of succession) Good (1965) to estimate the probability as follows:

$$p_c = \frac{N(c) + 1}{N + k} \tag{4}$$

k is the cardinality of the sentiment class, where $k = 3$, in our case. Table 2 shows some examples of $\mathbf{p_c}$ in negative, neutral and positive sentiment classes for some emoji.

Lastly, the sentiment score $\overline{S}$ of the emoji was computed as the mean of the distribution as follows:

$$\overline{S} = (-1 \, . \, p_-) \, + \, (0 \, . \, p_0) \, + \, (+1 \, . \, p_+) \tag{5}$$

The approach of Hakami et al. (2021) was followed to convert the resultant sentiment scores into sentiment labels. We classified three scaled-groups of sentiment scores under three sentiment norms (negative, neutral and positive). Emoji with sentiment score i, where -1 $\leq i <$ -0.0625, was classified as negative. Emoji with sentiment score i, where $1 \geq i >$ 0.0625, was classified as positive. Lastly, an emoji was classified as neutral when its sentiment score i was in the range where -0.0625 $\leq i \leq$ 0.0625. Table 2 shows some examples of sentiment scores and labels for some emoji in our lexicon.

4. Results and Discussion

4.1. Demographic Information Results

As is shown in Figure 2, the largest group of participants was from the Gulf region with 45%. The age of the majority of the participants (86%) was in the range 18-34 years old; and almost all of them are Muslims (96%). Regarding health conditions, only one of the participants had dyslexia (and was excluded); and none of them had colour blindness. Also, most of the participants were living in their native countries (75%); and all of them were highly educated. For the annotation, as is demonstrated in Table 3, 74% of the participants used a mobile phone while 26% used a personal laptop. Furthermore, 53% undertook the annotation using the *iOS* operating system, and 47% used the *Chrome*

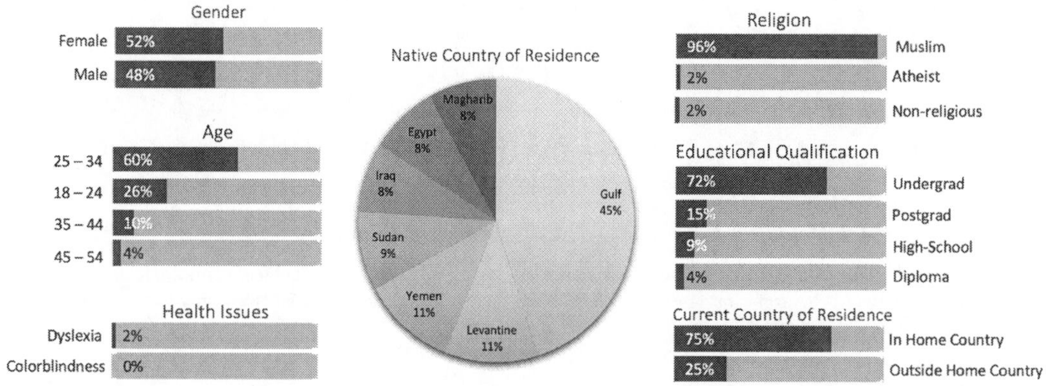

Figure 2: Summary of participants' demographic information.

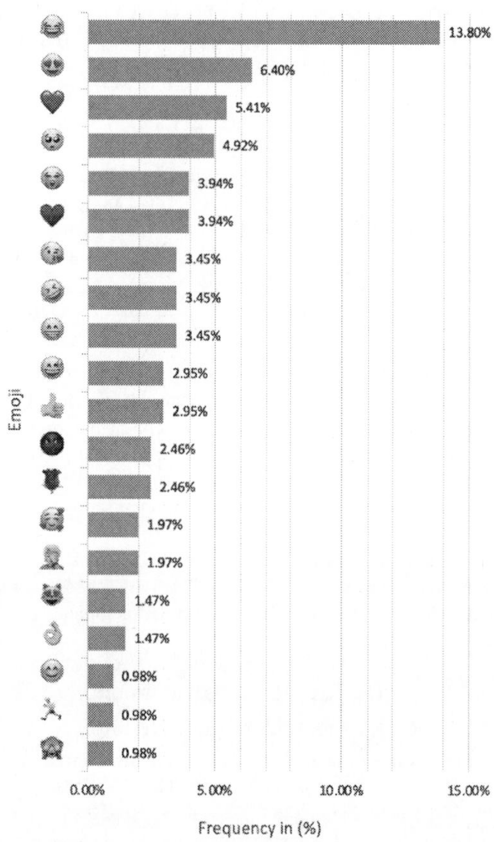

Figure 3: The most 20 commonly used emoji.

web browser. The most frequently used social media platform was *WhatsApp* with 16%, and the least used was the *SMS* with 7%. Lastly, Figure 3 shows that the most frequent emoji used by the participants is (😂); while the least frequent used emoji are (😊, 🏃, and 🙀).

Category	Hardware / Software	Usage in (%)
Device	Mobile Phone	74%
	Laptop	26%
Operating System	iOS	53%
	Android	28%
	Windows OS	19%
Web Browser	Google Chrome	47%
	Safari	42%
	Mozilla Firefox	9%
	Unmentioned Browser	2%

Table 3: Technical setup for the annotation by the participants.

4.2. Sentiment Annotation Results

Regarding the inclusion of emoji descriptions (i.e., emoji official names) during the sentiment annotation process, 53% of the participants reported that this was partially important, 25% that it was very important, 17% that it was not important, and only 5% of them that it was confusing.

In these, context free, emoji sentiment annotations, Arabic users (perhaps like other users from different cultures) agreed on a specific sentiment for a subset of emoji that obviously represent that sentiment. For example, our participants agreed on the positivity of positive facial expressions represented by emoji like: 😂, 😊, and 😎; as well as their agreement on the positivity of (almost) any emoji containing a heart in its graphical representation, like: 🥰, 😘, 😍, 💕, 💌, and ❣. Furthermore, positive concepts such as motherhood, represented by emoji like 'Breastfeeding' (i.e., 🤱) and 'Pregnant Woman' (i.e., 🤰); or childhood that is represented by emoji like 'Baby' (i.e., 👶) and 'Baby Bottle' (i.e., 🍼), were annotated as positive. Likewise, our

Emoji	Unicode Name	Sentiment Label
🇸🇦	Saudi Arabia	positive
🇪🇬	Egypt	positive
🇲🇦	Morocco	positive
🇹🇳	Tunisia	positive
🇰🇼	Kuwait	positive
🇦🇪	United Arab Emirates	positive
🇶🇦	Qatar	positive
🇴🇲	Oman	positive
🇮🇶	Iraq	positive
🇾🇪	Yemen	positive
🇩🇿	Algeria	positive
🇯🇴	Jordan	positive
🇱🇧	Lebanon	positive
🇸🇩	Sudan	positive
🇱🇾	Libya	positive
🇸🇾	Syria	positive
🇧🇭	Bahrain	positive
🇵🇸	Palestinian Territories	positive

Table 4: The flag emoji of Arabic countries in our lexicon.

annotators agreed on the negativity of the negative body language emoji, like: 👎, 🖕, 🙅, and 🙎. Also, emoji that represent prohibition symbols, such as 🔞, ❌, ⛔, and 🚫 were annotated as negative.

Focusing on the Arabian cultural effect on how our participants perceived emoji, we recognized interesting sentiment annotation results.

First, since all of our annotators are Arabic native speakers, they annotated all Arabic countries' flags with positive sentiment as a sense of national affiliation. Table 4 displays all of the emoji of Arabic countries' flags (i.e., 18 emoji flags) in our lexicon.

Second, usually, black color indicates negativity in Arabic culture. Therefore, we found emoji rendered in black colour like 'Black Heart' (i.e., 🖤), 'Black Flag' (i.e., 🏴), and many meaningless symbols, such as 'Black Circle' (i.e., ⚫), 'Black Medium Square' (i.e., ◼), 'Black Medium-Small Square' (i.e., ◾) were annotated as negative.

Third, there are many animals that indicate positivity in Arabic culture, such as camel (i.e., 🐪), lion (i.e., 🦁), horse (i.e., 🐎), and eagle (i.e., 🦅), which are annotated as positive for the emoji representing them. In contrast, there are other animals that indicate negativity in Arabic culture, such as snake (i.e., 🐍), pig (i.e., 🐖), and lizard (i.e., 🦎), and emoji representing them were annotated as negative by the Arabic annotators.

Fourth, rainy weather is considered positive in Arabic regions. Hence, we found that all emoji representing rainy or cloudy weather like 'Cloud' (i.e., ☁), 'Cloud with Rain' (i.e., 🌧), 'Cloud with Lightning and Rain' (i.e., ⛈), and 'Sun Behind Cloud' (i.e., ⛅); besides objects related to rain that are represented in emoji like 'Umbrella with Rain Drops' (i.e., ☔) and 'Closed Umbrella' (i.e., 🌂) were annotated positively.

Fifth, since the majority of the participant were Muslim, the Islamic religious impact was reflected in their sentiment annotation of some emoji. For example, emoji that represent Islamic religious rituals like 'Prayer Beads' (i.e., 📿), 'Woman with Headscarf' (i.e., 🧕), and 'Palms Up Together' (i.e., 🤲); or Islamic temples like 'Mosque' (i.e., 🕌), and 'Kaaba' (i.e., 🕋) were annotated as positive.

On the other hand, pork (i.e., the culinary name for the meat of the domestic pig) is prohibited to be eaten in Islam. Thus, we found that all the emoji that represent the pig animal (🐖); any part of it (i,e,. its face (🐷) and its nose (🐽)); or its related species (i.e., boar (🐗)) were annotated as negative. Similarly, drinking alcoholic beverages is prohibited in Islam. Thus, the 'Beer Mug' emoji (i.e., 🍺) was annotated as negative. However, we noticed that there are another three alcoholic drinks emoji named as 'Wine Glass' (i.e., 🍷), 'Tumbler Glass' (i.e., 🥃), and 'Cocktail Glass' (i.e., 🍸), which were annotated as neutral, neutral, and positive, respectively. This is, probably, due to either their neutral graphical appearances that might look like non-alcoholic drinks; or their neutral names that might indicate non-alcoholic drinks as well. We should clarify here that the non-alcoholic mixed-fruits drinks can be called 'Cocktail' in Arabic regions. Moreover, the sentiment annotation results show that the glasses-clink celebration behavior as it is represented by emoji such as 'Clinking Glasses' (i.e., 🥂) and 'Clinking Beer Mugs' (i.e., 🍻) was annotated as positive; even though these emoji are actually representing alcoholic drinks.

5. Conclusion and Future Work

In this work, we constructed a context-free sentiment emoji lexicon, annotated by 53 Arabic native speakers, from most Arabic regions. The sentiment annotation process, along with the annotators' personal characteristics are described in detail. We analyzed the resulting annotations to see how Arabic cultural-background was reflected in the sentiments of the annotated emoji. We discussed this cultural effect regarding national affiliation, colour indication, animal indication, weather indication, and religious impact.

This work is limited to an analysis of manual sentiment annotations of stand-alone emoji out of any context. In the future, it would be interesting to compare this resulting context-free lexicon with a context-sensitive emoji sentiment lexicon, in the Arabic language. This kind of comparison can help understanding the differences between how the sentiment of an emoji is perceived when it is stand-

alone and how it is interpreted differently, when it is presented in an accompanying context. Another limitation is the recruitment of a small number of participants as representatives for a specific Arabic region. Similar future investigations with more participants would be advantageous.
In the future, we intend to make the resulting emoji sentiment lexicon more fine grain for further, focused and detailed analytical studies of emoji within the Arabic language. In addition, the lexicon provided in this study may also be informative for Arabic socio-linguistics researchers interested in emoji usage and sentiment expression on social media by Arabic users. Also, the correlation between sentiment and meaning of emoji evolves over time. It might be important to explore the change in the meaning of controversial emoji, and how they are affected by the corresponding social processes.

6. Bibliographical References

Abdellaoui, H. and Zrigui, M. (2018). Using Tweets and Emojis to Build TEAD: an Arabic Dataset for Sentiment Analysis. *Computación y Sistemas*, 22:777 – 786.

Al-Azani, S. and El-Alfy, E.-S. (2018a). Emojis-based sentiment classification of arabic microblogs using deep recurrent neural networks. In *2018 International Conference on Computing Sciences and Engineering (ICCSE)*, pages 1–6.

Al-Azani, S. and El-Alfy, E.-S. M. (2018b). Combining emojis with arabic textual features for sentiment classification. In *2018 9th International Conference on Information and Communication Systems (ICICS)*, pages 139–144.

Al-Azani, S. and El-Alfy, E.-S. M. (2018c). Emoji-based sentiment analysis of arabic microblogs using machine learning. In *2018 21st Saudi Computer Society National Computer Conference (NCC)*, pages 1–6.

Al Rashdi, F. (2018). Functions of emojis in whatsapp interaction among omanis. *Discourse, Context & Media*, 26:117–126.

Al–Azani, S. and El–Alfy, E. M. (2018). Imbalanced sentiment polarity detection using emoji-based features and bagging ensemble. In *2018 1st International Conference on Computer Applications Information Security (ICCAIS)*, pages 1–5.

Badaro, G., Baly, R., Hajj, H., Habash, N., and El-Hajj, W. (2014). A large scale arabic sentiment lexicon for arabic opinion mining. In *Proceedings of the EMNLP 2014 workshop on arabic natural language processing (ANLP)*, pages 165–173.

Danesi, M. (2017). *The semiotics of emoji: The rise of visual language in the age of the internet*. Bloomsbury Publishing.

Donato, G. and Paggio, P. (2017). Investigating redundancy in emoji use: Study on a twitter based corpus. In *Proceedings of the 8th Workshop on Computational Approaches to Subjectivity, Sentiment and Social Media Analysis*, pages 118–126.

Dresner, E. and Herring, S. C. (2010). Functions of the nonverbal in cmc: Emoticons and illocutionary force. *Communication theory*, 20(3):249–268.

Gao, B. and VanderLaan, D. P. (2020). Cultural influences on perceptions of emotions depicted in emojis. *Cyberpsychology, Behavior, and Social Networking*.

Good, I. J. (1965). The estimation of probabilities: An essay on modern bayesian methods, vol. 30.

Hakami, S. A. A., Hendley, R., and Smith, P. (2020). Emoji as sentiment indicators: An investigative case study in arabic text. In *The Sixth International Conference on Human and Social Analytics*, pages 26–32. IARIA.

Hakami, S. A. A., Hendley, R., and Smith, P. (2021). Arabic emoji sentiment lexicon (Arab-ESL): A comparison between Arabic and European emoji sentiment lexicons. In *Proceedings of the Sixth Arabic Natural Language Processing Workshop*, pages 60–71, Kyiv, Ukraine (Virtual). Association for Computational Linguistics.

Husain, F. (2020). Osact4 shared task on offensive language detection: Intensive preprocessing-based approach. In *Proceedings of the 4th Workshop on Open-Source Arabic Corpora and Processing Tools, with a Shared Task on Offensive Language Detection*, pages 53–60, Marseille, France. European Language Resource Association.

Hussien, W. A., Tashtoush, Y. M., Al-Ayyoub, M., and Al-Kabi, M. N. (2016). Are emoticons good enough to train emotion classifiers of arabic tweets? In *2016 7th International Conference on Computer Science and Information Technology (CSIT)*, pages 1–6.

Kralj Novak, P., Smailović, J., Sluban, B., and Mozetič, I. (2015). Sentiment of emojis. *PloS one*, 10(12):e0144296.

Krippendorff, K. (2004). Measuring the reliability of qualitative text analysis data. *Quality and quantity*, 38:787–800.

Mubarak, H., Hassan, S., and Chowdhury, S. A. (2022). Emojis as anchors to detect arabic offensive language and hate speech. *CoRR*, abs/2201.06723.

Nielsen, F. Å. (2011). A new anew: Evaluation of a word list for sentiment analysis in microblogs. *arXiv preprint arXiv:1103.2903*.

Njenga, K. (2018). Social media information security threats: Anthropomorphic emoji analysis on social engineering. In *IT Convergence and Security 2017*, pages 185–192. Springer.

Refaee, E. and Rieser, V. (2014). Can we read emotions from a smiley face? emoticon-based distant supervision for subjectivity and sentiment analysis of arabic twitter feeds. In *5th International Workshop on Emotion, Social Signals, Sentiment and Linked Open Data, LREC*.

Riordan, M. A. (2017). The communicative role of non-face emojis: Affect and disambiguation. *Computers in Human Behavior*, 76:75–86.

Shiha, M. and Ayvaz, S. (2017). The effects of emoji in sentiment analysis. *Int. J. Comput. Electr. Eng.(IJCEE.)*, 9(1):360–369.

Skovholt, K., Grønning, A., and Kankaanranta, A. (2014). The communicative functions of emoticons in workplace e-mails::-. *Journal of Computer-Mediated Communication*, 19(4):780–797.

Su, L. T. (1994). The relevance of recall and precision in user evaluation. *Journal of the American Society for Information Science*, 45(3):207–217.

Proceedings of the OSACT 2022 Workshop @LREC2022, pages 60–70
Marseille, 20 June 2022

Sa`7r: A Saudi Dialect Irony Dataset

Najla AlHazzani, Amaal AlDawod, Hala AlMazrou, Lama AlAwlaqi, Noura AlReshoudi, Hend Al-Khalifa, Luluh AlDhubayi
Information Technology Department, College of Computer and Information Sciences
King Saud University
Riyadh, Saudi Arabia
{442204257, 442203073, 442203082, 442202911, 442203043}@student.ksu.edu.sa,
{Hendk, laldubaie}@ksu.edu.sa

Abstract

In sentiment analysis, detecting irony is considered a major challenge. The key problem with detecting irony is the difficulty to recognize the implicit and indirect phrases which signifies the opposite meaning. In this paper, we present Sa`7r ساخر the Saudi irony dataset, and describe our efforts in constructing it. The dataset was collected using Twitter API and it consists of 19,810 tweets, 8,089 of them are labeled as ironic tweets. We trained several models for irony detection task using machine learning models and deep learning models. The machine learning models include: K-Nearest Neighbor (KNN), Logistic Regression (LR), Support Vector Machine (SVM), and Naïve Bayes (NB). While the deep learning models include BiLSTM and AraBERT. The detection results show that among the tested machine learning models, the SVM outperformed other classifiers with an accuracy of 0.68. On the other hand, the deep learning models achieved an accuracy of 0.66 in the BiLSTM model and 0.71 in the AraBERT model. Thus, the AraBERT model achieved the most accurate result in detecting irony phrases in Saudi Dialect.

Keywords: Irony detection, Twitter, Arabic tweets, Saudi Dialect, Arabic NLP, Transformer, Neural networks

1 Introduction

The content of social media networks such as Twitter shows unlimited daily feeds of millions of users' interactions (Rajadesingan et al., 2015). The massive amount of data attracts researchers to conduct several types of data and textual analysis for different purposes, such as detecting opinions, sentiment and irony. One of the fundamental NLP tasks is detecting ironic expressions which is considered one of the complex language phenomena and was widely studied in linguistics, philosophy, and psychology (Sigar, et.al;2012, Grice, et. al; 1975).

Although several studies were conducted on irony from different perspectives, the definition of irony has not reached a consensus yet (Filatova, 2012). One of the obstacles to defining irony is that irony has various vocabularies that undergo language changes (Nunberg,2001). In addition, the irony definition is affected by the variation of regional languages and dialects (Dress et al. 2008).

On the other hand, the literature shows a similar term to irony, which is sarcasm, and some studies used both terms interchangeably (Buschmeier et al., 2014, Duden, 2014). On the contrary, many studies tackled the delusion problem of sarcasm and irony, such as Kreuz and Glucksberg (1989). Kreuz and his colleague defined sarcasm as a prominent victim and the target of ridicule, whereas, in irony, there is no individual or victim.

In addition, Ironic language is usually less cruel, harmful, and aggressive than sarcasm. However, due to the high similarity between sarcasm and irony definitions and the complexity of distinguishing between the two phonenma, we considered, in this paper, both terms as synonym to define any expression in which a person uses words that deliver the opposite of literal meaning.

Detecting ironic expressions is important and fundamental, especially in sentiment analysis (Rosso et al., 2018). The automatic detection of irony can assist many essential domains, such as gaining business insights into public opinion to improve certain services. Moreover, detecting ironic expressions can help identify threats and distinguish between fake and real threatening messages (Al-Ghadhban et al., 2017).

Although social media companies provide analytic tools to analyze the vast amount of data available, these tools do not provide the best accuracy when applied to some text that contains irony and sarcasm or hidden meaning (Ghanem et al., 2019). Detecting this type of speech is considered difficult, especially in the Arabic language, because of its complexity and variations of the Arabic written styles. Additionally, Arabic language is also considered a challenging language in the field of NLP, due to its morphological richness, orthographic ambiguity and inconsistency, and dialectal variations (Darwish et al., 2021).

In this paper, we focus on collecting tweets for Saudi dialect to build an irony dataset extracted from Twitter. This work has two main contributions:

1. Creation of a public Saudi dialect dataset of 19,810 tweets with irony and non-irony labels.
2. Comparison of different neural network and machine learning models and reporting the best accurate model.

The rest of the paper is organized as follows: Section 2 gives an overview of related work in the area of irony and sarcasm detection for Arabic language. Section 3 presents the dataset generation stages, including data collection, dataset annotation, dataset statistics, and dataset evaluation. The experiment results and evaluation are described in Section 4. We then discuss the challenges faced through the experiment in Section 5. Finally, in section 6, we concluded the paper with suggestions for future works.

2 Related Work

Detecting Sarcasm and irony in the textual contents has been extensively studied in different languages, especially the English language. The increasing popularity of shared tasks for irony detection and sentiment analysis has increased the interest in this field and attracted more researchers to develop robust irony detection tools. The first shared task for irony detection in English tweets was proposed in 2018 (Van Hee, Lefever, and Hoste 2018, 20), the organizers proposed fine-grained multiclassification task on different types of irony instead of binary classification.

A more profound analysis of linguistic phenomena of the ironic expression has been proposed by (Karoui et al. 2017) that analyzes different linguistic categories of irony in different languages in the social media contents. This approach was established by implementing a multilingual corpus annotated based on a multi-layered schema to measure the impact of different pragmatic phenomena used in the expression of irony in three Indo-European languages, including English, French, and Italian.

The efficiency of neural networks has been investigated to detect sarcastic texts (Ghosh and Veale 2016) by implementing a model composed of Convolutional Neural networks (CNN), Long Short Term Memory (LSTM), and Deep Neural Network (DNN) to detect sarcasm over social media contents, the proposed model compared against SVM-based models and showed an improvement for the neural networks. Another work (Dutta and Mehta 2021) applying deep learning techniques to detect sarcasm in the Twitter news dataset, the proposed model was implemented based on the Convolutional-Recurrent Neural network (C-RNN) to discover sarcastic pattern detection and achieved an accuracy of 84.73%.

For the Arabic language, there have been few papers that tackled Sarcasm and irony detection in the Arabic language. Twitter is the most widely used source for data collection for detecting irony due to the huge amount of textual and the large availability of ironic texts among different languages and cultures.

One of the earliest studies was conducted by Al-Ghadhban et al., (2017) and Karoui et al., (2017) where they both used supervised learning algorithm to develop a classifier model. Al-Ghadhban et al., (2017) used Naïve Bayes Multinomial Text algorithm for detecting tweets and the model evaluation achieved 0.659 in recall, 0.71 in precision, and 0.676 in f-score. While Karoui et al., (2017) used Random Forest with GainRatio algorithm to detect irony in Arabic tweets and achieved an accuracy of 72.36%.

Similarly, Allaith et al. (2019) proposed a system based on several language models: word-n-grams, topic models, sentiment models, statistical models, and embeddings of words. In addition, Bi-LSTM, Random Forest, and XGBoost were some of the classifiers that were used to evaluate the system. Based on the F1-score, the proposed system achieved 0.85. Also another submission has achieved 81.7% and 79.4% for two different neural networks models for word embedding respectively.

Recently, there has been renewed interest in detecting sarcasm and irony with a dedication on constructing datasets for Arabic ironic language. In a shred task conducted by (Abu Farha et al., 2021), they released ArSarcasm-v2 dataset, which consists of 15,548 tweets labelled for sarcasm, sentiment and dialect. The shared task received 27 submissions for the sarcasm detection subtask. Among the techniques used in the shared task is the work by El Mahdaouy et al. (2021). They used a deep multitask learning model to develop a model that allows knowledge to be accessed for sarcasm detection. Their work incorporated BERT model and multitask attention interaction module into a single model architecture which produced a better performance in detecting sarcasm. Furthermore, Wadhawan (2021) proposed an approach which consists of two phases: the dataset preprocessing phase which involves inserting, deleting, and segmenting various fragments of the text. The second phase was experimenting with two transformer-based models AraELECTRA and AraBERT. Author found out that AraBERT has the highest weighted F1-score while AraELECTRA has the worst weighted F1-score and accuracy. In addition, Abuzayed and Al-Khalifa (2021) employed seven BERT-based models which are: MARBERT, ArBERT, QARiB, AraBERTv02, GigaBERT, Arabic BERT and mBERT, also to fix the problem of imbalanced data they combined the shared task dataset with additional information.

Ameur and Aliane (2021) created a sarcasm and sentiment detection dataset for Arabic tweets during the pandemic, the dataset is called "AraCOVID19-SSD". They collected 5,162 tweets that are annotated with two labels related to the two tasks: Sarcasm detection (Yes or No) and sentiment analysis (Positive, negative, or neutral). They used three pre-trained transformer models for classification (AraBERT, mBERTm and XLM-Roberta) and other supervised models (SVM, LR, and Random Forest). Their experiments showed that the SVM and AraBERT models performed better than other models by reaching an F1-score of more than 95%. Another work proposed by Talafha et al. (2021), they collected Arabic tweets for sarcasm detection. The prediction task was tackled as a regression problem instead of a classification problem by quantifying the level of sarcasm for a given tweet instead of deciding if a tweet is sarcastic or not. The experiment was evaluated using Mean Squared Error (MSE) as a loss function and it obtained a 0.011 loss value.

Table 1 summarizes the available Arabic irony datasets. We can see that few dialectical datasets tackled irony and sarcasm detection specifically in Saudi dialect. Most of these datasets collected tweets using hashtags only. Therefore, this paper proposes a new Arabic dataset for Saudi irony tweets collected from hashtags, phrases and words annotated by humans.

Table 1: Summary of Arabic irony corpora

Datasets	Dialect	Number of Tweets	Number of Ironic/ Sarcastic Tweets
(Al-Ghadhban et al., 2017)	Saudi dialect	350	238
Soukhria (Karoui et al., 2017)	MSA, Egyptian, Syrian and Saudi dialect	5479	1733
IDAT (Ghanem et al., 2019)	MSA, Egypt, Gulf, Levantine and Maghrebi dialects.	22, 318	6, 809
DAICT (Abbes et al., 2020)	MSA, Egypt, Gulf, Levantine and Maghrebi dialects.	5358	4,809
ArSarcasm (Abu Farha and Magdy, 2020)	Egyptian, Gulf, LevantineMaghrebi and MSA	10,547	1682
ArSarcasm-v2 (Abu Farha et al., 2021)		15,548	2989
AraCOVID 19-SSD (Ameur and Aliane, 2021)	Multiple Arabic dialects (not specified) and MSA	5,162	1802
(Talafha et al., 2021)		1554	1165

3 Dataset Generation

3.1 Data Collection

The data collection was conducted using an open-source Python package called Twint[1]. Twint library enables scraping the raw data of interest from Twitter using a set of keywords. We aimed to collect Twitter data generated between 2011-03-16 and 2021-09-21 and the total collected tweets were 26,349 records. Hence, the date range specification was according to Twint library capability, which fixes the oldest date by default to 2011-03.

As for the keywords, we used 35 keywords that indicated irony in Saudi Dialect such as: كوميديا مسخرة, #سخرية, # سوداء, تعبير ساخر and hashtags like #دعابة, #تهكم and we searched for some words in phrases like: طبختيه يالرفلا to find tweets related to the ironic phrase: طبخ طبختيه يالرفلا اكليه. We also searched for the derivatives of the word, for example: تهكم، اتهكم. We found that Twint normalizes hamza and ta marbuta 'ة' or ha 'ه'. This means that there is no need to search for the same word in different orthographic forms.

The hashtags used along with their Buckwalter Arabic transliteration and translation and the keywords that inspired us to come up with other keywords are listed in Table 2.

Table 2: Hashtags and keywords used for data collection process

Hashtags		
Arabic text	**Transliteration**	**English translation**
#مزحة	mazha	Joke

[1] https://github.com/twintproject/twint

#دعابة	dueaba	Joke
#تهكم	tahakam	Irony
استهزيء| # #استهزاء	aistihzi' | aistihza'	Mockery
مسخرة | # #سخرية | #مصخرة	maskhara | sukhria | maskhara	Mockery
#اتهكم	aitahakum	Being ironic
#المضحك_المبكي	almudhik almabkiu	Laughing at the irony
#أمزح	'amzah	Joking
#أنكت	'ankat	Joking
#اتشمت	āttashamat	Gloated
#سخرية_القدر	sukhriat alqadr	Ironically
#كوميديا_سوداء	kumidia sawda'	Dark humor
Keywords		
Arabic text	**Transliteration**	**English translation**
لا ياشيخ | لايشيخ | لا يشيخ | لاياشيخ | لا يا شيخ	la yashykh | layshikh | la yashikh | layashykh | la ya shaykh	Oh Really!
اصفق لك	aisfaq lak	Should I clap for you?

اذا حجت البقرة على قرونها	adha hajat albaqarat ealaa quruniha	when a cow pilgrimage on its horns
قال تيس قال احلبه	qal tis qal ahlibh	I say this's a bull, he says milk it
طبخ طبختيه يالرفلا اكليه	tabkh tabkhatayh yalrafla akilih	hey bad cook, eat up what you cooked

اطقطق | طقطقة	aitqataq | taqtiqa	Mocking
الحمدلله والشكر	alhamudalaluh walshukr	Thank God
بس يابابا	bas yababa	Enough papa
بس ياشاطر | بس ياشاطرة	bas yashatir | bas yashatira	Stop it Smarty
خزياه بس	khizyah bas	Oh shameful
قل قسم	qul qasam	Swear to God
اتطنز	aitatanz	Making fun
جاب العيد | جابت العيد	jab aleid | jabat aleid	screwed up
هيا خدلك | هيا خذلك | يلا خذلك	hayaa khadalak | hayaa khadhalik | yala khadhalik	Oh here we go again
ياللهول	Yalllhwl	Oh my God
سوبهان الله	Subhan Allah	Subhan Allah (in mis-spilling)
Phrases		
Arabic text	**Transliteration**	**English translation**
اما حبى اما برك	ama habaa ama birak	Either crawling or sitting!

عنز لو طارت	aanz law tarat	Goat is a goat even if it flies

3.2 Dataset Description

As mentioned in the dataset collection section, the collected tweets file was about 3.7 MB in size. It is stored as a CSV file in which each row represents a tweet. Each tweet has five columns in which it is separated by a separator to ensure its correctness.

3.3 Dataset Annotation

As a first step, the tweets are classified based on two labels, "ironic" and "non-ironic". Nevertheless, we found that some tweets could not be clearly classified as ironic or non-ironic, such as: " هه زيي سهرانة اطقطق واناام". Moreover, other tweets are written with different contexts, which are difficult for annotators to understand and interpret. To solve these problems, we decided to use the labeling criteria proposed by (Abbes et al., 2020), which classify the tweets into three labels: "ironic", "non-ironic" and "ambiguous". The ambiguous label helps annotators when they cannot decide with certainty whether a tweet is ironic or not.

The collected tweets were first cleaned by removing URLS, new lines "\n", punctuation, numbers, non-Arabic words, and duplicate tweets. Emojis were replaced with a decoded format using a python package[2]. We also performed the following normalization process using CAMeL tools [3], and PyArabic[4]:

- Unicode normalization, for example: ﷺ to صلى الله عليه وسلم.
- Normalize teh marbuta 'ة' to heh 'ه'.
- Normalize alef variants to 'ا'.
- Normalize double characters, for example: ههههه.
- Remove elongation 'ـ'.
- Remove diacritics 'Tashkeel' (ً ، ٌ ، ٍ ، َ ، ُ ، ِ).

After the preprocessing step we got 19,810 unique tweets. The annotation process was crowdsourced by dividing this task among different numbers of volunteers as needed.

However, we need to maintain a certain level of quality and reliability in the annotation process, therefore the annotators must be qualified for these conditions:

- Annotators must be familiar with the communication style of social media, especially Twitter.
- The age range of annotators is between 16 and 40 years old.
- The annotators must be Saudis so that they can understand the ambiguity behind the written words.
- The annotators should read the "annotators guideline".

The annotation has gone through two rounds as explained in Figure 1.

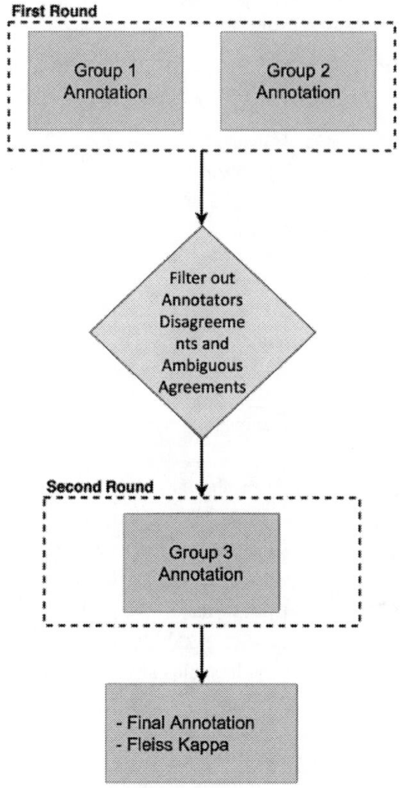

Figure 1: The annotation process

In the first round, we split the annotation process into two different groups to annotate 19,810 unique tweets. Each group consists of 7 annotators, with each annotator responsible for annotating 3,000 tweets, except for the seventh annotator who annotated the remaining 1,853 tweets. The number of annotated tweets with ironic tags was 7,425 and 8,573 for group one and two, respectively, while the number of non-ironic tweets is 11,026 for group one and 10671 for group two. This round of annotation took ten days and resulted in two annotations for each tweet. We then combined the annotations of the two groups and extracted the mismatched annotations; around 7753 tweets, and the tweets annotated as ambiguous; around 221 tweets. We offered the label "Ambiguous" to the annotators so that they could use it in case of uncertainty. After aggregation, we instructed five more annotators to perform the second round on a of total 7974 tweets to check for discrepancies, delete the "ambiguous" label, and clarify the new annotation considering emojis, punctuations, English words, and numbers for each tweet since they help to understand the tone of the tweet. Tables 3-6 show examples from the current dataset to proof that numbers, emojis,

[2] https://pypi.org/project/emojis/

[3] https://github.com/CAMeL-Lab/camel_tools

[4] https://pypi.org/project/PyArabic/

punctuations, and non-Arabic words are clarifying the tone of the tweet :

Table 3: Keep numbers in tweet example

Cleaned tweet with removing numbers:
تكفون يا عيال ارسلو له رابط
Tweet with keeping numbers:
٢٠٢١ تكفون يا عيال ارسلو له رابط
Translation of tweet with keeping numbers:
Please guys give him 2021 link
Transliteration of tweet with keeping numbers:
takufun ya eial arslu lah rabit 2021

Table 4: Keep emojis in tweet example

Cleaned tweet with removing emojis:
الحمد لله والشكر لله ع وجودنا في حياتك لولانا كانت حياتك
Tweet with keeping emojis:
الحمد لله والشكر لله ع وجودنا في حياتك لولانا كانت حياتك 😆 😭 😂 😂
Translation of tweet with keeping emojis:
Thank God for our presence in your life, if it were not for us, your life would have been 😭 😆 😂 😂
Transliteration of tweet with keeping emojis:
alhamd lilah walshukr lilah e wujuduna fi hayatik lawlana kanat hayatuk 😭 😆 😂 😂

Table 5: Keep punctuations in tweet example

Cleaned tweet with removing punctuations :
الحب لا يشيخ الحب لا يا شيخ
Tweet with removing punctuations:
؟ الحب لا يشيخ = الحب ... لا يا شيخ
Translation of tweet with keeping punctuations:
Love seriously = love … seriously?
Transliteration of tweet with keeping punctuations:
alhubu la yashikh = alhubu ... la ya shaykh ?

Table 6: Keep non-Arabic languages example

Cleaned tweet with removing non-Arabic languages:
من اقوال سيخلدها التاريخ لا ياشيخ
Tweet with keeping non-Arabic language:
People who are dying who have " :من اقوال سيخلّدها التاريخ "لا_ياشيخ never been died before. Donald trump 😂 😭
Translation of tweet with keeping non-Arabic language:
Sayings that will be immortalized by history: "People who are dying who have never been died before. Donald trump " Seriously 😭 😂
Transliteration of tweet with keeping non-Arabic language:
min aqwal sykhlldha altaarikhu: "People who are dying who have never been died before. Donald trump "la_yashikh 😭 😂

The second round lasted for five days. We measured the inter-annotator agreement between the two annotators using Fleiss's Kappa which is a statistical measure of agreement between categorical values. It is commonly used to measure the inter-annotator reliability of the annotation of a dataset (Abbes et al., 2020). The Fleiss's Kappa inter-annotator agreement value was 0.54 which is a moderate level. The final annotated collection consists of 8,089 ironic tweets, and 11,715 non-ironic tweets.

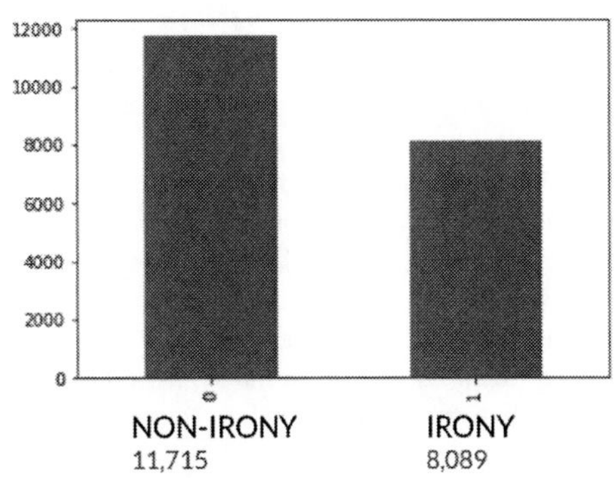

Figure 2 shows the distribution of the final corpus, we can see that the dataset has about 10% more on the non-irony class.

4 Experiments and Results

In this section we conducted different experiments to set a baseline system for the new dataset. We started with a set of machine learning algorithms, then a classifier built using word embeddings vectorization technique with BiLSTM, lastly, we tested a BERT-based model. We have split the dataset into two parts, the first is the training set, which represents 80% of the data which equals 15843 entries, while the testing set represents the remaining 20% of the data which equals 3961 entries. For the evaluation, we used the F1-score to compare the results of all the models, since F1-score delivers a realistic score that does not get affected by the data imbalance (Ibrahim, Torki, and El-Makky 2018).

4.1 Machine Learning Models

There are many options for classification algorithms that can be used for binary classification of tweets into irony or non-irony. We implemented K-Nearest Neighbor (KNN), Logistic Regression (LR), Support Vector Machine (SVM), and Naïve Bayes (NB) with several variations (Bernoulli, Multinomial and Gaussian).

4.1.1 K-Nearest Neighbor (KNN)

For this algorithm, we set the k value as 10, as it is a reasonable value to avoid noise, as well as avoiding the reduction of boundaries between each neighbor and the other (Ikram and Chakir, 2019).

4.1.2 Logistic Regression (LR)

LR is another classification algorithm that can be employed to classify text, this algorithm measures the statistical significance of each independent variable in accordance with the probability (Shah et al., 2020), we set the inverse of regularization strength (c parameter) to 0.01, to increase the regularization.

4.1.3 Naïve Bayes (NB)

Naive Bayes is a classification method based on the Bayes theorem (Lewis, 1998). NB has different types of classifiers, including Multinomial, Gaussian, and Bernoulli. In this experiment, we validated all three NB variations to identify which one gives better accuracy. Multinomial gained the best accuracy of 0.66 compared to others. To optimize accuracy, tuning the hyperparameters will affect the performance of the model and it might improve it (Yang and Shami, 2020). Hence, we changed the value of the Bernoulli hyperparameter (binarize) to be 0.1 to optimize the accuracy and then its accuracy increased to 0.67.

4.1.4 Support Vector Machine (SVM)

In this experiment, we used the linear SVM algorithm with the linear kernel and regularization parameter equals to 2 to determine how much misclassification should be avoided in the SVM optimization.

4.2 Deep Learning Models

Our aim in this experiment is to use an algorithm that can deal with the peculiarities of text data, as in the experimentations of (Abu Farha et al., 2021), and (Allaith et al., 2019). Where the Bidirectional Long-short-term memory (BiLSTM) model has proven its ability in dealing with sequential data.

This model was implemented by utilizing a pretrained Arabic word embeddings "AraVec" which is trained using skip-gram algorithm, these word embeddings are then fed into deep learning model of BiLSTM, its hyperparameters are described in Table 7. This model resulted in 0.66 accuracy and F1 score of 0.59.

Table 7: AraVec BiLSTM model hyperparameters

Embedding layer	300
Bidirectional LSTM	128
Dropout	0.2
Activation	Sigmoid
Optimizer	SGD
Loss	Binary_crossentropy
Learning Rate	0.001
Epochs	5
Batch Size	100

4.3 Transformers Model

In this experiment, we used AraBERT which is a pretrained language model that was trained with large data from Twitter (Antoun, Baly, and Hajj 2021). We used AraBERTv0.2-Twitter-base, which was trained using 60 million multi-dialect words obtained from Twitter, which suits the problem of irony classification, since our dataset was obtained from twitter as well. The AraBERT model was fine-tuned using our dataset and the resulted accuracy was 71%.

4.4 Models' Results

All models used were configured manually, using random values to initialize the hyperparameters. Table 8 shows the performance all the developed classifiers.

Table 8: Comparison of evaluation results using A: accuracy, P: precision, R: recall, and F1: F1-score macro.

Model	A	P	R	F1
KNN	0.65	0.63	0.62	0.62
LR	0.61	0.66	0.53	0.44
SVM	0.68	0.67	0.67	0.67
Bernoulli NB	0.67	0.66	0.67	0.66
Multinomial NB	0.66	0.65	0.61	0.61
Gaussian NB	0.53	0.56	0.56	0.53
AraVec BiLSTM	0.69	0.59	0.58	0.59
AraBERT	0.71	0.70	0.70	0.70

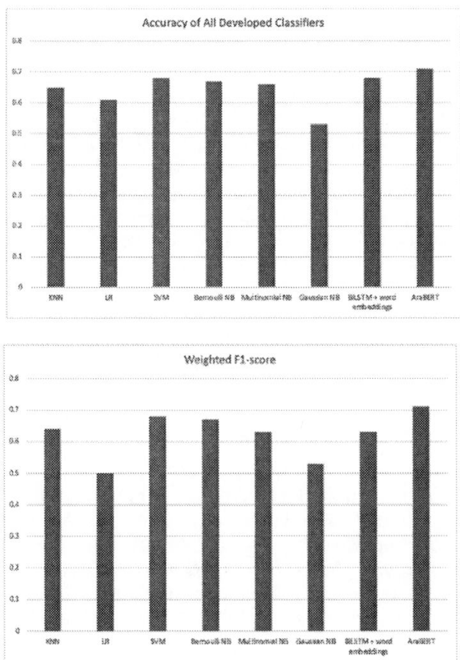

Figure 3: Comparison of the classifiers' accuracies and F1-Score

5 Discussion and Limitation

Figure 3 shows that the AraBERT-based model yielded the highest result of 71% F1-score macro, also it has the highest f1-score on the irony class detection with 65% as shown in Table 9, this indicates the power of transformers in handling text classification issues. The second-best model is the SVM model with F1-score of 68%. Followed by Bernoulli NB, KNN, Multinomial NB and BiLSTM, Gaussian NB and lastly logistic regression. We hypothesize that the fine-tuning of the hyperparameters would be in favor of improving the performance of the models, also increasing the number of annotated data for the training process could benefit the classifiers in general.

In terms of challenges, the collected tweets are based on Dialectal Arabic (DA) words that are common among Saudis; to obtain Arabic tweets from Saudi dialects it is important to mention that we totally relied on the words that are commonly used in the colloquial Saudi dialects, since lots of tweets were retrieved with no location tag. Pre-processing may affect the meaning, but its main benefit is to remove duplicate tweets and normalize the text. Even though the usage of some phrases would cause collecting similar tweets, the context of these phrases is still different, and a single emoji or punctuation or number or non-Arabic characters could change the whole meaning as shown in Table 3, Table 4, Table 5 and Table 6.

Also, it is unavoidable to collect tweets from another dialect or languages, but since these keywords are common in Saudi dialects, in addition to the fact that Saudis represent the largest number of users within the Arab region on Twitter ("Twitter: Most Users by Country" 2022), we have considered these collected tweets as Saudi tweets. However, the ironic words and phrases are huge, and this work is limited to only 35 keywords, more keywords may be included in future work.

In addition, the misspelled words such as (سوبهان الله) gave more ironic results than direct ironic words such as (تهكم). We noticed that misspelled words are intentionally used in the context of irony. The existence of English words and punctuation have high impact on understanding tweets, especially in dialects.

Moreover, the dataset is imbalanced where the number of non-ironic tweets is larger than ironic ones which requires further consideration during the model training and evaluation, therefore, we relied on F1-score for evaluation purposes and avoided accuracy.

Another issue is that ironic tweets depend on the topic; this issue should be considered when hiring annotators. Also, the annotator's personalities and mood is another issue, this could affect the annotation process. Yet, we mitigated this issue by making multiple annotation rounds.

Table 9 F1-score per class, for each model.

Model	**class**	**F1**

KNN	Non-irony	0.73
	Irony	0.51
LR	Non-irony	0.75
	Irony	0.13
SVM	Non-irony	0.74
	Irony	0.60
Bernoulli NB	Non-irony	0.71
	Irony	0.61
Multinomial NB	Non-irony	0.75
	Irony	0.46
Gaussian NB	Non-irony	0.52
	Irony	0.54
AraVec BiLSTM	Non-irony	0.79
	Irony	0.38
AraBERT	Non-irony	0.75
	Irony	0.65

6 Conclusion

In the era of social media, irony detection is considered a challenging and important task to understand a person's intentions. In this paper, we presented a new Arabic irony detection dataset for the Saudi dialects called Sa`7r[5]. We collected the corpus from Twitter using specific hashtags, keywords, and phrases related to irony based on the Saudi dialects. We plan to expand this dataset to include more linguistic content in the future. Additionally, we would like to determine whether there are any similarities and differences between ironic Arabic expressions used by speakers in other countries. In terms of modelling, we aim to solve the dataset imbalance in order to obtain more accurate results with a model trained with balanced dataset, we also aim to manipulate the hyperparameters of the BiLSTM model so that we can enhance the models learning abilities. For the transformer-based model, other options of pretrained Arabic BERT-based models do exist, and it is worth to experiment with such different models to find the best fit with the Saudi dialect dataset.

[5] https://github.com/iwan-rg/Saudi-Dialect-Irony-Dataset

7 References

Ibrahim Abu Farha, Wajdi Zaghouani, and Walid Magdy. 2021. Overview of the WANLP 2021 Shared Task on Sarcasm and Sentiment Detection in Arabic. In Proceedings of the Sixth Arabic Natural Language Processing Workshop, pages 296–305, Kyiv, Ukraine (Virtual), April. Association for Computational Linguistics.

Abeer Abuzayed and Hend Al-Khalifa. 2021. Sarcasm and Sentiment Detection In Arabic Tweets Using BERT-based Models and Data Augmentation. In Proceedings of the Sixth Arabic Natural Language Processing Workshop, pages 312–317, Kyiv, Ukraine (Virtual), April. Association for Computational Linguistics.

Hadj Ameur, Mohamed & Aliane, Hassina. (2021). AraCOVID19-SSD: Arabic COVID-19 Sentiment and Sarcasm Detection Dataset.

Kareem Darwish, Nizar Habash, Mourad Abbas, Hend Al-Khalifa, Huseein T. Al-Natsheh, Houda Bouamor, Karim Bouzoubaa, Violetta Cavalli-Sforza, Samhaa R. El-Beltagy, Wassim El-Hajj, Mustafa Jarrar, and Hamdy Mubarak. 2021. A panoramic survey of natural language processing in the Arab world. Communications of the ACM, 64(4):72–81, March.

Abdelkader El Mahdaouy, Abdellah El Mekki, Kabil Essefar, Nabil El Mamoun, Ismail Berrada, and Ahmed Khoumsi. 2021. Deep Multi-Task Model for Sarcasm Detection and Sentiment Analysis in Arabic Language. In Proceedings of the Sixth Arabic Natural Language Processing Workshop, pages 334–339, Kyiv, Ukraine (Virtual), April. Association for Computational Linguistics.

Talafha, B., Za'Ter, M. E., Suleiman, S., Al-Ayyoub, M., & Al-Kabi, M. N. (2021, November). sarcasm detection and quantification in arabic tweets. In *2021 IEEE 33rd International Conference on Tools with Artificial Intelligence (ICTAI)* (pp. 1121-1125). IEEE.

Wadhawan, A. (2021, April). AraBERT and Farasa Segmentation Based Approach For Sarcasm and Sentiment Detection in Arabic Tweets. In *Proceedings of the Sixth Arabic Natural Language Processing Workshop* (pp. 395-400).

Ines Abbes, Wajdi Zaghouani, Omaima El-Hardlo, and Faten Ashour. 2020. DAICT: A dialectal Arabic irony corpus extracted from Twitter. In Proceedings of the 12th language resources and evaluation conference, pages 6265–6271, Marseille, France, May. European Language Resources Association. Citation Key: abbes-etal-2020-daict.

Ibrahim Abu Farha and Walid Magdy. 2020. From Arabic Sentiment Analysis to Sarcasm Detection: The ArSarcasm Dataset. In Proceedings of the 4th Workshop on Open-Source Arabic Corpora and

Processing Tools, with a Shared Task on Offensive Language Detection, pages 32–39, Marseille, France, May. European Language Resource Association.

Kanish Shah, Henil Patel, Devanshi Sanghvi, and Manan Shah. 2020. A Comparative Analysis of Logistic Regression, Random Forest and KNN Models for the Text Classification. Augmented Human Research, 5(1):12, March.

Li Yang and Abdallah Shami. 2020. On hyperparameter optimization of machine learning algorithms: Theory and practice. Neurocomputing, 415:295–316, November.

Ali Allaith, Muhammad Shahbaz, and Mohammed Alkoli. 2019. Neural network approach for irony detection from arabic text on social media. In Parth Mehta, Paolo Rosso, Prasenjit Majumder, and Mandar Mitra, editors, Working notes of FIRE 2019 - forum for information retrieval evaluation, kolkata, india, december 12-15, 2019, volume 2517, pages 445–450. CEUR-WS.org.

Bilal Ghanem, Jihen Karoui, Farah Benamara, Véronique Moriceau, and Paolo Rosso. 2019. IDAT at FIRE2019: Overview of the Track on Irony Detection in Arabic Tweets. In Proceedings of the 11th Forum for Information Retrieval Evaluation, pages 10–13, New York, NY, USA, December. Association for Computing Machinery.

AIT YAHIA Ikram and LOQMAN Chakir. 2019. Arabic Text Classification in the Legal Domain. In 2019 Third International Conference on Intelligent Computing in Data Sciences (ICDS), pages 1–6. October.

Paolo Rosso, Francisco Rangel, Irazu Hernández Farías, Leticia Cagnina, Wajdi Zaghouani, and Anis Charfi. 2018. A survey on author profiling, deception, and irony detection for the Arabic language. Language and Linguistics Compass, 12(4):e12275.

Dana Al-Ghadhban, Eman Alnkhilan, Lamma Tatwany, and Muna Alrazgan. 2017. Arabic sarcasm detection in Twitter. In 2017 International Conference on Engineering MIS (ICEMIS), pages 1–7. May.

Ilseyar Alimova, Elena Tutubalina, Julia Alferova, and Guzel Gafiyatullina. 2017. A Machine Learning Approach to Classification of Drug Reviews in Russian. In 2017 Ivannikov ISPRAS Open Conference (ISPRAS), pages 64–69. November.

Jihen Karoui, Farah Banamara Zitoune, and Véronique Moriceau. 2017. SOUKHRIA: Towards an Irony Detection System for Arabic in Social Media. Procedia Computer Science, 117:161–168, January.

Ashwin Rajadesingan, Reza Zafarani, and Huan Liu. 2015. Sarcasm Detection on Twitter: A Behavioral Modeling Approach. In Proceedings of the Eighth ACM International Conference on Web Search and Data Mining, pages 97–106, New York, NY, USA, February. Association for Computing Machinery.

Buschmeier, K., Cimiano, P., & Klinger, R. (2014, June). An impact analysis of features in a classification approach to irony detection in product reviews. In Proceedings of the 5th workshop on computational approaches to subjectivity, sentiment and social media analysis (pp. 42-49).

Duden. 2014. Duden Verlag. Online: http://www. duden.de/rechtschreibung/Ironie. ac- cessed April 28, 2014.

Sigar, A., Taha, Z., 2012. A contrastive study of ironic expressions in english and arabic. College of Basic Education Researchers Journal.

Aurangzeb Khan, Baharum Baharudin, Lam Hong Lee, and Khairullah Khan. 2010. A review of machine learning algorithms for text-documents classification. Journal of advances in information technology, 1(1):4–20.

David D. Lewis. 1998. Naive (Bayes) at forty: The independence assumption in information retrieval. In Claire Nédellec and Céline Rouveirol, editors, Machine Learning: ECML-98, pages 4–15, Berlin, Heidelberg. Springer.

Kreuz, R. J., & Glucksberg, S. (1989). How to be sarcastic: The echoic reminder theory of verbal irony. Journal of experimental psychology: General, 118(4), 374.

Grice, H. P., Cole, P., & Morgan, J. L. (1975). Syntax and semantics. Logic and conversation 3,41–58.

Torki, Marwan & Ibrahim, Mai & El-Makky, Nagwa. (2018). Imbalanced Toxic Comments Classification Using Data Augmentation and Deep Learning. 10.1109/ICMLA.2018.00141.

Dutta, Shawni, and Akash Mehta. 2021. "Unfolding Sarcasm in Twitter Using C-RNN Approach." *Bulletin of Computer Science and Electrical Engineering* 2 (1): 1–8. https://doi.org/10.25008/bcsee.v2i1.1134.

Ghosh, Aniruddha, and Tony Veale. 2016. "Fracking Sarcasm Using Neural Network." In *Proceedings of the 7th Workshop on Computational Approaches to Subjectivity, Sentiment and Social Media Analysis*, 161–69. San Diego, California: Association for Computational Linguistics. https://doi.org/10.18653/v1/W16-0425.

Karoui, Jihen, Farah Benamara, Veronique Moriceau, Viviana Patti, Cristina Bosco, and Nathalie Aussenac-Gilles. 2017. "Exploring the Impact of Pragmatic Phenomena on Irony Detection in Tweets: A Multilingual Corpus Study." In *15th Conference of the European Chapter of the Association for Computational Linguistics*, 1:262–72. Valencia, Spain. https://hal.archives-ouvertes.fr/hal-01686475.

"Twitter: Most Users by Country." 2022. Statista. 2022. https://www.statista.com/statistics/242606/number-of-active-twitter-users-in-selected-countries/.

Van Hee, Cynthia, Els Lefever, and Véronique Hoste. 2018. "SemEval-2018 Task 3: Irony Detection in English Tweets." In

Proceedings of The 12th International Workshop on Semantic Evaluation, 39–50. New Orleans, Louisiana: Association for Computational Linguistics. https://doi.org/10.18653/v1/S18-1005.

Proceedings of the OSACT 2022 Workshop @LREC2022, pages 71–78
Marseille, 20 June 2022

Classifying Arabic Crisis Tweets using Data Selection and Pre-trained Language Models

Alaa Alharbi, Mark Lee
University of Birmingham, UK
Taibah University, KSA
{axa1314, m.g.lee}@bham.ac.uk
alaharbi@taibahu.edu.sa

Abstract

User-generated Social Media (SM) content has been explored as a valuable and accessible source of data about crises to enhance situational awareness and support humanitarian response efforts. However, the timely extraction of crisis-related SM messages is challenging as it involves processing large quantities of noisy data in real-time. Supervised machine learning methods have been successfully applied to this task but such approaches require human-labelled data, which are unlikely to be available from novel and emerging crises. Supervised machine learning algorithms trained on labelled data from past events did not usually perform well when classifying a new disaster due to data variations across events. Using the BERT embeddings, we propose and investigate an instance distance-based data selection approach for adaptation to improve classifiers' performance under a domain shift. The K-nearest neighbours algorithm selects a subset of multi-event training data that is most similar to the target event. Results show that fine-tuning a BERT model on a selected subset of data to classify crisis tweets outperforms a model that has been fine-tuned on all available source data. We demonstrated that our approach generally works better than the self-training adaptation method. Combing the self-training with our proposed classifier does not enhance the performance.

Keywords: Crisis Detection, Domain Adaptation, Data Selection, Self-training, BERT

1. Introduction

In the last decade, Social Media (SM) content has been explored by Natural Language Processing (NLP) and data mining researchers as a valuable and accessible source of data. Many of these studies have investigated the problem of mining social media (notably microblogging sites such as Twitter) to extract emergency events. They have demonstrated that SM posts contain actionable and time-critical information that can be leveraged to respond effectively to disasters (Olteanu et al., 2015; Imran et al., 2016). The automatic extraction of crises from SM as they unfold can enhance situational awareness and support humanitarian response efforts.

While SM event detection is challenging because of noisy language, several studies have demonstrated the possibility of identifying crisis-related data from Twitter and categorising these into different information types using conventional supervised Machine Learning (ML) techniques (Imran et al., 2013; Rudra et al., 2015; Rudra et al., 2018; Singh et al., 2017) and Deep Neural Networks (DNNs) (Caragea et al., 2016; Nguyen et al., 2017; Neppalli et al., 2018; Alharbi and Lee, 2019; Kozlowski et al., 2020). Annotated training datasets are unlikely to be available in real-time from current events since obtaining sufficient human-labelled data is time-consuming and labour intensive. The unavailability of training data from newly occurred crises and the growing generation of SM content challenge the timely processing of crisis data by the emergency responders. Researchers proposed to use data from historical events. Several studies have shown that DNNs generalise better than conventional ML approaches (Nguyen et al., 2017; Neppalli et al., 2018; Alharbi and Lee, 2019). However, DNNs are still challenged by out-of-distribution learning when classifying unseen crises – especially if they are trained on data from cross-type crises due to data variations across such events. Out-of-distribution (covariate shift) refers to the different probability distributions of input features across the training (source) and test (target) data.

Textual data varies across SM events in two main aspects: topic and language. Messages from two events of the same type can discuss various topics emerging from the event properties and its distinct aspects such as time, cause, related entities and impact. Such topic variations across events can lead to substantially different feature distributions. Events on SM are discussed with varying levels of formality, in various dialects and languages, resulting in more challenges to handle the out-of-distribution problem when learning from cross-event historical data. Supervised classifiers' performance drops on test data if it does not follow the training set distribution as many ML algorithms assume (Ramponi and Plank, 2020).

Recent works on Domain Adaptation (DA) show that training on a domain similar to the target data results in performance gains for various NLP tasks. Ruder et al. (2017) explored the performance of several domain similarity metrics on different text representations for data selection in the sentiment analysis context. The authors also proposed a subset-level data selection approach that outperforms instance-level selection. In the same vein, Guo et al. (2020) studied different domain distance measures and presented a bandit-based multi-source domain adaptation model for sentiment classification. Ma et al. (2019) presented a domain adaptation method based on data selection and curriculum learning to fine-tune BERT models for text classification. Leveraging pre-trained Language Model (LM) representations, Aharoni and Goldberg (2020) proposed data selection approaches for multi-domain Machine Translation (MT) using cosine similarity in embedding space.

This study aims at improving the cross-crisis (cross-domain) classification tasks using DA methods. We adopt a data selection approach to train a classifier on the best matching data for the target emergency event instead of using all multi-event source data. Training a classifier using examples that are dissimilar to the target data can adversely affect the model performance. As pre-trained contextualised LMs have achieved state-of-the-art results in various NLP tasks, we exploit their representation to propose a data selection approach based on the document similarity in the embedding space. The selected data has been used to fine-tune a Bidirectional Encoder Representation from Transformer (BERT) model to identify crisis-related posts from Twitter and classify the messages into different information types. We took advantage of transfer learning and used BERT as a classifier. Fine-tuning a model pre-trained on large data eliminates the need for massive training examples that are required to train a DNN from scratch. The presented adaptation strategy is unsupervised as it does not require labelled data from the target domain. It can also be adopted during the early hours of a crisis when small unlabelled data is available from the target event. To the best of our knowledge, we are the first to adopt the data selection with pre-trained LMs in the crisis detection domain. This work is also the first to investigate DA approaches to perform cross-domain crisis Arabic Twitter classification.

2. Related Work

Recently, researchers have adopted DA approaches to improve the generalisation of supervised models trained on past crisis data to classify unseen new crises. They showed that learning from both the labelled source and unlabelled target data is better than learning only from source labelled data. Several studies adopted an unsupervised DA approach using self-training (Li et al., 2015; Li et al., 2017; Li et al., 2018a; Li et al., 2018b; Li et al., 2021). Earlier work showed that an iterative self-training improved the performance of a NB classifier (Li et al., 2015; Li et al., 2017; Li et al., 2018a; Li et al., 2018b). Li et al. (2018b) demonstrated that the self-training strategy outperformed a feature-based correlation alignment method. Mazloom et al. (2018) proposed a hybrid feature-instance DA method using matrix factorisation and the k-nearest neighbours algorithm to learn a NB classifier for the target event. The work was extended by Mazloom et al. (2019) who combined the feature-instance approach with the self-training algorithm presented by Li et al. (2017). Li et al. (2021) used self-training with CNN and BERT models and highlighted that self-training improved the performance of the Deep Learning (DL) models. For retraining the base classifier, they used a soft-labelling strategy.

Alam et al. (2018) proposed an approach based on adversarial training and graph embeddings in a single DL framework. The adversarial training minimises the distribution shift across domains, whereas graph-based learning encodes similarity between source and target instances. Krishnan et al. (2020) created a multi-task domain adversarial attention network based on a shared Bi-LSTM layer to filter Twitter posts for crisis analytics under domain shift. The tasks are relevancy, priority level, sentiment and factoid detection. Chen et al. (2020) used a BERT-based adversarial model to classify tweets gathered during a disaster into different information categories. ALRashdi and O'Keefe (2019) proposed to use a distant supervision-based framework to label the data from emerging disasters. The pseudo-labelled target data is then used with labelled data from past crises of a similar type to train a classifier. Li and Caragea (2020) explored the use of the domain reconstruction classification approach on disaster tweets, which aims at reducing the covariate shift between source and target data distributions using an autoencoder. The authors showed that this approach outperformed the DA method proposed by Alam et al. (2018). To contribute to this line of research, we have adopted a selection-based DA approach that leverages pre-trained LMs. Our approach is an unsupervised DA as it does not require any labelled instances from the target event and can be utilised during the early hours of a disaster when small unlabelled data is available from the target event. We also explored whether combining the selection method with the self-training DA approach improves the performance. The evaluation was conducted on two crisis-related tasks as described in the next sections.

3. Methodology

3.1. Domain Definition and Tasks Description

In the NLP literature, the notion of domain typically refers to a specific corpus that differs from other domains in the topic, genre, style, etc. (Ramponi and Plank, 2020). In this work, a domain is defined as a dataset that has been collected from SM for a specific crisis. Hence, each crisis data represents a distinct domain. A crisis is a real-world emergency event that occurs at a particular time and location and is characterised by a main topic representing its type (flood, shooting, etc.). In this research, experiments will be performed using Arabic SM data which poses an additional challenge as they include several dialects that can vary across events based on their geographical locations. We consider two main SM crisis-related tasks as follows.

3.1.1. Relevancy Detection

This task aims at identifying crisis messages from SM by classifying them as relevant (on-topic) or irrelevant (off-topic). Twitter crisis datasets are usually collected by tracking specific relevant keywords and hashtags. Such a process captures lots of relevant data but can also include some irrelevant posts with various distribution across crises. Unrelated posts include advertisements, jokes, political views, unrelated personal messages or posts related to other disasters. Such posts usually exploit trending hashtags to be more visible. Other off-topic tweets were crawled due to the keywords' ambiguity. Relevancy detection is challenging because of the unbalanced datasets.

3.1.2. Information Classification

The task categorises relevant messages into one or more information categories that support situational awareness, such as infrastructure damage, caution, etc. This task is modelled as either a multi-class or multi-label problem. In this work, we used data that has been annotated using a multi-label scheme.

3.2. Multi-source Data Selection for SM Crisis Classification

This work proposes an unsupervised multi-source data selection approach using the K-nearest neighbours algorithm. The strategy aims at building a good model for target data by leveraging labelled data from several related source domains and unlabelled data from a target domain. We hypothesise that fine-tuning LMs on the most similar data can produce more accurate results on crisis classification tasks than using all multi-source training data.

We mimic the real scenario and assume that we are given labelled data from several historical emergency events (multi-source datasets) and only unlabelled data from an emerging crisis, representing the source and target domains, respectively. The goal is to find an optimal set of training data from a multi-source domain that enhances the model generalisation for the target data. Finding this set can be achieved by identifying the examples from training source data that are similar (as close as possible) to the target domain. Hence, we consider an instance-level data selection strategy using cosine similarity in the embedding space of the pre-trained LMs. The selected instances are expected to have similar feature distribution to the target domain of interest.

In our approach, we selected the data only from the crisis-related messages. Due to the unbalanced dataset, we used all off-topic posts for the relevancy detection task. Messages labelled irrelevant to a particular crisis but related to other emergency events were excluded from the off-topic set as depicted in Figure 1. For example, the Jordanian flood data contain two tweets about the Kuwait flood. Those posts were labelled irrelevant to Jordan flood because the annotation was performed per event level. We filtered out such posts from the off-topic training set. Therefore, the classifier will be trained to learn whether or not a post represents a crisis, as the aim is to build a model for cross-event crisis detection.

We leveraged the contextualised text representations produced by pre-trained LMs. In this work, we used Sentence-BERT (S-BERT) (Reimers and Gurevych, 2019). The authors created S-BERT by fine-tuning BERT using Siamese network architecture to produce fixed-sized sentence embeddings that can be compared using similarity measures. As there is no monolingual Arabic S-BERT, we used the multilingual S-BERT (Reimers and Gurevych, 2020). We used the K-nearest neighbours algorithm to select the K most similar instances for each example in the target set based on the cosine similarity on the S-BERT embedding space. The selected data was used to fine-tune a BERT model for classifying target tweets as outlined in Algorithm 1.

Algorithm 1: Multi-source instance-level data selection

Input:
    S_L: { $S_1 \cup S_2 \cup \cdots \cup S_n$ } Labelled source domain examples from n historical crisis data
    T_U: Unlabelled target domain data for a new crisis
SET $trainset$ to [ ]
S_R = S_L[label=relevant]
S_I = S_L[label=irrelevant]
Remove duplicates in T_U
Encode data in S_R using S-BERT
FOR EACH instance in T_U **DO:**
    Encode instance using S-BERT
    Select the nearest k instances S_k from S_R
    $trainset.append(S_k)$
END LOOP
Remove duplicates in $trainset$
$trainset.append(S_I)$
Output: $trainset$ to **Fine-tune** a BERT model M for classifying T_U

3.3. Self-training

We investigated the effect of combining the data selection approach with self-training. Self-training is a semi-supervised learning approach that learns a base classifier from source data and then uses that classifier to label the unseen target data. The classifier is then retrained utilising the source and pseudo-labelled target data. The self-training continues for a fixed number of iterations or until convergence. For retraining, we used a hard-labelled approach, in which most confidently classified instances are added with their predicted labels (e.g. 0 or 1) to the training set in subsequent training iterations. Figure 1 illustrates the DA framework that combines data selection and self-training.

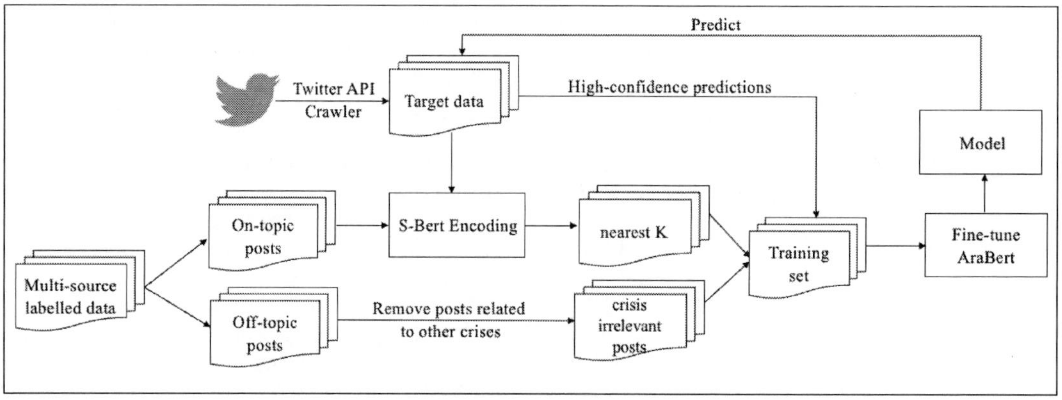

Figure 1: The DA approach with data selection and self-training.

4. Experimental Setup

For data selection, instances are encoded using the distiluse-base-multilingual-cased-v1 multilingual model[1] that supports 15 languages, including Arabic. We experimented with different values of K when choosing the nearest neighbours (3, 5 and 10). We evaluated the binary classification model on each selected set. The information type classifier was assessed on the last chosen dataset (K=10) as some classes can be under-represented in the smaller training set. AraBERT (Antoun et al., 2020) (trained on news corpus) was used as a classification model as it slightly outperforms other Arabic BERT variants (trained on Twitter corpora) on crisis tasks. We fine-tune AraBERT using the same parameters and text pre-processing steps introduced by Alharbi and Lee (2021). The batch size and the number of epochs were set to 32 and 3, respectively. For reproducibility, the random seed was set to 1. For self-training, we set the confidence threshold and the number of iterations to 0.99 and 2, respectively.

We experimented with different source and target crisis pairs using the leave-one-out strategy. In other words, the evaluation was performed by choosing one target event as the test set and the rest events for training. For self-training, the evaluation was performed using 3-folds cross-validation. The target data was split into three parts: one for testing and the rest (two-thirds) for adaptation. We report the average score. We used the weighted F1 and macro F1 to evaluate the models' performance on the relevancy detection task as the dataset is unbalanced. For information classification, we used the accuracy (Godbole and Sarawagi, 2004; Sorower, 2010) and macro F1 score.

The current study used the Kawarith (Alharbi and Lee, 2021) corpus, an Arabic crisis-related Twitter dataset, to evaluate our proposed DA approach. Table 1 shows the number of relevant and irrelevant messages per event in the dataset, while Table 2 presents the distribution of information types (for relevant posts) per event. We manually removed those messages related to other crises from the off-topic set in the source data. We found 30 such tweets in the dataset, most of which (18 posts) were in the Dragon storm data. We did not handle the imbalanced class distribution in this work.

In the following section, we will present the results of classifiers with the data selection method and the data selection with self-training. We will compare the performance of the two proposed models with the same classifier fine-tuned using the entirety of the historical source data (baseline-1). Besides that, we compare them against the self-training model (baseline-2) as self-training with BERT shows promising results in one of the most recent works on English crisis detection (Li et al., 2021). It is worth emphasising that we used a hard-labelling self-training strategy, while Li et al. (2021) adopted soft-labelling.

5. Results and Discussion

Table 3 presents the results of the proposed models and baselines. We found that fine-tuning BERT on the most similar data (BERT-DS models) improves performance in all cases over BERT(all) despite using smaller training data. On average, choosing different values of K results in slightly different performance. BERT-DS(k=10) achieved the best scores in four out of seven cases. We compared the best model with the baseline. BERT-DS(k=10) improved the average weighted F1 and macro F1 over BERT(all) by 3.67% and 4.57%, respectively. The improvement in weighted F1 scores ranges from 1% to 7.53, whereas the macro F1 improved by values ranging from 1.38 to 9.93. We observed that the macro F1 was enhanced by 9.93%, 6% and 5.79% when classifying KF, HF and CD, respectively. The pronounced enhanced performance for classifying CD emphasised the usefulness of DA based on data selection, as the features differ substantially between COVID-19 data and other crises.

[1]https://www.sbert.net/docs/pretrained_models.html

Crisis	Relevant posts	Irrelevant posts	Total
Jordan floods (JF)	1882	118	2000
Kuwait floods (KF)	3701	399	4100
Hafr Albatin floods (HF)	978	637	1615
Cairo bombing (CB)	700	6	706
COVID-19 (CD)	1782	223	2005
Dragon storms (DS)	701	309	1010
Beirut explosion (BE)	833	177	1010

Table 1: Distribution of tweets by relevancy in the Kawarith dataset

Label	JF	KF	HF	CB	DS	BE
Affected individuals & help	331	414	83	138	70	186
Infrastructure & utilities damage	39	271	100	17	105	64
Caution, preparations & other crisis updates	268	980	475	214	252	170
Emotional support, prayers & supplications	709	816	202	222	120	277
Opinions & criticism	604	1355	189	181	221	198

Table 2: Distribution of tweets by information types in the Kawarith dataset

The self-training (BERT-ST(all)) model achieved higher results than BERT(all) in four cases and comparable results in two cases. The BERT-ST(all) model improved the weighted F1 by 12.18% in the COVID-19 case. On average, it enhanced the weighted F1 and macro F1 by 1.82% and 2.27%, respectively. BERT(all) worked better than BERT-ST(all) for the HF data. The reason was that many irrelevant tweets from HF were misclassified and added to the classifier in the next iteration as ground truth data, which degraded the performance.

The DS models generally worked better than the BERT-ST(all) model. The BERT-ST(all) achieved comparable scores in two cases. However, the ST worked better for the CD data. It improved the weighted F1 by 5.54% over the best DS model. The self-training works well when there is a significant feature distribution gap between the source and target, shifting the weights gradually towards the target data.

Finally, we explore whether self-training enhanced the performance of the DS models. To do that, we combine the self-training strategy with the best DS model BERT-DS(K=10). We found that BERT-DS(K=10)+ST achieved the highest scores on CD data. It enhanced the weighted F1 and macro F1 by 12.53% and 10.36%, respectively. However, BERT-DS(K=10) produced a higher performance for KF and HF. Otherwise, they achieved comparable results in two cases. Hence, adding the pseudo-labels to the training data does not constantly improve the performance. We recommend using self-training on the relevancy detection task when the target event is very different from the source data, as in the case of COVID-19 and other disasters.

For the relevancy detection task, we excluded the crisis messages from the off-topic set to reduce the false negatives (crisis messages classified as not crisis). However, we still need to handle the irrelevant messages detected as relevant because they are about another crisis. For example, we found instances related to Covid-19 were classified as on-topic in the DS data because examples of CD were chosen as the most similar data and were added to the selected set with their positive labels. This results in false positives. We can solve this by following the crisis detection task with a message type classification to filter out such posts. We left this for future work.

Regarding the information category classification, we set the K value to 10. This task has been assessed separately, i.e. we suppose that we managed to filter out all irrelevant posts and need to categorise the crisis-related tweets into pre-defined information types. Table 4 displays the results of our experiments. When training the model on the chosen data, we obtained further improvements in macro F1 scores ranging from 1.17% to 6.73% absolute gains. Overall, data selection improved the performance in most cases. Similarly, BERT-ST(all) worked generally better than the BERT(all) model. The average of all scores showed that BERT-ST(all) and BERT-SD achieved comparable results, while BERT-SD(K=10)+ST resulted in lower performance on this task. We generally recommend using the data selection DA for information type classification as the self-training could damage the performance as in the KF event, which failed to detect many cases related to the 'affected individuals' class.

6. Conclusion

This paper proposed a selection-based multi-source domain adaptation approach to identify crisis Twitter messages for new events. Data was selected using the cosine similarity metric in the embedding that has been generated from transformer-based models. Selecting a subset of data that is semantically similar to the target

Target Data	Model	No. of human-labelled examples	Weighted F1	Mac. F1
JF	BERT(all)	10418	93.26	73.52
	BERT-DS(K=3)	3901	94.08	73.89
	BERT-DS(K=5)	4724	94.19	76.32
	BERT-DS(K=10)	6082	94.45	76.14
	BERT-ST(all)	10418	94.85	75.95
	BERT-DS(K=10)+BERT-ST	6082	**95.06**	**77.83**
KF	BERT(all)	8317	87.40	72.39
	BERT-DS(K=3)	3552	90.95	78.34
	BERT-DS(K=5)	4227	90.50	76.83
	BERT-DS(K=10)	5329	93.69	**82.32**
	BERT-ST(all)	8317	**95.83**	77.51
	BERT-DS(K=10)+BERT-ST	5329	**95.18**	77.94
HF	BERT(all)	10801	76.39	78.36
	BERT-DS(K=3)	3107	**85.25**	**84.54**
	BERT-DS(K=5)	3850	80.34	81.69
	BERT-DS(K=10)	5137	82.40	83.63
	BERT-ST(all)	5137	71.07	67.99
	BERT-DS(K=10)+BERT-ST	10801	73.86	85.25
CB	BERT(all)	11710	96.51	55.43
	BERT-DS(K=3)	2783	97.63	56.58
	BERT-DS(K=5)	3169	**98.21**	**65.39**
	BERT-DS(K=10)	3966	97.94	58.01
	BERT-ST(all)	3966	96.96	61.52
	BERT-DS(K=10)+BERT-ST	11710	97.29	63.46
CD	BERT(all)	10412	64.11	49.88
	BERT-DS(K=3)	4071	69.56	52.95
	BERT-DS(K=5)	5044	69.20	53.82
	BERT-DS(K=10)	6484	71.64	55.67
	BERT-ST(all)	6484	76.29	61.21
	BERT-DS(K=10)+BERT-ST	10412	**84.17**	**66.03**
DS	BERT(all)	11424	77.71	71.24
	BERT-DS(K=3)	3115	**84.55**	**80.81**
	BERT-DS(K=5)	3809	81.36	76.31
	BERT-DS(K=10)	5092	78.70	72.62
	BERT-ST(all)	11424	77.60	71.13
	BERT-DS(K=10)+BERT-ST	5092	79.45	73.66
BE	BERT(all)	11414	86.72	78.1
	BERT-DS(K=3)	3019	87.8	79.04
	BERT-DS(K=5)	3628	**90.54**	**82.76**
	BERT-DS(K=10)	4824	89.72	81.75
	BERT-ST(all)	11414	87.77	77.49
	BERT-DS(K=10)+BERT-ST	4824	89.01	79.32

Table 3: The weighted F1 and macro F1 for the relevancy detection task. DS and ST refer to the data selection and self-training techniques, respectively. The keyword (all) indicates training on the whole labelled data.

for fine-tuning BERT LMs showed promising results and outperformed two baselines: training on all data and self-training. We suppose that using monolingual Arabic S-BERT for data representation may achieve better results, so we left that for future work. We think that our instance-level DA approach is useful during the early hours of a crisis when no large unlabelled data is available from an emerging disaster.

7. Bibliographical References

Aharoni, R. and Goldberg, Y. (2020). Unsupervised domain clusters in pretrained language models. *arXiv preprint arXiv:2004.02105*.

Alam, F., Joty, S., and Imran, M. (2018). Domain adaptation with adversarial training and graph embeddings. *arXiv preprint arXiv:1805.05151*.

Alharbi, A. and Lee, M. (2019). Crisis detection from arabic tweets. In *Proceedings of the 3rd workshop*

Target Data	Model	No. of human-labelled examples	Accuracy	Mac. F1
JF	BERT(all)	6913	82	75.97
	BERT-DS(K=10)	3743	87.44	81.65
	BERT-ST(all)	6913	**88.78**	**82.42**
	BERT-DS(K=10)+BERT-ST	3743	87.36	79.29
KF	BERT(all)	5094	79.01	77.32
	BERT-DS(K=10)	3148	**81.23**	**78.86**
	BERT-ST(all)	5094	73.09	68.84
	BERT-DS(K=10)+BERT-ST	3148	71.45	56.55
HF	BERT(all)	7817	84.27	81.56
	BERT-DS(K=10)	3397	83.73	82.98
	BERT-ST(all)	7817	**85.18**	**82.97**
	BERT-DS(K=10)+BERT-ST	3397	83.35	79.65
CB	BERT(all)	8095	77.05	71.36
	BERT-DS(K=10)	1851	77.48	72.53
	BERT-ST(all)	8095	78.20	72.58
	BERT-DS(K=10)+BERT-ST	1851	**79.09**	**74.92**
DS	BERT(all)	8094	78.14	75.08
	BERT-DS(K=10)	3023	**81.88**	**81.18**
	BERT-ST(all)	8094	79.87	81.06
	BERT-DS(K=10)+BERT-ST	3023	**81.83**	**81.46**
BE	BERT(all)	7962	78.14	75.08
	BERT-DS(K=10)	2694	79.89	80.41
	BERT-ST(all)	7962	**83.44**	**77.72**
	BERT-DS(K=10)+BERT-ST	2694	76.70	65.01

Table 4: The accuracy and macro F1 for the information classification task. DS and ST refer to the data selection and self-training techniques, respectively. The keyword (all) indicates training on the whole labelled data.

on arabic corpus linguistics, pages 72–79.

Alharbi, A. and Lee, M. (2021). Kawarith: an arabic twitter corpus for crisis events. In *Proceedings of the Sixth Arabic Natural Language Processing Workshop*, pages 42–52.

ALRashdi, R. and O'Keefe, S. (2019). Robust domain adaptation approach for tweet classification for crisis response. In *International Conference Europe Middle East & North Africa Information Systems and Technologies to Support Learning*, pages 124–134. Springer.

Antoun, W., Baly, F., and Hajj, H. (2020). Arabert: Transformer-based model for arabic language understanding. *arXiv preprint arXiv:2003.00104*.

Caragea, C., Silvescu, A., and Tapia, A. H. (2016). Identifying informative messages in disaster events using convolutional neural networks. In *International conference on information systems for crisis response and management*, pages 137–147.

Chen, Q., Wang, W., Huang, K., De, S., and Coenen, F. (2020). Adversarial domain adaptation for crisis data classification on social media. In *2020 International Conferences on Internet of Things (iThings) and IEEE Green Computing and Communications (GreenCom) and IEEE Cyber, Physical and Social Computing (CPSCom) and IEEE Smart Data (SmartData) and IEEE Congress on Cybermatics (Cybermatics)*, pages 282–287. IEEE.

Godbole, S. and Sarawagi, S. (2004). Discriminative methods for multi-labeled classification. In *Pacific-Asia conference on knowledge discovery and data mining*, pages 22–30. Springer.

Guo, H., Pasunuru, R., and Bansal, M. (2020). Multi-source domain adaptation for text classification via distancenet-bandits. In *Proceedings of the AAAI Conference on Artificial Intelligence*, volume 34, pages 7830–7838.

Imran, M., Elbassuoni, S., Castillo, C., Diaz, F., and Meier, P. (2013). Practical extraction of disaster-relevant information from social media. In *Proceedings of the 22nd International Conference on World Wide Web*, pages 1021–1024. ACM.

Imran, M., Mitra, P., and Castillo, C. (2016). Twitter as a lifeline: Human-annotated twitter corpora for nlp of crisis-related messages. *arXiv preprint arXiv:1605.05894*.

Kozlowski, D., Lannelongue, E., Saudemont, F., Benamara, F., Mari, A., Moriceau, V., and Boumadane, A. (2020). A three-level classification of french tweets in ecological crises. *Information Processing & Management*, 57(5):102284.

Krishnan, J., Purohit, H., and Rangwala, H. (2020). Unsupervised and interpretable domain adaptation to rapidly filter tweets for emergency services. In *2020 IEEE/ACM International Conference on Advances in Social Networks Analysis and Mining (ASONAM)*, pages 409–416. IEEE.

Li, X. and Caragea, D. (2020). Domain adaptation with reconstruction for disaster tweet classification. In *Proceedings of the 43rd International ACM SIGIR Conference on Research and Development in Information Retrieval*, pages 1561–1564.

Li, H., Guevara, N., Herndon, N., Caragea, D., Neppalli, K., Caragea, C., Squicciarini, A. C., and Tapia, A. H. (2015). Twitter mining for disaster response: A domain adaptation approach. In *ISCRAM*.

Li, H., Caragea, D., and Caragea, C. (2017). Towards practical usage of a domain adaptation algorithm in the early hours of a disaster. In *ISCRAM*.

Li, H., Caragea, D., Caragea, C., and Herndon, N. (2018a). Disaster response aided by tweet classification with a domain adaptation approach. *Journal of Contingencies and Crisis Management*, 26(1):16–27.

Li, H., Sopova, O., Caragea, D., and Caragea, C. (2018b). Domain adaptation for crisis data using correlation alignment and self-training. *International Journal of Information Systems for Crisis Response and Management (IJISCRAM)*, 10(4):1–20.

Li, H., Caragea, D., and Caragea, C. (2021). Combining self-training with deep learning for disaster tweet classification. In *The 18th International Conference on Information Systems for Crisis Response and Management (ISCRAM 2021)*.

Ma, X., Xu, P., Wang, Z., Nallapati, R., and Xiang, B. (2019). Domain adaptation with bert-based domain classification and data selection. In *Proceedings of the 2nd Workshop on Deep Learning Approaches for Low-Resource NLP (DeepLo 2019)*, pages 76–83.

Mazloom, R., Li, H., Caragea, D., Caragea, C., and Imran, M. (2018). Classification of twitter disaster data using a hybrid feature-instance adaptation approach. In *Proceedings of the 15th Annual Conference for Information Systems for Crisis Response and Management (ISCRAM)*.

Mazloom, R., Li, H., Caragea, D., Caragea, C., and Imran, M. (2019). A hybrid domain adaptation approach for identifying crisis-relevant tweets. *International Journal of Information Systems for Crisis Response and Management (IJISCRAM)*, 11(2):1–19.

Neppalli, V. K., Caragea, C., and Caragea, D. (2018). Deep neural networks versus naïve bayes classifiers for identifying informative tweets during disasters.

Nguyen, D. T., Al Mannai, K. A., Joty, S., Sajjad, H., Imran, M., and Mitra, P. (2017). Robust classification of crisis-related data on social networks using convolutional neural networks. In *Eleventh International AAAI Conference on Web and Social Media*.

Olteanu, A., Vieweg, S., and Castillo, C. (2015). What to expect when the unexpected happens: Social media communications across crises. In *Proceedings of the 18th ACM conference on computer supported cooperative work & social computing*, pages 994–1009. ACM.

Ramponi, A. and Plank, B. (2020). Neural unsupervised domain adaptation in nlp—a survey. *arXiv preprint arXiv:2006.00632*.

Reimers, N. and Gurevych, I. (2019). Sentence-bert: Sentence embeddings using siamese bert-networks. *arXiv preprint arXiv:1908.10084*.

Reimers, N. and Gurevych, I. (2020). Making monolingual sentence embeddings multilingual using knowledge distillation. *arXiv preprint arXiv:2004.09813*.

Ruder, S., Ghaffari, P., and Breslin, J. G. (2017). Data selection strategies for multi-domain sentiment analysis. *arXiv preprint arXiv:1702.02426*.

Rudra, K., Ghosh, S., Ganguly, N., Goyal, P., and Ghosh, S. (2015). Extracting situational information from microblogs during disaster events: a classification-summarization approach. In *Proceedings of the 24th ACM international on conference on information and knowledge management*, pages 583–592.

Rudra, K., Ganguly, N., Goyal, P., and Ghosh, S. (2018). Extracting and summarizing situational information from the twitter social media during disasters. *ACM Transactions on the Web (TWEB)*, 12(3):1–35.

Singh, J. P., Dwivedi, Y. K., Rana, N. P., Kumar, A., and Kapoor, K. K. (2017). Event classification and location prediction from tweets during disasters. *Annals of Operations Research*, pages 1–21.

Sorower, M. S. (2010). A literature survey on algorithms for multi-label learning.

Proceedings of the OSACT 2022 Workshop @LREC2022, pages 79–87
Marseille, 20 June 2022

Qur'an QA 2022: Overview of The First Shared Task on Question Answering over the Holy Qur'an

Rana Malhas, Watheq Mansour, Tamer Elsayed
Qatar University, Doha, Qatar
{rana.malhas, wm1900793, telsayed}@qu.edu.qa

Abstract

Motivated by the resurgence of the machine reading comprehension (MRC) research, we have organized the first Qur'an Question Answering shared task,"Qur'an QA 2022". The task in its first year aims to promote state-of-the-art research on Arabic QA in general and MRC in particular on the Holy Qur'an, which constitutes a rich and fertile source of knowledge for Muslim and non-Muslim inquisitors and knowledge-seekers. In this paper, we provide an overview of the shared task that succeeded in attracting 13 teams to participate in the final phase, with a total of 30 submitted runs. Moreover, we outline the main approaches adopted by the participating teams in the context of highlighting some of our perceptions and general trends that characterize the participating systems and their submitted runs.

1. Introduction

The Holy Qur'an is sacredly held by more than 1.9B Muslims across the world.[1] It is the major source of knowledge, teachings, wisdom, and legislation in Islam. This makes it a rich and fertile source for Muslim and non-Muslim knowledge-seekers pursuing answers to questions raised for learning, out of curiosity, or skepticism. The Qur'an is composed of 114 chapters (Suras) and 6236 verses (Ayas) of different lengths, with a total of about 80k Arabic words. The words, revealed more than 1,400 years ago, are in *classical Arabic* (CA) (Atwell et al., 2011). It is a phenomenal yet challenging document collection due to its long-chained anaphoric-structures and unstructured topic diversity. A Qur'anic verse may relate to one or more topics, and the same topic may be tackled in different verses and chapters, but in variant contexts.

Extractive question answering (QA) approaches are recently being formulated as machine reading comprehension (MRC) tasks (Chen et al., 2017; Chen, 2018). MRC was initially used (in the 1970s) to evaluate the task of language understanding by computer systems (Chen, 2018). Given a passage of text, a system is evaluated based on its ability to correctly answer a set of questions over the given text. The resurgence of the MRC field (after being dormant for decades) is mainly attributed to the release of relatively large MRC datasets (Rajpurkar et al., 2016; Joshi et al., 2017) that facilitated exploiting and training of intelligent deep learning neural MRC models with better understanding capability. We believe that such MRC intelligence should be harnessed to address the permanent interest in the Holy Qur'an and the information needs of its inquisitors and knowledge seekers (Atwell et al., 2011; Bashir et al., 2021).

To this end, the main goal of the Qur'an QA shared task is to promote state-of-the-art research on Arabic QA and MRC tasks over the Holy Qur'an. At the same time, the main objective is to foster a common experimental test-bed for systems to showcase and benchmark their performance (Malhas and Elsayed, 2020).

To encourage quality participation in the task, we allotted four awards. The first 3 awards were $500, $350, and $250 allotted for the top 3 ranked teams, respectively, given that their papers are accepted. The fourth one was $150 allotted for the best paper.

The Qur'an QA shared task in its first round (2022)[2] has succeeded in attracting thirty teams to sign up for the task. In the final phase, 13 teams participated, with a total of 30 submitted runs on the test set. Ten out of the thirteen teams submitted system description papers.

The paper is organized as follows. In Section 2, we present the task description and briefly discuss its main challenges. Then we present the dataset used in the shared task in Section 3. The evaluation setup and evaluation measures, in addition to the leaderboard developed on Codalab, are described in Section 4. The results are presented in Section 5, which we follow with an overview of the methods and an analysis of some trends and results in Section 6. We conclude with final thoughts in Section 7.

2. Task Description

Our task is defined as follows. Given a Qur'anic passage that consists of consecutive verses in a specific surah of the Holy Qur'an, and a free-text question posed in Modern Standard Arabic (MSA) over that passage, a system is required to extract an answer to that question. The answer must be a *span* of text extracted from the given passage. The question can be a factoid or non-factoid question. Examples are shown in Figure 1 and 2. As the shared task is introduced for the first time, the task this year was relatively simplified such that a system may find *any* correct answer

[1] https://en.wikipedia.org/wiki/Islam_by_country

[2] https://sites.google.com/view/quran-qa-2022

Qur'anic Passage (38:41-44) الفقرة القرآنية
وَٱذْكُرْ عَبْدَنَآ أَيُّوبَ إِذْ نَادَىٰ رَبَّهُۥٓ أَنِّى مَسَّنِىَ ٱلشَّيْطَٰنُ بِنُصْبٍ وَعَذَابٍ. ٱرْكُضْ بِرِجْلِكَ هَٰذَا مُغْتَسَلٌۢ بَارِدٌ وَشَرَابٌ. وَوَهَبْنَا لَهُۥٓ أَهْلَهُۥ وَمِثْلَهُم مَّعَهُمْ رَحْمَةً مِّنَّا وَذِكْرَىٰ لِأُو۟لِى ٱلْأَلْبَٰبِ. وَخُذْ بِيَدِكَ ضِغْثًا فَٱضْرِب بِّهِۦ وَلَا تَحْنَثْ إِنَّا وَجَدْنَٰهُ صَابِرًا نِّعْمَ ٱلْعَبْدُ إِنَّهُۥٓ أَوَّابٌ.
السؤال/ Question: من هو النبي المعروف بالصبر؟
الإجابة الذهبية / Gold Answer:
1. أَيُّوبَ

Figure 1: An example of a factoid question whose answer is a single span of text.

Qur'anic Passage (74:32-48) الفقرة القرآنية
كَلَّا وَٱلْقَمَرِ. وَٱلَّيْلِ إِذْ أَدْبَرَ. وَٱلصُّبْحِ إِذَآ أَسْفَرَ. إِنَّهَا لَإِحْدَى ٱلْكُبَرِ. نَذِيرًا لِّلْبَشَرِ. لِمَن شَآءَ مِنكُمْ أَن يَتَقَدَّمَ أَوْ يَتَأَخَّرَ. كُلُّ نَفْسٍۭ بِمَا كَسَبَتْ رَهِينَةٌ. إِلَّآ أَصْحَٰبَ ٱلْيَمِينِ. فِى جَنَّٰتٍ يَتَسَآءَلُونَ. عَنِ ٱلْمُجْرِمِينَ. مَا سَلَكَكُمْ فِى سَقَرَ. قَالُوا۟ لَمْ نَكُ مِنَ ٱلْمُصَلِّينَ. وَلَمْ نَكُ نُطْعِمُ ٱلْمِسْكِينَ. وَكُنَّا نَخُوضُ مَعَ ٱلْخَآئِضِينَ. وَكُنَّا نُكَذِّبُ بِيَوْمِ ٱلدِّينِ. حَتَّىٰٓ أَتَىٰنَا ٱلْيَقِينُ. فَمَا تَنفَعُهُمْ شَفَٰعَةُ ٱلشَّٰفِعِينَ.
السؤال/ Question: ما هي الدلائل التي تشير بأن الانسان مخير؟
الإجابات الذهبية / Gold Answers:
1. لِمَن شَآءَ مِنكُمْ أَن يَتَقَدَّمَ أَوْ يَتَأَخَّرَ 2. كُلُّ نَفْسٍۭ بِمَا كَسَبَتْ رَهِينَةٌ

Figure 2: An example of a non-factoid question whose answers are two spans of text.

from the accompanying passage, even if the question has more than one answer in the given passage.

The systems of participating teams were required to return up to 5 potential answers, ranked from 1 (top/best) to 5 (lowest), from the accompanying passage for the given question. Therefore, the system is rewarded for returning any of the correct answers as higher as possible in the returned ranked list of answers.

The task is relatively challenging given the challenges of the Qur'an that are posed by its long anaphoric verse structures and unstructured topic diversity. Moreover, the vocabulary mismatch problem (that is typical for any QA or MRC task) is compounded here due to the literary style of the Qur'anic Classical Arabic. Such style would tend to make the answers evidence-based rather than natural language answers, especially for non-factoid questions. For example, answers to evidence questions (Figure 2) or yes/no questions necessitate finding evidence that asserts or negates the question. Such evidence answers are highly likely to include Classical Arabic words that have no overlap with the posed MSA question.

More importantly, the sacredness and unstructured topic diversity of the Qur'an pose a very critical challenge to machine learning (ML) and artificial intelligence (AI) approaches, not to generate results out of their intended context. As such, we should be extra cautious of using the results of learned models without the involvement of Qur'an scholars. (Bashir et al., 2021) discuss the caveats and potential pitfalls in Qur'anic NLP research that we should be wary of.

3. Dataset

The dataset for the task is the Qur'anic Reading Comprehension Dataset (or *QRCD* for short) (Malhas and Elsayed, 2022). It is an extension of the *AyaTEC* dataset (Malhas and Elsayed, 2020). It is composed of 1,093 tuples of question-passage pairs that are coupled with their extracted answers to constitute 1,337 question-passage-answer triplets. It is split into training (65%), development (10%), and test (25%) sets as shown in Table 1. *QRCD* is formatted as a JSON Lines (JSONL) file; each line is a JSON object that comprises a question-passage pair, along with its answers extracted from the accompanying passage.

Each Qur'anic passage in *QRCD* may have more than one occurrence; and each passage occurrence is paired with a different question. Likewise, each question in *QRCD* may have more than one occurrence; and each question occurrence is paired with a different Qur'anic passage. The source of the Qur'anic text in *QRCD* is the Tanzil project,[3] which provides verified versions of the Holy Qur'an in several scripting styles. Although we have chosen the simple-clean text style of Tanzil v1.0.2 for processing, it was later brought to our attention that the Uthmani orthography[4] should be used when quoting and printing Qur'an verses (Al-Azami, 2020).

[3]`https://tanzil.net/download/`

[4]Al-rasm al-Uthmani (or rasm al-mushaf) is the convention adopted for writing the Qur'anic text during the ruling of Caliph Uthman bin Affan (Al-Azami, 2020; Bashir et al., 2021).

Table 1: Distribution of question-passage pairs in QRCD

Dataset	%	# Question-Passage Pairs	#Question-Passage-Answer Triplets
Training	65%	710	861
Development	10%	109	128
Test	25%	274	348
All	100%	1,093	1,337

4. Evaluation Setup

4.1. Evaluation Measures

The task is viewed as a ranking task. Therefore, we used three rank-based evaluation measures, namely, partial Reciprocal Rank (pRR), Exact Match (EM), and $F_1@1$. We choose pRR as the main evaluation measure to give credit to a QA system that may retrieve an answer that is not necessarily at the first rank and/or *partially* (i.e., not exactly) match one of the gold answers (Malhas and Elsayed, 2020). However, EM and $F_1@1$ are applied only to the *top* predicted answer. While EM measure is binary, i.e., gives 1/0 score based on whether or not the top predicted answer *fully* matches the gold answer, $F_1@1$ measure is computed based on the overlap between the top predicted answer and the best matching gold answer (Rajpurkar et al., 2016). To get an overall evaluation score, each of the above measures is averaged over all questions.

To enable public research and allow participants to evaluate their runs, we made the dataset publicly available over the official repository of the shared task.[5] We also shared the following scripts with the teams:

- A reader script, which simply reads the tuples in the QRCD dataset.
- A submission checker script, which verifies the correctness of the run file. The run file should be in JSON format and has a list of passage-question ids along with their respective ranked lists of returned answers.
- An evaluation (scorer) script, which evaluates the run file according to the adopted different evaluation measures.

4.2. Leaderboard and Run Submission

For ease of submission and comparison, we hosted the task on Codalab platform.[6] A participating team is required to write answers to all questions (of the development or the test sets) in one file in a specific format, denoted as a "run file" or a "run" in short. A run typically constitutes the results of a different system or a model. We allow participants to submit up to 30 runs in the development phase, and up to 3 runs only in the test phase. Each team was allowed to submit its runs by its designated team leader only. In both development and test phases, we rank the teams based on their best run. However, teams were encouraged to describe their systems created for this task in their papers.

To give participants a reference point over the leaderboard, we created a simple (and *naïve*) baseline that just answers each question by returning the corresponding full passage as an answer.

5. Results

Thirty teams registered for the task. We received more than 100 submissions in both phases; 30 submissions were for the test phase. Among the 30 teams registered for the task, 13 teams participated in the final (test) phase. Table 2 presents the names of participating teams in the task, their size in terms of number of members, and their affiliations. We noticed a wide diversity in the participating teams. The participants are affiliated with 21 different institutes; all but one are universities. We also note that six of the teams are composed of at least two collaborating institutes.

The pRR score of the best run per team is used to rank the teams. Table 3 shows the evaluation results of the best run of each team ranked by pRR metric. Also, Table 4 illustrates the evaluation results of all submitted runs ranked by pRR metric as well. We underline the rows of the median runs. The top three teams are TF200, TCE, and QQATeam. The highest pRR score is 0.586 and the highest $F_1@1$ is 0.537, and both of them were achieved by TF200. However, the highest EM score is 0.269 which is achieved by TCE.

We noticed that all teams used transformer-based models that support Arabic to build their systems. The top teams used AraBERT and AraElectra in their systems, demonstrating high performance for these models. More details and analysis about the used approaches and their performance are in Section 6.

To see the performance distribution of all submitted runs across different test questions, Figure 3 shows the boxplots for them. It illustrates very diverse performance across the test questions for most of the runs.

6. Methods and Analysis

In this section, we give an overview of the main approaches adopted by the 13 participating teams in their 30 submitted runs on the test set. We do that in the context of highlighting some of our perceptions and general trends that characterize the participating systems and their submitted runs.

[5] https://gitlab.com/bigirqu/quranqa

[6] https://codalab.lisn.upsaclay.fr/competitions/2536

Table 2: Participating teams in Qur'an QA 2022

Team	Size	Affiliations
TF200	2	King Fahd University of Petroleum and Minerals
stars (Wasfey et al., 2022)	4	Tactful AI, Alexandria University, University of central Punja, Al-Azhar.
TCE (ElKomy and Sarhan, 2022)	3	Tanta University
QQATeam (Ahmed et al., 2022)	3	Alaqsa University, The Islamic University of Gaza, Jazan University
eRock (Aftab and Malik, 2022)	2	Punjab University
GOF (Mostafa and Mohamed, 2022)	3	Helwan University
LARSA22 (Mellah et al., 2022)	6	National School of Applied Sciences (ENSAH), Superior School of Technology (Meknes)
Rootroo	2	École Normale Supérieure, University of Helsinki
UM6P	3	Mohammed VI Polytechnic University
DTW (Premasiri et al., 2022)	3	University of Wolverhampton, Hamad Bin Khalifa University
SMASH (Keleg and Magdy, 2022)	2	The University of Edinburgh
LK2022 (Alsaleh et al., 2022)	6	University of Leeds, King Abdulaziz University
niksss (Singh, 2022)	1	Manipal University Jaipur

Table 3: Evaluation results of the best run for each team sorted by pRR

Team	Best Run	pRR	EM	$F_1@1$
TF200	TF200_run03	0.586	0.261	0.537
TCE (ElKomy and Sarhan, 2022)	MatMulMan_rejectAll	0.567	0.269	0.502
QQATeam (Ahmed et al., 2022)	QQATeam_Run02	0.559	0.244	0.513
GOF (Mostafa and Mohamed, 2022)	GOF_run01	0.546	0.239	0.525
stars (Wasfey et al., 2022)	stars_run06	0.528	0.256	0.507
DTW (Premasiri et al., 2022)	DTW_04	0.495	0.227	0.476
LK2022 (Alsaleh et al., 2022)	LK2022_run22	0.445	0.160	0.418
LARSA22 (Mellah et al., 2022)	LARSA22_run02	0.430	0.197	0.399
Rootroo	Rootroo_run03	0.409	0.092	0.364
SMASH (Keleg and Magdy, 2022)	SMASH_run03	0.400	0.151	0.382
eRock (Aftab and Malik, 2022)	eRock_testrun03	0.308	0.088	0.268
UM6P	NLPUM6P_run01	0.249	0.000	0.218
niksss (Singh, 2022)	niksss_run01	0.191	0.042	0.091

Pre-training transformer-based Language models trends. As expected, all of the 30 systems of the submitted runs leveraged variants of pre-trained transformer-based language models (LMs), with the majority using an encoder-only BERT-based model architecture. In contrast, only the LARSA22 team (Mellah et al., 2022) used a multilingual T5 (or mT5) encoder-decoder model architecture (Xue et al., 2021). Although such an architecture intrinsically supports sequence-to-sequence generative rather than extractive QA and MRC tasks, the best performing run for this team attained a pRR score of 0.430, which is very close to the median of all the pRR scores for the 30 runs in Table 4.

Naturally, the Arabic language was the main constituent of the dataset(s) used in pre-training the 30 models, 20 of which were pre-trained using MSA-only resources, and the remaining 10 were pre-trained using either multilingual resources, CA-only resources, or a mix of MSA, CA, and dialectal Arabic (DA) resources. Surprisingly, none of the LMs pre-trained using CA resources (exclusively or partially) have their respective systems/runs achieve pRR scores above the median (0.4375) of all pRR scores in Table 4). In Table 5, we list 2 runs of the SMASH team and two runs of the DTW team that belong to systems whose LMs were pre-trained using CA resources (exclusively as the case for the SMASH runs, and partially as the case of the DTW runs). All the attained scores are below the median. This is counter-indicative given that the Qur'an is in Classical Arabic. We speculate that adopting pre-trained models using CA-only resources or CA-resources combined with DA resources would prohibit or impede chances of transfer learning from

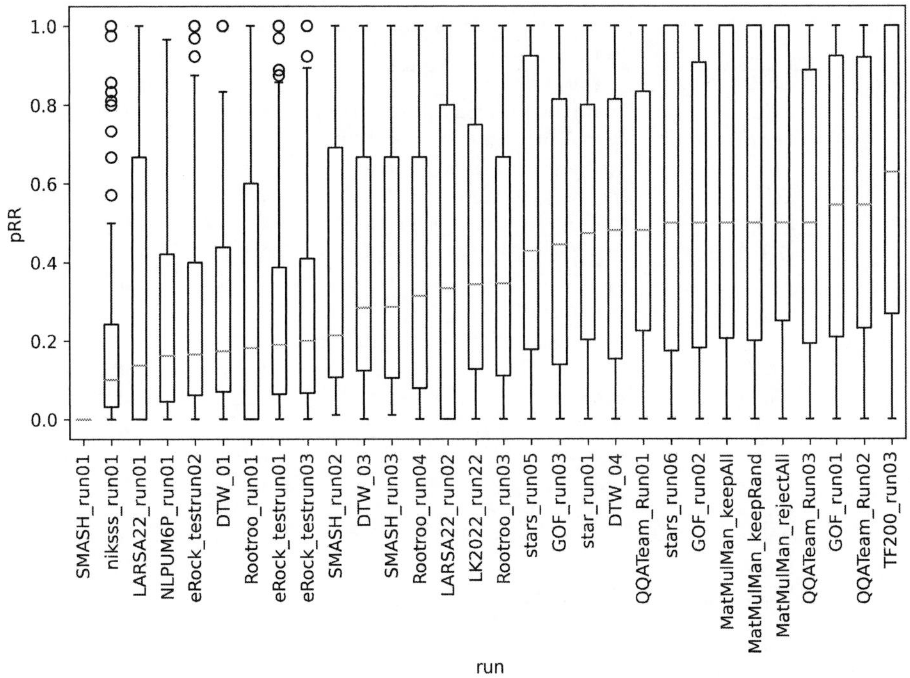

Figure 3: Boxplots for pRR metric for all submitted runs for Qur'an QA 2022 task. The plot illustrates the median and inter-quartile distance across questions.

MSA to CA. Albeit, this is needed given that the questions are in MSA and the answers are in CA.

Interestingly, only three of the 30 systems further pre-trained their language models using CA resources in an attempt to make them a better fit for the Qur'an QA task. The Rootroo team further pre-trained two multilingual BERT (mBERT) models (Devlin et al., 2019) using their crawled large corpus of Islamic and Fatwa websites, in addition to the verses of the Holy Qur'an. Whereas the Stars team (Wasfey et al., 2022) further pre-trained an AraBERT model using only the verses of Qur'an for their relatively least performing run (among their other two runs). This is not expected to make a significant improvement due to the relatively modest size of the Holy Qur'an to be used as the only CA resource in pre-training. Also, the performance of the submitted runs of the Rootroo team remained below the median (0.4375) of pRR scores in (Table 4), which may question the feasibility of further pre-training multilingual rather than monolingual MSA-only pre-trained models. This is a path worth further exploring.

Fine-tuning pre-trained language models trends. With respect to fine-tuning, all the systems used the *QRCD* training dataset in fine-tuning their pre-trained language models, either exclusively or in a pipelined fine-tuning procedure, where other MRC datasets were used in fine-tuning prior to using *QRCD*.

The 10 systems/runs of the following 5 teams only used *QRCD* in fine-tuning: TCE, LK2022, LARSA22, niksss, and SMASH (Table 4). Except for the TCE team (ElKomy and Sarhan, 2022), none of these teams had runs with pRR scores exceeding the median (though LK2022_run22's pRR is almost equal to the median). In contrast, the three runs of the TCE team ranked second, fourth, and fifth, respectively, with respect to their pRR scores. However, the systems of these runs used variant combinations of effective post-processing schemes to improve their predicted answers. The excelling results of these runs may have out shadowed the importance of using large MRC datasets in a pipelined fine-tuning procedure, such as that adopted by the top performing run/system of the TF200 team. The latter team achieved the highest pRR score of **0.586** among all runs (Tables 3 and 4). Their system simply leveraged the MSA-only pre-trained AraELECTRA by Antoun et al. (2021) that was fine-tuned using the Arabic subset of the multilingual TyDiQA dataset (Clark et al., 2020), which they further fine-tuned using the *QRCD* dataset. Similarly, the QQATeam team (Ahmed et al., 2022) adopted a hybrid of the two MSA-only pre-trained AraELECTRA models, namely, AraELECTRA-ArTyDiQA and AraELECTRA-ARCD. The latter model was fine-tuned using the Arabic-SQuAD and the ARCD datasets by Mozannar et al. (2019) prior to fine-tuning using *QRCD*. They also adopted a data augmentation ap-

Table 4: Performance of all submitted runs ranked by pRR metric. Underlined rows are median runs.

Team	**Run**	pRR	EM	$F_1@1$
TF200	TF200_run03	**0.586**	0.261	**0.537**
TCE	MatMulMan_rejectAll	0.567	0.269	0.502
QQATeam	QQATeam_Run02	0.559	0.244	0.513
TCE	MatMulMan_keepAll	0.557	0.269	0.486
TCE	MatMulMan_keepRand	0.548	**0.273**	0.473
GOF	GOF_run01	0.546	0.239	0.525
QQATeam	QQATeam_Run03	0.535	0.231	0.500
Stars	stars_run06	0.528	0.256	0.507
QQATeam	QQATeam_Run01	0.526	0.223	0.462
stars	stars_run05	0.522	0.248	0.497
GOF	GOF_run02	0.521	0.244	0.501
stars	star_run01	0.502	0.181	0.483
DTW	DTW_04	0.495	0.227	0.476
GOF	GOF_run03	0.485	0.210	0.466
LK2022	LK2022_run22	0.445	0.160	0.418
LARSA22	LARSA22_run02	0.430	0.197	0.399
Rootroo	Rootroo_run03	0.409	0.092	0.364
DTW	DTW_03	0.408	0.139	0.390
SMASH	SMASH_run03	0.400	0.151	0.382
Rootroo	Rootroo_run04	0.392	0.113	0.354
SMASH	SMASH_run02	0.380	0.134	0.359
Rootroo	Rootroo_run01	0.323	0.113	0.282
LARSA22	LARSA22_run01	0.323	0.130	0.290
eRock	eRock_testrun03	0.308	0.088	0.268
DTW	DTW_01	0.290	0.084	0.258
eRock	eRock_testrun01	0.287	0.076	0.268
eRock	eRock_testrun02	0.280	0.076	0.246
UM6P	NLPUM6P_run01	0.249	0.000	0.218
niksss	niksss_run01	0.191	0.042	0.091
SMASH	SMASH_run01	0.000	0.000	0.000

Table 5: Runs of teams with language models pre-trained using CA resources exclusively (CAMeLBERT-CA) or partially (CAMeLBERT-Mix). The suffix "Mix" denotes MSA, CA and DA resources.

Team	Runs	Pre-trained Language Model	pRR
SMASH	SMASH_run03	CAMeLBERT-CA	0.400
SMASH	SMASH_run02	CAMeLBERT-CA	0.380
DTW	DTW_03	CAMelBERT-Mix	0.408
DTW	DTW_01	CAMelBERT-Mix	0.290

proach by paraphrasing the questions in *QRCD* to increase its size. The best run for this team ranked third with a pRR score of 0.559 3. Likewise, the GOF team adopted the same pipelined fine-tuning procedure and datasets employed by the QQATeam team, to have their best run rank fourth with a pRR score of 0.546 (Table 3). Mostafa and Mohamed (2022) experimented with two loss functions other than cross-entropy, one of which is a dynamically scaled cross-entropy loss that applies a modulating term to focus the learning process on low confidence examples (hard misclassified) and down-weigh the contribution of the high confidence examples (easy classified).

Among the multilingual MRC datasets that were used in fine-tuning are the MLQA (Lewis et al., 2020) and the XSQuAD (Artetxe et al., 2020) datasets. The Rootroo team fine-tuned their further pre-trained multilingual models (mentioned above) using the latter two datasets, in addition to the English SQuAD dataset. Thus, persisting in their attempts to explore the multilingual path they adopted.

Lastly, we describe the independent attempts by the Stars and the eRock teams to augment the *QRCD* training dataset prior to fine-tuning their respective models. Wasfey et al. (2022) and Aftab and Malik (2022) used the Annotated Corpus of Arabic Al-Qur'an Question and Answer (AQQAC) (Alqahtani and Atwell, 2018). The dataset is composed of 1,224 publicly available

QA pairs (in addition to 1000 unpublished ones) that have natural language answers *generated* from a Tafseer book, with each accompanied by its respective verse-based answer. Both teams were able to select and exploit about 500-740 questions. Questions were selected only if their respective answers could be extracted from the accompanying verse-based answer. For each selected QA pair, a context passage was generated for its verse-based answer from the Qur'an such that it matched the format of the *QRCD* dataset. Using the augmented dataset, the best performing run of the Stars team ranked fifth with a pRR score of 0.528 (well above the median), while the best run for the eRock team was much lower (0.308). The difference in performance could be mainly attributed to eRock's use of only the *QRCD* and the augmented dataset to fine-tune an ArabicBERT model (Safaya et al., 2020), as opposed to an AraBERT model (Antoun et al., 2020) that was fine-tuned using additional MSA MRC datasets (the Arabic SQuAd and ARCD) by the Stars team.

Ensemble Learning Trends. From a machine learning perspective, ensemble learning is regarded as the wisdom of the crowd, where multiple models vote towards a prediction (Sagi and Rokach, 2018). Three teams adopted an ensemble approach, namely, the TCE, Stars, and DTW, with the best performing run of the TCE team ranking second with a score of 0.567 (Table 3). They used an ensemble of three pre-trained language models, namely, AraBERTv0.2-Base and AraBERTv0.2-Large by Antoun et al. (2021) in addition to ARBERT (Abdul-Mageed et al., 2021), to vote for answer span predictions. Interestingly, we note that all three models are MSA-only pre-trained models; and models pre-trained using a mix of DA and MSA were excluded from their final runs. This may suggest (as we speculated above) that using Dialect Arabic may impede effective transfer learning from MSA to CA (though further exploration is needed). Similarly, the Stars team also used an ensemble of MSA-only pre-trained models in the system of their second submitted run, which attained a score of 0.522 (well above the median as shown in Table4).
In contrast, the DTW team adopted a self-ensemble approach to address the limitation of transformer models being prone to random seed initialization that may cause prediction fluctuations. As such, they trained their models using different random seeds and ensembled the prediction results over those models. Although self-ensemble may have marginally degraded their results, they still used it to ensure more stable predictions. Their best-performing run attained a score of 0.495.

7. Conclusion

The resurgence of the machine reading comprehension (MRC) field and the recent advances in intelligent deep learning models have motivated the organization of the first Qur'an Question Answering shared task, Qur'an QA 2022. The task aims at promoting state-of-the-art research on Arabic QA in general and MRC in particular on the Holy Qur'an.
We consider the first year of the shared task a big success, as it attracted 13 teams from 21 different institutes to participate in the final phase, with a total of 30 submitted runs. That clearly shows a relatively strong interest from the research community, despite the narrow domain of the task and its first-ever offering.
We have shed light on the main approaches adopted by the participating teams in the context of highlighting some of our perceptions and general trends of those approaches. All teams leveraged variants of pre-trained transformer-based language models. The majority used AraBERT and AraELECTRA, which were both pre-trained using MSA-only resources. The three top performing teams used AraELECTRA that was fine-tuned using large MRC datasets in MSA prior to fine-tuning using the *QRCD* dataset. We note that the second best team used an ensemble of two MSA-only pre-trained AraBERT models as well as an AraELECTRA model.
Our prospects towards the next version of the Qur'an QA shared task is to entail more challenging tasks that will attract a larger number of participants. A potential task is a QA task that requires systems to return answers from a given Surah or even the entire Qur'an.

8. References

Abdul-Mageed, M., Elmadany, A., et al. (2021). Arbert & marbert: Deep bidirectional transformers for arabic. In *Proceedings of the 59th Annual Meeting of the Association for Computational Linguistics and the 11th International Joint Conference on Natural Language Processing (Volume 1: Long Papers)*, pages 7088–7105.

Aftab, E. and Malik, M. K. (2022). eRock at Qur'an QA 2022: Contemporary Deep Neural Networks for Qur'an based Reading Comprehension Question Answers. In *Proceedings of the 5th Workshop on Open-Source Arabic Corpora and Processing Tools (OSACT5) at the 13th Language Resources and Evaluation Conference (LREC 2022)*.

Ahmed, B. H., Saad, M. K., and Refaee, E. A. (2022). QQATeam at Quran QA 2022: Fine-Tunning Arabic QA Models for Quran QA Task. In *Proceedings of the 5th Workshop on Open-Source Arabic Corpora and Processing Tools (OSACT5) at the 13th Language Resources and Evaluation Conference (LREC 2022)*.

Al-Azami, M. (2020). *The History of the Qur'anic Text from Revelation to Compilation: A Comparative Study with the Old and New Testaments, 2nd ed.* Turath Publishing, UK.

Alqahtani, M. and Atwell, E. (2018). Annotated corpus of Arabic al-quran question and answer.

Alsaleh, A., Althabiti, S., Alshammari, I., Alnefaie, S., Alowaidi, S., Alsaqer, A., Atwell, E., Altahhan, A., and Alsalka, M. A. (2022). LK2022 at Qur'an QA 2022: Simple Transformers Model for Finding Answers to Questions from Qur'an. In *Proceedings of the 5th Workshop on Open-Source Arabic Corpora and Processing Tools (OSACT5) at the 13th Language Resources and Evaluation Conference (LREC 2022)*.

Antoun, W., Baly, F., and Hajj, H. (2020). Arabert: Transformer-based model for arabic language understanding. In *LREC 2020 Workshop Language Resources and Evaluation Conference 11–16 May 2020*, page 9.

Antoun, W., Baly, F., and Hajj, H. (2021). Araelectra: Pre-training text discriminators for arabic language understanding. In *Proceedings of the Sixth Arabic Natural Language Processing Workshop*, pages 191–195. Association for Computational Linguistics.

Artetxe, M., Ruder, S., and Yogatama, D. (2020). On the cross-lingual transferability of monolingual representations. In *Proceedings of the 58th Annual Meeting of the Association for Computational Linguistics*, pages 4623–4637. Association for Computational Linguistics, July.

Atwell, E., Brierley, C., Dukes, K., Sawalha, M., and Sharaf, A.-B. (2011). An artificial intelligence approach to arabic and islamic content on the internet. In *Proceedings of NITS 3rd National Information Technology Symposium*, pages 1–8. Leeds.

Bashir, M. H., M. Azmi, A., Nawaz, H., Zaghouani, W., Diab, M., Al-Fuqaha, A., and Qadir, J. (2021). Arabic natural language processing for qur'anic research: A systematic review. April.

Chen, D., Fisch, A., Weston, J., and Bordes, A. (2017). Reading wikipedia to answer open-domain questions. In *Proceedings of the 55th Annual Meeting of the Association for Computational Linguistics (Volume 1: Long Papers)*, page 1870–1879. Association for Computational Linguistics.

Chen, D. (2018). *Neural Reading Comprehension and Beyond*. Ph.D. thesis, Stanford University.

Clark, J. H., Choi, E., Collins, M., Garrette, D., Kwiatkowski, T., Nikolaev, V., and Palomaki, J. (2020). Tydi qa: A benchmark for information-seeking question answering in typologically diverse languages. *Transactions of the Association for Computational Linguistics*, 8:454–470.

Devlin, J., Chang, M.-W., Lee, K., and Toutanova, K. (2019). Bert: Pre-training of deep bidirectional transformers for language understanding. In *Proceedings of the 2019 Conference of the North American Chapter of the Association for Computational Linguistics: Human Language Technologies, Volume 1 (Long and Short Papers)*, page 4171–4186. Association for Computational Linguistics, June.

ElKomy, M. and Sarhan, A. M. (2022). TCE at Qur'an QA 2022: Arabic Language Question Answering Over Holy Qur'an Using a Post-Processed Ensemble of BERT-based Models. In *Proceedings of the 5th Workshop on Open-Source Arabic Corpora and Processing Tools (OSACT5) at the 13th Language Resources and Evaluation Conference (LREC 2022)*.

Joshi, M., Choi, E., Weld, D., and Zettlemoyer, L. (2017). Triviaqa: A large scale distantly supervised challenge dataset for reading comprehension. In *Proceedings of the 55th Annual Meeting of the Association for Computational Linguistics (Volume 1: Long Papers)*, page 1601–1611. Association for Computational Linguistics.

Keleg, A. and Magdy, W. (2022). Smash at qur'an qa 2022: Creating better faithful data splits for low-resourced question answering scenarios. In *Proceedings of the 5th Workshop on Open-Source Arabic Corpora and Processing Tools (OSACT5) at the 13th Language Resources and Evaluation Conference (LREC 2022)*.

Lewis, P., Oguz, B., Rinott, R., Riedel, S., and Schwenk, H. (2020). MLQA: Evaluating cross-lingual extractive question answering. In *Proceedings of the 58th Annual Meeting of the Association for Computational Linguistics*, pages 7315–7330. Association for Computational Linguistics, July.

Malhas, R. and Elsayed, T. (2020). AyaTEC: Building a Reusable Verse-based Test Collection for Arabic Question Answering on the Holy Qur'an. *ACM Transactions on Asian and Low-Resource Language Information Processing*, 19(6):1–21, Nov.

Malhas, R. and Elsayed, T. (2022). Official Repository of Qur'an QA Shared Task. `https://gitlab.com/bigirqu/quranqa`.

Mellah, Y., Touahri, I., Kaddari, Z., Haja, Z., Berrich, J., and Bouchentouf, T. (2022). LARSA22 at Qur'an QA 2022: Text-to-Text Transformer for Finding Answers to Questions from Qur'an. In *Proceedings of the 5th Workshop on Open-Source Arabic Corpora and Processing Tools (OSACT5) at the 13th Language Resources and Evaluation Conference (LREC 2022)*.

Mostafa, A. and Mohamed, O. (2022). GOF at Qur'an QA 2022: Towards an Efficient Question Answering For The Holy Qu'ran In The Arabic Language Using Deep Learning-Based Approach. In *Proceedings of the 5th Workshop on Open-Source Arabic Corpora and Processing Tools (OSACT5) at the 13th Language Resources and Evaluation Conference (LREC 2022)*.

Mozannar, H., Maamary, E., El Hajal, K., and Hajj, H. (2019). Neural arabic question answering. In *Proceedings of the Fourth Arabic Natural Language Processing Workshop*, page 108–118. Association for Computational Linguistics, Aug.

Premasiri, D., Ranasinghe, T., Zaghouani, W., Mitkov, R., Berrich, J., and Bouchentouf, T. (2022). DTW at Qur'an QA 2022: Utilising Transfer Learning with Transformers for Question Answering in a Low-resource Domain . In *Proceedings of the 5th Work-*

shop on Open-Source Arabic Corpora and Processing Tools (OSACT5) at the 13th Language Resources and Evaluation Conference (LREC 2022).

Rajpurkar, P., Zhang, J., Lopyrev, K., and Liang, P. (2016). Squad: 100, 000+ questions for machine comprehension of text. In *EMNLP*.

Safaya, A., Abdullatif, M., and Yuret, D. (2020). Kuisail at semeval-2020 task 12: Bert-cnn for offensive speech identification in social media. In *Proceedings of the Fourteenth Workshop on Semantic Evaluation*, pages 2054–2059.

Sagi, O. and Rokach, L. (2018). Ensemble learning: A survey. *Wiley Interdisciplinary Reviews: Data Mining and Knowledge Discovery*, 8(4):e1249.

Singh, N. (2022). niksss at Qur'an QA 2022: A Heavily Optimized BERT Based Model for Answering Questions from the Holy Qu'ran. In *Proceedings of the 5th Workshop on Open-Source Arabic Corpora and Processing Tools (OSACT5) at the 13th Language Resources and Evaluation Conference (LREC 2022).*

Wasfey, A., Elrefai, E., Marwa, M., and Haq, N. (2022). Stars at Qur'an QA 2022: Building Automatic Extractive Question Answering Systems for the Holy Qur'an with Transformer Models and Releasing a New Dataset. In *Proceedings of the 5th Workshop on Open-Source Arabic Corpora and Processing Tools (OSACT5) at the 13th Language Resources and Evaluation Conference (LREC 2022).*

Xue, L., Constant, N., Roberts, A., Kale, M., Al-Rfou, R., Siddhant, A., Barua, A., and Raffel, C. (2021). mt5: A massively multilingual pre-trained text-to-text transformer. In *NAACL-HLT*.

Proceedings of the OSACT 2022 Workshop @LREC2022, pages 88–95
Marseille, 20 June 2022

DTW at Qur'an QA 2022: Utilising Transfer Learning with Transformers for Question Answering in a Low-resource Domain

Damith Premasiri[1], Tharindu Ranasinghe[1], Wajdi Zaghouani[2], Ruslan Mitkov[1]
[1]University of Wolverhampton, UK
[2]Hamad Bin Khalifa University, Qatar
{damith.premasiri, tharindu.ranasinghe, r.mitkov}@wlv.ac.uk
wzaghouani@hbku.edu.qa

Abstract

The task of machine reading comprehension (MRC) is a useful benchmark to evaluate the natural language understanding of machines. It has gained popularity in the natural language processing (NLP) field mainly due to the large number of datasets released for many languages. However, the research in MRC has been understudied in several domains, including religious texts. The goal of the Qur'an QA 2022 shared task is to fill this gap by producing state-of-the-art question answering and reading comprehension research on Qur'an. This paper describes the DTW entry to the Quran QA 2022 shared task. Our methodology uses transfer learning to take advantage of available Arabic MRC data. We further improve the results using various ensemble learning strategies. Our approach provided a partial Reciprocal Rank (pRR) score of 0.49 on the test set, proving its strong performance on the task.

Keywords: Machine Reading Comprehension, Transformers, Transfer Learning, Ensemble Learning, Qur'an

1. Introduction

Machine Reading Comprehension (MRC) is a challenging Natural Language Processing (NLP) application (Baradaran et al., 2022). The concept of MRC is similar to how humans are evaluated in examinations where a person should understand the text and answer questions based on the text. Similarly, the goal of a typical MRC task requires a machine to read a set of text passages and then answer questions about the passages. MRC systems could be widely applied in many NLP systems such as search engines and dialogue systems. Therefore, the NLP community has shown a great interest in MRC tasks over recent years.

The most common way of dealing with MRC tasks is to train a machine learning model on an annotated dataset. Over the years, researchers have experimented with different machine learning approaches ranging from traditional algorithms such as support vector machines (Suzuki et al., 2002; Yen et al., 2013) to embedding based neural approaches such as transformers, with the latter providing state-of-the-art results in many datasets. We discuss them thoroughly in Section 2. However, an annotated dataset is an essential requirement for these machine learning models. Identifying this, the NLP community has developed several datasets in recent years. The most popular MRC dataset is the Stanford Question Answering Dataset (SQuAD), which contains more than 100,000 annotated examples (Rajpurkar et al., 2016). SQuAD dataset has been extended to several languages including Arabic (Mozannar et al., 2019), Dutch (Rouws et al., 2022), Persian (Abadani et al., 2021) and Sinhala (Jayakody et al., 2016). However, MRC datasets have been limited to common domains such as Wikipedia and MRC in low-resource domains, including religious books, have not been explored widely by the community (Baradaran et al., 2022). Moreover, most researchers focus on a few popular MRC datasets, while most other MRC datasets are not widely known and studied by the community (Zeng et al., 2020).

Qur'an QA 2022 shared task(Malhas et al., 2022) has been organised to address these gaps in MRC research. The goal of the shared task is to trigger state-of-the-art question answering and reading comprehension research on a book that is sacredly held by more than 1.8 billion people across the world. The shared task relies on a recently released dataset of 1,337 question-passage-answer triplets extracted from the holy Qur'an (Malhas and Elsayed, 2020). Despite the novelty, the dataset poses several challenges. Firstly, since the dataset contains texts from Qur'an, modern embedding models would have problems encoding them. Therefore, we experimented with different pre-processing techniques to handle the texts from Qur'an. Secondly, the dataset is small compared to other MRC datasets such as SQuAD (Rajpurkar et al., 2016), and it would be difficult to fine-tune the state-of-the-art neural models. We experiment with different techniques such as transfer learning and ensemble learning to overcome this. We show that state-of-the-art neural models can be applied in smaller MRC datasets utilising the above methods.

We address two research questions in this paper:

RQ1: Do ensemble models provide better results compared to single models?

RQ2: Can other Arabic MRC resources such as SOQAL (Mozannar et al., 2019) be used to improve the results for Qur'an MRC?

The code of the experiments has been released as an open-source Github project[1]. The project has been released as a Python package[2] and the pre-trained machine learning models are freely available to download in HuggingFace model hub[3]. Furthermore, we have created a docker image of the experiments adhering to the ACL reproducibility criteria[4].

The rest of the paper is structured as follows. Section 2 presents an overview of MRC datasets and machine learning models. Section 3 describes the data we used in the experiments. In Section 4 we explain the experiments carried out. Section 5 discusses the results answering the research questions. Finally, the paper outlines future works and provides conclusions.

2. Related Work

Machine reading comprehension is not newly proposed. The earliest known MRC system dates back to 1977 when (Lehnert, 1977) developed a question answering program called the QUALM. In 1999 (Hirschman et al., 1999) constructed a reading comprehension system exploiting a corpus of 60 development and 60 test stories of 3rd to 6th-grade material. Due to the lack of high-quality MRC datasets and the poor performance of MRC models, this research field was understudied until the early 2010s. However, with the creation of large MRC datasets and with the success of word embedding based neural models in the NLP field, research in MRC has been popular in recent years. We present the related work in MRC in two broad categories; datasets and models.

Datasets In 2013, (Richardson et al., 2013) created the MCTest dataset which contained 500 stories and 2000 questions. This dataset can be considered the first big MRC dataset. A breakthrough in MRC was achieved in 2015 when (Hermann et al., 2015) defined a new dataset generation method that provides large-scale supervised reading comprehension datasets. This was followed by the creation of large scale MRC datasets such as SQuAD(Rajpurkar et al., 2016). Later the SQuAD dataset has been expanded to many languages including Arabic (Mozannar et al., 2019), Dutch (Rouws et al., 2022), French (d'Hoffschmidt et al., 2020) and Russian (Efimov et al., 2020). Furthermore, SQuAD has been extended to low-resource languages such as Persian (Abadani et al., 2021) and Sinhala (Jayakody et al., 2016) proving that SQuAD has been an important benchmark in MRC research. MRC datasets have been compiled on different domains such as news (Trischler et al., 2017), publications (Dasigi et al., 2021) and natural sciences (Welbl et al., 2017). As far as we know, Qur'an Reading Comprehension Dataset used in this shared task is the first dataset created on religious texts (Malhas and Elsayed, 2020).

Methods Most MRC systems in the early 2000s were rule-based or statistical models (Riloff and Thelen, 2000; Charniak et al., 2000). These models do not provide good results compared to the neural methods introduced in recent years (Baradaran et al., 2022). (Hermann et al., 2015) developed a class of attention based deep neural networks that learn to read real documents and answer complex questions with minimal prior knowledge of language structure. Since 2015, with the emergence of various large scale, supervised datasets, neural network models have shown state-of-the-art results in MRC tasks. The recently introduced transformer models such as BERT (Devlin et al., 2019) have already exceeded human performance over the related MRC benchmark datasets (Zeng et al., 2020). A critical contribution of the SQuAD benchmark is that it provides a system to submit the MRC models and a leaderboard to display the top results[5]. This has enabled the NLP community to keep track of the state-of-the-art MRC systems. Other languages have also followed this approach[6]. However, the NLP community has focused mainly on improving system performance on popular benchmarks such as SQuAD and has not focused on improving results on benchmarks with limited coverage, which we address in this research paper.

3. Data

MRC tasks are usually divided into four categories: cloze style, multiple-choice, span prediction, and free form (Liu et al., 2019). The Qur'an QA 2022 shared task[7] belongs to the span prediction category where the MRC system needs to select the correct beginning and end of the answer text from the context. The event organisers provided the QRCD (Quran Reading Comprehension Dataset), which contained 1,093 tuples of question-passage pairs that are coupled with their extracted answers to constitute 1,337 question-passage-answer triplets. QRCD is a JSON Lines (JSONL) file; each line is a JSON object that comprises a question-passage pair and its answers extracted from the accompanying passage. Figure 1 shows a sample training tu-

[1]The Github project is available on https://github.com/DamithDR/QuestionAnswering

[2]The Python package is available on https://pypi.org/project/quesans/

[3]The pre-trained models are available on https://huggingface.co/Damith/AraELECTRA-discriminator-SOQAL and https://huggingface.co/Damith/AraELECTRA-discriminator-QuranQA

[4]The docker image is available on https://hub.docker.com/r/damithpremasiri/question-answering-quran

[5]SQuAD leaderboard is available on https://rajpurkar.github.io/SQuAD-explorer/

[6]Korean MRC leaderboard is available on https://korquad.github.io/

[7]More information on the Qur'an QA 2022 shared task is available on https://sites.google.com/view/quran-qa-2022/

ple. The distribution of the dataset into training, development and test sets is shown in Table 1.

```
{
  "pq_id": "33:60-62_400",
  "passage": "لئن لم ينته المنافقون والذين في قلوبهم مرض
    والمرجفون في المدينة لنغرينك بهم ثم لا يجاورونك فيها إلا
    قليلا. ملعونين أينما ثقفوا أخذوا وقتلوا تقتيلا. سنة الله
    في الذين خلوا من قبل ولن تجد لسنة الله تبديلا.",
  "surah": 33,
  "verses": "60-62",
  "question": "متى يحل الإسلام دم الشخص؟",
  "answers": [
    {
      "text": "لئن لم ينته المنافقون والذين في قلوبهم مرض
        والمرجفون في المدينة لنغرينك بهم",
      "start_char": 0
    }
  ]
}
```

Figure 1: Sample Json object from the QRCD dataset (Malhas and Elsayed, 2020)

Dataset	%	Q-P Pairs	Q-P-A Triplets
Training	65%	710	861
Development	10%	109	128
Test	25%	274	348
All	100%	1,093	1,337

Table 1: Shared Task Data Composition. Column Q-P Pairs shows the number of Question Passage pairs, Column Q-P-A Triplets shows the number of Question Passage Answer triplets in the dataset

SOQAL contains two Arabic MRC datasets; Arabic Reading Comprehension Dataset (ARCD) (Mozannar et al., 2019), composed of 1,395 questions posed by crowdworkers on Wikipedia articles, and a machine translation of the SQuAD (Mozannar et al., 2019) containing 48,344 questions. SQuAD is widely used as the standard dataset in English MRC tasks, therefore using the machine translation of the same dataset will be helpful for the learning process. Compared to QRCD, SOQAL is a large dataset and both of these datasets belong to the span prediction MRC category. Therefore, they can be used to perform transfer learning which we describe in Section 4.

4. Methodology

With the introduction of BERT (Devlin et al., 2019), transformer models have achieved state-of-the-art results in different NLP applications such as text classification (Ranasinghe and Hettiarachchi, 2020), information extraction (Plum et al., 2022) and event detection (Giorgi et al., 2021). Furthermore, the transformer architectures have shown promising results in SQuAD dataset (Zhang et al., 2021; Zhang et al., 2020; Yamada et al., 2020; Lan et al., 2020). In view of this, we use transformers as the basis of our methodology. Transformer architectures have been trained on general tasks like language modelling and then can be fine-tuned for MRC tasks. (Devlin et al., 2019). For the MRC task, transformer models take an input of a single sequence that contains the question and paragraph separated by a [SEP] token. Then the model introduces a start vector and an end vector. The probability of each word being the start-word is calculated by taking a dot product between the final embedding of the word and the start vector, followed by a softmax over all the words. The word with the highest probability value is considered. The architecture of transformer-based MRC model is shown in Figure 2.

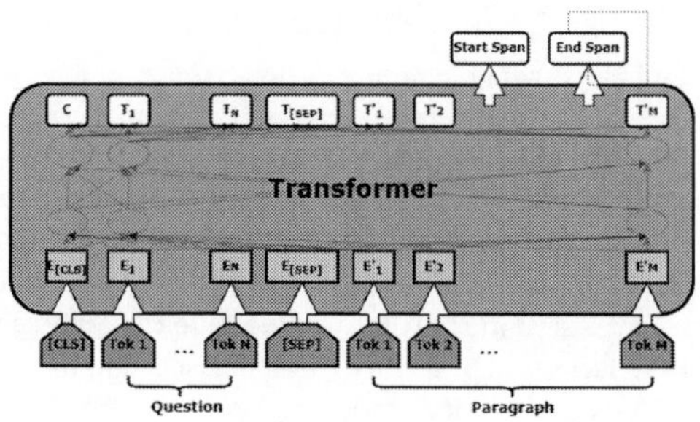

Figure 2: Transformer Architecture for MRC

We experimented with seven popular pre-trained transformer models that supports Arabic; camelbert-mix (Inoue et al., 2021), camelbert-ca (Inoue et al., 2021), mbert-cased (Devlin et al., 2019) , mbert-uncased (Devlin et al., 2019), AraELECTRA-generator (Antoun et al., 2021), AraELECTRA-discriminator (Antoun et al., 2021) and AraBERTv2 (Antoun et al., 2020). These models are available in HuggingFace model hub (Wolf et al., 2020). For all the experiments we used a batch-size of eight, Adam optimiser with learning rate 2e−5, and a linear learning rate warm-up over 10% of the training data. During the training process, the parameters of the transformer model, as well as the parameters of the subsequent layers, were updated. The models were trained using only training data. All the models were trained for five epochs. For some of the experiments, we used an Nvidia GeForce RTX 2070 GPU, whilst for others we used a GeForce RTX 3090 GPU. This was purely based on the availability of the hardware and it was not a methodological decision.
We further used following fine-tuning strategies to improve the performance.

4.1. Ensemble Learning

Ensemble learning is a popular technique in machine learning, where different machine learning models contribute to a single solution. As different machine learning algorithms tend to learn differently, the final predictions each one of them provides can be slightly different. However, they have the potential to contribute to the final output with ensemble learning. Usually,

ensemble learning provides better results compared to single models (Sagi and Rokach, 2018).
Transformer models that we used as the base model are prone to the random seed (Hettiarachchi and Ranasinghe, 2020). The same architecture can provide different results for different random seeds (Uyangodage et al., 2021). To avoid the impact of this, we performed self ensemble. We trained the same architecture using five different random seeds and ensembled the output files using Algorithm 1.

Algorithm 1 Ensemble Learning Algorithm for MRC

$R \leftarrow$ *all results files*
$r_i \leftarrow$ *i(th) result file*
$Q \leftarrow$ *all questions*
$q_j \leftarrow$ *j(th) question*
$A \leftarrow$ *all answers*
$a_{i,j} \leftarrow$ *answer for question j in files file i*
$a_j \leftarrow$ *all unique answers for question j in all files*
$a_{j,k} \leftarrow$ *answer k from unique answers for question j*
$a_{i,j,m} \leftarrow$ *answer m from file i to question j*
$answer_{j,k} \leftarrow$ *temporary score*
repeat
  for each $a_{j,k} \in a_j$ **do**
    repeat
      for each $a_{i,j,m} \in r_i$ **do**
        if $a_{i,j,m} = a_{j,k}$ **then**
          $score_{j,k} \leftarrow average(score_{a_{i,j,m}}, score_{a_{j,k}})$
          $answer_{j,k} \leftarrow a_{j,k}, score_{j,k}$
        end if
      end for
    until *all items iterated in R*
    final_answers $\leftarrow answer_{j,k}$
  end for
until *all unique answers iterated in for question j*
answers $\leftarrow$ **sort(answers)**
repeat
  for each $q_j \in Q$ **do**
    repeat
      for each $answer_{j,k} \in final_answers$ **do**
        $rank_{j,k} \leftarrow$ *assign rank*
      end for
    until *iterate all answers for question j*
  end for
until *iterate all questions iterated in Q*

4.2. Transfer Learning

One limitation of the QRCD dataset is that training set only contains 710 annotated QnA pairs and as a result transformer models would find it difficult to properly fine-tune their weights in the training process. A common practice to overcome this is to utilise transfer learning. The main idea of transfer learning is that we train a machine learning model on a resource rich setting, save the weights of the model and when we initialise the training process for a lower resource setting, start with the saved weights from the resource rich setting . Transfer learning has improved results for many NLP tasks such as offensive language identification (Ranasinghe and Zampieri, 2020), machine translation (Nguyen and Chiang, 2017) and named entity recognition (Lee et al., 2018).
For this task, we first trained a transformer-based MRC model on SOQAL dataset which contained more training data compared to the QRCD dataset as mentioned in Section 3. Then when we started the training for QRCD dataset we started from the saved weights from the SOQAL dataset.

5. Results and Discussion

In this section, we report the experiments we conducted and their results. As advised by the task organisers, we used partial Reciprocal Rank (pRR) score to measure the model performance. It is a variant of the traditional Reciprocal Rank evaluation metric that considers partial matching. We also report Exact Match (EM), and F1@1 in the results tables, which are evaluation metrics applied only to the top predicted answer. The EM metric is a binary measure that rewards a system only if the top predicted answer matches exactly one of the gold answers. In comparison, the F1@1 metric measures the token overlap between the top predicted answer and the best matching gold answer. The reported results are for the dev set.
As can be seen in Table 2, camelbert-mix model produced the best results with 0.549 pRR value. This was closely followed by camelbert-ca and AraELECTRA-discriminator. Transformer models built specifically for Arabic generally outperformed multilingual models.

Model	pRR	EM	F1@1
AraELECTRA-discriminator	**0.516**	0.303	0.495
AraELECTRA-generator	0.355	0.339	0.324
camelbert-mix	**0.549**	0.193	0.529
camelbert-ca	**0.535**	0.119	0.516
mbert-cased	0.425	0.321	0.405
mbert-uncased	0.440	0.220	0.424
AraBERTv2	0.501	0.294	0.472

Table 2: Results of different transformer models without ensemble learning or transfer-learning. Column **pRR** shows the partial Reciprocal Rank score, Column **EM** shows results for exact match and Column **F1@1** shows F1@1 score. The top three results are highlighted in Bold.

To answer our **RQ1**, we performed self ensemble learning. Table 3 shows the results of different models with results ensemble. Even though there was a slight improvement in AraELECTRA-discriminator, the overall impact for the results from the ensemble was very low. And we noticed that some of the models had performed less when using ensemble. However, the results were stable compared to the single models. Therefore, we used self ensemble learning even though it did not contribute to improving the results. With these findings, we answer our **RQ1**, ensemble models do not provide better results compared to single models; however, they provide more consistent results.

Model	pRR	EM	F1@1
AraELECTRA-discriminator	**0.528**	0.321	0.500
AraELECTRA-generator	0.364	0.128	0.335
camelbert-mix	**0.520**	0.303	0.497
camelbert-ca	**0.495**	0.239	0.467
mbert-cased	0.438	0.220	0.417
mbert-uncased	0.424	0.220	0.399
AraBERTv2	0.475	0.239	0.436

Table 3: Results of different transformer models with self ensemble learning. Column **pRR** shows the partial Reciprocal Rank score, Column **EM** shows results for exact match and Column **F1@1** shows F1@1 score. The top three results are highlighted in Bold.

To answer our **RQ2**, we performed transfer learning from SOQAL (Mozannar et al., 2019) to QRCD dataset as mentioned in Section 4. We only conducted the experiments for the best model from the self ensemble setting. As can be seen in the results in Table 4, transfer learning improved the results for AraELECTRA-discriminator. Without transfer learning, AraELECTRA-discriminator scored only 0.528 pRR, while with transfer learning, it provided 0.616 pRR. We did not observe improvements in other transformer models. However, the 0.616 pRR we got with performing transfer learning with AraELECTRA-discriminator was the best result for the dev set. With this, we answer our **RQ2**, other Arabic MRC resources such as SOQAL (Mozannar et al., 2019) can be used to improve the results for Qur'an MRC. We believe that this finding will be important to the researchers working on low-resource MRC datasets.

Model	pRR	EM	F1@1
AraELECTRA-discriminator	0.616	0.394	0.609
camelbert-mix	0.520	0.284	0.494
AraBERTv2	0.430	0.138	0.412

Table 4: Results of different transformer models after transfer learning. Column **pRR** shows the partial Reciprocal Rank score, Column **EM** shows results for exact match and Column **F1@1** shows F1@1 score.

Based on the results of the dev set, we selected three models for the final submission; camelbert-mix with ensemble learning but without transfer learning, camelbert-mix with transfer learning and ensemble learning and AraELECTRA-discriminator with transfer learning and ensemble learning. Table 5 shows the results that the organisers provided on the test set for our submitted models.

AraELECTRA-discriminator performed best in the test set too. The camelbert-mix mode without transfer

Model	TL	EN	pRR	EM	F1@1
camelbert-mix	✗	✓	0.290	0.084	0.258
camelbert-mix	✓	✓	0.408	0.138	0.390
AraELECTRA-discriminator	✓	✓	**0.495**	0.226	0.476

Table 5: Results of different transformer models on the test set. Column **TL** implies whether we performed transfer learning or not and the Column **EN** shows whether we performed ensemble learning. Column **pRR** shows the partial Reciprocal Rank score, Column **EM** shows results for exact match and Column **F1@1** shows F1@1 score.

learning has decreased its performance from 0.549 to 0.290, which is a 47% decrease. However, the models with transfer learning have performed comparatively high, confirming our answer to the **RQ2**.

6. Conclusion

In this paper, we have presented the system submitted by the DTW team to the Qur'an QA 2022 shared task in the 5th Workshop on Open-Source Arabic Corpora and Processing Tools. We have shown that AraELECTRA-discriminator with transfer learning from an Arabic MRC dataset is the most successful transformer model from several transformer models we experimented with. Our best system scored 0.495 pRR in the test set. With our **RQ1**, we showed that transformer models based on self ensemble provided stable results than single models in Qur'an QA task. Revisiting our **RQ2**, we showed that transfer learning could be used to improve the MRC results of the Qur'an. We believe that this finding would pave the way to enhance MRC in many low-resource domains. Our code, software and the pre-trained models have been made available freely to the researchers working on similar problems.

In future work, we would like to explore more to transfer learning. We will be exploring cross-lingual transfer learning with larger English MRC datasets such as SQuAD, as cross-lingual transfer learning has shown splendid results in many NLP tasks (Ranasinghe et al., 2021). Furthermore we will be exploring zero-shot and few-shot learning, which could benefit a multitude of low-resource languages.

7. Acknowledgements

This project was partially funded by the University of Wolverhampton's RIF4 Research Investment Funding provided for the Responsible Digital Humanities lab (RIGHT).

We would like to thank the Qur'an QA 2022 shared task organisers for running this interesting shared task and for replying promptly to all our inquiries. Furthermore, we thank the anonymous OSACT 2022 reviewers for their insightful feedback.

8. References

Abadani, N., Mozafari, J., Fatemi, A., Nematbakhsh, M. A., and Kazemi, A. (2021). Parsquad: Machine translated squad dataset for persian question answering. In *2021 7th International Conference on Web Research (ICWR)*, pages 163–168.

Antoun, W., Baly, F., and Hajj, H. (2020). AraBERT: Transformer-based model for Arabic language understanding. In *Proceedings of the 4th Workshop on Open-Source Arabic Corpora and Processing Tools, with a Shared Task on Offensive Language Detection*, pages 9–15, Marseille, France, May. European Language Resource Association.

Antoun, W., Baly, F., and Hajj, H. (2021). AraELECTRA: Pre-training text discriminators for Arabic language understanding. In *Proceedings of the Sixth Arabic Natural Language Processing Workshop*, pages 191–195, Kyiv, Ukraine (Virtual), April. Association for Computational Linguistics.

Baradaran, R., Ghiasi, R., and Amirkhani, H. (2022). A survey on machine reading comprehension systems. *Natural Language Engineering*, page 1–50.

Charniak, E., Altun, Y., Braz, R. d. S., Garrett, B., Kosmala, M., Moscovich, T., Pang, L., Pyo, C., Sun, Y., Wy, W., Yang, Z., Zeller, S., and Zorn, L. (2000). Reading comprehension programs in a statistical-language-processing class. In *Proceedings of the 2000 ANLP/NAACL Workshop on Reading Comprehension Tests as Evaluation for Computer-Based Language Understanding Sytems - Volume 6*, ANLP/NAACL-ReadingComp '00, page 1–5, USA. Association for Computational Linguistics.

Dasigi, P., Lo, K., Beltagy, I., Cohan, A., Smith, N. A., and Gardner, M. (2021). A dataset of information-seeking questions and answers anchored in research papers. In *Proceedings of the 2021 Conference of the North American Chapter of the Association for Computational Linguistics: Human Language Technologies*, pages 4599–4610, Online, June. Association for Computational Linguistics.

Devlin, J., Chang, M.-W., Lee, K., and Toutanova, K. (2019). BERT: Pre-training of deep bidirectional transformers for language understanding. In *Proceedings of the 2019 Conference of the North American Chapter of the Association for Computational Linguistics: Human Language Technologies, Volume 1 (Long and Short Papers)*, pages 4171–4186, Minneapolis, Minnesota, June. Association for Computational Linguistics.

d'Hoffschmidt, M., Belblidia, W., Heinrich, Q., Brendlé, T., and Vidal, M. (2020). FQuAD: French question answering dataset. In *Findings of the Association for Computational Linguistics: EMNLP 2020*, pages 1193–1208, Online, November. Association for Computational Linguistics.

Efimov, P., Chertok, A., Boytsov, L., and Braslavski, P. (2020). Sberquad – russian reading comprehension dataset: Description and analysis. In Avi Arampatzis, et al., editors, *Experimental IR Meets Multilinguality, Multimodality, and Interaction*, pages 3–15, Cham. Springer International Publishing.

Giorgi, S., Zavarella, V., Tanev, H., Stefanovitch, N., Hwang, S., Hettiarachchi, H., Ranasinghe, T., Kalyan, V., Tan, P., Tan, S., Andrews, M., Hu, T., Stoehr, N., Re, F. I., Vegh, D., Atzenhofer, D., Curtis, B., and Hürriyetoğlu, A. (2021). Discovering black lives matter events in the United States: Shared task 3, CASE 2021. In *Proceedings of the 4th Workshop on Challenges and Applications of Automated Extraction of Socio-political Events from Text (CASE 2021)*, pages 218–227, Online, August. Association for Computational Linguistics.

Hermann, K. M., Kocisky, T., Grefenstette, E., Espeholt, L., Kay, W., Suleyman, M., and Blunsom, P. (2015). Teaching machines to read and comprehend. In C. Cortes, et al., editors, *Advances in Neural Information Processing Systems*, volume 28. Curran Associates, Inc.

Hettiarachchi, H. and Ranasinghe, T. (2020). InfoMiner at WNUT-2020 task 2: Transformer-based covid-19 informative tweet extraction. In *Proceedings of the Sixth Workshop on Noisy User-generated Text (W-NUT 2020)*, pages 359–365, Online, November. Association for Computational Linguistics.

Hirschman, L., Light, M., Breck, E., and Burger, J. D. (1999). Deep read: A reading comprehension system. ACL '99, page 325–332, USA. Association for Computational Linguistics.

Inoue, G., Alhafni, B., Baimukan, N., Bouamor, H., and Habash, N. (2021). The interplay of variant, size, and task type in Arabic pre-trained language models. In *Proceedings of the Sixth Arabic Natural Language Processing Workshop*, pages 92–104, Kyiv, Ukraine (Virtual), April. Association for Computational Linguistics.

Jayakody, J. A. T. K., Gamlath, T. S. K., Lasantha, W. A. N., Premachandra, K. M. K. P., Nugaliyadde, A., and Mallawarachchi, Y. (2016). "mahoshadha", the sinhala tagged corpus based question answering system. In Suresh Chandra Satapathy et al., editors, *Proceedings of First International Conference on Information and Communication Technology for Intelligent Systems: Volume 1*, pages 313–322, Cham. Springer International Publishing.

Lan, Z., Chen, M., Goodman, S., Gimpel, K., Sharma, P., and Soricut, R. (2020). Albert: A lite bert for self-supervised learning of language representations. In *International Conference on Learning Representations*.

Lee, J. Y., Dernoncourt, F., and Szolovits, P. (2018). Transfer learning for named-entity recognition with neural networks. In *Proceedings of the Eleventh International Conference on Language Resources and Evaluation (LREC 2018)*, Miyazaki, Japan, May.

European Language Resources Association (ELRA).

Lehnert, W. G. (1977). *The process of question answering*. Yale University.

Liu, S., Zhang, X., Zhang, S., Wang, H., and Zhang, W. (2019). Neural machine reading comprehension: Methods and trends. *Applied Sciences*, 9(18).

Malhas, R. and Elsayed, T. (2020). Ayatec: Building a reusable verse-based test collection for arabic question answering on the holy qur'an. *ACM Trans. Asian Low-Resour. Lang. Inf. Process.*, 19(6), oct.

Malhas, R., Mansour, W., and Elsayed, T. (2022). Qur'an QA 2022: Overview of the first shared task on question answering over the holy qur'an. In *Proceedings of the 5th Workshop on Open-Source Arabic Corpora and Processing Tools (OSACT5) at the 13th Language Resources and Evaluation Conference (LREC 2022)*.

Mozannar, H., Maamary, E., El Hajal, K., and Hajj, H. (2019). Neural Arabic question answering. In *Proceedings of the Fourth Arabic Natural Language Processing Workshop*, pages 108–118, Florence, Italy, August. Association for Computational Linguistics.

Nguyen, T. Q. and Chiang, D. (2017). Transfer learning across low-resource, related languages for neural machine translation. In *Proceedings of the Eighth International Joint Conference on Natural Language Processing (Volume 2: Short Papers)*, pages 296–301, Taipei, Taiwan, November. Asian Federation of Natural Language Processing.

Plum, A., Ranasinghe, T., Jones, S., Orasan, C., and Mitkov, R. (2022). Biographical: A semi-supervised relation extraction dataset. In *Proceedings of the 45th International ACM SIGIR Conference on Research and Development in Information Retrieval*, Madrid, Spain. Association for Computing Machinery.

Rajpurkar, P., Zhang, J., Lopyrev, K., and Liang, P. (2016). SQuAD: 100,000+ questions for machine comprehension of text. In *Proceedings of the 2016 Conference on Empirical Methods in Natural Language Processing*, pages 2383–2392, Austin, Texas, November. Association for Computational Linguistics.

Ranasinghe, T. and Hettiarachchi, H. (2020). BRUMS at SemEval-2020 task 12: Transformer based multilingual offensive language identification in social media. In *Proceedings of the Fourteenth Workshop on Semantic Evaluation*, pages 1906–1915, Barcelona (online), December. International Committee for Computational Linguistics.

Ranasinghe, T. and Zampieri, M. (2020). Multilingual offensive language identification with cross-lingual embeddings. In *Proceedings of the 2020 Conference on Empirical Methods in Natural Language Processing (EMNLP)*, pages 5838–5844, Online, November. Association for Computational Linguistics.

Ranasinghe, T., Orasan, C., and Mitkov, R. (2021). An exploratory analysis of multilingual word-level quality estimation with cross-lingual transformers. In *Proceedings of the 59th Annual Meeting of the Association for Computational Linguistics and the 11th International Joint Conference on Natural Language Processing (Volume 2: Short Papers)*, pages 434–440, Online, August. Association for Computational Linguistics.

Richardson, M., Burges, C. J., and Renshaw, E. (2013). MCTest: A challenge dataset for the open-domain machine comprehension of text. In *Proceedings of the 2013 Conference on Empirical Methods in Natural Language Processing*, pages 193–203, Seattle, Washington, USA, October. Association for Computational Linguistics.

Riloff, E. and Thelen, M. (2000). A rule-based question answering system for reading comprehension tests. In *Proceedings of the 2000 ANLP/-NAACL Workshop on Reading Comprehension Tests as Evaluation for Computer-Based Language Understanding Sytems - Volume 6*, ANLP/NAACL-ReadingComp '00, page 13–19, USA. Association for Computational Linguistics.

Rouws, N. J., Vakulenko, S., and Katrenko, S. (2022). Dutch squad and ensemble learning for question answering from labour agreements. In Luis A. Leiva, et al., editors, *Artificial Intelligence and Machine Learning*, pages 155–169, Cham. Springer International Publishing.

Sagi, O. and Rokach, L. (2018). Ensemble learning: A survey. *WIREs Data Mining and Knowledge Discovery*, 8(4):e1249.

Suzuki, J., Sasaki, Y., and Maeda, E. (2002). SVM answer selection for open-domain question answering. In *COLING 2002: The 19th International Conference on Computational Linguistics*.

Trischler, A., Wang, T., Yuan, X., Harris, J., Sordoni, A., Bachman, P., and Suleman, K. (2017). NewsQA: A machine comprehension dataset. In *Proceedings of the 2nd Workshop on Representation Learning for NLP*, pages 191–200, Vancouver, Canada, August. Association for Computational Linguistics.

Uyangodage, L., Ranasinghe, T., and Hettiarachchi, H. (2021). Transformers to fight the COVID-19 infodemic. In *Proceedings of the Fourth Workshop on NLP for Internet Freedom: Censorship, Disinformation, and Propaganda*, pages 130–135, Online, June. Association for Computational Linguistics.

Welbl, J., Liu, N. F., and Gardner, M. (2017). Crowdsourcing multiple choice science questions. In *Proceedings of the 3rd Workshop on Noisy User-generated Text*, pages 94–106, Copenhagen, Denmark, September. Association for Computational Linguistics.

Wolf, T., Debut, L., Sanh, V., Chaumond, J., Delangue, C., Moi, A., Cistac, P., Rault, T., Louf, R., Funtowicz, M., Davison, J., Shleifer, S., von Platen, P., Ma,

C., Jernite, Y., Plu, J., Xu, C., Le Scao, T., Gugger, S., Drame, M., Lhoest, Q., and Rush, A. (2020). Transformers: State-of-the-art natural language processing. In *Proceedings of the 2020 Conference on Empirical Methods in Natural Language Processing: System Demonstrations*, pages 38–45, Online, October. Association for Computational Linguistics.

Yamada, I., Asai, A., Shindo, H., Takeda, H., and Matsumoto, Y. (2020). LUKE: Deep contextualized entity representations with entity-aware self-attention. In *Proceedings of the 2020 Conference on Empirical Methods in Natural Language Processing (EMNLP)*, pages 6442–6454, Online, November. Association for Computational Linguistics.

Yen, S.-J., Wu, Y.-C., Yang, J.-C., Lee, Y.-S., Lee, C.-J., and Liu, J.-J. (2013). A support vector machine-based context-ranking model for question answering. *Information Sciences*, 224:77–87.

Zeng, C., Li, S., Li, Q., Hu, J., and Hu, J. (2020). A survey on machine reading comprehension—tasks, evaluation metrics and benchmark datasets. *Applied Sciences*, 10(21).

Zhang, Z., Wu, Y., Zhou, J., Duan, S., Zhao, H., and Wang, R. (2020). Sg-net: Syntax-guided machine reading comprehension. *Proceedings of the AAAI Conference on Artificial Intelligence*, 34(05):9636–9643, Apr.

Zhang, Z., Yang, J., and Zhao, H. (2021). Retrospective reader for machine reading comprehension. *Proceedings of the AAAI Conference on Artificial Intelligence*, 35(16):14506–14514, May.

Proceedings of the OSACT 2022 Workshop @LREC2022, pages 96–103
Marseille, 20 June 2022

eRock at Qur'an QA 2022: Contemporary Deep Neural Networks for Qur'an based Reading Comprehension Question Answers

Esha Aftab, Muhammad Kamran Malik
Department of Computer Science, Department of Information Technology
Faculty of Computing and Information Technology, University of the Punjab, Lahore, Pakistan
esha.aftab@pucit.edu.pk, kamran.malik@pucit.edu.pk

Abstract

Question Answering (QA) has enticed the interest of NLP community in recent years. NLP enthusiasts are engineering new Models and fine-tuning the existing ones that can give out answers for the posed questions. The deep neural network models are found to perform exceptionally on QA tasks, but these models are also data intensive. For instance, BERT has outperformed many of its contemporary contenders on SQuAD dataset. In this work, we attempt at solving the closed domain reading comprehension Question Answering task on QRCD (Qur'anic Reading Comprehension Dataset) to extract an answer span from the provided passage, using BERT as a baseline model. We improved the model's output by applying regularization techniques like weight-decay and data augmentation. Using different strategies we had 59% and 31% partial Reciprocal Ranking (pRR) on development and testing data splits respectively.

1. Introduction

Question Answering (QA) is a longstanding task in Natural Language Processing that aims at providing a reliable, precise and well-formed natural language answer to a meaningful question from a given text body. The resurgence of Question Answering as an appealing problem in recent years, can be mainly attributed to the following factors; a) efficient Information Retrieval (IR) systems; b) neural Reading Comprehension (RC) models; c) availability of large scale annotated datasets. Another aspect that makes the QA task worth the effort is its wide range of potential applications. Some of the thriving and far reaching utilities are in personal assistant apps and chat bots to respond frequently asked questions in real time. Google Assistant [1] and FAQ Bot [2] are a few examples of such systems.

With ever increasing online resources and a large number of users looking for reliable and exact answers to their queries, it is a pressing need of time for modern search engines to employ intelligent automated QA models. It will expedite the process of examining the massive amount of data from web or local repositories and fetch rational and relevant responses to queries with higher degree of precision.

In classic search engines, the information retrieval systems extract keywords from a query and look them up by crawling through web documents to find similar resources. The algorithms like TF-IDF and BM25 are used to determine keyword frequency in crawled web documents and rank them with respect to their relevance to the query, respectively. The resulting links are displayed in the order of their computed relevancy. Many popular search engines like Google (Falconer, 2011) and Bing have shifted their paradigm towards providing precise answers to the queries rather than just links.

The Question Answering systems can be divided into two major categories: a) Open-domain Question Answering (OpenQA) – where the questions may belong to any topic or genre from a knowledge base e.g. Wikipedia; b) Closed-domain Question Answering (ClosedQA)– where the questions belong to a specific knowledge field or a particular genre e.g. law, education, finance, weather etc. The OpenQA tasks are more prevalent in studies, than closedQA, owing to their wider topic range and numerous resources.

The operational pipeline of either type of QA system, may undergo following sequential steps a) Query analysis b) Search and information retrieval and c) Answer formulation. The pipeline subtask 'Answer Formulation' further divides the Question Answering systems into two categories: a) Abstractive Question Answering – with well-formed natural language answers abstracted from the relevant text without copying exact phrases from it, b) Extractive Question Answering – with answers derived as a consecutive sequence of tokens from the relevant documents. Abstractive Question Answering is more suitable when complex reasoning is required over multiple paragraphs/documents to answer a question (Chen et al., 2019).

Machine Reading Comprehension (MRC) is a sub-task of OpenQA (Ruder, 2021). According to (Chen, 2018) MRC is a task of understanding unstructured text and precisely answer any questions about it. The answer is extracted from the context document by highlighting the start and end of the span. In this work, we attempt at solving the a closed domain MRC task released in 5th workshop on Open-Source Arabic Corpora and Corpora Processing Tools (OSACT) in LREC 2022 (Malhas et al., 2022). An annotated Qur'anic Reading Comprehension Dataset (QRCD) is shared at the gitlab repository[3] containing question-answer-passage tuples. The task objective is to extract an answer span against a question, from the provided passage of Quran. It is required to generate 5 possible answer spans ranked according to the scores assigned by our specific

[1] https://assistant.google.com/

[2] https://www.theta.co.nz/technologies/faq-bot/

[3] Rana Malhas and Tamer Elsayed. Official Repository of Qur'an QA Shared Task. https://gitlab.com/bigirqu/quranqa. February 2022

model. The performance of the model is evaluated over three metrics; Exact Match (EM), F1 score and partial Reciprocal Ranking (pRR). We contribute to effectively solve the task by adopting following approaches:

- Using a BERT (Devlin et al., 2018) pre-trained language model and fine tuning it for the specific dataset QRCD.
- Using regularization technique, Decoupled Weight Decay (Loshchilov and Hutter, 2017), to avoid overfitting.
- Using two different pre-trained models: a) BERT pre-trained Arabic model, b) BERT pre-trained multilingual model; showing that the first pre-trained model has an edge over the second one and out performs it.
- Using data augmentation to increase training data. For this purpose, we used Annotated Corpus of Arabic Al-Quran Question and Answer (AQQAC) (Alqahtani and Atwell, 2018a), filtered it to select the question answer tuples that matched in style to that of QRCD. For each tuple, we took the sequence of Quran verses present in answer and generated their context passage from Quran's simple text downloaded from Tanzil project [4].
- Finally, we analyze that how much a model can hatch improved results using regularization techniques like weight decay and data-augmentation. (Note: the augmented data being collected with an altogether different methodology might not be true representative of the testing data).

2. Related Work

Neural Machine Reading Comprehension (MRC) has gained success over answer retrieval from unstructured text. Many statistical systems like AskMSR (Banko et al., 2002) exploit the answer redundancy in the source data. In MRC, the answer might not be redundant or might occur just once, thus leading to undesired results. Thus a model needs to acquire deeper understanding of the question, the context passage and their mutual relationship. The neural models address this need by learning question and context similarities. One such model is BiDAF (Seo et al., 2016) based on Recurrent Neural Network (RNN) and uses bidirectional attention flow to generate query-aware-context representations. It took lead on SQuAD (Rajpurkar et al., 2016) dataset at the time of submission, with Exact Match (EM) and F1 scores of 68% and 77% respectively. DrQA (2017) (Chen et al., 2017) is a multi-layer RNN model. It presents pipeline architecture with document retriever, employing TF-IDF algorithm, and the document reader modules. The DrQA reader module showed EM score of 69% and F1 score of 78.8% on SQuAD. QANet (Yu et al., 2018) uses convolution and self-attention mechanisms making it more efficient than counterpart RNN based models. Being faster the model trains on more data generated through back translation.

[4] https://tanzil.net/download/

Generative Pre-trained Transformer (GPT-1) (Radford et al., 2018) model, with 117M parameters, introduced the approach of pre-training on unlabeled data with unsupervised tasks and fine-tuned on downstream tasks with remarkable results regardless of the limited size of task specific training data. Many more powerful models followed the pursuit. A few to name are BERT (Devlin et al., 2018), XLNET (Yang et al., 2019) and T5 (Raffel et al., 2019). GPT-2 (Radford et al., 2019) and GPT-3 (Brown et al., 2020), the successors of GPT-1, were trained on even larger data and with significantly more parameters, 1.5 billion and 175 billion parameters respectively.
BERT (Devlin et al., 2018) has multilayer bidirectional transformer encoder architecture that pre-trains on two unsupervised tasks Masked Language Model (MLM) or Next Sequence Prediction(NSP) model. RoBERTa (Liu et al., 2019) an extension of BERT is trained for longer period over longer sequences, with NSP loss removed under the observation that it is only useful if input sequences are individual sentences instead of passages with multiple sentences. A significant improvement is observed in the performance on SQUAD 1.1/2.0, MNLI-m, SST-2 and RACE datasets in comparison to original BERT and even exceeds many of the successors of BERT.

Dataset	Source	Size
DAWQUAS (Ismail and Homsi, 2018)	News, social, women, science and technology websites	3205
AQQAC (Alqahtani and Atwell, 2018a)	Book: 1000 Su'al Wa Jawab Fi ALKORAN, Website based on Al-Quran and Tafseer	2224 public: 1224
Arabic SQuAD (Mozannar et al., 2019)	Wikipedia translation of original SQuAD1.1	48,344
ARCD (Mozannar et al., 2019)	Arabic Wikipedia	1,395
TyDiQA-GoldP (Clark et al., 2020)	Wikipedia	204K
Ayatec (Malhas and Elsayed, 2020)	The Holy Quran verified text from Tanzil Project	1,762
AQAD (Atef et al., 2020)	Arabic Wikipedia articles matching SQuAD1.1 articles	17,911

Table 1: Arabic Question Answering Datasets

As mentioned earlier in section 1 that one of the driving forces in popularity of QA task is availability of the benchmark datasets. . SQuAD (Rajpurkar et al., 2016) is the most popular MRC dataset in English with 107,785 question-answer pairs over 23,125 paragraphs extracted from 536 Wikipedia articles selected after multiple ranking and random sampling. SQuAD2.0 (Rajpurkar et al., 2018) contains 53,775 unanswerable questions but seemingly answerable authored by crowd workers. English being a resourceful language has numerous evaluation datasets publically available both for MRC and OpenQA e.g. HotpotQA (Yang et al., 2018), Natural Questions (NQ) (Kwiatkowski et al., 2019), triviaQA (Joshi et al., 2017) etc. However QA research in resource poor languages like Arabic, Persian and Urdu is severely hampered. One ingenious resort to overcome this deficiency is through machine translation now much more advance and accurate owing to neural machine translation (NMT) models. For instance some of the datasets constructed using this method are PQuAD (Darvishi et al., 2022), K-QuAD (Lee et al., 2018) and SQuAD-es (Carrino et al., 2019) that are the respective translations of SQuAD dataset in Persian, Korean and Spanish languages.

(Mozannar et al., 2019) presents the Arabic translation of a subset of SQuAD containing 48,344 questions on 10,364 paragraphs. In addition to Arabic-SQuAD, the study also contributes another smaller Arabic Reading Comprehension Dataset (ARCD) containing 1,395 questions compiled over Arabic Wikipedia articles through crowdsourcing. It presents system for open domain question answering in Arabic (SOQAL) having Retriever and Reader modules. On both Arabic-SQuAD and ARCD, the reader module employs BERT-Base un-normalized multilingual model and QANet fastText, with the former taking the lead. Independent testing on ARCD and Arabic-SQuAD using BERT shows very insignificant difference in results, increasing confidence in data generated through NMT. DAWQUAS (Ismail and Homsi, 2018) is a collection of 3205 why-question-answers pair collected using Google Search API to look up for web pages in general as well as some specific news and social sites that contained the Arabic word ***'limadha'*** (meaning: why). TyDiQA-GoldP (Clark et al., 2020) is multi-lingual collection of 204K question-answer pairs for 11 languages. The data source is Wikipedia and questions are authored by human annotators with little access to article's content. Answers are generated later by annotators with full access to the content of article by selecting best answer passage and a minimal span in that passage if possible. Arabic Question-Answer dataset contains 17,911 questions from 3,381 paragraphs out of 299 Arabic Wikipedia articles. Only those articles and paragraphs are selected from Arabic Wikipedia that are also present in English-to-Arabic translation of SQuAD2.0 articles and paragraphs. The questions are generated for selected paragraphs through machine translation of SQuAD2.0 questions.

Annotated Corpus of Arabic Al-Quran Question and Answer (AQQAC) (Alqahtani and Atwell, 2018a) is a collection of 2224 question-answers and other helpful details about the Holy Quran from two authentic sources, the book "1000 Su'al Wa Jawab Fi ALKORAN" and a website on information about Quran.

AyaTEC is a test collection of verse based question-answers from the Holy Quran comprising of 207 question over 11 categories of the Holy Quran. The questions are gathered from Arabic QA systems on Quran and the users. Two user categories are defined: Curious – asking questions related to teachings of the Quran, Skeptical – asking controversial questions. The answer space is restricted to Qura'nic verses. The dataset provides all verses of Quran, exhaustively that may answer a question, collected by two freelancers with the knowledge of Quran. The relevance of selected verses of Quran to the question was verified by three specialists in the Holy Quran.

All the Arabic datasets discussed in this section are summarized in Table-1

3. Approach for Quran QA Task:

We use BERT (Devlin et al., 2018) for QuranQA task as our baseline model. BERT input can represent both a single sequence of text and a pair of two sequences separated by a special token '[SEP]' depending on the nature of downstream task. For instance, in our case we pass on the question-passage pair for our QA task.

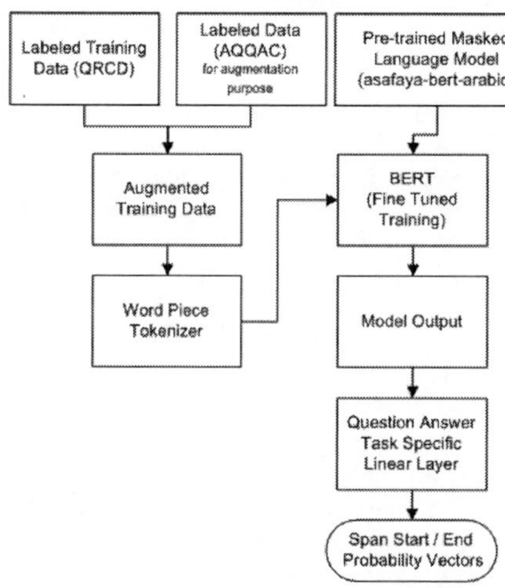

Figure 1: Our BERT QA Pilpeline Approach

Our model has a pipeline architecture, as shown in Figure-1, starting off with data preparation. The QRCD training data needs to be processed to transform into a format that can be fed as input to BERT. The given dataset has 118 unique questions, accompanied by multiple context passages from Quran and multiple possible answers from each passage. The answer text and its starting position in the passage is listed in the dataset. The ending position of an answer in the context needs to be known too for model to yield a span in terms of probabilities of start and end indices of the passage. Therefore the data is processed to create unique question-answer-passage tuples in a format consistent with BERT input.

After the pre-processing step QRCD training data resolves into 861 unique question-answer-passage tuples. Due to the limited size of training data and BERT being a hefty model, it tends to over fit very quickly. In order to keep this problem at bay, we augmented the training data with 473 additional tuples acquired from AQQAC dataset after careful sampling and building context passages from Quran which were deficit in the original dataset.

Entailing step was to initialize BERT either with some initial configurations or with some generic pre-trained checkpoint. For pre-training, BERT opt for two unsupervised learning schemes: Masked Language Modeling (MLM) and Next Sequence Prediction (NSP). We initialized BERT with two different pre-trained MLM models, 1) BERT multilingual base model[5], 2) asafaya/bert-base-arabic[6]. We empirically show that mono-lingual model is best fitting in our case.

In the subsequent step, question-passage pairs in the training data undergo tokenization routine. The Word Piece tokenizer is employed to generate the word embeddings with a special opening token '[CLS]', and another special token ['SEP'] parting the question and context tokens as well as indicating the end of input sequence. The model feeds off the word embeddings to fine-tune and learns query to context segmentation and positional embeddings. The model outputs are two vocabulary sized vectors representing probabilities of each token as a potential start and end positions of the answer span in the context.

4. Experimental Setup

This section describes the datasets used, model's output and evaluation measures used for experiments.

4.1. Dataset

We evaluate our models on the QRCD (Qur'anic Reading Comprehension Dataset) dataset (Malhas and Elsayed, 2020) shared at gitlab repository of Qur'an QA Task. The dataset includes 1093 question-passage pairs and along with their exhaustively extracted answers which results in 1,337 question-passage-answer triplets. The dataset is split into training (65%) , validation/development (10%) and test (25%) sets. The dataset is shared in JSON file with each line having passage, question, answer/answer-list, chapter number and list of verse numbers from passage.

4.2. Model Settings

The BERT pre-trained models **bert-base-multilingual-uncased**, supporting 102 languages, and **asafaya/bert-base-arabic** are both trained with 12 hidden layers, 768 hidden size, 12 attention heads, 0.1 dropout on each hidden layer and 110 parameters. For fine-tuning the Model, we run 30 epochs to train, using a batch size of 8.

4.3. Model Output

The QuranQA task requirement is to provide 5 probable answer spans ranked 1 (highest) to 5 (lowest) according to their scores. Each answer is listed in order of its rank providing following information: anwer text, rank and the score computed by the model.

[5]https://huggingface.co/bert-base-multilingual-uncased

[6]https://huggingface.co/asafaya/bert-base-arabic

4.4. Evaluation Method

For evaluation purpose, three metrics are used.

- Exact Match metric is applied only to the highest ranking answer. It awards a binary score 1 or 0. The score is 1 on finding output answer text in the context passage, 0 otherwise. Arabic prefixes and punctuations are removed from the answer and the passage, before finding exact match.

- The F1 metric, again applied to the highest ranking answer only, measures the average word overlap between the predicted and the ground truth answer.

$$F1 = 2 \times \frac{precision \times recall}{precision + recall} \tag{1}$$

$$precision = \frac{overlapping\_token\_count}{token\_count\_in\_predicted\_answer} \tag{2}$$

$$recall = \frac{overlapping\_token\_count}{token\_count\_in\_ground\_truth} \tag{3}$$

- pRR is the official metric of Qur'an QA Task. If an answer is assigned zero F1 score against any of the ground-truth answers then the average F1 scores of answers next in rank are taken into account. While coursing through answers with lower ranks, the F1 score of each answer is penalized by taking its product with the reciprocal of answer's rank.

5. Experiments

This section emphasizes on our experiments for QuranQA task. We begin with a baseline BERT model to extract preliminary results and improve results with subsequent modifications to the baseline model. We employ fine-tuning, a transfer learning strategy, using two differently pre-trained models. Finally we apply regularization strategies, data augmentation and weight-decay to achieve enhanced results.

5.1. Baseline Model

A BERT model is set up from scratch, with initial default settings same as mentioned for pre-trained models in section 4.2. The model is supplied with training data token embeddings, generated as discussed in section 3, as input.

5.2. Pre-trained Models and Fine-Tuning

Taking into account the size of training dataset, initializing BERT from pre-trained checkpoints give a reasonably enhanced kick start. The model can fine-tune with task specific training data and reaps astounding results. We selected two pre-trained BERT models for this task. First is the **bert-base-multilingual-uncased** pre-trained for 102 different languages comprising a vocabulary of 105879 tokens, open sourced at Hugging Face online library. The second pre-trained model is **asafaya/bert-base-arabic** (Safaya et al., 2020), for Arabic only with 32000 tokens, downloaded from Hugging Face.

5.3. Data Augmentation

The magnitude of our training data has its limitations to fully exploit the strength of a deep neural network model like BERT and is prone to over-fit. We regularize the model by supplementing it with additional training data. This additional data may not be the true representative of the development and test data splits of QRCD; nevertheless, it supports more generalized learning of the model parameters and keep it from over-fitting. We've used AQQAC (Alqahtani and Atwell, 2018a) originally containing 2224 annotated questions-answer pairs and only 1224 released publically due to copyright concerns. Each question-answer pair also provides ancillary information like question ID, question opening word, relevant chapter and verse numbers, question topic, question type, Al-Quran ontology concepts (Alqahtani and Atwell, 2018b) and question source.

The two datasets, QRCD and AQQAC, are collected using different methodologies and annotated for different objectives. Therefore we filter AQQAC to extract only those data points that best match in style to QRCD. We also construct the context passages as they are not already available in the original dataset.

For question-answer sampling from AQQAC we observed following salient features of the data. Unlike QRCD, the answer to a question is not necessarily a Quranic verse or a part of it. Many of the answers to questions are in plain language using Modern Standard Arabic (MSA) and supplement their argument with Quranic verses. Another very common type of questions are those seeking an explanation or interpretation to Quranic verses. The corresponding answers simply explain the verses but does not explicitly contain or refer to other relevant verses. Pertaining to these dissimilarities some preprocessing on AQQAC is inevitable.

Our objective is to identify the pairs where the answer is a part of a verse, a complete verse, or a continuous sequence of multiple verses. We use following steps to achieve this.

- On examining the data property **'question type'** we found that the two categories in this field ***'ashrah'*** (meaning: explain) and ***'fasr'*** (meaning: interpret) are mostly an explanation or interpretation of the given Quranic text, in modern standard Arabic. Therefore we omit these questions.
- In the remaining data, we use an automated routine to search the questions with answers containing no verse from the Holy Quran or any reference to one. We omit such question-answers too as our minimal criteria of selection is that the answer should contain at least one verse from the Holy Quran.
- After the first two steps, remaining questions have at least one or multiple continuous verses either as a direct answer or as a reference to support the answer. In either case, any plain text appended before and after the verses is removed. In the severed text, the verse numbers are replaced by sentence delimiters.

We get a set of 473 question-answers out of 1224. To make the selected set usable in QuranQA task we need a context passage along with question answer pairs. We use this idea that each answer is either a single verse or a set of continuous verses from Quran so their context can be taken from Quran too. We used simple text of Quran from the Tanzil project for this purpose. To build the passage for each data point, we take verses from the answer and locate them in the text of Quran. Then we select two verses from the preceding and following contexts each and concatenate them before and after the verses taken from the answer respectively. This gives a reasonable context for our task.

We also provide the index of passage after the preceding context, from where the original answer begins as a starting position of the answer span. After curating this information for each data point we save it in the same format as the QRCD training data, ready to use.

5.4. Weight Decay Regularization

Apart from data augmentation, to train model more generically we attempted at using the weight-decay (Loshchilov and Hutter, 2017) with Adam optimizer. The range of values we tested it for are 0.1, 0.01 and 0.001 with 0.01 giving the best results of the three.

6. Results and Discussions

In this section we shall discuss the results of our approach and analyze the impact of settings and techniques we applied to make it better. We refer to each model setting with a short code name as follows:

R0: Baseline model trained from scratch
R1: Fine-tuning (*bert-base-arabic*)
R2(a): Fine-tuning (*bert-base-arabic*) + Data augmentation
R2(b): Fine-tuning (*bert-base-multilingual-uncased*) + Data augmentation
R3: Fine-tuning (*bert-base-arabic*) + Weight decay (0.01)
R4(a): Fine-tuning (*bert-base-arabic*)+ Weight decay (0.01) + Data augmentation + Shuffled training data
R4(b): Fine-tuning (*bert-base-arabic*)+ Weight decay (0.01) + Data augmentation
R5: Fine-tuning (*bert-base-arabic*)+ Weight decay regularization (at value 0.01) + Data augmentation + Training data inclusive of Development data for training

Table 2, Table 3 and Table 4 show the pRR, EM and F1 scores respectively for each data split. Scores for QRCD training data, validation data and testing data are represented in respective columns with headers 'Training', 'Development' and 'Test'. The best scores are in bold font.

Model	Training	Development	Test
R0	0.7803	0.5146	-
R1	**0.9739**	0.55809	-
R2(a)	0.9526	0.5711	-
R2(b)	0.4870	0.3872	-
R3	0.9721	0.5685	-
R4 (a)	0.9675	0.5829	**0.3075** (run03)
R4 (b)	0.9643	**0.5888**	0.2795 (run02)
R5	0.9287	0.9217	0.2873 (run01)

Table 2: Models R1-R5 pRR Scores for Train, Development and Test Data

Model	Training	Development	Test
R0	0.6394	0.2660	-
R1	**0.9478**	0.3211	-
R2(a)	0.8957	0.3394	-
R2(b)	0.2774	0.1284	-
R3	0.9352	0.3302	-
R4 (a)	0.9267	**0.3486**	**0.0882** (run03)
R4 (b)	0.9282	0.3119	0.0756 (run02)
R5	0.8690	0.7889	0.0756 (run01)

Table 3: Models R1-R5 Exact-Match Scores for Train, Development and Test Data

Model	Training	Development	Test
R0	0.7549	0.4834	-
R1	**0.9728**	0.5305	-
R2(a)	0.9509	0.5409	-
R2(b)	0.4501	0.3507	-
R3	0.9702	0.5276	-
R4 (a)	0.9657	0.5544	**0.2676** (run03)
R4 (b)	0.9629	**0.5677**	0.2465 (run02)
R5	0.9246	0.9213	0.2684 (run01)

Table 4: Models R1-R5 F1 Scores for Train, Development and Test Data

In the last model setting **R5** the training and development data are merged thereby giving best results on development data. Therefore, we deliberately do not highlight **R5** scores on development data as best. Only its results for the test data are taken into account. For development data, we select **R4(a)** giving best EM score and **R4(b)** giving best pRR and F1 scores.

We observed that the model **R1** fine-tuned over the BERT pre-trained model, asafaya/bert-base-arabic using Masked Language Model, secured a better pRR score of 55.80% on development data compared to two other models; model **R0** trained from scratch giving 51.46% pRR and the model **R2(b)** fine-tuned over bert-base-multilingual-uncased, pre-trained on 102 languages, giving 38.72% pRR.

We also note the fine-tuned model **R1** has strikingly higher scores, on all three metrics, for training data as compared to development data. This indicates its tendency towards over-fitting. We use the data augmentation scheme that curbs the problem to some extent, improving the results relatively in the models using this scheme i.e. **R2(a)**, **R3**, **R4(a)**, **R4(b)** and **R5**. However, during training the augmented data, sampled from AQQAC dataset, is not true representative of the development data and therefore its impact is small if not insignificant. Figure-3 shows the effect of data augmentation at the time of fine-tuning as compared to the model in Figure-2 fine-tuned on data without any augmentation.

We observed that the model **R2(a)** using data augmentation and fine-tuned over pre-trained BERT model for Arabic only out performs **R2(b)** also using data augmentation but fine-tuned over multi-lingual pre-trained BERT model. We used settings of **R2(a)** as base settings for later models R3 to R5 along with additional enhancements.

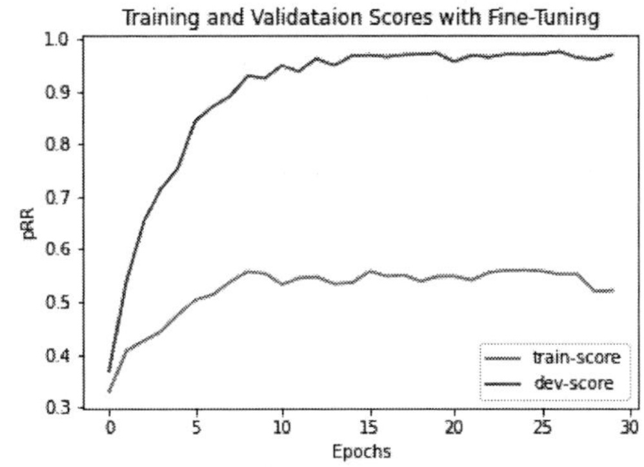

Figure 2: Model-R1 (Fine-tuned on bert-base-arabic) pRR Scores for Training and Development Data

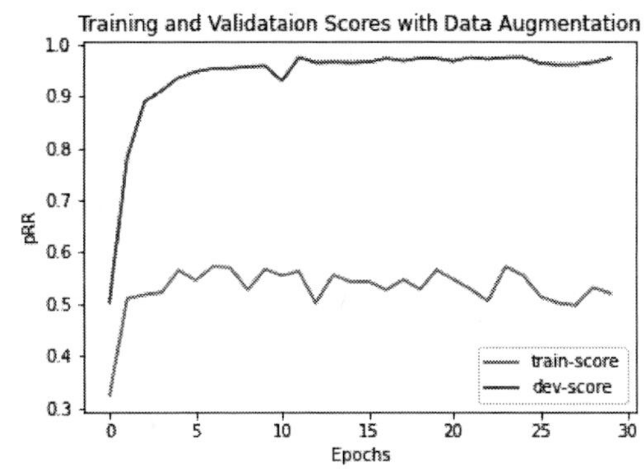

Figure 3: Model-R2(a) (Fine-tuned on bert-base-arabic with Augmented Training Data) pRR Scores for Training and Development Data

The model **R4** gave different results on two different training executions stated as **R4(a)** and **R4(b)**, which is due to permitting the shuffling of the training data for **R4(a)**. In both cases, we evaluated results after each epoch and saved the model at a checkpoint with best results. The execution of **R4(a)** shows best score of 30.75% pRR on test data, while **R5** stood second best with 28.73% pRR. Although, R5 included validation data for training, but its lack of showing improved results on test data could be attributed to one minor difference in saving the trained model state. Unlike other models, R5 was saved after 30 epochs and we did not evaluate it on validation data after every epoch to find the best checkpoint to save. This might have caused us to miss the best model state at some point during the course of epochs. Another reason could be that the augmented data size was not very significant.

Overall, in our approach the fine-tuning in combination with data augmentation technique and weight-decay value 0.01 generated the best scores of 58.88% pRR on development data and 30.75% on test data amongst all our settings and runs.

7. Conclusion and Future Work

We attempted to solve QuranQA shared task using BERT (Devlin et al., 2018) from scratch as well as fine-tuned over two different pre-trained variants. Moreover we opted for data augmentation and weight-decay regularization techniques to improve performance over the task.

Our key finding are thus summarized as follows:

- Fine-tuning over a pre-trained model specifically for Arabic language has leverage over the multi-lingual pre-trained model as well as training from scratch.
- Regularization methods like data augmentation and weight-decay enhance the performance by keeping the model from over-fitting.

In future work, we intend to apply following techniques in anticipation of improving the performance of our approach on QuranQA task.

- We expect to get enhanced performance by making architectural level changes in the model.
- We intend to increase the training data using techniques like back translation to generate rephrased questions or by replacing words in questions with synonyms.
- We intend to use different activation functions on hidden layers or even employ a different loss function that can help the model improve results to some extent.

8. Bibliographical References

Alqahtani, M. and Atwell, E. (2018a). Annotated corpus of arabic al-quran question and answer.

Alqahtani, M. M. and Atwell, E. (2018b). Developing bilingual arabic-english ontologies of al-quran. In *2018 IEEE 2nd International Workshop on Arabic and Derived Script Analysis and Recognition (ASAR)*, pages 96–101. IEEE.

Atef, A., Mattar, B., Sherif, S., Elrefai, E., and Torki, M. (2020). Aqad: 17,000+ arabic questions for machine comprehension of text. In *2020 IEEE/ACS 17th International Conference on Computer Systems and Applications (AICCSA)*, pages 1–6. IEEE.

Banko, M., Brill, E., Dumais, S., and Lin, J. (2002). Askmsr: Question answering using the worldwide web. In *Proceedings of 2002 AAAI Spring Symposium on Mining Answers from Texts and Knowledge Bases*, pages 7–9.

Brown, T., Mann, B., Ryder, N., Subbiah, M., Kaplan, J. D., Dhariwal, P., Neelakantan, A., Shyam, P., Sastry, G., Askell, A., et al. (2020). Language models are few-shot learners. *Advances in neural information processing systems*, 33:1877–1901.

Carrino, C. P., Costa-jussà, M. R., and Fonollosa, J. A. (2019). Automatic spanish translation of the squad dataset for multilingual question answering. *arXiv preprint arXiv:1912.05200.*

Chen, D., Fisch, A., Weston, J., and Bordes, A. (2017). Reading wikipedia to answer open-domain questions. *arXiv preprint arXiv:1704.00051.*

Chen, J., Lin, S.-t., and Durrett, G. (2019). Multi-hop question answering via reasoning chains. *arXiv preprint arXiv:1910.02610.*

Chen, D. (2018). *Neural reading comprehension and beyond.* Stanford University.

Clark, J. H., Choi, E., Collins, M., Garrette, D., Kwiatkowski, T., Nikolaev, V., and Palomaki, J. (2020). Tydi qa: A benchmark for information-seeking question answering in typologically diverse languages. *Transactions of the Association for Computational Linguistics*, 8:454–470.

Darvishi, K., Shahbodagh, N., Abbasiantaeb, Z., and Momtazi, S. (2022). Pquad: A persian question answering dataset. *arXiv preprint arXiv:2202.06219.*

Devlin, J., Chang, M.-W., Lee, K., and Toutanova, K. (2018). Bert: Pre-training of deep bidirectional transformers for language understanding. *arXiv preprint arXiv:1810.04805.*

Falconer, J. (2011). Google: Our new search strategy is to compute answers, not links. `https://thenextweb.com/news/google-our-new-search-strategy-is-to-compute-a` [Online; accessed 10-May-2022].

Ismail, W. S. and Homsi, M. N. (2018). Dawqas: A dataset for arabic why question answering system. *Procedia computer science*, 142:123–131.

Joshi, M., Choi, E., Weld, D. S., and Zettlemoyer, L. (2017). Triviaqa: A large scale distantly supervised challenge dataset for reading comprehension. *arXiv preprint arXiv:1705.03551.*

Kwiatkowski, T., Palomaki, J., Redfield, O., Collins, M., Parikh, A., Alberti, C., Epstein, D., Polosukhin, I., Devlin, J., Lee, K., et al. (2019). Natural questions: a benchmark for question answering research. *Transactions of the Association for Computational Linguistics*, 7:453–466.

Lee, K., Yoon, K., Park, S., and Hwang, S.-w. (2018). Semi-supervised training data generation for multilingual question answering. In *Proceedings of the Eleventh International Conference on Language Resources and Evaluation (LREC 2018).*

Liu, Y., Ott, M., Goyal, N., Du, J., Joshi, M., Chen, D., Levy, O., Lewis, M., Zettlemoyer, L., and Stoyanov, V. (2019). Roberta: A robustly optimized bert pretraining approach. *arXiv preprint arXiv:1907.11692.*

Loshchilov, I. and Hutter, F. (2017). Decoupled weight decay regularization. *arXiv preprint arXiv:1711.05101.*

Malhas, R. and Elsayed, T. (2020). Ayatec: building a reusable verse-based test collection for arabic question answering on the holy qur'an. *ACM Transactions on Asian and Low-Resource Language Information Processing (TALLIP)*, 19(6):1–21.

Malhas, R., Mansour, W., and Elsayed, T. (2022). Qur'an QA 2022: Overview of the first shared task on question answering over the holy qur'an. In *Proceedings of the 5th Workshop on Open-Source Arabic Corpora and Pro-*

cessing Tools (OSACT5) at the 13th Language Resources and Evaluation Conference (LREC 2022).

Mozannar, H., Hajal, K. E., Maamary, E., and Hajj, H. (2019). Neural arabic question answering. *arXiv preprint arXiv:1906.05394.*

Radford, A., Narasimhan, K., Salimans, T., and Sutskever, I. (2018). Improving language understanding by generative pre-training.

Radford, A., Wu, J., Child, R., Luan, D., Amodei, D., Sutskever, I., et al. (2019). Language models are unsupervised multitask learners. *OpenAI blog*, 1(8):9.

Raffel, C., Shazeer, N., Roberts, A., Lee, K., Narang, S., Matena, M., Zhou, Y., Li, W., and Liu, P. J. (2019). Exploring the limits of transfer learning with a unified text-to-text transformer. *arXiv preprint arXiv:1910.10683.*

Rajpurkar, P., Zhang, J., Lopyrev, K., and Liang, P. (2016). Squad: 100,000+ questions for machine comprehension of text. *arXiv preprint arXiv:1606.05250.*

Rajpurkar, P., Jia, R., and Liang, P. (2018). Know what you don't know: Unanswerable questions for squad. *arXiv preprint arXiv:1806.03822.*

Ruder, S. (2021). Multi-domain multilingual question answering. `https://ruder.io/multi-qa-tutorial/index.html#open-retrieval-qa-vs-reading-comprehension`. [Online; accessed 25-April-2022].

Safaya, A., Abdullatif, M., and Yuret, D. (2020). Kuisail at semeval-2020 task 12: Bert-cnn for offensive speech identification in social media. In *Proceedings of the Fourteenth Workshop on Semantic Evaluation*, pages 2054–2059.

Seo, M., Kembhavi, A., Farhadi, A., and Hajishirzi, H. (2016). Bidirectional attention flow for machine comprehension. *arXiv preprint arXiv:1611.01603.*

Yang, Z., Qi, P., Zhang, S., Bengio, Y., Cohen, W. W., Salakhutdinov, R., and Manning, C. D. (2018). Hotpotqa: A dataset for diverse, explainable multi-hop question answering. *arXiv preprint arXiv:1809.09600.*

Yang, Z., Dai, Z., Yang, Y., Carbonell, J., Salakhutdinov, R. R., and Le, Q. V. (2019). Xlnet: Generalized autoregressive pretraining for language understanding. *Advances in neural information processing systems*, 32.

Yu, A. W., Dohan, D., Luong, M.-T., Zhao, R., Chen, K., Norouzi, M., and Le, Q. V. (2018). Qanet: Combining local convolution with global self-attention for reading comprehension. *arXiv preprint arXiv:1804.09541.*

Proceedings of the OSACT 2022 Workshop @LREC2022, pages 104–111
Marseille, 20 June 2022

GOF at Qur'an QA 2022: Towards an Efficient Question Answering For The Holy Qu'ran In The Arabic Language Using Deep Learning-Based Approach

Aly Mostafa, Omar Mohamed
Department Of Computer Science, Faculty of Computers and Artificial Intelligence, Helwan University
Helwan, Egypt
{alymostafa, omar_20170353 }@fci.helwan.edu.eg

Abstract

Recently, significant advancements were achieved in Question Answering (QA) systems in several languages. However, QA systems in the Arabic language require further research and improvement because of several challenges and limitations, such as a lack of resources. Especially for QA systems in the Holy Qur'an since it is in classical Arabic and most recent publications are in Modern Standard Arabic. In this research, we report our submission to the Qur'an QA 2022 Shared task-organized with the 5th Workshop on Open-Source Arabic Corpora and Processing Tools Arabic (OSACT5). We propose a method for dealing with QA issues in the Holy Qur'an using Deep Learning models. Furthermore, we address the issue of the proposed dataset's limited sample size by fine-tuning the model several times on several large datasets before fine-tuning it on the proposed dataset achieving 66.9% pRR 54.59% pRR on the development and test sets, respectively.
Keywords: Holy Qur'an, Question Answering System, Information retrieval,

1. Introduction

Extractive Question Answering is essential for extracting a span of text from a given context paragraph as the answer to a specified question. It is a subset of Natural Language Processing and Information Retrieval. Question Answering has made significant development in recent years with applications in search engines. This is because large pre-trained language models and self-supervised learning, such as BERT(Devlin et al., 2018), T5 (Raffel et al., 2019), MT5 (Xue et al., 2020), ALBERT(Lan et al., 2019), and BART(Lewis et al., 2019), which use the Transformer architecture (Vaswani et al., 2017) to develop robust language models for a range of NLP tasks specified by benchmarks, such as GLUE (Wang et al., 2018). Furthermore, new datasets, such as SQuAD (Rajpurkar et al., 2016), have brought more complicated questions with inference-based context to the question answering task. Arabic is a Semitic language spoken by about 250 million people in the Middle East and North Africa. It is the official language of 26 countries and one of the six official languages of the United Nations. Classical Arabic (CA), Modern Standard Arabic (MSA), and Colloquial Arabic are the three main variants of Arabic (Arabic,). CA is the style that illustrates the Holy Qur'an. The Holy Qur'an came to fruition in the sixth century CE, and Arabic has evolved over the centuries, but not significantly. CA is the basis of the mediaeval languages of Arab tribes. The phrase structure is the same as in MSA's current form. Several minor variations exist between the CA and MSA, like grammar and phrase punctuation. More than 1.8 billion Muslims around the world revere the Qur'an. It is the primary source of Islamic knowledge. The Holy Qur'an consists of 114 chapters and 6,236 verses of varying lengths, totalling around 80k Arabic words. An Ayah-meaning verse in the Qur'an- might refer to one or more topics, and several Ayahs might address the same topic in similar contexts. Because of the Arabic word structure, many regards a morphological study of the Arabic language as an involute endeavour; Arabic words consist of a maximum of four letters root verb. Also, each word consists of a root and other affixes (prefix, infix, suffix) and can have many interpretations depending on the diacritics marks that make the word two-dimensional. Finally, while the Arabic language is one of the most widespread globally, it is a low-resource language by many standers since it suffers from a scarcity of resources, such as lacking large pre-trained models and corpora. These problems make Arabic NLP, NLU, and IR research more challenging than in other languages like English or Chinese. Most of the attention in the Arabic literature research is towards Modern Standard Arabic due to the availability of its resources compared with CA, especially the QA systems on the Holy Qur'an (Abdelnasser et al., 2014), (Adany and others, 2017), (Hamdelsayed et al., 2017), (Hakkoum and Raghay, 2016), (Hamdelsayed and Atwell, 2016b), where a question is likely to be posed in MSA since it is the most common Arabic version used in Arabic-speaking countries today. While significant efforts have been made to offer dependable QA systems for other applications in the Arabic language (Brini et al., 2009), (Mohammed et al., 1993), (Nabil et al., 2017), (Abdelmegied et al., 2017), there have been few attempts to research QA for the Holy Qur'an. In this work, we present a method for dealing with QA in the Holy Qur'an. We analyzed the existing pre-trained models, namely MARBERTv2 and AraBERTv2, for QA in Arabic and found that the AraELECTRA model produces cutting-edge outcomes in a variety of Arabic

Set	Percentage	#Question-Passage Pairs	#Question-Passage-Answer Triplets
Training	65%	710	861
Development	10%	109	128
Test	25%	274	348

Table 1: QRCD Distribution

QA datasets (Antoun et al., 2020)(Abdul-Mageed et al., 2021). Our approach consists of three stages. First, the chosen model is fine-tuned using the Ar-TyDi QA dataset (Clark et al., 2020a). Second, we improved its efficiency by fine-tuning it on a larger corpora (Arabic-SQuAD and ARCD) (Mozannar et al., 2019). Finally, we fine-tuned the same model using QRCD (Qur'anic Reading Comprehension Dataset), achieving 66.9%, 54.59% partial Reciprocal Rank (pRR) (Malhas and Elsayed, 2020) on the development and test set, respectively. The rest of the paper is organized as follows. section 2 provides a review of previous Question Answering systems in the Holy Qur'an literature. section 3 describes the proposed dataset. section 4 proposes the model of the QA. section 5 discusses the results and performance evaluation. Finally, we conclude in section 6.

2. Related Work

This section discusses previous research and applications addressing Question-Answering challenges in the Holy Qur'an, as well as the methodologies, datasets, strengths employed, and drawbacks.
(Shmeisani et al., 2014) Their model is composed of three layers that apply a semantic approach of Arabic ontology for Qur'anic content and analyze user inquiries expressed in Arabic. A Question processing layer, based on POS tagging, a semantic layer, and a query builder, enhancing query keywords. Their method was able to retrieve answers even when the user's precise words were not found in the Holy Qur'an.

(Abdelnasser et al., 2014) Their model is a Question-Answering System that comprises two modules. The first module accepts the input in the form of a question and retrieves the appropriate verses based on their semantics. The second module returns the extracted answer from the retrieved verses alongside their Tafseer. Their method achieved 85% accuracy in the top three rankings.

(Adany and others, 2017) The authors proposed six distinct ways of dealing with the problem of question-answering in the Holy Qur'an. Approaches were eliminating stopwords, diacritics, and special symbols, using Lucene indexing patterns, exaggeration formulas patterns, and single, dual, and plural patterns. They test their model on a corpus of only two chapters (AlBagrah and Alfatihah chapters)

(Hakkoum and Raghay, 2016) Introduce a Holy Qur'an Q&A system based on the development of an ontology that comprises a set of concepts and semantic relations between distinct inquiries and responses. The model has a precision of 95% and a recall of 73%.

(Hamed and Aziz, 2016) The authors propose a QAS based on identifying verses based on their content by utilizing the Neural Network (NN) approach. Based on N-gram and similarity scores, the model retrieves the ranking verses. The dataset used was Abdullah Yusuf Ali's translation of the English version of the Holy Qur'an (Ali, 2000).

(Hamoud and Atwell, 2016) They presented a Question Answering System for the Holy Qur'an that retrieves answers based on the contextual meaning of the keywords in the user's query, with the used corpus consisting of queries and their answers. They also used question paraphrasing as a data augmentation method to improve Question Answering (QA) performance. For the Arabic version, they attained a precision of 79% and a recall of 76%.
(Hamdelsayed and Atwell, 2016a) Their method improved the retrieved responses by adding additional semantic meaning to the words. Thye achieved this by manipulating several aspects of the Arabic language such as numbering, single, dual, and plural. They tested their method to the test using a corpus of questions and answers from the Holy Qur'an.

According to the results of this survey, we identified many flaws. To begin, several of the approaches for Q&A in the Holy Qur'an operate poorly. In addition, numerous studies aim to develop a static Qur'an ontology or hierarchical tree based on Qur'anic ontology. There is a scarcity of dynamic tools that prompt users to query using an abstract statement or a question. While there is a lot of research on developing Qur'an ontologies, there is little research on experimenting with state-of-the-art Deep Learning models for Q&A. In addition, there is a scarcity of structured, reusable, and publicly accessible gold standard test datasets for the Q&A in the Holy Qur'an. As a result, there are limitations in comparing the performance of different Q&A systems for the Holy Qur'an. The goal of this study is to solve previous

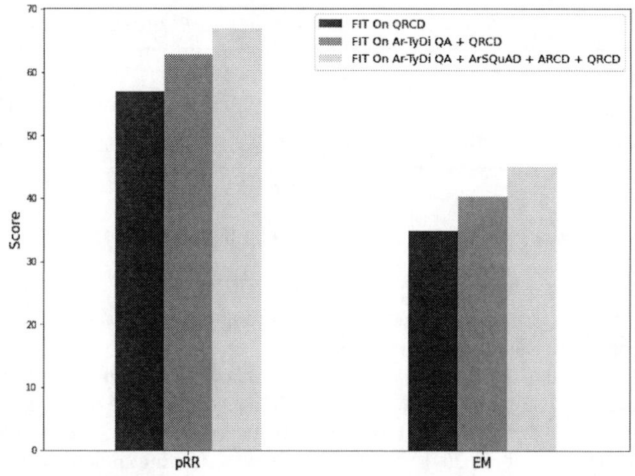

Figure 1: ARAELECTRA Fine-tuned (FIT) on different datasets. X-axis shows the pRR and EM of the different models. Y-axis shows the Score of each model

limitations by applying and analyzing state-of-the-art models and training those models on QRCD (Qur'anic Reading Comprehension Dataset) (Malhas and Elsayed, 2020)(Malhas and Elsayed, 2022)(Malhas et al., 2022).

3. Dataset

QRCD (Qur'anic Reading Comprehension Dataset) (Malhas and Elsayed, 2020)(Malhas and Elsayed, 2022) is a publically accessible dataset for extractive Question-Answering tasks (Machine Reading Comprehension) for the Holy Qur'an. There are two types of question passages in the dataset: question-passage pairs (1,093 records) and question-passage-answer triplets (1,337 records). Since the same question in the QRCD can be presented in multiple Qur'anic chapters, each passage may have multiple occurrences. Furthermore, the same passage may accompany different questions. The source of the Qur'anic text in QRCD is the Tanzil project download page, which provides validated versions of the Holy Qur'an in a variety of programming techniques. The simple-clean text style was chosen for convenience of usage. The proposed dataset is divided into three sets: training, development, and test; the dataset distribution is illustrated in Table 1

4. Methodology

In this section, we discuss the essential components of the proposed method, starting with an overview of the pre-trained models used and going over the fine-tuning process on the various datasets to overcome the dataset's small sample size problem. Finally, we present the fine-tuning of the QRCD.

4.1. ELECTRA

The Electra pre-training (Clark et al., 2020b) method involves training two neural networks, a generator G and a discriminator D. Each one essentially consists of a bi-directional encoder (e.g., Small BERT). The generator has been conditioned to conduct masked language modelling (MLM). MLM initially chooses a random set of positions (integers between 1 and n) to mask out m given an input. The generator's learning goal is to anticipate the original identities of the masked-out tokens. The discriminator is trained to discriminate between tokens in the data and tokens substituted by generator samples. While the Electra pre-training approach appears to be similar to GAN (Goodfellow et al., 2014), there are key variations. First, it was observed that changing the token status from "fake" to "real" after generating the correct token improves the results on downstream tasks. Second, GANs have trained adversarially to deceive the discriminator, whereas the Electra model is trained with maximum probability. Finally, The Electra pre-training's loss is a combination of MLM loss and discriminator loss as follows:

$$\min_{\theta_G,\theta_D} \sum_{\in \mathcal{X}} \mathcal{L}_{\text{MLM}}(,\theta_G) + \lambda \mathcal{L}_{\text{Disc}}(,\theta_D)$$

4.2. ARAELECTRA

The ARAELECTRA model (Antoun et al., 2020) is an ELECTRA-based Arabic language representation model. The goal of developing this model for the Arabic language is to improve current Arabic reading comprehension. The model is a bidirectional transformer encoder model with 136M parameters that includes 12 encoder layers, 12 attention heads, 768 hidden sizes, and 512 maximum input sequence lengths. As stated in the previous section, the ARAELECTRA pre-training objective replaced token detection (RTD). The pre-training dataset is identical to that of ARABERTV0.2 (Antoun et al.,). The dataset used is a collection of Arabic corpora

Model	Dataset	Loss Function	pRR
MARBERTv2	QRCD	Cross-Entropy	50.46
ARAELECTRA	QRCD	Cross-Entropy	56.07
		Focal-Loss + Label Smoothing	57.60
		Focal-Loss	**59.84**
ARAELECTRA	Ar-TyDi QA + QRCD	Cross-Entropy	62.88
ARAELECTRA	**Ar-TyDi QA + ArSQuAD + ARCD + QRCD**	**Cross-Entropy**	**66.9**
		Focal-Loss	61.2
		Dice-Loss	61.4

Table 2: The Results Of Applying Different Models on Development Set

totalling 8.8 billion words, the majority of which are news articles.

4.3. Fine-Tuning On Ar-TyDi QA

TyDi QA (Clark et al., 2020a) is a question-answer dataset with 204K question-answer pairs that covers 11 typologically diverse languages. TyDi QA's typology includes a wide range of languages. TyDi QA has a significant benefit in that data is collected directly in each language without the usage of neural machine translation. Furthermore, to give a realistic information-seeking activity, the questions are written by individuals who want to know the answer but do not yet know the answer, as opposed to SQuAD. We trained our model in the Arabic subset of the TyDi QA, the training examples were 15,364 and testing 941 with a total of 16305 samples. The model achieved an F1 score of 85.7% and an exact match of 72.9%.

4.4. Fine-Tuning On Arabic SQuAD and ARCD

Arabic-SQuAD: (Mozannar et al., 2019) The Arabic-SQuAD was obtained by a neural machine translation from the English version; the translation was carried out using the Google Translate neural machine translation (NMT) API; the authors chose to translate SQuAD version 1.1 because it was the most popular benchmark for Machine Reading Comprehension (MRC). Out of the 536 articles in the SQuAD training set, they only translated the first 231. The final distribution of the dataset is 48,344 questions on 10,364 paragraphs.

Arabic Reading Comprehension Dataset (ARCD): (Mozannar et al., 2019) ARCD's questions was written by proficient Arabic speakers. They retrieved the top 1000 viewed articles on Wikipedia in 2018 and then randomly sampled 155 articles. They tried to make the articles' topics as diverse as possible, including religious and historical figures, sports celebrities, countries, and companies. Finally, they requested a worker to create three question-answer pairs for each paragraph in unambiguous Modern Standard Arabic, with the answer to each question being an exact span of text from the article's paragraph. ARCD is composed of 1,395 questions along with their passages and answers.

Model Training: To train the proposed model, we merged the previous datasets, Arabic SQuAD and ARCD. The model was initially fine-tuned on Ar-TyDiQA, then the same model was used to fine-tune on the combined two datasets, yielding 49,739 questions, with the training set including 39,791 questions and the test set containing 9,948 questions, together with their passages and answers. The model obtained an F1 score of 70.05% and an exact match score of 36.47%.

4.5. Fine-Tuning On QRCD

Following the previous phases of fine-tuning the model on the Ar-TyDi QA and Arabic SQuAD + ARCD, we acquired the model's weights and fine-tuned it again on QRCD to improve performance. On the Development and Test sets, the model achieved 66.9% pRR and 54.59% pRR, respectively. We follow this approach due to the QRCD's small sample size because it is known that Deep Learning models require a large sample size even if it is pre-trained on a large corpus, and the transferred knowledge from previous dataset training helped the model retrieve better answers because the MSA(the style in which Ar-TyDi QA, Arabic SQuAD, and ARCD are written) is similar in many characteristics to CA (the style in which the Holy Qu'ran is written). This method is used in a variety of fields (Thrun and Pratt, 2012), (Menegola et al., 2017), (Jang et al., 2019), (Silver et al., 2013), not just in the Machine Reading Comprehension task. Even if the model suffers from catastrophic forgetting (McCloskey and Cohen, 1989) during the different phases of our training pipeline, which is split into three phases as detailed in the previous section, it may benefit from the transferred knowledge.

5. Results and Discussion

5.1. Performance Metrics

Because this is considered a ranking task, the QA system is needed to return up to 5 potential answers. The pRR

Question من هم الملائكة المذكورون في القرآن؟
واتبعوا ما تتلو الشياطين على ملك سليمان وما كفر سليمان ولكن الشياطين كفروا يعلمون الناس السحر وما أنزل على الملكين ببابل هاروت وماروت وما يعلمان من أحد حتى يقولا إنما نحن فتنة فلا تكفر فيتعلمون منهما ما يفرقون به بين المرء وزوجه وما هم بضارين به من أحد إلا بإذن الله ويتعلمون ما يضرهم ولا ينفعهم ولقد علموا لمن اشتراه ما له في الآخرة من خلاق ولبئس ما شروا به أنفسهم لو كانوا يعلمون. ولو أنهم آمنوا واتقوا لمثوبة من عند الله خير لو كانوا يعلمون
أرأيت الذي ينهى. عبدا إذا صلى. أرأيت إن كان على الهدى. أو أمر بالتقوى. أرأيت إن كذب وتولى. ألم يعلم بأن الله يرى. كلا لئن لم ينته لنسفعا بالناصية. ناصية كاذبة خاطئة. فليدع ناديه. سندع الزبانية. كلا لا تطعه واسجد واقترب
Question ما هي منزلة من يقتل في سبيل الله؟
فليقاتل في سبيل الله الذين يشرون الحياة الدنيا بالآخرة ومن يقاتل في سبيل الله فيقتل أو يغلب فسوف نؤتيه أجرا عظيما. وما لكم لا تقاتلون في سبيل الله والمستضعفين من الرجال والنساء والولدان الذين يقولون ربنا أخرجنا من هذه القرية الظالم أهلها واجعل لنا من لدنك وليا واجعل لنا من لدنك نصيرا. الذين آمنوا يقاتلون في سبيل الله والذين كفروا يقاتلون في سبيل الطاغوت فقاتلوا أولياء الشيطان إن كيد الشيطان كان ضعيفا
Question هل يجب ذكر اسم الله على المأكل والمشرب؟
فكلوا مما ذكر اسم الله عليه إن كنتم بآياته مؤمنين. وما لكم ألا تأكلوا مما ذكر اسم الله عليه وقد فصل لكم ما حرم عليكم إلا ما اضطررتم إليه وإن كثيرا ليضلون بأهوائهم بغير علم إن ربك هو أعلم بالمعتدين. وذروا ظاهر الإثم وباطنه إن الذين يكسبون الإثم سيجزون بما كانوا يقترفون. ولا تأكلوا مما لم يذكر اسم الله عليه وإنه لفسق وإن الشياطين ليوحون إلى أوليائهم ليجادلوكم وإن أطعتموهم إنكم لمشركون
إن الذين كفروا ويصدون عن سبيل الله والمسجد الحرام الذي جعلناه للناس سواء العاكف فيه والباد ومن يرد فيه بإلحاد بظلم نذقه من عذاب أليم. وإذ بوأنا لإبراهيم مكان البيت أن لا تشرك بي شيئا وطهر بيتي للطائفين والقائمين والركع السجود. وأذن في الناس بالحج يأتوك رجالا وعلى كل ضامر يأتين من كل فج عميق. ليشهدوا منافع لهم ويذكروا اسم الله في أيام معلومات على ما رزقهم من بهيمة الأنعام فكلوا منها وأطعموا البائس الفقير. ثم ليقضوا تفثهم وليوفوا نذورهم وليطوفوا بالبيت العتيق.

Figure 2: Samples Of Questions Combined With Context and Predicted Answers(in Green).

is best for measuring the retrieving performance of the system. pRR is a Reciprocal Rank variation in which the system may retrieve answers that partially match the gold ground-truth answers at different rankings. The suggested approach gives credit to responses at any rank but adds a penalty as the rank of the answers increases (1 top/best to 5 lowest), as shown below.

$$pRR(R) = \frac{m_{r_k}}{k}; k = min\{k|m_{r_k} > 0\},$$

where k denotes the rank position (in our case k = $\{1$ to $5\}$). m_r is computed as follows:

$$m_r = \max_{a \in A} f_m(r, a)$$

Where $f_m(r, a)$ is an answer-match function that matches a system answer r with the answer a in our case, we utilise the F1 measure applied across questions.

5.2. Experimental Results

In this section, we will present the results of experimenting with various models and architectures trained on different datasets, as well as the impact on performance. We analyzed multiple pre-trained models tailored for Arabic QA and found that the best performing models were MARBERTv2 and ARAELECTRA on multiple datasets. The results of our experiments showed that ARAELECTRA greatly outperformed MARBERTv2 on QRCD, which incentivised our choice to continue using ARAELECTRA in our pipeline.

MARBERTv2: (Abdul-Mageed et al., 2021) was trained using the same data as MARBERT and ARBERT, as well as the AraNews dataset (**?**), but with a longer sequence length of 512 tokens over 40 epochs, totalling 29B tokens. MARBERTv2 didn't obtain competitive results on QRCD, yielding 50.46, 32.11, and 50.5 pRR, exact match, and F1 on the development set, respectively .

Datasets: We fine-tuned ARAELECTRA on three datasets(Ar-TyDi QA, Arabic SQuAD, ARCD, and QRCD) as described in the previous sections. ARAELECTRA fine-tuned in the three datasets yielded the best performance of all the experiments. The comparison between the model's performance was fine-tuned on different datasets and tested on the development set illustrated in Figure 1.

Loss Functions: We experimented with several loss functions to see how they affected performance because the data imbalance issue is more severe for MRC tasks (Rajpurkar et al., 2016), (Bajaj et al., 2016), (Rajpurkar et al., 2018), with a negative-positive ratio of 200-50. Because the MRC task is thought to anticipate the start and end indices of the answer based on the query and context, only two tokens (start and end) are considered positive, while the others are considered negative. We tested Focal-loss (Lin et al., 2017) which is a dynamically scaled cross-entropy loss by applying a modulating term to focus the learning process on low confidence examples (hard misclassified) and down-weight the contribution of the high confidence examples (easy classified). Also, we applied Dice-Loss (Sorensen, 1948), (Dice, 1945), which is an F1- oriented statistic used to gauge the similarity of two sets. We only evaluated those losses in the last phase (fine-tune on QRCD), because we didn't have enough time to experiment with it in the early phases. But, we believe applying those loss functions in the early phases may enhance overall performance (Li et al., 2019). The results of different experiments are shown in Table 2

5.3. Results Analysis

The test set has 238 samples. We analysed the results across all competition participants. For each sample in the test set, we have the minimum, median, and maximum pRR across all submitted runs from all teams. We obtained 73 samples equal to the maximum pRR, 124 samples larger than the median, 52 samples less than the median, 62 samples equal to the median, and 21 samples equal to the minimum pRR from all 238 samples. Figure 2 Samples of the test set questions and their context are illustrated, with the predicted answers highlighted in green.

6. Conclusion and Future Works

In this study, We proposed a method for dealing with QA in the Holy Qur'an. The ARAELECTRA model's efficiency and performance were improved by fine-tuning it on the Ar-TyDi QA, Arabic-SQuAD, and ARCD datasets before fine-tuning it on the competition dataset (QRCD). Furthermore, because the dataset is imbalanced, experimenting with different loss functions to observe how they affect the model performance resulted in a higher model pRR score using the Cross-Entropy loss, which achieved 66.9% on the development set and 54.59% on the test set. In future work, we aim to experiment with alternative loss functions in the early stages of our technique to see whether it improves model performance and efficiency. Moreover, Increasing the dataset size may improve the model's robustness.

Code Availability: The code that was used to conduct the experiments in this work can be found at the following GitHub repository:`https://github.com/Alymostafa/GOF-Qur-an-QA-2022-Shared-Task-Code`

7. Bibliographical References

Abdelmegied, A., Ayman, Y., Eid, A., El-Makky, N., Fathy, A., Khairy, G., Nagi, K., Nabil, M., and Yousri, M. (2017). A modified version of alquans: An arabic language question answering system. In *International Joint Conference on Knowledge Discovery, Knowledge Engineering, and Knowledge Management*, pages 184–199. Springer.

Abdelnasser, H., Ragab, M., Mohamed, R., Mohamed, A., Farouk, B., El-Makky, N. M., and Torki, M. (2014). Al-bayan: an arabic question answering system for the holy quran. In *Proceedings of the EMNLP 2014 Workshop on Arabic Natural Language Processing (ANLP)*, pages 57–64.

Abdul-Mageed, M., Elmadany, A., and Nagoudi, E. M. B. (2021). ARBERT & MARBERT: Deep bidirectional transformers for Arabic. In *Proceedings of the 59th Annual Meeting of the Association for Computational Linguistics and the 11th International Joint Conference on Natural Language Processing (Volume 1: Long Papers)*, pages 7088–7105, Online, August. Association for Computational Linguistics.

Adany, M. A. H. et al. (2017). *An automatic question answering system for the Arabic Quran*. Ph.D. thesis, Sudan University of Science and Technology.

Ali, A. Y. (2000). *The holy Qur'an*. Wordsworth Editions.

Antoun, W., Baly, F., and Hajj, H.). Arabert: Transformer-based model for arabic language understanding. In *LREC 2020 Workshop Language Resources and Evaluation Conference 11–16 May 2020*, page 9.

Antoun, W., Baly, F., and Hajj, H. (2020). Araelectra: Pre-training text discriminators for arabic language understanding.

Arabic.). Arabic language.

Bajaj, P., Campos, D., Craswell, N., Deng, L., Gao, J., Liu, X., Majumder, R., McNamara, A., Mitra, B., Nguyen, T., et al. (2016). Ms marco: A human generated machine reading comprehension dataset. *arXiv preprint arXiv:1611.09268*.

Brini, W., Ellouze, M., Mesfar, S., and Belguith, L. H. (2009). An arabic question-answering system for factoid questions. In *2009 International Conference on Natural Language Processing and Knowledge Engineering*, pages 1–7. IEEE.

Clark, J. H., Choi, E., Collins, M., Garrette, D., Kwiatkowski, T., Nikolaev, V., and Palomaki, J. (2020a). Tydi qa: A benchmark for information-seeking question answering in typologically diverse languages. *Transactions of the Association for Computational Linguistics*, 8:454–470.

Clark, K., Luong, M.-T., Le, Q. V., and Manning, C. D. (2020b). Electra: Pre-training text encoders as discriminators rather than generators. *arXiv preprint arXiv:2003.10555*.

Devlin, J., Chang, M.-W., Lee, K., and Toutanova, K. (2018). Bert: Pre-training of deep bidirectional transformers for language understanding. *arXiv preprint arXiv:1810.04805*.

Dice, L. R. (1945). Measures of the amount of ecologic association between species. *Ecology*, 26(3):297–302.

Goodfellow, I., Pouget-Abadie, J., Mirza, M., Xu, B., Warde-Farley, D., Ozair, S., Courville, A., and Bengio, Y. (2014). Generative adversarial nets. *Advances in neural information processing systems*, 27.

Hakkoum, A. and Raghay, S. (2016). Semantic q&a system on the qur'an. *Arabian Journal for Science and Engineering*, 41(12):5205–5214.

Hamdelsayed, M. A. and Atwell, E. (2016a). Using arabic numbers (singular, dual, and plurals) patterns to enhance question answering system results. In *IMAN'2016 4th International Conference on Islamic Applications in Computer Science and Technologies*. Leeds.

Hamdelsayed, M. A. and Atwell, E. (2016b). Islamic applications of automatic question-answering.

Hamdelsayed, M. A., Mohamed, E. M. E., Saeed, M. T. M., Ai, A. M., Mhmoud, E. B. E. M., Mahmoud, M. A., Shamat, A., and Atwell, E. (2017). Islamic application of question answering systems: Comparative study. *Journal of Advanced Computer Science and Technology Research*, 7(1):29–41.

Hamed, S. K. and Aziz, M. J. A. (2016). A question answering system on holy quran translation based on question expansion technique and neural network classification. *J. Comput. Sci.*, 12:169–177.

Hamoud, B. and Atwell, E. (2016). Using an islamic question and answer knowledge base to answer questions about the holy quran. *International Journal on Islamic Applications in Computer Science And Technology*, 4(4):20–29.

Jang, Y., Lee, H., Hwang, S. J., and Shin, J. (2019). Learning what and where to transfer. In *International Conference on Machine Learning*, pages 3030–3039. PMLR.

Lan, Z., Chen, M., Goodman, S., Gimpel, K., Sharma, P., and Soricut, R. (2019). Albert: A lite bert for self-supervised learning of language representations. *arXiv preprint arXiv:1909.11942*.

Lewis, M., Liu, Y., Goyal, N., Ghazvininejad, M., Mohamed, A., Levy, O., Stoyanov, V., and Zettlemoyer, L. (2019). Bart: Denoising sequence-to-sequence pre-training for natural language generation, translation, and comprehension. *arXiv preprint arXiv:1910.13461*.

Li, X., Sun, X., Meng, Y., Liang, J., Wu, F., and Li, J. (2019). Dice loss for data-imbalanced nlp tasks. *arXiv preprint arXiv:1911.02855*.

Lin, T.-Y., Goyal, P., Girshick, R., He, K., and Dollár, P. (2017). Focal loss for dense object detection. In *Proceedings of the IEEE international conference on computer vision*, pages 2980–2988.

Malhas, R. and Elsayed, T. (2020). Ayatec: building a reusable verse-based test collection for arabic question answering on the holy qur'an. *ACM Transactions on Asian and Low-Resource Language Information Processing (TALLIP)*, 19(6):1–21.

Malhas, R. and Elsayed, T. (2022). Official repository of qur'an qa shared task. `https://gitlab.com/bigirqu/quranqa`.

Malhas, R., Mansour, W., and Elsayed, T. (2022). Qur'an QA 2022: Overview of the first shared task on question answering over the holy qur'an. In *Proceedings of the 5th Workshop on Open-Source Arabic Corpora and Processing Tools (OSACT5) at the 13th Language Resources and Evaluation Conference (LREC 2022)*.

McCloskey, M. and Cohen, N. J. (1989). Catastrophic interference in connectionist networks: The sequential learning problem. In *Psychology of learning and motivation*, volume 24, pages 109–165. Elsevier.

Menegola, A., Fornaciali, M., Pires, R., Bittencourt, F. V., Avila, S., and Valle, E. (2017). Knowledge transfer for melanoma screening with deep learning. In *2017 IEEE 14th international symposium on biomedical imaging (ISBI 2017)*, pages 297–300. IEEE.

Mohammed, F., Nasser, K., and Harb, H. M. (1993). A knowledge based arabic question answering system (aqas). *ACM SIGART Bulletin*, 4(4):21–30.

Mozannar, H., Maamary, E., El Hajal, K., and Hajj, H. (2019). Neural Arabic question answering. In *Proceedings of the Fourth Arabic Natural Language Processing Workshop*, pages 108–118, Florence, Italy, August. Association for Computational Linguistics.

Nabil, M., Abdelmegied, A., Ayman, Y., Fathy, A., Khairy, G., Yousri, M., El-Makky, N. M., and Nagi, K. (2017). Alquans-an arabic language question answering system. In *KDIR*, pages 144–154.

Raffel, C., Shazeer, N., Roberts, A., Lee, K., Narang, S., Matena, M., Zhou, Y., Li, W., and Liu, P. J. (2019). Exploring the limits of transfer learning with a unified text-to-text transformer. *arXiv preprint arXiv:1910.10683*.

Rajpurkar, P., Zhang, J., Lopyrev, K., and Liang, P. (2016). Squad: 100,000+ questions for machine comprehension of text. *arXiv preprint arXiv:1606.05250*.

Rajpurkar, P., Jia, R., and Liang, P. (2018). Know what you don't know: Unanswerable questions for squad. *arXiv preprint arXiv:1806.03822*.

Shmeisani, H., Tartir, S., Al-Na'ssaan, A., and Naji, M. (2014). Semantically answering questions from the holy quran. In *International Conference on Islamic Applications in Computer Science And Technology*, pages 1–8.

Silver, D. L., Yang, Q., and Li, L. (2013). Lifelong machine learning systems: Beyond learning algorithms. In *2013 AAAI spring symposium series*.

Sorensen, T. A. (1948). A method of establishing groups of equal amplitude in plant sociology based on similarity of species content and its application to analyses of the vegetation on danish commons. *Biol. Skar.*, 5:1–34.

Thrun, S. and Pratt, L. (2012). *Learning to learn*. Springer Science & Business Media.

Vaswani, A., Shazeer, N., Parmar, N., Uszkoreit, J., Jones, L., Gomez, A. N., Kaiser, Ł., and Polosukhin, I. (2017). Attention is all you need. *Advances in neural information processing systems*, 30.

Wang, A., Singh, A., Michael, J., Hill, F., Levy, O., and Bowman, S. R. (2018). Glue: A multi-task benchmark and analysis platform for natural language understanding. *arXiv preprint arXiv:1804.07461*.

Xue, L., Constant, N., Roberts, A., Kale, M., Al-Rfou, R., Siddhant, A., Barua, A., and Raffel, C. (2020). mt5: A massively multilingual pre-trained text-to-text transformer. *arXiv preprint arXiv:2010.11934*.

Proceedings of the OSACT 2022 Workshop @LREC2022, pages 112–119
Marseille, 20 June 2022

LARSA22 at Qur'an QA 2022: Text-to-Text Transformer for Finding Answers to Questions from Qur'an

[*]Youssef Mellah, [•]Ibtissam Touahri, [*]Zakaria Kaddari, [*]Zakaria Haja, [*]Jamal Berrich, [*]Toumi Bouchentouf
[*]LARSA Laboratory of National School of Applied Sciences, [2]Department of computer science, Superior School of Technology, Meknes
[*]Oujda, Morocco, [•]Meknes, Morocco
y.mellah@ump.ac.ma, i.touahri@umi.ac.ma, kadzaki@gmail.com, zakaria.haja@ump.ac.ma, jberrich@gmail.com, t.bouchentouf@ump.ac.ma

Abstract
Question Answering (QA) is one of the main focuses of Natural Language Processing (NLP) research. However, Arabic Question Answering is still not within reach. The challenges of the Arabic language and the lack of resources have made it difficult to provide powerful Arabic QA systems with high accuracy. While low accuracy may be accepted for general purpose systems, it is critical in some fields such as religious affairs. Therefore, there is a need for specialized accurate systems that target these critical fields. In this paper, we propose a Transformer-based QA system using the mT5 Language Model (LM). We finetuned the model on the Qur'anic Reading Comprehension Dataset (QRCD) which was provided in the context of the Qur'an QA 2022 shared task. The QRCD dataset consists of question-passage pairs as input, and the corresponding adequate answers provided by expert annotators as output. Evaluation results on the same DataSet show that our best model can achieve 0.98 (F1 Score) on the Dev Set and 0.40 on the Test Set. We discuss those results and challenges, then propose potential solutions for possible improvements. The source code is available on our repository[1].

Keywords: Question Answering (QA), Natural Language Processing (NLP), Transformer, mT5, Language Model (LM), QRCD

1. Introduction

The Holy Quran is the primary reference for about 1.6 billion Muslims around the world. The Qur'anic classical Arabic text is either instructive or narrative and it is composed of 114 chapters, 6,236 verses and 80k words (Malhas and Elsayed, 2020), the entire text is joined into one whole related concept which underlies a deep connection between the ideas and meaning that overlap whithin chapters and verses. Different researches have been conducted on the holy Quran, either to construct datasets, perform automatic text classification, Question answering (QA), semantic search based on ontology, topic assignment or optical text recognition tasks (Adeleke et al., 2019) (Alqahtani and Atwell, 2016) (Mohamed and Shokry, 2020) (Mohd et al., 2021). There is a need for automatic Qur'anic QA (Alsubhi et al., 2021) that helps to facilitate and improve the time of Qur'an knowledge acquirement since the holy Qur'an is the trustful legislated text used for teaching purposes and to respond to Muslim requests.The search engines are an automatic way to get information as they provide documents rich of relevant information to the user request. However, it doesn't pinpoint the answer. Hence, there is still a lack of methods that answer directly the user demands which makes answer search troubleshooting. In this context, reliable Question answering systems turn important to deal with this in different languages, while there are few attempts for Arabic QA investigation. QA is an interactive automatic process that belongs to the natural language processing field. QA systems provide the user with a solution that helps them to achieve the exact answer to a natural language question. The performance of a QA system is influenced by the size of training data, its quality as well as the used techniques. The Arabic language is still of scarce resources in comparison to English (Alsubhi et al., 2021) (Alanazi et al., 2021) (Maraoui et al., 2021) and yet the QA task needs more preprocessing and deep linguistic knowledge when extracting answers from the holy Qur'an.

In the following, we describe our participation in Qur'an QA 2022 Shared Task that aims to answer questions in the holly Qur'an. The task organizers provide participating systems with a consecutive passage from the Holy Qur'an based on which they answer questions raised in Modern Standard Arabic by selecting one or many ranked text spans from the passage. For this, they provided the Qur'anic Reading Comprehension Dataset (QRCD) composed of 1,337 question-passage-answer triplets.

Our paper proposed a model based on sequence to sequence (Seq2Seq) transformers using the mT5 Language Model that is fed by Arabic question and its corresponding passage (context), then extract the most relevant answers. The task starts by preprocessing and matching the question to the passage that contains the response, then we fine-tune the mT5 LM to get the adequate answer.

The paper is organized as follows, we present the related works, and afterward, we define the task steps and dataset as described by the organizers, we describe afterward the proposed approach besides analyzing the obtained results on both dev and test sets, then we give a conclusion with further work.

2. Related Work

Many studies have been interested in providing reliable linguistic resources for the Holy Qur'an automatic annotation, processing and interpretation. In this context, (Osman et al., 2015) provided a Quranic Dataset that may be exploited by researches aiming to explore the holy Quran. (Dukes et al., 2013) presented the Quranic Arabic Corpus that includes morphological segmentation, part-of-speech, and syntactic analysis annotations. (Al-Salhi and Abdullah, 2022) constructed the ontology of Quranic stories which construction depends on the MappingMaster

[1] https://github.com/mellahysf/Quran-QA

domain-specific language technology. (Malhas and Elsayed, 2020) introduced AyaTEC, a collection of verse-based questions answering on the Holy Qur'an. The dataset covers 11 topic categories of the Holy Qur'an and includes 207 questions and 1,762 answers covering that target the information needs of both curious and skeptical users.

Question answering(QA) aims to search for an answer to given questions is one widely investigated task among the most challenging ones in Natural Language Processing (NLP) (Alsubhi et al., 2021). A large volume of QA studies was devoted to the English language. However, it is not the case when it comes to the Arabic language due to its scarce resources. (Alanazi et al., 2021) provided a systematic review of QA research. They have examined English relevant studies and techniques. (Maraoui et al., 2021) have used standardized hadith, narrators, and Tafsir to develop a QA system. The system reached an accuracy of 92%. Current studies Investigated advanced techniques achieving state-of-the-art results. The language pre-trained transformers models helped to achieve significant progress in many NLP tasks. (Xue et al., 2021) used pre-trained multilingual T5 (mT5) as a generative model to generate multilingual question and answer pairs. (Alsubhi et al., 2021) have evaluated the fine-tuned AraBERTv2-base (Antoun et al., 2021a), AraBERTv0.2-large, and AraELECTRA (Antoun et al., 2021b) models using Arabic-SQuAD (Mozannar et al., 2019), ARCD (Mozannar et al., 2019), AQAD (Atef et al., 2020), and TyDiQA-GoldP (Clark et al., 2020) datasets. (Alsaleh et al., 2021) applied AraBERT language model with its two versions to binary classify the QurSim dataset pairs of verses. The best result was AraBERTv0.2 with 92% accuracy.

Imbalanced classification techniques have been applied widely in the field of data mining. It is used to classify the imbalanced classes that are not equal in the number of samples. The problem with imbalanced classes is that the classification performance tends to the class with more samples while the class with few samples will obtain poor performance. This problem can be occurred in the Qur'anic classification due to the difference in the number of verses (B. S. Arkok and Zeki, 2021) (B. Arkok and Zeki, 2021). (B. S. Arkok and Zeki, 2021) applied methods for under-sample (RUS), random oversample (ROS), synthetic minority oversampling technique (SMOTE), and random methods to classify the Qur'anic topics that are imbalanced. Many metrics were used in this research to evaluate the experimental results. (B. Arkok and Zeki, 2021) aimed to address balanced classification. They performed the Qur'anic text classification using SVM, Naïve Bayes, KNN, and J48. (Abdelnasser et al., 2014) provided an Arabic QA system for the Holy Quran that retrieves the most relevant verses corresponding to a question, then extracts the passage that contains the answer from the Quran and its interpretation books (Tafseer). Their system reached an accuracy of 85%. (Samy et al., 2019) provided a review of the Arabic Question Answering Systems, their approaches and challenges.

3. Shared Task and DataSet

In this section, we introduce the context of our paper which is the "Qur'an QA 2022 Shared Task", and we describe the given dataset in the task.

3.1 Qur'an QA 2022 Shared Task

Modern Standard Arabic (MSA) is the most understandable and common language in the Middle East and North Africa (by more than 400M people), and it is the official language used in media such as TV shows and newspapers. For this reason, it is encouraging for the scientific community to exert more effort to build systems specialized in solving situations related to the Arabic language. "Qur'an QA 2022 Shared Task" (Malhas et al, 2022) is shown in the efforts of developing the field of Arabic NLP and it is an attempt to enrich it, especially QA in the Qur'an script context.
The task is defined to find the correct answer(s) to a question in each passage (Figure 1), the questions are written in an MSA language, while the passage consists of verses from the Holy Qur'an written in Classical Arabic.


```
{
  "pq_id": "38:41-44_105",
  "passage": "واذكر عبدنا أيوب إذ نادى ربه أني مسني الشيطان بنصب وعذاب
              اركض برجلك هذا مغتسل بارد وشراب
              ووهبنا له أهله ومثلهم معهم رحمة منا وذكرى لأولي الألباب
              وخذ بيدك ضغثا فاضرب به ولا تحنث إنا وجدناه صابرا نعم العبد إنه أواب",
  "surah": 38,
  "verses": "41-44",
  "question": "من هو النبي المعروف بالصبر؟",
  "answers": [
    {
      "text": "أيوب",
      "start_char": 12
    }
  ]
}
{
  "pq_id": "74:32-48_330",
  "passage": "كلا والقمر. والليل إذ أدبر. والصبح إذا أسفر. إنها لإحدى الكبر
              نذيرا للبشر. لمن شاء منكم أن يتقدم أو يتأخر. كل نفس بما كسبت رهينة
              إلا أصحاب اليمين. في جنات يتساءلون. عن المجرمين. ما سلككم في سقر
              قالوا لم نك من المصلين. ولم نك نطعم المسكين
              وكنا نخوض مع الخائضين. وكنا نكذب بيوم الدين. حتى أتانا اليقين. فما تنفعهم شفاعة الشافعين",
  "surah": 74,
  "verses": "32-48",
  "question": "ما هي الدلائل التي تشير بأن الانسان مخير؟",
  "answers": [
    {
      "text": "لمن شاء منكم أن يتقدم أو يتأخر",
      "start_char": 76
    },
    {
      "text": "كل نفس بما كسبت رهينة",
      "start_char": 108
    }
  ]
}
```


Figure 1: Structure of the QRCD Dataset

From the accompanying passage for the given question, the model must return up to 5 possible responses, sorted from 1 (best) to 5 (lowest). Therefore, the partial Reciprocal Rank (pRR) will be the primary criterion for evaluating the competing models. Exact Match (EM) and F1@1, which are evaluation metrics applied only to the top predicted answer, will also be reported. The EM metric is a binary metric that only rewards a system if the top predicted answer exactly matches one of the gold answers. The F1@1 measurement, on the other hand, measures the token overlap between the best matching gold answer and the top predicted answer.

3.2 Dataset

The AyaTEC dataset was built with the help of three Islamic specialists in holy Qur'an interpretation (tafsir), and the questions were collected from different sources, questions were prepared by experts or asked by ordinary people on Islamic websites (Malhas and Elsayed, 2020), in the given dataset we have two types of samples, the single answer question samples, and the multi-answer question samples the first type is the questions that have only one answer for the question in the passage, the multi-answer type is those which have multiple answers for the question in the same passage. The dataset is divided into training, development, and test set. Figure *2* shows that the question-passage-answer triplets represent the greatest count compared to the question-passage pairs, which is also greater than the count of passages. We note that the questions take the least part. Our model is trained on the question passage pair as input, and it is expected to provide the answer(s) to the question extracted from the given passage.

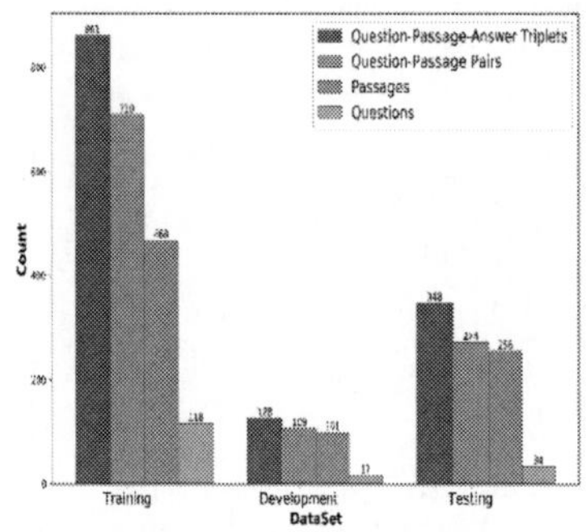

Figure 2: Task dataset parts distribution

4. Approach

Our approach consists of a Sequence-to-Sequence (Seq2Seq) model (Sutskever et al., 2014), based on the mT5 Language Model (Xue et al., 2021). We leverage the task as a Text-to-Text problem, which accepts an Arabic question and the passage as input, then extract the most relevant answers. Firstly, we preprocess and concatenate the question and the passage, then we fine-tune the mT5 LM to get an adequate answer. Figure *3* shows the general architecture of our approach.

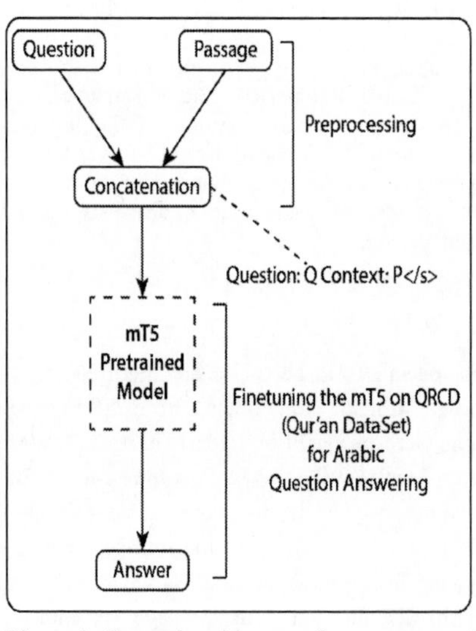

Figure 3: General architecture for our approach

We used mT5, which was pre-trained on a new Common Crawl-based DataSet covering 101 languages, Arabic language included. This model achieves top results on many NLP benchmarks while being flexible enough to be fine-tuned for a variety of important downstream tasks (Jawahar et al., 2021) (Agarwal et al., 2020) (Farahani et al., 2021) (Rothe et al., 2021). Another reason for choosing mT5 is that it is based on an encoder-decoder (Seq2Seq), which makes it appropriate for the Qur'an shared task. AraT5 (Nagoudi et al., 2021), is also a powerful Seq2Seq model which has better or comparable performance to mT5, but the source code is still not yet ready to use, at the time of writing this paper. In this sense, we fine tune mT5 on QRCD considering the input sequence (question + passage) as text and the output answer as text also.

4.1 Preprocessing

Given a question Q and a passage P from the Qur'an text, we form the input sequence as follows:

Question : Q Context : P</s>

Where </s> tag denotes the end of the input sequence. For all text in the dataset, we removed some stop words and since the original format of QRCD DataSet files is JSON, we converted the input and the output sequences to Tabulate-Separated Values in TSV files, the favorite format for fine-tuning mT5.

4.2 Fine-Tuning of mT5

In recent years, Transfer Learning (TL) has led to a new wave of cutting-edge results in Natural Language Processing (NLP). The power of TL comes from pretraining a model on abundantly available unlabeled text data with a self-supervised task. After that, the model can be refined on smaller labeled data sets, which often results in (much) better performance than training on the labeled data alone. The recent success of transfer learning was sparked in 2018 by ULMFiT (Howard and Ruder, 2018), ELMo and BERT (Devlin et al., 2019). The 2019 year saw the development of a wide variety of new methods like GPT (Radford et al., 2019), XLNet (Yang et al., 2019), RoBERTa, ALBERT (Lan et al., 2019), Reformer and MT-DNN (Liu et al., 2019). The pace of progress on the ground has made it difficult to assess the most significant improvements and their effectiveness when combined.

After a preliminary study that we did, we did not use these models because most of them do not deal with the Arabic language. Or, for for multilingual models (which also process Arabic), their architectures do not help to use them for seq2seq tasks (text generation or extraction task, the case of the task being processed), which led us to fine-tune the mT5 pretrained model.

Our implementation details are explained in the next section.

5. Experimentation and Results

Using the original mT5 recipe, we consider three model sizes: Base (580M), Large (1.2B) and XL (3.7B). The increase in parameters comes from the larger vocabulary used in mT5 (covering 101 languages).

The following setup is used across all our experiments. We used a global batch size of 64 with a max input length of 354 and a max target length of 150. AdamW was used as the optimizer with a constant learning rate set to 0.003. Models were trained for 15k steps and we saved the best checkpoint every 5k steps. We kept the other default hyperparameters suggested by T5 (Raffel et al., 2019) and mT5 papers. Finally, we selected the best checkpoint based on the Dev Set validation results. The training was performed on a TPU v3, using Google Colab Pro, with Google Cloud Platform (GCP) for storage.

We finetuned our models on the Train Set of QRCD Dataset, then we evaluated them on the Development Set. Finally, we generated predictions on the Test Set and submitted our runs for evaluation by the community of the Qur'an QA 2022 shared task using Codalab platform.

Table *1* shows the results of our experimentations over the Development Set and Table *2* shows our best run result on the Test Set.

Model	pRR	Exact Match	F1 Score
mT5-Base	0.79	0.65	0.79
mT5-Large	0.91	0.71	0.91
mT5-XL	0.98	0.97	0.98

Table 1: Results of evaluation on the Dev Set

Model	pRR	Exact Match	F1 Score
mT5-XL	0.43	0.20	0.40

Table 2: Best result of evaluation on the Test Set

As shown in the results tables, our best model achieves 0.98, 0.97 and 0.98 (pRR, EM and F1 scores respectively) on the Development Set, which are very good results, but it decreases on the Test Set, mainly on the EM metric.

6. Analysis and discussion

We have achieved good results in the Developpement set. However, there was a degradation when applying the model to the test set. This may be due to many reasons among which the ones presented in Table *3*, in which we give some examples of our model prediction and its interpretation based on our estimated human response since the gold answers aren't released yet. The model has a high performance when it comes to extractive answers such as in the first example. Moreover, it may generate singular terms from plurals such as in the second example. In the third example, our model generates close answers. However, the system may generate distant responses since sometimes the names of Prophets and messengers may be considered angels, which raises the need for named entities recognition. Our model may generate the same verse as the given passage if the response is difficult to be extracted as in the fifth example. Moreover, sometimes our model is not only extractive but it may become generative as in example six. The model can generate the best answer but with a low rank which has been fixed to five as the organizers of the competition consider the top five ranked answers. At this level, the right answer may be not reached yet. Increasing the number of estimated answers causes an increase in execution time and computational requirements.

N	Passage	Question	Response	Interpretation
1	والذين يتوفون منكم ويذرون أزواجا يتربصن بأنفسهن أربعة أشهر وعشرا فإذا بلغن أجلهن فلا جناح عليكم فيما فعلن في أنفسهن بالمعروف والله بما تعملون خبير. ولا جناح عليكم فيما عرضتم به من خطبة النساء أو أكننتم في أنفسكم علم الله أنكم ستذكرونهن ولكن لا تواعدوهن سرا إلا أن تقولوا قولا معروفا ولا تعزموا عقدة النكاح حتى يبلغ الكتاب أجله واعلموا أن الله يعلم ما في أنفسكم فاحذروه واعلموا أن الله غفور حليم. لا جناح عليكم إن طلقتم النساء ما لم تمسوهن أو تفرضوا لهن فريضة ومتعوهن على الموسع قدره وعلى المقتر قدره متاعا بالمعروف حقا على المحسنين. وإن طلقتموهن من قبل أن تمسوهن وقد فرضتم لهن فريضة فنصف ما فرضتم إلا أن يعفون أو يعفو الذي بيده عقدة النكاح وأن تعفوا ".أقرب للتقوى ولا تنسوا الفضل بينكم إن الله بما تعملون بصير As for those among you who die and leave widows behind, their widows shall wait by themselves for four months and ten days. When they have reached their term, there is no blame on you regarding what they might honorably do with themselves. God is fully acquainted with what you do. You commit no error by announcing your engagement to women, or by keeping it to yourselves. God knows that you will be thinking about them. But do not meet them secretly, unless you have something proper to say. And do not confirm the marriage tie until the writing is fulfilled. And know that God knows what is in your souls, so beware of Him. And know that God is Forgiving and Forbearing. You commit no error by divorcing women before having touched them, or before having set the dowry for them. And compensate them—the wealthy according to his means, and the poor according to his means—with a fair compensation, a duty upon the doers of good. If you divorce them before you have touched them, but after you had set the dowry	? كم مدة عدة الأرملة /kam mudat eidat al'armala/ How long is a widow's waiting period?	أربعة أشهر وعشرا / 'arbaeat 'ashhur waeashran/ four months and ten	Our model extracts the correct answer from a complicated paragraph

	for them, give them half of what you specified—unless they forego the right, or the one in whose hand is the marriage contract foregoes it. But to forego is nearer to piety. And do not forget generosity between one another. God is seeing of everything you do[2].			
2	ولقد ذرأنا لجهنم كثيرا من الجن والإنس لهم قلوب لا يفقهون بها ولهم أعين لا يبصرون بها ولهم آذان لا يسمعون بها أولئك كالأنعام بل هم ".أضل أولئك هم الغافلون We have destined for Hell multitudes of jinn and humans. They have hearts with which they do not understand. They have eyes with which they do not see. They have ears with which they do not hear. These are like cattle. In fact, they are further astray. These are the heedless.	هل أشار القرآن إلى العضو الذي يعقل به الإنسان؟ / hal 'ashar alquran 'iilaa aleudw aladhi yueqil bih al'iinsan / Did the Qur'an refer to the organ with which a person can reason?	الأذن / al'udhun/ Ear	Generate Singular terms
3	يا أيها النبي لم تحرم ما أحل الله لك تبتغي مرضات أزواجك والله غفور رحيم. قد فرض الله لكم تحلة أيمانكم والله مولاكم وهو العليم الحكيم. وإذ أسر النبي إلى بعض أزواجه حديثا فلما نبأت به وأظهره الله عليه عرف بعضه وأعرض عن بعض فلما نبأها به قالت من أنبأك هذا قال نبأني العليم الخبير. إن تتوبا إلى الله فقد صغت قلوبكما وإن تظاهرا عليه فإن الله هو مولاه وجبريل وصالح المؤمنين والملائكة بعد ذلك ظهير. عسى ربه إن طلقكن أن يبدله أزواجا خيرا منكن مسلمات مؤمنات قانتات ",تائبات عابدات سائحات ثيبات وأبكارا O prophet! Why do you prohibit what God has permitted for you, seeking to please your wives? God is Forgiving and Merciful. God has decreed for you the dissolution of your oaths. God is your Master. He is the All-Knowing, the Most Wise. The Prophet told something in confidence to one of his wives. But when she disclosed it, and God made it known to him; he communicated part of it, and he avoided another part. Then, when he informed her of it, she said, “Who informed you of this?” He said, “The All-Knowing, the All-Informed, informed me.” If you repent to God, then your hearts have listened. But if you band together against him, then God is his Ally, as is Gabriel, and the righteous believers. In addition, the angels will assist him. Perhaps, if he divorces you, his Lord will give him in exchange wives better than you: submissive, believing, obedient, penitent, devout, fasting—previously married, or virgins.	من هم الملائكة المذكورون في القرآن /man humm almalayikat almadhkurun fi alquran/ Who are the angels mentioned in the Qur’an?	جبريل وصالح المؤمنين / جبريل وصالح المؤمنين / Gabriel and the righteous believers	The need for named entities recognition
4	وكذلك أنزلناه آيات بينات وأن الله يهدي من يريد. إن الذين آمنوا والذين هادوا والصابئين والنصارى والمجوس والذين أشركوا إن الله يفصل بينهم يوم القيامة إن الله على كل شيء شهيد. ألم تر أن الله يسجد له من في السماوات ومن في الأرض والشمس والقمر والنجوم والجبال والشجر والدواب وكثير من الناس وكثير حق عليه العذاب ومن يهن الله فما له من .مكرم إن الله يفعل ما يشاء Thus We revealed it as clarifying signs, and God guides whomever He wills. Those who believe, and those who are Jewish, and the Sabeans, and the Christians, and the Zoroastrians, and the Polytheists—God will judge between them on the Day of Resurrection. God is witness to all things. Do you not realize that to God prostrates everyone in the heavens and everyone on earth, and the sun, and the moon, and the stars, and the mountains, and the trees, and the animals, and many of the people? But many are justly deserving of punishment. Whomever God shames, there is none to honor him. God does whatever He wills.	ما الدلائل على أن القرآن ليس من تأليف سيدنا محمد (ص)؟ / ma aldalayil ealaa 'ana alquran lays min talif sayidina muhamad (s)?/ What is the evidence that the Qur’an was not written by our master Muhammad (PBUH)?	من يهن الله فما له من مكرم / man yahin allah fama lah min makram / Whomever God shames, there is none to honor him.	The wrong answer is repeated for all ranks.

[2] https://www.quranful.com/

<table>
<tr><td>5</td><td>ولقد آتينا موسى تسع آيات بينات فاسأل بني إسرائيل إذ جاءهم فقال له فرعون إني لأظنك يا موسى مسحورا. قال لقد علمت ما أنزل هؤلاء إلا رب السماوات والأرض بصائر وإني لأظنك يا فرعون مثبورا. فأراد أن يستفزهم من الأرض فأغرقناه ومن معه جميعا. وقلنا من بعده لبني إسرائيل اسكنوا الأرض فإذا جاء وعد الآخرة جئنا بكم لفيفا."
We gave Moses nine clear signs—ask the Children of Israel. When he went to them, Pharaoh said to him, “I think that you, Moses, are bewitched.” He said, “You know that none sent these down except the Lord of the heavens and the earth—eye openers; and I think that you, Pharaoh, are doomed.” He resolved to scare them off the land, but We drowned him, and those with him, altogether. After him, We said to the Children of Israel, “Inhabit the land, and when the promise of the Hereafter arrives, We will bring you all together.”</td><td>ما هي معجزات النبي موسى عليه السلام؟
/ ma hi muejizat alnabii musaa ealayh alsalam /
What are the miracles of Prophet Moses, peace be upon him?</td><td>-</td><td>The difficulty of response extraction</td></tr>
<tr><td rowspan="2">6</td><td rowspan="2">ويوم نحشرهم جميعا ثم نقول للذين أشركوا أين شركاؤكم الذين كنتم تزعمون. ثم لم تكن فتنتهم إلا أن قالوا والله ربنا ما كنا مشركين. انظر كيف كذبوا على أنفسهم وضل عنهم ما كانوا يفترون. ومنهم من يستمع إليك وجعلنا على قلوبهم أكنة أن يفقهوه وفي آذانهم وقرا وإن يروا كل آية لا يؤمنوا بها حتى إذا جاءوك يجادلونك يقول الذين كفروا إن هذا إلا أساطير الأولين. وهم ينهون عنه وينأون عنه وإن يهلكون إلا أنفسهم وما يشعرون.
On the Day when We gather them all together, then say to the idolaters, “Where are your idols, those you used to claim?” Then their only argument will be to say, “By God, our Lord, we were not idolaters.” Look how they lied to themselves. And what they invented deserted them. Among them are those who listen to you; but We place covers over their hearts, to prevent them from understanding it, and heaviness in their ears. Even if they see every sign, they will not believe in it. Until, when they come to you, to argue with you, those who disbelieve will say, “These are nothing but myths of the ancients.” They keep others from it, and avoid it themselves; but they ruin only their own souls, and they do not realize.</td><td rowspan="2">هل أشار القرآن إلى العضو الذي يعقل به الإنسان؟
/ hal 'ashar alquran 'iilaa aleudw aladhi yueqil bih al'iinsan /
Did the Qur’an refer to the organ with which a person can reason?</td><td>العضو من العضو
/ aleudw min aleudw/
Organ from organ</td><td>Generate new terms</td></tr>
<tr><td>قلوبهم أكنة
/qulubuhum 'akuna /
Their hearts are veils</td><td>The correct answer hasn’t the first rank</td></tr>
</table>

Table 3: Error analysis

We have performed an in depth analysis of the proposed model and the obtained results and we have concluded the following points. Our model can be improved by addressing stemming, lemmatization, or word root and using synonyms to match a large set of similar questions. Also, the analysis done on the false predictions may be affined according to the questions using association rules. Since QRCD is a dataset of limited size yet imbalanced, we can use external Arabic data mainly Qur’an data and Tafsir to pretrain T5 from scratch then do fine tuning and explore data augmentation to augment the number of entries in the dataset. The data augmentation will be mainly applied to questions for preserving the meaning of the Qur’an verses. We assume also that larger base models could provide even more improvement. In fact, we can use mT5-XXL (about ×4 larger than mT5-XL), but this requires more resources precisely in terms of TPU and RAM. We have tested this model on Google Colab Pro (with 32G RAM) but it gives Coda out of memory.

7. Conclusion

In this paper, we presented our approach based on the Language Model mT5. We have finetuned it on the QRCD DataSet proposed by the Qur’an QA 2022 shared task. We fine-tuned our model using the Train Set, then we evaluated our model on the Development Set. After that, we generated predictions on the Test Set and then get an official evaluation from the community of the shared task. The result are compared in the overview paper (Malhas et al, 2022). Our best model can achieve very good results on the Development Set but less on the Test Set.

Finally, we discussed obtained results and challenges, then proposed potential solutions for possible improvements, that we can leverage as future works.

8. Bibliographical References

Abdelnasser, H., Ragab, M., Mohamed, R., Mohamed, A., Farouk, B., El-Makky, N.M. and Torki, M., 2014, October. Al-Bayan: an Arabic question answering system for the Holy Quran. *In Proceedings of the EMNLP 2014 Workshop on Arabic Natural Language Processing (ANLP)* (pp. 57-64).

Adeleke, A., Samsudin, N.A., Othman, Z.A. and Khalid, S.A., 2019. A two-step feature selection method for quranic text classification. Indones. *J. Electr. Eng. Comput. Sci*, 16(2), pp.730-736.

Agarwal, O., Kale, M., Ge, H., Shakeri, S. and Al-Rfou, R., 2020. Machine translation aided bilingual data-to-text generation and semantic parsing. *In Proceedings of the 3rd International Workshop on Natural Language*

Generation from the Semantic Web (WebNLG+) (pp. 125-130).

Alanazi, S.S., Elfadil, N., Jarajreh, M., Algarni, S., 2021. Question Answering Systems: A Systematic Literature Review. *Int. J. Adv. Comput. Sci. Appl. 12.* https://doi.org/10.14569/IJACSA.2021.0120359

Alqahtani, M. and Atwell, E., 2016, June. Arabic quranic search tool based on ontology. *In International Conference on Applications of Natural Language to Information Systems* (pp. 478-485). Springer, Cham.

Alsaleh, A.N., Atwell, E. and Altahhan, A., 2021, April. Quranic Verses Semantic Relatedness Using AraBERT. *In Proceedings of the Sixth Arabic Natural Language Processing Workshop* (pp. 185-190). Leeds.

Al-Salhi, R.Y. and Abdullah, A.M., 2022. Building Quranic stories ontology using MappingMaster domain-specific language. *International Journal of Electrical & Computer Engineering* (2088-8708), 12(1).

Alsubhi, K., Jamal, A. and Alhothali, A., 2021. Pre-trained transformer-based approach for Arabic question answering: A comparative study. arXiv preprint arXiv:2111.05671.

Alwaneen, T.H., Azmi, A.M., Aboalsamh, H.A., Cambria, E. and Hussain, A., 2022. Arabic question answering system: a survey. *Artificial Intelligence Review*, 55(1), pp.207-253.

Antoun, W., Baly, F., Hajj, H., 2021a. AraBERT: Transformer-based Model for Arabic Language Understanding. ArXiv200300104 Cs.

Antoun, W., Baly, F., Hajj, H., 2021b. AraELECTRA: Pre-Training Text Discriminators for Arabic Language Understanding. ArXiv201215516 Cs.

Arkok, B. and Zeki, A.M., 2021, June. Classification of Quranic Topics Using Ensemble Learning. In *2021 8th International Conference on Computer and Communication Engineering (ICCCE)* (pp. 244-248). IEEE.

Arkok, B.S. and Zeki, A.M., 2021. Classification of Quranic topics based on imbalanced classification. *Indones. J. Electr. Eng. Comput. Sci*, p.678.

Atef, A., Mattar, B., Sherif, S., Elrefai, E. and Torki, M., 2020, November. AQAD: 17,000+ Arabic Questions for Machine Comprehension of Text. In *2020 IEEE/ACS 17th International Conference on Computer Systems and Applications (AICCSA)* (pp. 1-6). IEEE.

Clark, J.H., Choi, E., Collins, M., Garrette, D., Kwiatkowski, T., Nikolaev, V. and Palomaki, J., 2020. TyDi QA: A benchmark for information-seeking question answering in typologically diverse languages. *Transactions of the Association for Computational Linguistics*, *8*, pp.454-470.

Devlin, J., Chang, M.W., Lee, K. and Toutanova, K., 2018. Bert: Pre-training of deep bidirectional transformers for language understanding. *arXiv preprint arXiv:1810.04805*.

Dukes, K., Atwell, E. and Habash, N., 2013. Supervised collaboration for syntactic annotation of Quranic Arabic. *Language resources and evaluation*, *47*(1), pp.33-62.

Farahani, M., Gharachorloo, M. and Manthouri, M., 2021, March. Leveraging ParsBERT and Pretrained mT5 for Persian Abstractive Text Summarization. In *2021 26th International Computer Conference, Computer Society of Iran (CSICC)* (pp. 1-6). IEEE.

Howard, J. and Ruder, S., 2018. Universal language model fine-tuning for text classification. *arXiv preprint arXiv:1801.06146*.

Jawahar, G., Nagoudi, E.M.B., Abdul-Mageed, M. and Lakshmanan, L.V., 2021. Exploring text-to-text transformers for english to hinglish machine translation with synthetic code-mixing. *arXiv preprint arXiv:2105.08807*.

Lan, Z., Chen, M., Goodman, S., Gimpel, K., Sharma, P. and Soricut, R., 2019. Albert: A lite bert for self-supervised learning of language representations. *arXiv preprint arXiv:1909.11942*.

Liu, X., He, P., Chen, W. and Gao, J., 2019. Multi-task deep neural networks for natural language understanding. *arXiv preprint arXiv:1901.11504*.

Malhas, R. and Elsayed, T., 2020. Ayatec: building a reusable verse-based test collection for arabic question answering on the holy qur'an. *ACM Transactions on Asian and Low-Resource Language Information Processing (TALLIP)*, *19*(6), pp.1-21.

Maraoui, H., Haddar, K. and Romary, L., 2021. Arabic factoid Question-Answering system for Islamic sciences using normalized corpora. *Procedia Computer Science*, *192*, pp.69-79.

Mohamed, E.H. and Shokry, E.M., 2020. QSST: A Quranic Semantic Search Tool based on word embedding. *Journal of King Saud University-Computer and Information Sciences*.

Mohd, M., Qamar, F., Al-Sheikh, I. and Salah, R., 2021. Quranic optical text recognition using deep learning models. *IEEE Access*, *9*, pp.38318-38330.

Mozannar, H., Hajal, K.E., Maamary, E. and Hajj, H., 2019. Neural Arabic question answering. *arXiv preprint arXiv:1906.05394*.

Nagoudi, E.M.B., Elmadany, A. and Abdul-Mageed, M., 2021. AraT5: Text-to-Text Transformers for Arabic Language Understanding and Generation. *arXiv preprint arXiv:2109.12068*.

Osman, M., Hilal, A., Alhawarat, M., 2015. Fine-Grained Quran Dataset. *Int. J. Adv. Comput. Sci. Appl.* 6. https://doi.org/10.14569/IJACSA.2015.061241

Radford, A., Wu, J., Child, R., Luan, D., Amodei, D. and Sutskever, I., 2019. Language models are unsupervised multitask learners. *OpenAI blog*, *1*(8), p.9.

Raffel, C., Shazeer, N., Roberts, A., Lee, K., Narang, S., Matena, M., Zhou, Y., Li, W., Liu, P.J., 2019. Exploring the Limits of Transfer Learning with a Unified Text-to-Text Transformer. https://doi.org/10.48550/ARXIV.1910.10683

Rajpurkar, P., Zhang, J., Lopyrev, K., Liang, P., 2016. SQuAD: 100,000+ Questions for Machine Comprehension of Text. https://doi.org/10.48550/ARXIV.1606.05250

Rothe, S., Mallinson, J., Malmi, E., Krause, S., Severyn, A., 2021. A Simple Recipe for Multilingual Grammatical Error Correction. https://doi.org/10.48550/ARXIV.2106.03830

Samy, H., E., E., Shaalan, K., 2019. Arabic Question Answering: A Study on Challenges, Systems, and Techniques. *Int. J. Comput. Appl.* 181, 6–14. https://doi.org/10.5120/ijca2019918524

Sutskever, I., Vinyals, O. and Le, Q.V., 2014. Sequence to sequence learning with neural networks. *Advances in neural information processing systems*, 27.

Xue, L., Constant, N., Roberts, A., Kale, M., Al-Rfou, R., Siddhant, A., Barua, A., Raffel, C., 2021. mT5: A massively multilingual pre-trained text-to-text transformer. *ArXiv201011934 Cs.*

Yang, Z., Dai, Z., Yang, Y., Carbonell, J., Salakhutdinov, R.R. and Le, Q.V., 2019. Xlnet: Generalized autoregressive pretraining for language understanding. *Advances in neural information processing systems*, 32.

Proceedings of the OSACT 2022 Workshop @LREC2022, pages 120–125
Marseille, 20 June 2022

LK2022 at Qur'an QA 2022: Simple Transformers Model for Finding Answers to Questions from Qur'an

Abdullah Alsaleh[1][2], Saud Althabiti[1][2], Ibtisam Alshammari[1][3], Sarah Alnefaie[1][2], Sanaa Alowaidi[1][2], Alaa Alsaqer[1][4], Eric Atwell[1], Abdulrahman Altahhan[1], Mohammad Ammar Alsalka[1]
[1]University of Leeds, [2]King Abdulaziz University, [3]University of Hafr Al-Batin, [4]King Faisal University
{scanaa, scssal, ml18ikfa, scsaln, ml20sara, scafa, e.s.atwell, a.altahhan, m.a.alsalka}@leeds.ac.uk

Abstract

Question answering is a specialized area in the field of NLP that aims to extract the answer to a user question from a given text. Most studies in this area focus on the English language, while other languages, such as Arabic, are still in their early stage. Recently, research tend to develop question answering systems for Arabic Islamic texts, which may impose challenges due to Classical Arabic. In this paper, we use Simple Transformers Question Answering model with three Arabic pre-trained language models (AraBERT, CAMeL-BERT, ArabicBERT) for Qur'an Question Answering task using Qur'anic Reading Comprehension Dataset. The model is set to return five answers ranking from the best to worst based on their probability scores according to the task details. Our experiments with development set shows that AraBERT V0.2 model outperformed the other Arabic pre-trained models. Therefore, AraBERT V0.2 was chosen for the the test set and it performed fair results with 0.45 pRR score, 0.16 EM score and 0.42 F1 score.

Keywords: NLP, Simple-Transformers, AraBERT, Question-Answering, Quran

1. Introduction

Natural Language Processing (NLP) is widely used for English language tasks; however, in case of Arabic language, it is still a challenging task especially for The Holy Qu'ran as it is considered a Classical Arabic and the Quranic terms have distinct meanings that differ from all Arabic variants, which make it more challenging for researchers (Altammami et al., 2020). Recent studies concentrate on Arabic language tasks such as Quranic Question Answering Systems, which plays significant role on NLP generally and Arabic language processing field specially. One of these recent studies is the 2022 Qur'an Question Answering shared task, where researchers can participate in teams to develop solutions to improve Question Answering Systems in terms of partial Reciprocal Rank (pRR) score (Malhas and Elsayed, 2020) (Malhas et al., 2022).

Recently, one of the most emerging NLP techniques is applying transformers-based models on Question Answering systems, which entails retrieving the required information from particular text according to a specific query or question (Rajpurkar et al., 2016) (Yang et al., 2015) (Mahdi, 2021). Therefore, we aim in this paper to utilize one of the transformers-based model, which is Simple Transformers model, on the Shared Task Question Answering over the Holy Qur'an. It mainly focuses on adapting Simple Transformers model to obtain the needed information from Qur'an passages and improve the accuracy of results using three Arabic pre-trained language models that are based on Bidirectional Encoder Representations from Transformers (BERT) (Devlin et al., 2018).

The paper structure as follows: In section 2, the related work are discussed. In section 3, the Qur'anic Reading Comprehension Dataset (QRCD) is presented. Section 4 describes the methodology that includes Simple Transformers model, dataset formation and Arabic pre-trained language models. Followed by section 5 as the results gained over the experiments given and supported by the discussion and analysis in section 6.

2. Related Work

2.1. Quranic Questions and Answers Systems

Many studies have been conducted to retrieve answers from the Holy Quran for the user's questions using information retrieval techniques such as semantic similarity and pattern matching. Abdelnasser et al. (2014) developed Al-Bayan system to answer Arabic Quranic questions. Al-Bayan represents verses by concept vectors and then uses cosine semantic similarity to retrieve the related verses for the user query. The system achieved 65% in terms of accuracy.

Moreover, AbuShawar and Atwell (2016) used the ALICE platform to implement a simple Quranic chatbot model based on the pattern matching technique. The model allows the user to ask questions in English and answer them in Arabic and English Quran verses. The experiment demonstrated that 54% of the results were wrong Answers.

In addition, Alqahtani (2019) built a model to answer the Arabic Quranic questions. This model enriched the user query with semantic features using the word2Vec algorithm. Then it extracted the most related concepts to the query from Quranic ontology using the cosine similarity. After that, it displayed the verses of the matched concepts to the user. The evaluation results

showed 41% in terms of recall.
These studies have contributed significantly to enriching the field of Quranic research. However, they can extract the required answer from the verse for only specific types of questions or answer the questions with the whole verse.

2.2. Arabic Questions and Answers Systems

The research on Arabic Question Answering systems has recently tended to apply deep learning transformers models such as the BERT model. According to Devlin et al. (2018) , it proved its effectiveness in several NLP tasks. Mozannar et al. (2019) trained the BERT model using an Arabic dataset. They constructed a specialized Arabic Reading Comprehension Dataset (ARCD) for the question and answering task consisting of 1,395 questions from Wikipedia. In addition, they created an Arabic version of the SQuAD 1.1 QA dataset by translating about 2,966 question pairs. The resulting datasets were used to train the BERT model. The experimental results achieved 61.3% in terms of F1 score. Additionally, Antoun et al. (2020) created an Arabic language model based on BERT named AraBERT by pre-trained the model using an extensive Arabic dataset. The dataset includes about 70 million sentences from available Arabic corpora and news websites. In addition, they tested the AraBERTv0.1 in question answering application using Arabic-SQuAD and ARCD datasets. This model showed better performance than the multilingual BERT (mBERT) by 1.4% and 3.0% improvement in F1 score and sentence match. The proposed model is available online for public use. Furthermore, Alsubhi et al. (2021) compared the performance of two transformer models, AraBERTv2-base and AraBERTv0.2-large. These models are trained on four Arabic QA datasets Arabic-SQuAD, ARCD, Arabic TyDiQA-GoldP, and AQAD, that generally are extracted from Wikipedia articles. The results showed that general AraBERTv0.2-large outperforms the other models, and the best results were achieved using the Arabic TyDiQA-GoldP dataset with 86.49% F1 score and 75.14% exact matches.
The current Arabic research train BERT models to answer questions in different domains. As far as we know, no conducted study train BERT models to the Quranic questions and answering systems.

3. Data

This section provides an overview of the dataset used in this paper. Quran QA shared task dataset is called QRCD [1] (Malhas and Elsayed, 2020), an Arabic Question Answering dataset. For each record, it includes a passage in plain text style that is derived from the Tanzil project [2], a question that is presented in Modern Standard Arabic (MSA), and one or more answers that are extracted from the given passage. It also includes PQ_ID, Surah number and verse numbers of the given passage. Ultimately, the structure of the QRCD is a JSON Line, as shown in Figure 1.


```
{ "pq_id": "74:32-48_330",
"passage": "كلا والقمر. والليل إذ أدبر. والصبح إذا أسفر. إنها لإحدى الكبر.
نذيرا للبشر. لمن شاء منكم أن يتقدم أو يتأخر. كل نفس بما كسبت رهينة.
إلا أصحاب اليمين. في جنات يتساءلون. عن المجرمين. ما سلككم في سقر. قالوا لم نك من المصلين.
ولم نك نطعم المسكين. وكنا نخوض مع الخائضين. وكنا نكذب بيوم الدين.
حتى أتانا اليقين. فما تنفعهم شفاعة الشافعين.",
"surah": 74, "verses": "32-48",
"question": "ما هي الدلائل التي تشير بأن الانسان مخير؟",
"answers":
[ {
"text": "لمن شاء منكم أن يتقدم أو يتأخر", "start_char": 76 }
{ "text": "كل نفس بما كسبت رهينة", "start_char": 108 }
] }
```


Figure 1: QRCD Structure

Figure 2 illustrates the distribution of the provided dataset. As it can be seen, the dataset contains 1093 question-passage pairs with their extracted answers. The training and development (validation) sets divided as 710, and 109 respectively. Furthermore, the test set includes 274 pairs of questions and passages without answers. However, through our experiments, we noticed that 99 questions in the training set and 15 in the development set have more than one answer. For example, this question (من هو قارون؟) meaning (Who is Qarun?) in the training set, has five answers from the Sura Al-Qasas (سورة القصص) verses (76-81 أيات). The same question was mentioned in other IDs and they have different answers from other passages.

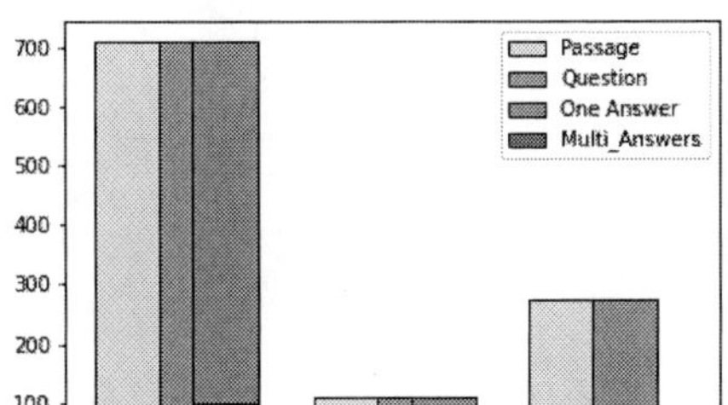

Figure 2: Distribution of QRCD

4. Method

This section outlines the methodology that has been utilised for this shared task. The model that was used

[1]The dataset can be accessed via this GitLab page: https://gitlab.com/bigirqu/quranqa/-/tree/main/datasets

[2]Tnazil Project contains a number of text styles including the plain text: https://tanzil.net/download/

for this task is Simple Transformers Question Answering model. The Question Answering model requires specific format that will be entailed in this section. Since the model is compatible with BERT, we applied three Arabic pre-trained language models with their weights and different sizes (base or large). Finally, the experiments were run on Google Colab with cuda for faster processing.

4.1. Simple Transformers

Simple Transformers model is a library that is built on Transformers architecture to solve downstream tasks such as binary or multi-class text classification. The library has since been developed to include question answering model, named-entity recognition, and language generations. The Question Answering model can be trained, evaluated and tested using different parameters that suit specific tasks and may improve performances. During training, the parameters that we focused on for this task are: batch size, learning rate and number of epochs. As for the prediction, we set the model to return five answers for each question. Finally, the output of the model is two lists that contain the answers and their probability scores.

4.2. Dataset Formation

Simple Transformers model requires specific data format prior feeding it to the model. The model expects a dictionary with two attributes `context` and `qas`, where "context" in this case is the verse. As for the "qas", it is a list that contains the ID, question and its answers. So, we have modified the existing scripts, given by the organisers, to convert the current QRCD format to the structure that Simple Transformers requires. The end format is shown in figure 3. Finally, there has been no pre-processing or pre-treatment on the dataset.

4.3. Arabic Pre-trained Language Models

There are three Arabic pre-trained language models that have been implemented in our experiments. They are AraBERT (Antoun et al., 2020), CAMeL-BERT (Inoue et al., 2021) and ArabicBERT (Safaya et al., 2020).

4.3.1. AraBERT

AraBERT is a BERT based language model with pre-trained corpus that includes 1.5 billion words from Arabic corpora (El-Khair, 2016) and Open-Sourced International Arabic News Corpus (Zeroual et al., 2019). AraBERT has two models which are AraBERT V2 and AraBERT V0.2 and the only difference is the use of Farasa Segmenter on V2. So for the model, AraBERT V0.2 was chosen since it performed better on recent Quran semantic similarity research (Alsaleh et al., 2021). Also, AraBERT provides base and large variants, and we opted with the latter since it performed better in the initial experiments on the development set.

4.3.2. CAMeL-BERT

CAMeL-BERT is a deep learning Arabic language model that is based on BERT architecture. The model provides more than 8 variants that are specific for Classical Arabic, Modern Standard Arabic and dialects. The pre-trained corpus for Classical Arabic is OpenITI (Nigst et al., 2020), which is an Arabic corpus that pertain to pre-modern Islamic texts. For our experiments, we have opted for the Classical Arabic base variant.

4.3.3. ArabicBERT

ArabicBERT is an Arabic language model that is based on BERT architecture with pre-trained corpus that includes Open Super-large Crawled Aalanch coRpus (OSCAR) (Ortiz Suárez et al., 2020), which includes Modern Standard Arabic, dialect texts and latest Arabic Wikipedia dump. The model provides different sizes including base, large and mega. We opted for the large model since we could not run our experiments with mega due to hardware limitations.

```
{'context': 'كلا والقمر. والليل إذ أدبر. والصبح إذا أسفر. إنها لإحدى الكبر. نذيرا للبشر. لمن شاء منكم أن يتقدم أو يتأخر. كل نفس بما كسبت رهينة. إلا أصحاب اليمين. في جنات يتساءلون. عن المجرمين. ما سلككم في سقر. قالوا لم نك من المصلين. ولم نك نطعم المسكين. وكنا نخوض مع الخائضين. وكنا نكذب بيوم الدين. حتى أتانا اليقين. فما تنفعهم شفاعة الشافعين.',
'qas': [
        {'id': '74:32-48_330',
        'surah': 74,
        'verses': '32-48',
        'question': 'ما هي الدلائل التي تشير بأن الانسان مخير؟',
        'answers': [
                {'text': 'لمن شاء منكم أن يتقدم أو يتأخر',
                'answer_start': 76},
                {'text': 'كل نفس بما كسبت رهينة',
                'answer_start': 108}
                ]
        }
]
}
```

Figure 3: Dataset Formation

5. Results

5.1. Validation

In this competition, we conducted various experiments using the development set on multiple transformer-based models, namely ArabicBERT, CAMeL-BERT, and AraBERT. On each model, we further investigated different versions of these models large or based. In addition, we fine-tuned our models on three parameters batch size, learning rate, and number of epochs. We chose these hyper parameters to minimise losses, avoid overfitting, and try to reach the local optima. After training our models over 25 epochs, we concluded that five to seven epochs are sufficient and could provide promising results. The obtained results from these various experiments with the different selected hyperparameters indicate that the AraBERT model usually outperforms other transformers-based models and could provide promising results, as illustrated in Figure 4.

Table 1 shows the highest scores acquired from each model. Within each model, we demonstrated the

Model	Batch Size	Learning Rate	Epochs	pRR	EM	F1@1
CAMeL-BERT	50	1e-4	15	0.53	0.31	0.49
	10	2e-5	20	0.52	0.30	0.47
	25	1e-4	15	0.51	0.28	0.47
AraBERT V0.2	**15**	**1e-4**	**5**	**0.59**	**0.34**	**0.55**
	15	1e-4	5	0.56	0.36	0.53
	15	4e-5	5	0.55	0.31	0.52
ArabicBERT	20	2e-4	30	0.51	0.33	0.47
	15	1e-4	5	0.49	0.30	0.46
	20	1e-4	20	0.48	0.28	0.43

Table 1: Summary of development set results, which includes the models with their arguments and evaluation scores

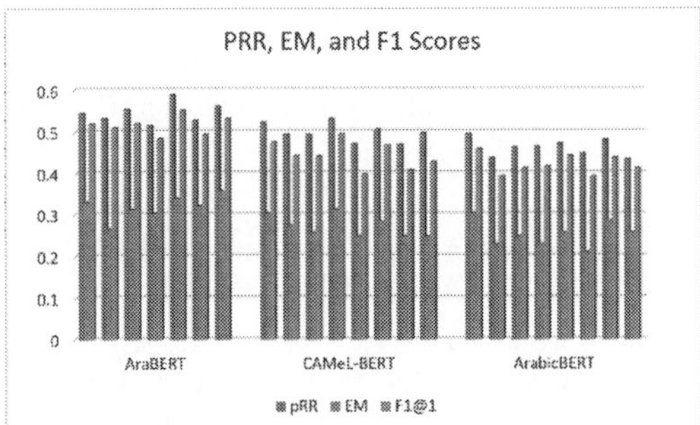

Figure 4: Overview of the experiments

used values of the three parameters manipulated in the employed transformer-based models (CAMeL-BERT, AraBERT, and ArabicBERT) to obtain the highest pRR scores (0.53, 0.59, and 0.48), respectively. We also attempt to adopt the best combination of parameters used with AraBERT (batch size of 15, learning rate of 1e-4, and five epochs) to the other two models. However, the comparison still indicates that this combination provides higher scores with AraBERT.

5.2. Testing

Accordingly, we employed these evaluated parameters in our final model's performance on the test dataset, and we got a fair result, with a 0.45 pRR score, 0.16 EM score and a 0.42 F1 score compared to the average scores of all participated teams with a 0.41 pRR score, 0.12 EM score and a 0.37 F1 score.

6. Discussion and Analysis

This section will discuss and analyse the development set as the true answers were not provided in the test set when publishing this paper.

The best result of the development set were using AraBERT V0.2 language model with parameters shown in table 1. When we analysed the results, we found that the model did not always return 5 answers. Also, there were 9 empty answers for the following IDs (9:1-6_400, 7:19-25_257, 22:30-37_313, 29:61-69_313, 20:95-98_163, 39:11-20_373, 31:12-19_132, 4:12-14_415, 33:36-40_415). The reason is that the model could not work out an answer for these questions based on given passage [3]. To avoid the warnings set in the official evaluation script on empty answers, we created a function to remove any empty answers except if the empty answer is the only answer that the model predicted.

According to the development set results, the model can predict the answer when there are matched words and/or synonyms between the questions and the passage; otherwise, it may face some difficulties. For example, in figure 5 the correct answer for the question "من الذي صنع عجلا من الحلي لبني إسرائيل؟" "Who made a calf out of jewelry for Israelites?" is "Samaritan" (السامري). In the first passage, there is a matching word "calf" (عجلا) , and "ornaments" (زينة) which is an Arabic synonyms for the word (الحلي) in the question. Therefore, the model successfully answered it when retrieving the answer from the passage.

In contrast, in the second passage in figure 6, the model could not predict the correct answer and produced empty answer. We notice that there are no matched words, although there are phrases that have related meanings, such as "إلهك الذي ظلت عليه عاكفا لنحرقنه" meaning (your 'god' to which you remained devoted. We will surely burn it), which points to the "calf", and "فقبضت قبضة من أثر الرسول فنبذتها" meaning (so I took a handful [of dust] from the track of the messenger and threw it), which is referred to how the "calf" was built according to Ibn-Kathir explication.

Moreover, the model predicts correct answers for some questions, but it was not mentioned in the gold answers. For example, in question 2:190-194_400 "متى يحل الإسلام دم الشخص؟" meaning "When does Islam allow the blood of a person?", the gold answer is "قاتلوا في سبيل الله الذين يقاتلونكم" which translates "Fight in the way of Allah those who fight you", while the model predicted this answer

[3]Please refer to https://simpletransformers.ai/docs/qa-specifics/

"فمن اعتدى عليكم فاعتدوا عليه بمثل ما اعتدى عليكم" which translates to "So whoever has assaulted you, then assault him in the same way that he has assaulted you". According to the scholar Al-Tabari (1954), the interpretation of the predicted answer "فقاتلوهم فيه كما قاتلوكم" meaning "fight them in it as they fought you" which has a similar meaning to the gold answer. Therefore, there maybe other correct answers that could potentially be added as gold answers in the datasets.

7. Conclusion

This paper presented Simple Transformers model to retrieve the best answer of particular questions related to the Holy Qur'an Shared Task competition. The experiments have been conducted using three Arabic language models AraBERT, CAMeL-BERT, and ArabicBERT. As the results shown that the AraBERT V0.2 model outperforms the other transformers-based models in this task with a 0.59 pRR score, 0.34 EM score and a 0.55 F1 score for the development set. As a consequence, in the test set shown fair results with 0.45 pRR score, 0.16 EM score and 0.42 F1 score.

Moreover, our findings shown that our developed model not only retrieves matching words as correct answers, but also predicts other additional answers that could be considered as accurate answers and potentially be added as gold answers to the datasets.

PQ_ID: 20:86-94_163

Passage:
فرجع موسى إلى قومه غضبان أسفا قال يا قوم ألم يعدكم ربكم وعدا حسنا أفطال عليكم العهد أم أردتم أن يحل عليكم غضب من ربكم فأخلفتم موعدي. قالوا ما أخلفنا موعدك بملكنا ولكنا حملنا أوزارا من زينة القوم فقذفناها فكذلك ألقى السامري. فأخرج لهم عجلا جسدا له خوار فقالوا هذا إلهكم وإله موسى فنسي. أفلا يرون ألا يرجع إليهم قولا ولا يملك لهم ضرا ولا نفعا. ولقد قال لهم هارون من قبل يا قوم إنما فتنتم به وإن ربكم الرحمن فاتبعوني وأطيعوا أمري. قالوا لن نبرح عليه عاكفين حتى يرجع إلينا موسى. قال يا هارون ما منعك إذ رأيتهم ضلوا. ألا تتبعن أفعصيت أمري. قال يا ابن أم لا تأخذ بلحيتي ولا برأسي إني خشيت أن تقول فرقت بين بني إسرائيل ولم ترقب قولي.

Question: من الذي صنع عجلا من الحلي لبني إسرائيل؟

Gold Answer:
1- السامري

Predicted Answer:
1- السامري. فأخرج لهم عجلا جسدا له خوار فقالوا هذا إلهكم وإله موسى فنسي
2- السامري
3- السامري.
4- السامري. فأخرج لهم عجلا جسدا له خوار
5- فأخرج لهم عجلا جسدا له خوار فقالوا هذا إلهكم وإله موسى فنسي

Figure 5: Example of predicting correct answers when the question has same words or synonyms in the passage

PQ_ID: 20:95-98_163

Passage:
قال فما خطبك يا سامري. قال بصرت بما لم يبصروا به فقبضت قبضة من أثر الرسول فنبذتها وكذلك سولت لي نفسي. قال فاذهب فإن لك في الحياة أن تقول لا مساس وإن لك موعدا لن تخلفه وانظر إلى إلهك الذي ظلت عليه عاكفا لنحرقنه ثم لننسفنه في اليم نسفا. إنما إلهكم الله الذي لا إله إلا هو وسع كل شيء علما.

Question: من الذي صنع عجلا من الحلي لبني إسرائيل؟

Gold Answer:
1- سامري

Predicted Answer:
1- "empty"

Figure 6: Example of incorrect prediction when there is no matching words or phrases in the question and in the passage

8. Acknowledgements

Authors, would like to express their deepest gratitude to King Abdulaziz University, University of Hafr Al-Batin, and King Faisal University for the support. We thank the reviewers for their constructive comments.

9. Bibliographical References

Abdelnasser, H., Ragab, M., Mohamed, R., Mohamed, A., Farouk, B., El-Makky, N. M., and Torki, M. (2014). Al-bayan: an arabic question answering system for the holy quran. In *Proceedings of the EMNLP 2014 Workshop on Arabic Natural Language Processing (ANLP)*, pages 57–64.

AbuShawar, B. and Atwell, E. (2016). Usefulness, localizability, humanness, and language-benefit: additional evaluation criteria for natural language dialogue systems. *International Journal of Speech Technology*, 19(2):373–383.

Al-Tabari, M. B. J. (1954). جامع البيان عن تاويل اي القرآن. Dar Al-Fikr.

Alqahtani, M. M. A. (2019). *Quranic Arabic Semantic Search Model Based on Ontology of Concepts*. Ph.D. thesis, University of Leeds.

Alsaleh, A., Atwell, E., and Altahhan, A. (2021). Quranic verses semantic relatedness using AraBERT. In *Proceedings of the Sixth Arabic Natural Language Processing Workshop*, pages 185–190, Kyiv, Ukraine (Virtual), April. Association for Computational Linguistics.

Alsubhi, K., Jamal, A., and Alhothali, A. (2021). Pre-trained transformer-based approach for arabic question answering: A comparative study. *arXiv preprint arXiv:2111.05671*.

Altammami, S., Atwell, E., and Alsalka, A. (2020). Towards a joint ontology of quran and hadith. *International Journal on Islamic Applications in Computer Science And Technology*.

Antoun, W., Baly, F., and Hajj, H. (2020). AraBERT: Transformer-based model for Arabic language understanding. In *Proceedings of the 4th Workshop on Open-Source Arabic Corpora and Processing Tools, with a Shared Task on Offensive Language Detection*, pages 9–15, Marseille, France, May. European Language Resource Association.

Devlin, J., Chang, M.-W., Lee, K., and Toutanova, K. (2018). Bert: Pre-training of deep bidirectional transformers for language understanding. *arXiv preprint arXiv:1810.04805*.

El-Khair, I. A. (2016). 1.5 billion words arabic corpus. *ArXiv*, abs/1611.04033.

Inoue, G., Alhafni, B., Baimukan, N., Bouamor, H., and Habash, N. (2021). The interplay of variant, size, and task type in Arabic pre-trained language models. In *Proceedings of the Sixth Arabic Natural Language Processing Workshop*, Kyiv, Ukraine (Online), April. Association for Computational Linguistics.

Mahdi, A. F. (2021). Survey: using bert model for arabic question answering system. *Turkish Journal of Computer and Mathematics Education (TURCOMAT)*, 12(13):723–729.

Malhas, R. and Elsayed, T. (2020). Ayatec: building a reusable verse-based test collection for arabic question answering on the holy qur'an. *ACM Transactions on Asian and Low-Resource Language Information Processing (TALLIP)*, 19(6):1–21.

Malhas, R., Mansour, W., and Elsayed, T. (2022). Qur'an QA 2022: Overview of the first shared task on question answering over the holy qur'an. In *Proceedings of the 5th Workshop on Open-Source Arabic Corpora and Processing Tools (OSACT5) at the 13th Language Resources and Evaluation Conference (LREC 2022)*.

Mozannar, H., Hajal, K. E., Maamary, E., and Hajj, H. (2019). Neural arabic question answering. *arXiv preprint arXiv:1906.05394*.

Nigst, L., Romanov, M., Savant, S. B., Seydi, M., and Verkinderen, P. (2020). Openiti: a machine-readable corpus of islamicate texts, Jun.

Ortiz Suárez, P. J., Romary, L., and Sagot, B. (2020). A monolingual approach to contextualized word embeddings for mid-resource languages. *Proceedings of the 58th Annual Meeting of the Association for Computational Linguistics*.

Rajpurkar, P., Zhang, J., Lopyrev, K., and Liang, P. (2016). Squad: 100,000+ questions for machine comprehension of text. *arXiv preprint arXiv:1606.05250*.

Safaya, A., Abdullatif, M., and Yuret, D. (2020). KUISAIL at SemEval-2020 task 12: BERT-CNN for offensive speech identification in social media. In *Proceedings of the Fourteenth Workshop on Semantic Evaluation*, pages 2054–2059, Barcelona (online), December. International Committee for Computational Linguistics.

Yang, Y., Yih, W.-t., and Meek, C. (2015). Wikiqa: A challenge dataset for open-domain question answering. In *Proceedings of the 2015 conference on empirical methods in natural language processing*, pages 2013–2018.

Zeroual, I., Goldhahn, D., Eckart, T., and Lakhouaja, A. (2019). Osian: Open source international arabic news corpus - preparation and integration into the clarin-infrastructure. In *WANLP@ACL 2019*.

Proceedings of the OSACT 2022 Workshop @LREC2022, pages 126–129
Marseille, 20 June 2022

niksss at Qur'an QA 2022: A Heavily Optimized BERT Based Model for Answering Questions from the Holy Qu'ran

Nikhil Singh
nikhil3198@gmail.com

Abstract

This paper presents the system description by team niksss for the Qur'an QA 2022 Shared Task. The goal of this shared task was to evaluate systems for Arabic Reading Comprehension over the Holy Quran. The task was set up as a question-answering task, such that, given a passage from the Holy Quran (consisting of consecutive verses in a specific surah(Chapter)) and a question (posed in Modern Standard Arabic (MSA)) over that passage, the system is required to extract a span of text from that passage as an answer to the question. The span was required to be an exact sub-string of the passage. We attempted to solve this task using three techniques namely conditional text-to-text generation, embedding clustering, and transformers-based question answering. The codes for the submitted system are available at: `https://github.com/nikhilbyte/Quran-Question-Answering`

Keywords: Question Answering,Machine Reading Comprehension, Arabic

1. Introduction

The Holy Quran is the central religious text of Islam and is held by over 1.8 billion[[1]] people in 47 languages and specific verses available in 114 languages across the world. This makes it one of the most popular books in the history of mankind. This shared task (Malhas et al., 2022) addresses the challenge of answering the questions in Modern Standard Arabic by inculcating the knowledge from the verses of the Holy Quran. Moreover most of the studies dealt with factoid (what, where, who, when, which, and how much/many) questions (Abdelnasser et al., 2014),(Gusmita et al., 2014),(Hakkoum and Raghay, 2016) and a very few non-factoid questions (Hakkoum and Raghay, 2015),(Alqahtani and Atwell, 2016). This task contains questions from both factoid and non-factoid types making it a harder task.

Closed domain information retrieval pertaining to the Holy Quran has been seldom explored. Techniques such as String Matching, Probabilistic Model, and Natural Language Processing have been used in the past to extract the answers from the holy Quran. These techniques, however, give inaccurate results when the user inputs their query in natural language as these techniques retrieve the answers on the basis of keywords provided by the users. This sprouts the need for a Question Answering System(QAS) which provides slightly accurate results when compared to the techniques mentioned above.

Due to the recent advancement of the transformer architecture in QAS in multiple languages and multiple domains, we decided to experiment with transformers based models to tackle this challenge.

[1]ThoughtC (`https://www.thoughtco.com`)

2. Dataset

The dataset for the task is called Qur'anic Reading Comprehension Dataset, abbreviated as QRCD[2] (Malhas and Elsayed, 2020). It is composed of 1,093 tuples of question-passage pairs that are coupled with their extracted answers to constitute 1,337 question-passage-answer triplets. Out of these 1337 triplets, 65% were allowed to train the model, 10% triplets were kept as a development set and the rest 25% triplets were reserved to evaluate the performance of the submitted system. The data distribution can be seen in Table **??**.

Dataset	#Question-Passage-Answer Triplets
Training	861
Development	128
Test	348

Table 1: Data Distribution

3. Experiments

3.1. Semantic Embeddings and Clustering(SEC)

The first experiment involved the creation of a basic sentence embedding that contained all the semantic information of a given sentence in a 786-dimensional feature vector which was generated by passing the sentence through 12 layers of transformer blocks. The transformers architecture used in all of our experiments is AraBERT(Antoun et al., 2020). The detailed steps involved in this experiment is presented below.

- Of a given Question-Answer-Passage triplet, the passage was first tokenized sentence-wise using the nltk's sent-tokenize function from the nltk library[3].

[2]`https://gitlab.com/bigirqu/quranqa`
[3]`https://www.nltk.org/`

- Sentence embeddings were extracted from the [CLS] token from the layer of BERT model for each sentence.

- The correlation between individual sentences and the result of Principal component analysis after applying K-Means Clustering(Lloyd, 1982) is visualized. A different number of clusters were found in different passages.

- Finally the text pair of Question-Answer were passed through the same model individually and were projected onto the same Euclidean space as the tokenized passage sentences.

- This Euclidean space was then optimized using the K- Nearest Neighbors (Fix and Hodges, 1989) for bringing the question embedding closer to the cluster containing the answer sentence.

- The question and passages were passed for inference and top 5 sentences from the nearest clusters were taken as predictions.

3.2. Seq2Seq based text span extraction(S2S)

In this experiment, we treated this problem as a text2text generation problem where the input for the model model was the Question and Passage pair separated by a [SEP] token and the model was required to generate the text span from the passage as the answer.State of the art generative models such as, mT5(Xue et al., 2020) and mBART(Liu et al., 2020) were used as the Seq2Seq models for this experiment. These models performed the best for "Exact-Match" metric out of all the experiments we conducted, however we couldn't bring them to generate more than one text sentence as required for evaluation on this shared task.

3.3. Fine-Tuning and Optimizing BERT model

This experiment constitutes our final experiment. In this, we fine-tune a BERT-based model which takes the question-passage pair as a singe-packed sequence which is converted into the input embedding by taking a sum of the token embedding and the segment embedding to distinguish between the two as shown in Figure 1.

The fine-tuning of a BERT-based QAS involves optimization of finding the start and end word of the text span inside the passed reference text. To find the probability of a particular word being the starting and the ending word of the answer span, it takes the dot-product between the final embedding of the words in the sequence and the start/end vector, which is a 768-dimensional vector and is the same for all the words. The vector obtained after the dot product is passed to a classification layer, which outputs the probability of the word being the starting token and ending token. The complete working of our model is shown in Figure 1.

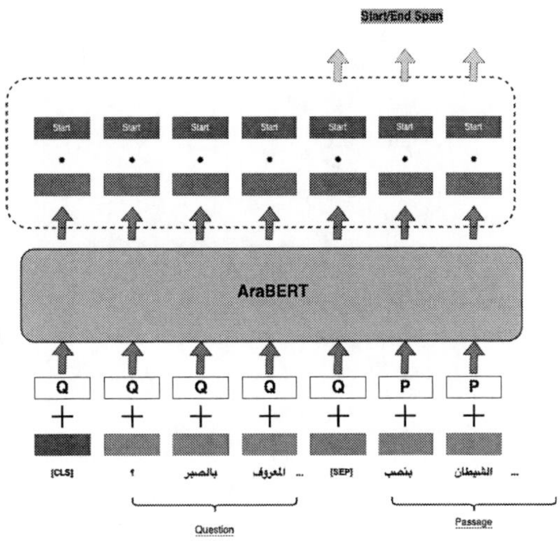

Figure 1: Model Architecture

We use Simple Transformers[4] for Conducting this Experiment.

3.3.1. Hyperparameter Optimization

We took the following Hyperparameters into consideration:

- Learning Rate
- Max Sequence Length
- Number of Epochs
- Train Batch Size

And we judged the performance of the model by the following parameters as Highlighted in Figure 2:

- Evaluation Loss
- Training Loss
- Number of Correct Answers
- Number of Incorrect answers

The results on validation set is shown in the Table 2:

Method	pRR	exact match	f1
SEC	0.236	0.0262	0.112
S2S	-	0.306	-
FT-Arabert	0.250	0.0834	0.139

Table 2: Performance on Evaluation set

The best hyperparameters are shown below:

- Learning Rate: 3e-4
- Max Sequence Length: 128

[4] https://simpletransformers.ai/

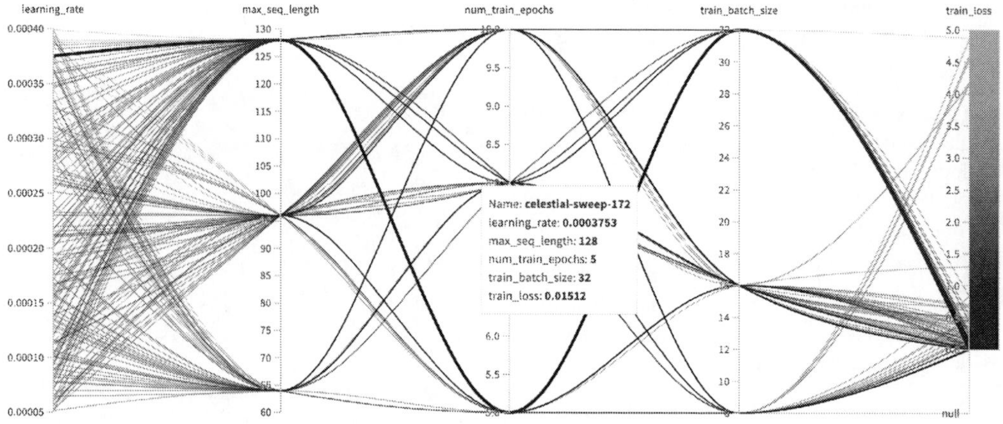

Figure 2: Hyper-Parameters(The Selected HP is the one used for submission.

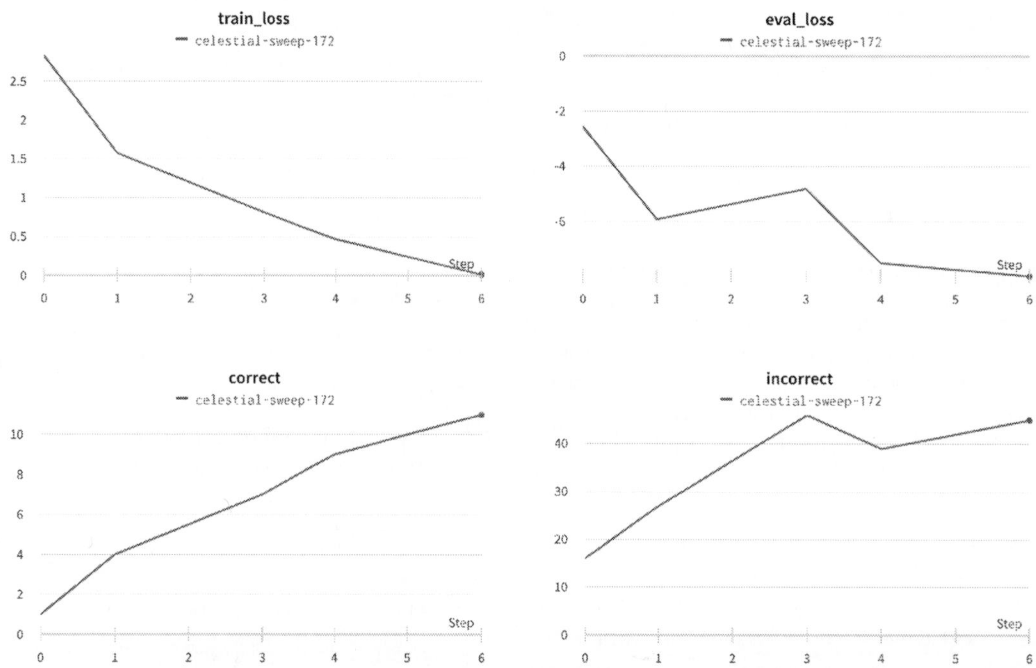

Figure 3: Results from the best performing Model on evaluation data.

- Number of Epochs: 5
- Training batch Size: 32

We Use Weights & Biases Sweeps for producing the visualizations. [5]

4. Results

The official evaluation measure of this shared task is Partial Reciprocal Rank. It is similar to Reciprocal Rank evaluation metric only that it considers partial matching with any of the gold labels. Two more metrics, Exact Match (EM) and F1@1 were also measured for checking if the top predicted answer matches one of the gold answers and the token overlap between the predicted and gold labels. Our best performing model has a pRR of 0.1913, Exact match of 4.2% and an F1@1 score of 9.1% .

[5] `https://docs.wandb.ai/guides/sweeps`

5. Error Analysis

After examining the predictions from the submitted model, we saw that our systems struggled significantly in answering the non-factoid questions whereas it did decently on factoid questions. The models for generating the contextual embeddings were traditional models used for resource-rich languages like English or German which receive an ample amount of domain-specific fine-tuning to do the closed domain retrieval task. The main reason we identify for the performance is the limited training data for a deep model like AraBERT. The model doesn't know the concept of question answering and has the weights adjusted as per the Self-Supervised MLM technique. Using just a 1000 samples to do the weight updations would have confused the model, leading to poor performance.

6. Conclusion and Future Work

Advancing the research on Under represented languages is very important and this Shared-Task seems to do just that. Arabic is a low resource language even though the number of people who use it is not low. We submit a simple method using a simple BERT based model with Arabic Corpus Pretraining. Due to the limited compute resources we just experimented with the mentioned hyper-parameters. However, we can optimize the number of layers of transformers in the model. Or, we can create custom parameter groups which can be used to set different learning rates for different layers in a model. Freeze layers or train only the final layer.

7. Bibliographical References

Abdelnasser, H., Ragab, M., Mohamed, R., Mohamed, A., Farouk, B., El-Makky, N., and Torki, M. (2014). Al-bayan: An Arabic question answering system for the holy quran. In *Proceedings of the EMNLP 2014 Workshop on Arabic Natural Language Processing (ANLP)*, pages 57–64, Doha, Qatar, October. Association for Computational Linguistics.

Alqahtani, M. and Atwell, E. (2016). Arabic quranic search tool based on ontology, June. © 2016, Springer International Publishing. This is an author produced version of a paper published in 21st International Conference on Applications of Natural Language to Information Systems, NLDB 2016 Proceedings, Natural Language Processing and Information Systems, Lecture Notes in Computer Science.. Uploaded in accordance with the publisher's self-archiving policy. The final publication is available at Springer via http://dx.doi.org/10.1007/978-3-319-41754-7_52.

Antoun, W., Baly, F., and Hajj, H. (2020). Arabert: Transformer-based model for arabic language understanding. *arXiv preprint arXiv:2003.00104*.

Fix, E. and Hodges, J. L. (1989). Discriminatory analysis. nonparametric discrimination: Consistency properties. *International Statistical Review / Revue Internationale de Statistique*, 57(3):238–247.

Gusmita, R. H., Durachman, Y., Harun, S., Firmansyah, A. F., Sukmana, H. T., and Suhaimi, A. (2014). A rule-based question answering system on relevant documents of indonesian quran translation. *2014 International Conference on Cyber and IT Service Management (CITSM)*, pages 104–107.

Hakkoum, A. and Raghay, S. (2015). Advanced search in the qur'an using semantic modeling. *2015 IEEE/ACS 12th International Conference of Computer Systems and Applications (AICCSA)*, pages 1–4.

Hakkoum, A. and Raghay, S. (2016). Semantic qa system on the qur'an. *Arabian Journal for Science and Engineering*, 41:5205–5214, 06.

Liu, Y., Gu, J., Goyal, N., Li, X., Edunov, S., Ghazvininejad, M., Lewis, M., and Zettlemoyer, L. (2020). Multilingual denoising pre-training for neural machine translation. *Transactions of the Association for Computational Linguistics*, 8:726–742.

Lloyd, S. P. (1982). Least squares quantization in pcm. *IEEE Trans. Inf. Theory*, 28:129–136.

Malhas, R. and Elsayed, T. (2020). ¡i¿ayatec¡/i¿: Building a reusable verse-based test collection for arabic question answering on the holy qur'an. *ACM Trans. Asian Low-Resour. Lang. Inf. Process.*, 19(6), oct.

Malhas, R., Mansour, W., and Elsayed, T. (2022). Qur'an QA 2022: Overview of the first shared task on question answering over the holy qur'an. In *Proceedings of the 5th Workshop on Open-Source Arabic Corpora and Processing Tools (OSACT5) at the 13th Language Resources and Evaluation Conference (LREC 2022)*.

Xue, L., Constant, N., Roberts, A., Kale, M., Al-Rfou, R., Siddhant, A., Barua, A., and Raffel, C. (2020). mt5: A massively multilingual pre-trained text-to-text transformer. *arXiv preprint arXiv:2010.11934*.

Proceedings of the OSACT 2022 Workshop @LREC2022, pages 130–135
Marseille, 20 June 2022

QQATeam at Qurán QA 2022: Fine-Tunning Arabic QA Models for Qurán QA Task

Basem H. Ahmed, Motaz K. Saad, Eshrag A. Refaee
Alaqsa University, The Islamic University of Gaza, Jazan University
Dept. of computer science, Faculty of Information Technology, Dept. of Info Technology & Security
basem@alaqsa.edu.ps, msaad@iugaza.edu.ps, erefaie@jazanu.edu.sa

Abstract

The problem of auto-extraction of reliable answers from a reference text like a constitution or holy book is a real challenge for the natural languages research community. Qurán is the holy book of Islam and the primary source of legislation for millions of Muslims around the world, which can trigger the curiosity of non-Muslims to find answers about various topics from the Qurán. Previous work on Question Answering (Q&A) from Qurán is scarce and lacks the benchmark of previously developed systems on a testbed to allow meaningful comparison and identify developments and challenges. This work presents an empirical investigation of our participation in the Qurán QA shared task (2022) that utilizes a benchmark dataset of 1,093 tuples of question-Qurán passage pairs. The dataset comprises Qurán verses, questions and several ranked possible answers. This paper describes the approach we follow with our participation in the shared task and summarises our main findings. Our system attained the best score at 0.63 pRR and 0.59 F1 on the development set and 0.56 pRR and 0.51 F1 on the test set. The best results of the Exact Match (EM) score at 0.34 indicate the difficulty of the task and the need for more future work to tackle this challenging task.

Keywords: Question Answering, Classic Arabic, Qurán question answering, fine-tuning, pre-trained models

1. Introduction

The enormous amount of data readily available and the advances in machine learning and computer-based systems in the past two decades have created the need for auto-extraction of answers for any given question. The domain of automatic extraction of answers to questions spanning various topics is a sub-field of Natural Language Processing (NLP). Specifically, QA is an NLP task concerned with querying information from content available in multiple formats, including structured and unstructured data (Bouziane et al., 2015). Research on QA is motivated by satisfying the users' need for obtaining answers across a variety of topics using computer-based and machine learning means to enhance the efficiency of this task.

A question-answering (QA) system is an application program that takes a user ś natural-language input question and attempts to return a precise answer (Prager, 2014). Figure 1 shows a typical QA model, where the inputs are the question and the passage, and the output is the answer extracted from the text.

QA as a task consists of three distinct NLP and IR subtasks: question analysis, passage retrieval, and answer extraction. Parsing the question is essential to extract its category, the type of answer required, and whether it is a name, place, quantity, or date. This early categorization of the question facilitates the answer extraction phase to select the best possible answer. The process can involve pre-processing steps like eliminating stop words, extracting named entities, and categorizing questions.

The application of QA to different languages has shown other performance mainly depending on how

Figure 1: Typical QA Model

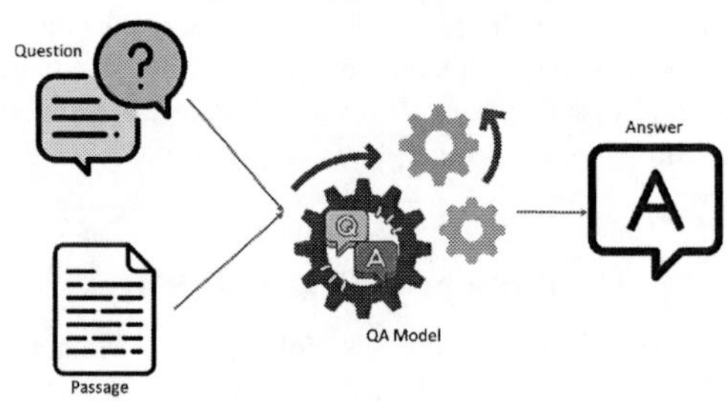

well-resourced is the language under consideration. According to the United Nations Educational, Scientific and Cultural Organisation (UNESCO), the Arabic language is the native tongue of more than 400 million people around the world.[1] The primary challenge when working on most NLP tasks for Arabic is the fact that Arabic is a morphological-rich language (Refaee, 2016). Another challenge is that, as compared to English, Arabic is still an under-resourced language with an increasing effort to address this issue.

QA can be applied to a wide range of text content, including web documents, constitutions and holy books. When it comes to Qurán as the major source of legislation for nearly 1.9 billion Muslims (Meters, 2022) and the way it attracts the curiosity of non-Muslims, QA becomes even more interesting. Several attempts have been made in this area to tackle the difficulty of auto-

[1] Available at `https://en.unesco.org/commemorations/worldarabiclanguageday` Accessed on 09/04/2022.

matically extracting answers regarding different questions from Qurán verses. However, previous QA work on Qurán is limited and lacks a reasonable and meaningful benchmark on a common testset. For this purpose, a shared task, namely Quraán QA 2022, has been launched.[2] The added value of the shared task, besides allowing several parallel attempts to develop QA systems, is the availability of a benchmark testset that has been released as a part of the shared task (Malhas et al., 2022). The competition of several teams worldwide on a benchmark test set allows for achieving remarkable improvements and identifying challenges associated with QA on Qurán. The work (Malhas et al., 2022) presents an overview of the shared task and outlines the approaches employed and results attained by the participating teams.

2. Related Work

The task of auto-extraction of answers for a given question is not new for Natural Language Processing (NLP) researchers. Literature has revealed considerable interest in this task for more than two decades. Research in this area has been highly motivated by computer-based methods and tools to extract reliable answers from a given text automatically. In most cases, the text used to extract answers is considered a reference, like the constitution or the holy textbook. However, the source for extracting answers can be merely news websites in other cases. The results of question answering have shown to be varied across different languages. This section outlines the previous work that has addressed the problem of automatic question-answering in Arabic.

In early work by (Hammo et al., 2002), traditional Information Retrieval (IR) techniques were used with an NLP approach. Specifically, the authors used a keyword matching strategy and matching simple structures extracted from both the question and the candidate documents selected by the IR system. The authors utilized a morphological analyzer and an existing tagger to identify proper names and build lexical entries for them. As for word-level, they used root stemming and identified the query type (What, when, where, who, etc.).

(Magdy and Shaheen, 2012) presented a survey on exciting efforts to tackle the main challenges associated with the question answering task in Arabic. The work outlined the approaches and tools utilized, including the early classification of the questions into Name, Date, and Quantity to determine the question type. This classification involves defining the type of a given question according to the question word used to extract the expected answer type, question focus and important question keywords. Common pre-processing steps involved question tokenization, normalization, removing stop words and stemming. A common practice was to determine the question focus, which is the proper noun phrase that the question mainly revolves around, which usually leads to choosing the answer type based on question words like who and when. Another common practice revealed by the authors is the utilization of Named Entity (NE) recognition tools. In addition, the passage retrieval technique utilized in QA mainly was the co-occurrence of question and answer keywords within the same context. Finally, semantic reasoning was accomplished by exploiting existing platforms like Amine to score and rerank the retrieved passages semantically using concept graphs to find the most relevant answer passage. Specifically, they used the semantic similarity between the focus of the question and the candidate's answer using N-grams.

Arabic has limited resources for the QA task, unlike English and other well-resourced languages where multiple large QA datasets are freely available (Rajpurkar et al., 2016). The linguistic resources are even more scarce when finding a dataset of Qurán versus annotated for QA. A recent effort (Malhas and Elsayed, 2020) has addressed this issue and introduced a publicly available reusable test collection for Arabic question answering on the Holy Qurán, namely AyaTEC. According to the authors, their test collection for verse-based question answering on the Holy Qur'an serves as a standard experimental testbed for QA. The dataset AyaTEC includes 207 questions with their corresponding 1,762 answers, spanning 11 topic categories. The authors stated that the dataset of the Holy Qurán targets the information needs of both curious and sceptical users. They proposed several evaluation measures to support the different types of questions and the nature of verse-based answers while integrating the concept of partial matching of answers in the evaluation. The dataset was used in the shared task to allow multiple systems to be implemented and compared.

In (Abdelnasser et al., 2014), the authors proposed an Arabic QA system specializing in the Holy Qurán. The system takes an Arabic question about the Qurán, retrieves the most relevant Qurán verses, and then extracts the passage that contains the answer from the Qurń. They utilized the Quranic Corpus Ontology to obtain and manually revise 1200 data instances. The authors reported up to 85% accuracy using the top-3 results.

(Hamdelsayed and Atwell, 2016) presented a rule-based system for the Holy Qurán that retrieves the correct verse from the Holy Qurán. The authors utilized their dataset and reported an improvement due to simple pre-processing of removing stop words.

In (Hamed and Ab Aziz, 2016), the authors used an Existing English translation of Qurán verses to develop a system utilizing neural networks (NN) for QA. They expanded the question by using WordNet. In addition, they utilized the NN classifier to reduce the retrieval of irrelevant verses using the word N-gram technique. The following step included ranking the re-

[2] Available at `shorturl.at/dlFH6` Accessed on 12/03/2022.

trieved verses based on the highest similarity score to fulfil the user question. The authors reported an F-score up to 87% on classification and recommended employing classification as an initial stage for retrieving verses as answers for a given question.
the authors in (Mozannar et al., 2019a) tackled the problem of open domain factual Arabic question answering (QA) using Wikipedia as our knowledge source. The authors reported that Open-domain QA for Arabic entails three challenges: annotated QA datasets in Arabic, large scale efficient information retrieval and machine reading comprehension. They addressed the first challenge by compiling The Arabic Reading Comprehension Dataset (ARCD). To address the second and the third challenge, the authors presented an open domain question-answering in Arabic (SOQAL) that is based on two components: (1) a document retriever using a hierarchical TF-IDF approach and (2) a neural reading comprehension model using the pre-trained bi-directional transformer BERT.
(Su et al., 2019) addressed the problem of generalizing QA models with pre-trained models fine-tuning. They fine-tuned a large pre-trained language model (XLNet) on multiple RC datasets. The results suggest that fine-tuning is effective.
On the other side, several attempts have been made to address the problem of QA in Arabic in general, not only in Qurán. Recent work (Alsubhi et al., 2021) has thoroughly highlighted the task of QA in Arabic. The authors evaluated the state-of-the-art pre-trained transformers models for Arabic QA using four datasets (Arabic-SQuAD, ARCD, AQAD, and TyDiQA-GoldP). They fine-tuned three pre-trained models (AraBERTv2-base, AraBERTv0.2-large, and AraELECTRA). The authors address the impact of the size and quality of the dataset on the performance of their proposed QA model. They also tried to improve the performance by fine-tuning hyper-parameters. The authors reported that the best F-score was 61%, obtained using AraBERTv0.2-large on Arabic-SQuAD dataset.
A more comprehensive view of QA in Arabic can be found in a recent survey (Alwaneen et al., 2021). To sum up, previous works lack benchmark comparison on a standard testbed.

3. Dataset

The shared-task data comprises 1,093 tuples of question-passage pairs coupled with their extracted answers to constitute 1,337 question-passage-answer triplets (Malhas and Elsayed, 2022). The benchmark dataset has been accessible for the teams registered in the competition (Malhas and Elsayed, 2020). The dataset distribution into training, development and test sets is shown below.

4. Approach

In this task, the approach uses Arabic QA pre-trained models and fine-tunes them with the Qurán QA dataset.

Dataset	%	# Question Passage Pairs	# Question Passage Answer Triplets
Training	65%	710	861
Dev	10%	109	128
Test	25%	274	348
All	100%	1,093	1,337

We use two pre-trained Arabic QA models listed in Table1, hosted on Hugging Face (Wolf et al., 2020). We used these models because they are the only existing pre-trained models that support the Arabic language on Hugging Face. In addition, these models can be fine-tuned easily.

Table 1: Arabic QA pre-trained Models

Arabic QA Model	Trained on	Reference
Salti Ara-Electra base fine-tuned ARCD (AraElectra-ARCD)	Arabic Reading Comprehension Dataset (ARCD) composed of 1,395 questions posed by crowd-workers on Wikipedia articles	(Mozannar et al., 2019b)
Wissam Antoun Ara-Electra base Artydiqa (AraElectra-Artydiqa)	TyDi QA is a question answering dataset covering 11 topologically diverse languages with 204K question-answer pair (Clark et al., 2020)	(Antoun et al., 2020)

The fine-tuning is done on the training data and the training, development, and augmented data merge. We manually applied data augmentation to the training and development parts of the dataset by paraphrasing only the question part on the QA dataset. Paraphrasing is done by changing word order, using different synonyms when asking about an object, using function words, and using a different questioning tool. Our hypothesis here is that data augmentation may help fine-tune the model to correct answers to different question forms in the test set. Augmented Data is described in Table 2, and can be found on `https://github.com/motazsaad/Quran-QA`.
Besides fine-tuning the two pre-trained models, we combine these two models and choose the best scores from both models for the answers obtained from them. So we made three submissions to the shared task. The first one uses *AraElectra-ARCD*, and the second uses

Table 2: Augmented Data

Dataset	Size
Training Question Passage Answer Triplets (training only)	861
Training Question Passage Answer Triplets (training and Dev)	989
augmented Question Passage Answer Triplets (training and Dev)	657
Training Question Passage Answer Triplets (training and dev and augmented)	1646

AraElectra-Artydiqa. The third attempt uses the Hybrid model, in which the two fined-tuned models are used to get the answers with their scores (weights), and then answer scores from both models are normalized and ranked together. The top 5 answers that have the highest scores are selected.
We use Colab Pro for fine-tuning, and the "*Salti Ara-Electra base fine-tuned ARCD*" model stopped at epoch 8, while the "*Wissam Antoun Ara-Electra base Artydiq*" model stopped at epoch 4.
Data is pre-processed by applying the normalization function that is provided by the maintainer of this shared task `https://gitlab.com/bigirqu/quranqa/-/blob/main/code/quranqa22_eval.py`, where the stopwords (only Arabic prepositions), and punctuation are removed. In addition, a predefined list of prefixes is removed.

5. Results and Discussion

Table 3delivers the performance of the QA pre-trained models fine-tuned on train data and tested on Dev data. Table 4 shows the performance of the QA pre-trained models fine-tuned on train, Dev and augmented data and tested on Test data. Figures 2 and 3 show the performance of *"AraElectra-ARCD"* and *"AraElectra-Artydiqa"* models, respectively. The figures indicate the pRR, Exact Match and F1@1 metrics with training epochs.

Table 3: Dev data Results using fine-tuned using training data

Model	pRR	Exact Match	F1@1
AraElectra-ARCD	0.60544	0.33027	0.57807
AraElectra-Artydiqa	0.61828	0.32110	0.57804
Hybrid	**0.62571**	**0.33944**	**0.59145**

Table 4 shows the test data results fine-tuned using Dev and augmented data. It can be noted from the Table 3 that the best fine-tuned QA model is the combined model with the following scores 0.62 pRR, 0.33 Exact Match, 0.59 F1@1. On the other hand, Table 4 shows that the best fine-tuned QA model is *AraElectra-Artydiqa*, with the following scores; 0.55 pRR, 0.24 Exact match, and 0.51 F1@1. The result suggests that

Figure 2: Performance of AraElectra-ARCD model

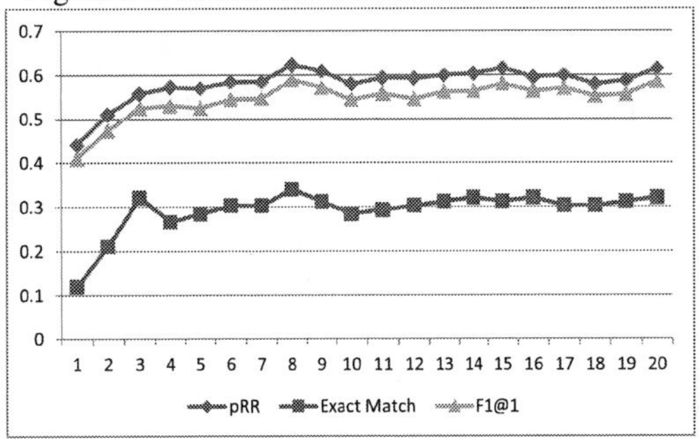

Figure 3: Performance of AraElectra-Artydiqa Model

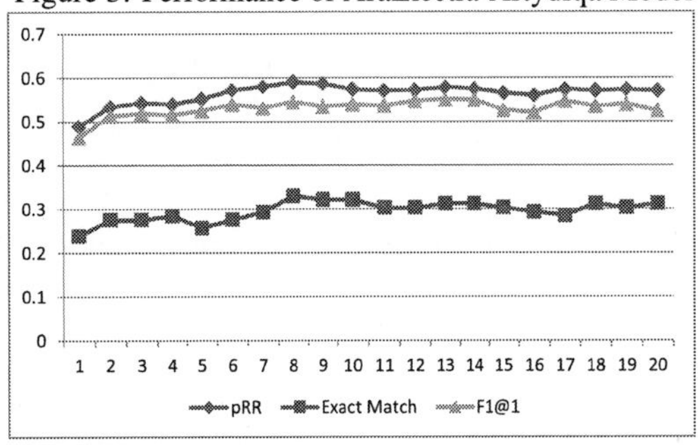

the combined model worked well when applied to the Dev dataset and obtained the best results, but the result was not the same on the model used on the test set. The best performing model on the test set was the *AraElectra-Artydiqa*, trained initially on more extensive data than the *AraElectra-ARCD* model. The performance of *AraElectra-Artydiqa* was even better than the combined model on the test set. This suggests that picking the trained model on a large dataset can be best for fine-tuning.
Comparing the best results in the two tables, we can see that When the models are applied to the test set (Table 4), the pRR score dropped 7%, the exact match dropped 9%, and the F1@1 dropped 8%. This performance is expected and suggests that the models need more fine-tuning, and the training data should be enlarged. Moreover, the domain of both models is Wikipedia, which is away from the Qurán QA domain, and the fine-tuning was not enough to get promising results because the QA training data is small.

6. Conclusion and Future Work

The ability to automatically extract answers from a user input natural text is one of the leading NLP tasks with plenty of real-life applications. QA task comes with several challenges, and performance on this task can vary across different languages. Obtaining answers from references like a constitution or holy textbooks can be more challenging than getting answers from other sources like news websites. That includes the limited linguistic resources available (i.e., annotated

Table 4: Test data Results fine-tuned using training and Dev and augmented data

Model	pRR	Exact Match	F1@1
AraElectra-ARCD	0.52600	0.22269	0.46228
AraElectra-Artydiqa	**0.55889**	**0.24370**	**0.51326**
Hybrid	0.53486	0.23109	0.49997

data) and the need to have the answers as accurate as possible. For example, Qurán is the primary source of legislation in Islam and having systems that accurately extract answers regarding laws and Islamic-based concepts is critical.

This paper presents the participation of our team, namely QQATeam, in the Qurán shared task (2022). The shared task released a benchmark Qurán dataset of 1,093 tuples of question-passage pairs. The shared task aims to allow different teams to participate in developing other systems using the benchmark dataset in combination with various NLP resources, tools, and techniques that the teams wish to employ. Unlike previous work that has been done on QA from Qurán lacks the meaningful comparison of different QA approaches on a shared testset to allow identifying a baseline performance. The work produced by the shared task can help identify the QA task's state-of-the-art performance and reveal the opportunities and challenges associated with this task. By fine-tuning pre-trained models, our system attained the best performance at 0.56 pRR and 0.51 F1. A detailed explanation of approaches used and results achieved by participating teams can be found at (Malhas et al., 2022).

The overall results indicate the need for further developments to tackle the challenges identified in the QA task on the Qurán text. Future directions can involve using Information Retrieval (IR) to improve the results by passing the question as a query and ranking passages according to this query. Then the question and the top-ranked passage can be fed to the QA model. In addition, Qurán commentaries for each verse to determine the best verse that contains the answer.

7. Bibliographical References

Abdelnasser, H., Ragab, M., Mohamed, R., Mohamed, A., Farouk, B., El-Makky, N. M., and Torki, M. (2014). Al-bayan: an arabic question answering system for the holy quran. In *Proceedings of the EMNLP 2014 Workshop on Arabic Natural Language Processing (ANLP)*, pages 57–64.

Alsubhi, K., Jamal, A., and Alhothali, A. (2021). Pre-trained transformer-based approach for Arabic question answering: A comparative study. *arXiv preprint arXiv:2111.05671*.

Alwaneen, T. H., Azmi, A. M., Aboalsamh, H. A., Cambria, E., and Hussain, A. (2021). Arabic question answering system: a survey. *Artificial Intelligence Review*, pages 1–47.

Antoun, W., Baly, F., and Hajj, H. (2020). Araelectra: Pre-training text discriminators for arabic language understanding.

Bouziane, A., Bouchiha, D., Doumi, N., and Malki, M. (2015). Question answering systems: Survey and trends. *Procedia Computer Science*, 73:366–375. International Conference on Advanced Wireless Information and Communication Technologies (AWICT 2015).

Clark, J. H., Choi, E., Collins, M., Garrette, D., Kwiatkowski, T., Nikolaev, V., and Palomaki, J. (2020). TyDi QA: A benchmark for information-seeking question answering in typologically diverse languages. *Transactions of the Association for Computational Linguistics*.

Hamdelsayed, M. A. and Atwell, E. (2016). Islamic applications of automatic question-answering.

Hamed, S. K. and Ab Aziz, M. J. (2016). A question answering system on holy quran translation based on question expansion technique and neural network classification. *J. Comput. Sci.*, 12(3):169–177.

Hammo, B., Abu-Salem, H., Lytinen, S. L., and Evens, M. (2002). QARAB: A: Question answering system to support the arabic language. In *Proceedings of the ACL-02 workshop on Computational approaches to semitic languages*.

Magdy, A. and Shaheen, M. (2012). A survey of arabic question answering: Challenges, tasks, approaches, tools, and future trends. 10.

Malhas, R. and Elsayed, T. (2020). AyaTEC: building a reusable verse-based test collection for arabic question answering on the holy qur'an. *ACM Transactions on Asian and Low-Resource Language Information Processing (TALLIP)*, 19(6):1–21.

Malhas, R. and Elsayed, T. (2022). official repository of Qur'an QA Shared Task. `https://gitlab.com/bigirqu/quranqa`, February.

Malhas, R., Mansour, W., and Elsayed, T. (2022). Qurán QA 2022: Overview of the first shared task on question answering over the holy qurán. In *Proceedings of the 5th Workshop on Open-Source Arabic Corpora and Processing Tools (OSACT5) at the 13th Language Resources and Evaluation Conference (LREC 2022)*.

Meters, C. (2022). Religion of the world. `https://countrymeters.info/en/World#religion`, journal=Religion of the World, Apr.

Mozannar, H., Maamary, E., El Hajal, K., and Hajj, H. (2019a). Neural Arabic question answering. In *Proceedings of the Fourth Arabic Natural Language Processing Workshop*, pages 108–118, Florence, Italy, August. Association for Computational Linguistics.

Mozannar, H., Maamary, E., El Hajal, K., and Hajj, H. (2019b). Neural Arabic question answering.

In *Proceedings of the Fourth Arabic Natural Language Processing Workshop*, pages 108–118, Florence, Italy, August. Association for Computational Linguistics.

Prager, J. (2014). Question answering. https://www.oxfordhandbooks.com/view/10.1093/oxfordhb/9780199573691.001.0001/oxfordhb-9780199573691-e-003, journal=Oxford Handbooks Online, Apr.

Rajpurkar, P., Zhang, J., Lopyrev, K., and Liang, P. (2016). SQuAD: 100,000+ questions for machine comprehension of text. In *Proceedings of the 2016 Conference on Empirical Methods in Natural Language Processing*, pages 2383–2392, Austin, Texas, November. Association for Computational Linguistics.

Refaee, E. A. A. (2016). *Sentiment analysis for microblogging platforms in Arabic*. Ph.D. thesis, Heriot-Watt University.

Su, D., Xu, Y., Winata, G. I., Xu, P., Kim, H., Liu, Z., and Fung, P. (2019). Generalizing question answering system with pre-trained language model fine-tuning. In *Proceedings of the 2nd Workshop on Machine Reading for Question Answering*, pages 203–211, Hong Kong, China, November. Association for Computational Linguistics.

Wolf, T., Debut, L., Sanh, V., Chaumond, J., Delangue, C., Moi, A., Cistac, P., Rault, T., Louf, R., Funtowicz, M., Davison, J., Shleifer, S., von Platen, P., Ma, C., Jernite, Y., Plu, J., Xu, C., Scao, T. L., Gugger, S., Drame, M., Lhoest, Q., and Rush, A. M. (2020). Transformers: State-of-the-art natural language processing. In *Proceedings of the 2020 Conference on Empirical Methods in Natural Language Processing: System Demonstrations*, pages 38–45, Online, October. Association for Computational Linguistics.

Proceedings of the OSACT 2022 Workshop @LREC2022, pages 136–145
Marseille, 20 June 2022

SMASH at Qur'an QA 2022: Creating Better Faithful Data Splits for Low-resourced Question Answering Scenarios

Amr Keleg and Walid Magdy
School of Informatics, University of Edinburgh
Edinburgh, UK
a.keleg@sms.ed.ac.uk, wmagdy@inf.ed.ac.uk

Abstract

The Qur'an QA 2022 shared task aims at assessing the possibility of building systems that can extract answers to religious questions given relevant passages from the Holy Qur'an. This paper describes SMASH's system that was used to participate in this shared task. Our experiments reveal a data leakage issue among the different splits of the dataset. This leakage problem hinders the reliability of using the models' performance on the development dataset as a proxy for the ability of the models to generalize to new unseen samples. After creating better faithful splits from the original dataset, the basic strategy of fine-tuning a language model pretrained on classical Arabic text yielded the best performance on the new evaluation split. The results achieved by the model suggests that the small scale dataset is not enough to fine-tune large transformer-based language models in a way that generalizes well. Conversely, we believe that further attention could be paid to the type of questions that are being used to train the models given the sensitivity of the data.

Keywords: Question Answering, Reading Comprehension Question Answering, Arabic NLP

1. Introduction

Automatic Question Answering (QA) task is gaining increased attention in recent years. The task aims at building models that can provide answers to various user-generated questions by utilizing a large set of curated documents. The type of understanding and reasoning required to answer these questions automatically is challenging. Open-domain QA aims at extracting answers using knowledge graphs and information retrieval systems, or generating answers using large pre-trained transformer-based architectures (Chen and Yih, 2020). Conversely, Reading Comprehension QA (RCQA) aims at extracting a span from a specified passage as the answer to a question. Training models for RCQA generally depends on building large scale datasets of question (Q), answer (A), passage (P) triples in which the answer (A) is a span of contiguous text extracted from the passage (P). For example, the SQUAD dataset was built by crowdsourcing more than 100k triples of Question/Answer/Passage where human annotators were asked to pose questions, and extract their answers from 536 English Wikipedia articles (Rajpurkar et al., 2016). The availability of such large datasets allows researchers to train models that can better generalize to unseen questions, thus advancing the field of Question Answering.

The Qur'an QA 2022 shared-task is another example of the RCQA tasks (Malhas et al., 2022). The Qur'an QA task provides 1,337 triples of questions, passages, and their answers (Malhas et al., 2022). In addition to the small size of the dataset, having questions written in Modern Standard Arabic (MSA), and passages written in Classical Arabic (CA) makes it more challenging. For instance, questions such as ما هي الإشارات للدماغ أو لأجزاء من الدّماغ في القرآن؟, and هل أشار القرآن الى نقص الأكسجين في المرتفعات؟ contain lexical terms that are not part of CA.

In this paper, we provide the system description of the SMASH[1] team of the University of Edinburgh in the task. We built a system for answering questions given passages from the holy Qur'an and make our code available for public[2]. In addition, we provide our general thoughts on the task and potential suggestions for improvements. Our team achieved a pRR score of 0.4004 in the official submitted run to the task.

The remaining sections of the paper are organized as follows: §2 shows the steps we took to create better faithful splits of the dataset, §3 describes the model's architecture, §4 reports the results achieved by the different model variants that were tested, and finally §5 gives some directions that might help with building better models.

2. Data Preparation

Rogers et al. (2020) argues that dataset creators need to provide an additional annotation for each triple to indicate the type of reasoning needed in order to answer the question. Providing such taxonomy allows for analyzing the performance of models trained using the dataset. Depending on a single aggregated metric for evaluating a model will neglect the fact that the model might be poorly performing on some question types, given that the datasets might be skewed in a way such that some question types are over-represented, while other types are under-represented.

Automatic categorization of question types: starting from the aforementioned recommendation, we classified the questions in the Qur'an QA dataset according to the interrogative article that appears in the question as a proxy for the type of reasoning needed to answer these

[1] `https://smash.inf.ed.ac.uk/`

[2] We release the code through: `https://github.com/AMR-KELEG/SMASH-QuranQA`

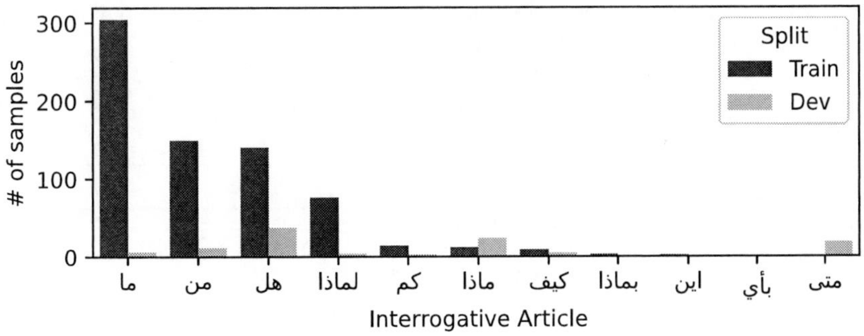

Figure 1: The distribution of question types among the train and development splits.

Shared Answer	Shared Passage	Question (Dev)	Question (Train)
من شاء فليؤمن ومن شاء فليكفر	وقل الحق من ربكم فمن شاء فليؤمن ومن شاء فليكفر إنا أعتدنا للظالمين نارا أحاط بهم سرادقها وإن يستغيثوا يغاثوا بماء كالمهل يشوي الوجوه بئس الشراب وساءت مرتفقا. إن الذين آمنوا وعملوا الصالحات إنا لا نضيع أجر من أحسن عملا. أولئك لهم جنات عدن تجري من تحتهم الأنهار يحلون فيها من أساور من ذهب ويلبسون ثيابا خضرا من سندس وإستبرق متكئين فيها على الأرائك نعم الثواب وحسنت مرتفقا.	هل سمح الإسلام بحرية الاعتقاد بالدخول إلى الإسلام؟	اتهم القرآن بأنه السبب في الدكتاتورية الإسلامية لكونه أباح التكفير وقتال الكفار حتى يسلموا، كيف نرد على ذلك؟
أطيعوا الرسول لعلكم ترحمون	وعد الله الذين آمنوا منكم وعملوا الصالحات ليستخلفنهم في الأرض كما استخلف الذين من قبلهم وليمكنن لهم دينهم الذي ارتضى لهم وليبدلنهم من بعد خوفهم أمنا يعبدونني لا يشركون بي شيئا ومن كفر بعد ذلك فأولئك هم الفاسقون. وأقيموا الصلاة وآتوا الزكاة وأطيعوا الرسول لعلكم ترحمون. لا تحسبن الذين كفروا معجزين في الأرض ومأواهم النار ولبئس المصير.	هل هناك إسلام بدون الحديث الشريف؟	لماذا لا يكتفي المسلمون بالقرآن الكريم ويلجأون للسنة أيضاً؟
ما كان قولهم إلا أن قالوا ربنا اغفر لنا ذنوبنا وإسرافنا في أمرنا وثبت أقدامنا وانصرنا على القوم الكافرين	وما كان لنفس أن تموت إلا بإذن الله كتابا مؤجلا ومن يرد ثواب الدنيا نؤته منها ومن يرد ثواب الآخرة نؤته منها وسنجزي الشاكرين. وكأين من نبي قاتل معه ربيون كثير فما وهنوا لما أصابهم في سبيل الله وما ضعفوا وما استكانوا والله يحب الصابرين. وما كان قولهم إلا أن قالوا ربنا اغفر لنا ذنوبنا وإسرافنا في أمرنا وثبت أقدامنا وانصرنا على القوم الكافرين. فآتاهم الله ثواب الدنيا وحسن ثواب الآخرة والله يحب المحسنين.	ماذا يشمل الإحسان؟	من هم المحسنون؟
قل يا عباد الذين آمنوا اتقوا ربكم	أمن هو قانت آناء الليل ساجدا وقائما يحذر الآخرة ويرجو رحمة ربه قل هل يستوي الذين يعلمون والذين لا يعلمون إنما يتذكر أولو الألباب. قل يا عباد الذين آمنوا اتقوا ربكم للذين أحسنوا في هذه الدنيا حسنة وأرض الله واسعة إنما يوفى الصابرون أجرهم بغير حساب.	ماذا يشمل الإحسان؟	من هم المحسنون؟

Table 1: Examples of data leakage in the original training and development splits. Leakage is sometimes caused by having paraphrased questions in the two splits that refer to the same passages, and have the same answer span.

questions.First, we manually compiled a list of twelve interrogative articles by investigating their occurrences in the training and development dataset splits. These articles are لماذا، كيف، بأي، بماذا، من، كم، كيف، ما، ماذا، هل، اين، متى. Since the word من can be either a preposition or an interrogative article, it is discarded in case the question contains another interrogative article. In case the question contains more than one interrogative article, the one occurring first is selected as the question type. An "NA" article is used in case a question contains none of the interrogative articles listed above. Figure 1 shows how the distribution of questions types is different between the train and development splits. It is also clear that polar interrogative questions (هل), what questions (ماذا), and when questions (متي) are frequent in the development split.

While fine-tuning an Arabic BERT model to extract the answer span (as described in §3), we noticed that the model's performance on what (ماذا) and polar interrogative questions (هل) is much better than the other question types. Our initial interpretation was that the model is able to reason about these types of questions in a way that generalizes to new unseen questions in the development dataset split. However, manually investigating the data showed that most of the questions of these types in the development dataset are paraphrases of questions in the training dataset that have exactly the same answer spans (A) from the same passages (P). Table 1 provides some examples demonstrating the issue of having questions in the development split that are mere paraphrases of other questions in the training split. These questions refer to the same passage, are paraphrases of each others, and thus have the exact same answer span. Questions belonging to these two question types represent 60% of the development dataset. A model that overfits the training data can achieve high scores by just generating the same answer span for a passage that was seen in the training data without doing any kind of reasoning. Consequently, a high performance on the provided development set might be misleading which does not help in reaching a robust optimized model for the task. On the other hand, we noticed that 17.5% of the development dataset belongs to the question type 'when متى' that is not part of the training dataset. One can argue that it is nearly impossible to expect the model to generalize to question types that were not encountered in the training data. A similar issue was flagged by Lewis et al. (2021) as they showed that there exists an overlap between the training and testing splits of multiple open-domain QA datasets, which in turn affects the ability of these datasets to be used as benchmarks for the various QA models.

Building faithful splits: based on limitations discussed above in the original training and the development datasets, we decided to generate new training and development splits by concatenating both the original training and development splits then dividing the dataset into four mutually exclusive datasets: (1) context in domain with leakage (i.e. training and development set share questions that have the same passage and answer) $D_{(1)\ in+leakage}$, (2) context in domain without leakage $D_{(2)\ in+no\ leakage}$, (3) hard out of domain $D_{(3)\ ood+hard}$, and (4) easy out of domain $D_{(4)\ ood+easy}$. First, $D_{(1)\ in+leakage}$ is formed by selecting all samples having repeated (passage, answer) pairs or (question, answer) pairs[3]. This type represents samples that the model can memorize, and thus are not useful for evaluating the generalization abilities of the model. $D_{(2)\ in+no\ leakage}$ contains samples of repeated passages that are not part of $D_{(1)\ in+leakage}$. All the remaining samples have unique passages (i.e.: passages that occur only once in the concatenated datasets).

Split name	Train	Dev	Total
$D_{(1) in+leakage}$	119	181	300
$D_{(2) in+no\ leakage}$	209	32	241
$D_{(3) ood+hard}$	0	60	60
$D_{(4) ood+easy}$	189	29	218
Total	517	302	819

Table 2: Number of triples in the new faithful splits of the dataset.

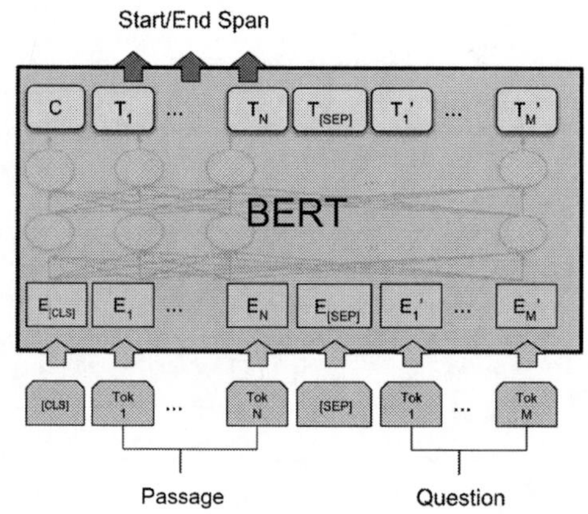

Figure 2: Using BERT for Reading Comprehension Question Answering (Devlin et al., 2019). In our implementation, the passage (P) followed by the question (Q) is fed to the BERT model.

These samples are split by assigning the ones having their question appearing three times or less to $D_{(3)\ ood+hard}$. These questions are rare, and thus the model should find it tricky to overfit them. Lastly, samples of unique passages which have their question appearing four or more times are assigned to $D_{(4)\ ood+easy}$.

After categorizing the samples, the four datasets were split into training, and development splits as follows. For $D_{(2)\ in+no\ leakage}$, and $D_{(4)\ ood+easy}$, each dataset was randomly shuffled and split into training and development datasets using 86.7/13.3 splitting percentages which are the same ratios used in the original dataset[4]. For $D_{(1)\ in+leakage}$, only one question is kept for each repeated (question, answer) and (passage, answer) pairs in the training dataset. The remaining samples of $D_{(1)\ in+leakage}$ are added to the development split. On the other hand, the whole $D_{(3)\ ood+hard}$ is used as a development split in order to measure the ability of the model to reason about the different question types without relying on memorizing answers that are frequent for specific questions or specific passages. Table 2 shows the number of the training and development samples

[3]We use full-match to consider two strings to be matching, which implies that for instance the following answers ناقة, الناقة are not considered to be repeated.

[4]The number of samples in the development dataset of each type is rounded to the nearest integer. The remaining samples are used as the training dataset

within the new faithful splits[5].

Detecting overfitting using the new faithful splits: We hypothesize that splitting the original dataset into four splits provides a proxy for predicting whether a model is still learning, or is just overfitting the training examples. Knowing that models need large number of samples to operate effectively, training samples from the four splits are compiled, and used as a whole to train/fine-tune models. Irrespective of the model being deployed, we think that a model which is overfitting the samples of the compiled training data would have the following performance trend on the development samples of the different splits (sorted in a descending order):

- $\mathbf{D}_{\mathbf{(1)in+leakage}}$: Samples within this split either share the same passage-answer pair or the same question-answer with one sample of the compiled training dataset. An overfitting model might be tempted to yield high probabilities for the answer's tokens, irrespective of the passage or the question.
- $\mathbf{D}_{\mathbf{(4)ood+easy}}$: While passages within this split are unique and are not encountered in the training data, the fact that the questions are previously encountered in the dataset, would in some cases imply that the answers needed to be extracted from this unique passage have lexical overlap with the answers of the same questions within the training data.
- $\mathbf{D}_{\mathbf{(3)ood+hard}}$: The fact that both the questions and passages are unique implies that the model would need to achieve good generalization in order to be able to properly answer these questions.
- $\mathbf{D}_{\mathbf{(2)in+no\ leakage}}$: This split is the most challenging one, since the model has encountered the passages within this split in the training dataset, however the new questions imply that the model should be able to understand the question in order to generate the right answer instead of just recalling the answer of the question in the training dataset.

3. Model Architecture

3.1. Model used in our submission

Given the success of BERT models with the RCQA task (Devlin et al., 2019), we fine-tuned the CAMELBERT-CA (Inoue et al., 2021) to predict the span of the answer given both the passage and the questions as an input to the model separated by the special $[SEP]$ token as shown in Figure 2. While there is a large number of avaialbe Arabic BERT models that showed their quality peformance on several tasks (Farha and Magdy, 2021), we decided to use the CAMELBERT-CA model for our task since it is pretrained on the OpenITI dataset, which is a large curated corpus of books written in Classical Arabic, including the Holy Quran (Nigst et al., 2020). The fact that the model's pretraining corpus contains text written in Classical Arabic makes it more suitable to the Qur'an QA task.

After tokenizing the input into subwords, the model $Vanilla + CA$ is fine-tuned to independently predict the probability that the answer span starts at each subword and the probability that the answer span ends at each subword. In inference time, a simple greedy decoding method is used to predict the right answer span. More specifically, the subwords at which the answer span begins/ends are these subwords having the highest start/end probabilities, respectively. In case the answer span is invalid (i.e.: the subword at which the span ends precedes the subword at which it starts), then the answer span is considered to start at the start index and end at the last subword of the passage (i.e.: the subword just before the $[SEP]$ token). The model was fine-tuned for 16 epochs, while saving checkpoints of the weights at the end of each epoch. An Adam optimizer was used with a learning rate set to 10^{-5}, beta values set to 0.9, and 0.98, and batches of 32 passagelquestion sequences having a maximum length of 512 subwords[6]. A single NVIDIA Quadro-RTX-8000 GPU of 48 GB VRAM was used to fine-tune the models. In order to simplify the fine-tuning process, no hyper-parameter tuning was performed. Since the task allows providing five different answers to each sample and being motivated by keeping our solution simple, the whole passage was used as the second ranked trivial answer.

3.2. Abandoned experiments

As an attempt to improve the performance of the fine-tuned BERT-based model, we tested different independent tricks that did not manage to improve the performance of the basic fine-tuned CAMELBERT-CA model ($Vanilla + CA$).

Using a pretrained MSA model ($Vanilla + MSA$) Since the questions are written in MSA and given that CAMELBERT-MSA is pretrained on larger data than CAMELBERT-CA, then fine-tuning CAMELBERT-MSA might give the model a better understanding of the questions, and thus better reasoning.

Embedding Named Entities (NER) Motivated by the fact that some questions are about the prophets, angels and other religious named entities, the intuition was that giving the model an extra signal might help in extracting spans that are related to these entities. First, a list of named-entities was compiled from multiple Wikipedia pages related to the Qur'an[7]. Then, a learnable entity embedding

[5]Examples of triples from the four splits are listed in the Appendix.

[6]Padding was used in case a sequence is shorter. Only two sequences in the training/development data had longer lengths than 512 subwords, and these sequences were truncated to the maximum length of 512 subwords.

[7]https://ar.wikipedia.org/wiki/قائمة_أشخاص_ذكروا_في_الكتاب_المقدس_والقرآن,

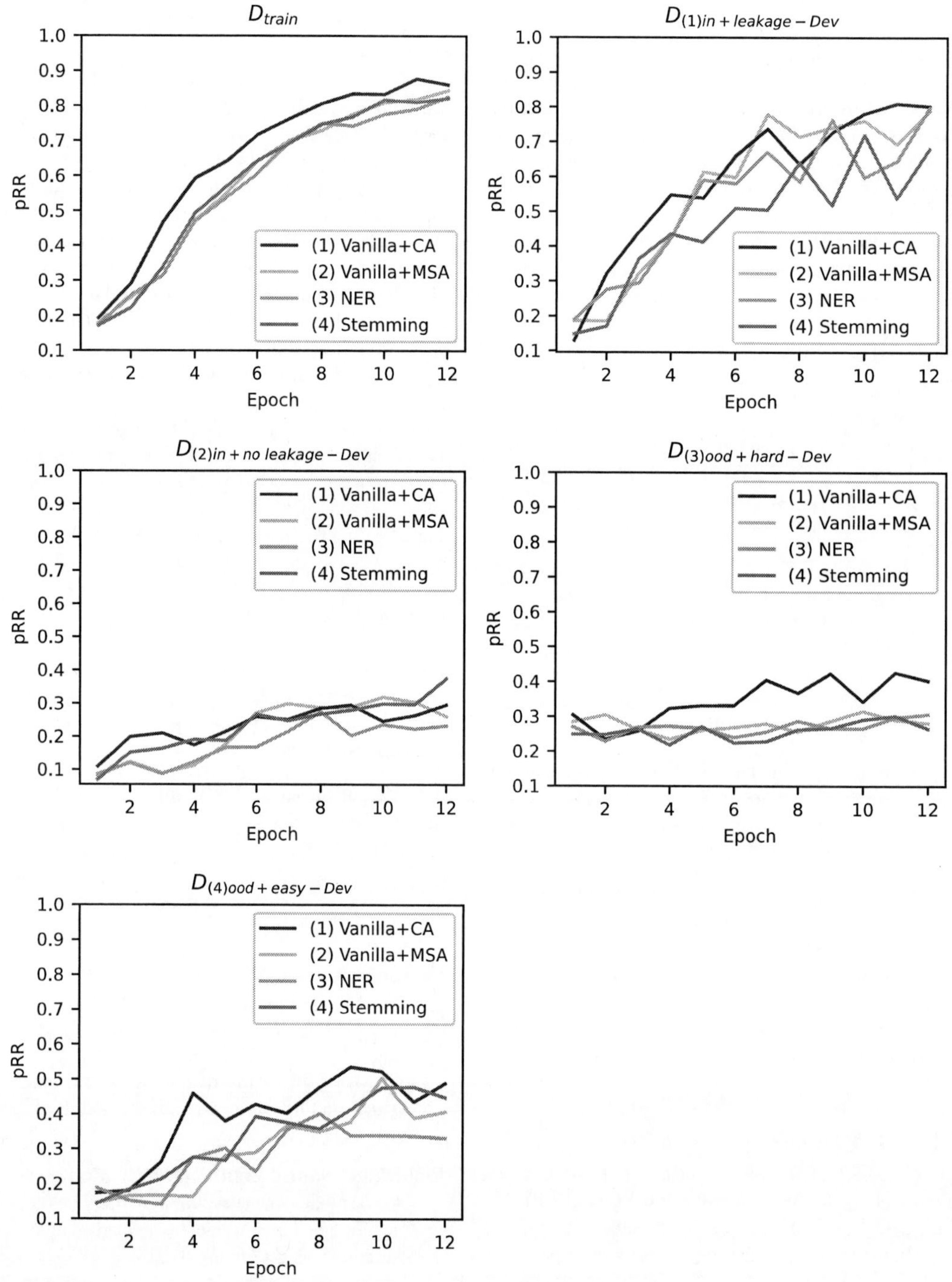

Figure 3: pRR scores computed at the end of each training epoch on the different data splits. D_{train} refers to the compiled training sets from all the data splits. This compiled dataset is used to fine-tune the models. On the other hand, models are evaluated on the development samples of each split independently.

was added to the input embeddings of the tokens that are among the list of compiled named-entities. The entity embedding is a parameter similar to positional embeddings used to encode the position of subtokens in the input sentence.

https://ar.wikipedia.org/wiki/حيوانات_ذكرت_في_القرآن, https://ar.wikipedia.org/wiki/شخصيات_ذكرت_في_القرآن

Stemming the text ($Stemming$) As a way to reduce the morphological diversity of Arabic tokens that might hinder the model's ability to find connections between the question and the passage, Farasa (Abdelali et al., 2016) was used to stem the text before feeding it into the CAMELBERT-CA. In order to be able to extract a span from the raw passage, mapping needed to be done between the span of tokens before and after stemming. It is worth mentioning that stemming does not affect the number of tokens.

More complex answer span decoding methods We tested with decoding multiple answer spans based on the start/end probabilities of the passage subtokens. Our empirical results showed that just depending on the start/end probabilities is not enough to rank the decoded spans. Therefore, we opted to using the greedy decoding method mentioned at the beginning of this section.

4. Results

Using the new faithful splits of the dataset described in §2, the four variants of the model (namely $(1)Vanilla + CA$, $(2)Vanilla + MSA$, $(3)NER$, and $(4)Stemming$) were fine-tuned on the compiled training samples of all the four splits. Figure 3 shows pRR scores computed at the end of each fine-tuning epoch. The model is typically evaluated on the compiled set of training samples in addition to the development samples of each of the four splits.

Analyzing the models' performance: Looking at the pRR scores, we observe that the four variants of the model perform better on samples that are similar to the ones found in the training dataset. More specifically, the scores on the $D_{(1)in+leakage}$ split are nearly on par with these achieved on the compiled set of training samples D_{train}. While the scores on the other three splits are lower than these achieved on the $D_{(1)in+leakage}$ split, the models are show higher performance on the $D_{(4)ood+easy}$ split in compared to the harder $D_{(3)ood+hard}$, and $D_{(2)in+no\ leakage}$ splits. Given that the number of evaluation samples in the $D_{(3)ood+hard}$ split is nearly double these in the $D_{(2)in+no\ leakage}$ split, the $D_{(3)ood+hard}$ split was used to guide the selection of the best performing variant. Surprisingly, the vanilla CAMELBERT-CA model ($Vanilla + CA$) fine-tuned on the training samples outperform all the other variants by an absolute difference of nearly 0.1. This can be attributed to the fact that the training set is too small for the models to generalize to new samples. Consequently, using more complex models might be not beneficial since it is hard to tune the parameters using such small dataset.

Error analysis on the official testing dataset: The pRR scores achieved by the model indicate that it is unable to reason about all the questions in the testing dataset. Manual inspection of the answers extracted from passages within the testing data reveals that the model sometimes tend to ignore the question, and extract the same answer span for specific passages that occurred in the training dataset. For example, the model predicts the same answer span of the following question in the training datasets كيف اهلك الله قوم عاد؟ when it is fed the same passage with a different question كيف اهلك الله قوم ثمود؟.

Assessing the stability of the models: Reimers and Gurevych (2017) showed how deep learning models are susceptible to achieve unstable performances when spurious parameters such as the random seed are changed. Therefore, we are reporting the distribution of the pRR scores achieved by the four model variants when evaluated on the $D_{(1)in+leakage}$, and $D_{(3)ood+hard}$ splits in Figure 4. Focusing our attention first on the performance of the models on the $D_{(3)ood+hard}$ split reveals the superior performance achieved by the $Vanilla + CA$ model in compared to all the other model variants. Moreover, the box plots show a non-negligible variance in the pRR achieved by the models as an effect of just changing the random seed. Conversely, the pRR scores achieved on the $D_{(1)in+leakage}$ split yields different conclusions, with having the $Vanilla + MSA$ model outperforming the $Vanilla + CA$ one. We think that these contradicting observations demonstrate the harmful impact that data leakage might have in case design decisions are blindly taken based on the performance on the development split without investigating the samples represented within the split, and comparing them to the ones in the training split.

Results of our submissions: Following these observations, we made two submissions based on the $Vanilla + CA$ model in which the model was fine-tuned using 1, and 3 as the random seeds respectively. The pRR scores reported in Table 3 indicate that the official results on the hidden test set, and these achieved on the $D_{(3)ood+hard}$ split are similar to a great extent, which in turn might mean that the $D_{(3)ood+hard}$ split can be reliably used to evaluate the ability of the model to generalize to unseen data.

5. Going Further

Given how models are sensitive to the samples within the training dataset, we believe that researchers interested in extending the dataset should be mindful of the types of questions and the passages of these new samples. A potential way of preventing the models from overfitting would be to have multiple questions of different types referring to different spans from the same passage. Doing so might prevent the models from extracting the same answer span for a passage while ignoring the question. This strategy is employed in large RCQA datasets such as SQUAD, where more than 100,000 questions were generated from 23,215 paragraphs extracted from only 536 Wikipedia articles (i.e.: The average number of questions for each paragraph is 4.31) (Rajpurkar et al., 2016). On the other hand, the training split of the QRCD dataset

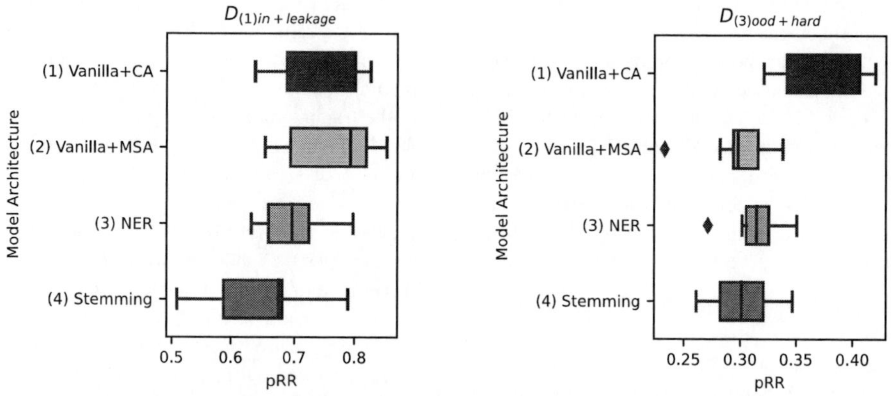

Figure 4: Distribution of pRR scores on the development samples of the $D_{(1)in+leakage}$, and $D_{(3)ood+hard}$ splits for 10 different random seeds of each architecture.

Model name	Official pRR score on the hidden test set	pRR score on the $\mathbf{D_{(3)ood+hard}}$ Dev split
$Vanilla + CA_{seed=1}$	0.3801	0.4073
$Vanilla + CA_{seed=3}$	0.4004	0.4083

Table 3: pRR scores of the submitted systems on the hidden test set, and the $D_{(3)ood+hard}$ dataset

has 468 unique passages, and 710 questions (i.e.: The average number of questions for each passage is 1.51). It is worth mentioning that for SQUAD, the paragraphs were first compiled, and then annotators were asked to pose questions that are answered by spans within these paragraphs. Conversely, the AyaTEC dataset, from which the QRCD dataset is created, was built by first compiling a list of questions, and then searching for Quranic verses that answer such questions (Malhas and Elsayed, 2020). Moreover, providing annotations for the reasoning type required to answer the questions would be beneficial for analyzing the performance of the model on different types of questions and interpreting the behavior of these models.

Finally, and given the sensitivity of this task, it might be better to avoid questions that can have multiple interpretations, and would create unnecessary controversy. For example, "متى يحل الإسلام دم الشخص؟" is a question that appears 19 times in the original development dataset, where some answer spans are specific to some contexts, and can not be provided as an answer to this question in general. For instance, the following answer span "فإذا انسلخ الأشهر الحرم فاقتلوا المشركين حيث وجدتموهم وخذوهم واحصروهم واقعدوا لهم كل مرصد" that Muslims should defend themselves against a group that attack them. This does not in turn imply by any means that Islam urges Muslims to kill each and every person who participated in this war. Consequently, extracting the following answer span for the specified extreme question would be misleading. Given the diversity of topics in the Quran and the small size of the dataset, it might be better to train models to answer factoid questions. Answers to such questions do not depend on the context, and therefore will not cause any unnecessary controversy. This is also motivated by the fact that the answers extracted by models are not generally interpretable, and thus one will not be able to reason about why a model is behaving in a specific way.

6. Conclusion

Despite the advancements researchers have achieved in solving a diverse set of Natural Language Processing (NLP) tasks using the (pretrain then fine-tune) paradigm, our experiments show that using a relatively small-sized Reading Comprehension Question Answering (RCQA) dataset for fine-tuning a large pretrained language model is challenging, especially if we are aiming at having models that can generalize to different types of questions that require complex reasoning. Moreover, we indicate that the dataset used for fine-tuning the models might have a data leakage problem between the training and developments splits. This problem hinders the possibility of using the model's performance on the development set as a reliable proxy for the model's generalization abilities to new unseen samples.

7. Acknowledgements

This work was supported in part by the UKRI Centre for Doctoral Training in Natural Language Processing, funded by the UKRI (grant EP/S022481/1) and the University of Edinburgh, School of Informatics and School of Philosophy, Psychology & Language Sciences.

8. Bibliographical References

Abdelali, A., Darwish, K., Durrani, N., and Mubarak, H. (2016). Farasa: A fast and furious segmenter for

Arabic. In *Proceedings of the 2016 Conference of the North American Chapter of the Association for Computational Linguistics: Demonstrations*, pages 11–16, San Diego, California, June. Association for Computational Linguistics.

Chen, D. and Yih, W.-t. (2020). Open-domain question answering. In *Proceedings of the 58th Annual Meeting of the Association for Computational Linguistics: Tutorial Abstracts*, pages 34–37, Online, July. Association for Computational Linguistics.

Devlin, J., Chang, M.-W., Lee, K., and Toutanova, K. (2019). BERT: Pre-training of deep bidirectional transformers for language understanding. In *Proceedings of the 2019 Conference of the North American Chapter of the Association for Computational Linguistics: Human Language Technologies, Volume 1 (Long and Short Papers)*, pages 4171–4186, Minneapolis, Minnesota, June. Association for Computational Linguistics.

Farha, I. A. and Magdy, W. (2021). Benchmarking transformer-based language models for arabic sentiment and sarcasm detection. In *Proceedings of the sixth Arabic natural language processing workshop*, pages 21–31.

Inoue, G., Alhafni, B., Baimukan, N., Bouamor, H., and Habash, N. (2021). The interplay of variant, size, and task type in Arabic pre-trained language models. In *Proceedings of the Sixth Arabic Natural Language Processing Workshop*, pages 92–104, Kyiv, Ukraine (Virtual), April. Association for Computational Linguistics.

Lewis, P., Stenetorp, P., and Riedel, S. (2021). Question and answer test-train overlap in open-domain question answering datasets. In *Proceedings of the 16th Conference of the European Chapter of the Association for Computational Linguistics: Main Volume*, pages 1000–1008, Online, April. Association for Computational Linguistics.

Malhas, R. and Elsayed, T. (2020). AyaTEC. *ACM Transactions on Asian and Low-Resource Language Information Processing (TALLIP)*, 19:1 – 21.

Malhas, R., Mansour, W., and Elsayed, T. (2022). Qur'an QA 2022: Overview of the first shared task on question answering over the holy Qur'an. In *Proceedings of the 5th Workshop on Open-Source Arabic Corpora and Processing Tools (OSACT5) at the 13th Language Resources and Evaluation Conference (LREC 2022)*.

Nigst, L., Romanov, M., Savant, S. B., Seydi, M., and Verkinderen, P. (2020). OpenITI: a Machine-Readable Corpus of Islamicate Texts, June.

Rajpurkar, P., Zhang, J., Lopyrev, K., and Liang, P. (2016). SQuAD: 100,000+ questions for machine comprehension of text. In *Proceedings of the 2016 Conference on Empirical Methods in Natural Language Processing*, pages 2383–2392, Austin, Texas, November. Association for Computational Linguistics.

Reimers, N. and Gurevych, I. (2017). Reporting score distributions makes a difference: Performance study of LSTM-networks for sequence tagging. In *Proceedings of the 2017 Conference on Empirical Methods in Natural Language Processing*, pages 338–348, Copenhagen, Denmark, September. Association for Computational Linguistics.

Rogers, A., Kovaleva, O., Downey, M., and Rumshisky, A. (2020). Getting closer to AI complete question answering: A set of prerequisite real tasks. *Proceedings of the AAAI Conference on Artificial Intelligence*, 34(05):8722–8731, Apr.

Appendix

Tables 4, and 5 showcase some samples from the new faithful splits, along with the original splits of these examples. The first set of examples demonstrates how questions that share the same passages and answer spans are grouped together in the $D_{(1)in+leakage}$ split. The second set shows the difficulty of the $D_{(2)\ in+no\ leakage}$ split, since the model needs to extract an answer span from a passage that is used to answer another unrelated question. This is particularly hard in case the model has overfitted the training data in a sense that it generates the same answer span for the same passage irrespective of the question being asked. Examples of questions in $D_{(3)ood\ +\ hard}$ in Table 5 showcase the complexity of these rare questions that are not part of the training dataset. The model will need to have superior generalization in order to be able to have proper reasoning, and consequently answer these questions. The last example shows two questions referring to different passages yet having some lexical overlap. We think that large models such as BERT have the ability to consider وعمل صالحاً and وعملوا الصالحات are inflections of the same lexical items, and consequently will be to some extent able to extract the correct answer span for both cases even if one of them is not part of the training dataset.

Answer	Passage	Question	Original Split	New Split
إبراهيم وإسماعيل	وإذ ابتلى إبراهيم ربه بكلمات فأتمهن قال إني جاعلك للناس إماما قال ومن ذريتي قال لا ينال عهدي الظالمين. وإذ جعلنا البيت مثابة للناس وأمنا واتخذوا من مقام إبراهيم مصلى وعهدنا إلى إبراهيم وإسماعيل أن طهرا بيتي للطائفين والعاكفين والركع السجود. وإذ قال إبراهيم رب اجعل هذا بلدا آمنا وارزق أهله من الثمرات من آمن منهم بالله واليوم الآخر قال ومن كفر فأمتعه قليلا ثم أضطره إلى عذاب النار وبئس المصير. وإذ يرفع إبراهيم القواعد من البيت وإسماعيل ربنا تقبل منا إنك أنت السميع العليم. ربنا واجعلنا مسلمين لك ومن ذريتنا أمة مسلمة لك وأرنا مناسكنا وتب علينا إنك أنت التواب الرحيم. ربنا وابعث فيهم رسولا منهم يتلو عليهم آياتك ويعلمهم الكتاب والحكمة ويزكيهم إنك أنت العزيز الحكيم.	من هم الأنبياء الذين ذكروا في القرآن على أنهم مسلمون؟	Train	$D_{(1)in+leakage-Train}$
		من بنى الكعبة؟	Dev	$D_{(1)in+leakage-Dev}$
من اهتدى فلنفسه ومن ضل فإنما يضل عليها	ولئن سألتهم من خلق السماوات والأرض ليقولن الله قل أفرأيتم ما تدعون من دون الله إن أرادني الله بضر هل هن كاشفات ضره أو أرادني برحمة هل هن ممسكات رحمته قل حسبي الله عليه يتوكل المتوكلون. قل يا قوم اعملوا على مكانتكم إني عامل فسوف تعلمون. من يأتيه عذاب يخزيه ويحل عليه عذاب مقيم. إنا أنزلنا عليك الكتاب للناس بالحق فمن اهتدى فلنفسه ومن ضل فإنما يضل عليها وما أنت عليهم بوكيل.	اتهم القرآن بأنه السبب في الدكتاتورية الإسلامية لكونه أباح التكفير وقتال الكفار حتى يسلموا، كيف نرد على ذلك؟	Train	$D_{(1)in+leakage-Train}$
		ما هي الدلائل التي تشير بأن الانسان مخير؟	Dev	$D_{(1)in+leakage-Dev}$
		إن كان الله قدّر علي أفعالي فلماذا يحاسبني؟	Dev	$D_{(1)in+leakage-Dev}$
		لماذا سيُحاسب ويُعذب الضال يوم القيامة ان كان """من يضلل الله فما له من هاد""" كما ورد من قوله تعالى في آية 32 و آية 63 من سورة الزمر؟	Dev	$D_{(1)in+leakage-Dev}$
		هل سمح الإسلام بحرية الاعتقاد بالدخول إلى الإسلام؟	Dev	$D_{(1)in+leakage-Dev}$
مدين	إذ أوحينا إلى أمك ما يوحى. أن اقذفيه في التابوت فاقذفيه في اليم فليلقه اليم بالساحل يأخذه عدو لي وعدو له وألقيت عليك محبة مني ولتصنع على عيني. إذ تمشي أختك فتقول هل أدلكم على من يكفله فرجعناك إلى أمك كي تقر عينها ولا تحزن وقتلت نفسا فنجيناك من الغم وفتناك فتونا فلبثت سنين في أهل مدين ثم جئت على قدر يا موسى. واصطنعتك لنفسي. اذهب أنت وأخوك بآياتي ولا تنيا في ذكري. اذهبا إلى فرعون إنه طغى. فقولا له قولا لينا لعله يتذكر أو يخشى. قالا ربنا إننا نخاف أن يفرط علينا أو أن يطغى. قال لا تخافا إنني معكما أسمع وأرى. فأتياه فقولا إنا رسولا ربك فأرسل معنا بني إسرائيل ولا تعذبهم قد جئناك بآية من ربك والسلام على من اتبع الهدى. إنا قد أوحي إلينا أن العذاب على من كذب وتولى.	ما هي اسماء المدن المذكورة في القرآن؟	Train	$D_{(1)in+leakage-Train}$
لعله يتذكر أو يخشى		ما هو أثر الكلام الطيب؟	Train	$D_{(2)\ in+no\ leakage-Train}$

Table 4: Examples of samples showing the characteristics of the new four faithful splits.

Answer	Passage	Question	Original Split	New Split
من يرد الله أن يهديه يشرح صدره للإسلام ومن يرد أن يضله يجعل صدره ضيقا حرجا كأنما يصعد في السماء	فمن يرد الله أن يهديه يشرح صدره للإسلام ومن يرد أن يضله يجعل صدره ضيقا حرجا كأنما يصعد في السماء كذلك يجعل الله الرجس على الذين لا يؤمنون. وهذا صراط ربك مستقيما قد فصلنا الآيات لقوم يذكرون. لهم دار السلام عند ربهم وهو وليهم بما كانوا يعملون.	هل أشار القرآن الى نقص الأكسجين في المرتفعات؟	Train	$D_{(3)ood\,+\,hard-Dev}$
ناصيتها	وإلى عاد أخاهم هودا قال يا قوم اعبدوا الله ما لكم من إله غيره إن أنتم إلا مفترون. يا قوم لا أسألكم عليه أجرا إن أجري إلا على الذي فطرني أفلا تعقلون. ويا قوم استغفروا ربكم ثم توبوا إليه يرسل السماء عليكم مدرارا ويزدكم قوة إلى قوتكم ولا تتولوا مجرمين. قالوا يا هود ما جئتنا ببينة وما نحن بتاركي آلهتنا عن قولك وما نحن لك بمؤمنين. إن نقول إلا اعتراك بعض آلهتنا بسوء قال إني أشهد الله واشهدوا أني بريء مما تشركون. من دونه فكيدوني جميعا ثم لا تنظرون. إني توكلت على الله ربي وربكم ما من دابة إلا هو آخذ بناصيتها إن ربي على صراط مستقيم. فإن تولوا فقد أبلغتكم ما أرسلت به إليكم ويستخلف ربي قوما غيركم ولا تضرونه شيئا إن ربي على كل شيء حفيظ. ولما جاء أمرنا نجينا هودا والذين آمنوا معه برحمة منا ونجيناهم من عذاب غليظ. وتلك عاد جحدوا بآيات ربهم وعصوا رسله واتبعوا أمر كل جبار عنيد. وأتبعوا في هذه الدنيا لعنة ويوم القيامة ألا إن عادا كفروا ربهم ألا بعدا لعاد قوم هود.	ما هي الإشارات للدماغ أو لأجزاء من الدّماغ في القرآن؟	Train	$D_{(3)ood\,+\,hard-Dev}$
من دعا إلى الله وعمل صالحا وقال إنني من المسلمين	ومن أحسن قولا ممن دعا إلى الله وعمل صالحا وقال إنني من المسلمين. ولا تستوي الحسنة ولا السيئة ادفع بالتي هي أحسن فإذا الذي بينك وبينه عداوة كأنه ولي حميم. وما يلقاها إلا الذين صبروا وما يلقاها إلا ذو حظ عظيم. وإما ينزغنك من الشيطان نزغ فاستعذ بالله إنه هو السميع العليم.	من هم المحسنون؟	Train	$D_{(1)in+leakage-Dev}$
الذين آمنوا وعملوا الصالحات	وقل الحق من ربكم فمن شاء فليؤمن ومن شاء فليكفر إنا أعتدنا للظالمين نارا أحاط بهم سرادقها وإن يستغيثوا يغاثوا بماء كالمهل يشوي الوجوه بئس الشراب وساءت مرتفقا. إن الذين آمنوا وعملوا الصالحات إنا لا نضيع أجر من أحسن عملا. أولئك لهم جنات عدن تجري من تحتهم الأنهار يحلون فيها من أساور من ذهب ويلبسون ثيابا خضرا من سندس وإستبرق متكئين فيها على الأرائك نعم الثواب وحسنت مرتفقا.	من هم المحسنون؟	Train	$D_{(4)in+leakage-Train}$

Table 5: Examples of samples showing the characteristics of the new four faithful splits.

Proceedings of the OSACT 2022 Workshop @LREC2022, pages 146–153
Marseille, 20 June 2022

Stars at Qur'an QA 2022: Building Automatic Extractive Question Answering Systems for the Holy Qur'an with Transformer Models and Releasing a New Dataset

Ahmed Wasfey, Eman Elrefai , Marwa Muhammad, Haq Nawaz
Tactful AI , BambooGeeks , Freelancer , PUCIT
{ahmedsleemce, eman.lotfy.elrefai, marwa.mohammad.matar, haqnawaz99}@gmail.com

Abstract

The Holy Qur'an is the most sacred book for more than 1.9 billion Muslims worldwide, and it provides a guide for their behaviours and daily interactions. Its miraculous eloquence and the divine essence of its verses (Khorami, 2014)(Elhindi, 2017) make it far more difficult for non-scholars to answer their questions from the Qur'an. Here comes the significant role of technology in assisting all Muslims in answering their Qur'anic questions with state-of-the-art advancements in natural language processing (NLP) and information retrieval (IR). The task of constructing the finest automatic extractive Question Answering system from the Holy Qur'an with the use of the recently available Qur'anic Reading Comprehension Dataset(QRCD) was announced for LREC 2022 (Malhas et al., 2022) which opened up this new area for researchers around the world. In this paper, we propose a novel Qur'an Question Answering dataset with over 700 samples to aid future Qur'an research projects and three different approaches where we utilised self-attention based deep learning models (transformers) for building reliable intelligent question-answering systems for the Holy Qur'an that achieved a partial Reciprocal Rank (pRR) best score of 52% on the released QRCD test set.

Keywords: Qur'an, Extractive Question Ansewring , Deep Learning, NLP , Transformers

1. Introduction

Reading Comprehension, which is the skill of reading a text and then answering questions about it, is a difficult task for machines that continues to pique the interest of many academics and will continue to do so for many years to come (Rajpurkar et al., 2016). Unlike open domain question answering systems (Mishra and Jain, 2016) in extractive question answering, a passage or a context is provided so that the model can refer to it and predict where the answer is inside the passage as shown in Figure 4, and it is still a very challenging as it requires machines to have both natural language understanding and knowledge of the world or the domain in the case of domain-specific applications.

There are six official languages of the United Nations and the only Semitic language among these six languages is Arabic (Tahani et al., 2021). Mainly Arabic can be divided into three categories. Classical Arabic (CA) is the language of the Qur'an, Hadith and classical Islamic literature. Modern Standard Arabic (MSA) is the language used in the news, articles or modern Arabic era. Colloquial or dialectal Arabic is the variety of different dialects in different regions of Arabic speaking countries. Additionally, The grammatical structure of the Arabic language is exceedingly rich and complex(Khaled et al., 2018) as compared to the other languages. Arabic QA is addressed in a few studies since 2004(Bakari et al., 2016), and the existence of considerable, realistic datasets have always been crucial for propelling fields ahead, famous examples include SQUAD for English reading comprehension (Rajpurkar et al., 2016) and the Penn Tree-

Passage : "إن الله اصطفى آدم ونوحا وآل إبراهيم وآل عمران على العالمين. ذرية بعضها من بعض والله سميع عليم. إذ قالت امرأت عمران رب إني نذرت لك ما في بطني محررا فتقبل مني إنك أنت السميع العليم. فلما وضعتها قالت رب إني وضعتها أنثى والله أعلم بما وضعت وليس الذكر كالأنثى وإني سميتها مريم وإني أعيذها بك وذريتها من الشيطان الرجيم. فتقبلها ربها بقبول حسن وأنبتها نباتا حسنا وكفلها زكريا كلما دخل عليها زكريا المحراب وجد عندها رزقا قال يا مريم أنى لك هذا قالت هو من عند الله إن الله يرزق من يشاء بغير حساب. هنالك دعا زكريا ربه قال رب هب لي من لدنك ذرية طيبة إنك سميع الدعاء. فنادته الملائكة وهو قائم يصلي في المحراب أن الله يبشرك بيحيى مصدقا بكلمة من الله وسيدا وحصورا ونبيا من الصالحين. قال رب أنى يكون لي غلام وقد بلغني الكبر وامرأتي عاقر قال كذلك الله يفعل ما يشاء. قال رب اجعل لي آية قال آيتك ألا تكلم الناس ثلاثة أيام إلا رمزا واذكر ربك كثيرا وسبح بالعشي والإبكار."

Question : "كم ليلة امر الله زكريا الا يكلم الناس؟"
Answers : "ثلاثة أيام"

Question : "من هو ابن زكريا؟"
Answers : "يحيى"

Question : "من كفل السيدة مريم؟"
Answers : "زكريا"

Figure 1: : Question-answer pairs for a sample passage in the QRCD dataset. Each of the answers is a segment extracted from the passage.

bank for syntactic parsing (Marcus et al., 1994). To assist in meeting the need to improve the Qur'anic reading comprehension dataset in order to boost the use of state-of-the-art data intensive models, we propose a new dataset with more than 700 Qur'an questions extracted from the publicly available Annotated Corpus of Arabic Al-Qur'an Question and Answer(AQQAC) dataset (Alqahtani and Atwell, 2018) and reformatted sample by sample to be usable for the extractive Ques-

tion Answering task. We also conducted many experiments with transformers like araBERT(Antoun et al., 2020a) some experiments by using the vanilla model for direct Question Answering fine tuning with different configurations and combinations of data and in other experiments we created araBERT based Qur'an masked language model by fine tuning the model on bare Qur'an verses first then using it for building the Question Answering model further more we also tried ensemble of different transformers to strengthen each other for better results and acheived 52% best pRR score on the test set and 62% score on the development dataset.
The rest of the paper is organized as follows: Section 2 summaries some of the work done previously in this field. Section 3 discusses the data and its challenges. Section 4 presents the basic ideas that were used as building blocks for the final three systems used in the final submissions which are defined in section 5. We evaluate the three systems performance and conclude the paper in section 6 and section 7respectively.

2. Related Work

In this section, we shed light on the previous work for both the Qur'anic datasets has questions and answers from the Holy Qur'an and Arabic Question Answering (QA) Systems.

2.1. Qur'anic datasets:

Several studies have been made to understand the Qur'anic text and extract knowledge from it. AyaTEC (Malhas and Elsayed, 2020) is the dataset for Arabic QA on the Holy Qur'an. All of the Qur'anic verses that directly answer the questions were exhaustively extracted and annotated. The answers are divided into a single answer, multiple answers and no answers with evaluation for each type. it proposed several evaluation measures to integrate the concept of partial matching. Also, there is a dataset have a partial matching for the required structure of the Qur'an QA task called AQQAC (Alqahtani and Atwell, 2018). It was annotated corpus of Arabic Al-Qur'an QA using machine learning.

2.2. Arabic QA Systems:

(Alsubhi et al., 2021) evaluated the performance of three existing Arabic pre-trained models(AraBERTv2-base, AraELECTRA, AraBERTv0.2-large) on Arabic QA. Al-Bayan(Abdelnasser et al., 2014) proposed a novel Question Answering system for the Qur'an, that extracted the answer from the retrieved verses accompanied by their Tafseer. (Mozannar et al., 2019) proposed an approach for open domain Arabic QA and introduced the Arabic Reading Comprehension Dataset (ARCD) and ArabicSQuAD and consisted of a document retriever using hierarchical TF-IDF and a document reader using BERT.

3. Data

3.1. Existing Datasets

We begin by investigating existing Qur'anic Reading Comprehension with Question Answering (QA) datasets. We highlight their structure and the challenges for each dataset. QRCD (Qur'anic Reading Comprehension Dataset) (Malhas and Elsayed, 2020) (Malhas et al., 2022) is the dataset which was provided by the organizers of the Qur'an QA competition with 1,337 question-passage-answer. AQQAC (Alqahtani and Atwell, 2018) is annotated corpus of Arabic Al-Qur'an Question and Answer with 1,225 question-answer. The last existing dataset we used is Arabic SQuAD(Mozannar et al., 2019). It's a machine translation of the Stanford Question Answering.

3.1.1. QRCD

QRCD (Qur'anic Reading Comprehension Dataset) (Malhas and Elsayed, 2020) (Malhas et al., 2022)is the main dataset we used. It helped us for understanding the task and creating a similar dataset following the same structure. The passage is extracted from some specific verses from the Qur'an. The passage is about one page from Qur'an or less than that. QRCD may have multiple same questions for different passages from the Qur'an. For the same question, there are a single answer or multiple answers with ranking. The first answer is the gold answer and the other answers after that are partially exact answers. The answer must be included in the passage. It is composed of 1,093 tuples of question-passage pairs that are coupled with their extracted answers to constitute 1,337 question-passage-answer triplets.It is divided to training, validation and testing dataset. For the training dataset, it is 710 samples, the development dataset is 109 samples and the testing is 352 samples. QRCD consists of a question-passage pair and the answers retrieved from the accompanying text. The dataset is formatted as shown in Figure 1.

3.1.2. AQQAC

After searching for any open-source dataset that can work fine for Qur'an QA, The only related dataset we found is The Al-Qur'an Question and Answer Compilation (AQQAC) (Alqahtani and Atwell, 2018) is a collection of 1224 questions and answers regarding the Al-Qur'an. Combining more datasets, they can increase the dataset and get higher scores. AQQAC dataset consists of The question ID, question word (particles), chapter number, verse number, question topic, question type, Al-Qur'an ontology concepts (Alqahtani Atwell, 2018), and question source are all marked on each question and response. The goal of this corpus is to give a Question-Answering taxonomy for Al-Qur'an-related inquiries. This corpus might also be utilised as a data set for testing and evaluating Islamic IR systems. We aimed to use this dataset with the QRCD (Malhas and Elsayed, 2020) (Malhas et al., 2022) dataset but we couldn't use it directly. The problem with it is that most of the passages and the answers aren't extracted from the Qur'an. They are extracted from the Altabari Tafseer. Most of the questions are valid to get and follow the same structure as the QRCD dataset. We used about 500 questions from the AQQAC dataset and added them to our data. We added some small passages and answers that are extracted from Qur'an.

Question: "ما مصير المنافقين يوم القيامة ؟ اذكر الآية الكريمة."
Answer: "الدرك الأسفل من النار .إِنَّ الْمُنَافِقِينَ فِي الدَّرْكِ الأَسْفَلِ مِنَ النَّارِ وَلَن تَجِدَ لَهُمْ نَصِيراً{145}النساء."

Question: "ماذا تعلم آدم عليه السلام من الله جل جلاله وكان هذا العلم ليس عند الملائكة ؟"
Answer: "علم الأسماء . والدليل : وَعَلَّمَ آدَمَ الأَسْمَاء كُلَّهَا ثُمَّ عَرَضَهُمْ عَلَى الْمَلاَئِكَةِ فَقَالَ أَنبِئُونِي بِأَسْمَاء هَؤُلاء إِن كُنتُمْ صَادِقِينَ{31} البقرة"

Question: "ما هي السبع المثاني ؟"
Answer: "سورة الفاتحة .بِسْمِ اللهِ الرَّحْمنِ الرَّحِيمِ{1} الْحَمْدُ للهِ رَبِّ الْعَالَمِينَ{2} الرَّحْمـنِ الرَّحِيمِ{3} مَالِكِ يَوْمِ الدِّينِ{4} إِيَّاكَ نَعْبُدُ وإِيَّاكَ نَسْتَعِينُ{5} اهدِنَــــا الصِّرَاطَ المُستَقِيمَ{6} صِرَاطَ الَّذِينَ أَنعَمتَ عَلَيهِمْ غَيرِ المَغضُوبِ عَلَيهِمْ وَلاَ الضَّالِّينَ{7}الفاتحة"

Question: "اشرح الآية الكريمة.يَا أَيُّهَا الَّذِينَ آمَنُواْ عَلَيْكُمْ أَنفُسَكُمْ لاَ يَضُرُّكُم مَّن ضَلَّ إِذَا اهْتَدَيْتُمْ إِلَى اللهِ مَرْجِعُكُمْ جَمِيعاً فَيُنَبِّئُكُم بِمَا كُنتُمْ تَعْمَلُونَ{105}المائدة"
Answer: "يا أيها الذين آمنوا عليكم أنفسكم أي احفظوها وقوموا بصلاحها , لا يضركم من ضل إذا اهتديتم قيل المراد لا يضركم من ضل من أهل الكتاب وقيل المراد غيرهم لحديث أبي ثعلبة الخشني: سألت عنها رسول الله صلى الله عليه وسلم فقال: ائتمروا بالمعروف وتناهوا عن المنكر حتى إذا رأيت شحا مطاعا وهوى متبعا ودنيا مؤثرة وإعجاب كل ذي رأي برأيه فعليك نفسك إلى الله مرجعكم جميعا فينبئكم بما كنتم تعملون فيجازيكم به"رواه الحاكم وغيره

Figure 2: : Question-answer pairs with no passage in the AQQAC dataset.

3.1.3. Arabic SQuAD

Arabic SQuAD (Mozannar et al., 2019) is a dataset with 48,344 questions on 10,364 paragraphs. The paragraphs are extracted from Wikipedia articles so this dataset isn't related to Qur'an QA. We aimed to make the model deal with the Arabic question answer in general. After that, we expected the model can perform better when we apply the Qur'an QA.

When we trained the transformer model using QRCD

passage: '33 ASR عندما تلقى جهاز تيليتيبي ASR كونترول الأوتوماتيكي الشريط الورقي بقارئ المزود S XOFF ، الإرسال على تسبب في استئناف قارئ ، Q XON اختصار للإرسال ، تسبب في توقف قارئ الشريط تلقي كونترول الشريط . أصبحت هذه التقنية معتمدة من قبل العديد من أنظمة تشغيل الكمبيوتر في وقت مبكر باعتبارها إشارة المصافحة تحذير المرسل لوقف انتقال بسبب تجاوز الوشيكة يستمر حتى يومنا هذا في العديد من الأنظمة كتقنية التحكم ثانية S بـ كونترول Q بمعناها ولكن يتم استبدال كونترول S اليدوي في الإخراج . في بعض الأنظمة تحتفظ كونترول لبدء وإيقاف لكمة الشريط T DC4 و كونترول R DC2 لتعيين كونترول 33 ASR لاستئناف الإخراج . يمكن أيضا تكوين في بعض الوحدات المجهزة بهذه الوظيفة ، كان الحرف المقابل لحروف التحكم على كيكاب الموجود أعلى الحرف هو على التوالي TAPE و TAPE. '

question: 'ما انتهى قارئ الشريط الورقي التلقائي للتوقف؟'
answers: 'تحذير'

Figure 3: : Question-answer pairs for a sample passage in the Arabic SQuAD dataset. Each of the answers is a segment extracted from the passage.

(Malhas and Elsayed, 2020) (Malhas et al., 2022) only, the pRR scores were 44% or less than that. We did many experiments without adding any external data. The model performed well with adding more data and increased in pRR score by 10% when adding our data so our team decided to use Arabic SQuAD for two approaches.

One is to train the model using Arabic SQuAD only then using this pre-trained model for our task. This approach didn't perform better as expected. Another approach is to combine the QRCD dataset with the Arabic SQuAD dataset and our collected data. The reason to apply this is that modern Arabic isn't different so much from the Qur'an. We can increase more data with modern Arabic that enabling the model to train to extract more answers from different questions. This approach performed better sometimes than normal. We did random portions with different sizes and used them for the last advanced approaches.

3.2. Challenges

Previously available work combines many ways to produce their own data. However, there are certain obstacles to each strategy. We highlight the hurdles that must be solved in order to create a large-scale, high-quality dataset.

3.2.1. Limited question-answer for QRCD

QRCD (Malhas and Elsayed, 2020) (Malhas et al., 2022) is a small data which has about 700 questions. Most of them are repeated questions for different passages from Qur'an verses so the model is limited by a few questions to train and extract the answer. That changes our direction towards creating a similar data with following the same structure to add it to QRCD and all training data become doubled in size which QRCD is 710 samples and our data is about 730. We focus on adding more different types of questions.

3.2.2. Unavailability of open-source datasets

Qur'an QA is a hard task and collecting data can consume time with inaccurate answers. We are interested in doing a deep search to get any open-source data that can help us with this task. However, we found only annotated data with its passage and answer from tafsir and few of them from Qur'an AQQAC (Alqahtani and Atwell, 2018) as mentioned previously.

3.2.3. Automated vs Manual dataset

With the previous 2 challenges. We decided to collect our own data to combine it with QRCD (Malhas and Elsayed, 2020) (Malhas et al., 2022) and with the help of AQQAC (Alqahtani and Atwell, 2018). The first plan is to generate an automated dataset that enables us to create a large-scale dataset. Creating it manually means consuming time with generating a small-scale dataset. The challenges with AQQAC are that most of the answers aren't extracted from their specific passages, the passage and answers are mixed with Qur'an verses and tafsir, There are answers with the same meaning but with different words that aren't found in the Qur'an, and there are types of questions like" ما معني كلمة", " ما الدليل من القرآن" aren't related to Qur'an QA tasks. We couldn't solve all these issues so we decided to do it manually by using the questions of AQQAC.

3.2.4. Qur'an Experts to add accurate answers

The Holy Qur'an is a classical Arabic with Complex Word Structure. Before answering any questions from Qur'anic passage manually that requires knowing the tafsir and the meaning of the passage with related context events. The questions are in modern Arabic and understanding it easier. For that, we care about constructing it by Qur'an scholars despite it consuming time and cost but it was our only choice. We have in our team a Qur'an scholar who added the passage and answers for every question and created some similar questions. The constructed data by a Qur'an scholar in our team is about 730 questions with answers. It's called AQAQ (Arabic Question Answers from the Holy Qur'an dataset).

3.3. Dataset Collection

These previous challenges made us do it manually adding question by question. The source of questions in this dataset is Corpus of Arabic Al-Qur'an Question and Answer(AQQAC)(Alqahtani and Atwell, 2018) as mentioned previously. This data helped us to do authorized questions and answers. This data answers the question from the Qur'an and Tafseer. It consists of 1225 questions. We filtered about 500 questions and removed every answer from Tafsier because our task is to get the answers from the Qur'an only.

passage: 'يا أيها الناس إنا خلقناكم من ذكر وأنثى وجعلناكم شعوبا وقبائل لتعارفوا إن أكرمكم عند الله أتقاكم إن الله عليم خبير'

question: 'ما مقياس التفاضل عند الله تعالى بين الناس'

answers: 'إن أكرمكم عند الله أتقاكم'

Figure 4: : Question-answer pairs for a sample passage in the AQAQ dataset. Each of the answers is a segment extracted from the passage.

We structured it like the original dataset and added multiple same questions with other different passages. There are 2 versions. One was used for the first and second submissions with 625 questions. The second version has 732 questions and is used for the third submission. By this data, the scores are increased by 5% for the development evaluation for the first version. The second version is increased by 10% for the development evaluation.

4. Methodology

In this section, we illustrate the main components and ideas that we used for constructing our solution approaches explained in the upcoming section 5. We focus on the main four elements. First, **Masked Language Models** that were the basic building blocks for our approaches, we have not only made use of existing Arabic pre-trained MLM like BERT (Devlin et al., 2018) ,ELECTRA (Clark et al., 2020) and XLM-ROBERTA (Conneau et al., 2019), but also we created our Qur'anic MLM by fine-tuning araBERT (Antoun et al., 2020a) on the Holy Qur'an's verses only, the second step is **Preprocessing** where we put together the two sequence for tokenization and encode the tokens to be used for **fine tuning** the MLM for our task which is the third step, finally we tried using **ensemble** of many fine-tuned QA models and take a vote of the best answer to achieve better results, more details for every step in the following subsections.

4.1. Masked Language Models

Attention mechanisms have been proved to be extremely efficient for understanding context for natural languages (Hu, 2019). Consequently, Transformers (Vaswani et al., 2017) have shown qualitative superiority over previously used sequence models in most NLP tasks, so we tried to make the best use of them, especially with their availability and ease of fine-tuning.

4.1.1. Pre-trained Models

HuggingFace provides a wide variety of pretrained ready-for-use transformers for more than 175 languages For Arabic language araBERT (Antoun et al., 2020a) with 136 million parameters -for base version- is one of the best options, as it was trained on a combination of large Arabic corpora along with araELECTRA (Antoun et al., 2020b) and other publicly available Arabic question answering models on their hub, was the foundation for many experiments we did by directly fine-tuning them for extractive question answering with different configurations and combinations from datasets mentioned above in section 3.

4.1.2. Qur'anBERT

Because this task is very specific for only a set of verses we needed an MLM that really understands the Qur'an more than any corpus or Arabic text so We used a Qur'an dataset from Kaggle -The Holy Qur'an competition- that contained the Holy Qur'an verses with diacritics [1], we removed all diacritics and signs of stopping (like صلي ، مـ) and transformed it into a text file that contains all verses to be ready for training the model. We used this data to fine-tune araBERT as Qur'anic MLM with the help HugingFace Dataset utility we used DataCollatorForLanguageModeling with masked language probability of 0.1 and 0.15 for different trails to create our Qur'anBERT that was better at filling masks in Qur'an verses, for example, the original model was unable to predict the word "الدين" in surah 1 verse 4 " مالك يوم الدين " if we masked it with [MASK] spe-

[1]Kaggle the Holy Qur'an competition `https://www.kaggle.com/zusmani/the-holy-Qur'an`

cial token "ماﻟﻚ ﻳﻮم [MASK]" while the Qur'anBERT predicted it easily, this indicated more understanding-better attention weights- for the Qur'anic verses and words. so we used this model also in our experiments along with previously mentioned models.

4.2. Preprocessing

In preprocessing, the questions and passages are tokenized and converted into a suitable format that can be used to fine-tune transformers. The input to the tokenizer is the question and the passage of that question. The tokenizer output a dictionary containing the followings(pritesh1, 2022).

- input-ids: Stores the tokens ids of question and passage including the [CLS] and [SEP] tokens which indicate the beginning of the question, and SEP between question and the passage.
- token-type-ids: Stores 0s and 1s to differentiate between the passage and question borders. It has 0 for question tokens and 1s for passages tokens.
- attention-Mask: for every token indicates which tokens must not have attention like padding, and proceeding tokens.

Then, the start and the end position of the answer - index of the first and last tokens - have been added to the tokenizer output dictionary, after calculating it by comparing given start character with tokens' offset mapping returned from the tokenizer

4.3. Training

Fine-tuning large models like transformers on a small dataset like we have was challenging so we avoided using large batch sizes and kept our trails in the range [2, 4] and tried increasing the learning rate for faster convergence {2e-5, 1e-4, 2e-4}. in All experiments, we used the trainer API [2].

4.4. Model Ensemble

Ensemble models are a machine learning technique for combining multiple models in the prediction process. These models are known as base estimators or weak learners, and it is a solution to the many challenges of developing a single estimator like low accuracy and high sensitivity.

5. Solution Approaches for Our Submitted Results

As you know in the methodology section, our team developed different techniques to improve the system results. Let's discover their effect on this task.

[2] https://huggingface.co/docs/transformers/main_classes/trainer

5.1. Qur'anBERT

As mentioned earlier in section 4.1.2 we fine-tuned our masked language model for Qur'an that we named Qur'anBERT the first submitted results -stars_run01- were generated from the ensemble of many trained models most of them were Qur'anBERT based models, different combinations of data were used for training the weak learners, some were trained on QRCD (Malhas and Elsayed, 2020) (Malhas et al., 2022) data only other were trained on QRCD augmented by 625 sample unfinished AQAQ dataset or some other models with random portions of Arabic Squad dataset (Mozannar et al., 2019), also with variety of training configurations (epochs, batch sizes, learning rate, or weight decay) as explained with code in our repo [3]

5.2. Ensembling with K-Folds-Like Data Splitting

For the second submission -stars_run05- We have divided the competition dataset merged with our extracted AQAQ dataset into distinct 8-Folds instead of using normal bootstrapping as we might get more dissimilar weak learners for better final ensemble model. Then, the training of 8 transformers has been accomplished with distinct configurations per split of data. In the following table, all model names and configurations are shown. (Note, the list values are registered in the same order of running folds) We have 8 folds with different configurations as mentioned above. Each fold model has its own behavior on the development dataset (Figure 2). As noticed from the curves below that the model 2 has the best behavior across all metrics pRR, exact match, f1.

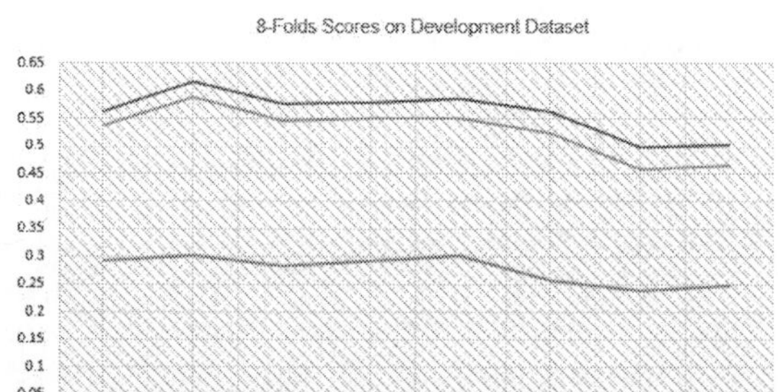

Figure 5: k-fold development results for the configurations mentioned in table 1

5.3. Expanding AQAQ dataset

For this approach, We focused on measuring the effect of the size of the data on the performance. We

[3] https://github.com/EmanElrefai/Qur'an_QA/tree/main/Qur'anBERT

Tokenization	token-model-name = "bert-base-arabertv02" max-length= 384 truncation="only-second" return_offsets_mapping=True padding="max_length"
Training	QA_model_name = ['bert-base-arabertv02', bert-base-arabertv02', 'AraElectra-base-finetuned-ARCD', 'AraElectra-base-finetuned-ARCD' 'AraElectra-base-finetuned-ARCD', 'AraElectra-base-finetuned-ARCD', 'arap_qa_bert_v2', 'arap_qa_bert_v2'] learning_rate=2e-5, per_device_train_batch_size= [2,3,2,2,2,2,2,2] per_device_eval_batch_size= 2 num _train_epochs= [5,5,5,4,3,2,7,10]
Inference	Extracting the highest 5 start and end scores from the all predicted scores returned from the model

Table 1: k-folds experiment details

worked on creating more examples during last moments of the competition's deadline. We reached about 732 samples instead of 625 samples. This combined with QRCD (Malhas and Elsayed, 2020) (Malhas et al., 2022) dataset is about 1,593 samples. We did shuffle for all data and used araBertv0.2 transformer base version. We clearly noticed during experiments that increasing AQAQ to be 732 samples worked better than AQAQ with 625 samples for the same model. This is for the third submission stars_run06. In Table 2 below are the configurations that are used for the third submission.

6. Results

In this section, we show the results of the three different approaches on both development dataset and test dataset, metrics used for evaluation are partial Reciprocal Rank (pRR) which is a variant of the traditional Reciprocal Rank evaluation metric that considers partial matching (Malhas and Elsayed, 2020) for 5 predicted answers , Exact Match (EM) and F1@1 the top predicted answer only. All three systems perform better than fine tuning araBERT base model with QRCD data which gives 44% pRR 24% exact match and 42% F1@1 on the development dataset. Throughout most of the experiments and as shown in table 3 and table 4, we noticed that ensemble and Qur'anBERT were not

Tokenization	token-model-name = "bert-base-arabertv02" max-length= 512 truncation="only-second" return_offsets_mapping=True padding="max_length"
Training	QA_model_name = 'aubmindlab/bert-base-arabertv02' learning_rate=2e-5, per_device_train_batch_size= 2 per_device_eval_batch_size= 2 num _train_epochs= 4

Table 2: Expanding AQAQ dataset experiment details

as effective as increasing the size of AQAQ data with fresh samples, which might be attributed to the following reasons.

We have only 1500 Qur'an training examples in the best case scenario -QRCD training set with AQAQ data - which makes the splits coming out of bootstrapping to be very similar, consequently, the weak learners of the ensemble will be almost identical, especially given that, transformers are known to be extremely data intensive.

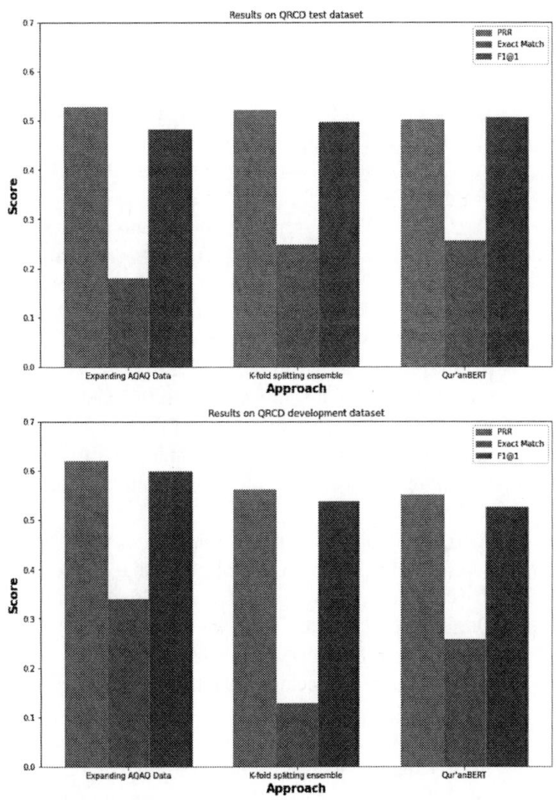

Figure 6: Results of the three approaches on QRCD development and test dataset.

On the other hand, Masked Language Models are known to be trained on a large corpus of the text so the 6236 verses of the Qur'an are tiny in size compared to that enormous amount of data that araBERT is trained on (Antoun et al., 2020a) for example. Additionally, in the Question Answering task model needs to learn the attention between the two different sequences of the passage -which is part of Qur'an- and the question -which is a *non-Qur'anic* sentence- unlike the single Qur'anic sequence in the Masked Language task.

Approach	pRR	EM	F1@1
Expanding AQAQ	0.6195	0.3394	0.5983
K-folds ensemble	0.562	0.128	0.537
Qur'anBERT	0.5495	0.2568	0.526

Table 3: Results of different approaches on development dataset

Approach	pRR	EM	F1@1
Expanding AQAQ	0.528	0.256	0.507
K-folds ensemble	0.521	0.247	0.4966
Qur'anBERT	0.502	0.18	0.483

Table 4: Results of different approaches on test dataset

7. Conclusion and Future Work

We proposed three different approaches with remarkable results. The best and the highest one was expanding AQAQ with 0.528 (pRR) in testing. Our data team did their best to add more to be 732 samples eventually. The second approach was ensembling the most three best models and it's called K-folds ensemble approach. Its pRR score was 0.521. The last one was training Bert model on Qur'an then we used this pretrained model for this specific task Qur'an QA. The pRR score of Qur'anBert was 0.502. The scores for the three approaches are similar. For all three approaches, we developed the system with transformer models. The task was difficult and need more time and effort to collect more data that made our scores couldn't excceed a half in pRR.

Also, we proposed a new Arabic Question Answers dataset from the Holy Qur'an called AQAQ about 625 question-answers. We used it for K-folds ensemble and Qur'anBert approach. Then we increased it to be 732 samples and it was used for expanding AQAQ dataset approach only. We achieved highest scores by expanding it.

In future work, The data team aims to increase the AQAQ dataset to be the biggest one related to this task. We plan to cover all kinds of questions with answers, add complex questions and increase the question with multiple answers. In order to improve the scores of the system, we plan to expand our experiments for more approaches in different directions as many different adaptations, tests, and experiments and achieve higher scores in pRR. We plan to make the system and AQAQ dataset publicly available to the research community.

8. Reproducibility

All code, data, and experiments for this paper are available at GitHub [4]

9. Bibliographical References

Abdelnasser, H., Ragab, M., Mohamed, R., Mohamed, A., Farouk, B., El-Makky, N. M., and Torki, M. (2014). Al-bayan: an arabic question answering system for the holy quran. In *Proceedings of the EMNLP 2014 Workshop on Arabic Natural Language Processing (ANLP)*, pages 57–64.

Alqahtani, M. and Atwell, E. (2018). Annotated corpus of arabic al-quran question and answer.

Alsubhi, K., Jamal, A., and Alhothali, A. (2021). Pretrained transformer-based approach for arabic question answering: A comparative study. *arXiv preprint arXiv:2111.05671.*

Antoun, W., Baly, F., and Hajj, H. (2020a). Arabert: Transformer-based model for arabic language understanding. *arXiv preprint arXiv:2003.00104.*

Antoun, W., Baly, F., and Hajj, H. (2020b). Araelectra: Pre-training text discriminators for arabic language understanding. *arXiv preprint arXiv:2012.15516.*

Bakari, W., Bellot, P., and Neji, M. (2016). Literature review of arabic question-answering: Modeling, generation, experimentation and performance analysis. In *Flexible Query Answering Systems 2015*, pages 321–334, cham. Springer International Publishing.

Clark, K., Luong, M.-T., Le, Q. V., and Manning, C. D. (2020). Electra: Pre-training text encoders as discriminators rather than generators. *arXiv preprint arXiv:2003.10555.*

Conneau, A., Khandelwal, K., Goyal, N., Chaudhary, V., Wenzek, G., Guzmán, F., Grave, E., Ott, M., Zettlemoyer, L., and Stoyanov, V. (2019). Unsupervised cross-lingual representation learning at scale. *arXiv preprint arXiv:1911.02116.*

Devlin, J., Chang, M.-W., Lee, K., and Toutanova, K. (2018). Bert: Pre-training of deep bidirectional transformers for language understanding. *arXiv preprint arXiv:1810.04805.*

Elhindi, Y. (2017). Metaphors in the quran: A thematic categorization. *QURANICA-International Journal of Quranic Research*, 9(1):1–20.

Hu, D. (2019). An introductory survey on attention mechanisms in nlp problems. In *Proceedings of SAI Intelligent Systems Conference*, pages 432–448. Springer.

[4]https://github.com/EmanElrefai/Qur'an_QA

Khaled, S., Siddiqui, S., Alkhatib, M., and Monem, A. A. (2018). Challenges in arabic natural language processing. *Computational Linguistics, Speech and Image Processing for Arabic Language*, pages 59—-83.

Khorami, M. (2014). Eloquence of repetition in quran and arabic old poetry. *Language Related Research*, 5(2):91–110.

Malhas, R. and Elsayed, T. (2020). Ayatec: building a reusable verse-based test collection for arabic question answering on the holy qur'an. *ACM Transactions on Asian and Low-Resource Language Information Processing (TALLIP)*, 19(6):1–21.

Malhas, R., Mansour, W., and Elsayed, T. (2022). Qur'an QA 2022: Overview of the first shared task on question answering over the holy qur'an. In *Proceedings of the 5th Workshop on Open-Source Arabic Corpora and Processing Tools (OSACT5) at the 13th Language Resources and Evaluation Conference (LREC 2022)*.

Marcus, M., Kim, G., Marcinkiewicz, M. A., MacIntyre, R., Bies, A., Ferguson, M., Katz, K., and Schasberger, B. (1994). The penn treebank: Annotating predicate argument structure. In *Human Language Technology: Proceedings of a Workshop held at Plainsboro, New Jersey, March 8-11, 1994*.

Mishra, A. and Jain, S. K. (2016). A survey on question answering systems with classification. *Journal of King Saud University-Computer and Information Sciences*, 28(3):345–361.

Mozannar, H., Hajal, K. E., Maamary, E., and Hajj, H. (2019). Neural arabic question answering. *arXiv preprint arXiv:1906.05394*.

pritesh1. (2022). An explanatory guide to bert tokenizer.

Rajpurkar, P., Zhang, J., Lopyrev, K., and Liang, P. (2016). Squad: 100, 000+ questions for machine comprehension of text. *CoRR*, abs/1606.05250.

Tahani, A., Azmi, A. M., Aboalsamh, H. A., Cambria, E., and Hussain, A. (2021). Arabic question answering system: A survey. *Artificial Intelligence Review*.

Vaswani, A., Shazeer, N., Parmar, N., Uszkoreit, J., Jones, L., Gomez, A. N., Kaiser, Ł., and Polosukhin, I. (2017). Attention is all you need. *Advances in neural information processing systems*, 30.

Proceedings of the OSACT 2022 Workshop @LREC2022, pages 154–161
Marseille, 20 June 2022

TCE* at Qur'an QA 2022: Arabic Language Question Answering Over Holy Qur'an Using a Post-Processed Ensemble of BERT-based Models

Mohammed ElKomy, Amany M. Sarhan
Computer and Control Engineering Department, Faculty of Engineering, Tanta University.
{mohammed.a.elkomy, amany_sarhan}@f-eng.tanta.edu.eg

Abstract

In recent years, we witnessed great progress in different tasks of natural language understanding using machine learning. Question answering is one of these tasks which is used by search engines and social media platforms for improved user experience. Arabic is the language of the Holy Qur'an; the sacred text for 1.8 billion people across the world. Arabic is a challenging language for Natural Language Processing (NLP) due to its complex structures. In this article, we describe our attempts at OSACT5 Qur'an QA 2022 Shared Task, which is a question answering challenge on the Holy Qur'an in Arabic. We propose an ensemble learning model based on Arabic variants of BERT models. In addition, we perform post-processing to enhance the model predictions. Our system achieves a Partial Reciprocal Rank (pRR) score of 56.6% on the official test set.

Keywords: Natural Language Processing, Extractive Question Answering, Holy Qur'an Computational Linguistics, Arabic SharedTask, Ensemble Bert

1. Introduction

Nowadays, the web and social media are integral parts of our modern digital life as they are the main sources of the unprecedented amounts of data we have. Thanks to the breakthrough in deep learning, search engines are no longer restricted to keyword matching; instead, they are currently able to understand queries in natural language and satisfy the intended information need of users. Question Answering (QA) is an essential task in information retrieval which is forming the basis for the new frontier of search engines. Plenty of studies on question answering systems has been performed on English and other languages. However, very few attempts have addressed the problem of Arabic question answering (Alwaneen et al., 2022).

Arabic NLP research in question answering is particularly challenging due to the scarcity of resources and the lack of processing tools available for Arabic. Arabic language, as well, has some unique characteristics by being a highly inflectional and derivational language with complex morphological structures (Abdelnasser et al., 2014). The Holy Qur'an is the sacred text for Muslims around the globe and it is the main source for teachings and legislation in Islam (Malhas and Elsayed, 2020), there are 114 chapters in Qur'an corresponding to 6,236 verses, every verse consists of a sequence of words in Classical Arabic (CA) dating back to 1400 years ago.

This paper describes our proposed solutions for OSACT5 Qur'an QA 2022 shared task. The shared task introduced QRCD (The Qur'anic Reading Comprehension Dataset), which is a dataset for extractive question answering. First, we experimented with a variety of Arabic pre-trained Bidirectional Encoder Representations from Transformers (BERT) models, then we implemented an Ensemble approach to get more robust results from a mixture of experts (MOEs). After that, we propose some post-processing operations to enhance the quality of answers according to the official evaluation measures. The task is evaluated as a ranking task according to the Partial Reciprocal Rank (pRR) metric.

The rest of this paper is organized as follows. In section 2, we describe the related work, in section 3, we outline the dataset details and official evaluation measures, in section 4, we explain the system design and the implementation details, in section 5, we report the system evaluation results, and finally section 6 concludes the paper. [1]

2. Related Work

Question answering systems have been an active point of research in recent years, particularly for highly-resourced languages such as English. (Rajpurkar et al., 2016) introduced SQuAD1.0 dataset which is a widely used dataset for question answering in English. To tackle the data scarcity in Arabic NLP, (Mozannar et al., 2019) presented Arabic Reading Comprehension Dataset (ARCD) which consists of 1,395 questions posed by crowdworkers. Moreover, (Mozannar et al., 2019) automatically translated SQuAD1.0 using google translation services. Only a little attention has been paid to question answering on Qur'an. (Abdel-

[1]The source code and trained models are available at https://github.com/mohammed-elkomy/quran-qa.

[2]To enable fair comparison among the teams, the organizers only considered 238 examples for the official test-split results and excluded 36 samples due to being very similar to public splits.

*Tanta Computer Engineering

nasser et al., 2014) proposed a Support Vector Machine (SVM) question answering system with hand-crafted features to extract answers from both Qur'an and its interpretation books (Tafseer). Recent work by (Malhas and Elsayed, 2020) introduced `AyaTEC` as the first fully reusable test collection for Arabic QA on the Holy Qur'an where questions are posed in Modern Standard Arabic (MSA) and their corresponding answers are qur'anic verses in CA.

3. Dataset and Task Description

In this section, we describe QRCD (The Qur'anic Reading Comprehension Dataset), the problem definition and official evaluation metrics of the Qur'an QA 2022 shared task of answering questions on the holy Qur'an (Malhas et al., 2022b).

3.1. Dataset Details

The Qur'anic Reading Comprehension Dataset (QRCD) (Malhas et al., 2022a) is the first large scale question answering dataset on the holy Qur'an text. It was introduced as a part of the Qur'an QA 2022 Shared Task for question answering (Malhas et al., 2022a). The dataset consists of 1,093 tuples of question-passage pairs that are coupled with their extractive answers to constitute 1,337 question-passage-answer triplets. The question-passage pairs are split into training, development and testing sets as shown in Table 1. The dataset follows the same format as the commonly used reading comprehension dataset SQuAD1.0 (Rajpurkar et al., 2016). However, QRCD is quite different in terms of size as it is much smaller than SQuAD1.0 which contains 100k unique pairs/questions. In addition, unlike SQuAD, the QCRD contains a small number of unique questions, each of which is repeated multiple times with different passage and answer pairs. As shown in Table 1, the number of unique questions in QRCD is much lower than the number of question-passage pairs. This poses an additional challenge for learning a question answering system which should be able to predict different answers to the same question under different passage contexts.

Split / Aspect	Train	Dev	Test
Question-passage pairs	710	109	274[2]
Unique questions	118	17	34

Table 1: Number of question-passage pairs and number of unique questions in each split of QRCD dataset.

The QRCD dataset draws its inspiration from the prior work `AyaTEC` by reformulating the test collection into an extractive question answering task (Malhas et al., 2022a). Each sample in QRCD is a question-passage-answer triplet which comprises a question in MSA, a passage taken from the Holy Qur'an [3] that spans one or more consecutive verses, and an answer to the question extracted from the passage. Figure 1 demonstrates an example from the QRCD dataset[4].

3.2. Qur'an QA Shared Task Description

The Qur'an QA 2022 shared task (Malhas et al., 2022a) aims to develop models for extractive question answering on the holy Qur'an passages. Given a Qura'nic passage and a question, the solution to the shared task should extract the answer to the question from the input passage. The answer always exists as a span within the given passage. Questions could be either factoid or non-factoid. Solutions to the shared task are required to extract any correct answer to the input question from the context passage even when the passage has more than one answer.

3.3. Task Evaluation Measures

This question answering task is evaluated as a *ranking* task. The QA system will return up to 5 potential answers ranked from the best to the worst according to their probability of correctness. The task evaluation measure produces a higher score when the correct answer is ranked at a higher position. When the correct answer is predicted among the 5 potential answers but it is at a lower rank, then the evaluation score is discounted. The task adopts the *partial Reciprocal Rank (**pRR**)* (Malhas and Elsayed, 2020) as the official evaluation metric. Partial Reciprocal Rank (**pRR**) is a variant of the *Reciprocal Rank* (RR) evaluation metric which is a commonly used metric for ranking tasks. Unlike *Reciprocal Rank* (RR), the *partial Reciprocal Rank (**pRR**)* will give credit to systems that predict answers with a partial inexact matching with the correct answer. Equation 1 formally describes the **pRR** metric evaluation for a ranked list of answers A, where m_{r_k} is the partial matching score for the returned answer at the kth rank, as k is taken to be equal to the rank position of the first answer with a non-zero matching score. More details can be found at (Malhas and Elsayed, 2020) 5.2.

$$pRR(A) = \frac{m_{r_k}}{k}; k = \min\{k \mid m_{r_k} > 0\} \quad (1)$$

In addition to the pRR scores, the task evaluation system reports other metrics such as the Exact Match (**EM**) and **F1@1**. The **EM** score is a binary measure that will be equal to one when the top predicted answer exactly matches the ground truth answer. The **F1@1** metric measures the degree of token overlap between the top predicted answer and any of the ground truth

[3]The Holy Qur'an is a very special classical Arabic text revealed 1,400 years ago, making it extremely challenging for computational linguistics tasks.

[4]The verses from the Holy Qur'an in the dataset come from the simple-clean text style (diacritics removed) from Tanzil Project.

Sample ID: 21:83-86_105
Passage
واذكر عبدنا أيوب إذ نادى ربه أني مسني الشيطان بنصب وعذاب. اركض برجلك هذا مغتسل بارد وشراب. ووهبنا له أهله ومثلهم معهم رحمة منا وذكرى لأولي الألباب. وخذ بيدك ضغثا فاضرب به ولا تحنث إنا وجدناه صابرا نعم العبد إنه أواب.
Question
من هو النبي المعروف بالصبر؟
Answer
أيوب

Figure 1: An example of question-passage-answer triplet from QRCD (Malhas et al., 2022a).

answers. Scores computed from individual passage-question-answer triplets are averaged to compute the overall score over the entire evaluation dataset.

4. QA System Design

Bidirectional **E**ncoder **R**epresentations from **T**ransformers (BERT) (Devlin et al., 2019) models achieve state-of-the-art results in many natural language understanding problems. Our solution is an ensemble of BERT based models pre-trained on Arabic language corpora and fine-tuned on the shared task dataset. We built an ensemble that merges predictions from individual models. Additionally, we also designed and implemented a set of post-processing operations that aim to improve the quality of predicted answers and boost the task evaluation measure. In this section, we describe our QA system developed to solve the Qur'an QA 2022 challenge. First, we give a brief background on BERT models and their usage for question answering tasks. Then we provide an overview of Arabic language BERT models that we used to build our ensemble. Finally, we provide the details of our ensemble building approach and the proposed post-processing operations to improve predicted answers quality.

4.1. BERT for Question Answering

4.1.1. BERT

BERT models achieve their state-of-the-art performance due to a procedure called pre-training which allows BERT to discover the language structures and patterns. BERT uses two pre-training tasks, namely masked language model (MLM) and next sentence prediction (NSP) (Devlin et al., 2019). After that, a second stage called fine-tuning, which is performed to adapt the model for a downstream task by making use of the features learnt during the pre-training phase.

4.1.2. Question Answering using BERT

As mentioned in 4.1.1, the fine-tuning phase takes a pre-trained model and stacks a randomly-initialized output layer suitable for a particular downstream task. For extractive question answering, both the question and passage are tokenized and packed into a single sequence and the output layer is required to give a probability for the ith token in the passage to be the start of the answer span P_i using the dot product of a start vector S and the ith token's hidden representation T_i as seen from equation 2, a similar analysis holds for the end of the answer span with an end vector E. The score of a candidate's answer span from the ith token to the jth token is defined in Equation 3. Answers are only accepted for $j \geq i$ since the two probability distributions are independent and not guaranteed to produce a valid span (Devlin et al., 2019). S and E are trainable weights and randomly initialized layers stacked on top of pre-trained BERT. In our case the system is not limited to just one answer as in SQuAD1.0 (Rajpurkar et al., 2016), instead, a ranked list of 20 answers is generated from the model and ranked based on the span score as in Equation 3.

$$P_i = \frac{e^{S \cdot T_i}}{\sum_j e^{S \cdot T_j}} \quad (2)$$

$$Span_{i,j} = ST_i + ET_j \quad (3)$$

4.2. Arabic variants of BERT model

The standard BERT model variants are not pre-trained on Arabic text which hinders the development of Arabic NLP. Nevertheless, various researchers working on the Arabic natural language understanding have developed variants of BERT models that were trained on Arabic corpora. We made use of those models, which are discussed later in this section, to build our ensemble.

4.2.1. AraBERT

The work by (Antoun et al., 2020) introduced AraBERT model which inherits the exact same architecture from BERT. However, being pre-trained on a large Arabic corpus of 24GB of text collected from news articles and Wikipedia dumps. In this work, we use **bert-large-arabertv02** and **bert-base-arabertv02** available on the huggingface community (Wolf et al., 2019).

4.2.2. QARiB

QARiB (Abdelali et al., 2021) is another Arabic BERT variant pretrained on a mixture of formal and informal

Arabic with state-of-the-art support for Arabic dialects and social media text, (Abdelali et al., 2021) released 5 BERT models to the community pre-trained on corpora of different sizes.

4.2.3. ARBERT and MARBERT

ARBERT and MARBERT (Abdul-Mageed et al., 2021) are two Arabic-specific Transformer-based MLM pre-trained on a widely large Modern Standard Arabic (MSA) corpus of 61GB of text for the case of ARBERT, while MARBERT is pre-trained on 128GB of text focused on both dialectal Arabic (DA) and MSA.

4.3. Training Details

We fine-tune a set of five Arabic BERT models as mentioned in 4.2, namely AraBERT-v02$_{\text{Large}}$[5], AraBERT-v02$_{\text{Base}}$, QARiB$_{\text{Base}}$, ARBERT and MARBERT [6].

The training objective is to maximize the log-likelihoods of the correct start and end token positions (Devlin et al., 2019). For the development phase, we train BERT$_{\text{Base}}$ and BERT$_{\text{Large}}$ for 50 and 65 epochs respectively, looking for the epoch at which the model performs best on the validation split. For the test phase, we train BERT$_{\text{Base}}$ and BERT$_{\text{Large}}$ for 32 and 40 respectively. We used a batch size of 8 for BERT$_{\text{Large}}$ and 16 for BERT$_{\text{Base}}$ and a learning rate of 2e-5 for all of our models.

4.4. Span Voting Ensemble

In this work, we build an ensemble from several different Arabic BERT models that we discussed earlier in 4.3. The ensemble approach is effective for cancelling the noise exhibited by individual models through majority voting among experts. i.e. Mixture of Experts (MOE). We treat the answer spans as discrete entities. For each sample, we consider the top 20 predictions made by each model along with its correctness probability. For each candidate prediction, we compute the sum of its associated correctness probabilities from all models. We formulate the voting process as follows.

$$\alpha_{s,e} = \sum_{j=0}^{M} \alpha_{s,e}^{j}$$

Where $\alpha_{s,e}$ represents the summed ensemble correctness probability for the answer span starting at token s and ending at token e, and $\alpha_{s,e}^{j}$ represents the correctness probability for the same answer span for the jth expert of the M experts taken into account.

After that, the set of all possible answers considered by the ensemble is sorted according to their summed ensemble correctness probabilities. Finally, the entire ranked list is post-processed and truncated for only the top 5 answers to be evaluated by **pRR@5**.

[5]A subscript Large and Base refers to the model size.

[6]ARBERT and MARBERT uses BERT$_{\text{Base}}$ architecture.

4.5. Post-processing

By carefully reviewing the answer spans predicted by the BERT models we fine-tuned, we found some systematic errors causing sub-optimal predictions. Here we propose some basic post-processing rules to improve the model predictions. The post-processing pipeline takes a ranked list of answer spans, it typically takes at least 20 answer spans from a single model or the span-voting ensemble. Figure 2 provides an illustrative example of the post-processing pipeline. Due to the limited space, we only consider the top 15 answer spans from the original system outputs.

4.5.1. Handling Sub-words

Before feeding the input to BERT, it must undergo the tokenization step. Tokenization is the process of splitting a sentence into tokens. For BERT, WordPiece tokenizer is commonly used as a subword tokenizer. This makes the system susceptible to producing an output with incomplete words like "وفي الرقاب والغارم" which will be penalized by the evaluation process; we perform a simple post-processing rule to extend or drop tokens such that we do not have broken words and this simple rule produces a corresponding output "وفي الرقاب والغارمين", for the previously mentioned example. In Figure 2, we dropped the sub-token "ون" at rank 12 which is part of "ينالون".

4.5.2. Redundancy Elimination

We analyzed the predictions of a variety of our fine-tuned models and discovered that most of the answer spans are highly overlapping with each other, making the ranked list suboptimal with respect to the pRR metric in 3.3. The rationale behind this is, the pRR metric *only* considers the (k+1)th prediction when there is no overlap with any of the ground-truth answer tokens for the kth prediction, This implies repeating any of the words from the kth prediction in the (k+1)th prediction is suboptimal, which is a common behaviour exhibited by BERT for QA. Here we present algorithm 1 which ensures the elimination of span overlap among the answers of a ranked list returned by the system. An illustrative example showing the predictions before and after the application of this rule is given in Figure 2, the colours used for highlighting text depict the high overlap between unprocessed answers, it clearly shows the span "ما كان لأهل المدينة" is common in the first few unprocessed answers. After applying this rule, the ranked list after post-processing better covers the text

Sample ID: 9:117-121_313
Passage
لقد تاب الله على النبي والمهاجرين والأنصار الذين اتبعوه في ساعة العسرة من بعد ما كاد يزيغ قلوب فريق منهم ثم تاب عليهم إنه بهم رءوف رحيم. وعلى الثلاثة الذين خلفوا حتى إذا ضاقت عليهم الأرض بما رحبت وضاقت عليهم أنفسهم وظنوا أن لا ملجأ من الله إلا إليه ثم تاب عليهم ليتوبوا إن الله هو التواب الرحيم. يا أيها الذين آمنوا اتقوا الله وكونوا مع الصادقين. ما كان لأهل المدينة ومن حولهم من الأعراب أن يتخلفوا عن رسول الله ولا يرغبوا بأنفسهم عن نفسه ذلك بأنهم لا يصيبهم ظمأ ولا نصب ولا مخمصة في سبيل الله ولا يطئون موطئا يغيظ الكفار ولا ينالون من عدو نيلا إلا كتب لهم به عمل صالح إن الله لا يضيع أجر المحسنين. ولا ينفقون نفقة صغيرة ولا كبيرة ولا يقطعون واديا إلا كتب لهم ليجزيهم الله أحسن ما كانوا يعملون.
Question
ماذا يشمل الإحسان؟
Ground Truth Answer
ما كان لأهل المدينة ومن حولهم من الأعراب أن يتخلفوا عن رسول الله ولا يرغبوا بأنفسهم عن نفسه ذلك بأنهم لا يصيبهم ظمأ ولا نصب ولا مخمصة في سبيل الله ولا يطئون موطئا يغيظ الكفار ولا ينالون من عدو نيلا إلا كتب لهم به عمل صالح

System Predictions After Post-Processing	System Predictions Before Post-Processing	Rank
ما كان لأهل المدينة ومن حولهم من الأعراب أن يتخلفوا عن رسول الله ولا يرغبوا بأنفسهم عن نفسه ذلك بأنهم لا يصيبهم ظمأ ولا نصب ولا مخمصة في سبيل الله	ما	1
نيلا إلا كتب لهم به عمل صالح	ما كان لأهل المدينة ومن حولهم من الأعراب أن يتخلفوا عن رسول الله ولا يرغبوا بأنفسهم عن نفسه ذلك بأنهم لا يصيبهم ظمأ ولا نصب ولا مخمصة في سبيل الله	2
من عدو	ما كان لأهل المدينة ومن حولهم من الأعراب	3
يا أيها الذين آمنوا اتقوا الله وكونوا مع الصادقين.	ما كان لأهل المدينة	4
ولا يطئون موطئا يغيظ الكفار ولا ينالون	ما كان لأهل المدينة ومن حولهم من الأعراب أن يتخلفوا عن رسول الله ولا يرغبوا بأنفسهم عن نفسه ذلك	5
pRR@5 Score: 0.76923	**pRR@5 Score:** 0.04878	
	ما كان لأهل المدينة ومن حولهم	6
	ما كان لأهل المدينة ومن حولهم من الأعراب أن يتخلفوا عن رسول الله ولا يرغبوا بأنفسهم عن نفسه ذلك بأنهم لا يصيبهم ظمأ ولا نصب ولا مخمصة	7
	ما كان لأهل المدينة ومن حولهم من الأعراب أن يتخلفوا عن رسول الله ولا يرغبوا بأنفسهم عن نفسه ذلك بأنهم لا يصيبهم ظمأ	8
	ما كان لأهل المدينة ومن حولهم من الأعراب أن يتخلفوا عن رسول الله ولا يرغبوا بأنفسهم عن نفسه	9
	ما كان لأهل المدينة ومن حولهم من الأعراب أن يتخلفوا عن رسول الله	10
	نيلا إلا كتب لهم به عمل صالح	11
	ون من عدو نيلا إلا كتب لهم به عمل صالح	12
	يا أيها الذين آمنوا اتقوا الله وكونوا مع الصادقين. ما	13
	بأنهم لا يصيبهم ظمأ ولا نصب ولا مخمصة في سبيل الله ولا يطئون موطئا يغيظ الكفار ولا ينالون من عدو نيلا إلا كتب لهم به عمل صالح	14
	لا يصيبهم ظمأ ولا نصب ولا مخمصة في سبيل الله ولا يطئون موطئا يغيظ الكفار ولا ينالون من عدو نيلا إلا كتب لهم به عمل صالح	15

Figure 2: A comprehensive example for post-processing. Here we present the outputs of the system before post-processing (original outputs) on the right and after post-processing on the left. We used green to highlight the ground truth answer or parts of it extracted by the system. Words and sub-words marked by red are dropped according to the rules 4.5.1 and 4.5.3. Other colours used for highlighting text depict the high overlap among the predictions before post-processing.

in the passage and the pRR score increases from 0.048 to 0.769 after post-processing. Figure 3 shows the distribution of the per-sample pRR score before and after post-processing, the percentage of development samples of the first two bins after post-processing is reduced, which means we are less observing completely wrong answers after post-processing.

4.5.3. Uninformative Answer Removal

In this post-processing rule, we remove the uninformative answers from the ranked list, We define an

Algorithm 1 Redundancy Elimination Algorithm

Input: P, passage text; A, input answers list.
Output: post-processed answers list.
$N_P \leftarrow$ Number of words in P.
$M_{seen} \leftarrow 0_{N_P}$ ▷ Initialized to Zero
▷ The mask used to track seen words
$A_{post} \leftarrow$: [] ▷ Output Initialized to an empty list

for each a **in** A **do**
  $s \leftarrow$ get start-word index of span a.
  $e \leftarrow$ get end-word index of span a.
  $a_{seen} \leftarrow M_{seen}[s{:}e]$
  ▷ Get seen slice of answer span a
  if a_{seen} has any zero **then**
   ▷ at least a word is not seen,
   ▷ marked by 1 in a_{seen}
   $a_{\text{unseen of } P} \leftarrow$ get_unseen_seqs(a_{seen},P)
  ▷ brings unseen contiguous sequences of words.
   for each seq_{unseen} **in** $a_{\text{unseen of } P}$ **do**
    ▷ seq_{unseen} is a subsequence of words
    ▷ with a_{seen} consisting of only zeros
    $s_{unseen} \leftarrow$ start-word index of seq_{unseen}.
    $e_{unseen} \leftarrow$ end-word index of seq_{unseen}.
    $seq_{text} \leftarrow$ text spanned by seq_{unseen}.
    $M_{seen}[s_{unseen}{:}\ e_{unseen}] = 1$
    ▷ Mark tokens as seen
    $A_{post} = A_{post} \smile seq_{text}$
   ▷ Append this unseen part of answer span a
   end for

  end if
end for

uninformative answer as having one of the following conditions:

1. All of the stemmed answer tokens exist in the stemmed question tokens, for example, a question like "لما هي شجرة الزقوم؟" with a complete answer span predicted by the system "الزقوم" is considered an uninformative answer.

2. The whole answer span consists of stop-words, which can never meet the information need of a question in QRCD, for example, answer spans like "اذا", "ليس", "ثم" are considered uninformative answers.

Uninformative answers come from two sources, first, the original output of the BERT model without post-processing and second, the post-processed outputs after removing redundant tokens as in 4.5.2. For the example in Figure 2, the answer at rank 1 "لما" is rejected due to being uninformative.

4.5.4. Updating the Ranked List

After performing the post-processing pipeline described in 4.5.2, 4.5.3 and 4.5.1 in order, we may end up with a new ranked list with more than 5 answer spans, we only consider the top 5 answer spans in the post-processed ranked list for the metric evaluation (pRR@5).

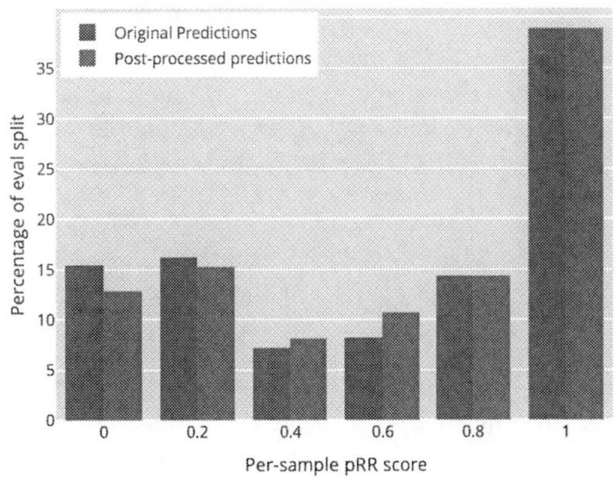

Figure 3: The post-processing impact on the per-sample pRR score distribution, for this plot, we used the ouputs of the models marked with † in Table 2.

5. Experimental Evaluation

In this section, we report our trained models' results along with the official scores and run details on the Codalab competition.

5.1. Development Phase

In this phase, we did not have access to the test dataset. We trained our models on the training set as in 4.3 while only saving the best performing model on the validation split. We observed a large variation (around ±3%) in the pRR score reported for the same starting checkpoint with different seeds, we relate this to the small size of the validation split. To enable fair comparison, we average the reported scores for the same model trained multiple times with different seeds as shown in Table 2. For the ensemble method, we considered 15 checkpoints with different seeds for each of AraBERT-v02$_{\text{Large}}$, AraBERT-v02$_{\text{Base}}$ and ARBERT (marked with † in the table), adding up to 45 experts, labelled as **Ensemble$_{\text{Vanilla}}$** in Table 2. After that, we performed the post-processing step on the ensemble outputs referred to as **Ensemble$_{\text{POST}}$** in Table 2. Also from the table, QARiB$_{\text{Base}}$ and MARBERT are performing worse on average, because of being primarily targeted for dialectal Arabic and social media text.

Single Models	EM (%)	F1 (%)	pRR (%)
†arabertv02$_{Large}$	37.2	59.0	**61.7**
†arabertv02$_{Base}$	36.5	58.5	60.7
†ARBERT	37.3	58.7	60.9
MARBERT	32.1	51.5	53.9
QARiB$_{Base}$	25.9	45.3	48.1

Ensemble	EM (%)	F1 (%)	pRR (%)
Ensemble$_{\textbf{Vanilla}}$	39.4	59.4	63.97
Ensemble$_{\textbf{POST}}$	38.5	59.4	**65.22**

Table 2: QRCD development split results, reported metrics for single models are averaged for a number of model checkpoints trained with different seeds, while for the ensemble case, it is a single instance produced from combining different checkpoints. **Ensemble**$_{\textbf{Vanilla}}$ refers to combining 45 checkpoints of models indicated by † (15 for each). **Ensemble**$_{\textbf{POST}}$ represents the **Ensemble**$_{\textbf{Vanilla}}$ output after post-processing.

Run ID	EM (%)	F1 (%)	pRR (%)
Ensemble$_{keep}$	26.8	48.5	55.7
Ensemble$_{remove}$	26.8	50.0	**56.6**

Table 3: Test phase official results on QRCD dataset, Each ensemble reported is a span-voting ensemble combining all models in Table 4. "keep" subscript refers to keeping uninformative answer spans as discussed in 4.5.3, on the other hand, "remove" subscript points to removing uninformative answer spans.

5.2. Competition Final Testing Phase

During the competition's final testing phase, we had access to the test dataset without labels, and participants were required to submit at most 3 submissions produced by their proposed systems. We trained our models on both the training and development datasets as in 4.3. The trained models were combined in an ensemble as discussed in 4.4, then we performed the post-processing. Table 4 shows the number of models used as experts for span-voting ensemble in the test phase. In Table 3, we outline the official results obtained for our submissions. All of them are ensemble-based due to the significant variations we observed in the development phase. Combining **all** of the models in Table 4 followed by post-processing the output predictions with uninformative span **removal** performs best, this is marked in the table as **Ensemble**$_{\textbf{remove}}$. There is a significant gap between the results in the development and test phases as in tables 2 and 3 respectively, we relate this to the small size of the validation split against the test split, another reason is excluding 36 samples from the test split since their questions were similar to the public splits as indicated by the organizers in the official test phase results.

Models	Num
arabertv02$_{Large}$	16
arabertv02$_{Base}$	18
ARBERT	17

Table 4: Number of models involved in the final ensemble of the test phase.

6. Conclusion and Future Work

In this work, we leveraged the pre-trained Arabic language models to solve the Qur'an QA 2022 Shared Task. We fine-tuned a variety of BERT models optimized for the Arabic language. We proposed some post-processing operations to enhance the quality of answers aligning with the official measure. Ensemble-based approaches are effective to produce more robust predictions. In the future, we will further study how to incorporate a stacking ensemble approach with multiple stages to achieve better performance rather than a voting ensemble as used in this study. We will also investigate why we observed huge variations in the reported results by performing extensive cross-validation.

7. Acknowledgements

We appreciate the efforts and assistance of Dr Moustafa Alzantot regarding the paper-writing phase, and recommendations during the implementation.

8. Bibliographical References

Abdelali, A., Hassan, S., Mubarak, H., Darwish, K., and Samih, Y. (2021). Pre-training bert on arabic tweets: Practical considerations.

Abdelnasser, H., Ragab, M., Mohamed, R., Mohamed, A., Farouk, B., El-Makky, N., and Torki, M. (2014). Al-bayan: An Arabic question answering system for the holy quran. In *Proceedings of the EMNLP 2014*

Workshop on Arabic Natural Language Processing (ANLP), pages 57–64, Doha, Qatar, October. Association for Computational Linguistics.

Abdul-Mageed, M., Elmadany, A., and Nagoudi, E. M. B. (2021). ARBERT & MARBERT: Deep bidirectional transformers for Arabic. In *Proceedings of the 59th Annual Meeting of the Association for Computational Linguistics and the 11th International Joint Conference on Natural Language Processing (Volume 1: Long Papers)*, pages 7088–7105, Online, August. Association for Computational Linguistics.

Alwaneen, T. H., Azmi, A. M., Aboalsamh, H. A., Cambria, E., and Hussain, A. (2022). Arabic question answering system: a survey. *Artificial Intelligence Review*, 55(1):207–253, Jan.

Antoun, W., Baly, F., and Hajj, H. (2020). AraBERT: Transformer-based model for Arabic language understanding. In *Proceedings of the 4th Workshop on Open-Source Arabic Corpora and Processing Tools, with a Shared Task on Offensive Language Detection*, pages 9–15, Marseille, France, May. European Language Resource Association.

Devlin, J., Chang, M.-W., Lee, K., and Toutanova, K. (2019). BERT: Pre-training of deep bidirectional transformers for language understanding. In *Proceedings of the 2019 Conference of the North American Chapter of the Association for Computational Linguistics: Human Language Technologies, Volume 1 (Long and Short Papers)*, pages 4171–4186, Minneapolis, Minnesota, June. Association for Computational Linguistics.

Malhas, R. and Elsayed, T. (2020). Ayatec: Building a reusable verse-based test collection for arabic question answering on the holy qur'an. *ACM Trans. Asian Low-Resour. Lang. Inf. Process.*, 19(6), oct.

Malhas, R., Mansour, W., and Elsayed, T. (2022a). Qur'an QA 2022: Overview of the first shared task on question answering over the holy qur'an. In *Proceedings of the 5th Workshop on Open-Source Arabic Corpora and Processing Tools (OSACT5) at the 13th Language Resources and Evaluation Conference (LREC 2022)*.

Malhas, R., Mansour, W., and Elsayed, T. (2022b). Qur'an qa 2022 shared task. `https://gitlab.com/bigirqu/quranqa`.

Mozannar, H., Maamary, E., El Hajal, K., and Hajj, H. (2019). Neural Arabic question answering. In *Proceedings of the Fourth Arabic Natural Language Processing Workshop*, pages 108–118, Florence, Italy, August. Association for Computational Linguistics.

Rajpurkar, P., Zhang, J., Lopyrev, K., and Liang, P. (2016). SQuAD: 100,000+ questions for machine comprehension of text. In *Proceedings of the 2016 Conference on Empirical Methods in Natural Language Processing*, pages 2383–2392, Austin, Texas, November. Association for Computational Linguistics.

Wolf, T., Debut, L., Sanh, V., Chaumond, J., Delangue, C., Moi, A., Cistac, P., Rault, T., Louf, R., Funtowicz, M., and Brew, J. (2019). Huggingface's transformers: State-of-the-art natural language processing. *CoRR*, abs/1910.03771.

Proceedings of the OSACT 2022 Workshop @LREC2022, pages 162–166
Marseille, 20 June 2022

Overview of OSACT5 Shared Task on Arabic Offensive Language and Hate Speech Detection

Hamdy Mubarak[1], Hend Al-Khalifa[2], AbdulMohsen Al-Thubaity[3]
[1] Qatar Computing Research Institute, HKBU, Doha, Qatar,
[2] Information Technology Department, King Saud University, Riyadh, KSA
[3] King Abdulaziz City for Science and Technology (KACST), Riyadh, KSA
humbarak@hbku.edu.qa, hendk@ksu.edu.sa, aalthubaity@kacst.edu.sa

Abstract

This paper provides an overview of the shard task on detecting offensive language, hate speech, and fine-grained hate speech at the fifth workshop on Open-Source Arabic Corpora and Processing Tools (OSACT5). The shared task comprised of three subtasks; Subtask A, involving the detection of offensive language, which contains socially unacceptable or impolite content including any kind of explicit or implicit insults or attacks against individuals or groups; Subtask B, involving the detection of hate speech, which contains offensive language targeting individuals or groups based on common characteristics such as race, religion, gender, etc.; and Subtask C, involving the detection of the fine-grained type of hate speech which takes one value from the following types: **(i)** race/ethnicity/nationality, **(ii)** religion/belief, **(iii)** ideology, **(iv)** disability/disease, **(v)** social class, and **(vi)** gender. In total, 40 teams signed up to participate in Subtask A, and 17 of them submitted test runs. For Subtask B, 26 teams signed up to participate and 12 of them submitted runs. And for Subtask C, 23 teams signed up to participate and 10 of them submitted runs. 10 teams submitted papers describing their participation in one subtask or more, and 8 papers were accepted. We present and analyze all submissions in this paper.

Keywords: OSACT, Arabic, Offensive Language, Hate Speech, Fine-Grained Hate Speech, Shared Task, CodaLab

1. Introduction

Disclaimer: Due to the nature of this work, some examples contain offensive language and/or hate speech. This does not reflect authors' opinions by any mean. Our aim is to detect and prevent such harmful content from spreading.

Detection of offensive language and hate speech is very important for content moderation, online safety, etc. Studies show that the presence of hate speech may be connected to hate crimes (Watch, 2014). In recent years, there has been a large amount of research on detecting offensive language and hate speech in the NLP and computational social sciences communities. Many shared tasks were created for this purpose such as OffensEval 2020 (Zampieri et al., 2020) to detect offensive language for five languages, and OSACT4 (Mubarak et al., 2020a) to detect offensive language and hate speech for Arabic.

OSACT5 shared task can be considered as an extension of OSACT4, where the target is to identify the fine-grained type of the hate speech in addition to detecting offensive language and hate speech on Arabic social media using a new dataset.

We considered any kind of socially unacceptable or impolite content as offensive language. This includes vulgar, swear words, and any kind of explicit or implicit insults or attacks against individuals or groups.

Hate speech contains offensive language targeting individuals or groups based on common characteristics such as Race (including also ethnicity and nationality),[1] Religion (including belief), Ideology (ex: political or sport affiliation), Disability (including diseases), Social Class, and Gender.[2]

The shared task has three subtasks. Subtask A involves the detection of offensive language, and Subtask B is concerned with detecting hate speech. Subtask C is concerned with detecting the hate speech type.

2. Dataset

We used the data set described in (Mubarak et al., 2022) which contains 12,698 tweets collected using emojis that commonly appear in offensive communications. These emojis are extracted from existing datasets of offensive tweets, namely (Zampieri et al., 2020) and (Chowdhury et al., 2020). Authors showed that using emojis is more efficient than keywords (ex, as in (Mubarak et al., 2017)) or patterns (as in (Mubarak et al., 2020b)) and this method can be applied to other languages to collect a large percentage of offensive and hate tweets regardless of their topics, dialects, or genres. Tweets were extracted from 4.4M Arabic tweets collected between June 2016 and November 2017 having one or more emojis from a predefined list.

Tweets were labeled using two jobs on Appen crowdsourcing platform with the following quality settings: 3 judgements per tweet, 200 test questions, and 80% threshold to pass test questions. Inter-Annotator Agreement agreement was 0.82 (Cohen's kappa value). In the first annotation job (Job1), annotators classified tweets into Offensive (OFF) or Clean (CLN). In Job2, offensive tweets obtained from Job1 were classified into one of the

[1] We merged close types to ease the task.

[2] Other hate speech types did not exist in the Arabic dataset.

fine-grained hate speech types. Examples and statistics are shown in Table 1.

The subtasks used the same splits as in (Mubarak et al., 2022) for training (70% of all tweets), development (10%), and testing (20%). For Subtask A (offensiveness detection), the labels are: OFF or NOT_OFF, and for Subtask B (hate speech detection), the labels are: HS or NOT_HS. For Subtask C (hate speech type), the labels are: HS1 (Race), HS2 (Religion), HS3 (Ideology), HS4 (Disability), HS5 (Social Class), and HS6 (Gender) in addition to NOT_HS.

Simple preprocessing steps were applied to tweets to replace user mentions with @USER, URLs with "URL", and empty lines with <LF>.

3. Task Settings and Evaluation

Given the strong imbalance in class distributions in all Subtasks, we used the macro-averaged F1-score ($\mathcal{F}$) as the official evaluation measure. Macro-averaging gives equal importance to all classes regardless of their size. We also used Precision ($\mathcal{P}$) and Recall ($\mathcal{R}$) on the positive class (offensive or hate speech tweets) in addition to the overall Accuracy ($\mathcal{A}$) as secondary evaluation measures.

Subtasks were hosted on CodaLab platform at the following competition links:
Subtask A: `https://codalab.lisn.upsaclay.fr/competitions/2324`
Subtask B: `https://codalab.lisn.upsaclay.fr/competitions/2332`
Subtask C: `https://codalab.lisn.upsaclay.fr/competitions/2334`

We allowed teams to submit up to 10 runs on the test set, and we asked them to specify two submissions as their official runs (primary/first and secondary/second submissions). If they didn't specify their official runs, the latest were considered as official. Teams had the freedom to describe the differences between these runs in their papers which gives the chance to examine the effectiveness of different approaches and setups.
The official score for all subtasks was the macro-average F1 ($\mathcal{F}$) of the first submission.

The shared task attracted a large number of participants. In all, 40, 26 and 23 teams signed up to Subtasks A, B and C respectively. From them, 17, 12 and 10 teams submitted test runs to Subtasks A, B and C in order. Of those teams, 10 submitted system description papers and 8 papers were accepted. Table 2 lists information about the accepted papers, teams and affiliations.

We received 142 submissions for Subtask A including 22 failed ones (due to incorrect format). For Subtask B, we received 70 submissions including 3 failed ones. And for Subtask C, we received 59 submissions including 4 failed ones. Competitions were open from March 1st, 2022 until March 30th, 2022. The test sets were available starting from March 26th, 2022.

4. Results and Methods

The highest F1 score for Subtask A was 0.852 (Accuracy = 0.867, Precision = 0.856, and Recall = 0.848) achieved by **GOF** team (Mostafa et al., 2022). For Subtask B, the highest F1 was 0.831 (Accuracy = 0.941, Precision = 0.869, and Recall = 0.801) achieved by **iCompass** team (Ben Nessir et al., 2022). And for Subtask C, the highest F1 was 0.528 (Accuracy = 0.919, Precision = 0.548, and Recall = 0.531) achieved also by **iCompass** team (Ben Nessir et al., 2022).

Most teams performed basic to extensive data preprocessing, which typically involved character normalization, removal of punctuation, diacritics, repeated letters, and non-Arabic tokens. As for learning methods, the teams used different fine-tuned transformer versions, such as mT5, AraBERT, ARBERT, MARBERT, AraElectra, QARiB, Albert-Arabic, AraGPT2, mBert, and XLMRoberta.

The highest ranking submissions used an ensemble of different transformers. Table 3 briefly lists the preprocessing and learning methods used by different teams. Tables 4, 5, and 6 list the results of all the teams for Subtasks A, B, and C in order ranked by F1-measure ($\mathcal{F}$).

5. Conclusion

This paper presented an overview of the OSACT5 shared task on offensive language and hate speech detection in the Arabic Twitter sphere. The shared task consists of three subtasks: A, B, and C. The most successful systems in the shared task performed Arabic specific preprocessing, with the winning system for hate speech detection (subtask A) performing an ensemble of different machine learning approaches, while the the winning system for offensive language detection (subtask B) used a multi-task of different pre-trained language models, and finally, the winning system for the detection of the fine-grained type of hate speech detection (subtask C) used task specific layers that were fine-tuned with Quasi-recurrent neural networks (QRNN).

6. References

AlKhamissi, B. and Diab, M. (2022). Meta ai at arabic hate speech 2022: Multitask learning with self-correction for hate speech classification. *OSACT*, 5.

Alzu'bi, S., Ferreira, T. C., Pavanelli, L., and Al-Badrashiny, M. (2022). aixplain at arabic hate speech 2022: An ensemble based approach to detecting offensive tweets. *OSACT*, 5.

Ben Nessir, M. A., Rhouma, M., Haddad, H., and Fourati, C. (2022). icompass at arabic hate speech 2022: Detect hate speech using qrnn and transformers. *OSACT*, 5.

Chowdhury, S. A., Mubarak, H., Abdelali, A., Jung, S.-g., Jansen, B. J., and Salminen, J. (2020). A multi-platform arabic news comment dataset for offensive language detection. In *Proceedings of the 12th Language Resources and Evaluation Conference*, pages 6203–6212.

de Paula, A. F. M., Rosso, P., Bensalem, I., and Zaghouani, W. (2022). Upv at the arabic hate speech 2022 shared task: Offensive language and hate speech detection using transformers and ensemble models. *OSACT*, 5.

Table 1: Statistics and examples from the annotated corpus

Class/Subclass	#	%	Example
Clean (CLN or NOT_OFF)	8,235	65	لن تحصل على غدٍ افضل مادمت تفكر بالامس You won't have a better tomorrow as long as you think about yesterday.
Offensive (OFF)	4,463	35	يلعن ابوك على هالسؤال. عساه ينقرض الكريه May God curse your father for this question! I hope this fool will die out!
Hate Speech	1,339	11	(Note: 30% of Offensive tweets are labeled as Hate Speech)
- Gender	641	48	بنات اليوم قليلات أدب. والله ما نوصل لعهر بعض الرجال Girls today are impolite. I swear to God, we don't reach for some men immorality.
- Race	366	27	شعبكم متخلف. الله ياخذك إنتي والفلبين People of your country are musty. May God take (kill) you and the Philippines.
- Ideology	190	14	ناديك وضيع لا شك في ذلك. حزبك لا يقدر إلا على النباح You club is vile, no doubt about that. Your party cannot do anything except barking.
- Social Class	101	8	دامك مقيم انكتم وخل اهل الأرض الاصليين يتكلمون. ابلع يا سباك! As you are a resident, shut up and let original citizens speak. Swallow, plumber!
- Religion	38	3	إنتوا بتعملوا ف ديك أبونا كده ليه هو إحنا كفرة ولايهود Why are you doing this to us? Are we disbelievers or Jews?
- Disability	3	0	ذا القزم طلعت جايزتن له بس ماعرف يعبر This dwarf got two prizes, but he does not know how to express.

Team	Affiliation	Subtasks
aiXplain (Alzu'bi et al., 2022)	aiXplain Inc, USA	A
iCompass (Ben Nessir et al., 2022)	iCompass, Tunisia	A, B, C
AlexU-AIC (Shapiro et al., 2022)	Alexandria University, Egypt	A, B, C
CHILLAX (Makram et al., 2022)	Helwan University, Egypt	A, B
GOF (Mostafa et al., 2022)	Helwan University, Egypt	A
GUCT (Elkaref and Abu-Elkheir, 2022)	German University in Cairo, Egypt	A
Meta-AI (AlKhamissi and Diab, 2022)	Meta, USA	A, B, C
UPV (de Paula et al., 2022)	Universitat Politecnica de Valencia, Spain	A, B, C

Table 2: List of participating teams in Subtasks A, B, and C (alphabetical order)

Elkaref, N. and Abu-Elkheir, M. (2022). Guct at arabic hate speech 2022: Towards a better isotropy for hate speech detection. *OSACT*, 5.

Makram, K. H., Nessim, K. G., Abd-Almalak, M. E., Roshdy, S. Z., Salem, S. H., Thabet, F. F., and Mohamed, E. H. (2022). Chillax - at arabic hate speech 2022: A hybrid machine learning and transformers based model to detect arabic offensive and hate speech. *OSACT*, 5.

Mostafa, A., Mohamed, O., and Ashraf, A. (2022). Gof at arabic hate speech 2022: Breaking the loss function convention for data-imbalanced arabic offensive text detection. *OSACT*, 5.

Mubarak, H., Darwish, K., and Magdy, W. (2017). Abusive language detection on arabic social media. In *Proceedings of the first workshop on abusive language online*, pages 52–56.

Mubarak, H., Darwish, K., Magdy, W., Elsayed, T., and Al-Khalifa, H. (2020a). Overview of osact4 arabic offensive language detection shared task. In *Proceedings of the 4th Workshop on open-source arabic corpora and processing tools, with a shared task on offensive language detection*, pages 48–52.

Mubarak, H., Rashed, A., Darwish, K., Samih, Y., and Abdelali, A. (2020b). Arabic offensive language on twitter: Analysis and experiments. *arXiv preprint arXiv:2004.02192*.

Mubarak, H., Hassan, S., and Chowdhury, S. A. (2022). Emojis as anchors to detect arabic offensive language and hate speech. *arXiv preprint arXiv:2201.06723*.

Shapiro, A., Khalafallah, A., and Torki, M. (2022). Alexu-aic at arabic hate speech 2022: Contrast to classify. *OSACT*, 5.

Watch, H. S. (2014). Hate speech watch. hate crimes: Consequences of hate speech. In *http://www.nohatespeechmovement.org/hate-speechwatch/focus/ consequences-of-hate-speech*.

Zampieri, M., Nakov, P., Rosenthal, S., Atanasova, P., Karadzhov, G., Mubarak, H., Derczynski, L., Pitenis, Z., and Çöltekin, Ç. (2020). Semeval-2020 task 12: Multilingual offensive language identification in social media (offenseval 2020). *arXiv preprint arXiv:2006.07235*.

Team	Preprocessing	Methods
aiXplain (Alzu'bi et al., 2022)	For the textual part of the tweet, they apply the following transformations sequentially on each tweet: 1. Remove URLs and mentions, 2. Remove diacritics and tatweel, 3. Remove punctuation. For the Emojis part, they translated emojis in a tweet to Arabic using (Junczys-Dowmunt et al., 2018) English to Arabic model. For some emojis, they inferred their intended meaning and provided their translation using the team's expertise in the Arabic language and the colloquial dialect used. Additionally, they extracted the relevant emojis from each tweet and used a classifier to predict their sentiment individually. They also used data augmentation (Semi-Supervised Learning and Contextual Augmentation based on Semantic Similarity).	Their system architecture involved feeding the predictions of an ensemble of classifiers combined with relative high-level features to a final meta-learner yielding a binary label of "OFF" to represent offensive or "NOT_OFF" to represent inoffensive speech. Each of the classifiers in the ensemble consist of a final linear layer the following pre-trained model as a backbone: AraBERTv0.2-Twitter-large - Mazajak 250M CBOW pre-trained embeddings - Character level N-gram + word level N-gram TF- IDF embeddings - MUSE. The predictions from the aforementioned models are then concatenated into a final vector.
iCompass (Ben Nessir et al., 2022)	1. Removing all non Arabic tokens, including ones like USER, URL, < LF >. Emojis were also removed. 2. Normalizing all the hashtags by simply decomposing them. 3. Removing white spaces.	Different pre-trained models were used in order to achieve the best results when fine-tuning it in a multi-task fashion (mT5, AraBERT, ARBERT, and MARBERT) and task specific layers that were fine-tuned with Quasi-recurrent neural networks (QRNN) for each down-stream subtask.
AlexU-AIC (Shapiro et al., 2022)	Arabic letters, punctuation and digit Normalization, Hashtag segmentation, diacritic and symbols removal and removal of repeated characters or emojis more than two times	AraBERT, MarBERT v1 and MarBERT v2 with multiple training paradigms such as: Classification Fine-tuning, Contrastive Learning and Multi-task Learning.
CHILLAX (Makram et al., 2022)	cleaning: all URLs and User mentions were removed. augmentation: generates new tweets from the minority classes using MARBERT Arabic model	MARBERT Arabic LM for features extraction and Logistic Regression and Random Forest for training.
GOF (Mostafa et al., 2022)	non-Arabic letters, punctuation marks, digits, Arabic diacritics and repeated characters removal and replacing URL, @USER, and Email with their Arabic translations (رابط، مستخدم، بريد)	seven language models: MARBERT(without emojis), AraBERT-Large-Twitter, QARiB, AraBERT-Base-Twitter, MARBERT, MARBERTV2, LightGBM(QARiB Embeddings) and ensemble learning approach : Ensemble(LightGBM+ MARBERT+MARBERTV2) ,Ensemble(AraBERT-B-T+ MARBERT+QARiB) and Ensemble(MARBERTV2+ MARBERT+QARiB)
GUCT (Elkaref and Abu-Elkheir, 2022)	replace any instances of Twitter mentions with "@USER" and URLs by "URL". diacritics and non-Arabic letters removal.	1. calculate MARBERT's isotropy. 2. refine MARBERT's isotropy. 3. pass refined isotropic representations to a Bidirectional Long-Short Term Memory (biLSTM) to be learned and perform classification.
Meta-AI (AlKhamissi and Diab, 2022)	user mentions are reduced to @USER, URLs are replaced with URL , and empty lines in original tweets are replaced with <LF>.	the input text is encoded using MARBERTv2 and is then passed to 3 task-specific classification heads. Each class specific head is made up of a multi-layered feed forward neural network with layer normalization.
UPV (de Paula et al., 2022)	No preprocessing	six different transformer versions: Arabert, Ara-Electra, Albert-Arabic, AraGPT2, mBert, and XLMRoberta. In addition, two ensemble methods were employed: Majority vote and Highest sum

Table 3: Methods used by different teams (alphabetical order)

	First Submission				Second Submission			
Team	$\mathcal{A}$	$\mathcal{P}$	$\mathcal{R}$	$\mathcal{F}$	$\mathcal{A}$	$\mathcal{P}$	$\mathcal{R}$	$\mathcal{F}$
GOF (Mostafa et al., 2022)	**0.867**	**0.856**	**0.848**	**0.852**	0.864	0.853	0.844	0.848
Meta AI (AlKhamissi and Diab, 2022)	0.860	0.846	0.843	0.845	0.852	0.839	0.834	0.836
aiXplain (Alzu'bi et al., 2022)	0.858	0.845	0.840	0.843	0.864	0.852	0.847	0.849
AlexU-AIC (Shapiro et al., 2022)	0.856	0.842	0.839	0.841				
iCompass (Ben Nessir et al., 2022)	0.854	0.841	0.837	0.839	-	-	-	-
UPV (de Paula et al., 2022)	0.837	0.821	0.818	0.819	0.841	0.824	0.831	0.827
CHILLAX (Makram et al., 2022)	0.803	0.784	0.779	0.781	0.740	0.716	0.723	0.719
GUCT (Elkaref and Abu-Elkheir, 2022)	0.765	0.742	0.750	0.745	-	-	-	-
BASELINE	0.651	0.325	0.500	0.394	-	-	-	-

Table 4: Subtask A results

	First Submission				Second Submission			
Team	$\mathcal{A}$	$\mathcal{P}$	$\mathcal{R}$	$\mathcal{F}$	$\mathcal{A}$	$\mathcal{P}$	$\mathcal{R}$	$\mathcal{F}$
iCompass (Ben Nessir et al., 2022)	**0.941**	0.869	**0.801**	**0.831**				
Meta-AI (AlKhamissi and Diab, 2022)	**0.941**	**0.870**	0.795	0.827	0.938	0.845	0.819	0.832
AlexU-AIC (Shapiro et al., 2022)	0.937	0.855	0.787	0.817				
CHILLAX (Makram et al., 2022)	0.891	0.728	0.809	0.759	0.869	0.694	0.792	0.727
UPV (de Paula et al., 2022)	0.925	0.845	0.711	0.757	0.932	0.858	0.751	0.792
BASELINE	0.893	0.447	0.500	0.472	-	-	-	-

Table 5: Subtask B results

	First Submission				Second Submission			
Team	$\mathcal{A}$	$\mathcal{P}$	$\mathcal{R}$	$\mathcal{F}$	$\mathcal{A}$	$\mathcal{P}$	$\mathcal{R}$	$\mathcal{F}$
iCompass (Ben Nessir et al., 2022)	0.919	0.548	**0.531**	**0.528**				
Meta-AI (AlKhamissi and Diab, 2022)	**0.926**	**0.551**	0.508	0.519				
AlexU-AIC (Shapiro et al., 2022)	0.923	0.490	0.470	0.476				
UPV (de Paula et al., 2022)	0.920	0.543	0.369	0.423	0.917	0.382	0.294	0.325
BASELINE	0.893	0.128	0.143	0.135	-	-	-	-

Table 6: Subtask C results

Proceedings of the OSACT 2022 Workshop @LREC2022, pages 167–175
Marseille, 20 June 2022

GOF at Arabic Hate Speech 2022: Breaking The Loss Function Convention For Data-Imbalanced Arabic Offensive Text Detection

Aly Mostafa, Omar Mohamed, Ali Ashraf
Department Of Computer Science, Faculty of Computers and Artificial Intelligence, Helwan University
Helwan, Egypt
{alymostafa, omar_20170353, aliashraf }@fci.helwan.edu.eg

Abstract

With the rise of social media platforms, we need to ensure that all users have a secure online experience by eliminating and identifying offensive language and hate speech. Furthermore, detecting such content is challenging, especially in the Arabic language, due to several challenges and limitations. Generally, one of the challenging issues in real-world datasets is long-tailed data distribution. We report our submission to the Offensive Language and hate-speech Detection shared task organized with the 5th Workshop on Open-Source Arabic Corpora and Processing Tools Arabic (OSACT5). In our approach, we focused on how to overcome such a problem by experimenting with alternative loss functions rather than using the traditional weighted cross-entropy loss. Finally, we evaluated various pre-trained deep learning models using the suggested loss functions to determine the optimal model. On the development and test sets, our final model achieved 86.97% and 85.17%, respectively.
Keywords: Arabic, Offensive Language Detection, Class imbalance

1. Introduction

Offensive speech has expanded at an unprecedented rate in today's digital age since most communication has transitioned to digital. Because of the lack of limits on users on social media platforms, the role of detecting offensive speech arises. In general, offensive speech is a public communication that displays hatred or urges violence against a person or group based on characteristics such as race or religion. Detecting offensive speech can be beneficial for filtering out inappropriate content. However, the detection process is difficult for several reasons. First, offensive information is classified into several categories, and not all of them have the same negative impact. Second, most research efforts are directed toward the English language (Hada et al., 2021), (Gupta et al., 2021), (Agrawal and Awekar, 2018), (Davidson et al., 2017); however, offensive detection research in the Arabic language is still in its early stages, with very few notable works (Mubarak and Darwish, 2019), (Mubarak et al., 2017), (Mubarak et al., 2020), (Mubarak et al., 2022). This is due to several challenges, namely a lack of pre-trained models, a small dataset size, and multiple dialects with no dataset that spans all of them; additionally, most social media content is written in Colloquial Arabic, which is not a formal language. It is written in Colloquial Arabic, which differs significantly from Modern Standard Arabic (MSA) since it does not always follow certain grammatical rules and has various word pronunciations. Finally, the Arabic offensive datasets have a long-tailed data distribution (i.e., a few classes account for the majority of the data, while most classes are under-represented), which adds difficulty because most learners will exhibit bias towards the majority class, and in extreme cases, may ignore the minority class entirely. Most offensive/hate speech classification researches ignore this issue since they utilize the traditional/naive technique of assigning sample weights inversely proportionately to the class frequency in the cross-entropy loss. This basic heuristic strategy is commonly used (Huang et al., 2016), (Wang et al., 2017). However, when training deep neural networks on large-scale, real-world, long-tailed datasets, weighted cross-entropy reveals poor performance (Mahajan et al., 2018), (Mikolov et al., 2013). In addition, recent studies (Cao et al., 2019) (Kini et al., 2021) suggest that weighted cross-entropy has little value for balanced accuracy and that alternative strategies based on margin adjustment can be more beneficial, mainly by ensuring that minority classes are further away from the decision boundary. As a result of the aforementioned causes, an important question is raised: How can we address this issue through improved class-balanced loss? In this study, we analyze five distinct loss functions and their variants in the text classification task across three different pre-trained Arabic language models. The experiments revealed that employing the suggested loss functions instead of standard weighted cross-entropy improved the model's macro f1 score metric by 0.5-2.0%. To summarise, our final model was an ensemble learning model composed of three different models (MARBERT, MARBERTV2, and QARiB) (Abdul-Mageed et al., 2021), (Abdelali et al., 2021a), all of which were trained using suggested loss functions and achieved 86.97% and 85.17% on the development and test sets, respectively.

The rest of the paper is organized as follows. section 2 provides a review of previous Arabic offensive text detection literature. section 3 describes the proposed dataset. section 4 proposes the model of the offensive detection. section 5 discusses the results and performance evaluation. Finally, we conclude in section 6.

2. Related Works

This section discusses previous research addressing offensive detection challenges in the Arabic language, the methodologies, strengths, and drawbacks. All of the following studies were conducted on SemEval 2020 Arabic offensive language dataset (Mubarak et al., 2020).

(Husain, 2020) An intensive cleaning strategy was proposed. First, emojis and emoticons are converted to an Arabic textual label that explains their content. Second, they normalise Arabic words with diacritics. Then, stopwords, HTML tags, URLs, mentions, and punctuation marks are removed. Finally, they employ Count Vectorizer as a feature extractor and character-based features to train a Support Vector Machine (SVM)-based classifier. For offensive language detection, they obtained an F1 score of 89.82%.

(Hassan et al., 2020), An ensemble learning model was proposed using four distinct classifiers, two of which are SVM as a classifier and a combination of Mazajak word embedding, character level, and word-level features. The Feed-forward Neural Network (FFNN) was the third classifier, and it used a combination of character-level and word-level features. The final classifiers were Convolutional Neural Network (CNN) and Mazajak as pre-trained word embeddings. As an ensemble learning technique, they used Majority voting and achieved an F1 score of 90.51%.

(Keleg et al., 2020) BERT-generated contextualised word embeddings were used for Arabic offensive detection. Furthermore, a morphological technique for augmentation strategy was used to increase the dataset sample size by employing a list of 87 bad words that were augmented to reach 5497 unique terms. Their strategy yielded an 89.57% of F1 score.

(Saeed et al., 2020) As the stacking classifier, they propose an ensemble of multiple models created from four different Deep Learning models. First and foremost, CNN, Bi-LSTM, Bi-GRU, and CNN-Bi-LSTM are trained as Deep Learning Architectures. Second, they experiment with several word embeddings to see which one may improve the classifier's performance. According to their findings, they combined FastText word embeddings (Bojanowski et al., 2017) with existing Deep Learning architectures. Finally, they use an ensemble stacking approach using five distinct Machine Learning classifiers to obtain the final predictions. Their methodology received an F1 score of 87.37%.

(Haddad et al., 2020) A Deep Learning technique for detecting offensive language is proposed. With the Word2Vec Arabic embedding, they use a bidirectional Gated Recurrent Unit (GRU) with attention layers (AraVec) (Soliman et al., 2017). Also, they employed an oversampling strategy. They added some offensive and inoffensive comments from an already created Arabic dataset derived from YouTube comments (Alakrot et al., 2018). Their strategy received an F1 score of 85.90%.

(Abdellatif and Elgammal, 2020) They proposed ULMFiT (Howard and Ruder, 2018) pre-trained from scratch on the Arabic Wikipedia corpus, then they fine-tuned their model on the Arabic offensive dataset achieving a 77.83% F1 score.

(Djandji et al., 2020) Due to the limited sample size in both tasks, they presented a multi-task learning strategy to train jointly offensive and hate speech detection. Their multi-task learning architecture goes as follows: They apply data pre-processing methods to the offensive tweet input before using the AraBERT model as a shared layer between the two tasks. Finally, for each task, two dense layers are used as task-specific layers. Their architecture achieved an f1 score of 90.04%.

(Elmadany et al., 2020) They used the BERT Multilingual model to leverage an effective offensive detection method. In addition, they use an oversampling approach to obtain negative sentiment tweets and label them as offensive or hate speech based on a lexical seed. Their method received 77.38% of the f1 score.

(Farha and Magdy, 2020) They presented a CNN-BiLSTM-based multi-task learning architecture. Their architecture is as follows: First, they used pre-trained skip-gram word2vec embedding on a corpus of 250 million tweets to embed the input tweets. Second, they pass the embedding to the CNN layer and performed Max Pooling. Third, pass the feature vectors to the BiLSTM layer; all previous stages are considered shared layers. Finally, three dense layers are employed as task-specific layers, one for offensive speech detection, one for hate speech identification, and one for the sentiment. The reason for incorporating sentiment in offensive and hate speech detection is that sentiment may include additional information for the model since offensive language or hate speech are often sentimental and express negative emotion towards the target. Their model achieved 87.87% of the f1 score.

According to the findings of this survey, most studies did not make further research to address the problem of data imbalance; instead, they relied on the standard weighted cross-entropy. However, only two of them addressed the issue in data-level methods with oversampling techniques by augmenting the dataset to the positive class (offensive class). The purpose of this research is to overcome previous limitations by using and assessing various loss functions to better address the problem of data imbalance.

3. Dataset

The proposed dataset (Mubarak et al., 2022) for the OSACT-2022 Shared challenge comprises 13k Arabic tweets collected using a set of emojis with a high malicious effect independent of the tweet text. As a result, they chose tweets that had one or more emojis. The data is classified into three categories: offensive, hate speech, and fine-grained hate speech, and divided into 70% for training, 10% for development, and 20% for testing. However, the dataset's distribution is severely imbalanced and skewed, with 35% being offensive and 11% being hate speech. Offensive tweets and violent account for 1.5% and 0.7% of the total corpus, respectively. To address this challenge, we used the proposed approach of experimenting with different loss functions rather than simply adopting standard weighted loss cross-entropy.

4. Methodology

In this section, we will go over the key components of the proposed method, starting with the data pre-processing techniques used, then a discussion of the suggested loss functions, followed by an overview of the pre-trained models used, finally the ensemble learning approach of the three pre-trained models is presented.

4.1. Data Pre-Processing

We eliminated non-Arabic letters, punctuation marks, digits, and Arabic diacritics during the pre-processing. Following the removal of unnecessary characters, the text is normalized into its unified form. Because social media material is written in unconventional ways and is not a formal language, some users choose to repeat the same word characters to emphasize its meaning, such as "جوووووول" instead of "جول" which means GOAL. We addressed this problem by eliminating duplicate letters from each word (elongation removal) (Hegazi et al., 2021). We did not remove emojis or emotions as they can significantly aid the tweet classification decision. The final step is to replace selected terms with meaningful tokens in order to unify them throughout the dataset, as seen below:

- Replace URL with "رابط"
- Replace mentions @USER with "مستخدم"
- Replace Email with "بريد"

4.2. Loss Functions

In this subsection, we discuss five different loss functions with their variations as follows :

- Weighted Cross-Entropy loss(CE)
- Weighted CE combined with label smoothing
- Focal Loss
- Focal Loss combined with label smoothing
- Dice Loss
- Tversky Loss
- Focal Tversky Loss
- Vector Scaling(VS) Loss
- VSLoss combined with label smoothing
- Weighted VSLoss
- Weighted VSLoss combined with label smoothing

4.2.1. Weighted Cross-Entropy Loss

Standard Cross-Entropy loss: is calculated as follows:

$$\text{CE} = -\frac{1}{N}\sum_{i}\sum_{j\in\{0,1\}} y_{ij}\log p_{ij} \quad (1)$$

As shown in Eq.1, each x_i contributes equally to the overall objective. The standard technique for dealing with the case when we don't want all x_i to be regarded equally is to provide various weighting factors to distinct classes. Eq.1 is modified as follows for the former:

$$\text{Weighted CE} = -\frac{1}{N}\sum_{i}\alpha_i\sum_{j\in\{0,1\}} y_{ij}\log p_{ij} \quad (2)$$

where $\alpha_i \in [0,1]$ may be set by assigning sample weights inversely proportionately to the class frequency. Empirically, these methods are extensively used as the training objective for data-imbalanced NLP problems(Lample et al., 2016), (Meng et al., 2019), (Devlin et al., 2018), (Yu et al., 2018), (McCann et al., 2018), (Ma and Hovy, 2016), (Chen et al., 2017).

Weighted Cross-Entropy loss + Label Smoothing: The use of a smoothing parameter $\epsilon \in [0,1]$ is the only difference between standard weighted cross-entropy and weighted cross-entropy paired with label smoothing (Szegedy et al., 2016), (Müller et al., 2019). Label smoothing is a regularization technique that solves the overconfidence and overfitting issues. The cross-entropy with label smoothing is calculated as follows:

$$H(y_{i,j}, p_{i,j}) = (1-\epsilon)H(y,p) + \epsilon H(y,p) \quad (3)$$

4.2.2. Focal Loss

Standard Focal Loss: (Lin et al., 2017) it is a dynamically scaled cross-entropy loss created by adding a modulating term to the cross-entropy loss so that the scaling factor decays to zero as confidence in the correct class increases (easily classified examples) and increases on low confidence cases (hard misclassified, examples). This procedure is used to quickly focus the learning process on difficult examples. The modulating factor $(1-p_t)^\gamma$ is added to the cross-entropy loss. Configure $\gamma > 0$ lowers the relative loss for cases that have been correctly classified $p_t > .5$, emphasising challenging, misclassified cases. There is a focusing parameter that may be adjusted here $\gamma \geq 0$. The equation of Focal loss as follows:

$$\text{FL}(p_t) = -(1-p_t)^\gamma \log(p_t) \quad (4)$$

Focal loss + Label Smoothing: The Focal loss is edited to add label smoothing parameter, as stated before the label smoothing aids to tackle the problem of overconfidence.

Model	Weighted CE		Weighted CE + LS[‡]		Focal Loss		Focal Loss+LS[‡]		Dice Loss		Tversky Loss		Focal Tversky Loss		VS Loss	
	F_1	PR - RR	F_1	PR - RR	F_1	PR - RR	F_1	PR - RR	F_1	PR - RR	F_1	PR - RR	F_1	PR - RR	F_1	PR - RR
MARBERT	83.7	83.2 - 84.2	83.6	83.3 - 84.1	84.5	84.4 - 84.6	84.4	84.3 - 84.4	83.2	82.8 - 83.5	84.1	84.7 - 83.6	83.7	84.6 - 83.0	**85.6**	**85.8 - 85.4**
MARBERT(v2)	84.5	83.6 - 85.9	84.7	83.8 - 86.1	84.9	84.8 - 85.1	**85.2**	**85.1 - 85.2**	84.3	84.0 - 84.8	83.7	83.1 - 84.5	83.7	83.0 - 84.6	84.6	84.3 - 85.0
QARiB	85.4	84.7 - 86.3	85.2	84.6 - 86.1	85.4	85.2 - 85.6	85.4	85.2 - 85.6	**85.7**	**85.5 - 85.8**	84.9	84.8 - 85.1	85.0	85.7 - 84.3	83.6	84.8 - 82.6

Table 1: Comparsion Between Different Loss Functions. [‡] Refer to Label Smoothing, PR for Precision rate, and RR for Recall rate.

4.2.3. Dice Loss

The Sørensen–Dice coefficient (Dice, 1945), (Sorensen, 1948), often known as the dice coefficient (DSC), is a harmonic mean of precision and recall thus weighs false positives (FPs) and false negatives (FNs) equally. Furthermore, (Milletari et al., 2016) proposed to convert the denominator to the square form for faster convergence, which results in the dice loss (DL) shown below:

$$\mathrm{DL} = 1 - \frac{2\sum_i p_{i1} y_{i1} + \gamma}{\sum_i p_{i1}^2 + \sum_i y_{i1}^2 + \gamma} \tag{5}$$

In our context, p is the set of all positive cases predicted by a certain model, and y is the set of all golden positive examples in the dataset. When applied to boolean data, the definitions of true positive (TP), false positive (FP), and false-negative (FN) are used (FN). It is usual to apply a γ factor to both the nominator and the denominator for smoothing reasons.

4.2.4. Tversky Loss

The Tversky index (Tversky, 1977), (Hashemi et al., 2018) is a broadening of the Dice similarity coefficient and F_β scores. The Tversky index is defined as where and govern the level of penalties for FPs and FNs. One of the Dice loss function's shortcomings is that it equally weights false positive (FP) and false negative (FN) detections. To improve the recall rate, FN detections should be weighted higher than FPs. The following formulation is used to define the Tversky loss function:

$$T(\alpha, \beta) = \frac{\sum_{i=1}^{N} p_{0i} g_{0i}}{\sum_{i=1}^{N} p_{0i} g_{0i} + \alpha \sum_{i=1}^{N} p_{0i} g_{1i} + \beta \sum_{i=1}^{N} p_{1i} g_{0i}} \tag{6}$$

4.2.5. Focal Tversky Loss

The focal Tversky loss function (FTL) is a combination of the regular Tversky loss and focal loss (modulating term). FTL is parametrized by γ, for control between easy and hard training examples. In (Lin et al., 2017), the focal parameter exponentiates the cross-entropy loss to focus on hard classes detected with a lower probability. The focal Tversky Loss (FTL) function is defined as follows:

$$FTL = (T)^{1/\gamma} \tag{7}$$

4.2.6. Vector Scaling Loss

Vector-scaling (Vs) loss (Kini et al., 2021) is an improved form of cross-entropy with three additional parameters that integrate additive and multiplicative logit modifications, which had previously been proposed in the literature but in isolation. The following is the **binary VS-loss** for labels $y \in \{\pm 1\}$, weight parameters $\omega_\pm > 0$, additive logit parameters $\iota_\pm \in \mathbb{R}$, and multiplicative logit parameters $\Delta_\pm > 0$:

$$\ell_{\mathrm{VS}}(y, f_w(x)) = \omega_y \cdot \log\left(1 + e^{\iota_y} \cdot e^{-\Delta_y y f_w(x)}\right) \tag{8}$$

The VS-loss for imbalanced datasets with C > 2 classes is as follows:

$$\ell_{\mathrm{VS}}(y, f_w(x)) = -\omega_y \log\left(e^{\Delta_y f_y(x) + \iota_y} / \sum_{c \in [C]} e^{\Delta_c f_c(x) + \iota_c}\right) \tag{9}$$

Here $f_w : R^d \to R^C$ and $f_w(x) = [f_1(x), \ldots, f_C(x)]$ is the vector of logits. The various modifications include adding a label smoothing parameter, applying sample weights inversely related to the class frequency, and combining the previous settings together.

4.3. Pre-Trained Models

Because the dataset is a collection of tweets, selecting pre-trained models that have been trained on Twitter data with diverse dialects was critical. Following the literature (Abdul-Mageed et al., 2021), utilising models pre-trained on social media data (e.g., Twitter data) improves finetuning performance over training on standard data (e.g., Wikipedia) if the finetuning procedure is done on a dataset that is mostly composed of tweets. The details about the employed models are described below.

QARiB: (Abdelali et al., 2021b) QCRI Arabic and Dialectal BERT model was trained on 420 million tweets and 180 million sentences of text comprised of 14B tokens. The data for the tweets was gathered using the Twitter API. The text data was derived from a mix of Arabic GigaWord, Abulkhair Arabic Corpus (El-Khair, 2016), and OPUS (Lison and Tiedemann, 2016). The model is a bidirectional transformer encoder model (BERT) (Devlin et al., 2018) with 110M parameters that contains 12 encoder layers, 12 attention heads, and 768 hidden sizes. The QARiB model trained with Dice-Loss (Dice, 1945), (Li et al., 2019) achieved 85.717% on F1-score.

MARBERT & MARBERTv2: MARBERT (Abdul-Mageed et al., 2021) was trained on 1 billion Arabic tweets by randomly picking tweets from a huge in-house dataset of around 6 billion tweets made up of 15.6 billion tokens and with a sequence length of just 128. The model was trained using the same network architecture as BERT Base (masked language model) but without the next sentence prediction (NSP) component. Because the model has been pre-trained on a variety of tweets, it can recognize a variety of dialects, not only Modern Standard Arabic (MSA). The model incorporates 163M parameters, including 12 encoder layers, 12 attention heads, and 768 hidden sizes. Because the model was trained with a sequence length of just 128, it is inadequate for Question Answering. As a result, they re-train the model using a different collection of MSA resources, including Books (Hindawi), El-Khair (El-Khair, 2016), Gigaword, OSCAR (Suárez et al., 2019), OSIAN (Zeroual et al., 2019), and AraNews dataset (Nagoudi et al., 2020) with a longer sequence length of 512 tokens totaling 29B tokens. The MARBERT model trained using Focal loss + Label smoothing achieved an f1 score of 85.66%, while the MARBERTV2 model trained with VSLoss obtained an f1 score of 85.21%.

4.4. Ensemble Learning Model

We employed the ensemble learning approach to enhance and improve model performance. We noticed that the three models generate different mistakes on different samples; so, we used Ensemble learning approaches since the ensemble's ability to correct the errors of some of its members is entirely dependent on the diversity of the classifiers that comprise the ensemble. Our final ensemble model is based on a majority voting technique between the following models: 1). QARiB trained with Dice loss. 2). MARBERT trained with VS loss. 3). MARBERTV2 trained with Focal loss + label smoothing.

5. Results and Discussion

5.1. Performance Metrics

We employed different metrics to assess the model performance and to understand/analyse its efficiency and errors. We calculated Precision, recall, and F1-score in the macro setting. We used Macro F1-score instead of Accuracy to assess the model's performance since the proposed dataset is highly imbalanced, making the Accuracy unsuitable for this task.

5.2. Experimental Results

In this section, we present the results of experimenting with various models and architectures trained with different loss functions and the impact on performance.

Different Models: We evaluated many pre-trained models to determine the most effective one for achieving the best results individually or as part of an ensemble group. The majority of the pre-trained models that were fine-tuned on the proposed data generated outcomes that were comparable to each other. Among all models tested, Light Gradient Boosting Machine (LGBM) trained on QARiB embeddings fine-tuned on the proposed data yielded the best results individually. In addition, we eliminated the emojis and emotions from the proposed dataset and trained the MARBERT model, however, the results were not competitive. Furthermore, we tested two versions of AraBERT, a base and a large version trained on Twitter data, and they achieved 85.54% and 85.15% on the F1-score measure, respectively. Finally, we tried a different model combination in an ensemble approach; the first experiment consisted of Arabert-base-Twitter, MARBERT, and QARiB and obtained 86.73% on the F1-score. The second was a combination of MARBERTV2, MARBERT, and QARiB that resulted in an f1-score of 87.04%. The final experiment obtained an f1-score of 86.43% by combining LightGBM trained on QARiB embeddings, MARBERT, and MARBERTV2. The experiments are shown in Table 2.

Different Loss Functions: According to the no-free lunch, theory (Wolpert and Macready, 1997), there is no optimum solution for all problems. Furthermore, after experimenting with various loss functions on the selected models, we observed that some loss functions perform better for some models but not others. However, under the f1-score metric, most of the suggested loss functions exceeded the standard weighted cross-entropy. The comparison between different loss functions and models is presented in Table 1.

Models	Macro-F1(%)
MARBERT(Without emojis)	85.077
AraBERT-Large-Twitter	85.158
QARiB	85.424
AraBERT-Base-Twitter	85.548
MARBERT	85.574
MARBERTV2	85.723
LightGBM(QARiB Embeddings)	**85.798**
Ensemble(LightGBM+ MARBERT+MARBERTV2)	86.432
Ensemble(AraBERT-B-T+ MARBERT+QARiB)	86.733
Ensemble(MARBERTV2+ MARBERT+QARiB)	**87.044**

Table 2: Different Models With an F1-score On Development Set.

5.3. Discussion

Results show in Table 1 that Weighted CE was not the best performer compared to the rest of the loss functions. Its best result was on the QARiB model, yielding an F1 score of 84.4%, higher than MARBERT-v2's result of 84.5% and MARBERT's of 83.7%. Even with the addition of Label Smoothing, Weighted CE still failed to outperform the rest of the loss functions while not making any significant difference from the standard Weighted CE. For MARBERT, results were quite similar between the loss functions, namely Weighted CE, Weighted CE with Label Smoothing and Focal Tversky

True Label	Predicted Label	Attribution Score	Word Importance
OFF	+1 (0.79)	0.22	[CLS] يلعنهم الله [UNK] [SEP]
OFF	+1 (0.71)	0.32	[CLS] بعينك شيطان 😡 [SEP]
OFF	+1 (0.81)	0.87	[CLS] ابح النار كلب يا 😂 اتراك لقاح اسمك من [UNK] [SEP]
NOT OFF	-1 (0.20)	-1.90	[CLS] اصرار عندك يكون لازم بحياتك ناجح تكون عشان [SEP]
NOT OFF	-1 (0.20)	-0.51	[CLS] زين اعلانات من كانه زينه 😂 [SEP]
NOT OFF	-1 (0.21)	-2.22	[CLS] ياجماعه الله ماشاء قولوا [SEP]

Table 3: Word Attributions In Dataset's Tweets (Not Offensvie -1 , Offensive +1)

loss, yielding an F1 score of 83.7%, 83.6%, and 83.7%, respectively, while Focal loss and Focal loss with Label Smoothing had close results with an F1 score of 84.5% and 84.4%, respectively. MARBERT's best performer was VS loss, yielding an F1 score of 85.6. For MARBERT-v2, results were also quite similar between the loss functions, namely Tversky loss and Focal Tversky loss, both yielding an F1 score of 83.7%, while Weighted CE, Weighted CE with label Smoothing, Focal loss, Dice loss, and VS loss had close results with an F1 score of 84.5%, 84.7%, 84.9%, 84.3%, and 84.6%, respectively. MARBERT-v2's best performer was Focal loss with Label Smoothing, yielding an F1 score of 85.2%. For QARiB, results were close between the loss functions, but with significant improvements compared to the other models. Weighted CE, Weighted CE with Label Smoothing, Focal loss, and Focal loss with Label Smoothing yielded an F1 score of 85.4, 85.2%, 85.4%, and 85.4%, respectively. MARBERT's best performer was Dice loss, yielding an F1 score of 85.7%.

5.4. Model Interpretability

We used Captum (Kokhlikyan et al., 2020), a model interpretability and understanding library for PyTorch (Paszke et al., 2019), to interpret the final model decision or predicted class. It allows researchers and developers to efficiently understand which features are contributing to the model's outputs using tools such as integrated gradients, smooth-grad, and others. Furthermore, Captum solves the lack of transparency in deep learning models, or as their called, Black Boxes. This term refers to how difficult it is to understand and explain the behaviour of a model. Captum looks at a single prediction and identifies features leading to that prediction through Integrated Gradients. In our case, the features are the words or emojis in the tweet that led the model to a specific predicted outcome. Green indicates that the tokens are pulling towards offensiveness, while red indicates that they are pulling toward inoffensiveness. The colour intensity represents the magnitude of the signal. Table 3 illustrates the word attributions for selected examples of the proposed dataset using Captum.

6. Conclusion and Future Works

In this work, we proposed a method for dealing with Arabic Offensive text detection. Our final model is a Deep Learning ensemble learning system consisting of three different Deep Learning models. Furthermore, because the dataset distribution is highly skewed, testing with alternative loss functions to observe how they affect model performance revealed that simply replacing the standard weighted cross-entropy with different loss functions enhanced the model's Macro F1-score by 0.5-2%. On the development set, the proposed pipeline achieved 87.04%, while on the test set, it obtained 85.17%. In future work, we aim to test the effectiveness of those loss functions on a wide range of tasks in the Arabic language. This result would also support our findings that standard cross-entropy loss is ineffective for long-tailed data distribution. Because most real-world datasets in various tasks are highly imbalanced, such a study would assist the researcher in better addressing the problem of highly imbalanced datasets.

7. References

Abdelali, A., Hassan, S., Mubarak, H., Darwish, K., and Samih, Y. (2021a). Pre-training bert on arabic tweets: Practical considerations.

Abdelali, A., Hassan, S., Mubarak, H., Darwish, K., and Samih, Y. (2021b). Pre-training bert on arabic tweets: Practical considerations. *arXiv preprint arXiv:2102.10684*.

Abdellatif, M. and Elgammal, A. (2020). Offensive language detection in arabic using ulmfit. In *Proceedings of the 4th Workshop on Open-Source Arabic Corpora and Processing Tools, with a Shared Task on Offensive Language Detection*, pages 82–85.

Abdul-Mageed, M., Elmadany, A., and Nagoudi, E. M. B. (2021). ARBERT & MARBERT: Deep bidirectional transformers for Arabic. In *Proceedings of the 59th Annual Meeting of the Association for Computational Linguistics and the 11th International Joint Conference on Natural Language Processing (Volume 1: Long Papers)*, pages 7088–7105, Online, August. Association for Computational Linguistics.

Agrawal, S. and Awekar, A. (2018). Deep learning for detecting cyberbullying across multiple social media platforms. In *European conference on information retrieval*, pages 141–153. Springer.

Alakrot, A., Murray, L., and Nikolov, N. S. (2018). Dataset construction for the detection of anti-social behaviour in online communication in arabic. *Procedia Computer Science*, 142:174–181.

Bojanowski, P., Grave, E., Joulin, A., and Mikolov, T. (2017). Enriching word vectors with subword information. *Transactions of the association for computational linguistics*, 5:135–146.

Cao, K., Wei, C., Gaidon, A., Arechiga, N., and Ma, T. (2019). Learning imbalanced datasets with label-distribution-aware margin loss. *Advances in neural information processing systems*, 32.

Chen, D., Fisch, A., Weston, J., and Bordes, A. (2017). Reading wikipedia to answer open-domain questions. *arXiv preprint arXiv:1704.00051*.

Davidson, T., Warmsley, D., Macy, M., and Weber, I. (2017). Automated hate speech detection and the problem of offensive language. In *Proceedings of the International AAAI Conference on Web and Social Media*, volume 11, pages 512–515.

Devlin, J., Chang, M.-W., Lee, K., and Toutanova, K. (2018). Bert: Pre-training of deep bidirectional transformers for language understanding. *arXiv preprint arXiv:1810.04805*.

Dice, L. R. (1945). Measures of the amount of ecologic association between species. *Ecology*, 26(3):297–302.

Djandji, M., Baly, F., Antoun, W., and Hajj, H. (2020). Multi-task learning using arabert for offensive language detection. In *Proceedings of the 4th Workshop on Open-Source Arabic Corpora and Processing Tools, with a Shared Task on Offensive Language Detection*, pages 97–101.

El-Khair, I. A. (2016). 1.5 billion words arabic corpus. *arXiv preprint arXiv:1611.04033*.

Elmadany, A., Zhang, C., Abdul-Mageed, M., and Hashemi, A. (2020). Leveraging affective bidirectional transformers for offensive language detection. *arXiv preprint arXiv:2006.01266*.

Farha, I. A. and Magdy, W. (2020). Multitask learning for arabic offensive language and hate-speech detection. In *Proceedings of the 4th workshop on open-source Arabic corpora and processing tools, with a shared task on offensive language detection*, pages 86–90.

Gupta, A., Pal, A., Khurana, B., Tyagi, L., and Modi, A. (2021). Humor@IITK at SemEval-2021 task 7: Large language models for quantifying humor and offensiveness. In *Proceedings of the 15th International Workshop on Semantic Evaluation (SemEval-2021)*, pages 290–296, Online, August. Association for Computational Linguistics.

Hada, R., Sudhir, S., Mishra, P., Yannakoudakis, H., Mohammad, S. M., and Shutova, E. (2021). Ruddit: Norms of offensiveness for English Reddit comments. In *Proceedings of the 59th Annual Meeting of the Association for Computational Linguistics and the 11th International Joint Conference on Natural Language Processing (Volume 1: Long Papers)*, pages 2700–2717, Online, August. Association for Computational Linguistics.

Haddad, B., Orabe, Z., Al-Abood, A., and Ghneim, N. (2020). Arabic offensive language detection with attention-based deep neural networks. In *Proceedings of the 4th Workshop on Open-Source Arabic Corpora and Processing Tools, with a Shared Task on Offensive Language Detection*, pages 76–81.

Hashemi, S. R., Salehi, S. S. M., Erdogmus, D., Prabhu, S. P., Warfield, S. K., and Gholipour, A. (2018). Tversky as a loss function for highly unbalanced image segmentation using 3d fully convolutional deep networks. *arXiv preprint arXiv:1803.11078*.

Hassan, S., Samih, Y., Mubarak, H., Abdelali, A., Rashed, A., and Chowdhury, S. A. (2020). Alt submission for osact shared task on offensive language detection. In *Proceedings of the 4th Workshop on Open-Source Arabic Corpora and Processing Tools, with a Shared Task on Offensive Language Detection*, pages 61–65.

Hegazi, M. O., Al-Dossari, Y., Al-Yahy, A., Al-Sumari, A., and Hilal, A. (2021). Preprocessing arabic text on social media. *Heliyon*, 7(2):e06191.

Howard, J. and Ruder, S. (2018). Universal language model fine-tuning for text classification. *arXiv preprint arXiv:1801.06146*.

Huang, C., Li, Y., Loy, C. C., and Tang, X. (2016). Learning deep representation for imbalanced classification. In *Proceedings of the IEEE conference on computer vision and pattern recognition*, pages 5375–5384.

Husain, F. (2020). Osact4 shared task on offensive language detection: Intensive preprocessing-based approach. *arXiv preprint arXiv:2005.07297*.

Keleg, A., El-Beltagy, S. R., and Khalil, M. (2020). Asu_opto at osact4-offensive language detection for arabic text. In *Proceedings of the 4th Workshop on Open-Source Arabic Corpora and Processing Tools, with a Shared Task on Offensive Language Detection*, pages 66–70.

Kini, G. R., Paraskevas, O., Oymak, S., and Thrampoulidis, C. (2021). Label-imbalanced and group-sensitive classification under overparameterization. *Advances in Neural Information Processing Systems*, 34.

Kokhlikyan, N., Miglani, V., Martin, M., Wang, E., Alsallakh, B., Reynolds, J., Melnikov, A., Kliushkina, N., Araya, C., Yan, S., et al. (2020). Captum: A unified and generic model interpretability library for pytorch. *arXiv preprint arXiv:2009.07896*.

Lample, G., Ballesteros, M., Subramanian, S., Kawakami, K., and Dyer, C. (2016). Neural architectures for named entity recognition. *arXiv preprint arXiv:1603.01360*.

Li, X., Sun, X., Meng, Y., Liang, J., Wu, F., and Li, J. (2019). Dice loss for data-imbalanced nlp tasks. *arXiv preprint arXiv:1911.02855*.

Lin, T.-Y., Goyal, P., Girshick, R., He, K., and Dollár, P. (2017). Focal loss for dense object detection. In *Proceedings of the IEEE international conference on computer vision*, pages 2980–2988.

Lison, P. and Tiedemann, J. (2016). OpenSubtitles2016: Extracting large parallel corpora from movie and TV subtitles. In *Proceedings of the Tenth International Conference on Language Resources and Evaluation (LREC'16)*, pages 923–929, Portorož, Slovenia, May. European Language Resources Association (ELRA).

Ma, X. and Hovy, E. (2016). End-to-end sequence labeling via bi-directional lstm-cnns-crf. *arXiv preprint arXiv:1603.01354*.

Mahajan, D., Girshick, R., Ramanathan, V., He, K., Paluri, M., Li, Y., Bharambe, A., and Van Der Maaten, L. (2018). Exploring the limits of weakly supervised pretraining. In *Proceedings of the European conference on computer vision (ECCV)*, pages 181–196.

McCann, B., Keskar, N. S., Xiong, C., and Socher, R. (2018). The natural language decathlon: Multitask learning as question answering. *arXiv preprint arXiv:1806.08730*.

Meng, Y., Wu, W., Wang, F., Li, X., Nie, P., Yin, F., Li, M., Han, Q., Sun, X., and Li, J. (2019). Glyce: Glyph-vectors for chinese character representations. *Advances in Neural Information Processing Systems*, 32.

Mikolov, T., Sutskever, I., Chen, K., Corrado, G. S., and Dean, J. (2013). Distributed representations of words and phrases and their compositionality. *Advances in neural information processing systems*, 26.

Milletari, F., Navab, N., and Ahmadi, S.-A. (2016). V-net: Fully convolutional neural networks for volumetric medical image segmentation. In *2016 fourth international conference on 3D vision (3DV)*, pages 565–571. IEEE.

Mubarak, H. and Darwish, K. (2019). Arabic offensive language classification on twitter. In *International Conference on Social Informatics*, pages 269–276. Springer.

Mubarak, H., Darwish, K., and Magdy, W. (2017). Abusive language detection on Arabic social media. In *Proceedings of the First Workshop on Abusive Language Online*, pages 52–56, Vancouver, BC, Canada, August. Association for Computational Linguistics.

Mubarak, H., Darwish, K., Magdy, W., Elsayed, T., and Al-Khalifa, H. (2020). Overview of osact4 arabic offensive language detection shared task. In *Proceedings of the 4th Workshop on open-source arabic corpora and processing tools, with a shared task on offensive language detection*, pages 48–52.

Mubarak, H., Hassan, S., and Chowdhury, S. A. (2022). Emojis as anchors to detect arabic offensive language and hate speech. *arXiv preprint arXiv:2201.06723*.

Müller, R., Kornblith, S., and Hinton, G. E. (2019). When does label smoothing help? *Advances in neural information processing systems*, 32.

Nagoudi, E. M. B., Elmadany, A., Abdul-Mageed, M., and Alhindi, T. (2020). Machine generation and detection of Arabic manipulated and fake news. In *Proceedings of the Fifth Arabic Natural Language Processing Workshop*, pages 69–84, Barcelona, Spain (Online), December. Association for Computational Linguistics.

Paszke, A., Gross, S., Massa, F., Lerer, A., Bradbury, J., Chanan, G., Killeen, T., Lin, Z., Gimelshein, N., Antiga, L., Desmaison, A., Kopf, A., Yang, E., DeVito, Z., Raison, M., Tejani, A., Chilamkurthy, S., Steiner, B., Fang, L., Bai, J., and Chintala, S. (2019). Pytorch: An imperative style, high-performance deep learning library. In H. Wallach, et al., editors, *Advances in Neural Information Processing Systems 32*, pages 8024–8035. Curran Associates, Inc.

Saeed, H. H., Calders, T., and Kamiran, F. (2020). Osact4 shared tasks: Ensembled stacked classification for offensive and hate speech in arabic tweets. In *Proceedings of the 4th Workshop on Open-Source Arabic Corpora and Processing Tools, with a Shared Task on Offensive Language Detection*, pages 71–75.

Soliman, A. B., Eissa, K., and El-Beltagy, S. R. (2017). Aravec: A set of arabic word embedding models for use in arabic nlp. *Procedia Computer Science*, 117:256–265.

Sorensen, T. A. (1948). A method of establishing groups of equal amplitude in plant sociology based on similarity of species content and its application to analyses of the vegetation on danish commons. *Biol. Skar.*, 5:1–34.

Suárez, P. J. O., Sagot, B., and Romary, L. (2019). Asynchronous pipeline for processing huge corpora on medium to low resource infrastructures. In *7th Workshop on the Challenges in the Management of Large Corpora (CMLC-7)*. Leibniz-Institut für Deutsche Sprache.

Szegedy, C., Vanhoucke, V., Ioffe, S., Shlens, J., and Wojna, Z. (2016). Rethinking the inception architecture for computer vision. In *Proceedings of the IEEE conference on computer vision and pattern recognition*, pages 2818–2826.

Tversky, A. (1977). Features of similarity. *Psychological review*, 84(4):327.

Wang, Y.-X., Ramanan, D., and Hebert, M. (2017). Learning to model the tail. *Advances in Neural Information Processing Systems*, 30.

Wolpert, D. H. and Macready, W. G. (1997). No free lunch theorems for optimization. *IEEE transactions on evolutionary computation*, 1(1):67–82.

Yu, A. W., Dohan, D., Luong, M.-T., Zhao, R., Chen, K., Norouzi, M., and Le, Q. V. (2018). Qanet: Combining local convolution with global self-attention for reading comprehension. *arXiv preprint arXiv:1804.09541*.

Zeroual, I., Goldhahn, D., Eckart, T., and Lakhouaja, A. (2019). OSIAN: Open source international Arabic news corpus - preparation and integration into the CLARIN-infrastructure. In *Proceedings of the Fourth Arabic Natural Language Processing Workshop*, pages 175–182, Florence, Italy, August. Association for Computational Linguistics.

Proceedings of the OSACT 2022 Workshop @LREC2022, pages 176–180
Marseille, 20 June 2022

iCompass at Arabic Hate Speech 2022: Detect Hate Speech Using QRNN and Transformers

Mohamed Aziz Ben Nessir, Malek Rhouma, Hatem Haddad, Chayma Fourati
iCompass, 49, rue de Marseille, Tunis, Tunisia
mohamedaziz.bennessir@etudiant-isi.utm.tn, {malek, haddad}@gmail.com,
{haddad, chayma}@icompass.digital

Abstract

This paper provides a detailed overview of the system we submitted as part of the OSACT2022 Shared Tasks on Fine-Grained Hate Speech Detection on Arabic Twitter, its outcome, and limitations. Our submission is accomplished with a hard parameter sharing Multi-Task Model that consisted of a shared layer containing state-of-the-art contextualized text representation models such as MARBERT, AraBERT, ARBERT and task specific layers that were fine-tuned with Quasi-recurrent neural networks (QRNN) for each down-stream subtask. The results show that MARBERT fine-tuned with QRNN outperforms all of the previously mentioned models.

Keywords: Multi-Task,QRNN, MARBERT, Hate Speech Detection, Arabic

1. Arabic Hate Speech Detection

Hate Speech (HS) is particularly widespread in online communication due to users' anonymity and the lack of hate speech detection tools on social media platforms. Consequently, HS detection has determined a growing interest in using Machine/Deep Learning techniques to address this issue (Schmidt and Wiegand, 2017).

We describe our submitted system to the 2022 Shared Task Fine-Grained Hate Speech Detection on Arabic Twitter. We tackled the three subtasks, namely Detect whether a tweet is offensive or not (Subtask A), Detect whether a tweet has hate speech or not (Subtask B) and Detect the fine-grained type of hate speech (Subtask C). We used state-of-the-art pretrained contextualized text representation models and fine-tuned them according to the downstream subtasks in hand. As a first approach, we used the multilingual mT5 (Xue et al., 2020) and three Arabic Language models variants: AraBERT (Antoun et al., 2020), ARBERT (Abdul-Mageed et al., 2020) and MARBERT (Abdul-Mageed et al., 2020). The achieved performances on the development dataset showed that MARBERT outperforms all of the previously mentioned models overall, either on the three subtasks. In addition, we used the Quasi-recurrent neural networks (QRNN) (Stosic et al., 2016) model combined with MARBERT to achieve the best performances.

HS Detection tasks in Arabic are challenging ones because of the lack of the labelled data and the complexity of the Arabic language (Mulki et al., 2019; Haddad et al., 2019). In addition, Hate Speech is highly dependent on the culture, political and religious background and other aspects like Arabic dialects that are different from the Modern Standard Arabic (MSA). As the provided dataset is mainly based on dialect used in the area located in the Eastern Mediterranean, we used the Levantine Hate Speech and Abusive (L-HSAB) (Mulki et al., 2019) Twitter dataset as extra resources that we added to the provided training dataset.

Examples labelled labelled as normal, offensive, and hate from the OSACT Fine-Grained Hate Speech Detection dataset are presented in Table 1.

The paper is structured as follows: Section 2 provides a description of the OSACT Fine-Grained Hate Speech Detection dataset, the used external resource and the pre-processing step. Section 3 and section 4 describe the used pre-trained models and the quasi-recurrent neural network. Section 5 presents our submitted system description. Section 6 presents our development and test results compared to the baseline results provided by OSACT2022 Shared Tasks on Fine-Grained Hate Speech Detection on Arabic Twitter. Section 7 and 8 present the discussion and the conclusion with points to possible directions for future work.

2. Data Description

The provided training dataset of the OSACT Fine-Grained Hate Speech Detection task (Mubarak et al., 2022) is about 13k tweets, labelled with the 6 Hate Speech types: race/ethnicity/nationality, religion/belief, ideology, disability/disease, social class, and gender. 35% of the tweets are offensive and 11% are hate speech as shown in Table 2.

2.1. External Resources and Pre-processing

Levantine Hate Speech and Abusive (L-HSAB) dataset is a publicly available hate and abusive speech dataset collected from twitter and labeled with 3 types: 468 Hate speech, 1728 Offensive speech and 3650 Normal speech. In order to increase the size of the provided datasets, we manually relabelled samples from the L-HSAB (Mulki et al., 2019) and the samples have been used as extra resource.

Label	Example
Normal	بوين الحش ؟اذا فهمته هو واشكاله ان زمن جل
Offensive	هيلق و جحلط غير كذا مافي
Hate	شغالتك هي من حرر الكويت

Table 1: Examples from the OSACT Fine-Grained Hate Speech Detection dataset.

Type	Train	Dev.	Total
Offensive	3172	404	3576
Hate - Race	260	28	288
Hate - Religion	27	4	31
Hate - Ideology	144	14	158
Hate - Disability	0	1	1
Hate - Social Class	72	10	82
Hate - Gender	456	52	508
Normal	5715	866	6581

Table 2: Provided datasets Statistics.

After adding L-HSAB, we preformed multiple re-sampling strategies. Mainly focusing on over-sampling the minority type and under-sampling the majority type to prevent the model from over-fitting. Table 3 presents statistics of the final dataset used in our three subtasks submissions.

Type	Train	Dev	Total
Offensive	4155 (+984)	404	4559
Hate - Race	1644 (+1384)	28	439
Hate - Religion	64 (+37)	4	68
Hate - Ideology	195 (+51)	14	209
Hate - Disability	5 (+5)	1	6
Hate - Social Class	78 (+6)	10	88
Hate - Gender	471 (+15)	52	523
Normal	5715 (+0)	866	6581

Table 3: Final dataset statistics used in our three subtasks submissions.

2.2. Pre-Processing

Several pre-processing pipelines from intensive strategies like translating emojis to fairly light pre-processing and removing the English tokens were experimented with. The best performances were achieved when:

1. Removing all non Arabic tokens, including ones like USER, URL, $< LF >$. Emojis were also removed.
2. Normalizing all the hashtags by simply decomposing them.
3. Removing white spaces.

Table 4 presents examples before and after the pre-processing step.

3. Pre-trained Models

Different pre-trained models were used in order to achieve the best results when fine-tuning it in a multi-task fashion.

3.1. mT5

mT5 (Xue et al., 2020) is a massive multilingual pre-trained text-to-text transformer with 57B tokens Arabic tokens gather from 53M Arabic pages. The model leverages a unified text-to-text format and scale to attain state-of-the-art results on a wide variety of NLP tasks.

3.2. AraBERT

AraBERT (V2) (Antoun et al., 2020), is a BERT based model for Modern Standard Arabic Language understanding, trained on 70M sentences from several public Arabic datasets and news websites. It was fine-tuned on 3 tasks: Sequence Classification, Named Entity Recognition and Question Answering. It was reported to achieve state-of-the-art performances even on Arabic dialects after fine-tuning by (Abu Farha and Magdy, 2020).

3.3. ARBERT

ARBERT (Abdul-Mageed et al., 2020) is also a Bert based model trained on 61GB of Modern Standard Arabic text (6.5B tokens) gathered from books, news articles, crawled data and Wikipedia.

3.4. MARBERT

MARBERT (Abdul-Mageed et al., 2020) is a large-scale pretrained language model using the BERT base's architecture. MARBERT is trained on on 128 GB of tweets from various Arabic dialects containing at least 3 Arabic words. With very light preprocessing the tweets were almost kept at their initial state to retain a faithful representation of the naturally occurring text.

4. Quasi-recurrent Neural Network

Quasi-recurrent neural network (QRNN) (Stosic et al., 2016) represents an architecture that combines the sequential manner of treating the input tokens from Recurrent Neural Networks (RNNs) and the parallel processing fashion of Convolutional Neural Networks (CNNs) to allow a longer term dependency window while also addressing several issues faced when using both architectures separately. Stacked QRNNs are reported to have a better predictive accuracy than stacked LSTMs of the same hidden size. Figure 1 represents details of the QRNN architecture.

Before Pre-processing	After Pre-processing
#بكل_عنف_وقوة	بكل عنف و قوة
☺ ☺ URL وصارت فطاير البقالات غذاء صحي	وصارت فطاير البقالات غذاء صحي
☹ لا اثق القلوب متقلبة لا تثبت على حال RT USER	لا اثق القلوب متقلبة لا تثبت على حال

Table 4: Examples before and after pre-processing.

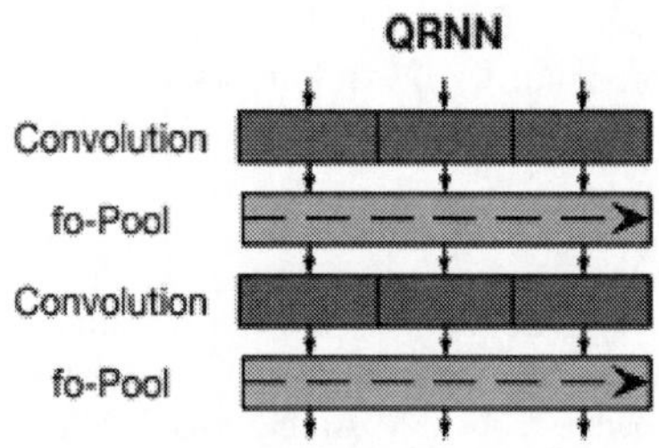

Figure 1: QRNN architecture.(Stosic et al., 2016)

5. System Description

The final submitted system is represented as in Figure 6.

5.1. Shared Layer

Preliminary results on the development dataset showed that a fine-tuned MARBERT achieved the best performances compared to the other language models. Hence, MARBERT was used as the shared part of the QRNN model and we focused our efforts on better squeezing out its performance by experimenting with different hyper-parameters values.

5.2. Subtasks Specific Layers

All of the three subtasks specific layers were essentially the same:

1. 1-dimensional convolution neural network with 128 units and a kernel size of 3.
2. 0.3 Dropout layer.
3. Bidirectional QRNN with 256 units.
4. 0.2 Dropout layers.
5. Dense layer with a Relu activation function and 64 units.

The architectures used for each subtask:

- Subask A: a dense layer with a Sigmoid activation function, 1 unit, and a threshold of 0.75.
- Subtask B and subtask C: a dense layer with a Softmax activation function and 7 units.

Given the fact that multi-task models learn better from closely related tasks, we added another output to penalize the model when it mistakes offensive comments for hate speech. This gave a 0.04 performance boost mainly for subtask C without much affecting other tasks.

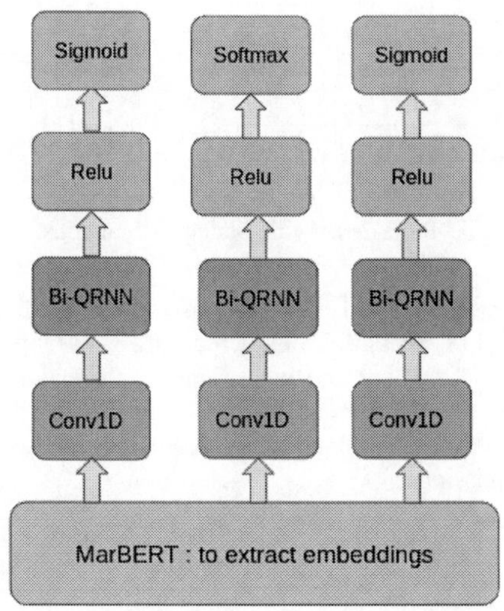

Figure 2: Submitted System Architecture.

6. Results

The submitted model was trained with a total of 16 epochs. The first 6 epochs were only used to warm up the QRNN layers, we froze MARBERT and trained them with a learning rate of 10-3, Adam optimizer, and a batch size of 350. As for the loss functions, we experimented with focal loss and categorical/binary crossentropy and submitted with categorical/binary crossentropy. In the last 10 epochs where we unfroze MARBERT, we lowered the learning rate to 10-4 keeping the same configuration.

Baseline results provided by OSACT2022 Shared Tasks on Fine-Grained Hate Speech Detection on Arabic Twitter (Mubarak et al., 2022) are presented in Table 5.

Subtask	Accuracy	Precision	Recall	F1-macro
Subtask A	0.651	0.325	0.5	0.394
Subtask B	0.893	0.447	0.5	0.472
Subtask C	0.893	0.128	0.143	0.135

Table 5: Baseline results on the development dataset.

Our results on the development datset with and without extra resources are presented in Table 6 where * refers to results after adding the extra resources.

Subtask	Accuracy	Precision	Recall	F1-macro
Subtask A*	0.825	0.855	0.812	0.845
Subtask A	0.848	0.808	0.834	0.819
Subtask B*	0.943	0.824	0.823	0.820
Subtask B	0.930	0.792	0.778	0.784
Subtask C*	0.931	0.558	0.559	0.555
Subtask C	0.918	0.382	0.480	0.734

Table 6: Results on the development dataset without and with using extra resources.

the confusion matrix for Subtask A on the validation is presented in figure 3

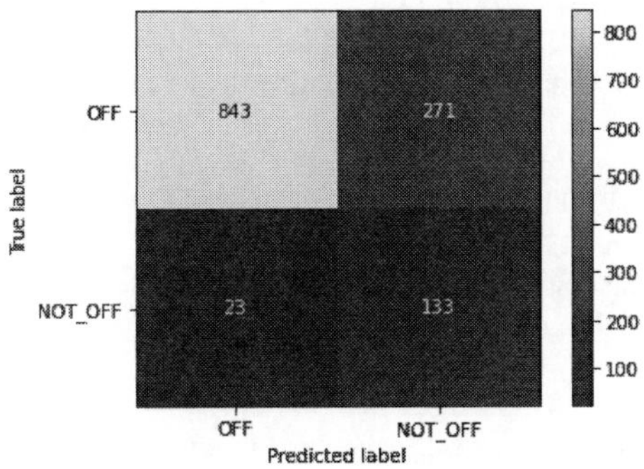

Figure 3: SubtaskA confusion matrix.

the confusion matrix for Subtask B on the validation is presented in figure 4

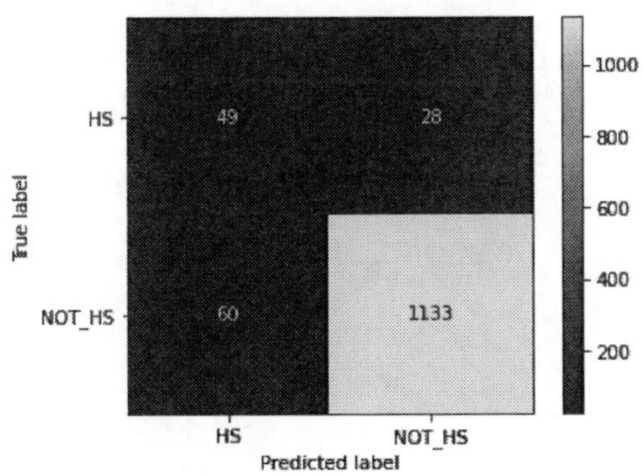

Figure 4: SubtaskB confusion matrix.

the confusion matrix for Subtask C on the validation is presented in figure 5

Our results on the test dataset are presented in Table 7.

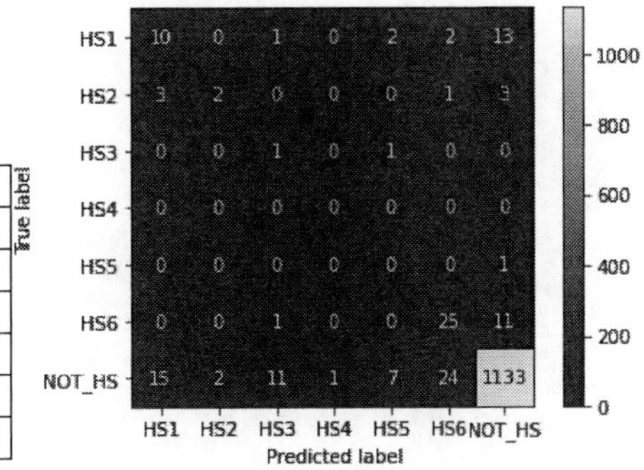

Figure 5: SubtaskC confusion matrix.

Subtask	Accuracy	Precision	Recall	F1-macro
Subtask A	0.854	0.841	0.837	0.839
Subtask B	0.941	0.869	0.801	0.831
Subtask C	0.919	0.548	0.531	0.528

Table 7: Results on the test dataset.

7. Discussion

Different language models were used in this work. However, MARBERT achieved the best results. This was the case because it was pre-trained on various Arabic dialects and therefore works better with dialectal data.

In addition, the data imbalance decreased the model performance. In fact, the training data set presents skewed class proportions. Relating to offensiveness, "Not Offensive" is the most frequent value with a count of 5,715 labels over a total of 8887. As for hate speech, the majority of samples fall under "Not Hate Speech" with a count of 7928 over 8887.

Category	Top Label	Label Frequency
OFF Label	NOT OFF	5715
HS label	NOT HS	7928
Vulgar label	NOT VLG	8753
Violence label	NOT VIO	8826

Table 8: Top labels and their frequencies in provided the training dataset.

The data imbalance in provided the training dataset further illustrated in Figure 7 .

Indeed, class proportions vary substantially, especially among hate speech classes. As illustrated in Table 2, there are 27 instances of "HS2" (i.e. hate speech based on religion) versus 456 instances of "HS6" (i.e. hate speech based on gender). In particular, there are no instances of "HS4" (i.e. hate speech based on disability). The data imbalance problem has a substantial effect on subtask C (i.e. multi-class classification) and explains the resulting relatively-low macro-averaged F1 score. Indeed, it stems from limited data relating to (from least to most available) hate speech based on disability/disease, hate speech based on religion/belief, and

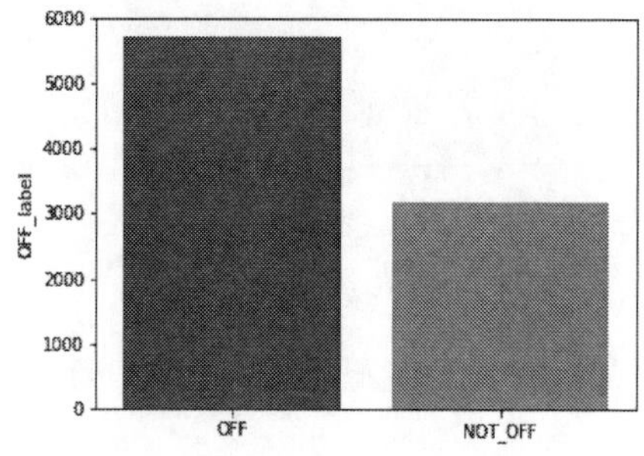

Figure 6: Offensive speech statistics.

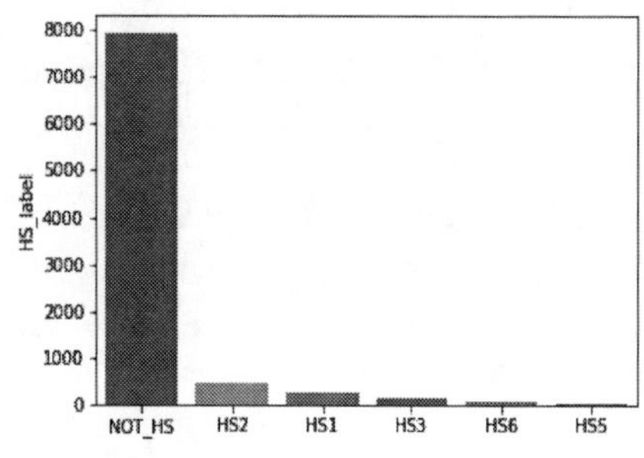

Figure 7: Hate speech statistics.

hate speech based on social class.

8. Conclusion

In this paper, we demonstrated how promising Multi-Tasking is for Hate & Abusive speech detection by fine-tuning the pre-trained model MARBERT with quasi-recurrent neural networks. Despite the small sized annotated data and the presence of different Arabic dialects, the model achieved satisfactory results.

With respect to the model, further work should explore meta-learning, Focal loss, semi-supervised learning, and ways to make use of violent and vulgar labels in the multi-task architecture.

As for the data, further work should focus on the need for disability data collection, disaggregation, and analysis. Indeed, persons with disabilities and their representative organizations must be at the core of data collection. The same goes for religious minorities in order to address the data gap.

9. Bibliographical References

Abdul-Mageed, M., Elmadany, A., and Nagoudi, E. M. B. (2020). Arbert & marbert: deep bidirectional transformers for arabic. *arXiv preprint arXiv:2101.01785*.

Abu Farha, I. and Magdy, W. (2020). Multitask learning for Arabic offensive language and hate-speech detection. In *Proceedings of the 4th Workshop on Open-Source Arabic Corpora and Processing Tools, with a Shared Task on Offensive Language Detection*, pages 86–90, Marseille, France, May. European Language Resource Association.

Antoun, W., Baly, F., and Hajj, H. (2020). Arabert: Transformer-based model for arabic language understanding. *arXiv preprint arXiv:2003.00104*.

Haddad, H., Mulki, H., and Oueslati, A. (2019). T-hsab: A tunisian hate speech and abusive dataset. In *Proceedings of 7th International Conference on Arabic Language*, pages 1251–263, Nancy, France. Springer Nature.

Mubarak, H., Hassan, S., and Chowdhury, S. A. (2022). Emojis as anchors to detect arabic offensive language and hate speech. *arXiv preprint arXiv:2201.06723*.

Mulki, H., Haddad, H., Ali, C. B., and Alshabani, H. (2019). L-hsab: A levantine twitter dataset for hate speech and abusive language. In *Proceedings of the third workshop on abusive language online*, pages 111–118.

Schmidt, A. and Wiegand, M. (2017). A survey on hate speech detection using natural language processing. In *Proceedings of the Fifth International Workshop on Natural Language Processing for Social Media*, pages 1–10, Valencia, Spain, April. Association for Computational Linguistics.

Stosic, D., Stosic, D., Zanchettin, C., Ludermir, T., and Stosic, B. (2016). Qrnn: q-generalized random neural network. *IEEE transactions on neural networks and learning systems*, 28(2):383–390.

Xue, L., Constant, N., Roberts, A., Kale, M., Al-Rfou, R., Siddhant, A., Barua, A., and Raffel, C. (2020). mt5: A massively multilingual pre-trained text-to-text transformer. *arXiv preprint arXiv:2010.11934*.

Proceedings of the OSACT 2022 Workshop @LREC2022, pages 181–185
Marseille, 20 June 2022

UPV at the Arabic Hate Speech 2022 Shared Task: Offensive Language and Hate Speech Detection using Transformers and Ensemble Models

Angel Felipe Magnossão de Paula[1], Paolo Rosso[1], Imene Bensalem[2,3], Wajdi Zaghouani[4]
[1]Universitat Politècnica de València,
[2]MISC-Lab – Constantine 2 University, [3]ESCF de Constantine,
[4]Hamad Bin Khalifa University
adepau@doctor.upv.es, prosso@dsic.upv.es, ibensalem@escf-constantine.dz, wzaghouani@hbku.edu.qa

Abstract

This paper describes our participation in the shared task Fine-Grained Hate Speech Detection on Arabic Twitter at the 5th Workshop on Open-Source Arabic Corpora and Processing Tools (OSACT). The shared task is divided into three detection subtasks: (i) Detect whether a tweet is offensive or not; (ii) Detect whether a tweet contains hate speech or not; and (iii) Detect the fine-grained type of hate speech (race, religion, ideology, disability, social class, and gender). It is an effort toward the goal of mitigating the spread of offensive language and hate speech in Arabic-written content on social media platforms. To solve the three subtasks, we employed six different transformer versions: AraBert, AraElectra, Albert-Arabic, AraGPT2, mBert, and XLM-Roberta. We experimented with models based on encoder and decoder blocks and models exclusively trained on Arabic and also on several languages. Likewise, we applied two ensemble methods: Majority vote and Highest sum. Our approach outperformed the official baseline in all the subtasks, not only considering F1-macro results but also accuracy, recall, and precision. The results suggest that the Highest sum is an excellent approach to encompassing transformer output to create an ensemble since this method offered at least top-two F1-macro values across all the experiments performed on development and test data.

Keywords: Deep Learning, Transformers, Offensive Language, Hate Speech, Arabic, Twitter

1. Introduction

The detection of offensive language and hate speech is becoming an important element when it comes to reducing the spread of the toxicity online. Despite some efforts done to address this issue, the automatic detection of hate speech is still considered a challenge, especially when it comes to detecting hate speech written in low-resources languages and varieties such as the several Arabic dialects used in social media nowadays. In this paper, we present our approach to offensive language and hate speech detection for the Arabic language using transformers and ensemble models. To train our models, we used the data set shared by the organizers of the Arabic Hate Speech 2022 shared task on Fine-Grained Hate Speech Detection on Arabic Twitter (Mubarak et al., 2022).

We address the problem of detecting hate speech and offensive language by applying six different transformer models and two ensemble methods. Within the transformers, we tried models based on encoder and decoder blocks and models exclusively trained on Arabic and others trained on several languages. Furthermore, we also combine the transformer results employing the Majority vote and Highest sum ensemble methods. Our code is open and available on Github [1].

The rest of the paper is structured as follows. Section 2 provides an overview on the problem of hate speech and offensive language detection in Arabic. Sections 3 and 4 present the task details and the used dataset. The created models are described in Section 5. Finally, we wrap up our paper with the discussion of the results and some conclusions.

2. Hate Speech and Offensive Language Detection in Arabic

Literature on the identification of hate speech and offensive language in Arabic deals with the two following main tasks:

(i) The identification of the hateful or offensive language. Most of the works in this task propose *binary classification* solutions able to distinguish between two classes: (Hate and Not hate) or (Offensive and Not offensive). See, for example, the methods described in (Albadi et al., 2018; Guellil et al., 2020; Mubarak et al., 2020). Some works proposed datasets that allow addressing the problem as a *multi-class classification* where the hateful or offensive discourse has to be distinguished not only from the clean text but also from other similar discourses categorized as obscene (Mubarak et al., 2017), vulgar (Chowdhury et al., 2020), abusive (Haddad et al., 2019; Mulki et al., 2019), or disrespectful (Ousidhoum et al., 2019).

(ii) The fine-grained categorization of hate speech according to its type or target. To the best of our knowledge, only a few works addressed this task in the Arabic language. Below, we summarized the works that employed Arabic datasets involving fine-grained categories of hate speech.

[1] https://github.com/AngelFelipeMP/Transformers-for-Arabic-hate-speech-and-offensive-language

Mulki and Ghanem (2021) addressed the problem of detecting misogyny, i.e., hatred against women. The authors built a dataset composed of 6550 tweets in the Levantine dialect. They collected them from the accounts of female journalists who were active during the Lebanon protest of October 2019. The tweets have been labelled as misogynistic or not. In addition, seven categories of misogyny have been used to label the misogynistic tweets (for instance, sexual harassment, stereotyping, threat of violence, etc). The authors employed the dataset in a set of experiments where the best results in misogyny identification and categorization, respectively, have been obtained by using AraBert and an ensemble technique combining the predictions of Naïve Bayes, SVM, and Logistic Regression classifiers.

Ousidhoum et al. (2019) created a multilingual dataset comprising more than 3000 tweets in Arabic among others in French and English. Tweets are labelled with five tags indicating (1) the hostility type i.e., whether the tweet is abusive, hateful, offensive, disrespectful, fearful or normal (2) whether the tweet is direct or indirect hate speech, (3) the personal attribute targeted by the hostility such as the origin, the disability, and the gender (4) the target group such as Arabs, refugees, Christians, women among others (5) the feeling that the annotator gets when reading the hateful tweet. The authors used the dataset to evaluate five tasks corresponding to the above five label sets. Apart from the task of classifying tweets as direct or indirect, which is a binary classification, the four other tasks are multi-class classification tasks. The conducted experiments compare a traditional approach based on logistic regression and bag-of-words features with deep learning approaches based on bidirectional LSTM trained under multi-/mono- task and language settings. The results show the outperformance of the deep learning approaches in most of the multi-class classification tasks.

Albadi et al. (2018) created a dataset of 6000 tweets involving religious hate speech referring to the different beliefs in the Middle East. Tweets are labelled as hateful or not. The dataset has been annotated as well with the religious groups targeted by the hateful tweets (Muslims, Jews, Christians, Atheists, Sunnis, Shia, other). The inter-annotator agreement concerning the target-group labels was only 55%. These labels are not available in the published dataset, but have been leveraged by the authors to obtain statistics on the religious groups most targeted by hate speech. The authors conducted binary-classification experiments to identify hateful tweets using three approaches. The first approach is lexicon-based. It consists in summing the sentiment scores of the tweet words. The second approach applies traditional machine learning to character n-grams features. The third approach relies on deep learning. It uses the GRU-based RNN with pre-trained embeddings. Results showed the outperformance of the deep learning approach.

To sum up, the existing approaches to hateful/offensive language identification and categorization use a range of traditional machine learning classifiers (such as SVM, Logistic Regression, Naïve Bayes ...etc) and deep learning methods including transformers, such as AraBert and multilingual Bert (mBert). Some works combine different methods in multitask learning or ensemble settings (Husain and Uzuner, 2021). While the performance of the identification task is promising (most notably, when it comes to a binary classification), the categorization task is still challenging.

3. Task Description

The task presented in this paper is another iteration of the previous similar tasks presented in OSACT 2020. This year, the OSACT 2022 has three subtasks to identify and categorize hate speech in the Arabic language given that the dataset was collected from Twitter with a large amount written in dialectal Arabic. The goal of the first subtask A is to detect whether a tweet is offensive or not with two possible labels: OFF (Offensive) or NOT OFF (Not Offensive).

The second subtask B is similar to task A but with a focus on hate speech. The two possible labels are HS (Hate Speech) or NOT HS (Not Hate Speech). According to the organizers, subtask B is more challenging given the low number of tweets falling into the hate speech class. Finally, the last task is subtask C in which the systems are expected to detect hate speech on fine-grained types this time. The organizers provided six possible labels for this subtask: race, religion, ideology, disability, social class, and gender. The first one is HS1 and is used to label hate speech targeting a specific race. HS2 is reserved for any kind of religious hate targeting either religion or religious groups. HS3 on the other hand is reserved for hate expressions targeting ideologies, while HS4 is reserved for expressions used against people with disabilities. Finally, HS5 and HS6 are the labels for hate targeting people based on their social classes or gender, respectively. The three tasks will be evaluated through the submissions made to the dedicated shared task platform (Codalab).

4. Dataset

The annotated dataset shared by the organizers of this shared task was collected from Twitter. The dataset can be considered among the largest publicly available annotated Arabic datasets released so far for offensiveness, along with fine-grained hate speech types, vulgarity, and violence. The annotation process went through a rigorous process, wherein each tweet is annotated by three annotators to ensure the quality of the annotation. In case of disagreement between the annotators, the label with the majority is taken into consideration. The organizers used a crowdsourcing platform to annotate their data for offensiveness and to classify each tweet into one of the hate speech types (religion, race, disability, ideology, social class, and gender). Moreover, the data was annotated for containing or not vulgar language or violent terms.

The dataset contains around 13K tweets in total, with 35% annotated as offensive and only 11% marked as hate speech. Furthermore, the tweets annotated as vulgar and violent represent only around 1.5% and 0.7% of the dataset, respectively. According to the organizers, the provided dataset can be considered one of the highest in terms of the percentages of offensive language and hate speech. They claimed also that it is not biased toward specific topics, dialects, or genres since its creation did not rely on specific keywords. The dataset is split into 70% for training, 10% for development, and 20% for testing.

5. Transformer Models

This section introduces the transformer models applied to solve the three OSACT 2022 subtasks. Table 1 shows their main features: (i) transformer's version, (ii) model size, (iii) originating block, and (iv) trained input language

Transformer models are massive deep learning architectures constructed for dealing with natural language processing tasks (Vaswani et al., 2017; Ravichandiran, 2021; Lin et al., 2021). These models are trained, in an unsupervised way, on enormous datasets by performing different tasks, such as mask language modelling, next sequence prediction, and many others (Devlin et al., 2019; Mohammed and Ali, 2021).

Usually, the transformers are available in three different sizes: base, medium, and large. The term size is related to the number of trainable parameters in the model. We used the large size for Albert-Arabic, and, for all the other transformers, we used the base version due to computational constraints.

The original transformer model designed by Google researchers (Vaswani et al., 2017) encompasses encoder and decoder blocks. However, the new versions, currently, contain only either one encoder or one decoder block. We used four models based only on the encoder block: AraBert (Antoun et al., 2020), AraElectra (Antoun et al., 2021a), mBert, and XLM-Roberta (Conneau et al., 2020), and one based only on the decoder block, AraGT2 (Antoun et al., 2021b).

There are transformer models trained on different languages. AraBert, AraElectra, Albert-Arabic, and AraGT2 were trained on a collection of Arabic datasets (Ravichandiran, 2021). mBert and XLM-Roberta belong to a subclass of transformers that we call multilingual. mBert was trained on a dataset including texts written in 104 different languages, and XLM-Roberta was trained on one dataset gathering documents from 100 different languages.

On the top of each transformer model, we added a linear layer classifier which computes a probability distribution based on the possible classes in the subtask, which varied among the three subtasks.

Version	Size	Block	Language
AraBert AraElectra	base	Encoder	Arabic
Albert-Arabic	large		
AraGPT2	base	Decoder	
mBert XLM-Roberta	base	Encoder	Multilingual

Table 1: Transformers used for the OSACT 2022 tasks

6. Results and Discussion

This section explains the hyper-parameter selection and the performance of the models through the validation and test. In addition, we present how we combine the transformer results by means of two ensembles methods: (i) Majority vote; and (ii) Highest sum.

We were concerned about the number of training epochs, learning rate, and dropout percentage for the transformer's fine-tuning. Therefore, we applied a 5-fold cross-validation on the training data to find suitable parameters for each model based on the OSACT 2022 official metric, F1-macro. Table 2 shows the best number of training epochs for the transformers in each subtask. Coincidentally, the appropriate dropout and learning rates found are the same for all the models, respectively equal to 0.3 and 0.00005. We adopted a max length of 64 tokens and a batch size of 32 samples during all experiments.

	Epochs		
Model	**Subtask A**	**Subtask B**	**Subtask C**
AraBert	5	4	4
AraElectra	4	2	5
Albert-Arabic	2	4	5
AraGPT2	5	5	5
mBert	3	5	5
XLM-Roberta	5	1	4

Table 2: Transformer's suitable number of epochs

OSACT 2022 allowed only two submissions of the predictions on the test data. Thus, we trained the transformers on the training data and evaluated them on the development data to find the two best models for each subtask. In addition, we applied two ensemble methods: Majority vote and Highest sum. The Majority vote selects the most predicted class among the transformers, and if there is a tie, it randomly selects one of the classes among the tied classes. The Highest sum aggregates the output values by each transformer separately for each class and selects the class with the highest sum. Table 3 shows the F1-macro results obtained by the two best models in each subtask on the development data.

In order to make the final predictions on the test data for all the subtasks, we applied the two models that obtained the best results on the development data. However, the inferences for subtask C were dependent on the inferences for subtask B. Considering this fact, we must detect whether a tweet has hate speech or not

Subtask	Model	Accuracy	F1-macro
A	**Highest sum**	**0.837**	**0.814**
	AraBert	0.829	0.808
B	**AraElectra**	0.932	**0.795**
	Highest sum	**0.938**	0.794
C	**AraBert**	**0.979**	**0.582**
	Highest sum	0.981	0.513

Table 3: Results of our two best models in the development data

(subtask B), and only in case it belongs to the positive class we detect the type of hate speech (subtask C). Therefore, we used subtask B predictions from our best model to pass the tweets detected with hate content to the subtask C models, with the aim of identifying the type of hate speech in the tweets. Table 4 shows our final results on the test data and the OSACT 2022 baseline for each subtask.

Subtask	Model	F1-macro	Accuracy	Precision	Recall
A	**AraBert**	**0.827**	**0.841**	**0.824**	**0.831**
	Highest sum	0.819	0.837	0.821	0.818
	Baseline	0.394	0.651	0.325	0.500
B	**Highest sum**	**0.792**	**0.932**	**0.858**	**0.751**
	AraElectra	0.757	0.925	0.845	0.711
	Baseline	0.472	0.893	0.447	0.500
C	**AraBert**	**0.423**	**0.920**	**0.542**	**0.369**
	Highest sum	0.325	0.917	0.382	0.294
	Baseline	0.135	0.893	0.128	0.143

Table 4: Final results in the test data

The differences between the results of our worst models and the baselines for the F1-macro are 0.425 subtask A, 0.285 subtask B, and 0.190 subtask C. Thus, we can conclude that all our models (even the worst ones) obtained results significantly superior to the baselines for the OSACT 2022 official metric. The results also suggest that the Highest sum is suitable for aggregating transformers' outputs to create an ensemble. It offered at least the top-two F1-macro across development and test data experiments.

Looking again at table 4, we can see a discrepancy between accuracy and F1-macro for tasks B and C. The F1-macro is computed as the unweighted mean of the F1-score calculated for each class. The recall is one of the factors that compose the F1-score calculation, which is sensitive to false negatives. We hypothesize that because, since the number of positive samples for task B is low - only 11% -, the models achieved high accuracy but had an increased number of false negatives which degraded the F1-macro. Thus, because of the imbalanced proportion of the classes in the training data, the model overfits the distribution and ended up tending to select more the negative class. Task C was affected by the same phenomenon as mentioned for task B, and, besides that, it also suffered a decrease in the F1-macro results because of the multiple labelling of the target variable.

7. Conclusions

In this paper, we proposed to solve the problems of offensive language detection, hate speech detection, and fine-grained hate speech classification by employing six different transformer versions: Arabert, AraElectra, Albert-Arabic, AraGPT2, mBert, and XLM-Roberta. In addition, we also employed two ensemble methods: Majority vote and Highest sum. Our approach outperformed the official OSACT 2020 baselines in all the subtasks.

8. Acknowledgements

This publication was made possible by NPRP grant 13S-0206-200281 (Resources and Applications for Detecting and Classifying Polarized and Hate Speech in Arabic Social Media) from the Qatar National Research Fund (a member of Qatar Foundation). The findings achieved herein are solely the responsibility of the authors.

9. Bibliographical References

Albadi, N., Kurdi, M., and Mishra, S. (2018). Are they our brothers? analysis and detection of religious hate speech in the Arabic twittersphere. In *2018 IEEE/ACM International Conference on Advances in Social Networks Analysis and Mining (ASONAM)*, Barcelona. IEEE.

Antoun, W., Baly, F., and Hajj, H. (2020). AraBERT: Transformer-based model for Arabic language understanding. In *Proceedings of the 4th Workshop on Open-Source Arabic Corpora and Processing Tools, with a Shared Task on Offensive Language Detection*, pages 9–15, Marseille, France, May. European Language Resource Association (ELRA).

Antoun, W., Baly, F., and Hajj, H. (2021a). AraELECTRA: Pre-training text discriminators for Arabic language understanding. In *Proceedings of the Sixth Arabic Natural Language Processing Workshop*, pages 191–195, Kyiv, Ukraine (Virtual), April. Association for Computational Linguistics (ACL).

Antoun, W., Baly, F., and Hajj, H. (2021b). AraGPT2: Pre-trained transformer for Arabic language generation. In *Proceedings of the Sixth Arabic Natural Language Processing Workshop*, pages 196–207, Kyiv, Ukraine (Virtual), April. Association for Computational Linguistics (ACL).

Chowdhury, S. A., Mubarak, H., Abdelali, A., Jung, S.-G., Jansen, B. J., and Salminen, J. (2020). A multi-platform arabic news comment dataset for offensive language detection. In *Proceedings of the 12th Language Resources and Evaluation Conference*, pages 6203–6212, Marseille. European Language Resources Association (ELRA).

Conneau, A., Khandelwal, K., Goyal, N., Chaudhary, V., Wenzek, G., Guzmán, F., Grave, É., Ott, M., Zettlemoyer, L., and Stoyanov, V. (2020). Unsupervised cross-lingual representation learning at scale. In *Proceedings of the 58th Annual Meeting of the*

Association for Computational Linguistics, pages 8440–8451, Online. Association for Computational Linguistics (ACL).

Devlin, J., Chang, M.-W., Lee, K., and Toutanova, K. (2019). BERT: Pre-training of deep bidirectional transformers for language understanding. In *Proceedings of the 2019 Conference of the North American Chapter of the Association for Computational Linguistics: Human Language Technologies, Volume 1 (Long and Short Papers)*, pages 4171–4186, Minneapolis, Minnesota, June. Association for Computational Linguistics (ACL).

Guellil, I., Adeel, A., Azouaou, F., Chennoufi, S., Maafi, H., and Hamitouche, T. (2020). Detecting hate speech against politicians in arabic community on social media. *International Journal of Web Information Systems*, 16(3):295–313.

Haddad, H., Mulki, H., and Oueslati, A. (2019). T-HSAB: A tunisian hate speech and abusive dataset. In *International Conference on Arabic Language Processing*, pages 251–263. Springer.

Husain, F. and Uzuner, O. (2021). A survey of offensive language detection for the Arabic language. *ACM Transactions on Asian and Low-Resource Language Information Processing (TALLIP)*, 20(1):1–44.

Lin, T., Wang, Y., Liu, X., and Qiu, X. (2021). A survey of transformers. *arXiv preprint arXiv:2106.04554*.

Mohammed, A. H. and Ali, A. H. (2021). Survey of BERT (bidirectional encoder representation transformer) types. *Journal of Physics: Conference Series*, 1963(1):012173.

Mubarak, H., Darwish, K., and Magdy, W. (2017). Abusive language detection on Arabic social media. In *Proceedings of the First Workshop on Abusive Language Online*, pages 52–56, Vancouver. Association for Computational Linguistics (ACL).

Mubarak, H., Darwish, K., Magdy, W., and Al-Khalifa, H. (2020). Overview of OSACT4 arabic offensive language detection shared task. In *Proceedings of the 4th Workshop on Open-Source Arabic Corpora and Processing Tools, with a Shared Task on Offensive Language Detection. Language Resources and Evaluation Conference (LREC 2020)*, pages 48–52, Marseille. European Language Resources Association (ELRA).

Mubarak, H., Hassan, S., and Chowdhury, S. A. (2022). Emojis as anchors to detect arabic offensive language and hate speech. *arXiv preprint arXiv:2201.06723*.

Mulki, H. and Ghanem, B. (2021). Let-Mi: An arabic levantine twitter dataset for misogynistic language. In *Proceedings of the Sixth Arabic Natural Language Processing Workshop*, pages 154–163, Kyiv.

Mulki, H., Haddad, H., Bechikh Ali, C., and Alshabani, H. (2019). L-HSAB: A levantine twitter dataset for hate speech and abusive language. In *Proceedings of the Third Workshop on Abusive Language Online*, pages 111–118, Florence. Association for Computational Linguistics (ACL).

Ousidhoum, N., Lin, Z., Zhang, H., Song, Y., and Yeung, D.-Y. (2019). Multilingual and multi-aspect hate speech analysis. In *Proceedings of the 2019 Conference on Empirical Methods in Natural Language Processing and the 9th International Joint Conference on Natural Language Processing (EMNLP-IJCNLP)*, pages 4675–4684, Stroudsburg, PA, USA. Association for Computational Linguistics (ACL).

Ravichandiran, S. (2021). *Getting Started with Google BERT: Build and train state-of-the-art natural language processing models using BERT*. Packt Publishing Ltd.

Vaswani, A., Shazeer, N., Parmar, N., Uszkoreit, J., Jones, L., Gomez, A. N., Kaiser, Ł., and Polosukhin, I. (2017). Attention is all you need. *Advances in neural information processing systems*, 30.

Proceedings of the OSACT 2022 Workshop @LREC2022, pages 186–193
Marseille, 20 June 2022

Meta AI at Arabic Hate Speech 2022: MultiTask Learning with Self-Correction for Hate Speech Classification

Badr AlKhamissi, Mona Diab
Responsible AI, Meta
Seattle, USA
{bkhmsi, mdiab}@fb.com

Abstract

In this paper, we tackle the Arabic Fine-Grained Hate Speech Detection shared task and demonstrate significant improvements over reported baselines for its three subtasks. The tasks are to predict if a tweet contains (1) *Offensive* language; and whether it is considered (2) *Hate Speech* or not and if so, then predict the (3) *Fine-Grained Hate Speech* label from one of six categories. Our final solution is an ensemble of models that employs multitask learning and a self-consistency correction method yielding 82.7% on the hate speech subtask—reflecting a 3.4% relative improvement compared to previous work.

1. Introduction

Disclaimer: *Due to the nature of this work, some examples contain offensiveness and hate speech. This does not reflect authors' values, however our aim is to help in detecting and preventing spread of such harmful content.*

The advent of online social networks have created a platform for billions of people to express their thoughts freely on the internet. This has enormous benefits for advancing culture. However, it also can be used by malicious actors to distribute misinformation and offensive content. This led to an increasing interest in the NLP community for the automatic detection of *Hate Speech* (HS) (Waseem and Hovy, 2016; Schmidt and Wiegand, 2017; Zampieri et al., 2019; MacAvaney et al., 2019; League, 2020; Vogels, 2021). Its dangers are becoming more apparent with studies showing its connection to hate crimes around the globe (Paz et al., 2020). Further, the spread of hateful content on the internet has also been linked to degenerate effects on peoples' psychological well-being (Gülaçti, 2010; Waldron, 2012).

HS is defined as any kind of abusive or offensive language (e.g. insults, threats, etc.) that expresses prejudice against a specific person or a group based on common characteristics such as race, religion or sexual orientation (Davidson et al., 2017; Mollas et al., 2020). Despite the growing body of HS research, few have focused on it in the context of the Arabic language.

Arabic is the mother tongue of more than 420M people, and is spoken in the fastest growing markets (Tinsley and Board, 2013). Arabic content is rapidly growing on the internet during the past couple of years (Abdelali et al., 2021). For instance, studies have shown that there are more than 27 million tweets per day in the Arab region (Alshehri et al., 2018).

In this work, we focus on the Arabic language by participating in the three subtasks of the *Arabic Fine-Grained Hate Speech Detection* shared task (Mubarak et al., 2022). The three subtasks use the same dataset from (Mubarak et al., 2022) (see Section 3 for more details.) The goal of the first subtask is to detect whether a tweet is offensive or not, while the second subtask focuses on HS detection. The third subtask further classifies a HS post into one of six fine-grained categories: Race/Ethnicity/Nationality, Religion/Belief, Ideology, Disability/Disease, Social Class, and Gender. Table 1 shows an example with its corresponding label for each subtask. An offensive post is not necessarily HS, while a HS post is always offensive. If offensive speech is not targeting an individual or a group based on common characteristics, then it is not HS.

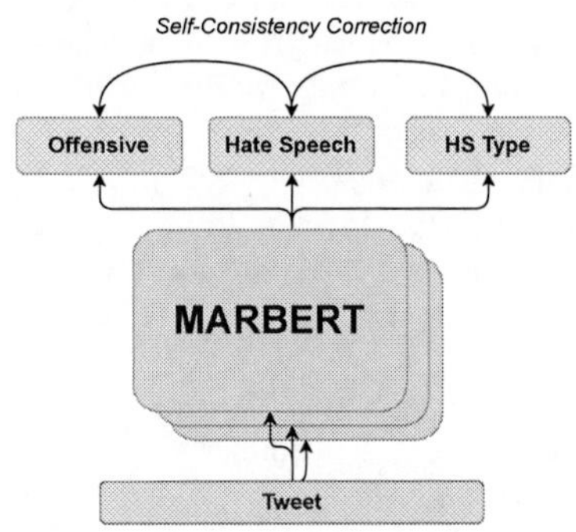

Figure 1: **System Architecture** The input tweet is encoded using a fine-tuned MARBERT model and the output embedding is given to 3 task-specific classifiers. The final prediction is computed using an ensemble of those models.

The contributions of this paper are as follows: (1) We present a solution that outperforms the baseline models of (Mubarak et al., 2022) on every reported metric; (2) We propose the self-consistency correction method that improves the fine-grained HS subtask even further; (3) We conduct an ablation study and further analysis illustrating the importance of multi-task learning for Arabic HS detection.

Class	Example
Clean	1. لن تحصل على غدٍ افضل ما دمت تفكر بالامس (Non-Off) You won't have a better tomorrow as long you are thinking about yesterday.
Offensive	2. يلعن ابوك على هالسؤال. عساه ينقرض الكريه. (Off/Non-HS) May your father be damned for this question! I hope this fool will just wither!
Hate Speech	3. لذا القزم طلعت جايزتن له بس ماعرف يعبر (Off/HS) This dwarf got two prizes, but he does not know how to express.

Table 1: Here we show examples and their translation in English adapted from (Mubarak et al., 2022). Example 1 is non offensive (Non-Off), Example 2 is Offensive but not Hate speech (Off/Non-HS), Example 3 is offensive and hate speech (Off/HS).

2. Motivation

There has been a growing body of research in recent years for the automatic detection of offensive language and HS online (Waseem and Hovy, 2016; Davidson et al., 2017; Schmidt and Wiegand, 2017; Fortuna and Nunes, 2018; Founta et al., 2018). Studies have shown that 41% of internet users have been harassed online with a third of these cases being targeted for something related to their inherent identity such as race or sexual orientation (Vogels, 2021; League, 2020). The massive amount of content shared on social media platforms renders manual filtering out of such malicious content impossible, driving platform providers to resort to automated means for detecting hateful content. On the other hand, machine learning based methods are data hungry and require large amounts of labelled data in order to train reliable HS classification systems. Moreover, such data has been proven hard to collect especially for low-resource languages such as Arabic. For example, (Mubarak et al., 2017) show that only 1-2% of a randomly collected sample of Arabic tweets are abusive, and only a small percentage of these are considered HS. Therefore, generalizable and robust systems for detecting offensive and HS content are direly needed.

Previous work has framed this problem as a binary classification task. However, binary judgments of HS are known to be unreliable (Sanguinetti et al., 2018; Assimakopoulos et al., 2020a). Therefore, in order to collect higher quality HS datasets researchers resorted to more complex annotation schema. For example, (Sap et al., 2020; Assimakopoulos et al., 2020b) proposed to decompose a post into several subtasks (such as the HS class and group targeted) in an effort to minimize subjectivity when deciding the HS label.

Here, we leverage the task decomposed dataset provided by (Mubarak et al., 2022) to train an Arabic transformer in a multitask manner for improving the performance of fine-grained HS detection.

3. Dataset

We use the dataset from (Mubarak et al., 2022). It consists of $\sim$ 13k tweets in both Modern Standard Arabic (MSA) and Dialectal forms of Arabic (DA). It is the largest annotated corpus of Arabic tweets that is not biased towards specific topics, genres, or dialects (Mubarak et al., 2022). Each tweet was judged by 3 annotators using crowd-sourcing. Table 2 shows the number and percentages of each annotated category. The data was split into 70% for training, 10% for development, and 20% for test. The dataset has also annotations for vulgar and violent tweets representing 1.5% and 0.7% of the whole corpus, respectively, however we are not using them in this work. Moreover, one or more user mentions are reduced to `@USER`, URLs are replaced with `URL`, and empty lines in original tweets are replaced with `<LF>`. See Table 1 for an example of each annotated class.

One limitation of this dataset is that the classes are highly imbalanced. Moreover, the *Disability/Disease* subclass does not exist in the training set. There are only 3 tweets related to this category and they appear in the validation and test sets only.

Class - Subclass	# of Tweets	Percentage (%)
Clean	8,235	64.85%
Offensive	4,463	35.15%
Hate Speech	1,339	10.54%
HS - Gender	641	5.05%
HS - Race	366	2.88%
HS - Ideology	190	1.50%
HS - Social Class	101	0.80%
HS - Religion	38	0.30%
HS - Disability	3	0.02%

Table 2: **Dataset Statistics** The number and percentages of tweets as represented in the entire corpus of each annotated category used in this work as described in (Mubarak et al., 2022).[1]

[1]The percentages do not add up to 100 since all HS tweets are a subset of the offensive ones.

Subtask	Model	Accuracy	Precision	Recall	F1 Macro
OFFD	QARiB	84.0%	82.5%	82.1%	82.3%
	AraHS	**86.0%**	**84.6%**	**84.3%**	**84.5%**
HSD	QARiB	93.0%	83.0%	77.7%	80.0%
	AraHS	**94.1%**	**87.0%**	**79.5%**	**82.7%**
HSC	AraHS	92.6%	55.1%	50.8%	51.9%

Table 3: Performance on Test for each of the subtasks Offensive Detection (OFFD), Hate Speech Detection (HSD), Hate Speech Classification (HSC) in comparison with the QARiB baseline models reported in (Mubarak et al., 2022). Our model, AraHS, outperforms the baseline QARiB on every metric. **NB:** no baseline was reported for the HSC subtask.

4. System Description

In this work, we use MARBERTv2 (Abdul-Mageed et al., 2021) as our core model. It is publicly available in the HuggingFace library (Wolf et al., 2019). It is pretrained with 1B multi-dialectal Arabic (DA) tweets which includes both MSA and DA. MARBERTv2 has the same architecture as $\text{BERT}_{\text{BASE}}$ (Devlin et al., 2019) with $\sim$ 163M parameters, similarly using Word-Piece tokenization (Wu et al., 2016).

We frame the 3 subtasks as a multi-task classification problem. Specifically, the input text is encoded using MARBERTv2 and is then passed to 3 task-specific classification heads as shown in Figure 1. Each class specific head is made up of a multi-layered feed forward neural network with layer normalization (Ba et al., 2016). Concretely, the `[CLS]` embedding of the final MARBERTv2 transformer block is forwarded to a dense layer with 768 units, which is then passed through a GELU activation function (Hendrycks and Gimpel, 2016), the output of which is normalized using layer normalization, and this is finally given to a linear layer that maps it to the corresponding number of classes.

The final model is an ensemble of several trained models each of which uses a different set of hyperparameters. To obtain the final prediction we perform element-wise multiplication of the corresponding probabilities across the different models then take the argmax.

Self-Consistency Correction Since we are training one model for all three subtasks, and the subtasks themselves are interdependent, we leverage that to our advantage. We perform a post-processing step where errors of one classification head are corrected by the others. Concretely, the fine-grained HS prediction is corrected in the following cases: the tweet is predicted to be offensive and contains HS using the first two classification heads respectively, while the fine-grained classifier predicted that it is not HS. In that case, we take the second most probable class prediction as the label since there is an inconsistency. The other scenario in which it is corrected is when the tweet is predicted as not offensive and does not contain HS while the fine-grained classifier predicted it as one of the HS classes.

5. Experimental Setup

To train the AraHS model, we use the AdamW optimzier (Loshchilov and Hutter, 2019) and a learning rate scheduler that is warmed-up linearly for 500 steps to some initial learning rate. This is then decayed linearly to zero over the course of 10 epochs. The model is evaluated on the validation-set 4 times every epoch with equal intervals, and a checkpoint for the corresponding subtask is saved when its F1-macro score improves. The objective function is the sum of the negative log-likelihood of the three classification heads. The tokenizer encodes the input text using a maximum length of 256 tokens. The model is trained 12 times over a grid of $\{2, 4, 8, 16\}$ batch-sizes and $\{1e-5, 5e-6, 1e-6\}$ initial learning rates.

For the fine-grained HS detection subtask, we further finetune the best single model on only this subtask, using the same experimental setup described above.

6. Results

Table 3 shows the performance on the test-set for each subtask. Our method (AraHS) outperforms the baseline models reported in (Mubarak et al., 2022) on every metric: Offensive Detection subtask (OFFD) (accuracy: AraHS 86% vs. QARiB 84%; F1-Macro: AraHS 84.5% vs. QARiB 82.3%); Hate Speech Detection (HSD) subtask (accuracy: AraHS 94.1% vs. QARiB 93%; F1-Macro: AraHS 82.7% vs. QARiB 80%). Only the HS Classification (HSC) uses the self-consistency correction method. Since the dataset used in this work does not contain the disability class in the training set, the final HSC F1-macro score degrades considerably.

6.1. Ablation Study

In order to demonstrate the importance of training the subtasks jointly, we train each subtask on its own. Specifically, Table 4 compares the validation performance of each subtask with its multitask counterpart. Performance improves when using multitask learning (MTL) for the HS subtasks. However, for the offensive subtask we observe similar performance to the single-task trained models. Similar to Table 3, only the HSC is using self-consistency correction, improving the F1-macro score from 54.8% to 56.6%.

Subtask	Model	Accuracy	Precision	Recall	F1 Macro
OFFD	Single-task	**88.7%**	**87.4%**	**86.1%**	**86.7%**
	Multitask	88.5%	87.1%	**86.1%**	86.6%
HSD	Single-task	95.8%	87.2%	85.7%	86.4%
	Multitask	**96.2%**	**87.7%**	**88.4%**	**88.1%**
HSC	Single-task	**95.3%**	**72.4%**	46.8%	51.0%
	Multitask	95.0/94.4%	58.5/54.8%	52.5/**58.8%**	54.8/**56.6%**

Table 4: The validation performance on each subtask. The single-task models are trained on the subtask alone, while the multitask model trains all subtasks jointly. The results before and after applying the self-consistency correction as a post-processing step is shown for the HSC subtask. **Bold** shows the best result for each subtask.

7. Error Analysis

The subtasks we are training are not independent of one another, even though we are modelling them that way. For example, as previously mentioned, a tweet that is considered HS is automatically offensive as well, and needless to say that each of the fine-grained HS classes (e.g. race, gender, etc.) are HS. Therefore, in this section we want to measure the degree of self-consistency within the trained multitask model. Specifically, we take the predictions of the best ensemble of models and calculate the percentage of contradiction between each classification head (see Table 5). Concretely, we compute the number of times in which the OFFD head yielded a negative prediction whereas the HSD or the HSC yielded a positive one. This is a contradiction since each HS post must be offensive as well. Similarly, we calculate the number of times the HSD head predicted negative while the HSC predicted positive and vice versa. As illustrated in Table 5, correcting the HSC head based on the two other subtasks reduces the contradiction considerably (from 2.6% to 0.79%) while achieving a better performance overall.

Subtask	Contradiction (%)
OFFD	2.44%
HSD	2.60%
HSC	2.60% / 0.79%

Table 5: Percentage of contradiction between classification heads before and after self-correction for the HSC. Each row correspond to the best checkpoint achieved for that subtask.

Furthermore, Table 6 shows two examples where the classification heads disagreed with one another. For example, the first tweet was detected as HS but the fine-grained classification head classified it as non-HS leading to a disagreement. Using our self-consistency correction method, the model was able to correct itself and yield the correct label, which was the *Ideology* subclass in this case. Example 1 in the table is a modification of an Arabic adage: "الطيور على اشكالها تقع", corresponding to "`Birds of a feather flock together`. Changing *birds* to *frogs* implies ugliness. Such tweets are not straight forward to classify since they require an understanding of cultural knowledge and implicit social nuance that is not explicitly encoded in language models such as MARBERT. One way to mitigate this is to finetune the model on a corpus that contains such information explicitly incorporating such inductive bias. Another method would be training the language model to generate the implication of the tweet as an additional subtask. The other example in the table implies that people of a certain nationality are ignorant. We believe that the provided gold label is incorrect (not HS). We believe that this tweet constitutes HS because it is offensive (a certain group of people is ignorant since they parrot rather than understand information) and it targets a group. Accordingly, the model was able to successfully predict it as HS, and even yield the correct class for it using the self-consistency method.

In Table 7 we report the percentage of false positives (FP) and false negatives (FN) of the best checkpoint of each subtask. To compute the percentage of FP and FN for the HSC subtask we convert it into a binary variable with negative implying that the prediction is not-HS and positive otherwise. Interestingly, the self-consistency correction method increases the percentage of FPs, as it takes the second top prediction as its label when both the HSD and OFFD are positive. We note that HS systems can tolerate more false positives (i.e. over enforcement) than false negatives (i.e. under enforcement), since the latter will lead to more propagation of harm. This highlights the advantage of self-consistency correction.

8. Related Work

Datasets The first Arabic HS dataset was collected by (Albadi et al., 2018) and consisted of $\sim$ 6.6k Arabic HS tweets. In an effort to collect a more dialect specific dataset, (Haddad et al., 2019) compiled 6k tweets of the Tunisian dialect containing both abusive language and HS. (Mulki et al., 2019) similarly collected a Levantine HS dataset. In the multilingual front, (Ousidhoum et al., 2019) created a HS dataset made up of 13k Arabic, English and French tweets with fine-grained labels

Tweet	OFFD	HSD	HSC
الضفادع على اشكالها تقع Frogs settle with their own kind.	✓—✓	✓—✓	✗— Ideology
أستغفر الله العظيم شعب حافظ مش فاهم The people of this country memorize without understanding.	✓—✗	✓—✗	✗—✗
ضروري من الطقوس في هذا المجتمع القائم على النفاق الاجتماعي Necessary rituals in this community that is based on social hypocrisy.	✗—✓	✗—✓	✗— Nationality

Table 6: The first two are examples that led to a disagreement between the classification heads, while the third one show a false negative example. Below each example is a rough English translation that is used to convey the meaning. On the right-side of the table, the prediction of the model is shown first followed by the ground truth label for each subtask. Note that the self-consistency correction method was able to correct the first two examples among others.

	False +ve (%)	False -ve (%)
OFFD	4.96%	6.54%
HSD	1.97%	1.81%
HSC	2.52%/3.86%	2.44%/1.73%

Table 7: Percentage of false positives and false negatives for the best checkpoint for each subtask. In the HSC we report the percentage before and after applying the self-consistency correction method.

covering different aspects such as target groups, directness, target attributes and hostility types.

Models Early work tackled this problem by extracting n-gram features using term frequency weighting, which was then passed to a Support Vector Machine (SVM) and Naive Bayes (NB) classifiers (Mulki et al., 2019). Other work used a gated recurrent unit (GRU) coupled with an SVM trained on the AraVec embeddings (Ashi et al., 2018) to classify HS (Albadi et al., 2018). (Hassan et al., 2020) used an ensemble of SVM, CNN-BiLSTM and feed-forward neural networks for HS detection. (Duwairi et al., 2021) showed that CNN models outperform their CNN-LSTM and CNN-BiLSTM counterparts in detecting HS when treated as a binary classification task on the ArHS dataset.

Multitask Learning In the Offensive Detection shared task co-located with the 4th Workshop on Open-Source Arabic Corpora and Processing Tools (OSACT4) (Al-Khalifa et al., 2020), (Djandji et al., 2020) trained AraBERT (Antoun et al., 2020) on multiple tasks simultaneously achieving the best score on the shared task. (El Mahdaouy et al., 2021) used a model based on MARBERT that employed MTL. In another line of work, a CNN-BiLSTM based architecture was trained using MTL to detect HS and OFF language (Abu Farha and Magdy, 2020). That model used extra sentiment information (Abu Farha and Magdy, 2019) during training. Finally, (Aldjanabi et al., 2021) explore a multi-corpus-based learning approach built on top of MARBERT. It uses MTL from three datasets for improving OFF and HS detection. Unlike previous work, our paper focuses on improving fine-grained Arabic HS classification using MTL and self-consistency correction on the new dataset introduced in (Mubarak et al., 2022).

9. Conclusion

In this paper, we propose MTL as an approach to Hate Speech Classification. Our proposed model, AraHS, outperforms the baseline models. AraHS is an ensemble of MARBERT (Abdul-Mageed et al., 2021) models trained with different hyperparameters using MTL. The fine-grained HS subtask is then finetuned on its own for a couple of epochs. We demonstrate the importance of training the three subtasks jointly through an ablation study and propose the self-consistency correction method that improves the final result even further. In future work, we would like to explore the limits of combining multilingual models (e.g. mBART (Liu et al., 2020)) with Arabic monolingual models such as MARBERT. Further, we would like to explore treating the problem as a conditional generation task using the AraT5 model (Nagoudi et al., 2021) that has been shown to outperform MARBERT on the Arabic language understanding evaluation benchmark (ARLUE) (Abdul-Mageed et al., 2021).

10. Ethics and Social Impact

Modern deep learning models are energy intensive and can cause environmental damage due to the carbon dioxide emissions required for running modern hardware. Studies have shown that training a BERT model on GPU has a comparable carbon footprint to a trans-American flight (Strubell et al., 2019). In this work, even though we do not pre-train the model, we still run multiple experiments across a grid of hyperparameters, that when combined consumes significant energy. Therefore, one of the reasons we chose multitask learning (MTL) is that we can reduce the amount of training substantially by training one model on multiple tasks. MTL does not only offer energy efficiency, but is also more data efficient, it has been shown to converge faster by leveraging auxiliary information and reduces over-fitting through shared representations (Crawshaw, 2020).

Further, building models for detecting OFF language and HS can help improve the moderation of hateful content on the internet. This can potentially lead to less hate crimes and better psychological well-being for users receiving such content. However, the authors are aware of potential misuse of HS models, such as propagating the spread of HS rather than suppressing it. Therefore, human moderation is required for preventing such misuse.

11. Bibliographical References

Abdelali, A., Mubarak, H., Samih, Y., Hassan, S., and Darwish, K. (2021). QADI: Arabic dialect identification in the wild. In *Proceedings of the Sixth Arabic Natural Language Processing Workshop*, pages 1–10, Kyiv, Ukraine (Virtual), April. Association for Computational Linguistics.

Abdul-Mageed, M., Elmadany, A., and Nagoudi, E. M. B. (2021). ARBERT & MARBERT: Deep bidirectional transformers for Arabic. In *Proceedings of the 59th Annual Meeting of the Association for Computational Linguistics and the 11th International Joint Conference on Natural Language Processing (Volume 1: Long Papers)*, pages 7088–7105, Online, August. Association for Computational Linguistics.

Abu Farha, I. and Magdy, W. (2019). Mazajak: An online Arabic sentiment analyser. In *Proceedings of the Fourth Arabic Natural Language Processing Workshop*, pages 192–198, Florence, Italy, August. Association for Computational Linguistics.

Abu Farha, I. and Magdy, W. (2020). Multitask learning for Arabic offensive language and hate-speech detection. In *Proceedings of the 4th Workshop on Open-Source Arabic Corpora and Processing Tools, with a Shared Task on Offensive Language Detection*, pages 86–90, Marseille, France, May. European Language Resource Association.

Al-Khalifa, H., Magdy, W., Darwish, K., Elsayed, T., and Mubarak, H. (2020). Proceedings of the 4th workshop on open-source arabic corpora and processing tools, with a shared task on offensive language detection. Marseille, France, May. European Language Resource Association.

Albadi, N., Kurdi, M., and Mishra, S. (2018). Are they our brothers? analysis and detection of religious hate speech in the arabic twittersphere. *2018 IEEE/ACM International Conference on Advances in Social Networks Analysis and Mining (ASONAM)*, pages 69–76.

Aldjanabi, W., Dahou, A., Al-qaness, M. A. A., Elsayed Abd Elaziz, M., Helmi, A., and Damasevicius, R. (2021). Arabic offensive and hate speech detection using a cross-corpora multi-task learning model. *Informatics*, 8:69, 10.

Alshehri, A., Nagoudi, E. M. B., Alhuzali, H., and Abdul-Mageed, M. (2018). Think before your click: Data and models for adult content in arabic twitter.

Antoun, W., Baly, F., and Hajj, H. (2020). AraBERT: Transformer-based model for Arabic language understanding. In *Proceedings of the 4th Workshop on Open-Source Arabic Corpora and Processing Tools, with a Shared Task on Offensive Language Detection*, pages 9–15, Marseille, France, May. European Language Resource Association.

Ashi, M. M., Siddiqui, M. A., and Nadeem, F. (2018). Pre-trained word embeddings for arabic aspect-based sentiment analysis of airline tweets. In *AISI*.

Assimakopoulos, S., Muskat, R. V., van der Plas, L., and Gatt, A. (2020a). Annotating for hate speech: The maneco corpus and some input from critical discourse analysis. *arXiv preprint arXiv:2008.06222*.

Assimakopoulos, S., Vella Muskat, R., van der Plas, L., and Gatt, A. (2020b). Annotating for hate speech: The MaNeCo corpus and some input from critical discourse analysis. In *Proceedings of the 12th Language Resources and Evaluation Conference*, pages 5088–5097, Marseille, France, May. European Language Resources Association.

Ba, J., Kiros, J., and Hinton, G. E. (2016). Layer normalization. *ArXiv*, abs/1607.06450.

Crawshaw, M. (2020). Multi-task learning with deep neural networks: A survey. *ArXiv*, abs/2009.09796.

Davidson, T., Warmsley, D., Macy, M. W., and Weber, I. (2017). Automated hate speech detection and the problem of offensive language. In *ICWSM*.

Devlin, J., Chang, M.-W., Lee, K., and Toutanova, K. (2019). BERT: Pre-training of deep bidirectional transformers for language understanding. In *Proceedings of the 2019 Conference of the North American Chapter of the Association for Computational Linguistics: Human Language Technologies, Volume 1 (Long and Short Papers)*, pages 4171–4186, Minneapolis, Minnesota, June. Association for Computational Linguistics.

Djandji, M., Baly, F., Antoun, W., and Hajj, H. (2020). Multi-task learning using AraBert for offensive language detection. In *Proceedings of the 4th Workshop on Open-Source Arabic Corpora and Processing Tools, with a Shared Task on Offensive Language Detection*, pages 97–101, Marseille, France, May. European Language Resource Association.

Duwairi, R., Hayajneh, A., and Quwaider, M. (2021). A deep learning framework for automatic detection of hate speech embedded in arabic tweets. *Arabian Journal for Science and Engineering*, 46:1–14.

El Mahdaouy, A., El Mekki, A., Essefar, K., El Mamoun, N., Berrada, I., and Khoumsi, A. (2021). Deep multi-task model for sarcasm detection and sentiment analysis in Arabic language. In *Proceedings of the Sixth Arabic Natural Language Processing Workshop*, pages 334–339, Kyiv,

Ukraine (Virtual), April. Association for Computational Linguistics.

Fortuna, P. and Nunes, S. (2018). A survey on automatic detection of hate speech in text. *ACM Computing Surveys (CSUR)*, 51(4):1–30.

Founta, A. M., Djouvas, C., Chatzakou, D., Leontiadis, I., Blackburn, J., Stringhini, G., Vakali, A., Sirivianos, M., and Kourtellis, N. (2018). Large scale crowdsourcing and characterization of twitter abusive behavior. In *Twelfth International AAAI Conference on Web and Social Media*.

Gülaçti, F. (2010). The effect of perceived social support on subjective well-being. *Procedia - Social and Behavioral Sciences*, 2:3844–3849.

Haddad, H., Mulki, H., and Oueslati, A., (2019). *T-HSAB: A Tunisian Hate Speech and Abusive Dataset*, pages 251–263. 10.

Hassan, S., Samih, Y., Mubarak, H., Abdelali, A., Rashed, A., and Chowdhury, S. A. (2020). ALT submission for OSACT shared task on offensive language detection. In *Proceedings of the 4th Workshop on Open-Source Arabic Corpora and Processing Tools, with a Shared Task on Offensive Language Detection*, pages 61–65, Marseille, France, May. European Language Resource Association.

Hendrycks, D. and Gimpel, K. (2016). Bridging nonlinearities and stochastic regularizers with gaussian error linear units. *ArXiv*, abs/1606.08415.

League, A.-D. (2020). Online hate and harassment. the american experience 2021. *Center for Technology and Society. Retrieved from www. adl. org/media/14643/download.*

Liu, Y., Gu, J., Goyal, N., Li, X., Edunov, S., Ghazvininejad, M., Lewis, M., and Zettlemoyer, L. (2020). Multilingual denoising pre-training for neural machine translation. *Transactions of the Association for Computational Linguistics*, 8:726–742.

Loshchilov, I. and Hutter, F. (2019). Decoupled weight decay regularization. In *International Conference on Learning Representations*.

MacAvaney, S., Yao, H.-R., Yang, E., Russell, K., Goharian, N., and Frieder, O. (2019). Hate speech detection: Challenges and solutions. *PloS one*, 14(8):e0221152.

Mollas, I., Chrysopoulou, Z., Karlos, S., and Tsoumakas, G. (2020). Ethos: an online hate speech detection dataset. *ArXiv*, abs/2006.08328.

Mubarak, H., Darwish, K., and Magdy, W. (2017). Abusive language detection on Arabic social media. In *Proceedings of the First Workshop on Abusive Language Online*, pages 52–56, Vancouver, BC, Canada, August. Association for Computational Linguistics.

Mubarak, H., Hassan, S., and Chowdhury, S. A. (2022). Emojis as anchors to detect arabic offensive language and hate speech. *arXiv preprint arXiv:2201.06723*.

Mulki, H., Haddad, H., Bechikh Ali, C., and Alshabani, H. (2019). L-HSAB: A Levantine Twitter dataset for hate speech and abusive language. In *Proceedings of the Third Workshop on Abusive Language Online*, pages 111–118, Florence, Italy, August. Association for Computational Linguistics.

Nagoudi, E. M. B., Elmadany, A., and Abdul-Mageed, M. (2021). Arat5: Text-to-text transformers for arabic language generation.

Ousidhoum, N., Lin, Z., Zhang, H., Song, Y., and Yeung, D.-Y. (2019). Multilingual and multi-aspect hate speech analysis. In *Proceedings of the 2019 Conference on Empirical Methods in Natural Language Processing and the 9th International Joint Conference on Natural Language Processing (EMNLP-IJCNLP)*, pages 4675–4684, Hong Kong, China, November. Association for Computational Linguistics.

Paz, M. A., Montero-Díaz, J., and Moreno-Delgado, A. (2020). Hate speech: A systematized review. *SAGE Open*, 10(4):2158244020973022.

Sanguinetti, M., Poletto, F., Bosco, C., Patti, V., and Stranisci, M. (2018). An Italian Twitter corpus of hate speech against immigrants. In *Proceedings of the Eleventh International Conference on Language Resources and Evaluation (LREC 2018)*, Miyazaki, Japan, May. European Language Resources Association (ELRA).

Sap, M., Gabriel, S., Qin, L., Jurafsky, D., Smith, N. A., and Choi, Y. (2020). Social bias frames: Reasoning about social and power implications of language. In *ACL*.

Schmidt, A. and Wiegand, M. (2017). A survey on hate speech detection using natural language processing. In *Proceedings of the Fifth International Workshop on Natural Language Processing for Social Media*, pages 1–10, Valencia, Spain, April. Association for Computational Linguistics.

Strubell, E., Ganesh, A., and McCallum, A. (2019). Energy and policy considerations for deep learning in nlp. *ArXiv*, abs/1906.02243.

Tinsley, T. and Board, K. (2013). *Languages for the Future*. British Council.

Vogels, E. A. (2021). The state of online harassment. *Pew Research Center*, 13.

Waldron, J. (2012). *The Harm in Hate Speech*. Harvard University Press.

Waseem, Z. and Hovy, D. (2016). Hateful symbols or hateful people? predictive features for hate speech detection on Twitter. In *Proceedings of the NAACL Student Research Workshop*, pages 88–93, San Diego, California, June. Association for Computational Linguistics.

Wolf, T., Debut, L., Sanh, V., Chaumond, J., Delangue, C., Moi, A., Cistac, P., Rault, T., Louf, R., Funtowicz, M., and Brew, J. (2019). Huggingface's transformers: State-of-the-art natural language processing. *ArXiv*, abs/1910.03771.

Wu, Y., Schuster, M., Chen, Z., Le, Q., Norouzi,

M., Macherey, W., Krikun, M., Cao, Y., Gao, Q., Macherey, K., Klingner, J., Shah, A., Johnson, M., Liu, X., Kaiser, u., Gouws, S., Kato, Y., Kudo, T., Kazawa, H., and Dean, J. (2016). Google's neural machine translation system: Bridging the gap between human and machine translation. 09.

Zampieri, M., Malmasi, S., Nakov, P., Rosenthal, S., Farra, N., and Kumar, R. (2019). Predicting the type and target of offensive posts in social media. In *Proceedings of the 2019 Conference of the North American Chapter of the Association for Computational Linguistics: Human Language Technologies, Volume 1 (Long and Short Papers)*, pages 1415–1420, Minneapolis, Minnesota, June. Association for Computational Linguistics.

Proceedings of the OSACT 2022 Workshop @LREC2022, pages 194–199
Marseille, 20 June 2022

CHILLAX - at Arabic Hate Speech 2022: A Hybrid Machine Learning and Transformers based Model to Detect Arabic Offensive and Hate Speech

Kirollos Hany Makram, Kirollos George Nessim, Malak Emad Abd-Almalak,
Shady Zekry Roshdy, Seif Hesham Salem, Fady Fayek Thabet,
Ensaf Hussein Mohamed
Research Support Center in Computing and Informatics
Department of Computer Science, Faculty of Computers and Artificial Intelligence,
Helwan University, Cairo, Egypt.
kirollos_20180442@fci.helwan.edu.eg,
kirollos_20180437@fci.helwan.edu.eg, Malak_20180615@fci.helwan.edu.eg,
Shady_20180285@fci.helwan.edu.eg, seif_20180284@fci.helwan.edu.eg,
fady_20180413@fci.helwan.edu.eg, ensaf_hussein@fci.helwan.edu.eg

Abstract

Hate speech and offensive language have become a crucial problem nowadays due to the extensive usage of social media by people of different gender, nationality, religion and other types of characteristics, allowing anyone to share their thoughts and opinions. In this research paper, we proposed a hybrid model for the first and second tasks of OSACT2022. This model used the Arabic pre-trained Bert language model MARBERT for feature extraction of the Arabic tweets in the dataset provided by the OSACT2022 shared task, then fed the features to two classic machine learning classifiers (Logistic Regression, Random Forest). The best results achieved for the offensive tweet detection task were achieved by the Logistic Regression model with accuracy, precision, recall, and f1-score of 80%, 78%, 78%, and 78%, respectively. The results for the hate speech tweet detection task were 89%, 72%, 80%, and 76%.
The source code can be found on GitHub here (Hany, 2022)
Keywords: Arabic Tweets, Offensive language, Hate speech, Transformers, Text classification

1 Introduction

Twitter and similar social media platforms users are from every race, religion, nationality, and background communicate and freely share their opinions and beliefs. The down side to this is that it is easy to exploit these social media platforms by sharing offensive and hate speech content that targets and threatens individuals or groups based on common characteristics, or identities. Despite the considerable efforts that social media platforms are making to prevent such content from spreading, it is still threatening the online communities and users are still seeing it on many platforms. It is imperative to detect and prevent such content from appearing on social media platforms, thus motivating our research on Arabic offensive and hate speech detection. Pre-trained language models based on Transformer (Vaswani et al., 2017) such as GPT (Radford et al., 2018), Bert (Devlin et al., 2018), XLNet (Yang and Zhao, 2019), and RoBERTa (Zhuang et al., 2021) have been shown to be effective for learning contextualized language representation achieving state-of-the-art results on a wide variety of natural language processing tasks. Recent research has adopted the methodology of fine-tuning a pre-trained language model by simply adding a fully connected neural layer specific to the downstream task the model is being fine-tuned for, such as sarcasm detection (Farha and Magdy, 2021) and hate speech detection (Aldjanabi et al., 2021). Research has shown that due to the numerous layers present in Transformer models, simply feeding the output of the Transformer's encoder final layer to the fully connected neural layer would restrict the power of the pre-trained representations of the language (Yang and Zhao, 2019). (Devlin et al., 2018) shows that different combinations of different output layers of the Transformers encoder layers result in distinct performance on various tasks like Named Entity Recognition task. It is found that the most contextualized representations of input text tend to occur in the middle layers, while the top layers are for language modeling (Yang and Zhao, 2019). This research used different transformers' encoder layers as feature extractors. Then we used the extracted features to feed into two classical machine learning classifiers; Logistic Regression and Random Forest. We used the MARBERT pre-trained Transformer model as it was trained on a large Arabic tweets corpora and has proved to be efficient in similar tasks such as sentiment analysis, where it scored 0.93 F1-score on the ArSAS dataset ("Abdul-Mageed et al., 2021). Also, we used Logistic Regression as a classifier as it proved superior on binary classification problems as the current subtasks. We conducted our experiments on the OSACT2022 dataset for subtask 1: Arabic offensive, and subtask2: hate speech tweets detection. One of The challenges of the OSACT2022 dataset are that the dataset is imbalanced; the number of tweets on both subtasks aren't equal across the two classes, offensive and hate speech detection. We tackled this problem by using data augmentation techniques to achieve a balanced class distribution in the dataset to prevent the classifiers from biasing towards the majority class. The research paper is organized as follows. Section 2 gives a brief overview of related work. Section 3 explain in details our methodology and proposed model. Section 4 presents the experiment results and evaluation metrics. Section 5 concludes our research and our potential future work.

2 Related Work

Recently, the interest in detecting hate speech has increased rapidly, attracting the attention of many researchers trying to develop various models and methods to extract hate features and hateful content. Several research studies were conducted to study hate speech and offensive language in online communities and social media over Arabic content. (Abuzayed and Elsayed, 2020) investigate 15 classical and neural learning models with TF-IDF and word embedding as feature representations of the OSACT-2020 dataset; their best classifier (A joint architecture of CNN and RNN) achieved 73% macro F1-score on the development dataset and 69% on the test dataset with word embedding as feature representations. (Alshaalan and Al-Khalifa, 2020) investigate several neural network models that are based on CNN and RNN to detect hate speech in Arabic tweets and also evaluates recent BERT model on the task of Arabic hate speech detection. They built a hate speech dataset containing 9,316 annotated Arabic tweets. They conducted experiments on that dataset and an out-domain dataset showing that the CNN model achieves an F1-score of 79% and AUROC of 89%. (Faris et al., 2020) proposed an innovative deep learning approach for the detection of cyber hate speech. The detection of hate speech on Twitter in the Arabic region, in particular, using a word embedding mechanism for feature representation and fed to a hybrid CNN and LSTM neural network that achieved a 71% F1-score on a dataset that is collected from the Twitter API. (Al-khalifa et al., 2020) collected a 3,000 tweet dataset from Twitter where they experimented BOW and TF-IDF methods for feature representation and classical machine learning models (SVM, NB, RF) and concluded that TF-IDF with SVM achieved the best results of 82% F1-score. So far, related work shows that word embeddings, TF-IDF, and BOW have been used as the feature representation for text experimented with traditional machine learning models as well as deep learning neural networks. In most cases, deep learning neural networks show superior results to classical machine learning models. This further motivates our approach to experiment with the feature representation of the different combinations of hidden layers in pre-trained transformer models on classical machine learning models.

3 Methods and Materials

3.1 The dataset

We used the Arabic tweets dataset provided by the OSACT2022 shared task, which contains around 13,000 tweets, where 35% are offensive, and 11% are hate speech. Vulgar and violent tweets represent 1.5% and 0.7% of the dataset, respectively. The dataset was split into three parts train, development, and test, with percentages of 70%, 10%, and 20%, respectively. For the first task, offensive tweet detection, the training dataset contained 5,715 offensive and 3,172 not offensive tweets—figure 1 shows the class imbalance presented in the training dataset for our first task. The training dataset for the second task, hate speech tweet detection, contained 7,928 not hate speech and 959 hate speech tweets, which shows a significant class imbalance. Figure 2 shows the class imbalance presented in the training dataset for the second task.

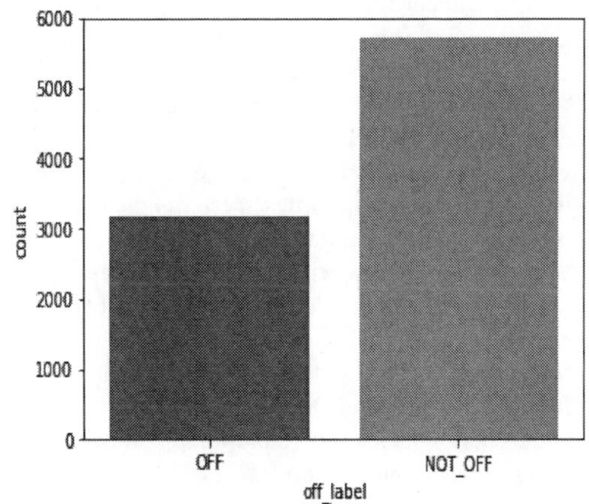

Figure 1: Offensive detection task label count plot

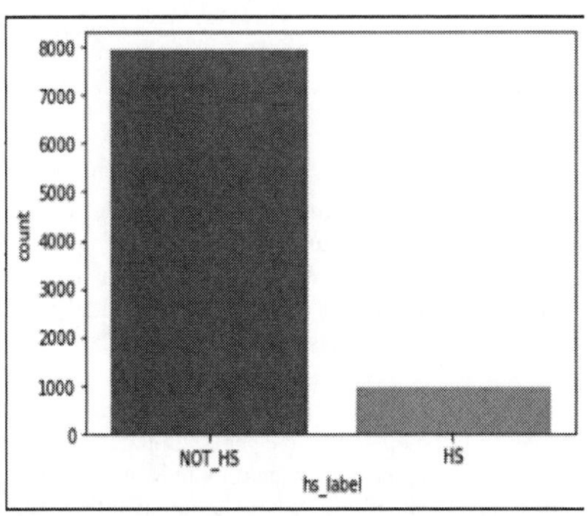

Figure 2: Hate speech detection task label count plot

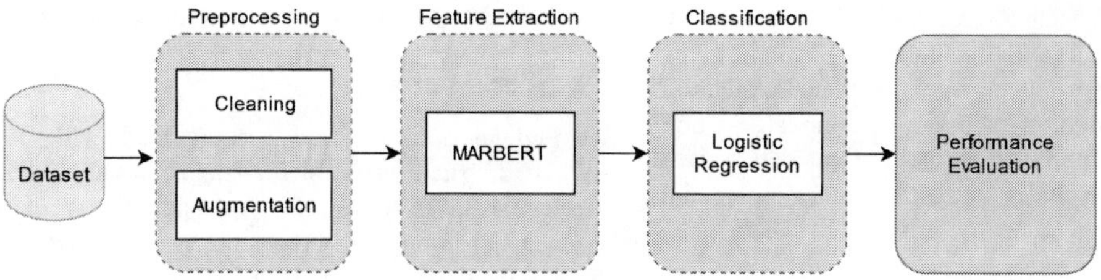

Figure 3: The proposed Model

3.2 Proposed Model

The proposed model consists of three modules; Preprocessing, Feature Extraction, and Classification. We will describe each module in detail in the following subsections. Figure 3 illustrates the proposed model pipeline.

3.2.1 Preprocessing

The preprocessing phase includes two submodules, cleaning and augmentation. In cleaning, all URLs and User mentions were removed. In augmentation, we solved the class imbalance problem in the two tasks. We used the contextual word embedding augmentation technique like the MARBERT Arabic model, which generates new tweets from the minority classes (offensive and hate speech) so that the class distribution in both tasks was balanced to prevent the model from biasing towards the majority classes (not offensive, not hate speech). Some of the augmented tweets had an unknown special token generated; these tokens were removed from the augmented tweets. The NLP aug (Alkhalifa et al., 2020) data augmentation library was used for the data augmentation. Table 1 and 2 show a sample of augmented offensive and hate speech tweets, respectively. It is worth mentioning that traditional text preprocessing methods like stemming, lemmatizing, and punctuation removal were experimented with but resulted in poor results as MARBERT was trained on Twitter text that was not preprocessed with these methods. Simply removing the URL and user mention tags achieved better results.

3.2.2 Feature Extraction

For the feature extraction phase, we used MARBERT pre-trained Arabic language model to extract features which will be later fed to the machine learning models Logistic Regression and Random Forest for training. The MARBERT model is a Bert-based model which consists of 12 hidden layers and a hidden size of 768. The output of the last four hidden layers was obtained, where each layer is of dimensions sentence length x hidden size. The output of each layer is summed to produce a single vector of sentence length x hidden size dimensions. The mean of this vector is computed to create a single vector of hidden size length representing the feature vector for the tweet that will be fed to the machine learning models.

Original Tweets	Augmented Tweets
جمهور الاهلي مضحوك عليهم الحين يصدقو ان عددهم كثير 🤭 😂	جمهور وجمهور الاهلي مضحوك عليهم الحين من يصدقو ان الاهلاويين عددهم كثير 🤭 😂
#بايع_الكليجا الله يفشلكم فشلتونا يالمراهقات انا استحيت من تصرفات البنات وتعليقاتهم وانا مالي دخل 😩	واحد [UNK] سعودي بايع [UNK] يبيع الكليجاالله يفشلكم فشلتونا يالمراهقاتانا استحيت من كثر تصرفات البنات وتعليقاتهم وانا مالي فيها دخل 😩
#بايع_الكليجا من العام اشوفه يبيع ويسترزق الله حاله حال نفسه سالفه التصوير والتشهير فيه قله أدب اللي 😩 قاعد يصير البنات م عاد يستحو	[UNK] ▪ بايع [UNK] الكليجا من العام اشوفه يبيع ويسترزق الله حاله حال نفسه ف سالفه التصوير والكلام والتشهير ذي فيه قله وسوء ادب اللي قاعد يصير البنات م عاد يستحو 😩 فيه

Table 1: Augmented Offensive tweets sample

Original Tweets	Augmented Tweets
الهندي قاعد يثبت للمعزّب إن الخروف صار صديقه علشان ما يذبحه 😂 🐑	الهندي قاعد يثبت للمعزب ان الخروف صار له صديقه علشان بس ما يذبحه 😂 🐑
قلبنا يابنت خلينا حلوين يعني انتم وش يجملكم غير الميك اب 🐑	قلبنا يابنت خلينا نكون حلوين يعني انتم وش اللي يجملكم من غير الميك اب 🐑
عاهات بزمنكم كانوا يصولون ويجولون شرق اسيا، ختاماً بعالمية ضد سوباولو البرازيلي، وانت بعز مستواك حققت الدوري بعد ٣٢ سنه عاجفه بالضحك والطقطقه عليكم؟	عاهات بزمنكم كانوا يصولون ويجولون شرق قارة اسيا الان ، ختاما فاز بعالمية ضد سوباولو البرازيلي ، تخيل وانت بعز مستواك حققت الدوري بعد ٣٢ سنه سنه عاجفه ، بالضحك عليه والطقطقه شلون عليكم ؟

Table 2: Augmented hate speech tweets sample

3.2.3 Classification

We used two classifiers; The Scikit-Learn library implementation of Logistic Regression and Random Forest were used in the training phase.

For the Logistic Regression model, a regularisation parameter of 1^{-3} was used, and for the optimization algorithm, the Saga solver was used. A max sample parameter of 0.4 was used for the Random Forest model, where max sample is the number of samples to be drawn from the inputs to train each base estimator.

4 Results and Discussion

Before training the model, the training dataset was split into 70% for training and 30% for testing to evaluate the model, along with the development and test datasets provided by the OSACT2022 shared task.

4.1 Performance Evaluation

The evaluation metrics used are macro averaged Precision, Recall, F1-score, and Accuracy, where Precision is the fraction of classified tweets that are relevant, which is formulated in equation 1. The recall is the fraction of relevant tweets that are classified, which is presented in equation 2. F1-score is the harmonic mean of Precision and Recall, which is presented in equation 3. Accuracy is the fraction of correct tweets that have been classified from actual classes as shown in Equation 4.

$$\text{Precision} = \frac{TP}{TP+FP} \tag{1}$$

$$\text{Recall} = \frac{TP}{TP+FN} \tag{2}$$

$$\text{F1-score} = \frac{2 \times \text{Precision} \times \text{Recall}}{\text{Precision} + \text{Recall}} \tag{3}$$

$$\text{Accuarcy} = \frac{TP+TN}{TP+FP+TN+FN} \tag{4}$$

where:
True Positive (TP): refers to a set of tweets that have been classified correctly to the task class (offensive, hate speech).
False Positive (FP): refers to a set of tweets that have been classified incorrectly and have been said to be related to the task class (offensive, hate speech) incorrectly.
True Negative (TN): refers to a set of tweets that have not been classified into the task class (offensive, hate speech) and are not labeled as task class (offensive, hate speech).
False Negative (FN): refers to a set of tweets that have not been classified correctly and have been said to be non-related to the task class (offensive, hate speech), but they are labeled as task class (offensive, hate speech).

4.2 Experimental Results

The baselines for evaluation provided by OSACT2022 are as following:

Task	Accuracy	Precision	Recall	F1-score
Offensive detection	65%	65%	50%	39%
Hate speech detection	89%	45%	50%	47%

For the offensive detection task, we applied two experiments. The First one, using MARABERT as a Feature extractor, then fed the feature vector into the Logistic regression classifier and in the second experiment, we used the same feature vector that was produced by MARABERT and then fed it into the Random Forest classifier. Each model was trained on 70% of the training dataset after augmentation and evaluated on the remaining 30% of the training dataset along with the development and the OSACT2022 test dataset. Best results were achieved by Logistic Regression on the test dataset with macro average accuracy, F1-score, of 80%, 78% respectively. The results obtained for each model and dataset for the offensive detection task are as shown in the following Table 3 and Table 4:

Model	Dataset	Accuracy	Precision	Recall	F1-score
Logistic Regression	Train	85%	85%	85%	85%
	Test(30% of train)	81%	81%	81%	81%
	Development	80%	77%	78%	78%
	OSACT-2022-Test	80%	78%	78%	78%

Table 3: Results of detecting offensive language using MARABERT and Logistic Regression

Model	Dataset	Accuracy	Precision	Recall	F1-score
Random Forest	Train	97%	97%	97%	97%
	Test(30% of train)	77%	77%	77%	77%
	Development	75%	72%	73%	72%
	OSACT-2022-Test	74%	72%	72%	72%

Table 4: Results of detecting offensive language using MARABERT and Random Forest

For the hate speech detection task, we applied two experiments. First one, using MARABERT as a Feature extractor then fed the feature vector into the Logistic regression classifer and in the second experiment, we used the same feature vector that was produced by MARABERT and then fed it into the Random Forest classifier. Each model was trained on 70% of the training dataset after augmentation and evaluated on the remaining 30% of the training dataset along with the development and the OSACT2022 test dataset. Best results were achieved by Logistic Regression on the test dataset with macro averaged accuracy, F1-score of 89%, 76% respectively. The results obtained for each model and dataset for the hate speech detection task are as follows in Table 5, Table 6:

Model	Dataset	Accuracy	Precision	Recall	F1-score
Logistic Regression	Train	91%	91%	91%	91%
	Test(30% of train)	91%	91%	91%	91%
	Development	89%	70%	81%	74%
	OSACT2022-Test	89%	73%	81%	76%

Table 5: Results of detecting Hate Speech using MARABERT and Logistic Regression

5 Conclusion

We proposed a hybrid machine learning and transformers based model for the detection of Arabic offensive and hate speech tweets. We leverage the superiority

Model	Dataset	Accuracy	Precision	Recall	F1-score
Random Forest	Train	98%	98%	98%	98%
	Test(30% of train)	90%	90%	90%	90%
	Development	87%	67%	81%	70%
	OSACT2022-Test	87%	69%	79%	73%

Table 6: Results of detecting Hate Speech using MARABERT and Random Forest

of transformers for text feature extraction and the excellence of Logistic Regression in binary classification tasks and data augmentation techniques for handling data imbalances. The best results achieved for the offensive tweet detection task were achieved by the Logistic Regression model with accuracy, precision, recall, and f1-score of 80%, 78%, 78%, and 78%, respectively. The results for the hate speech tweet detection task were 89%, 72%, 80%, and 76%. For future work we plan to further investigate the different representations that different combinations of transformer-based models layers have for extracting features of text and also investigate different machine learning classification models such as SVM and Naive Bayes for the binary classification tasks in hope to achieve higher scores and obtaining a more efficient model.

References

Abdul-Mageed, M., Elmadany, A., and Nagoudi, E. M. B. (2020). Arbert & marbert: deep bidirectional transformers for arabic. *arXiv preprint arXiv:2101.01785*.

"Abdul-Mageed, M., Elmadany, A., and Nagoudi, E. M. B. ("2021"). "ARBERT & MARBERT: Deep bidirectional transformers for Arabic". In *"Proceedings of the 59th Annual Meeting of the Association for Computational Linguistics and the 11th International Joint Conference on Natural Language Processing (Volume 1: Long Papers)"*, pages "7088–7105", "Online", aug. "Association for Computational Linguistics".

Abuzayed, A. and Elsayed, T. (2020). Quick and simple approach for detecting hate speech in arabic tweets. In *Proceedings of the 4th workshop on open-source Arabic Corpora and processing tools, with a shared task on offensive language detection*, pages 109–114.

Al-khalifa, S., Aljarah, I., and Abushariah, M. A. M. (2020). Hate speech classification in arabic tweets. *Journal of Theoretical and Applied Information Technology*, 98:1816–1831.

Aldjanabi, W., Dahou, A., Al-qaness, M. A., Abd Elaziz, M., Helmi, A. M., and Damaševičius, R. (2021). Arabic offensive and hate speech detection using a cross-corpora multi-task learning model. In *Informatics*, volume 8, page 69. Multidisciplinary Digital Publishing Institute.

Alshaalan, R. and Al-Khalifa, H. (2020). Hate speech detection in saudi twittersphere: A deep learning approach. In *Proceedings of the Fifth Arabic Natural Language Processing Workshop*, pages 12–23.

Devlin, J., Chang, M.-W., Lee, K., and Toutanova, K. (2018). Bert: Pre-training of deep bidirectional transformers for language understanding. *arXiv preprint arXiv:1810.04805*.

Farha, I. A. and Magdy, W. (2021). Benchmarking transformer-based language models for arabic sentiment and sarcasm detection. In *Proceedings of the sixth Arabic natural language processing workshop*, pages 21–31.

Faris, H., Aljarah, I., Habib, M., and Castillo, P. A. (2020). Hate speech detection using word embedding and deep learning in the arabic language context. In *ICPRAM*, pages 453–460.

Hany, K. (2022). Osact2022-source-code. `https://github.com/kirollos-hany/OSACT2022-source-code`.

Ma, E. (2019). Nlp augmentation. https://github.com/makcedward/nlpaug.

Mubarak, H., Hassan, S., and Chowdhury, S. A. (2022). Emojis as anchors to detect arabic offensive language and hate speech. *arXiv preprint arXiv:2201.06723*.

Radford, A., Narasimhan, K., Salimans, T., and Sutskever, I. (2018). Improving language understanding by generative pre-training.

Vaswani, A., Shazeer, N., Parmar, N., Uszkoreit, J., Jones, L., Gomez, A. N., Kaiser, Ł., and Polosukhin, I. (2017). Attention is all you need. *Advances in neural information processing systems*, 30.

Williams, M. L., B. P. J. A. L. H. and Ozalp. (2020). Hate in the machine: anti-black and anti-muslim social media posts as predictors of offline racially and religiously aggravated crime. *The British Journal of Criminology 60(1): 93–117.*

Yang, J. and Zhao, H. (2019). Deepening hidden representations from pre-trained language models. *arXiv preprint arXiv:1911.01940*.

Zhuang, L., Wayne, L., Ya, S., and Jun, Z. (2021). A robustly optimized bert pre-training approach with post-training. In *Proceedings of the 20th Chinese National Conference on Computational Linguistics*, pages 1218–1227.

Proceedings of the OSACT 2022 Workshop @LREC2022, pages 200–208
Marseille, 20 June 2022

AlexU-AIC at Arabic Hate Speech 2022: Contrast to Classify

Ahmad Shapiro, Ayman Khalafallah, Marwan Torki
Computer and Systems Engineering Department
Alexandria University
Alexandria, Egypt
{ahmad.shapiro, ayman.khalafallah, mtorki}@alexu.edu.eg

Abstract

Online presence on social media platforms such as Facebook and Twitter has become a daily habit for internet users. Despite the vast amount of services the platforms offer for their users, users suffer from cyber-bullying, which further leads to mental abuse and may escalate to cause physical harm to individuals or targeted groups. In this paper, we present our submission to the Arabic Hate Speech 2022 Shared Task Workshop (OSACT5 2022) using the associated Arabic Twitter dataset. The shared task consists of 3 sub-tasks, sub-task A focuses on detecting whether the tweet is offensive or not. Then, For offensive Tweets, sub-task B focuses on detecting whether the tweet is hate speech or not. Finally, For hate speech Tweets, sub-task C focuses on detecting the fine-grained type of hate speech among six different classes. Transformer models proved their efficiency in classification tasks, but with the problem of over-fitting when fine-tuned on a small or an imbalanced dataset. We overcome this limitation by investigating multiple training paradigms such as Contrastive learning and Multi-task learning along with Classification fine-tuning and an ensemble of our top 5 performers. Our proposed solution achieved 0.841, 0.817, and 0.476 macro F1-average in sub-tasks A, B, and C respectively.

Keywords: Offensive Language Detection, Contrastive Learning, Multi-task Learning

1. Introduction

The Internet has revolutionized the way humans communicate, providing organizations and people with many features to promote and express themselves. Social media platforms (e.g. Facebook, Twitter, etc.) became a daily habit and even a source of income for many individuals. As of (2021[1]) Twitter had 206 million monetizable daily active users worldwide who can interact with each other and freely express their opinions. Unfortunately, without proper moderation and prevention, offensive language and hate speech may result in mental abuse to users or groups of individuals, as a matter of fact, social media can act as a propagation mechanism for violent crimes by enabling the spread of extreme viewpoints (Müller and Schwarz, 2020).

Research community has been focused on identifying the offensive language on social media in multiple languages (such as English, German, etc.), but offensive language detection is a challenge for Arabic, not only because it's a morphologically rich language, but because Arabic is considered as "macrolanguage" with many dialects. Arabic dialects differ in various ways from MSA "Modern Standard Arabic". These include phonological, morphological, lexical, and syntactic differences (Abdul-Mageed et al., 2018).

To address those challenges, hate speech datasets for multiple dialects have been collected such as L-HSAB (Mulki et al., 2019) for Levantine Dialects, T-HSAB (Haddad et al., 2019) for Tunisian Dialects. Also, previous shared tasks such as : OffensEval 2020 (Zampieri et al., 2020) that focused on identifying offensive language from Tweets in Arabic and other multiple languages, OSACT4 2020 (Mubarak et al., 2020) that focused on the detection of both offensive Language and hate Speech as its two sub-tasks respectively.

OSACT5 2022 presents a fine-grained detection of hate speech on Arabic Twitter shared task that consists of three sub-tasks. Sub-task A focuses on detecting whether the tweet is offensive or not. Then, for offensive Tweets, sub-task B focuses on detecting whether the tweet is hate speech or not. Finally, for hate speech tweets, sub-task C focuses on detecting the fine-grained type of hate speech among six different classes.

We approach the problem by exploring pre-trained transformer models using Arabic corpus. Given the imbalanced small dataset of 8.8k labeled tweets, transformers models tend to over-fit easily under this setting. Hence, we explore different training strategies such as Contrastive learning with different losses and training paradigms. Also, we explore the Multi-task learning approach. We also do a comparative study to decide which training strategy succeed on each sub-task. Our proposed solution of an ensemble of our top five models for Sub-task A, and a Multi-task learner for both Sub-tasks B and C solution achieved 0.841, 0.817, and 0.476 macro F1-average in sub-tasks A, B, and C respectively. Our results show a significant improvement on the majority baselines of 0.394, 0.472, 0.135 macro F1-average.

The following abbreviations will be used throughout the paper : Offensive Language (OFF), Hate-Speech (HS), Hate-Speech Classes (HS-C), Multi-task Learning (MTL).

[1]https://www.statista.com/statistics/242606/number-of-active-twitter-users-in-selected-countries/

2. Related Work

Hugely influenced by (Aldjanabi et al., 2021) work, we were able to explore many previous approaches to Arabic (HS) and (OFF) detection using (MTL). The first Arabic Religious (HS) Twitter dataset was collected by (Albadi et al., 2018). Their model encoded the tweets using GRUs trained on AraVec embeddings (Ashi et al., 2018) and then the features are passed to SVM classifier. They achieved the best performance with 79% accuracy.

(Haddad et al., 2019) collected 6k tweets for (HS) and abusive language for Tunisian Dialect (T-HSAB). They used Term Frequency weighting to extract n-grams features from tweets. Features are then used to train Naive Bayes and SVM classifiers. Their proposed method achieved 0.836 F1-score.

Related work from OSACT2020 (Mubarak et al., 2020) submissions that incorporates (MTL) are (Djandji et al., 2020; Abu Farha and Magdy, 2020; Hassan et al., 2020).

(Djandji et al., 2020) fine-tuned AraBERT (Antoun et al., 2020) with (MTL). They obtained a great results with the small imbalanced dataset setting. Their proposed method achieved 0.9 macro-averaged F1-score.

(Hassan et al., 2020) Experimented with multiple Classical Machine learning and Deep learning approaches. They used CNN-BiLSTM, SVM and M-BERT for the (HS) sub-task. Their stacked SVMs achieved 0.806 F1-Score.

(Abu Farha and Magdy, 2020) trained CNN-BiLSTM with (MTL) on the two sub-tasks, in addition to Mazajak Arabic Sentiment Analysis dataset (Abu Farha and Magdy, 2019), detecting the sentiment of the text. We can deduce a correlation between negative sentiment and the tweet being (HS) or (OFF). Their proposed model achieved 0.904, 0.737 F1-score in the (OFF) and (HS) sub-tasks respectively.

Moving from OSACT2020 submissions, (Aldjanabi et al., 2021) explores (MTL) more widely. They use dataset from OSACT2020 (HS) and (OFF), T-HSAB (Haddad et al., 2019), and (L-HSAB) (Mulki et al., 2019). They experimented with both AraBERT (Antoun et al., 2020) and MarBERT (Abdul-Mageed et al., 2021) models. They train 6 different (MTL) models using OSAT2020 two sub-tasks (HS) and (OFF) as the main sub-tasks, in addition two (L-HSAB) or (T-HSAB) or both, on both MarBERT and AraBERT. They report their best results on both (OFF) and (HS) sub-tasks using MarBERT model trained on the (HS) sub-task, (OFF) sub-task, and (L-HSAB) which is 3 class classification (Abusive, HS, Normal). Their score was 0.9234, 0.8873 F1-Scores in (OFF), (HS) respectively.

In our work we focus on exploring different training paradigms using pre-trained Arabic Transformer models due to their efficiency in Natural Language Understanding (NLU) tasks instead of classical machine learning models. We use a different (MTL) approach by only considering the main 3 sub-tasks with under-sampled version of dataset, and balanced version of dataset using another datasets of the same tasks.

3. Approach

We follow a pragmatic study in model selection and training strategy selection for each sub-task.

We based our approaches on Encoder-Based Transformers models because of their efficiency on (NLU) tasks, but their only flaw is over-fitting on small and imbalanced data-sets. We overcome this problem by exploring multiple training paradigms such as :

- Classification Fine-tuning
- Contrastive Learning
- Multi-task Learning

Also, we use regularization techniques such as Dropout and Early-Stopping.

All of our models were developed using HuggingFace Library (Wolf et al., 2019), Sentence-Transformers Library (Reimers and Gurevych, 2019).

We had two choices of models that showed promising results on previous Arabic shared tasks, AraBERT (Antoun et al., 2020) and MarBERT (Abdul-Mageed et al., 2021). We loaded their latest checkpoints from hugging face.

In Section 3.4 we show how we chose only the best of those models - based on current task performance and pre-training data of the model - to use it as our main encoder that will run for the rest of the experiments.

3.1. Exploratory Data Analysis

The dataset (Mubarak et al., 2022) for the three sub-tasks is the same, containing 12.7K tweets that were annotated for :

- Sub-task A : OFF and NOT_OFF
- Sub-task B : HS and NOT_HS
- Sub-task C : NOT_HS, HS1 (Race), HS2 (Religion), HS3 (Ideology), HS4 (Disability), HS5 (Social Class), and HS6 (Gender).

With two extra labels expressing tweet being vulgar : NOT_VLG, VLG, and being violent : NOT_VIO, VIO. Dataset was split into 70% (8887 tweets) for training, 10% (1270 tweets) for development, and 20% (2541 tweets) for testing. Sub-task C (HS Classes) labels distribution was very imbalanced; with 89.2%, 2.9%, 0.3%, 1.6%, 0%, 0.8%, 5.13% for classes from NOT_HS, HS1 to HS6 respectively for training. We can see that HS4 (Religion) wasn't present in the training dataset. Development dataset follows a similar distribution but with only an extra example for HS4. Followed by sub-task B (HS) with only 10.8% (HS) labels in training and 8.5% in development. And, finally subtask A (OFF) with 35.7% (OFF) labels in training and 31.8% in development.

We discovered that only 2 out of the 8887 train tweets and 1270 development tweets combined didn't have emoji(s). This helped us in narrowing the search for Transformer models candidates to be used.

Our first candidate model was MarBERTv2 (Abdul-Mageed et al., 2021) for two reasons :

1. It was trained using 1B Arabic tweets which matches the text distribution of our dataset.
2. Emojis weren't filtered from the training dataset, as MarBERTv2 Vocabulary has 567 emoji.

Our second candidate was AraBERT (Antoun et al., 2020) due to its performance in our task as discussed in Section 2.

After submission, details about the dataset has been made public. We discovered that emojis were treated as anchors to build the dataset itself according to (Mubarak et al., 2022).

3.2. Data Pre-processing

Data pre-proccesing is an important step in classification tasks, many unnecessary tokens may not help in the given task, as a matter of fact, they may have bad influence on the final results. We ran the data-set through the following pre-processing steps :

- Arabic Letter Normalisation : We unify the Alef {أ} letter that may appear in different forms as following {آ إ أ} to {ا} .
- Punctuation Normalisation : We replace {؟} to {?}, {،} to {,}, {؛}to {;}.
- Digit Normalisation : We replace {...٠١٩٨٧٦٥٤٣٢١} to {1,2,3,4,5,6,7,8,9,10 ....}
- Hashtag segmentation : #هاش_تاج to هاش تاج
- Diacritic removal except shaddah.
- Removal of symbols such as : {—, /, #, [,], {, }, - , _, *, @, USER, LF }
- Removal of repeated characters or emojis more than two times.

While (Djandji et al., 2020; Haddad et al., 2020) removed emojis as pre-processing step, and (Husain, 2020) replaced emojis with their description in Arabic. Normalisation of digits and punctuation, and removal of symbols and repeated characters, emojis were done to reduce scarcity of the representations. We decided to keep emojis without any cleaning or pre-processing because they are an important data feature as discussed in Section 3.1.

We fine-tuned our models with and without pre-processing. We found that pre-processing improved the results as will be shown in Section 4.

3.3. Data Balancing and Additional Data Resources

We made a balanced version of our dataset (BALANCED) using dataset associated with OSACT2020 and OffenseEval2020 and (Chowdhury et al., 2020; Ousidhoum et al., 2019; Alakrot et al., 2018).

For Sub-task A , we used all samples from (Chowdhury et al., 2020; Alakrot et al., 2018; Ousidhoum et al., 2019) along with data associated with OSACT2020 and OffenseEval2020. We first took all OFF samples from OSACT2020 and then random under-sample all other data-sets, resulting in 19906 balanced data-set instead of the original 8887 associated with the task.

For Sub-task B, we used all samples from (Chowdhury et al., 2020; Ousidhoum et al., 2019) along with data associated with OSACT2020 and OffenseEval2020. We first took all HS samples from OSACT2020 and then random under-sampled all other data-sets. Which resulted in 4800 balanced data-set instead of the original 8887 associated with the task that had only 959 (HS) samples. We used (BALANCED) data only in Multi-task learning.

While other approaches (Ibrahim et al., 2020; Ibrahim et al., 2018) used data augmentation to tackle class imbalance. We chose to use extra data resources collected by different methods to study the effect of distribution mismatch.

3.4. Model Selection

As discussed in Section 3.1, we consider only two models in our Experiments : AraBERT (Antoun et al., 2020) and MarBERT (Abdul-Mageed et al., 2021). The introduction of Bidirectional Encoder Representation from Transformers (BERT) (Devlin et al., 2018) led to a revolution in the NLP world, as BERT-based models achieved state-of-the-art results in many tasks.

In the proposed architecture, we utilize a pre-trained language model and fine tune it for a specific task.

3.4.1. MarBERT

MarBERTv1 is a large-scale pre-trained masked language model focused on both Dialectal Arabic (DA) and Modern Standard Arabic (MSA). It was trained on 1B Arabic tweets (15.6B tokens), (Abdul-Mageed et al., 2021) using a BERT-base architecture but without the Next Sentence Prediction (NSP) objective since tweets length are naturally short.

MarBERTv2 differs from v1 in the training dataset only. They add multiple data-sets and train the model for 40 epochs, readers can refer to the original paper (Abdul-Mageed et al., 2021) for more details.

3.4.2. AraBERT

AraBERT differs from MarBERTv1 and v2 in the training data. Most of its training data is MSA instead of DA as in MarBERT. They also use Farasa (Darwish and Mubarak, 2016) Arabic morphological segmentation in the text pre-processing.
As discussed earlier in Section 2, AraBERT showed a good performance in (MTL).

3.5. Classification Fine-tuning

We use Huggingface library (Wolf et al., 2019) to fine-tune our BERT-Based Models on a binary classification task for Sub-task A and B. We use ADAM optimizer and fine-tune for 100 epochs with early stopping patience of 10 epochs and report the best checkpoint.
We fine-tune AraBERTv2, MarBERTv1, MarBERTv2 on Sub-task A data with and without pre-processing to choose the model we will proceed with, and whether we will pre-process our data or not. Results are reported in Section 4.

3.6. Contrastive Learning

Instead of classification fine-tuning which adds a linear layer after the BERT encoder to leverage the pooled BERT representation in classification. And then back propagate the cross entropy loss to fine tune both the linear layer, and the BERT encoder parameters for classification objective. We explore another training objective, contrastive learning. It's main objective is minimizing the distance of pooled BERT representations between similar sentence pairs, and maximizing distance between dissimilar pairs.
There are many distance metrics, such as Cosine Similarity, Euclidean Distance, and Manhattan Distance. All of our experiments uses Cosine Similarity as distance metric with 0.7 margin between positive pairs and negative pairs.
We use Sentence-Transformers Library (Reimers and Gurevych, 2019) for training which is built over HuggingFace (Wolf et al., 2019) library.
The main reason we chose contrastive learning is data imbalance. The construction of data-set for contrastive learning eliminates any imbalance and increase the dataset by order of n^2 as shown in Section 3.6.4. But it's very sensitive to annotation errors and differences in data distribution.
We experiment with different variants of contrastive loss and we use only the original data not the (BALANCED) 3.3.

3.6.1. Contrastive Loss

Contrastive loss (Hadsell et al., 2006) expects as input two texts and a label of either 0 or 1.
If the label = 1 (Positive/Similar Examples), then the distance between the two embeddings is minimized.
If the label = 0 (Negative/dissimilar Examples), then the distance between the embeddings is maximized. Loss is calculated for all examples in each batch.

3.6.2. Online Contrastive loss

Online Contrastive loss is similar to Constrative Loss 3.6.1, but it selects hard positive (positives that are far apart) and hard negative pairs (negatives that are close) and computes the loss only for these pairs.

3.6.3. Batch All Triplet Loss

Batch All Triplet Loss (Hermans et al., 2017) takes a batch with (label, sentence) pairs and computes the loss for all possible, valid triplets, i.e., anchor and positive must have the same label, anchor and negative a different label.

3.6.4. Contrastive Data Creation

We limit our experiments to only sub-task A (OFF). Positive examples are pair of sentences with the same label (OFF, OFF) and (NOT_OFF, NOT_OFF). Negative samples are pair of sentences with different labels (OFF, NOT_OFF). Let the number of examples with (OFF) label = n, (NOT_OFF) = m.
We make three pools of examples :

1. Negative Examples : product of set (OFF) and (NOT_OFF), resulting in size = $n * m$
2. Positive Examples (OFF) : product of set (OFF) with itself, resulting in size = n^2
3. Positive Examples (NOT_OFF) : product of set (NOT_OFF) with itself, resulting in size = m^2

We experiment with different data sizes. Let our selected data $size$ be 20K examples. To ensure balance between data, we sample 10K examples from the Negative Examples Pool, 5K from Positive Examples (OFF), Positive Examples (OFF) each respectively.
Generally, $size/2$ from Negative examples, $size/4$ from Positive Examples of (OFF) and (NOT_OFF) respectively.

3.7. Multitask Learning

We focused in contrastive learning to increase the amount of data we have and solve the data imbalance by changing the training objective to contrast instead of classifying without any additional examples.
Hugely influenced with the results of (MTL) as discussed in Section 2. We experiment with Multi-task learning with our two versions of data (BALANCED) and the original task data as will be discussed in Section 4.
Rather than training the model on a single task, multi-task learning enables the model to benefit from multiple tasks at the same time. Given the existence of relatedness between tasks, an inductive transfer of knowledge will take place in the process of multitask learning (Djandji et al., 2020). We can see that the 3 main sub-tasks are an extensions of each other. Not offensive (sub-task A) tweets are always not hate speech (sub-task B), and the class of hate speech (sub-task C) is an explicit extension of hate speech detection (sub-task B).

The tasks share the same encoder, but there's a task specific dense layer for prediction. We limit (MTL) tasks to Sub-tasks A, B, and C, as illustrated in Figure 1.

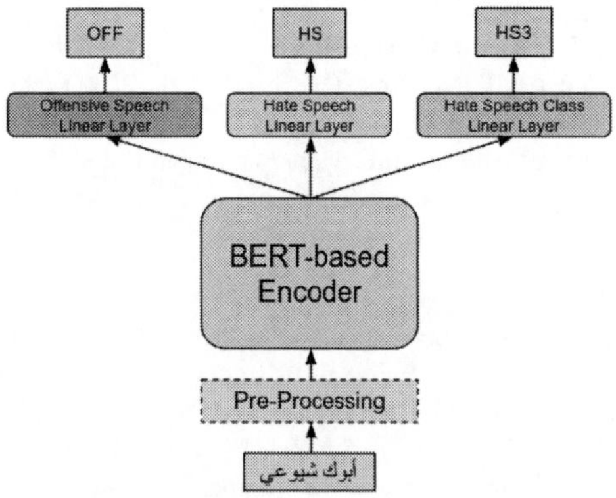

Figure 1: Multi-task Model Architecture.

4. Experimental Evaluation

In this section we report our results on both development set and test set for different approaches we used. We notice a quick over-fit while fine-tuning our models. All of the models achieve the best development set F1-score in the first 3 epochs.

4.1. Encoder Selection

We fine-tuned AraBERTv2, MarBERTv1, and MarBERTv2 on classification for Sub-task A, without pre-processing and a Dropout probability = 0.1 (Huggingface default) and learning rate = 2^{-5}.
As we can see in Table 1, both Versions of MarBERT performed better than AraBERT, so we moved forward with MarBERTv2.

Model	Dev F1
AraBERTv2	0.694
MarBERTv1	0.783
MarBERTv2	**0.841**

Table 1: Encoder Selection

4.2. Text Pre-processing

To test the effect of the pre-processing approach 3.2 we used. We fine-tuned both versions of MarBERT with and without pre-processing on Sub-task A.
We evaluated them on the development set, F1-Score is reported in Table 2.
As we can see that our pre-processing approach improved the results for both models.
Concluding this comparative study, we decided to move forward with MarBERTv2 as our encoder for the rest of the experiments, and with our text pre-processing approach.

Model	w/o PP	w/ PP
MarBERTv1	0.783	0.801
MarBERTv2	0.841	**0.850**

Table 2: Text Pre-Processing Effect

We tuned the dropout probability and found the best results with the default probability of 0.1 .

4.3. Contrastive Learning

As discussed in Earlier in Section 3.6.1, we fine-tuned our model using multiple contrastive objectives. Following the contrastive fine-tuning phase, we trained a linear layer and freezed MarBERT parameters using original data. All contrastive fine-tuning was done on Sub-task A, results are shown in Table 3.

Model	Data Size	Dev F1
Online Contrastive	50K	0.851
Online Contrastive	1M	0.849
Contrastive	50K	0.847
Contrastive	250K	0.833
Batch All	*	0.847

Table 3: Contrastive Training Results

We plot separation between classes using PCA as shown in Figures 2 through 4.
They key difference between contrastive, online contrastive and batch all triplet is the combination of losses and the creation of data. For both contrastive loss and online contrastive loss, data is created manually as discussed in Section 3.6.4. Therefore, at a given iteration we have pair of sentences as single example, and a label that corresponds of whether the two sentences are similar or not. If the label corresponds to the pair = 1 (positive), distance between two sentences are reduced, and minimized otherwise. Contrastive calculates the loss for all pairs, but online contrastive calculates only hard examples (positive that are far apart, and negative that are close).
In contrast, Batch All uses the original from of data : single sentence with one label (OFF = 1, NOT_OFF = 0). It creates valid triplets (Positive, Anchor, Negative) in a given batch and calculates the loss for triplet as whole not as single similarity between pair of sentences.
We noticed that contrastive learning is very sensitive to annotation errors and different text distributions. We also noticed that contrastive loss performance degrades with the increase of data size, unlike online contrastive loss which doesn't face the same rate of degradation. We noticed a similar results between online contrastive and batch all, this can be attributed to the fact that both losses doesn't take all data samples in consideration.
We've tried multiple classical machine learning classification algorithms, using BERT encoder output as our

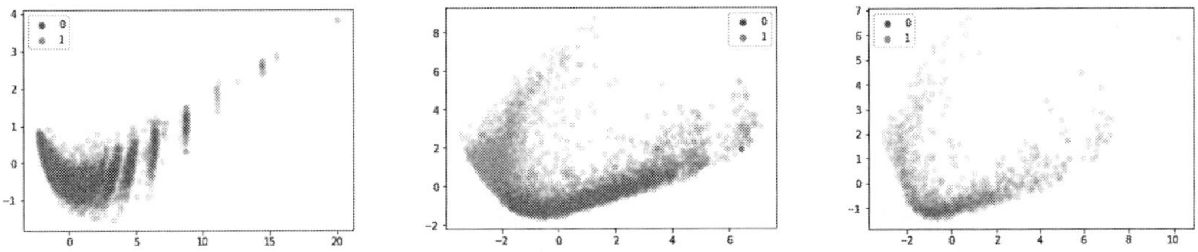

(a) Baseline MarBERT (b) Fine-tuned MarBERT : Train (c) Fine-tuned MarBERT : Dev

Figure 2: MarBERT vs Classification Fine-tuned MarBERT

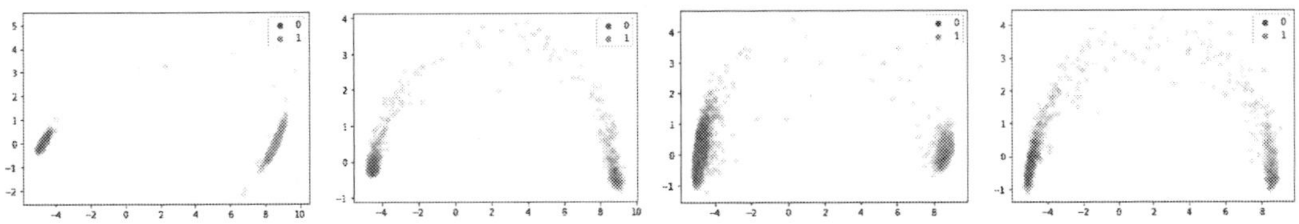

(a) Train (b) Development (c) Train (d) Development

Figure 3: Left: Contrastive 50K. Right: Online Contrastive 50K

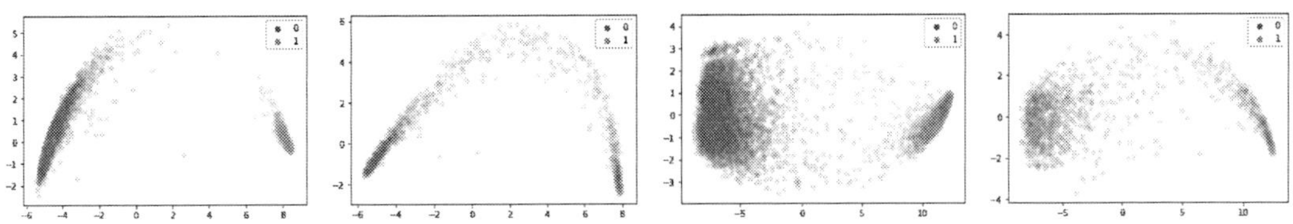

(a) Train (b) Development (c) Train (d) Development

Figure 4: Left: Online Contrastive 1M. Right: Batch All Triplet Loss

features. We didn't see any improvement in the results. We tried SMOTE oversampling after applying dimensionality reduction using PCA to the encoder outputs, but we didn't see any improvement too.

4.4. Multitask Learning

As discussed in Section 3.7, we fine-tuned MarBERT on multi-task learning objective using all 3 sub-tasks for 5 epochs and learning rate = 2^{-5}.
We used the original data and the (BALANCED) data. Results on development dataset are shown in Table 4.

Sub-task	Original Data	BALANCED
A (OFF)	**0.838**	0.830
B (HS)	0.810	**0.830**
C (HS-C)	**0.435**	0.431

Table 4: Multitask Learning Results

We noticed that training for extra epochs achieves better results in Sub-task C, but degrades the performance on Sub-task A, B respectively. This can be attributed to So we decided to use the checkpoint trained for 5 epochs. We tuned the learning rate and found that 2^{-5} achieved the best results.

As we can see in Table 4 that using (BALANCED) data didn't achieve better results in all sub-tasks, and it wasn't tied with data imbalance. Sub-task C had much extreme case of data imbalance than B, but when we used (BALANCED) data for A and B, C's result degraded. We can assume that this is due to the difference in distribution in data-sets used to construct the (BALANCED) dataset. And also due to the extreme class imbalance in sub-task C.

4.5. Our Submission

4.5.1. Sub-Task A

We used an ensemble of the following MarBERT based models:

1. Classification Fine-tuned
2. Batch All Fine-tuned.
3. Online Contrastive Fine-tuned with 50K examples.
4. Online Contrastive Fine-tuned with 1M examples.
5. Contrastive Fine-tuned with 50K examples.

We tried two ensemble techniques :

1. Summing positive and negative logits of ensembled models and the maximum between summed positive and summed negative is the classification result.
2. Using positive and negative logits of ensembled models as features to multiple classification algorithm to achieve a weighted voting.

Both methods achieved the same results on development set in terms of F1-Score. We moved forward with the former. We achieved 0.86 F1-Score on the development set. We report our results on the test set in Table 5.

Model	Majority Baseline	Ours
F1	0.394	**0.841**
Precision	0.325	**0.842**
Recall	0.5	**0.839**
Accuracy	0.651	**0.856**

Table 5: Sub-Task A (OFF) Test Results

4.5.2. Sub-Task B and C

We used multitask model trained with (BALANCED) data to submit our result. Sub-Task B, C results are shown in Tables 6 and 7 respectively.

Model	Majority Baseline	Ours
F1	0.472	**0.817**
Precision	0.447	**0.855**
Recall	0.5	**0.787**
Accuracy	0.893	**0.937**

Table 6: Sub-Task B (HS) Test Results

Model	Majority Baseline	Ours
F1	0.135	**0.476**
Precision	0.128	**0.49**
Recall	0.143	**0.47**
Accuracy	0.893	**0.923**

Table 7: Sub-Task C (HS Classes) Test Results

5. Conclusion and Future Work

In this paper, we experimented multiple approaches along with classification fine-tuning to approach the problems of offensive language detection, hate-speech detection, and fine-grained hate-speech classes classification.

We evaluated BERT-based models trained on Arabic corpus. We found that MarBERTv2 performed the best, and better with our pre-processing approach.

We found that contrastive learning achieved slightly better results than classification fine-tuning when data imbalance wasn't extreme, and an ensemble of models trained with contrastive objective and classification objective achieved better results than each of them solely. We used multitask learning to tackle extreme data imbalance. We found that training for more epochs benefits tasks with extreme data imbalance, but degrades the performance for tasks with mild and slight data imbalance.

For future work, we plan to investigate contrastive learning for extreme cases of data imbalance, accompanied with curriculum learning and a care-full selection of contrastive samples.

We also plan to tackle data imbalance by using data from multiple languages for the same task, using a language agnostic encoder trained with contrastive objective as LaBSE (Feng et al., 2020).

6. Acknowledgements

The authors would like to thank the Applied Innovation Center of Egyptian MCIT for providing necessary resources to complete the project presented in this paper.

7. Bibliographical References

Abdul-Mageed, M., Alhuzali, H., and Elaraby, M. (2018). You tweet what you speak: A city-level dataset of Arabic dialects. In *Proceedings of the Eleventh International Conference on Language Resources and Evaluation (LREC 2018)*, Miyazaki, Japan, May. European Language Resources Association (ELRA).

Abdul-Mageed, M., Elmadany, A. A., and Nagoudi, E. M. B. (2021). ARBERT & MARBERT: deep bidirectional transformers for arabic. *CoRR*, abs/2101.01785.

Abu Farha, I. and Magdy, W. (2020). Multitask learning for Arabic offensive language and hate-speech detection. In *Proceedings of the 4th Workshop on Open-Source Arabic Corpora and Processing Tools, with a Shared Task on Offensive Language Detection*, pages 86–90, Marseille, France, May. European Language Resource Association.

Aldjanabi, W., Dahou, A., Al-qaness, M. A. A., Elaziz, M. A., Helmi, A. M., and Damaševičius, R. (2021). Arabic offensive and hate speech detection using a cross-corpora multi-task learning model. *Informatics*, 8(4):69, October.

Antoun, W., Baly, F., and Hajj, H. M. (2020). Arabert: Transformer-based model for arabic language understanding. *CoRR*, abs/2003.00104.

Ashi, M. M., Siddiqui, M. A., and Nadeem, F. (2018). Pre-trained word embeddings for arabic aspect-based sentiment analysis of airline tweets. In *Advances in Intelligent Systems and Computing*, pages 241–251. Springer International Publishing, August.

Darwish, K. and Mubarak, H. (2016). Farasa: A new fast and accurate Arabic word segmenter. In *Proceedings of the Tenth International Conference on Language Resources and Evaluation (LREC'16)*, pages 1070–1074, Portorož, Slovenia, May. European Language Resources Association (ELRA).

Devlin, J., Chang, M., Lee, K., and Toutanova, K. (2018). BERT: pre-training of deep bidirectional transformers for language understanding. *CoRR*, abs/1810.04805.

Djandji, M., Baly, F., Antoun, W., and Hajj, H. (2020). Multi-task learning using AraBert for offensive language detection. In *Proceedings of the 4th Workshop on Open-Source Arabic Corpora and Processing Tools, with a Shared Task on Offensive Language Detection*, pages 97–101, Marseille, France, May. European Language Resource Association.

Feng, F., Yang, Y., Cer, D., Arivazhagan, N., and Wang, W. (2020). Language-agnostic BERT sentence embedding. *CoRR*, abs/2007.01852.

Haddad, B., Orabe, Z., Al-Abood, A., and Ghneim, N. (2020). Arabic offensive language detection with attention-based deep neural networks. In *Proceedings of the 4th Workshop on Open-Source Arabic Corpora and Processing Tools, with a Shared Task on Offensive Language Detection*, pages 76–81, Marseille, France, May. European Language Resource Association.

Hadsell, R., Chopra, S., and LeCun, Y. (2006). Dimensionality reduction by learning an invariant mapping. In *2006 IEEE Computer Society Conference on Computer Vision and Pattern Recognition (CVPR'06)*, volume 2, pages 1735–1742.

Hassan, S., Samih, Y., Mubarak, H., Abdelali, A., Rashed, A., and Chowdhury, S. A. (2020). ALT submission for OSACT shared task on offensive language detection. In *Proceedings of the 4th Workshop on Open-Source Arabic Corpora and Processing Tools, with a Shared Task on Offensive Language Detection*, pages 61–65, Marseille, France, May. European Language Resource Association.

Hermans, A., Beyer, L., and Leibe, B. (2017). In defense of the triplet loss for person re-identification. *CoRR*, abs/1703.07737.

Husain, F. (2020). OSACT4 shared task on offensive language detection: Intensive preprocessing-based approach. *CoRR*, abs/2005.07297.

Ibrahim, M., Torki, M., and El-Makky, N. (2018). Imbalanced toxic comments classification using data augmentation and deep learning. In *2018 17th IEEE International Conference on Machine Learning and Applications (ICMLA)*, pages 875–878.

Ibrahim, M., Torki, M., and El-Makky, N. (2020). AlexU-BackTranslation-TL at SemEval-2020 task 12: Improving offensive language detection using data augmentation and transfer learning. In *Proceedings of the Fourteenth Workshop on Semantic Evaluation*, pages 1881–1890, Barcelona (online), December. International Committee for Computational Linguistics.

Mubarak, H., Darwish, K., Magdy, W., Elsayed, T., and Al-Khalifa, H. (2020). Overview of OSACT4 Arabic offensive language detection shared task. In *Proceedings of the 4th Workshop on Open-Source Arabic Corpora and Processing Tools, with a Shared Task on Offensive Language Detection*, pages 48–52, Marseille, France, May. European Language Resource Association.

Mubarak, H., Hassan, S., and Chowdhury, S. A. (2022). Emojis as anchors to detect arabic offensive language and hate speech. *arXiv preprint arXiv:2201.06723*.

Müller, K. and Schwarz, C. (2020). Fanning the Flames of Hate: Social Media and Hate Crime. *Journal of the European Economic Association*, 19(4):2131–2167, 10.

Zampieri, M., Nakov, P., Rosenthal, S., Atanasova, P., Karadzhov, G., Mubarak, H., Derczynski, L., Pitenis, Z., and Çöltekin, c. (2020). SemEval-2020 Task 12: Multilingual Offensive Language Identification in Social Media (OffensEval 2020). In *Proceedings of SemEval*.

8. Language Resource References

Abu Farha, I. and Magdy, W. (2019). Mazajak: An online Arabic sentiment analyser. In *Proceedings of the Fourth Arabic Natural Language Processing Workshop*, pages 192–198, Florence, Italy, August. Association for Computational Linguistics.

Alakrot, A., Murray, L., and Nikolov, N. S. (2018). Dataset construction for the detection of anti-social behaviour in online communication in arabic. *Procedia Computer Science*, 142:174–181. Arabic Computational Linguistics.

Albadi, N., Kurdi, M., and Mishra, S. (2018). Are they our brothers? analysis and detection of religious hate speech in the arabic twittersphere. In *Proceedings of the 2018 IEEE/ACM International Conference on Advances in Social Networks Analysis and Mining*, ASONAM '18, page 69–76. IEEE Press.

Chowdhury, S. A., Mubarak, H., Abdelali, A., Jung, S.-g., Jansen, B. J., and Salminen, J. (2020). A multiplatform arabic news comment dataset for offensive language detection. In *Proceedings of the International Conference on Language Resources and Evaluation (LREC'20)*.

Haddad, H., Mulki, H., and Oueslati, A. (2019). T-hsab: A tunisian hate speech and abusive dataset. In *ICALP*.

Mulki, H., Haddad, H., Bechikh Ali, C., and Alshabani, H. (2019). L-HSAB: A Levantine Twitter dataset for hate speech and abusive language. In *Proceedings of the Third Workshop on Abusive Language Online*, pages 111–118, Florence, Italy, August. Association for Computational Linguistics.

Ousidhoum, N., Lin, Z., Zhang, H., Song, Y., and Yeung, D.-Y. (2019). Multilingual and multi-aspect hate speech analysis. In *Proceedings of EMNLP*. Association for Computational Linguistics.

Reimers, N. and Gurevych, I. (2019). Sentence-bert: Sentence embeddings using siamese bert-networks. In *Proceedings of the 2019 Conference on Empirical Methods in Natural Language Processing*. Association for Computational Linguistics, 11.

Wolf, T., Debut, L., Sanh, V., Chaumond, J., Delangue, C., Moi, A., Cistac, P., Rault, T., Louf, R., Funtowicz, M., and Brew, J. (2019). Huggingface's transformers: State-of-the-art natural language processing. *CoRR*, abs/1910.03771.

Proceedings of the OSACT 2022 Workshop @LREC2022, pages 209–213
Marseille, 20 June 2022

GUCT at Arabic Hate Speech 2022: Towards a Better Isotropy for Hate Speech Detection

Nehal Elkaref, Mervat Abu-Elkheir
German University in Cairo
nehal.elkaref@student.guc.edu.eg, mervat.abuelkheir@guc.edu.eg

Abstract

Hate Speech is an increasingly common occurrence in verbal and textual exchanges on online platforms, where many users, especially those from vulnerable minorities, are in danger of being attacked or harassed via text messages, posts, comments, or articles. Therefore, it is crucial to detect and filter out hate speech in the various forms of text encountered on online and social platforms. In this paper, we present our work on the shared task of detecting hate speech in dialectical Arabic tweets as part of the OSACT shared task on Fine-grained Hate Speech Detection. Normally, tweets have a short length, and hence do not have sufficient context for language models, which in turn makes a classification task challenging. To contribute to sub-task A, we leverage MARBERT's pre-trained contextual word representations and aim to improve their semantic quality using a cluster-based approach. Our work explores MARBERT's embedding space and assess its geometric properties in-order to achieve better representations and subsequently better classification performance. We propose to improve the isotropic word representations of MARBERT via clustering. we compare the word representations generated by our approach to MARBERT's default word representations via feeding each to a bidirectional LSTM to detect offensive and non-offensive tweets. Our results show that enhancing the isotropy of an embedding space can boost performance. Our system scores 81.2% on accuracy and a macro-averaged F1 score of 79.1% on sub-task A's development set and achieves 76.5% for accuracy and an F1 score of 74.2% on the test set.

Keywords: hate speech, isotropy, contextual word embeddings, pre-trained-models, representation degeneration problem

1. Introduction

Social media platforms are continuously being used as a medium for freedom of expression. However, users tend to abuse this liberty and disregard the possibility of their comments harbouring any sort of hate or offensive content. Hatespeesh could be considered as an umbrella-term for various expressions that can be offensive interms of one's gender, race, religion, disability, or ethnicity or simply encourage hatred towards certain groups and individuals. Such expressions can elevate to threats and can put users in the risk of being cyberbullied. Therefore, tackling the issue of classifying online content as containing any sort of hate is crucial to users safety.

2. Related Work

Previous research efforts and methods to detect hate-speech within the scope of Arabic language include a comparative study between word representations, distributed term representation and statistical bag of words (Abuzayed and Elsayed, 2020) where they showcased that the former outperforms the latter in a joint CNN and LSTM architecture. In the same vein (Saeed et al., 2020) compared between embeddings that support the Arabic language, amongst them are Word2Vec (Church, 2017), FastText (Joulin et al., 2016), BERT's multilingual vectors[1], and AraVec (Soliman et al., 2017). Their evaluation yielded Word2Vec and FastText as better suited for the task. They concatenated both embeddings and used deep learning models for the learning process in addition to a stack of classifiers fine-tuned for classification. Similarly, the study in (Saeed et al., 2020) explored the use of different word embeddings including Word2Vec, FastText and GloVe accompanied by different neural network models, those of which included LSTM, CNN and GRU, to find the best performing combination of word embeddings and neural network architecture. The research in (Husain, 2020) showed that substantial preprocessing of Arabic data could remarkably escalate performance, where they converted emojis in texts into their corresponding label, thus creating additional features. Moreover, they attempted to reduce dimensionality by neutralising the dialectical nature of the dataset and turning it into Modern Standard Arabic (MSA), in addition to the other basic cleaning and preprocessing techniques.

All the aforementioned systems aimed to give better representations either using different kind of embeddings or extensive preprocessing, and in the same vein to their work, we tackle this shared task by using and refining MARBERT's (Abdul-Mageed et al., 2020) contextual word representations. To give a general framework of our method, we firstly enhance MARBERT's embedding space by making it more isotropic, then we extract contextual representations from the improved geometric space to finally feed them to a Bidirectional LSTM to detect offensive tweets. We compare the performance of isotropic representations

[1] `https://github.com/google-research/bert/blob/master/multilingual.md`

against anisotropic or default representations of MARBERT.

3. Background

An isotropic embedding space is a space where all representations are scattered uniformly in all directions. Having this geometric property enhances expressiveness in the embedding space, enables an optimizer algorithm's an improved convergence rate(Rajaee and Sheikhi,), and improves overall performance.(Ioffe and Szegedy, 2015)(Wang et al., 2019) (Rajaee and Pilehvar, 2021a).
Multiple research efforts have shown that architectures that utilise contextual and non-contextual word representations lack isotropy (i.e anisotropic) (Devlin et al., 2018) (Rajaee and Pilehvar, 2021b)(Rajaee and Pilehvar, 2021a). This stems from what is known as the *Representation Degeneration Problem* discovered by (Gao et al., 2019), where they showed that when likelihood maximization is used with the weight tying to train a model on large corpora for language generation tasks, high frequency words are pushed towards hidden states while low frequency words are pushed in the negative direction of most hidden states. This creates a cluster in the embedding space of low frequency words, far away from the origin. This problem impacts the distribution of word vectors as they become dispersed into a cone-like shape making the embedding space *anisotropic*. Such property can negatively impact the training time (Huang et al., 2018) and can overestimate the cosine similarity between representations. (Gao et al., 2019). There have been multiple strategies to tweak embedding spaces to become more isotropic (Devlin et al., 2018) (Liang et al., 2021). We use (Rajaee and Pilehvar, 2021a)'s cluster-based approach in our work to achieve an embedding space with representations homogeneously dispersed.
The rest of the paper is organised as follows, in section 4 we describe the objective of the sub-task and the nature of the data. We also, quantify isotropy and prove numerically and visually that MARBERT has an anisotropic geometry. In section5 we explain the methodology to improving MARBERT's isotropy and the architecture used to learn representations and perform classification. Finally in section6 we reveal our results and findings and discuss additional settings used to attempt score better results.

4. Dataset and Sub-task

The OSACT5 Shared Task[2] consists of three sub-tasks, we contribute to one sub-task (sub-task A) which requires classifying a tweet as offensive or not offensive. The training samples are in dialectical Arabic and consist of 8.5K tweets for training and 1.2K tweets for development collected by (Mubarak et al., 2022). We provide below the number of offensive to non-offensive tweets. The dataset features a number of emojis per data sample that can relay the intention of the tweet as containing hate-speech generally or not.

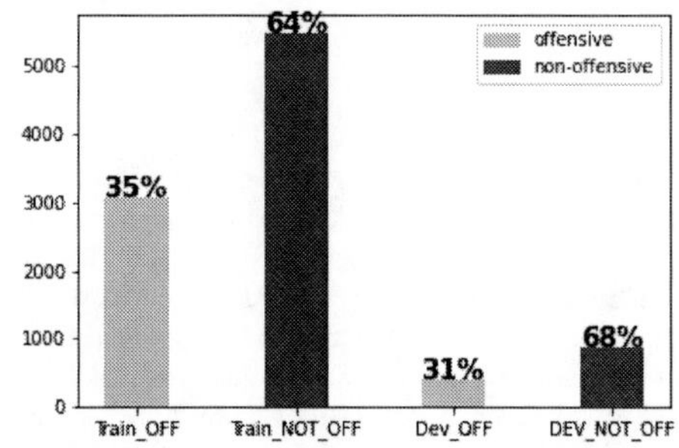

Figure 1: Offensive to non-offensive samples in training and development sets

Data samples are already partially pre-processed; any instances of twitter mentions are replaced with '@USER' and URLs by 'URL'. We remove these tokens along with diacritics, elongations and any instance of non-Arabic letters.

4.1. Isotropy

We begin our methodology by proving that MARBERT's embedding space lacks uniformity. We follow (Mu et al., 2017) (Rajaee and Pilehvar, 2021a) in quantifying isotropy using the metric in 1, and the partition function 2 by (Arora et al., 2016):

$$I(W) = \frac{min_{u \in U} F(u)}{max_{u \in U} F(u)} \tag{1}$$

$$F(u) = \sum_{i=1}^{N} e^{u^T w_i} \tag{2}$$

where:

- U: is the set of eigenvectors of the embedding matrix W
- u: is the unit vector
- $F(u)$: is the partition function
- w_i: is the contextual word representation of the ith word in embedding matrix W where $W \in \mathrm{R}^{N \times D}$ with N being the size of the vocabulary and D the size of the embedding

As cited by (Rajaee and Pilehvar, 2021a), (Arora et al., 2016) proved that using a constant for isotropic embedding spaces, $F(u)$ can be approximated. Thereby $I(w)$ serves as an approximation for isotropy, where the closer the value it yields is to one the more isotropic the embedding space is.

[2]https://sites.google.com/view/arabichate2022/home

5. System Description

An essential part of our methodology is proving firstly that MARBERT's embedding space is in need for a better distribution. To quantify this, we calculate MARBERT's isotropy by extracting the training samples corresponding representations from MARBERT and apply equations 1 & 2. Furthermore, we visualise the embedding space to display non-uniformity of representations in Figure 1.

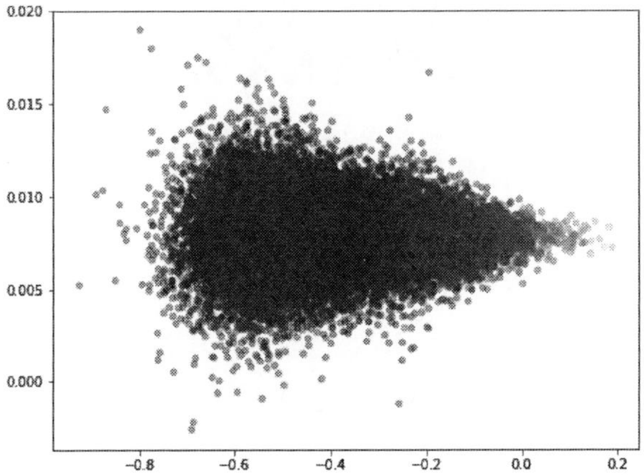

Figure 2: Visual of MARBERT's Cone-Shaped Embedding Space

We find MARBERT's isotropy value to be **2.88e-08**, which means that MARBERT has an extremely anisotropic embedding space, meaning that representations in MARBERT are not uniformly scattered around the origin. Figure 2 is an illustration of MARBERT's embedding space and shows that the model exhibits the representation degeneration problem. Darker colours in the figure indicate low frequency words while light colors are words with high frequency. When inspecting the figure we find the majority of low frequency words clustered together and shifting away from the origin. Moreover, the shape of the embedding takes the shape of a cone aligning with the depiction of an anisotropic space mentioned in 3.

5.1. Improving Isotropy

To refine MARBERT's isotropy, we use a cluster-based approach (Rajaee and Pilehvar, 2021a) which builds on top of (Mu et al., 2017) technique to improve isotropy in non-contextual word embeddings. Experiments in (Rajaee and Pilehvar, 2021a) illustrated the use of such method which improved classification performance and surpassed baseline values in pre-trained language models, particularly, BERT(Devlin et al., 2018).
The method is composed of the following steps:

1. cluster extracted features into k using K-means
2. zero-mean each cluster
3. remove a specified number of dominant directions D in each cluster. These dominant representations are the most occurring words per cluster

We set D according to (Devlin et al., 2018) approach.

$$D = \frac{d}{100} \tag{3}$$

where d is the dimension of a word embedding.
However for k we experiment with different ks and measure the isotropy for each k setting. Table 1 shows isotropy values after using cluster-based approach to enhance representations. Isotropy values show there is a significant increase starting with k=1 compared to the original baseline value. Isotropy values then sustain a small increase as the number of k clusters increases.

Baseline	**2.88e-08**
k =1	0.9564
k =3	0.9685
k = 5	0.9728
k =7	0.9719
k = 10	0.9743
k = 20	0.9767

Table 1: Isotropy Values for Different k Values

We illustrate in Figure 4 the embedding space post cluster-based approach. As shown, the geometry of representations completely changed from being cone-shaped to clusters scattered around the origin.

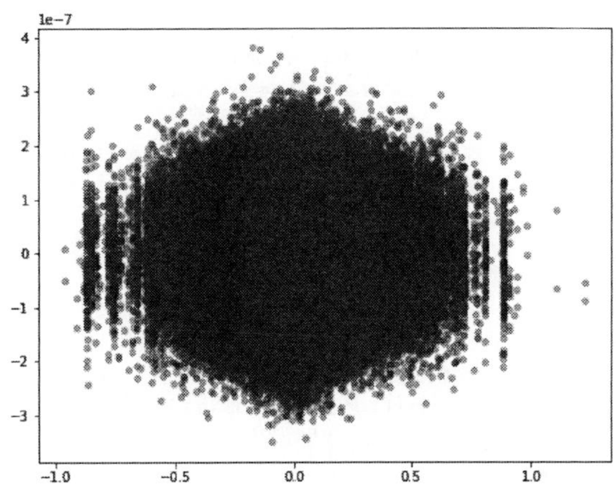

Figure 3: Representations post cluster-based processing

5.2. Training, Development & Testing

Next, We pass our isotropic representations to a Bidirectional Long-Short Term Memory (biLSTM) to be learned and perform classification.

5.2.1. Experimental Setup

We opt for using 10 clusters, and eight dominant directions to be removed per each according to the formula in 3. Naturally, we would not want to remove a larger number of directions not to lose linguistic features of the dataset.

Our biLSTM model is made up of two hidden layers each of size 102 and input sequence length of 768. We use Adam optimizer with decoupled weight regularization, a learning rate of 3e-5 and cross entropy loss. The development data undergoes the same preprocessing as the training data, meaning, we apply cluster based approach on development data as well with the same settings used with training samples. We validate our results using development data every epoch for 10 epochs of training and save the best performing checkpoint according to macro-averaged f1 score.

Additionally, we extract representations from MARBERT without any isotropic processing and compare development scores between isotropic representations and default ones.

6. Results & Discussion

Rep.	accuracy	precision	recall	f1
Isotropic	**81.2%**	71.5%	**71.5%**	**79.1%**
Default	81.2%	**74.9%**	61.5%	77.2%

Table 2: Development scores per type of Representations used

Table 2 shows results for the development data achieved by using isotropic representations in contrast to MARBERT's raw representations. Using better representations boosted f1 score by 1.9%.

Given these scores, we submit the better performing system of the two for the testing phase to achieve an accuracy of 76.5%, and 74.5% for f1. Additionally, our system scores 76.5% and 74.2% for precision and recall.

The confusion matrix of our better performing system (isotropic system) on the development set in figure 4 shows that it managed to predict 766 out of 898 non-offensive tweets correctly while predicting 271 offensive tweets correctly out of 368.

We employ different settings to our clustering approach in-order to enhance performance.

6.1. Additional Settings

We tried to anchor the number of dominant directions against distant values of k in order to check if the number of clusters in an embedding space can have an impact on the performance. We choose to compare between k = 2, 10, & 20 and we report below their respective validation results .

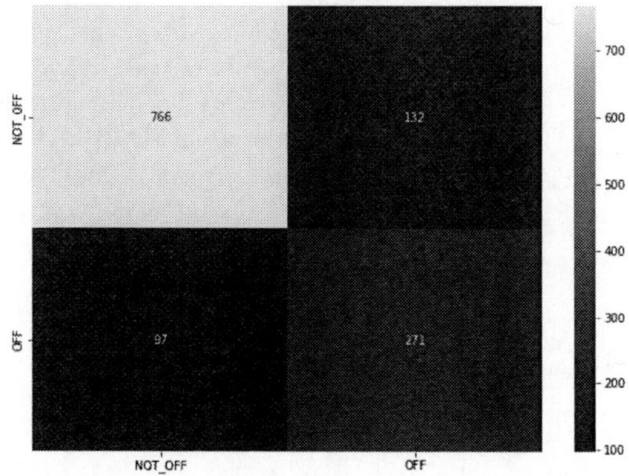

Figure 4:

K	Accuracy	F1
k =2	81.1%	71.1%
k =10	81.2%	79.1%
k = 20	81.0%	78.9%

Table 3: Development Results using k=2, 10 & 20

From table 3 we observe that scores are very close, and using all ks gives better performance than the default anisotropic representations. This means that increasing or lowering k may not impact performance significantly as long as the use of those k-values showcase isotropic properties in representations. Furthermore, we experimented with removing a larger number of dominant directions such as 16, and 30 directions, to find that the performance stays relatively the same.

This suggests one of two things, the first being is that we may have removed too many directions, thus some essential semantics were perished, or, given the nature of twitter data as we can see in figure 2, the majority of words are of low frequency (dark coloured points), hence, there is a limited number of dominant directions to be removed.

7. Conclusion

In this shared task we contributed to sub-task A, and in order to classify offensive and non-offensive tweets we aimed improve the geometric properties of MARBERT's embedding space, where we used a cluster-based approach to group representations into a number of clusters, removed a number of dominant directions per cluster which improved isotropy from being originally **2.88e-08** to **0.9743**. Moreover, we experiment the use of isotropic representations in contrast to

MARBERT's anisotropic embeddings by feeding each to a Bidirectional LSTM to find that isotropic representations achieve better scores. Our system for task A achieves an accuracy score of **81.2%** and f1 score of **79.1%** for development data and **76.5%** and **74.2%** for accuracy and f1 scores using test data respectively surpassing the baseline and outperforming MARBERT's default embeddings. Our code for the task can be found on github.[3]

8. Bibliographical References

Abdul-Mageed, M., Elmadany, A., and Nagoudi, E. M. B. (2020). Arbert & marbert: deep bidirectional transformers for arabic. *arXiv preprint arXiv:2101.01785*.

Abuzayed, A. and Elsayed, T. (2020). Quick and simple approach for detecting hate speech in arabic tweets. In *Proceedings of the 4th workshop on open-source Arabic Corpora and processing tools, with a shared task on offensive language detection*, pages 109–114.

Arora, S., Li, Y., Liang, Y., Ma, T., and Risteski, A. (2016). A latent variable model approach to pmi-based word embeddings. *Transactions of the Association for Computational Linguistics*, 4:385–399.

Church, K. W. (2017). Word2vec. *Natural Language Engineering*, 23(1):155–162.

Devlin, J., Chang, M.-W., Lee, K., and Toutanova, K. (2018). Bert: Pre-training of deep bidirectional transformers for language understanding. *arXiv preprint arXiv:1810.04805*.

Gao, J., He, D., Tan, X., Qin, T., Wang, L., and Liu, T.-Y. (2019). Representation degeneration problem in training natural language generation models. *arXiv preprint arXiv:1907.12009*.

Huang, L., Yang, D., Lang, B., and Deng, J. (2018). Decorrelated batch normalization. In *Proceedings of the IEEE Conference on Computer Vision and Pattern Recognition*, pages 791–800.

Husain, F. (2020). Osact4 shared task on offensive language detection: Intensive preprocessing-based approach. *arXiv preprint arXiv:2005.07297*.

Ioffe, S. and Szegedy, C. (2015). Batch normalization: Accelerating deep network training by reducing internal covariate shift. In *International conference on machine learning*, pages 448–456. PMLR.

Joulin, A., Grave, E., Bojanowski, P., Douze, M., Jégou, H., and Mikolov, T. (2016). Fasttext. zip: Compressing text classification models. *arXiv preprint arXiv:1612.03651*.

Liang, Y., Cao, R., Zheng, J., Ren, J., and Gao, L. (2021). Learning to remove: Towards isotropic pre-trained bert embedding. In *International Conference on Artificial Neural Networks*, pages 448–459. Springer.

Mu, J., Bhat, S., and Viswanath, P. (2017). All-but-the-top: Simple and effective postprocessing for word representations. *arXiv preprint arXiv:1702.01417*.

Mubarak, H., Hassan, S., and Chowdhury, S. A. (2022). Emojis as anchors to detect arabic offensive language and hate speech. *arXiv preprint arXiv:2201.06723*.

Rajaee, S. and Pilehvar, M. T. (2021a). A cluster-based approach for improving isotropy in contextual embedding space. *arXiv preprint arXiv:2106.01183*.

Rajaee, S. and Pilehvar, M. T. (2021b). An isotropy analysis in the multilingual bert embedding space. *arXiv preprint arXiv:2110.04504*.

Rajaee, S. and Sheikhi, M.). Isotropic contextual word representation in bert.

Saeed, H. H., Calders, T., and Kamiran, F. (2020). Osact4 shared tasks: Ensembled stacked classification for offensive and hate speech in arabic tweets. In *Proceedings of the 4th Workshop on Open-Source Arabic Corpora and Processing Tools, with a Shared Task on Offensive Language Detection*, pages 71–75.

Soliman, A. B., Eissa, K., and El-Beltagy, S. R. (2017). Aravec: A set of arabic word embedding models for use in arabic nlp. *Procedia Computer Science*, 117:256–265.

Wang, L., Huang, J., Huang, K., Hu, Z., Wang, G., and Gu, Q. (2019). Improving neural language generation with spectrum control. In *International Conference on Learning Representations*.

[3]https://github.com/nehalelkaref/Towards-a-Better-Isotropy-to-Detect-Hatespeech.git

Proceedings of the OSACT 2022 Workshop @LREC2022, pages 214–217
Marseille, 20 June 2022

aiXplain at Arabic Hate Speech 2022: An Ensemble Based Approach to Detecting Offensive Tweets

Salaheddin Alzu'bi, Thiago Castro Ferreira , Lucas Pavanelli, Mohamed Al-Badrashiny
aiXplain Inc.
Los Gatos, CA
(salah.alzubi, thiago, lucas.pavanelli, mohamed)@aixplain.com

Abstract

Abusive speech on online platforms has a detrimental effect on users' mental health. This warrants the need for innovative solutions that automatically moderate content, especially on online platforms such as Twitter where a user's anonymity is loosely controlled. This paper outlines aiXplain Inc.'s ensemble based approach to detecting offensive speech in the Arabic language based on OSACT5's shared **sub-task A**. Additionally, this paper highlights multiple challenges that may hinder progress on detecting abusive speech and provides potential avenues and techniques that may lead to significant progress.

Keywords: Offensive Language Detection, Arabic Shared Task, Abusive Language Detection

1. Introduction

The presence of abusive speech in online communities poses a detrimental effect to many users' mental health. This is particularly apparent in interactive platforms such as Twitter, where a user's anonymity is loosely moderated. This phenomenon warrants the need for models that automatically detect and handle abusive language; while solutions to this problem in the English language have been proposed, there is room for improvement for the Arabic language.

This paper presents aiXplain Inc.'s ensemble based approach to detecting offensive speech in Arabic for the OSACT5 shared sub-task A (Hassan et al., 2020). In particular, this paper outlines the individual approaches that were used in tackling this task and offers a final system architecture based on a combination of these models. Additionally, this paper offers insights into the challenging aspects of classifying offensive speech in Arabic and potential future directions that may bear fruit in tackling this problem.

2. Data & Task Description

In this section, we provide an overview of the data and a description of the sub-tasks available.

2.1. Data

The dataset provided for OSCAT5 Arabic hate speech task consists of 12698 annotated tweets that serve as the largest annotated database for the Arabic community. Each tweet is independently judged by 3 annotators that assign the following labels to them: offensive/not-offensive; hate-speech/not-hate-speech; type of hate-speech: race, religion, ideology, disability, social class, and gender; additionally, each tweet is labeled as vulgar/not-vulgar and violent/not-violent. The dataset is split into a training set, development set and testing set with the following distribution:

Train	Development	Test
8887	1270	2541

Table 1: OSACT5 Arabic Hate Speech Data Distribution

It is worth emphasizing that the dataset is heavily imbalanced for both available sub-tasks, with the second & third sub-tasks (hate speech classification) being more severe than the first.

Subtask	Label 0 (%)	Label 1 (%)
A	65	35
B	90	10

Table 2: Subtask Label Distribution

2.2. Shared Sub-tasks

This section provides an overview of the three different sub-tasks that are available. We would like to emphasize the fact that our submission involves participation in **Subtask A only**.

2.2.1. Subtask A: Offensive Speech Detection

The first subtask involves detecting whether a tweet contains offensive speech or not. Offensive speech is defined as any kind of implicit or explicit insults or attacks against individuals or groups.

2.2.2. Subtask B: Hate Speech Detection

The second sub-task involves detecting hate speech. Hate speech is defined as any kind of implicit or explicit speech that targets an individual's, or groups', race, religion, ideology, disability, social class, or gender.

2.2.3. Subtask C: Hate Speech Detection

The third sub-task is the same as the second sub-task, however, the problem is posed as a multi-class classification problem. The primary aim of this sub-task is to perform fine-grained classification of tweets that contain hate-speech into one of the six classes mentioned in the section above.

3. Approach

This section includes the primary approach we used to achieve the best results. Our approach consists of three main steps: Augmentation, Pre-processing and passing the data through an ensemble[1].

3.1. Preprocessing

This section discusses the pre-processing techniques that we apply on tweets. Our pre-processing technique involves dealing with text and emojis separately.

3.1.1. Textual Pre-processing

For the textual part of the tweet, we apply the following transformations sequentially on each tweet:

1. Remove URLs and mentions
2. Remove diacritics and tatweel
3. Remove punctuation

This simple approach ensures that the data remains faithful to the original distribution while removing noisy signals in the tweet.

3.1.2. Emoji Pre-processing

(Mubarak et al., 2022) show that emoji's provide invaluable information to detect a tweet's sentiment. Since most models are not directly trained to handle tweets, we translate emojis in a tweet to Arabic using (Junczys-Dowmunt et al., 2018) English to Arabic model.For some emojis, we infer their intended meaning (from how they are usually used in the region's context) and provide their translation using our expertise in the Arabic language and the colloquial dialect used. Additionally, we extract the relevant emojis from each tweet and use a classifier to predict their sentiment individually. These predictions are used as additional high-level features to other classifiers.

3.2. Data Augmentation

Since deep-learning models such as BERT (Devlin et al., 2018) are data hungry, a large amount of data from each class is required for any significant learning to occur. This section outlines the two methods that were used to augment the offensive dataset.

3.2.1. Semi-Supervised Learning

We use recent developments in semi-supervised learning to augment the classes with less support (in this case: offensive class). We fine-tune a pre-trained AraBERTv0.2-Twitter-base (Antoun et al., 2020) model on detecting offensive speech; this model is then used to classify a large set of tweets that have been scraped from external sources. We select the tweets that the model predicts as offensive with high confidence.

[1]https://github.com/aixplain/arabic-hate-speech

3.2.2. Contextual Augmentation based on Semantic Similarity

We use the Python package NLPAug (Ma, 2019) to augment the tweets. This technique consists of feeding surrounding words to AraBERTv0.2-Twitter-base (Antoun et al., 2020) to find out a semantically similar word that is suitable for augmentation. We run this augmentation for every offensive example, randomly substituting 30% of the words with the similar one and, thus, generating a new example. We apply this technique till we double the number of examples in the offensive class making the class distribution balanced. Based on our empirical observations, we have found that changing around 2-3 words in a tweet preserves the overall meaning whilst adding capturing a broader spectrum of the negative sentiment.

3.3. System Overview

This section provides a detailed overview of the approach that we use to make the final predictions on tweets. Our system's architecture involves feeding the predictions of an ensemble of classifiers combined with relative high-level features to a final meta-learner yielding a binary label of "OFF" to represent offensive or "NOT_OFF" to represent unoffensive speech.
Each of the classifiers in the ensemble consist of a final linear layer the following pre-trained model as a backbone:

- AraBERTv0.2-Twitter-large (Antoun et al., 2020)
- Mazajak 250M CBOW pre-trained embeddings (Abu Farha and Magdy, 2019)
- Character level N-gram + word level N-gram TF-IDF embeddings (Takase et al., 2019)
- MUSE (Conneau et al., 2017)

Additionally, we use our Emoji model to extract additional high level features from each tweet.
The predictions from the aforementioned models are then concatenated into a final vector which is fed into either a final XGBoost model or a linear layer to produce the final binary prediction.

3.4. Models

This section contains an overview of the models that we use as part of our ensemble.

3.4.1. AraBERTv0.2-Twitter-large

AraBERTv0.2-Twitter (Antoun et al., 2020) is a pre-trained transformer model that is based on Google's BERT (Devlin et al., 2018) model. Similar to BERT the model is pre-trained on an MLM task using a collection of 60M arabic tweets. This particular model contains emojis as part of its vocabulary making it suitable for this task. We use HuggingFace's API to fine-tune our model using Adam (Kingma and Ba, 2014) optimizer and a learning rate of 1e-5.

3.4.2. Mazajak Pre-trained Embeddings

Mazajak embeddings (Abu Farha and Magdy, 2019) are the largest available embeddings for the arabic langauge trained on 250M tweets. Mazajak embeddings were created by training a Continuous Bag-of-Words (CBOW) model to yield a 300-dimensional contextual vector for each word in the corpus. In our model, we use the mazajak embeddings for each word and apply average pooling to produce a final 300-dimensional vector that is fed into a linear layer to give a prediction.

3.4.3. Character + Word level N-gram TF-IDF Embeddings

In this model, we combine the tri-gram character level tf-idf embeddings of tweets with the bi-gram word level tf-idf embeddigs. We believe that lexical level features such as character level and word level embeddings add an extra dimension to the learning of our ensemble classifier.

3.4.4. MUSE

This model utilizes the word embeddings provided by FAIR's Multilingual Universal Sentence Encoder (Conneau et al., 2017). Given a tweet, we feed the pre-processed data to MUSE to generate a 512 word embedding vector; this vector is then fed into a logistic regression layer to provide a final prediction.

3.4.5. Emoji Score

Emoji score is the model we use to extract additional high-level features from the emoji's present in a tweet. In particular, we assign a score to each emoji based on how many times it is used in offensive tweets and how many times it is present in non-offensive ones. For each tweet, we aggregate the emoji-score of each emoji into a final score representing the emoji-score.

An additional approach we experimented with involved a bag-of-words model that calculated the offensiveness of a tweet based on the emoji scores in a tweet.

4. Model Evaluation

This section presents and discusses the performance of our models on the development set. We also present the final evaluation scores on the test set provided.

4.1. Dev Set Results

The development set is used as a benchmark for our model's generalization performance on unseen data; the table below shows the performance of each individual model and different combinations of the models on the most common metrics used to evaluate binary classification.

Model	P	R	Macro F1
Char-tfidf	0.79	0.72	0.74
Word-tfidf	0.75	0.65	0.66
Emoji	0.68	0.56	0.54
Muse	0.73	0.69	0.7
Emoji-Score	**0.68**	**0.55**	**0.51**
AraBERT	**0.84**	**0.83**	**0.84**
Mazajak	0.73	0.64	0.64
Char+word+MUSE	0.79	0.74	0.75
Char+word+MUSE +Emoji	**0.79**	**0.76**	**0.77**
Ensemble of Boldface Models	**0.86**	**0.85**	**0.85**

Table 3: Evaluation of different models on the Precision (P), Recall (R) and Macro F1-Score binary classification performance metrics

4.1.1. Results Discussion

The results above show that AraBERT outperforms all the other models by a large margin. We believe that this is due to the fact that AraBERT was specifically trained on a large number of tweets that captured the datas underlying distribution. A surprising result is the poor performance of the Mazajak pre-trained embeddings as they are also trained on 250M tweets, yet the Mazajak embeddings did not seem to represent the tweets in a successful manner. We believe that this may be due to a couple of reasons: (1) the underlying distribution of the data (in this case, the different dialects) is different from the distribution that the Mazajak model was trained on. (2) The pre-processing steps that the authors used are different from the steps that we used leading to a large discrepancy in the performance. Other models such as TF-IDF and MUSE show promise but are not up to par with the best result of AraBERT. Under the aforementioned, the final result which involves ensembling multiple models and high-level features only pushes the final result by .02 f1 points; this indicates that apart from AraBERT, the other feature extraction methods are either insignificant or provide weak signals to the final prediction.

4.1.2. Error Analysis

This section highlights some of the examples that our best model gets wrong and provides some insight as to why the model may be behaving the way it is.

	Tweet	Golden Label	Confidence
1	العامل يشرح للمعزب ان الخروف حيوان صار صديقه حتي ما يذبحه هههه	NOT_OFF	.92
2	بعض البشر اخلاقهم في غيبويه مدي الحياه زعلان	NOT_OFF	.93
3	ههه ههه ههه حبيبي	OFF	.99
4	بطلوا كذب بقي زعلان زعلان زعلان	OFF	.80

Figure 1: Examples the best model confidently misclassifies

The above results show that our best model struggles

to classify examples with no emojis; this supports the claim that language agnostic indicators such as emojis provide valuable insights to the models' predictions. The model also seems to fail to recognize offensive tweets that when placed in context count as offensive such as example (3).

4.2. Test Set Results

The table below shows our model's final result on the test set. The final models that were submitted involved using different meta-learners as the final classification layer. For the first submission, we use a auto-sklearn to select the best estimators; for the second submission, we use a linear layer as the classification layer.

Model	Acc	P	R	Macro F1
1	**0.864**	**0.852**	**0.847**	**0.849**
2	0.858	0.845	0.84	0.843
Baseline	0.651	0.325	0.5	0.394

Table 4: Accuracy (Acc), Precision (P), Recall (R) and Macro F1-Score of Our Best Models on the Test Set

These results are in line with the results achieved in the development phase. This shows that our best model is able to generalize well to unseen tweets from the same distribution.

5. Challenges & Future Directions

The biggest challenge we faced when attempting to detect offensive tweets was normalizing the dialect of the tweets. Most of the available pre-trained models or pre-processing libraries are trained on MSA or a particular Arabic dialect making a unified approach difficult. This limited our ability to extract relevant features from the tweets in a useful manner; for example, POS tags and NER. This lead us to look for relevant signals in emojis as they are, to a large extent, language agnostic. We believe that exploring emoji's and their relevance to classifying offensive speech in tweets can provide valuable signals to the overall prediction.

6. Bibliographical References

Abu Farha, I. and Magdy, W. (2019). Mazajak: An online Arabic sentiment analyser. In *Proceedings of the Fourth Arabic Natural Language Processing Workshop*, pages 192–198, Florence, Italy, August. Association for Computational Linguistics.

Antoun, W., Baly, F., and Hajj, H. (2020). Arabert: Transformer-based model for arabic language understanding. In *LREC 2020 Workshop Language Resources and Evaluation Conference 11–16 May 2020*, page 9.

Conneau, A., Lample, G., Ranzato, M., Denoyer, L., and Jégou, H. (2017). Word translation without parallel data. *arXiv preprint arXiv:1710.04087*.

Devlin, J., Chang, M.-W., Lee, K., and Toutanova, K. (2018). Bert: Pre-training of deep bidirectional transformers for language understanding.

Hassan, S., Samih, Y., Mubarak, H., Abdelali, A., Rashed, A., and Chowdhury, S. A. (2020). ALT submission for OSACT shared task on offensive language detection. In *Proceedings of the 4th Workshop on Open-Source Arabic Corpora and Processing Tools, with a Shared Task on Offensive Language Detection*, pages 61–65, Marseille, France, May. European Language Resource Association.

Junczys-Dowmunt, M., Grundkiewicz, R., Dwojak, T., Hoang, H., Heafield, K., Neckermann, T., Seide, F., Germann, U., Fikri Aji, A., Bogoychev, N., Martins, A. F. T., and Birch, A. (2018). Marian: Fast neural machine translation in C++. In *Proceedings of ACL 2018, System Demonstrations*, pages 116–121, Melbourne, Australia, July. Association for Computational Linguistics.

Kingma, D. P. and Ba, J. (2014). Adam: A method for stochastic optimization.

Ma, E. (2019). Nlp augmentation. https://github.com/makcedward/nlpaug.

Mubarak, H., Hassan, S., and Chowdhury, S. A. (2022). Emojis as anchors to detect arabic offensive language and hate speech.

Takase, S., Suzuki, J., and Nagata, M. (2019). Character n-gram embeddings to improve rnn language models.

Author Index

Association for Computational Linguistics
209 N. Eighth Street
Stroudsburg, Pennsylvania 18360

ISBN 978-1-7138-6131-7

CURRAN ASSOCIATES INC.
proceedings.com